Frommer's
Hawaii 2015

by Martha Cheng, Jeanne Cooper &
Shannon Wianecki

FrommerMedia LLC

Published by: Frommer Media LLC
Copyright © 2015

ISBN 978-1-62887-146-3 (paper), 978-1-62887-147-0 (e-book)

Editorial Director: Pauline Frommer
Editor: Alexis Lipsitz Flippin
Production Editor: Suzanna R. Thompson
Cartographer: Roberta Stockwell
Photo Editor: Seth Olenick

Front cover photo: Aerial view of the remote Na Pali coastline.
Back cover photo: Couple kayaking on Oahu.

For information on our other products and services or to obtain technical support, please contact support@frommers.com.

Frommer's also publishes its books in a variety of electronic formats. Some content that appears in print may not be available in electronic formats.

Manufactured in China

5 4 3 2 1

ABOUT THE AUTHORS

Martha Cheng is the food editor of "Honolulu Magazine." Originally from San Francisco, she's a former pastry chef, line cook, food-truck owner, Peace Corps volunteer, and Google techie. These days, she surfs, eats, and writes mostly in Honolulu, occasionally leaving her Hawaiian paradise to explore its other forms.

Jeanne Cooper fell in love with the real Hawaii on her first visit in 1998, after growing up with enchanting stories and songs of the islands from her mother, who had lived there as a girl. The former editor of the "San Francisco Chronicle" travel section, Jeanne writes frequently about Hawaii for the newspaper and its website, SFGate.com, home of her Aloha Friday column and Hawaii Insider blog, and for magazines such as "Sunset" and "Caviar Affair." She has also contributed to guidebooks on her former hometowns of Boston; Washington, D.C.; and San Francisco.

Shannon Wianecki grew up in Hawaii swimming in waterfalls, jumping off of sea cliffs, and breakfasting on ripe mangoes. An award-winning writer and editor, she writes feature stories for numerous travel and lifestyle magazines, including "Spirituality & Health," "Modern Luxury Hawaii," "Hawaii Business," "Honolulu," and "Hana Hou!," the Hawaiian Airlines magazine. Having served 8 years as food editor for "Maui No Ka 'Oi" magazine, she knows the island's restaurant scene as well as her own kitchen. She's an avid scuba diver who delights in finding frogfish and once won the Maui Dreams Dive Company's pumpkin-carving contest. Her book credits include "Top Maui Restaurants 2012" and "Simple Ayurvedic Recipes."

CONTENTS

LIST OF MAPS

ACKNOWLEDGMENTS

Thanks to Melissa Erb, Jesse Lee Burgess, and especially Ben Trevino.

—*Martha Cheng*

I would like to thank my editor, Alexis Lipsitz Flippin, and my husband, Ian Hersey, for their support, and all those in Hawaii who have shared their knowledge and aloha with me.

—*Jeanne Cooper*

Thanks to Roxie Pell, who contributed to this chapter.

—*Shannon Wianecki*

HOW TO CONTACT US

In researching this book, we discovered many wonderful places—hotels, restaurants, shops, and more. We're sure you'll find others. Please tell us about them so we can share the information with your fellow travelers in upcoming editions. If you were disappointed with a recommendation, we'd love to know that, too. Please email: support@frommers.com.

ADVISORY & DISCLAIMER

Travel information can change quickly and unexpectedly, and we strongly advise you to confirm important details locally before traveling, including information on visas, health and safety, traffic and transport, accommodations, shopping, and eating out. We also encourage you to stay alert while traveling and to remain aware of your surroundings. Avoid civil disturbances, and keep a close eye on cameras, purses, wallets, and other valuables.

While we have endeavored to ensure that the information contained within this guide is accurate and up-to-date at the time of publication, we make no representations or warranties with respect to the accuracy or completeness of the contents of this work and specifically disclaim all warranties, including without limitation warranties of fitness for a particular purpose. We accept no responsibility or liability for any inaccuracy or errors or omissions, or for any inconvenience, loss, damage, costs, or expenses of any nature whatsoever incurred or suffered by anyone as a result of any advice or information contained in this guide.

The inclusion of a company, organization, or website in this guide as a service provider and/or potential source of further information does not mean that we endorse them or the information they provide. Be aware that information provided through some websites may be unreliable and can change without notice. Neither the publisher nor author shall be liable for any damages arising herefrom.

FROMMER'S STAR RATINGS, ICONS & ABBREVIATIONS

Every hotel, restaurant, and attraction listing in this guide has been ranked for quality, value, service, amenities, and special features using a **star-rating system.** In country, state, and regional guides, we also rate towns and regions to help you narrow down your choices and budget your time accordingly. Hotels and restaurants are rated on a scale of one (recommended) to three stars (exceptional). Attractions, shopping, nightlife, towns, and regions are rated according to the following scale: one star (recommended), two stars (very highly recommended), and three stars (must-see).

TRAVEL RESOURCES AT FROMMERS.COM

Frommer's travel resources don't end with this guide. Frommer's website, **www.frommers. com**, has travel information on dozens of other destinations. We update features regularly, giving you access to the most current trip-planning information and the best airfare, lodging, and car-rental bargains. You can also listen to podcasts, connect with other Frommers.com members through our active-reader forums, share your travel photos, read blogs, and much more.

1

THE BEST OF HAWAII

There's no place on earth quite like this handful of sun-drenched Pacific islands. Here you'll find palm-fringed blue lagoons, lush rainforests, cascading waterfalls, soaring summits (some capped with snow), a live volcano, and beaches of every hue: gold, red, black, and even green. Roadside stands offer fruits and flowers for pocket change, and award-winning chefs deliver unforgettable feasts. Each of the six main islands possesses its own unique mix of natural and cultural treasures—and the possibilities for adventure, indulgence, and relaxation are endless.

THE best BEACHES

o **Lanikai Beach** (Oahu): Too gorgeous to be real, this stretch along the Windward Coast is one of Hawaii's postcard-perfect beaches—a mile of golden sand as soft as powdered sugar bordering translucent turquoise waters. The waters are calm year-round and excellent for swimming, snorkeling, and kayaking. Two tiny offshore islands complete the picture, functioning both as scenic backdrops and bird sanctuaries. See p. 88.

o **Hapuna Beach** (Big Island): A half-mile of tawny sand, as wide as a football field, gently slopes down to crystalline waters that in summer are usually excellent for swimming, snorkeling, and bodysurfing; in winter, the thundering waves should be admired from the shore, where the picnicking and state camping facilities are first-rate. See p. 192.

Lanikai Beach, Oahu.

Previous page: Hawaiian beach.

Hula.

○ **Waianapanapa State Park** (Maui): Maui has many terrific beaches to choose from, but this one is extra special: On the dramatic Hana coast, jet-black sand is pummeled by the azure surf, sea arches and caves dot the shoreline, and a forested path leads to a secret swimming hole, the hiding place of an ancient Hawaiian princess. Plan to picnic or camp here. See p. 283.

○ **Papohaku Beach Park** (Molokai): The currents are too strong for swimming here, but the light-blond strand of sand, nearly 300 feet wide and stretching for some 3 miles—one of Hawaii's longest beaches—is great for picnicking, walking, and watching sunsets, with Oahu shimmering in the distance. See p. 380.

○ **Hulopoe Beach** (Lanai): This large sprawl of soft, golden sand is one of the prettiest in the state. Bordered by the regal Four Seasons resort on one side and lava-rock tide pools on the other, this protected marine preserve offers prime swimming, snorkeling, tide-pool exploring, picnicking, camping, and the chance to spy on resident spinner dolphins. See p. 401.

○ **Poipu Beach** (Kauai): This popular beach on Kauai's sunny South Shore has something for everyone: protected swimming, snorkeling, bodyboarding, surfing, and plenty of sand for basking—with a rare Hawaiian monk seal joining sunbathers every so often. See p. 452.

THE best AUTHENTIC EXPERIENCES

○ **Eat Local:** People in Hawaii love food. Want to get a local talking? Ask for her favorite place to get poke or saimin or shave ice. The islands offer excellent fine-dining opportunities (see examples below), but they also have plenty of respectable hole-in-the-wall joints and beloved institutions that have hung around for half a century. On Oahu, eat poke at **Ono Seafood** (p. 122), enjoy true Hawaiian food at **Helena's Hawaiian Food** (p. 130), and join the regulars at **Liliha Bakery** (p. 130) for a loco moco. On Kauai, slurp saimin and shave ice at **Hamura's Saimin Stand** (p. 490).

○ **Feel History Come Alive at Pearl Harbor** (Oahu): On December 7, 1941, Japanese warplanes bombed Pearl Harbor, forcing the United States to enter World War II. Standing on the deck of the **USS *Arizona* Memorial**—the eternal tomb for the 1,177 sailors trapped below when the battleship sank—is a profound experience. You can also visit the USS *Missouri* Memorial, where the Japanese signed their surrender on September 2, 1945. See p. 61.

○ **Experience Hula:** Each year the city of Hilo on the Big Island hosts a prestigious competition celebrating ancient Hawaiian dance: the **Merrie Monarch Festival** (p. 40). The week after Easter, local *halau* (hula troupes) perform **free shows** at several shopping centers. On Oahu, check out the **Bishop Museum** (p. 58), which stages excellent performances on weekdays, or head to the Halekulani's **House Without a Key** (p. 142) at sunset to watch the enchanting Kanoelehua Miller dance beautiful hula under a century-old kiawe tree. On Maui, the **Old Lahaina Luau** (p. 364) is the real deal, showcasing Hawaiian dance and storytelling nightly on a gracious, beachfront stage.

○ **Ponder Petroglyphs:** More than 23,000 ancient rock carvings decorate the lava fields at **Hawaii Volcanoes National Park** (p. 182) on the Big Island. You can see hundreds more on a short hike through the **Puako Petroglyph Archaeological Preserve** (p. 165), near the Fairmont Orchid on the Kohala Coast. Go early in the morning or late afternoon, when the angle of the sun lets you see the forms clearly. On Lanai, fantastic birdmen and canoes are etched into rocks at **Shipwreck Beach** (p. 403) and **Kaunolu Village** (p. 400).

○ **Trek to Kalaupapa** (Molokai): The only access to this hauntingly beautiful and remote place is by foot, mule, or nine-seater plane. Hikers can descend the 26 switchbacks on the sea cliff's narrow 3-mile trail, but the **Kalaupapa Guided Mule Ride** (p. 376) is a once-in-a-lifetime adventure astride sure-footed mules. Once you've reached the peninsula, you'll board the **Damien Tours** bus (p. 378)—your transport back to a time when islanders with Hansen's Disease (leprosy) were exiled to Molokai and Father Damien devoted his life to care for them.

THE best OUTDOOR ADVENTURES

○ **Witness the Whales:** From December to April, humpback whales cruise Hawaiian waters. You can see these gentle giants from almost any shore; simply scan the horizon for a spout. You can hear them, too, by ducking your head below the surface and listening for their otherworldly music. Boats on every island offer whale-watching cruises, but Maui is your best bet for seeing the massive marine mammals up close. Try **Trilogy** (p. 285) for a first-class catamaran ride, or, if you're adventurous, climb into an outrigger canoe with **Hawaiian Paddle Sports** (p. 287).

Lava flowing into the sea.

○ **Visit Volcanoes:** The entire island chain is made of volcanoes; don't miss the opportunity to explore them. On Oahu, the whole family can hike to the top of ancient, world-famous **Diamond Head Crater** (p. 97). At **Hawaii Volcanoes National Park** (p. 182) on the Big Island, where Kilauea has been erupting since 1983, acres of new black rock and billowing sulfurous steam give hints of Pele's presence even when red-hot lava isn't visible. On Maui, **Haleakala National Park** (p. 294) provides a bird's-eye view into a long-dormant volcanic crater.

○ **Get Misted by Waterfalls:** Waterfalls thundering down into sparkling pools are some of Hawaii's most beautiful natural wonders. If you're on the Big Island, head to the spectacular 442-foot **Akaka Falls** (p. 170), north of Hilo. On Maui, the Road to Hana offers numerous viewing opportunities; at the end of the drive, you'll find **Oheo Gulch** (p. 274), with some of the most dramatic and accessible waterfalls on the islands. Kauai is laced with waterfalls, especially along the North Shore and in the Wailua area, where you can drive right up to 151-foot **Opaekaa Falls** (p. 433) and 80-foot **Wailua Falls** (p. 433). On Molokai, the 250-foot **Moaula Falls** (p. 374) can be visited only via a guided cultural hike through breathtaking Halawa Valley, but that, too, is a very special experience.

○ **Peer into Waimea Canyon** (Kauai): It may not share the vast dimensions of Arizona's Grand Canyon, but Kauai's colorful gorge—a mile wide, 3,600 feet deep, and 14 miles long—has a grandeur all its own, easily viewed from several overlooks just off Kokee Road. Hike to Waipoo Falls to experience its red parapets up close, or take one of the helicopter rides that swoop between its walls like the white-tailed tropicbird. See p. 443.

○ **Explore the Napali Coast** (Kauai): With the exception of the Kalalau Valley Overlook, the fluted ridges and deep, primeval valleys of the island's northwest portion can't be viewed by car. You must hike the 11-mile Kalalau Trail (p. 467), kayak (p. 456), take a snorkel cruise (p. 458), or book a helicopter ride (p. 445) to experience its wild, stunning beauty.

○ **Four-Wheel It on Lanai** (Lanai) Off-roading is a way of life on barely paved Lanai. Rugged trails lead to deserted beaches, abandoned villages, sacred sites, and valleys filled with wild game.

THE welcoming LEI

A lei is aloha turned tangible, communicating "hello," "goodbye," "congratulations," and "I love you" in a single strand of fragrant flowers. Leis are the perfect symbol for the islands: Their fragrance and beauty are enjoyed in the moment, but the aloha they embody lasts long after they've faded.

Traditionally, Hawaiians made leis out of flowers, shells, ferns, leaves, nuts, and even seaweed. Some were twisted, some braided, and some strung. Then, as now, they were worn to commemorate special occasions, honor a loved one, or complement a hula dancer's costume. Leis are available at all of the islands' airports, from florists, and even at supermarkets. You can find wonderful, inexpensive leis at the half-dozen lei shops on **Maunakea Street** in Honolulu's Chinatown, and at **Castillo Orchids,** 73-4310 Laui St., off Kaiminani Drive in the Kona Palisades subdivision, across from the Kona Airport on the Big Island (✆ **808/329-6070**). You can also arrange in advance to have a lei-greeter meet you as you deplane. **Greeters of Hawaii** (www.greetersof hawaii.com; ✆ **800/366-8559**) serves the major airports on Oahu, Maui, Kauai, and the Big Island.

THE best HOTELS

○ **Halekulani** (Oahu; www.halekulani.com; ✆ **800/367-2343**): When price is no object, this is really the only place to stay. A place of Zen amid the buzz, this beach hotel is the finest Waikiki has to offer. Even if you don't stay here, pop by for a sunset mai tai at House Without a Key to hear live Hawaiian music while a lovely hula dancer sways to the music. See p. 109.

○ **Royal Hawaiian** (Oahu; www.royal-hawaiian.com; ✆ **800/325-3535**): This flamingo-pink oasis, hidden away among blooming gardens within the concrete jungle of Waikiki, is a stunner. It's vibrant and exotic, from the

Four Seasons Resort Hualalai at Historic Kaupulehu, the Big Island.

Grand Hyatt Kauai.

Spanish-Moorish arches in the common spaces to the pink-and-gold pineapple wallpaper in the rooms in the Historic Wing. See p. 110.

o **Kahala Hotel & Resort** (Oahu; www.kahalaresort.com; ℂ 800/367-2525): Situated in one of Oahu's most prestigious residential areas, the Kahala provides the peace and serenity of a neighbor-island vacation, but with the conveniences of Waikiki just a 10-minute drive away. The lush, tropical grounds include an 800-foot, crescent-shaped beach and a 26,000-square-foot lagoon (home to two bottlenose dolphins, sea turtles, and tropical fish). See p. 114.

o **Four Seasons Resort Hualalai at Historic Kaupulehu** (Big Island; www.fourseasons.com/hualalai; ℂ 888/340-5662): The seven pools alone will put you in seventh heaven at this exclusive yet environmentally conscious oasis of understated luxury, which also offers a private, 18-hole golf course and an award-winning spa, exquisite dining, and impeccable service—with no resort fee. See p. 220.

o **Fairmont Orchid Hawaii** (Big Island; www.fairmont.com/orchid; ℂ 800/845-9905): Subtle elegance and warm service mark this recently renovated hotel on the Mauna Lanai Resort, which takes pride in the area's cultural treasures as well as its golf courses. See p. 225.

o **Hapuna Beach Prince Hotel** (Big Island; www.princeresortshawaii.com/hapuna-beach-prince-hotel; ℂ 888/977-4623): This is the sleeper on the Kohala Coast—boasting huge rooms, an enormous beach, and an exceptional restaurant, together with a relaxing, low-key atmosphere. See p. 226.

o **The Fairmont Kea Lani Maui** (Maui; www.fairmont.com/kealani; ℂ 800/659-4100): Each unit in this all-suites hotel has a kitchenette with granite countertop, living room with sofa bed (great for kids), spacious bedroom, and marble bathroom (head immediately for the deep soaking tub). Youngsters will enjoy building volcanoes in the 1,500-square-foot kids' club, while the entire family can get into rhythm paddling an outrigger canoe from the beach out front. See p. 319.

o **Travaasa Hana** (Maui; www.travaasa.com/hana; ℂ 808/248-8211): Nestled in the center of quaint Hana town, this 66-acre resort wraps around

Kauiki Head, the dramatic point where Queen Kaahumanu was born. You'll feel like royalty in one of the Sea Ranch Cottages here. Floor-to-ceiling sliding doors open to spacious lanais, some with private hot tubs. You'll be far from shopping malls and sports bars, but exotic red-, black-, and white-sand beaches are just a short walk or shuttle ride away. This is luxury in its purest form. See p. 327.

o **Four Seasons Resort Lanai at Manele Bay** (Lanai; www.fourseasons.com/lanai; © 800/321-4666): This gracious resort on Lanai's south coast overlooks Hulopoe Beach—one of the finest stretches of sand in the state. Each room has a semi-private lanai with a day bed from which you can gaze at the big blue Pacific to your heart's content. Other amenities include world-class restaurants, Adirondack chairs beneath swaying palms, and an exercise room with a view so grand that you'll forget you're burning calories on a stationary cycle. See p. 407.

o **Grand Hyatt Kauai Resort & Spa** (Kauai; www.kauai.hyatt.com; © 800/554-9288): At this sprawling, family-embracing resort in Poipu, the elaborate, multi-tiered fantasy pool and saltwater lagoon more than compensate for the rough waters of Shipwrecks (Keoneloa) Beach. Don't fret: Calmer Poipu Beach is just a short drive away. Anara Spa and Poipu Bay Golf Course offer excellent adult diversions, too. See p. 482.

o **Poipu Plantation B&B Inn and Vacation Rentals** (Kauai; www.poipubeach.com; © 800/643-0263): Just a short walk from Brennecke and Poipu beaches, a handsomely renovated 1938 cottage holds four bed-and-breakfast suites, with a half-dozen well-equipped cottage units sharing the quiet compound, managed by gracious innkeepers and their helpful staff. See p. 484.

THE best RESTAURANTS

o **Alan Wong's Restaurant** (Oahu; www.alanwongs.com; © 808/949-2526): Master strokes at this shrine of Hawaii Regional Cuisine include ginger-crusted fresh *onaga* (red snapper), a whole-tomato salad dressed with *li hing ume* (plum powder) vinaigrette, and *opihi* (limpet) shooters. Alan Wong reinvents local flavors for the fine-dining table in ways that continue to surprise and delight. See p. 131.

o **Izakaya Gaku** (Oahu; © 808/589-1329): The city is dotted with *izakayas*, Japanese pubs serving small plates made for sharing, and Izakaya Gaku is the best of them all. You'll discover life beyond maguro and hamachi nigiri with seasonal, uncommon seafood such as sea bass sashimi and grilled ray. Thanks to the large population of Japanese nationals living in Honolulu, the Japanese food here is some of the best outside of Japan. But it's not just straight-from-Tokyo fare at Gaku; the chefs here scour fish markets around town daily for the best local fish. See p. 131.

o **The Pig and the Lady** (Oahu; http://thepigandthelady.com; © 808/585-8255): This casual restaurant, with its traditional Vietnamese noodle soups and playful interpretations of Southeast Asian food, is both soulful and surprising. The soulful: the pho of the day, drawing on recipes from chef Andrew Le's mother. The surprising: hand-cut pasta with pork and *lilikoi* (passionfruit). The best of both worlds: a pho French dip banh mi, with slices of tender brisket and a cup of pho broth for dipping. See p. 129.

o **Vintage Cave** (Oahu; http://vintagecave.com; © **808/441-1744**): The interior is a bit odd: luxe-man-cave-meets-brick-lined art gallery (18 original Picasso drawings hang in the dining room), but the food is amazing. It's Honolulu's most stunning (and its priciest). There's only one menu a night, and it's constantly changing. The young chef, Chris Kajioka, sources near and far for his ingredients, from Big Island baby lettuces to *amadai* (tilefish) from Japan, and applies impeccable technique to it all. See p. 125.

o **Ka'ana Kitchen** (Maui; www.maui.andaz.hyatt.com; © **808/573-1234**): Treat Chef Isaac Bancaco's grid menu like a gourmet bingo card; every combo is a winner. Start off with a hand-mixed cocktail and the ahi tataki: ruby red tuna, heirloom tomato, and fresh burratta decorated with black salt and nasturtium petals. The $45 breakfast buffet grants you access to the kitchen's novel chilled countertops, stocked with every delicacy and fresh juice you could imagine. See p. 318.

o **Mama's Fish House** (Maui; www.mamasfishhouse.com; © **808/579-8488**): Overlooking Kuau Cove on Maui's north shore, this restaurant is a South Pacific fantasy. Every nook is decorated with some fanciful artifact of salt-kissed adventure. The menu lists the anglers who reeled in the day's catch; you can order ono "caught by Keith Nakamura along the 40-fathom ledge near Hana" or deep-water ahi seared with coconut and lime. The Tahitian Pearl dessert is almost too stunning to eat. Though pricey, a meal at Mama's is a complete experience. See p. 354.

o **Merriman's** (Waimea, Big Island, © **808/885-6822**; Kapalua, Maui, © **808/669-6400**; and Poipu, Kauai, © **808/742-8385**; www.merrimanshawaii. com): Chef Peter Merriman, one of the founders of Hawaii Regional Cuisine, oversees a locally inspired culinary empire that includes Merriman's and Monkeypod Kitchen outlets on Maui, Kauai (p. 498), and Oahu. He

Mama's Fish House, Maui.

completely renovated his original Waimea restaurant in 2014, adding a bar and Sunday brunch, but held onto his high standards under the direction of exciting young chef Zach Sato. See p. 240.

○ **Da Poke Shack** (Kailua-Kona, Big Island; www.dapokeshack.com; ✆ 808/ 329-7653): The islands' diced raw, marinated seafood specialty comes in many varieties at this hole in the wall, which prepares them so expertly that patrons make repeat visits just to try them all. See p. 234.

○ **Bar Acuda** (Hanalei, Kauai; www.restaurantbaracuda.com; ✆ 808/826-7081): When the sun goes down, the surfing set freshens up for a night on the town at this stylish tapas bar, created by a former star of San Francisco's culinary scene and centered around fresh seafood and seasonal pairings inspired by Mediterranean cuisine. See p. 492.

○ **The Beach House** (Poipu, Kauai; www.the-beach-house.com; ✆ 808/742-1424): Sunset should be listed as its own course on the menu here because everyone stops to ogle it or snap pictures from the oceanfront lawn. But the food, which is just as good at lunch, stands on its own merits, from a cracker-jack kitchen that was sourcing ingredients locally long before "farm-to-table" became a buzzword. See p. 495.

○ **Nobu Lanai** (Lanai; www.fourseasons.com/manelebay/dining; ✆ 808/565-2290): Lanai now ranks among New York, Milan, Budapest, and Mexico City as somewhere one can dine at a Nobu restaurant—a measure of how fun a place is, in the immortal words of pop star Madonna. The best way to experience this epicurean phenomenon is to order the *omakase*—the chef's tasting menu—for $120. Each dish is as delicious as it is artful. See p. 409.

THE best OF HAWAII FOR KIDS

○ **Aulani, a Disney Resort & Spa, Ko Olina, Hawaii** (Oahu; http://resorts. disney.go.com/aulani-hawaii-resort; ✆ 714/520-7001): Disney built this high-rise hotel and spa (with timeshare condos) on 21 acres on the beach, about an hour's drive from Waikiki. It's a great destination for families, with a full children's program, plus areas and activities for teens and tweens. Mickey, Minnie, Goofy, and other Disney characters walk the resort and stop to take photos with kids. See p. 116.

○ **Dole Pineapple Plantation** (Oahu; www.dole-plantation.com; ✆ 808/621-8408): Get the kids (and yourself!) a Dole Whip and fresh pineapple, and then take them through the main attraction: part maze, part scavenger hunt. They'll also enjoy the Pineapple Express, a short train ride on a single-engine diesel locomotive around the plantation's grounds. See p. 80.

○ **Build Sandcastles on Kailua Beach** (Oahu): This gorgeous beach is kid-friendly, with sand that slopes gently into the water. The waves vary in spots—perfect for the young ones to splash around and older kids to boogie board. The broad stretch of sand is also great for building castles. See p. 88.

○ **Slumber Party at the Aquarium** (Maui): Kids can book a sleepover in the Maui Ocean Center, staying up into the wee hours to watch glowing jellyfish and other nocturnal animals. See p. 263.

○ **Snorkel in Kealakekua Bay** (Big Island): Everyone can enjoy the dazzling display of marine life here on a **Fair Wind** cruise (www.fair-wind.com;

Dole Plantation, Oahu.

© **800/677-9461** or 808/322-2788), which offers inner tubes and underwater viewing boxes for little ones (or older ones) who don't want to get their faces wet. Two water slides and a spacious boat with a friendly crew also make this a treat. See p. 198.

○ **Play at Lydgate Park** (Kauai): If kids tire of snorkeling in the protected swimming area of Lydgate Beach, a giant wooden fantasy play structure and bridge to the dunes await, along with grassy fields and several miles of biking trails. See p. 432.

○ **Ride a Sugarcane Train** (Kauai): At **Kilohana Plantation** (p. 431), families can enjoy an inexpensive, narrated train ride through fields, forest, and orchards, with a stop to feed sheep, goats, and wild pigs.

2

SUGGESTED HAWAII ITINERARIES

F or most people, the fetching dollops of land in the middle of the Pacific Ocean are a dream destination—but their sheer distance from practically everywhere else makes getting here sometimes daunting. So once you finally arrive in the Hawaiian Islands, you'll want to make the most of your time. In this chapter we've built five 1-week itineraries for Oahu, the Big Island, Maui, and Kauai, each one designed to hit the highlights and provide a revealing window into the real Hawaii.

You can follow these itineraries to the letter or use them to build your own personalized trip. Whatever you do, *don't max out your days.* This is Hawaii, after all—allow time to do nothing but relax. Smell the sweet perfume of plumeria, listen to the wind rustling through a bamboo forest, and feel the caress of the gentle Pacific.

A WEEK ON OAHU

Oahu is so stunning that the *alii,* the kings of Hawaii, made it the capital of the island nation. Below, I've presumed that you are staying in Waikiki; if your hotel is in another location, be sure to factor in extra time for traveling.

DAY 1: Arrive & Hit Waikiki Beach ★★★

Unwind from your plane ride with a little sun and sand. Take a dip in the ocean at the most famous beach in the world: **Waikiki Beach** (p. 85). Catch the sunset with a mai tai, Hawaiian music, and some of the loveliest hula you'll ever see at **House Without a Key** (p. 142).

DAY 2: Visit Pearl Harbor ★★★ & Honolulu's Chinatown ★★★

Head to the **USS *Arizona* Memorial at Pearl Harbor** (p. 61), site of the infamous Pearl Harbor attack. You'll have reserved your ticket ahead of time online, so you'll skip the lines and head straight to the memorial. On your way back, stop in **Chinatown** for lunch and browse its trendy boutiques (p. 138). For dinner tonight, go local. Head to the **Highway Inn** (p. 126) for kalua pig, laulau, pipikaula, and poi.

DAY 3: Explore the North Shore ★★★

Fuel up on fresh fruit smoothies and chocolate banana bread at **Tucker & Bevvy** (p. 121) before heading to the **North Shore** (see "Central Oahu & the North Shore," on p. 80). Stop in the quaint town of **Haleiwa** for a pineapple-lilikoi-mango treat at **Matsumoto Shave Ice** (p. 83), and then grab a picnic lunch from **Beet Box Café** (p. 134). Pick one of the gorgeous North Shore beaches for a day of swimming and sunbathing. **Waimea Beach Park** (p. 90) is a favorite, no matter the season. In the winter, if the waves are

Facing page: Surfer in Waikiki.

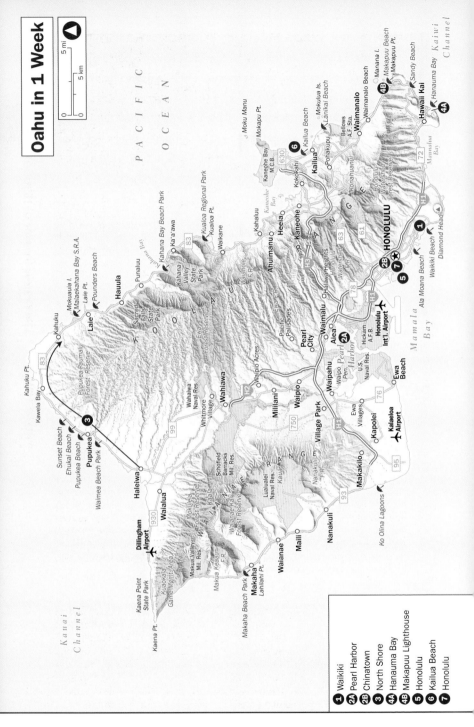

Oahu in 1 Week

1 Waikiki
2A Pearl Harbor
2B Chinatown
3 North Shore
4A Hanauma Bay
4B Makapuu Lighthouse
5 Honolulu
6 Kailua Beach
7 Honolulu

Waikiki Beach.

pumping and conditions are right, head to **Pipeline** (p. 83) and watch pro surfers ride this tube-like wave over razor-sharp reef. As you make your way back south, hit the **shrimp trucks at Kahuku** (p. 134). While there's still daylight, take the longer coastal road back into Honolulu. On the way back to Waikiki, stop at **Town** (p. 132) or **12th Ave Grill** (p. 132) for dinner.

DAY 4: Snorkel in Hanauma Bay ★★ & Hike the Makapuu Lighthouse Trail ★★

Head out early in the morning to grab a fried malasada dipped in sugar at **Leonard's Bakery** (p. 123) on your way to snorkeling at **Hanauma Bay** (p. 86). If you're a strong swimmer and the water is calm (check with the lifeguard), head out past the reef and away from the crowds, where the water's clearer and you'll see more fish and the occasional turtle. Continue beach-hopping down the coastline—check out **Sandy Beach** (p. 86) to watch body-surfing daredevils. Hike the **Makapuu Lighthouse** (p. 97), an easy trail with views to Molokai and Lanai on a clear day. In the winter, you may even see migrating humpback whales. Turn back to take the Pali Highway home to Waikiki—and be sure to stop at the **Nuuanu Pali Lookout** (p. 66).

DAY 5: Surf in Waikiki, Glimpse Historic Honolulu & Experience Hawaiian Culture

Waikiki has great waves for learning. Take an early-morning surf lesson (p. 95) and you'll be up on your board in no time. Poke at **Ono Seafood** (p. 122) makes a great post-surf meal. Then head to downtown Honolulu to see some of the city's historic sites, including the **Iolani Palace** (p. 60) and **Kawaiahao Church** (p. 61). Spend the afternoon at the **Bishop Museum** (p. 58) to immerse yourself in Hawaiian culture. Head up to **Puu Ualakaa State Park** (p. 67) to watch the sunset over Honolulu. For dinner, get a taste of Honolulu's spectacular Japanese cuisine at **Izakaya Gaku** (p. 131).

Iolani Palace.

DAY 6: Relax at Kailua Beach ★★★

On your last full day on Oahu, travel over the Pali Highway to the windward side of the island and spend a day at **Kailua Beach** (p. 88). Kailua is the perfect beach to kayak or stand-up paddle to the Mokulua Islands (or "the Mokes," as the locals call it) or simply relax. By now, you've gone native, cuisine-wise, so for your last dinner on Oahu, try local reinvented for fine dining at **Alan Wong's Restaurant** (p. 131).

DAY 7: Marvel at Shangri La ★★

Head to the **Honolulu Museum of Art** for your tour of **Shangri La** (p. 59), the private palace of tobacco heiress Doris Duke. Filled with Islamic art, the interior is stunning, but so is the location, on a cliff facing Diamond Head and overlooking a hidden surf break. Pick up souvenirs at the museum's gift shop. On your way to the airport, be sure to stop at one of the **Maunakea Street lei shops** (p. 140) in Chinatown to buy a sweet-smelling souvenir of your trip.

A WEEK ON THE BIG ISLAND OF HAWAII

Because of the distances involved, a week is barely enough time to see the entire Big Island; it's best to plan for 2 weeks—or even better, a return visit. Nevertheless, here is a way to see most of the highlights, changing hotels as you go.

DAY 1: Arrive & Amble Through Kailua-Kona ★★★

Since most flights arrive at lunchtime or later, check into your Kona Coast lodgings and go for a stroll through historic **Kailua-Kona,** including **Hulihee Palace** (p. 157) and **Mokuaikaua Church** (p. 159). Wear sandals so you can dip your feet in one of the pocket coves, such as Kamakahonu Bay,

5A Puukohola Heiau
National Historical Park

5B Lapakahi State Park

5C King Kamehameha's Statue

5D Pololu Valley Overlook

5E Puako Petroglyph
Archaeological District

6A Kohala Coast Beaches

6B Mauna Kea

7A Kekaha Kai State Park

7B Kona coffee farms

7C Spa Without Walls

1 Kailua-Kona

2A Kealakekua Bay

2B Puuhonua O Honaunau
National Historical Park

2C Kau Coffee Mill

3 Hawaii Volcanoes National Park

4A Hilo

4B Akaka Falls

4C Hamakua Coast

4D Waipio Valley Overlook

4E Waimea

within sight of **Kamehameha's historic compound,** and enjoy an early dinner at an ocean-view restaurant to view a spectacular sunset. Don't unpack—you'll be on the road early the next day, taking advantage of your internal clock's Mainland time.

DAY 2: A Morning Sail & Afternoon Drive ★★★

The day starts with a morning snorkel tour (plus breakfast and lunch) aboard the *Fair Wind II* (p. 198), sailing to the historic preserve of **Kealakekua Bay.** After returning to Keauhou Bay, head south to **Hawaii Volcanoes National Park** (p. 182), by way of **Puuhonua O Honaunau National Historical Park** (p. 163) and the **Kau Coffee Mill** (p. 185), for a pick-me-up. Check into **Volcano Village** lodgings (p. 231) or **Volcano House** (p. 232) in the park, where you'll dine in full view of Kilauea's fiery evening glow.

Hawaii Volcanoes National Park.

DAY 3: Explore an Active Volcano ★★★

Stop at the national park's **Kilauea Visitor Center** to learn about current lava viewing (if any) and the day's free ranger-led walks. Take **Crater Rim Road** past billowing **Halemaumau Crater** (p. 182) to see **Thurston Lava Tube** (p. 183), **Devastation Trail** (p. 215), and other sights before driving down **Chain of Craters Road,** leading to a vast petroglyph field and the 2003 lava flow that smothered the roadway. After sunset, visit the **Thomas A. Jaggar Museum** (open till 7:30pm; p. 183) and its observation deck for yet another look at Pele's power.

DAY 4: Tour Old Hawaii ★★★

It's just a 45-minute drive from Volcano to **Hilo** (p. 175), so after breakfast go to the **Imiloa: Astronomy Center of Hawaii** (p. 177), opening at 9am. Then explore **Banyan Drive** (p. 175), **Liliuokalani Gardens** (p. 175), and one of Hilo's small but intriguing museums, such as the free **Mokupapapa Discovery Center** (p. 178). Stroll through **Nani Mau Gardens** (p. 178) or **Hawaii Tropical Botanical Garden** (p. 171) before driving along the pastoral **Hamakua Coast** (p. 229), stopping at breathtaking **Akaka Falls** (p. 170) and the similarly stunning **Waipio Valley Lookout** (p. 173). Dine on farm-fresh cuisine in **Waimea** or **Kawaihae** (p. 239) before checking into your Kohala Coast hotel.

DAY 5: Step Back in Time on the Kohala Coast ★★★

Start by exploring **Puukohola Heiau National Historic Site** (p. 164), the temple Kamehameha built to the war god, Ku, and sign up for a free ride on a traditional outrigger sailing canoe. Continue north on Hwy. 270 to **Lapakahi State Historical Park** (p. 166) to see the outlines of a 14th-century Hawaiian village, and have lunch in Hawi or Kapaau, home of the original **King Kamehameha Statue** (p. 166) in Kapaau. The final northbound stop is the picturesque **Pololu Valley Lookout** (p. 167). Heading

The Pololu Valley Lookout.

south in the late afternoon, stop at the **Puako Petroglyph Archaeological Preserve** (p. 165). To learn more Hawaiian lore, book one of Kohala's evening **luaus** (p. 250).

DAY 6: Sand, Sea & Stars ★★★

You've earned a morning at the beach, and the Big Island's prettiest are on the Kohala Coast: **Anaehoomalu Bay (A-Bay), Hapuna,** and **Kaunaoa** (see "Beaches," p. 188). Skip the scuba, though, because in the afternoon you're heading up the 13,796-foot **Mauna Kea** (p. 167), sacred to Hawaiians and revered by astronomers. Let an expert with 4WD, cold-weather gear, and telescopes for stargazing take you there: **Mauna Kea Summit Adventures** (p. 169) or **Hawaii Forest & Trail** (p. 169).

DAY 7: Spa, Beach, or Coffee Time ★★★

On your last full day, visit one of North Kona's gorgeous beaches hidden behind lava fields, such as **Kekaha Kai State Park** (p. 190) or the tranquil cove at **Kaloko-Honokohau National Historical Park** (p. 157) in the morning. In the afternoon, relax with a spa treatment at the Fairmont Orchid Hawaii's **Spa Without Walls** (p. 225) or another Kohala resort spa, or tour a **Kona coffee farm** (p. 160), and pick up gourmet beans as souvenirs.

A WEEK ON MAUI

You'll need at least a week to savor Maui's best experiences. I recommend splitting your vacation between East and West Maui, starting with sultry, sunny beaches and ending in the rejuvenating rainforest. I've designed this itinerary around a stay in West Maui for the first 3 days, but it works just as well if you stay in Wailea or Kihei. To minimize driving, move your headquarters to lush East Maui on Day 4. Stay at one of the island's charming B&Bs or the exquisite Traavasa Hana resort.

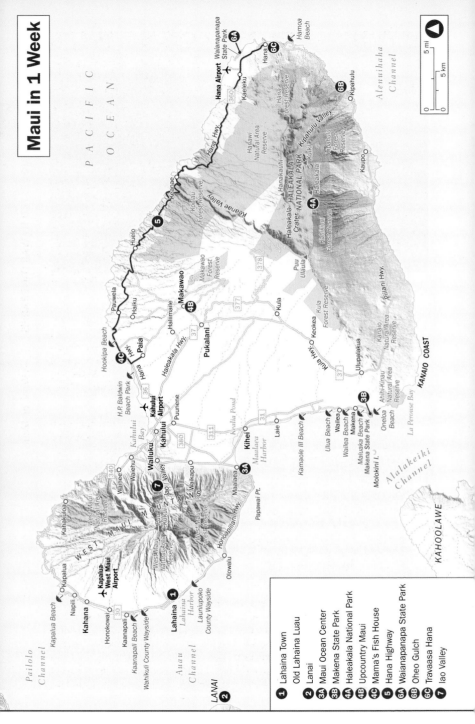

Maui in 1 Week

Legend:

1. Lahaina Town
2. Old Lahaina Luau
3A. Maui Ocean Center
3B. Makena State Park
4A. Haleakala National Park
4B. Upcountry Maui
4C. Mama's Fish House
5. Hana Highway
6A. Waianapanapa State Park
6B. Oheo Gulch
6C. Travaasa Hana
7. Iao Valley

Old Lahaina Luau.

DAY 1: Arrive & Explore West Maui

After checking into your hotel, head immediately for one of West Maui's prime beaches (p. 227). After a reviving dip in the ocean, spend a couple of hours walking around the historic old town of **Lahaina** (p. 254). As the sun sets, immerse yourself in Hawaiian culture at **Old Lahaina Luau** (p. 364).

DAY 2: Sail to Lanai

You'll likely wake up early on your first morning here, so take advantage and board an early-morning trip with **Trilogy** (p. 285) the best sailing/snorkeling operation in Hawaii. You'll spend the day (breakfast and lunch included) sailing to Lanai, snorkeling, touring the island, and sailing back to Lahaina. You'll have the afternoon free to shop or nap.

DAY 3: Sunbathe in South Maui

Take a drive out to **Makena State Beach Park** (p. 282) and soak in the raw beauty of this wild shore. On the way, pay a visit to the sharks and sea turtles at the **Maui Ocean Center** (p. 263), in Maalaea. Linger in South Maui to enjoy the sunset and dine at one of the area's terrific restaurants (recommendations start on p. 331).

DAY 4: Ascend a 10,000-Foot Volcano

Head to the 10,023-foot summit of **Haleakala,** the island's massive dormant volcano. Witnessing the sunrise here can be phenomenal (as well as mind-numbingly cold and crowded). Hiking in the **Haleakala National Park** (p. 266) is awe-inspiring any time of day. On your way back down the mountain, stop and tour **Upcountry Maui** (p. 265), particularly the communities of **Kula, Makawao,** and **Paia.** Plan for a sunset dinner in Paia at **Mama's Fish House** (p. 354). Stay at a nearby B&B or the chic **Paia Inn** (p. 324).

DAY 5: Drive the Hana Highway

Pack a lunch and spend the entire day driving the scenic **Hana Highway** (p. 269). Pull over often and get out to take photos, smell the flowers, and jump in mountain-stream pools. Wave to everyone, move off the road for those speeding by, and breathe in Hawaii. Spend the night in Hana (hotel recommendations start on p. 327).

DAY 6: Relax in Heavenly Hana

Take an early-morning hike along the black sands of **Waianapanapa State Park** (p. 283), and then explore the tiny town of **Hana** (p. 273). Be sure to see the **Hana Cultural Center & Museum** (p. 273), **Hasegawa General Store,** and **Hana Coast Gallery.** Get a picnic lunch and drive out to the Kipahulu end of Haleakala National Park at **Oheo Gulch** (p. 274). Hike to the waterfalls and swim in the pools. Splurge on dinner at the **Travaasa Hana** hotel (p. 327).

DAY 7: Relax & Shop

Depending on how much time you have on your final day, you can relax on the beach, get pampered in a spa, or shop for souvenirs. Spa-goers have a range of terrific spas to choose from, and fashionistas should check out the boutiques in **Makawao** and **Paia** (recommendations start on p. 361). If you have time, check out the gardens and waterfalls at **Iao Valley** (p. 260).

A WEEK ON KAUAI

Because much of the Garden Island, including the Napali Coast, is inaccessible to cars, a week will *just* suffice to view its beauty. To save driving time, split your stay between the North and South shores (detailed below) or stay on the East Side, but avoid the main road at rush hour.

DAY 1: Arrival, Lunch & a Scenic Drive ★★★

From the airport, stop by **Hamura's Saimin Stand** (p. 490) or another **Lihue** lunch counter (see "Plate Lunch, Bento & Poke," p. 490) for a classic taste of Kauai, before driving through the bustling Coconut Coast on your way to the serenity of the rural **North Shore** (p. 433). Soak in the views at the **Kilauea Point National Wildlife Refuge & Lighthouse** (p. 435), and then poke around Kilauea's **Kong Lung Historic Market Center** (p. 503). After checking in to your lodgings, pick up snorkel gear for the next day.

DAY 2: North Shore Hiking, Snorkeling & Exploring ★★★

Thanks to the time difference, you'll have a head start driving across the nine one-lane bridges on the way to the end of the road and popular **Kee Beach** (p. 450). If conditions permit, hike at least a half-hour out on the challenging **Kalalau Trail** (p. 467), for glimpses of the stunning **Napali Coast,** or tackle the first 2 miles to **Hanakapiai Beach,** 3 to 4 hours round-trip. After (or instead of) hiking, snorkel at **Kee** and equally gorgeous **Tunnels (Makua) Beach** (p. 451), accessed from **Haena Beach Park** (p. 451). Eat lunch in Haena, and then spend time in the jewel-box setting of **Limahuli Garden and Preserve** (p. 435). Return to Hanalei to explore

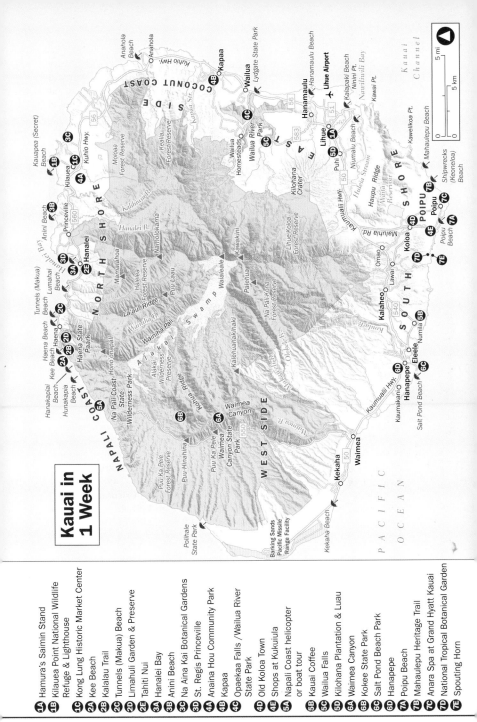

Kauai in
1 Week

- **1A** Hamura's Saimin Stand
- **1B** Kilauea Point National Wildlife
  Refuge & Lighthouse
- **1C** Kong Lung Historic Market Center
- **2A** Kee Beach
- **2B** Kalalau Trail
- **2C** Tunnels (Makua) Beach
- **2D** Limahuli Garden & Preserve
- **2E** Tahiti Nui
- **3A** Hanalei Bay
- **3B** Anini Beach
- **3C** Na Aina Kai Botanical Gardens
- **3D** St. Regis Princeville
- **4A** Anaina Hou Community Park
- **4B** Kapaa
- **4C** Opaekaa Falls /Wailua River
  State Park
- **4D** Old Koloa Town
- **4E** Shops at Kukuiula
- **5A** Napali Coast helicopter
  or boat tour
- **5B** Kauai Coffee
- **5C** Wailua Falls
- **6A** Kilohana Plantation & Luau
- **6B** Waimea Canyon
- **6C** Kokee State Park
- **6D** Salt Pond Beach Park
- **7A** Hanapepe
- **7B** Poipu Beach
- **7C** Mahaulepu Heritage Trail
- **7D** Anara Spa at Grand Hyatt Kauai
- **7E** National Tropical Botanical Garden
- **7E** Spouting Horn

23

Kayaking in Hanalei River.

shops and galleries; after dinner, enjoy live Hawaiian music at the venerable **Tahiti Nui** (p. 507).

DAY 3: More Adventures in & Around Hanalei ★★★

Taking advantage of the ocean's calmer morning conditions, the day begins on **Hanalei Bay, kayaking, surfing,** or **snorkeling** (see "Watersports," p. 454), or just frolicking at one of the three different beach parks (p. 446). If the waves are too rough, head instead to lagoon-like **Anini Beach** (p. 449). In the afternoon, try ziplining (p. 470) or horseback riding (p. 468) amid waterfalls and green mountains; the less adventurous (who've booked in advance) can tour delightful **Na Aina Kai Botanical Gardens** (p. 436). Savor views of Hanalei Bay and "Bali Hai" over cocktails at the **St. Regis Princeville** (p. 479) before dinner at **Bar Acuda** (p. 492).

DAY 4: Nature & Culture En Route to Poipu ★★

After breakfast, head south. Visit Kilauea's **Anaina Hou Community Park** (p. 433) for Kauai-themed mini-golf in a botanical garden or a hike or bike (rentals available) along the scenic Wai Koa loop trail. Stop for a bite to eat at a funky cafe in **Kapaa,** and then drive to **Opaekaa Falls** and see the cultural sites of **Wailua River State Park** (p. 433). After crossing through busy Lihue, admire the scenery on the way to **Old Koloa Town** (p. 504), where you can browse the quaint shops before checking into your Poipu lodgings. Pick a dinner spot from the many choices in the **Shops at Kukuiula,** such as **Merriman's Gourmet Pizza and Burgers** (p. 498).

DAY 5: Napali by Boat or Helicopter ★★★

Today you splurge on a **snorkel boat** or **Zodiac raft tour** (p. 454) to the fluted ridges and pristine valleys of the **Napali Coast,** or a **helicopter**

Napali Coast from helicopter.

tour (p. 445) that provides amazing views of Napali, Waimea Canyon, waterfalls, and more. In either case, it's an unforgettable experience—but don't book this for your last day, in case weather forces rescheduling. After your boat returns, hoist a draft beer at **Kauai Island Brewery & Grill** (p. 500) or try the free samples at nearby **Kauai Coffee.** For helicopter tours, most of which depart from Lihue, book a late-morning tour (after rush hour); have lunch in Lihue, and then drive to **Wailua Falls** (p. 420) before perusing the shops, tasting rum, or riding the train at **Kilohana Plantation** (p. 431), which also hosts the island's best **luau** (p. 432).

DAY 6: Waimea Canyon & Kokee State Park ★★★

Start your drive early to "the Grand Canyon of the Pacific," **Waimea Canyon** (p. 443), which you'll view from several breathtaking overlooks from Highway 550 (Kokee Rd.). Stay on the road through forested **Kokee State Park** (p. 441) to the **Kalalau Valley Lookout** (p. 437), and wait for any mists to part for a magnificent view. Stop by the **Kokee Museum** (p. 468) for trail information for a hike after lunch at **Kokee Lodge** (p. 501). If you're not a hiker, hit the waves at **Salt Pond Beach** or stroll through rustic **Hanapepe** (p. 505), home to a **Friday night art walk** (p. 508).

DAY 7: Beach, Sightseeing & Spa Time in Poipu ★★★

Spend the morning at glorious **Poipu Beach** (p. 452) before the crowds arrive, and then head over to **Shipwrecks (Keoneloa) Beach** (p. 453) to hike along the coastal **Mahaulepu Heritage Trail** (p. 467). Later, indulge in a spa treatment at Anara Spa at the **Grand Hyatt Kauai** (p. 482) or take a tour (booked in advance) at the **National Tropical Botanical Garden** (p. 439). Check out the flume of **Spouting Horn** (p. 441) before sunset cocktails at **RumFire Poipu Beach** in the **Sheraton Kauai** (p. 483) and dinner at the **Beach House** (p. 495) or **Red Salt** (p. 498).

HAWAII IN CONTEXT

by *Shannon Wianecki*

3

Since the Polynesians ventured across the Pacific to the Hawaiian Islands 1,000 years ago, these floating jewels have continued to call visitors from around the globe.

Located in one of the most remote and isolated places on the planet, the islands bask in the warm waters of the Pacific, where they are blessed by a tropical sun and cooled by gentle year-round trade winds—creating what might be the most ideal climate imaginable. Mother Nature has carved out verdant valleys, hung brilliant rainbows in the sky, and trimmed the islands with sandy beaches in a spectrum of colors. The indigenous Hawaiian culture embodies the "spirit of aloha," an easy-going generosity that takes the shape of flower leis freely given, monumental feasts shared with friends and family, and hypnotic Hawaiian melodies played late into the tropical night.

Visitors are drawn to Hawaii not only for its incredible beauty, but also for its opportunities for adventure. Go on, gaze into that fiery volcano, swim in a sea of rainbow-colored fish, tee off on a championship golf course, hike through a rainforest to hidden waterfalls, and kayak into the deep end of the ocean, where whales leap out of the water for reasons still mysterious. Looking for rest and relaxation? You'll discover that life moves at an unhurried pace here. Extra doses of sun and sea allow both body and mind to recharge.

Hawaii is a sensory experience that will remain with you, locked in your memory, long after your tan fades. Years later, a sweet fragrance, the sun's warmth on your face, or the sound of the ocean breeze will deliver you back to the time you spent in the Hawaiian Islands.

THE FIRST HAWAIIANS

The Hawaiian Islands were born of violent volcanic eruptions that took place deep beneath the ocean's surface about 70 million years ago and continue today. As each island emerged, the wind and rain began to carve beauty from barren rock. Molten mountains spewed forth rivers of fire that cooled into stone. Severe tropical storms battered and blasted the cooling lava rock. Ferocious earthquakes and persistent rains formed the islands into precipitous valleys, jagged cliffs, and recumbent flatlands. The result of several million years' worth of natural sculpture is a tropical dreamscape of flora and fauna, ringed by coral reefs.

Throughout the Middle Ages, while Western sailors clung to the edges of continents for fear of falling off the earth's edge, Polynesian voyagers crisscrossed the planet's largest ocean. The first people to colonize Hawaii were unsurpassed navigators. Using the stars, birds, and currents as guides, they sailed double-hulled canoes across thousands of miles, zeroing in on tiny islands in the center of the Pacific. They packed their vessels with food, plants, medicine, tools, and animals: everything necessary for building a new life on a distant shore. Over a

Facing page: Fire dancers.

span of 800 years, the great Polynesian migration connected a vast triangle of islands stretching from New Zealand to Hawaii to Easter Island and encompassing the many diverse archipelagos in between. Archaeologists surmise that Hawaii's first wave of settlers came via the Marquesas Islands sometime after A.D. 1000, though oral histories suggest a much earlier date.

Over the ensuing centuries, a distinctly Hawaiian culture arose. Sailors became farmers and fishermen. These early Hawaiians were as skilled on land as they had been at sea; they built highly productive fish ponds, aqueducts to irrigate terraced *kalo loi* (taro patches), and 3-acre *heiau* (temples) with 50-foot-high rock walls. Farmers cultivated more than 400 varieties of *kalo,* their staple food; 300 types of sweet potato; and 40 different bananas. Each variety served a different need—some were drought resistant, others medicinal, and others good for babies. Hawaiian women fashioned intricately patterned *kapa* (barkcloth)—some of the finest in all of Polynesia. Each of the Hawaiian Islands was its own kingdom, governed by *alii* (high-ranking chiefs) who drew their authority from an established caste system and *kapu* (taboos). Those who broke the *kapu* could be sacrificed.

The ancient Hawaiian creation chant, the *Kumulipo,* depicts a universe that began when heat and light emerged out of darkness, followed by the first life form: a coral polyp. The 2,000-line epic poem is a grand genealogy, describing how all species are interrelated, from gently waving seaweeds to mighty human warriors. It is the basis for the Hawaiian concept of *kuleana,* a word that simultaneously refers to privilege and responsibility. To this day, Native Hawaiians view the care of their natural resources as filial duty and honor.

WESTERN CONTACT
Cook's Ill-Fated Voyage

In the dawn hours of January 18, 1778, Captain James Cook of the HMS *Resolution* spotted an unfamiliar set of islands, which he later named for his benefactor, the Earl of Sandwich. The 50-year-old sea captain was already famous in Britain for "discovering" much of the South Pacific. Now on his third great voyage of exploration, Cook had set sail from Tahiti northward across uncharted waters. He was searching for the mythical Northwest Passage that was said to link the Pacific and Atlantic oceans. On his way, he stumbled upon Hawaii (aka the Sandwich Isles) quite by chance.

With the arrival of the *Resolution,* Stone Age Hawaii entered the age of iron. Sailors swapped nails and munitions for fresh water, pigs, and the affections of Hawaiian women. Tragically, the foreigners brought with them a terrible cargo: syphilis, measles, and other diseases that decimated the Hawaiian people. Captain Cook estimated the native population at 400,000 in 1778. (Later historians claim it could have been as high as 900,000.) By the time Christian missionaries arrived 40 years later, the number of Native Hawaiians had plummeted to just 150,000.

In a skirmish over a stolen boat, Cook was killed by a blow to the head. His British countrymen sailed home, leaving Hawaii forever altered. The islands were now on the sea charts, and traders on the fur route between Canada and China stopped here to get fresh water. More trade—and more disastrous liaisons—ensued.

Two more sea captains left indelible marks on the Islands. The first was American John Kendrick, who in 1791 filled his ship with fragrant Hawaiian sandalwood and sailed to China. By 1825, Hawaii's sandalwood groves were gone. The second was Englishman George Vancouver, who in 1793 left behind cows and sheep, which ventured out to graze in the islands' native forest and hastened the spread of invasive species. King Kamehameha I sent for cowboys from Mexico and Spain to round up the wild livestock, thus beginning the islands' *paniolo* (cowboy) tradition.

King Kamehameha.

King David Kalakaua.

King Kamehameha I was an ambitious *alii* who used western guns to unite the islands under single rule. After his death in 1819, the tightly woven Hawaiian society began to unravel. One of his successors, Queen Kaahumanu, abolished the *kapu* system, opening the door for religion of another form.

Staying to Do Well

In April 1820, missionaries bent on converting Hawaiians arrived from New England. The newcomers clothed the natives, banned them from dancing the hula, and nearly dismantled the ancient culture. The churchgoers tried to keep sailors and whalers out of the bawdy houses, where whiskey flowed and the virtue of native women was never safe. To their credit, the missionaries created a 12-letter alphabet for the Hawaiian language, taught reading and writing, started a printing press, and began recording the islands' history, which until that time had been preserved solely in memorized chants.

Children of the missionaries became business leaders and politicians. They married Hawaiians and stayed on in the islands, causing one wag to remark that the missionaries "came to do good and stayed to do well." In 1848, King Kamehameha III enacted the Great Mahele (division). Intended to guarantee Native Hawaiians rights to their land, it ultimately enabled foreigners to take ownership of vast tracts of land. Within two generations, more than 80 percent of all private land was in *haole* (foreign) hands. Businessmen planted acre after acre in sugarcane and imported waves of immigrants to work the fields: Chinese starting in 1852, Japanese in 1885, and Portuguese in 1878.

King David Kalakaua was elected to the throne in 1874. This popular "Merrie Monarch" built Iolani Palace in 1882, threw extravagant parties, and lifted the prohibitions on the hula and other native arts. For this, he was much loved. He proclaimed that "hula is the language of the heart and, therefore, the heartbeat of the Hawaiian people." He also gave Pearl Harbor to the United States; it became the westernmost bastion of the U.S. Navy. While visiting chilly San Francisco in 1891, King Kalakaua caught a cold and died in the royal suite of the Sheraton Palace. His sister, Queen Liliuokalani, assumed the throne.

IS EVERYONE hawaiian IN HAWAII?

The sugar and pineapple plantations brought so many different people to Hawaii that the state is now a remarkable potpourri of ethnic groups: Native Hawaiians were joined by **Caucasians, Japanese, Chinese, Filipinos, Koreans, Portuguese, Puerto Ricans, Samoans, Tongans, Tahitians,** and other **Asian and Pacific Islanders.** Add to that a sprinkling of **Vietnamese, Canadians, African Americans, American Indians, South** **Americans,** and **Europeans** of every stripe. Many people retain an element of the traditions of their homeland. Some Japanese Americans in Hawaii, generations removed from the homeland, are more traditional than the Japanese of Tokyo. The same is true of many Chinese, Koreans, and Filipinos, making Hawaii a kind of living museum of Asian and Pacific cultures.

The Overthrow

For years, a group of American sugar plantation owners and missionary descendants had been machinating against the monarchy. On January 17, 1893, with the support of the U.S. minister to Hawaii and the Marines, the conspirators imprisoned Queen Liliuokalani in her own palace. To avoid bloodshed, she abdicated the throne, trusting that the United States government would right the wrong. As the Queen waited in vain, she penned the sorrowful lyric "Aloha Oe," Hawaii's song of farewell.

U.S. President Grover Cleveland's attempt to restore the monarchy was thwarted by congress. Sanford Dole, a powerful sugar plantation owner, appointed himself president of the newly declared Republic of Hawaii. His fellow sugarcane planters, known as the Big Five, controlled banking, shipping, hardware, and every other facet of economic life on the islands. In 1898, through annexation, Hawaii became an American territory ruled by Dole.

Oahu's central Ewa Plain soon filled with row crops. The Dole family planted pineapple on its sprawling acreage. Planters imported more contract laborers from Puerto Rico (1900), Korea (1903), and the Philippines (1907–31). Many of the new immigrants stayed on to establish families and become a part of the islands. Meanwhile, Native Hawaiians became a landless minority. Their language was banned in schools and their cultural practices devalued, forced into hiding.

For nearly a century in Hawaii, sugar was king, generously subsidized by the U.S. government. Sugar is a thirsty crop, and plantation owners oversaw the construction of flumes and aqueducts that channeled mountain streams down to parched plains, where waving fields of cane soon grew. The waters that once fed taro patches dried up. The sugar planters dominated the territory's economy, shaped its social fabric, and kept the islands in a colonial plantation era with bosses and field hands. But the workers eventually went on strike for higher wages and improved working conditions, and the planters found themselves unable to compete with cheap third-world labor costs.

Tourism Takes Hold

Tourism in Hawaii began in the 1860s. Kilauea volcano was one of the world's prime attractions for adventure travelers. In 1865, a grass Volcano House was built on the rim of Halemaumau Crater to shelter visitors; it was Hawaii's first tourist hotel. But the visitor industry really got off the ground with the demise of the plantation era.

In 1901, W. C. Peacock built the elegant Beaux Arts Moana Hotel on Waikiki Beach, and W. C. Weedon convinced Honolulu businessmen to bankroll his plan to advertise Hawaii in San Francisco. Armed with a stereopticon and tinted photos of Waikiki, Weedon sailed off in 1902 for 6 months of lecture tours to introduce "those remarkable people and the beautiful lands of Hawaii." He drew packed houses. A tourism promotion bureau was formed in 1903, and about 2,000 visitors came to Hawaii that year.

The steamship was Hawaii's tourism lifeline. It took 4½ days to sail from San Francisco to Honolulu. Streamers, leis, and pomp welcomed each Matson liner at downtown's Aloha Tower. Well-heeled visitors brought trunks, servants, and Rolls-Royces and stayed for months. Hawaiians amused visitors with personal tours, floral parades, and shows spotlighting that naughty dance, the hula.

Beginning in 1935 and running for the next 40 years, Webley Edwards's weekly live radio show, "Hawaii Calls," planted the sounds of Waikiki—surf, sliding steel guitar, sweet Hawaiian harmonies, drumbeats—in the hearts of millions of listeners in the United States, Australia, and Canada.

By 1936, visitors could fly to Honolulu from San Francisco on the *Hawaii Clipper,* a seven-passenger Pan American Martin M-130 flying boat, for $360 one-way. The flight took 21 hours, 33 minutes. Modern tourism was born, with five flying boats providing daily service. The 1941 visitor count was a brisk 31,846 through December 6.

World War II & Its Aftermath

On December 7, 1941, Japanese Zeros came out of the rising sun to bomb American warships based at Pearl Harbor. This was the "day of infamy" that plunged the United States into World War II.

The attack brought immediate changes to the islands. Martial law was declared, stripping the Big Five cartel of its absolute power in a single day. Japanese Americans and German Americans were interned. Hawaii was "blacked out" at night, Waikiki Beach was strung with barbed wire, and Aloha Tower was painted in camouflage. Only young men bound for the Pacific came to Hawaii during the war years. Many came back to graves in a cemetery called Punchbowl.

SPEAKING hawaiian

Most everyone in Hawaii speaks English. But many folks now also speak *olelo Hawaii,* the native language of these Islands. You will regularly hear *aloha* and *mahalo* (thank you). If you've just arrived, you're a *malihini.* Someone who's been here a long time is a *kamaaina.* When you finish a job or your meal, you are *pau* (finished). On Friday, it's *pau hana,* work finished. You eat *pupu* (Hawaii's version of hors d'oeuvres) when you go *pau hana.*

The Hawaiian alphabet, created by the New England missionaries, has only 12 letters: the five regular vowels (*a, e, i, o,* and *u*) and seven consonants (*h, k, l, m, n, p,* and *w*). The vowels are pronounced in the Roman fashion: that is, *ah, ay, ee, oh,* and *oo* (as in "too")—not *ay, ee, eye, oh,* and *you,* as in English. For example, *huhu* is pronounced *who-who.* Most vowels are sounded separately, though some are pronounced together, as in Kalakaua: "kah-lah-*cow*-ah."

The postwar years saw the beginnings of Hawaii's faux culture. The authentic traditions had long been suppressed, and into the void flowed a consumable brand of aloha. Harry Yee invented the Blue Hawaii cocktail and dropped in a tiny Japanese parasol. Vic Bergeron created the mai tai, a drink made of rum and fresh lime juice, and opened Trader Vic's, America's first themed restaurant that featured the art, decor, and food of Polynesia. Arthur Godfrey picked up a ukulele and began singing *hapa-haole* tunes on early TV shows. In 1955, Henry J. Kaiser built the Hilton Hawaiian Village, and the 11-story high-rise Princess Kaiulani Hotel opened on a site where the real princess once played. Hawaii greeted 109,000 visitors that year.

Statehood

In 1959, Hawaii became the 50th state of the United States. That year also saw the arrival of the first jet airliners, which brought 250,000 tourists to the state. Aloha spirit began to buckle under the sheer force of numbers. Waikiki's room count nearly doubled in 2 years, from 16,000 units in 1969 to 31,000 in 1971, and kept increasing until city fathers finally clamped down on growth. By 1980, annual arrivals had reached 4 million.

In the early 1980s, the Japanese began traveling overseas in record numbers, bringing with them plenty of yen to spend. Their effect on sales in Hawaii was phenomenal: European boutiques opened branches in Honolulu, and duty-free shopping became the main supporter of Honolulu International Airport. Japanese investors competed for the chance to own or build part of Hawaii. Hotels sold so fast and at such unbelievable prices that heads began to spin with dollar signs.

In 1986, Hawaii's visitor count passed 5 million. Two years later, it went over 6 million. Fantasy megaresorts bloomed on the neighbor islands like giant artificial flowers, swelling the luxury market with ever-swanker accommodations. The visitor count was at a record 6.7 million in 1990 when the Gulf War and worldwide recessions burst the bubble in early 1991. The following year, Hurricane Iniki devastated Kauai. Airfare wars sent Americans to Mexico and the Caribbean. Overbuilt with luxury hotels, Hawaii slashed its room rates, giving middle-class consumers access to high-end digs at affordable prices—a trend that continues as Hawaii struggles to stay atop the tourism heap. Still, Hawaii's tourism industry had a record-breaking 2013, welcoming more than 8.2 million visitors, who spent a whopping $14.5 billion. The machine that runs Hawaii's economy appears to be back on track.

HAWAII TODAY
A Cultural Renaissance

Despite the ever-increasing influx of foreign people and customs, the Native Hawaiian culture is experiencing a rebirth. It began in earnest in 1976, when members of the Polynesian Voyaging Society launched *Hokulea,* a double-hulled canoe of the sort that hadn't been seen on these shores in centuries. The *Hokulea's* daring crew sailed her 2,500 miles to Tahiti without using modern instruments, relying instead on ancient navigational techniques. Most historians at that time discounted Polynesian wayfinding methods as rudimentary; the prevailing theory was that Pacific Islanders had discovered Hawaii by accident, not intention. The *Hokulea's* successful voyage sparked a fire in hearts of indigenous islanders across the Pacific, who reclaimed their identity as a sophisticated, powerful people with unique wisdom to offer the world.

Hula girls.

The Hawaiian language found new life, too. In 1984, a group of educators and parents recognized that, with fewer than 50 children fluent in Hawaiian, the language was dangerously close to extinction. They started a preschool where *keiki* (children) learned lessons purely in Hawaiian. They overcame numerous bureaucratic obstacles (including a law still on the books forbidding instruction in Hawaiian) to establish Hawaiian-language-immersion programs across the state that run from preschool through post-graduate education.

Hula—which never fully disappeared despite the missionaries' best efforts—is thriving. At the annual Merrie Monarch festival commemorating King Kalakaua, hula *halau* (troupes) from Hawaii and beyond gather to demonstrate their skill and artistry. Fans of the ancient dance form are glued to the live broadcast of what is known as the Olympics of hula. *Kumu hula* (hula teachers) have safeguarded many Hawaiian cultural practices as part of their art: the making of *kapa,* the collection and cultivation of native herbs, and the observation of *kuleana,* an individual's responsibility to the community.

In that same spirit, in May 2014, the traditional voyaging canoe *Hokulea* embarked on her most ambitious adventure yet: an international peace delegation. The crew's mission is "to weave a lei around the world" and chart a new course toward a healthier and more sustainable horizon for all of humankind. During the canoe's 3-year circumnavigation of the globe, the sailors hope to collaborate with political leaders, scientists, educators, and schoolchildren in each of the ports they visit.

The history of Hawaii has come full circle: the ancient Polynesians traveled the seas to discover these Islands. Today, their descendants set sail to share Hawaii with the world.

DINING IN HAWAII
The Gang of 12

In the early days of Hawaii's tourism industry, the food wasn't anything to write home about. Continental cuisine ruled fine-dining kitchens. Meats and produce arrived much the same way visitors did: jet-lagged after a long journey from

Ahi poke.

a far-off land. Island chefs struggled to revive limp iceberg lettuce and frozen cocktail shrimp—often letting outstanding ocean views make up for uninspired dishes. In 1991, 12 chefs staged a revolt. They partnered with local farmers, ditched the dictatorship of imported foods, and brought sun-ripened mango, crisp organic greens, and freshly caught *uku* (snapper) to the table. Coining the name "Hawaii Regional Cuisine," they gave the world a taste of what happens when passionate, classically trained cooks have their way with ripe Pacific flavors.

Two decades later, the movement to unite local farms and kitchens is still bearing fruit. The HRC heavyweights hold the culinary industry's top titles (James Beard awards and Mobil stars aplenty), and several have authored best-selling cookbooks. **Alan Wong** wows diners at his award-winning restaurants on Oahu, Maui, and the Big Island with deceptively simple hearts-of-palm salads and succulent strip loin poached in olive oil. At **Chef Mavro Restaurant** in Honolulu, George Mavrothalassitis serves transcendent *uni* (sea urchin) vichyssoise. Roy Yamaguchi's multiple restaurants feature the chef's personal sake brew paired with seafood potstickers doused in citrus ponzu sauce. Beverly Gannon dishes out fancy comfort foods at **Haliimaile General Store** on Maui and **Lanai City Grille** on Lanai, including her legendary crab dip and irresistible sashimi "Napoleon"—a stacked tower of translucent ahi and hamachi layered with wonton chips, pickled ginger, and wasabi cream.

Members of the original gang of 12 continue to keep things hot in Hawaii kitchens. But they aren't, by any means, the sole source of good eats in Hawaii. Fresh steaming noodle shops abound in Oahu's **Chinatown.** Francophiles will delight in the classic French cooking at **La Mer** on Oahu and **Gerard's** on Maui. You'll be hard-pressed to discover more authentic Japanese fare than can be had in the restaurants dotting Honolulu's side streets.

Plate Lunches, Shave Ice & Food Trucks

Haute cuisine is alive and well in Hawaii, but equally important in the culinary pageant are good-value plate lunches, shave ice, and food trucks.

The **plate lunch,** which is ubiquitous throughout the islands, can be ordered from a lunch wagon or a restaurant and usually consists of some protein—fried mahimahi, say, or teriyaki beef, shoyu chicken, or chicken or pork cutlets served katsu style: breaded and fried and slathered in a rich gravy— "two scoops rice," macaroni salad, and a few leaves of green, typically julienned cabbage. Chili water and soy sauce are the condiments of choice. Like **saimin**—the local version of noodles in broth topped with scrambled eggs, green onions, and sometimes pork—the plate lunch is Hawaii's version of comfort food.

Shave ice.

Because this is Hawaii, at least a few licks of **poi**—steamed, pounded taro (the traditional Hawaiian staple crop)—are a must. Mix it with salty *kalua* pork (pork cooked in a Polynesian underground oven known as an *imu*) or *lomi* salmon (salted salmon with tomatoes and green onions). Other tasty Hawaiian foods include *poke* (pronounced *"po-kay,"* this popular appetizer is made of cubed raw fish seasoned with onions, seaweed, and roasted *kukui* nuts), *laulau* (pork, chicken, or fish steamed in *ti* leaves), **squid *luau*** (cooked in coconut milk and taro tops), *haupia* (creamy coconut pudding), and *kulolo* (a steamed pudding of coconut, brown sugar, and taro).

For a sweet snack, the prevailing choice is **shave ice.** Particularly on hot, humid days, long lines of shave-ice lovers gather for heaps of finely shaved ice topped with sweet tropical syrups. Sweet-sour *li hing mui* is a favorite, and new gourmet flavors include calamansi lime and red velvet cupcake. Aficionados order shave ice with ice cream and sweetened adzuki beans on the bottom or sweetened condensed milk on top.

WHEN TO GO

Most visitors come to Hawaii when the weather is lousy most everywhere else. Thus, the **high season**—when prices are up and resorts are often booked to capacity—is generally from mid-December to March or mid-April. The last 2 weeks of December, in particular, are prime time for travel to Hawaii. Spring break is also jam-packed with families taking advantage of the school holiday. If you're planning a trip during peak season, make your hotel and rental car reservations as early as possible, expect crowds, and prepare to pay top dollar.

The **off season,** when the best rates are available and the islands are less crowded, is late spring (mid-Apr to early June) and fall (Sept to mid-Dec).

If you plan to travel in **summer** (June–Aug), don't expect to see the fantastic bargains of spring and fall—this is prime time for family travel. But you'll still find much better deals on packages, airfare, and accommodations in summer than in the winter months.

Climate

Because Hawaii lies at the edge of the tropical zone, it technically has only two seasons, both of them warm. There's a dry season that corresponds to **summer** (Apr–Oct) and a rainy season in **winter** (Nov–Mar). It rains every day

on location **IN HAWAII**

Hawaii's iconic landscapes serve as a backdrop for numerous TV shows and films. Fans of **"Lost"** might recognize Mokuleia Beach on Oahu's North Shore as the site of the fictional plane crash. Episode three of Lost was shot in Oahu's Ka'a'awa Valley, a lush and remote spot that appears in several movies, including **"50 First Dates,"** **"Godzilla,"** and **"Pearl Harbor."** Johnny Depp leaps into Kilauea Falls on Kauai in **"Pirates of the Caribbean: On Stranger Tides."** Adam Sandler and Jennifer Aniston luxuriate at the Grand Wailea's pool and pass through the lobby of the Mana Kai on Maui in **"Just Go With It."**

"The Descendants," Alexander Payne's film about a dysfunctional Hawaii *kamaaina* (long-time resident) family, features a wealth of island scenery and music. George Clooney (as Matt King) and the cast spent 11 weeks shooting in Hawaii; it's easy to trace their trail. Matt King's house is on Old Pali Road in Nuuanu. When King runs down the hill to visit a friend, he's greeted by Poppy, a pygmy goat standing beneath a 50-foot-tall lychee tree. Payne rented the plantation-style house—goat and all—from a local family and shot scenes there without changing a thing. Whether or not you're a film buff, you should definitely pick up a copy of **"The Descendants" soundtrack.** This gold mine of modern and classic Hawaiian music features the very best island voices, from Gabby Pahinui to Keola Beamer, and includes several versions of the hauntingly beautiful anthem, "Hiilawe." You won't find a better soundtrack for your Hawaiian vacation.

Scene from "The Descendants."

somewhere in the islands at any time of the year, but the rainy season can bring enough gray weather to spoil your tanning opportunities. Fortunately, it seldom rains in one spot for more than 3 days straight.

The **year-round temperature** doesn't vary much. At the beach, the average daytime high in summer is 85°F (29°C), while the average daytime high in winter is 78°F (26°C); nighttime lows are usually about 10° cooler. But how warm it is on any given day really depends on *where* you are on the island.

Each island has a **leeward** side (the side sheltered from the wind) and a **windward** side (the side that gets the wind's full force). The leeward sides (the west and south) are usually hot and dry, while the windward sides (east and north) are generally cooler and moist. When you want arid, sunbaked, desert-like weather, go leeward. When you want lush, wet, jungle-like weather, go windward.

Hawaii also has a wide range of **microclimates,** thanks to interior valleys, coastal plains, and mountain peaks. Kauai's Mount Waialeale is one of the wettest spots on earth, yet Waimea Canyon, just a few miles away, is almost a desert. On the Big Island, Hilo ranks among the wettest cities in the nation, with 180 inches of rainfall a year. At Puako, only 60 miles away, it rains less than 6 inches a year. The summits of Mauna Kea on the Big Island and Haleakala on Maui often see snow in winter—even when the sun is blazing down at the beach. The locals say if you don't like the weather, just drive a few miles down the road—it's sure to be different!

Average Temperature & Number of Rainy Days in Waikiki

	JAN	FEB	MAR	APR	MAY	JUNE	JULY	AUG	SEPT	OCT	NOV	DEC
HIGH (°F/°C)	80/27	80/27	81/27	82/28	84/29	86/30	87/31	88/31	88/31	86/30	84/29	81/27
LOW (°F/°C)	70/21	66/19	66/19	69/21	70/21	72/22	73/23	74/23	74/23	72/22	70/21	67/19
RAINY DAYS	10	9	9	9	7	6	7	6	7	9	9	10

Average Temperature & Number of Rainy Days in Hanalei, Kauai

	JAN	FEB	MAR	APR	MAY	JUNE	JULY	AUG	SEPT	OCT	NOV	DEC
HIGH (°F/°C)	79/26	80/27	80/27	82/28	84/29	86/30	88/31	88/31	87/31	86/30	83/28	80/27
LOW (°F/°C)	61/17	61/16	62/17	63/17	65/18	66/19	66/19	67/19	68/20	67/19	65/18	62/17
RAINY DAYS	8	5	6	3	3	2	8	2	3	3	4	7

Holidays

When Hawaii observes holidays (especially those over a long weekend), travel between the islands increases, interisland airline seats are fully booked, rental cars are at a premium, and hotels and restaurants are busier.

Federal, state, and county government offices are closed on all federal holidays. Federal holidays in 2015 include New Year's Day (Jan 1); Martin Luther King, Jr., Day (Jan 18); Washington's birthday (Feb 16); Memorial Day (May 25); Independence Day (July 4); Labor Day (Sept 7); Columbus Day (Oct 12); Veterans Day (Nov 11); Thanksgiving Day (Nov 26); and Christmas (Dec 25).

State and county offices are also closed on local holidays, including Prince Kuhio Day (Mar 26), honoring the birthday of Hawaii's first delegate to the U.S. Congress; King Kamehameha Day (June 11), a statewide holiday commemorating Kamehameha the Great, who united the islands and ruled from 1795 to 1819; and Admission Day (third Fri in Aug), which honors the admittance of Hawaii as the 50th state on August 21, 1959.

Hey, No Smoking in Hawaii

Well, not *totally* no smoking, but Hawaii has one of the toughest laws against smoking in the U.S. It's against the law to smoke in public buildings, including airports, shopping malls, grocery stores, retail shops, buses, movie theaters, banks, convention facilities, and all government buildings and facilities. There is no smoking in restaurants, bars, and nightclubs. Most bed-and-breakfasts prohibit smoking indoors, and more and more hotels and resorts are becoming smoke-free even in public areas. Also, there is no smoking within 20 feet of a doorway, window, or ventilation intake (so no hanging around outside a bar to smoke—you must go 20 ft. away). Even some beaches have no-smoking policies.

Hawaii Calendar of Events

Please note that, as with any schedule of upcoming events, the following information is subject to change; always confirm the details before you plan your trip around an event.

JANUARY

Waimea Ocean Film Festival, Waimea and the Kohala Coast, Big Island. Several days of films featuring the ocean, ranging from surfing and Hawaiian canoe paddling to ecological issues. Go to http://waimea oceanfilm.org or call ☎ **808/854-6095.** First weekend after New Year's Day.

PGA Hyundai Championship, Kapalua Resort, Maui. Top PGA golfers compete for $1.12 million purse. Go to http://kapalua.com/golf/hyundai-tournament-champions or call ☎ **808/665-9160.** Early January.

Pacific Islands Arts Festival, Kapiolani Park, Honolulu, Oahu. More than 100 artists and handicrafts artisans, entertainment, food, and demonstrations fill the day. Admission is free. Go to www.icb-web.net/haa or call ☎ **808/637-5337.** Mid-January.

Ka Molokai Makahiki, Kaunakakai Town Baseball Park, Mitchell Pauole Center, Kaunakakai, Molokai. Makahiki, a traditional time of peace in ancient Hawaii, is re-created with performances by Hawaiian music groups and *halau* (hula schools), ancient Hawaiian games, a sporting competition, and crafts and food. It's a wonderful chance to experience the Hawaii of yesteryear. Go to www.molokaievents.com or call ☎ **800/800-6367** or 808/553-3876. Late January.

FEBRUARY

Lanai Hawaiian Culture Film & Music Festival, Lanai City, Lanai. Enjoy 3 days of fascinating feature films, shorts, and documentaries about the people of the Pacific. Live music and cultural workshops round out the weekend's events, most of which are free. The Four Seasons Resorts Lanai offers special festival packages. Go to http://lanaifilmfestival.com or call ☎ **808/565-4000.** Early to mid-February.

Waimea Town Celebration, Waimea, Kauai. This annual 2-day party on Kauai's west side celebrates the Hawaiian and multiethnic history of the town where Captain Cook first landed. This is the island's biggest event, drawing some 10,000 people. Top Hawaiian entertainers, sporting events, rodeo, and hat lei contests are just some of the draws of this weekend celebration. Details at www.wkbpa.org/events.html or ☎ **808/338-1332.** Weekend after Presidents' Day weekend.

Sand Castle Building Contest, Kailua Beach Park, Oahu. Students from the University of Hawaii School of Architecture compete against professional architects to see who can build the best, most unusual, and most outrageous sand sculpture. Call ☎ **808/956-7225** for dates.

Whale Day Celebration, Kalama Park, Kihei, Maui. A daylong celebration in the park, with a "parade of whales," entertainment, a crafts fair, games, and food. Go to www.mauiwhalefestival.org or call ☎ **808/856-8304.** Early or mid-February.

Punahou School Carnival, Punahou School, Honolulu, Oahu. This 2-day event has everything you can imagine in a school carnival, from high-speed rides to homemade jellies. All proceeds go to scholarship funds for Hawaii's most prestigious private high school. Go to www.punahou.edu or call ☎ **808/944-5753.** Early to mid-February.

Chinese New Year, most islands. In 2015, lion dancers will be snaking their way around the state on February 19, the start of the Chinese Year of the Sheep. On Oahu, Honolulu's Chinatown rolls out the red carpet for this fiery celebration with parades, pageants, and street festivals (www.chinatownhi.com). On Maui, lion dancers perform at the historic Wo Hing Temple on Front Street (www.visit lahaina.com). Call ☎ **888/310-1117** or 808/667-9175. Also in Wailuku; call ☎ **808/244-3888** for location.

Narcissus Festival, Honolulu, Oahu. Taking place around the Chinese New Year, this cultural festival includes a queen pageant, cooking demonstrations, and a cultural fair. Call ☏ **808/533-3181.**

Buffalo's Big Board Classic, Makaha Beach, Oahu. Contest featuring classic Hawaiian-style surfing, with longboard, tandem, and canoe surfing heats. Go to www.buffalosurfingclassic.com or call ☏ **808/951-7877.** Mid-February or early March.

MARCH

Lanai Jazz Festival, Lanai City, Lanai. Jazz greats descend on Lanai for a weekend in March, performing free, intimate concerts around the island. The Four Seasons Resorts Lanai offers special festival packages. Go to www.lanaijazzfestival or call ☏ **808/565-4000.** Early to mid-March.

Lahaina Whale and Ocean Arts Festival, Lahaina. The entire town of Lahaina celebrates the annual migration of Pacific humpback whales with this festival in Banyan Tree Park. Artists offer their best ocean-themed art for sale, while Hawaiian musicians and hula troupes entertain. Enjoy marine-related activities, games, and a touch-pool exhibit for kids. Get details at www.visitlahaina.com or call ☏ **888/310-1117.** Mid-March.

Kona Brewers Festival, King Kamehameha's Kona Beach Hotel Luau Grounds, Kailua-Kona, Big Island. This annual event features microbreweries from around the world, with beer tastings, food, and entertainment. Go to www.konabrewersfestival.com or call ☏ **808/987-9196.** Mid-March.

St. Patrick's Day Parade, Waikiki (Fort DeRussy to Kapiolani Park), Oahu. Bagpipers, bands, clowns, and marching groups parade through the heart of Waikiki, with lots of Irish-style celebrating all day. Call ☏ **808/926-1777** (Kelley O'Neil's Pub). March 17.

Kamehameha III Birthday Celebration, Sheraton Keauhou Bay Resort & Spa, Big Island. Free concert under the stars and Hawaiian culture lectures capped by Sam Choy's celebrity chef poke-making contest. Go to www.samchoyskeauhoupokecontest.org or call ☏ **808/930-4900.** March 15 to 17, 2015.

Prince Kuhio Day Celebrations, all islands. On this state holiday, various festivals throughout Hawaii celebrate the birth of Jonah Kuhio Kalanianaole, who was born on March 26, 1871, and elected to Congress in 1902. Kauai, his birthplace, stages a huge celebration in Lihue; call ☏ **808/240-6369** for details. Molokai also hosts a celebration; go to www.molokaievents.com or call ☏ **808/567-6027.**

Celebration of the Arts, Ritz-Carlton Kapalua, Kapalua Resort, Maui. Contemporary and traditional Hawaiian artists give free hands-on lessons during this 2-day festival, which also features song contests and rousing debates on what it means to be Hawaiian. Go to www.celebrationofthearts.org or call ☏ **808/665-7084.** March 28 and 29, 2015.

APRIL

Maui County Ag Fest, Waikapu, Maui. Maui celebrates its farmers and their fresh bounty at this well-attended event. Kids enjoy barnyard games while parents

---

Daylight Saving Time

Most of the United States observes daylight saving time, which lasts from 2am on the second Sunday in March to 2am on the first Sunday in November. **Hawaii does not observe daylight saving time.** So when daylight saving time is in effect in most of the U.S., Hawaii is 3 hours behind the West Coast and 6 hours behind the East Coast. When the U.S. reverts to standard time in November, Hawaii is 2 hours behind the West Coast and 5 hours behind the East Coast.

duck into the "Grand Taste" tent to sample top chefs' collaborations with local farmers. Go to www.mauicountyfarm bureau.org/maui-county-agricultural-festival-2 or call ✆ **808/243-2290.** April 4, 2015.

Buddha Day, Lahaina Jodo Mission, Lahaina, Maui. Each spring this historic mission holds a flower festival pageant honoring the birth of Buddha. Go to www.lahainajodomission.org or call ✆ **808/661-4304.** Generally the first Sunday in April.

Easter Sunrise Service, National Memorial Cemetery of the Pacific, Punchbowl Crater, Honolulu, Oahu. For a century, people have gathered at this famous cemetery for Easter sunrise services. Call ✆ **808/532-3720.** April 5, 2015.

Merrie Monarch Hula Festival, Hilo, Big Island. Hawaii's biggest, most prestigious hula festival features 3 nights of modern *(auana)* and ancient *(kahiko)* dance competition in honor of King David Kalakaua, the "Merrie Monarch" who revived the dance. Tickets sell out by January, so reserve early. Go to www.merriemonarch. com or call ✆ **808/935-9168.** April 5 to 11, 2015.

East Maui Taro Festival, Hana, Maui. Taro, a Hawaiian staple food, is celebrated through music, hula, arts, crafts, and, of course, taro-inspired feasts. Go to www.tarofestival.org or call ✆ **808/264-1553.** Last weekend in April.

MAY

Outrigger Canoe Season, all islands. From May to September, canoe paddlers across the state participate in outrigger canoe races nearly every weekend. Go to www.ocpaddler.com for this year's schedule of events.

Big Island Chocolate Festival, Kona, Big Island. This celebration of chocolate (cacao) grown and produced in Hawaii features symposiums, candy-making workshops, and gala tasting events. Go to www.bigislandchocolatefestival.com or call ✆ **808/854-6769.** May 2, 2015.

Lei Day Celebrations, Waikiki, Oahu. May Day (May 1) is Lei Day in Hawaii, celebrated with lei-making contests, pageantry, arts, and crafts. On Oahu, the real highlight is the live concert from 9am to 5:30pm at the Queen Kapi'olani Regional Park Bandstand. Call ✆ **808/692-5118.**

Maui Onion Festival, Whalers Village, Kaanapali. The sweetest onions in the world have their day of fame each May. Sample onion truffles, enter the raw-onion eating contest, and watch chefs compete for the best onion-inspired dish. Go to www.whalersvillage.com/onion festival.htm or call ✆ **808/661-4567.** May 2, 2015.

World Fire-Knife Dance Championships & Samoa Festival, Polynesian Cultural Center, Laie, Oahu. Junior and adult fire-knife dancers from around the world converge on the center for one of the most amazing performances you'll ever see. Authentic Samoan food and cultural festivities round out the fun. Go to www.world fireknife.com or call ✆ **808/293-3333.** Mid-May.

Lantern Floating Hawaii, Magic Island at Ala Moana Beach Park, Honolulu, Oahu. Some 40,000 people gather at Shinnyo-en Temple's annual Memorial Day lantern ceremony, a beautiful appeal for peace and harmony. At sunset, hundreds of glowing lanterns are set adrift. Hula and music follow. Go to www.lanternfloating hawaii.com or call ✆ **808/947-2814.** May 25, 2014.

Memorial Day, National Memorial Cemetery of the Pacific, Punchbowl Crater, Honolulu, Oahu. The armed forces hold a ceremony recognizing those who died for their country, beginning at 10am. Call ✆ **808/532-3720.** Last Monday in May.

Molokai Ka Hula Piko Festival, Mitchell Pau'ole Center, Kaunakakai, Molokai. This 3-day hula celebration occurs on the island where the Hawaiian dance was born and features performances by hula schools, musicians, and singers from across Hawaii, as well as local food and Hawaiian crafts: quilting, woodworking, featherwork, and deer-horn scrimshaw.

Go to www.kahulapiko.com or call ✆ **800/800-6367** or 808/553-3876. Early May.

JUNE

Obon Season, all islands. This colorful Buddhist ceremony honoring the souls of the dead kicks off in June. Synchronized dancers circle a tower where Taiko drummers play, and food booths sell Japanese treats late into the night. Each weekend, a different Buddhist temple hosts the Bon Dance. Go to www.gohawaii.com for a statewide schedule.

Maui Windsurfing Race Series, Kanaha Beach Park, Kahului. This annual windsurfing slalom race takes place at Kanaha Beach Park, west of Kahului Airport in central Maui. Go to www.surfmaui.com or call ✆ **808/877-2111.** Early June.

Honolulu Pride Parade & Celebration, Waikiki, Oahu. Since 1990, Hawaii's capital has celebrated diversity. This annual rainbow-splashed parade features a gay military color guard, roller derby, and high-energy floats. Kapiolani Park hosts daylong festivities. Go to www.honolulupride.org or call ✆ **808/877-2111.** Early June.

King Kamehameha Celebration, all islands. This state holiday (officially June 11, but celebrated on different dates on each island) features a massive floral parade, *hoolaulea* (party), and much more. Oahu: ✆ **808/586-0333.** Kauai: ✆ **808/651-6419.** Big Island: www.kamehameha festival.org and www.konaparade.org. Maui: www.visitlahaina.com or ✆ **808/667-9194.** Molokai: ✆ **808/553-3876.**

Maui Film Festival, Wailea Resort, Maui. Five days and nights of premiere screenings, celebrity awards, and lavish parties under the stars. Go to www.mauifilm festival.com or call ✆ **808/579-9244.** June 17 to 21, 2015.

King Kamehameha Hula Competition, Neal Blaisdell Center, Honolulu, Oahu. This daylong hula competition features dancers from as far away as Japan. Call **808/586-0333.** Third weekend in June.

Kapalua Wine & Food Festival, Kapalua Resort, Maui. Big-time wine and food experts and oenophiles gather at the Ritz-Carlton Kapalua resort for formal tastings, panel discussions, and samplings of new releases. The seafood finale ranks among the state's best feasts. Go to www.kapalua.com or call ✆ **800/KAPALUA** [527-2582]. June or mid-July.

Lanai Pineapple Festival, Lanai City, Lanai. This festival celebrates Lanai's history of pineapple plantations and ranching, including a pineapple-eating contest, a pineapple-cooking contest, arts and crafts, food, music, and fireworks. Go to www.lanaipineapplefestival. com or call ✆ **808/565-7600.** Last Saturday in June or first Saturday in July.

JULY

Makawao Parade & Rodeo, Makawao, Maui. The annual parade and rodeo event has been taking place in this upcountry cowboy town for generations. Go to www.gohawaii.com/maui or call ✆ **808/572-9565.** July 4.

Ala Moana Fourth of July Spectacular, Ala Moana Center, Waikiki, Oahu. The 15-minute fireworks display is among the largest in the country. People gather on the Ewa parking deck at 4pm for the best view. A concert at 5pm is followed by fireworks at 8:30pm. Shoppers enjoy a 20-percent discount all week. Go to www.alamoanacenter.com/Events/4th-of-July or call ✆ **808/955-9517.** July 3 to 6, 2015.

Molokai to Oahu Paddleboard Race, starts on Molokai and finishes on Oahu. Some 200 international participants journey to Molokai to compete in this 32-mile race, considered to be the world championship of long-distance paddleboarding. The race begins at Kaluakoi Beach on Molokai at 7:30am and finishes at Maunaloa Bay on Oahu around 12:30pm. Go to www.molokai2oahu.com or call ✆ **760/944-3854.** Late July.

Ukulele Festival, Kapiolani Park Bandstand, Waikiki, Oahu. This free concert features a ukulele orchestra of some 800 students, ages 4 to 92. Hawaii's top musicians pitch in. Go to www.ukulelefestival hawaii.org. Late July.

Queen Liliuokalani Keiki Hula Competition, Neal Blaisdell Center, Honolulu, Oahu. More than 500 *keiki* (children) representing 22 *halau* (hula schools) from the islands compete in this dance-fest. The event is broadcast a week later on KITV-TV. Go to www.kpcahawaii.com or call ✆ **808/521-6905.** Mid- to late July.

50th State Fair, Aloha Stadium, Honolulu, Oahu. The annual state fair is a great one, with displays of Hawaii agricultural products (including orchids), educational and cultural exhibits, entertainment, and local food. Go to www.ekfernandez.com or call ✆ **808/682-5767.** June and July.

AUGUST

Hawaii State Windsurfing Championship, Kanaha Beach Park, Kahului, Maui. Top windsurfers compete in the final race of the series. Call ✆ **808/877-2111.** Late July or early August.

Puukohola Heiau National Historic Site Anniversary Celebration, Kawaihae, Big Island. This homage to authentic Hawaiian culture begins at 6am at Puukohola Heiau. It's a rugged, beautiful site where attendees make leis, weave lauhala mats, pound poi, and dance ancient hula. Bring refreshments and sunscreen. Go to www.nps.gov/puhe/planyourvisit/events.htm or call ✆ **808/882-7218.** Mid-August.

Duke's OceanFest Hoolaulea, Waikiki, Oahu. Nine days of water-oriented competitions and festivities celebrate the life of Duke Kahanamoku. Events include longboard surfing, paddleboard racing, swimming, tandem surfing, surf polo, beach volleyball, and stand-up paddling and a Hawaiian luau. Go to www.dukefoundation.org or call ✆ **808/545-4880.** Mid- to late August.

Admission Day, all islands. Hawaii became the 50th state on August 21, 1959. On the third Friday in August, the state takes a holiday (all state-related facilities are closed).

Hawaii Food & Wine Festival, Ko Olina Resort, Oahu. Co-founded by two of the state's most celebrated chefs, this 5-day feast includes wine tastings, cooking demos, field trips, and glitzy galas. See www.hawaiifoodandwinefestival.com or call ✆ **808/738-6245.** Late August.

SEPTEMBER

Waikiki Roughwater Swim, Waikiki, Oahu. This popular 2.5-mile, open-ocean swim goes from Sans Souci Beach to Duke Kahanamoku Beach in Waikiki. Early registration is encouraged, but last-minute entries on race day are allowed. Go to www.wrswim.com. Labor Day.

Queen Liliuokalani Canoe Race, Kailua-Kona to Honaunau, Big Island. Thousands of paddlers compete in the world's largest long-distance canoe race. Go to www.kaiopua.org or call ✆ **808/938-8577.** Labor Day weekend.

Parker Ranch Rodeo, Waimea, Big Island. This hot rodeo competition is in the heart of cowboy country. Go to www.parkerranch.com or call ✆ **808/885-7311.** Weekend before Labor Day.

Aloha Festivals, various locations on all islands. Parades and other events celebrate Hawaiian culture and friendliness throughout the state. Go to www.alohafestivals.com or call ✆ **808/589-1771.**

Maui County Fair, War Memorial Complex, Wailuku, Maui. The oldest county fair in Hawaii features a parade, amusement rides, live entertainment, and exhibits. Go to www.mauifair.com or call ✆ **808/280-6889.** Last weekend in September.

OCTOBER

Emalani Festival, Kokee State Park, Kauai. This festival honors Her Majesty Queen Emma, an inveterate gardener and Hawaii's first environmental queen, who made a forest trek to Kokee with 100 friends in 1871. Go to www.kokee.org or call ✆ **808/335-9975.** Second Saturday in October.

Ironman Triathlon World Championship, Kailua-Kona, Big Island. Some 1,500-plus world-class athletes run a full marathon, swim 2.5 miles, and bike 112 miles on the Kona-Kohala Coast of the Big Island. Spectators watch the action along the route for free. The best place to see the 7am start is along the Alii Drive seawall, facing Kailua Bay; arrive before 5:30am to get a seat. (Alii Dr. closes to traffic; park on a side street and walk down.) To watch finishers come in, line up along Alii Drive from Holualoa Street to Palani Road. The first finisher can arrive as early as 2:30pm. Go to www.ironmanworld championship.com or call ✆ **808/329-0063.** Saturday closest to the full moon in October (Oct 10, 2015).

Hana Hoohiwahiwa O Kaiulani, Sheraton Princess Kaiulani, Waikiki, Oahu. This hotel commemorates the birthday of its namesake, Princess Victoria Kaiulani, with a week of complimentary hula lessons, lei making, ukulele lessons, and more. The crowning touch is the Princess Kaiulani Keiki Hula Festival, which showcases performances by more than 200 *keiki* (children) from *halau* (schools) on the island of Oahu. Go to www.princess-kaiulani.com or call ✆ **808/931-4524.** Mid-October.

Xterra World Championship, Kapalua, Maui. Hundreds of gonzo athletes plunge into the Pacific, jump on mountain bikes, and race through the rainforest to be crowned Xterra world champion. After the race, athletes and friends celebrate at an awards dinner and adrenaline-fueled Halloween party. Go to www.xterra planet.com/maui or call ✆ **808/216-8606.** Late October.

Pacific Rim Jazz Festival, Hawaii Convention Center, Honolulu, Oahu. This festival features a lineup of big-time artists in evening concerts and daily jam sessions, plus scholarship giveaways. Go to www.pacificrimjazzfestival.com or call ✆ **808/941-9974.** Early November.

Hawaiian Slack Key Guitar Festival, Kauai Beach Resort, Lihue, Kauai. The best of Hawaii's folk music (slack key guitar) performed by the best musicians in Hawaii.

It's 6 hours long and free. Go to www.slackkeyfestival.com or call ✆ **808/226-2697.** Mid-November.

Kona Coffee Cultural Festival, Kailua-Kona, Big Island. Celebrate the coffee harvest with a bean-picking contest, lei contests, song and dance, and the Miss Kona Coffee Pageant. Go to www.kona coffeefest.com or call ✆ **808/326-7820.** Events throughout November.

Hawaii International Film Festival, various locations throughout the state. This cinema festival with a cross-cultural spin features filmmakers from Asia, the Pacific Islands, and the United States. Go to www.hiff.org or call ✆ **808/792-1577.** Mid-October to early November.

Na Mele O Maui, Maui. A traditional Hawaiian song competition for children in kindergarten through 12th grade, held at the Maui Arts & Cultural Center. Free admission. Go to www.kaanapaliresort.com or call ✆ **808/661-3271** or 808/242-7469.

EA Sports Maui Invitational Basketball Tournament, Lahaina Civic Center, Lahaina. Elite college teams battle in this intimate annual preseason tournament. Go to www.mauiinvitational.com or call ✆ **847/480-4886.** Thanksgiving weekend.

Invitational Wreath Exhibit, Volcano Art Center, Hawaii Volcanoes National Park, Big Island. Thirty-plus artists, including painters, sculptors, glass artists, fiber artists, and potters, produce both whimsical and traditional "wreaths" for this exhibit. Park entrance fees apply. Go to www.volcanoartcenter.org or call ✆ **808/967-7565.** Mid-November to early January.

Van's Triple Crown of Surfing, North Shore, Oahu. The world's top professional surfers compete in events for more than $1 million in prize money. Go to http://vanstriplecrownofsurfing.com or call ✆ **808/637-2245.** Held between mid-November and mid-December, depending on the surf.

Kona Surf Film Festival, Courtyard Marriott King Kamehameha's Kona Beach Hotel, Big Island. An outdoor screening of independent films focusing on waves and wave riders. Go to www.konasurffilm festival.org. Early December.

Festival of Lights, all islands. On Oahu, the mayor throws the switch to light up the 40-foot-tall Norfolk pine and other trees in front of Honolulu Hale, while on Maui, kids can play in a "snow zone" and make holiday crafts beneath the Lahaina Banyan tree, glowing with thousands of twinkle lights. Molokai celebrates with a host of activities in Kaunakakai; on Kauai, the lighting ceremony takes place in front of the former county building on Rice Street, in Lihue. Call ☎ **808/768-6622** on Oahu; ☎ **808/667-9175** on Maui; ☎ **808/553-4482** on Molokai; or

☎ **808/639-6571** on Kauai. Early December.

Honolulu Marathon, Honolulu, Oahu. More than 30,000 racers compete in this oceanfront marathon, one of the largest in the world. Check it out at www.honolulu marathon.org or call ☎ **808/734-7200.** December 13, 2015.

Sheraton Hawaii Bowl, Aloha Stadium, Honolulu, Oahu. A Pac 10 team plays a Big 12 team in this nationally televised collegiate football classic. Go to www. sheratonhawaiibowl.com or call ☎ **808/523-3688.** December 24.

First Light, Maui Arts & Cultural Center, Kahului, Maui. The Maui Film Festival screens Academy Award–contending films over the holidays. Go to www.maui filmfestival.com or call ☎ **808/579-9244.** Mid- to late December.

OAHU
by Martha Cheng

O ahu has it all: wide, sandy beaches; year-round surf; breathtaking ridge hikes; and, in Honolulu, a vibrant urban city. Home to Pearl Harbor and the only royal palace in the United States, Honolulu is imbued with history. Always deeply mindful of its past, it is also streaking into the future. The revitalization of old neighborhoods has sprouted trendy boutiques and attention-grabbing cuisine, and Waikiki, the world-famous vacation playground, gets more cutting-edge luxe every day. Sure, Oahu may be Hawaii's most crowded island, but its rich human tapestry—locals of myriad ethnic mixes, wealthy Japanese expats, Mainland sunseekers, surfers from around the globe—makes it unlike any other place in the world.

ESSENTIALS

Arriving

Even though more and more transpacific flights are going directly to the neighbor islands these days, chances are still good that you'll touch down on Oahu first and Honolulu will be your gateway to the Hawaiian Islands. **Honolulu International Airport** sits on the south shore of Oahu, west of downtown Honolulu and Waikiki near Pearl Harbor. Many major American and international carriers fly to Honolulu from the Mainland; for a list of airlines, see chapter 10, "Planning Your Trip to Hawaii."

LANDING AT HONOLULU INTERNATIONAL AIRPORT

The airport at Honolulu is probably the most cosmopolitan spot in the Pacific, bustling with passengers from every corner of the globe. You can walk or take the free airport shuttle from your arrival gate to the main terminal and baggage claim, on the ground level. Unless you're connecting to an interisland flight immediately, you'll exit to the palm-lined street, where uniformed attendants can either flag down a taxi or direct you to **TheBus** (www.thebus.org; see "By Bus," below). For Waikiki shuttles and rental-car vans, cross the street to the median and wait at the designated stop.

Passengers connecting to neighbor-island flights take the free shuttle or walk to the large interisland terminal serving Hawaiian Airlines or to the more distant commuter terminal, which serves smaller carriers such as Island Air and Mokulele Airlines. (For details on interisland flights, see "Getting Around Hawaii" on p. 511.)

GETTING TO & FROM THE AIRPORT

BY RENTAL CAR All major car-rental companies have vehicles available at the airport. Rental-agency vans will pick you up curbside at the center island outside

Previous page: USS *Arizona* Memorial.

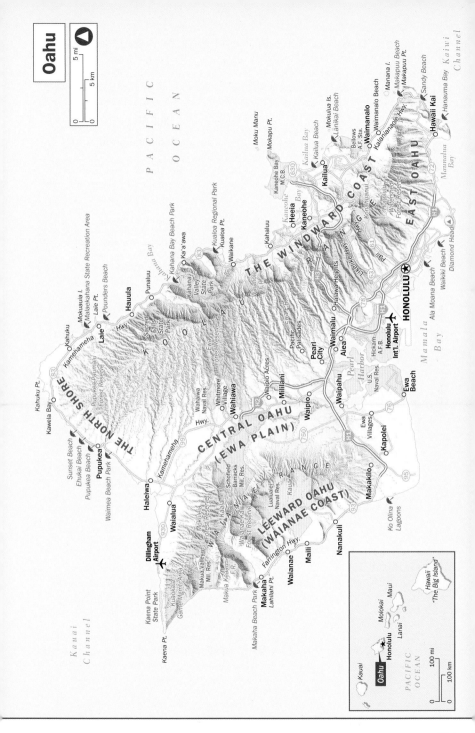

baggage claim and take you to their off-site lots. It's about a 20-minute drive from the airport to downtown Honolulu.

BY TAXI   Taxis are abundant at the airport; an attendant will be happy to flag one down for you. Taxi fare is about $25 from Honolulu International to downtown Honolulu and around $35 to $40 to Waikiki. If you need to call a taxi, see "Getting Around," later in this chapter, for a list of cab companies.

BY AIRPORT SHUTTLE   **SpeediShuttle** (www.speedishuttle.com; © **877/242-5777**) offers transportation in air-conditioned vans from the airport to Waikiki hotels; a one-way trip from the airport to Waikiki is $15 per person and $27 round-trip. You'll find the shuttle at street level outside baggage claim on the median. You can board with two pieces of luggage and a carry-on at no extra charge. Tips are welcome. For advance purchase of group tickets, call the number above.

BY BUS   **TheBus** (www.thebus.org; © **808/848-4500**) is a good option if you aren't carrying a lot of luggage. TheBus nos. 19 and 20 (Waikiki Beach and Hotels) run from the airport to downtown Honolulu and Waikiki. The first bus from Waikiki to the airport leaves at 4:55am Monday through Friday and 5:10am Saturday and Sunday; the last bus departs the airport for Waikiki at 1:22am Monday through Friday, 1:24am Saturday and Sunday. There are two bus stops on the main terminal's upper level; a third is on the second level of the interisland terminal. *Note:* You can board TheBus with a carry-on or small suitcase, as long as it fits under the seat and doesn't disrupt other passengers; otherwise, you'll have to take a shuttle or taxi. The travel time to Waikiki is approximately 1 hour. The one-way fare is $2.50 for adults and $1.25 for children 6 to 17, exact change only. For more on TheBus, see "Getting Around," later in this chapter.

Visitor Information

The **Hawaii Visitors & Convention Bureau (HVCB),** 2270 Kalakaua Ave., Suite 801, Honolulu, HI 96815 (www.gohawaii.com or www.hvcb.org; © **800/GO-HAWAII**), supplies free brochures, maps, accommodations guides, and "Islands of Aloha," the official HVCB magazine.

A number of free publications, such as **"This Week Oahu,"** are packed with money-saving coupons and good regional maps; look for them on racks at the airport and around town. *Another tip:* Snag one of the Japanese magazines scattered around Waikiki. Even if you can't read Japanese, you'll find out about the latest, trendiest, or best restaurants and shops around the island.

The Island in Brief

HONOLULU

Hawaii's largest city looks like any other big metropolitan center with tall buildings. In fact, some cynics refer to it as "Los Angeles West." But within Honolulu's boundaries, you'll find rainforests, deep canyons, valleys, waterfalls, a nearly mile-high mountain range, coral reefs, and gold-sand beaches. The city proper—where most of Honolulu's residents live—is approximately 12 miles wide and 26 miles long, running east-west roughly between **Diamond Head** and **Pearl Harbor.** Within the city are seven hills laced by seven streams that run to Mamala Bay.

A plethora of neighborhoods surrounds the central area. These areas are generally quieter and more residential than Waikiki, but they're still within minutes of beaches, shopping, and all the activities Oahu has to offer.

View from Diamond Head.

WAIKIKI ★★   Some say that Waikiki is past its prime—that everybody goes to Maui now. If it has fallen out of favor, you couldn't prove it by me. Waikiki is the very incarnation of Yogi Berra's comment about Toots Shor's famous New York restaurant: "Nobody goes there anymore. It's too crowded."

When King Kalakaua played in Waikiki, it was "a hamlet of plain cottages . . . its excitements caused by the activity of insect tribes and the occasional fall of a coconut." The Merrie Monarch, who gave his name to Waikiki's main street, would love the scene today. Some 5 million tourists visit Oahu every year, and 9 out of 10 of them stay in Waikiki. This urban beach is where all the action is; it's backed by 175 high-rise hotels with more than 33,000 guest rooms and hundreds of bars and restaurants, all in a 1½-square-mile beach zone. Waikiki means honeymooners and sun seekers, bikinis and bare buns, an around-the-clock beach party every day of the year. Staying in Waikiki puts you in the heart of it all, but also be aware that this is an on-the-go place with traffic noise 24 hours a day and its share of crime—and it's almost always crowded.

ALA MOANA ★★   A great beach as well as a famous shopping mall, Ala Moana is the retail and transportation heart of Honolulu, a place where you can both shop and suntan in one afternoon. All bus routes lead to the open-air **Ala Moana Center,** across the street from **Ala Moana Beach Park ★★**. This 200-store shopping behemoth is getting even bigger—a 650,000-square-foot expansion, anchored by Bloomingdale's, is expected to open in the Ala Moana Center by the end of 2015. For our purposes, the neighborhood called "Ala Moana" extends along Ala Moana Boulevard from Waikiki in the direction of Diamond Head to downtown Honolulu in the Ewa direction (west) and includes the **Ward Centers** and **Ward Warehouse** complexes, as well as **Restaurant Row.**

DOWNTOWN ★★   A tiny cluster of high-rises west of Waikiki, downtown Honolulu is the financial, business, and government center of Hawaii. On the waterfront stands the iconic 1926 **Aloha Tower.** The whole history of Honolulu can be seen in just a few short blocks: Street vendors sell papayas from trucks on skyscraper-lined concrete canyons; joggers and BMWs rush by a lacy palace where U.S. Marines overthrew Hawaii's last queen and stole her kingdom; burly bus drivers sport fragrant white ginger flowers on their dashboards; Methodist

churches look like Asian temples; and businessmen wear aloha shirts to billion-dollar meetings.

On the edge of downtown is the **Chinatown Historic District,** the oldest Chinatown in America and still one of Honolulu's liveliest neighborhoods, a non-stop pageant of people, sights, sounds, smells, and tastes—not all Chinese. Southeast Asians, including many Vietnamese, share the old storefronts, as do Honolulu's oldest bar (the divey **Smith's Union Bar**) and some of the city's hippest clubs and chic-est boutiques. Go on Saturday morning, when everyone shops for fresh goods such as mangoes (when in season), live fish (sometimes of the same varieties you saw while snorkeling), fresh tofu, and hogs' heads.

MANOA VALLEY ★   First inhabited by white settlers, the Manoa Valley, above Waikiki, still has vintage *kamaaina* (native-born) homes, one of Hawaii's premier

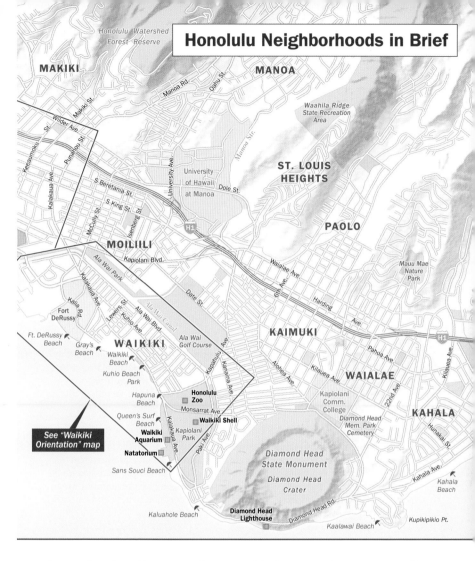

botanical gardens (the **Lyon Arboretum ★**), the ever-gushing **Manoa Falls,** and the 320-acre campus of the **University of Hawaii,** where 50,000 students hit the books when they're not on the beach.

TO THE EAST: KAHALA   Except for the estates of millionaires and the luxurious **Kahala Hotel & Resort ★★★**, there's not much out this way that's of interest to visitors.

EAST OAHU

Beyond Kahala lies East Honolulu and suburban bedroom communities like Aina Haina, Niu Valley, and Hawaii Kai, among others, all linked by the Kalanianaole Highway and loaded with homes, condos, fast-food joints, and shopping malls. It looks like Southern California on a good day. You'll drive through here if you take

51

Hanauma Bay.

the longer, scenic route to Kailua. Some reasons to stop along the way: to have dinner at **Roy's Restaurant** ★, the original and still-outstanding Hawaii Regional Cuisine restaurant, in Hawaii Kai; to snorkel at **Hanauma Bay** ★★ or watch daredevil body surfers and boogie boarders at **Sandy Beach** ★; or to just enjoy the natural splendor of the lovely coastline, which might include a hike to **Makapuu Lighthouse** ★★.

THE WINDWARD COAST

The windward side is the opposite side of the island from Waikiki. On this coast, trade winds blow cooling breezes over gorgeous beaches; rain squalls spawn lush, tropical vegetation; and miles of subdivisions dot the landscape. Bed-and-break-fasts, ranging from oceanfront estates to tiny cottages on quiet residential streets, are everywhere. Vacations here are spent enjoying ocean activities and exploring the surrounding areas. Waikiki is just a 15-minute drive away.

KAILUA ★★★   The biggest little beach town in Hawaii, Kailua sits at the foot of the sheer green Koolau mountain range, on a great bay with two of Hawaii's best beaches. The town is undergoing some redevelopment—there's now a strip mall anchored by the island's largest Whole Foods, and new condos are sprouting up. But, for the most part, it's still a funky low-rise cluster of timeworn shops and homes (at least for now). Kailua has become the B&B capital of Hawaii; it's an affordable alternative to Waikiki, with rooms and vacation rentals starting at $70 a day. With the prevailing trade winds whipping up a cooling breeze, Kailua attracts windsurfers from around the world. On calmer days, kayaking to the Mokulua Islands off the coast is a favorite adventure.

KANEOHE BAY ★   Helter-skelter suburbia sprawls around the edges of Kaneohe, one of the most scenic bays in the Pacific. After you clear the trafficky maze of town, Oahu returns to its more natural state. This great bay beckons you to get out on the water; you can depart from Heeia Boat Harbor on snorkel or fishing charters. From here, you'll have a panoramic view of the Koolau Range.

KUALOA/LAIE ★   The upper-northeast shore is one of Oahu's most sacred places, an early Hawaiian landing spot where kings dipped their sails, cliffs hold ancient burial sites, and ghosts still march in the night. Sheer cliffs stab the reef-fringed seacoast, while old fish ponds are tucked along the two-lane coast road that winds past empty gold-sand beaches around beautiful Kahana Bay. Thousands "explore" the South Pacific at the **Polynesian Cultural Center** in Laie, a Mormon settlement with its own Tabernacle Choir of sweet Samoan harmony.

THE NORTH SHORE ★★★   Here is the Hawaii of Hollywood—home to giant waves, surfers, tropical jungles, waterfalls, and mysterious Hawaiian temples. If you're looking for a quieter vacation that's closer to nature and filled with swimming, snorkeling, diving, and surfing, or just plain hanging out on some of the world's most beautiful beaches, the North Shore is your place. The artsy little beach town of **Haleiwa** ★★ and the surrounding shoreline seem a world away from Waikiki. The North Shore boasts good restaurants, shopping, and cultural activities—but they come with the quiet of country living. Vacation rentals are the most common accommodations, but there's also the first-class **Turtle Bay Resort** ★★. Be forewarned: It's a long trip—nearly an hour's drive—to Honolulu and Waikiki, and even longer during the surf season, when tourists and wave-seekers can jam up the roads.

CENTRAL OAHU: THE EWA PLAIN

Flanked by the Koolau and Waianae mountain ranges, the hot, sunbaked Ewa Plain runs up and down the center of Oahu. Once covered with sandalwood forests (hacked down for the China trade) and later the sugarcane and pineapple backbone of Hawaii, Ewa today sports a new crop: suburban houses stretching to the sea. But let your eye wander west to the Waianae Range and Mount Kaala, at 4,020 feet the highest summit on Oahu; up there in the misty rainforest, native birds thrive in the hummocky bog. In 1914, the U.S. Army pitched a tent camp on the plain; author James Jones would later call Schofield Barracks "the most beautiful army post in the world." Hollywood filmed Jones's "From Here to Eternity" here.

LEEWARD OAHU: THE WAIANAE COAST

The west coast of Oahu is a hot and dry place of dramatic beauty: white-sand beaches bordering the deep-blue ocean, steep verdant green cliffs, and miles of Mother Nature's wildness. Tourist services are concentrated in Ko Olina Resort, which has a Marriott and Disney hotel, pricey resort restaurants, golf course,

---

Finding Your Way Around, Oahu-Style

Mainlanders sometimes find the directions given by locals a bit confusing. Seldom will you hear the terms *east, west, north,* and *south;* instead, islanders refer to directions as either **makai** (ma-kae), meaning toward the sea, or **mauka** (*mow*-kah), toward the mountains. In Honolulu, people use **Diamond Head** as a direction meaning to the east (in the direction of the world-famous crater called Diamond Head), and **Ewa** as a direction meaning to the west (toward the town called Ewa, on the other side of Pearl Harbor).

So if you ask a local for directions, this is what you're likely to hear: "Drive 2 blocks makai (toward the sea), and then turn Diamond Head (east) at the stoplight. Go 1 block, and turn mauka (toward the mountains). It's on the Ewa (western) side of the street."

marina, and wedding chapel, should you want to get hitched. The funky west-coast villages of **Nanakuli, Waianae,** and **Makaha** are the last stands of native Hawaiians. This side of Oahu is seldom visited, except by surfers bound for **Yokohama Bay** ★ and those coming to see needle-nose **Kaena Point** ★ (the island's westernmost outpost), which has a coastal wilderness park.

GETTING AROUND

BY CAR Oahu residents own more than 686,000 registered vehicles, but they have only 1,500 miles of mostly two-lane roads to use. That's 450 cars for every mile, a fact that becomes abundantly clear during morning and evening rush hours. You can avoid the gridlock by driving between 9am and 2pm or after 7pm.

All of the major car-rental firms have agencies on Oahu, at the airport and in Waikiki. For listings, see chapter 10. For tips on insurance and driving rules in Hawaii, see "Getting Around Hawaii" (p. 511).

BY BUS One of the best deals anywhere, **TheBus** will take you around the whole island for $2.50 ($1.25 for children age 6–17)—if you have time. To get to the North Shore and back takes 4 hours, twice as long as a car. But for shorter distances, TheBus is great, and it goes almost everywhere almost all the time. If you're planning on sticking to the Waikiki–Ala Moana–Downtown region, go with TheBus, which will save you a lot of car hassle and expense. The most popular route is **no. 8,** which arrives every 10 minutes or so to shuttle people between Waikiki and Ala Moana Center (the ride takes 15–20 min.). The **no. 19** (Airport/Hickam), **no. 20** (Airport/Halawa Gate), and **no. 40** (Waipahu/Ala Moana) also cover the same stretch. Waikiki service begins daily at 5am and runs until midnight; most buses run about every 15 minutes during the day and every 30 minutes in the evening.

The Circle Island–North Shore route is **no. 52** (Wahiawa/Circle Island); the Circle Island–South Shore route is **no. 55** (Kaneohe/Circle Island). Both routes leave Ala Moana Center every 30 minutes and take about 4½ hours to circle the island. Be aware that at Turtle Bay Resort, just outside Kahuku, the 52 becomes the 55 and returns to Honolulu via the coast, and the 55 becomes the 52 and returns to Honolulu on the inland route. (Translation: You'll have to get off and switch buses to complete your island tour.) There are express buses available to some areas (for example, **no. 54** to Pearl City, **no. 85** to Kailua and to Kaneohe).

For more information on routes and schedules, call **TheBus** (© **808/848-5555,** or 808/296-1818 for recorded information) or check out **www.thebus.org**, which provides timetables and maps for all routes, plus directions to many local attractions and a list of upcoming events. Taking TheBus is often easier than parking your car.

BY TAXI Oahu's major cab companies offer 24-hour, islandwide, radio-dispatched service, with multilingual drivers and air-conditioned cars, limos, and vans, including vehicles equipped with wheelchair lifts (there's a $9 charge for wheelchairs). Fares are standard for all taxi firms. From the airport, expect to pay about $35 to $40 to Waikiki, about $25 to $35 to downtown, $60 and up to Kailua, about $60-plus to Hawaii Kai, and about $90 to $125 to the North Shore (plus tip). Plus there may be a $4.75 fee per piece of luggage.

Uber, the taxi-hailing app, has arrived in Honolulu. Use it on your phone to summon and pay for a taxi (standard taxi meter rates, plus a $1 surcharge; gratuity automatically added). If you prefer to go the old-fashioned route, try **The Cab** (☏ **808/422-2222**) or **EcoCab** (☏ **808/979-1010**), an all-hybrid taxi fleet. **Robert's Taxi and Shuttle** (☏ **808/261-8555**) serves windward Oahu, while **Hawaii Kai Hui/Koko Head Taxi** (☏ **808/396-6633**) serves east Honolulu/ southeast Oahu.

[FastFACTS] OAHU

Dentists If you need dental attention on Oahu, find a dentist near you through the website of the **Hawaii Dental Association** (www.hawaiidental association.net).

Doctors Straub Clinic & Hospital's **Doctors on Call** (www.straubhealth.org; ☏ **808/971-6000**) can dispatch a van if you need help getting to the main clinic or to any of its additional clinics at the Hilton Hawaiian Village and the Sheraton Princess.

Emergencies Call ☏ **911** for police, fire, and ambulance. If you need to call the **Poison Control Center** (☏ **800/222-1222**), you will automatically be directed to the Poison Control Center for the area code of the phone you are calling from; all are available 24/7 and very helpful.

Hospitals Hospitals offering 24-hour emergency care include **Queen's Medical Center**, 1301 Punchbowl St. (☏ **808/538-9011**); **Kuakini Medical Center,**

347 Kuakini St. (☏ 808/536-2236); **Straub Clinic & Hospital,** 888 S. King St. (☏ 808/522-4000); **Kaiser Permanente Medical Center,** 3288 Moanalua Rd. (☏ 808/432-0000), where the emergency room is open to Kaiser members only; **Kapiolani Medical Center for Women & Children,** 1319 Punahou St. (☏ 808/983-8633); and **Kapiolani Medical Center at Pali Momi,** 98–1079 Moanalua Rd. (☏ 808/486-6000). Central Oahu has **Wahiawa General Hospital,** 128 Lehua St. (☏ 808/621-8411). On the windward side is **Castle Medical Center,** 640 Ulukahiki St., Kailua (☏ 808/263-5500).

Internet Access Outside of your hotel, your best bet for Internet access is Starbucks. The Royal Hawaiian Center shopping mall also offers free Wi-Fi.

Newspapers Oahu's only daily paper is the "Honolulu Star Advertiser."

Post Office To find the location nearest you, call

☏ **800/275-8777.** The downtown location is in the old U.S. Post Office, Customs, and Court House Building (referred to as the Old Federal Building) at 335 Merchant St., across from Iolani Palace and next to the Kamehameha Statue (bus: 20, E, or 19). Other branch offices can be found in Waikiki, at 330 Saratoga Ave. (Diamond Head side of Fort DeRussy; bus: 19 or 20), and in the Ala Moana Center (bus: 8, 19, or 20).

Safety The Honolulu Police Department cautions that there has been a series of purse-snatching incidents in Oahu. Thieves work from slow-moving cars or on foot. The police advise that you carry your purse on the shoulder away from the street or, better yet, wear your bag with the strap across your chest instead of on one shoulder. If you're carrying a clutch bag, hold it close to your chest.

Weather For National Weather Service recorded forecasts for Oahu, call ☏ **808/973-4380.**

Honolulu Attractions

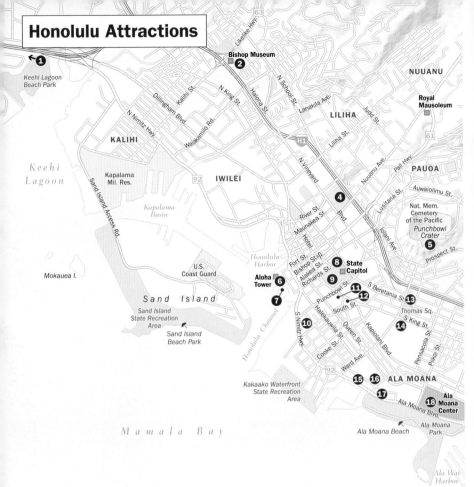

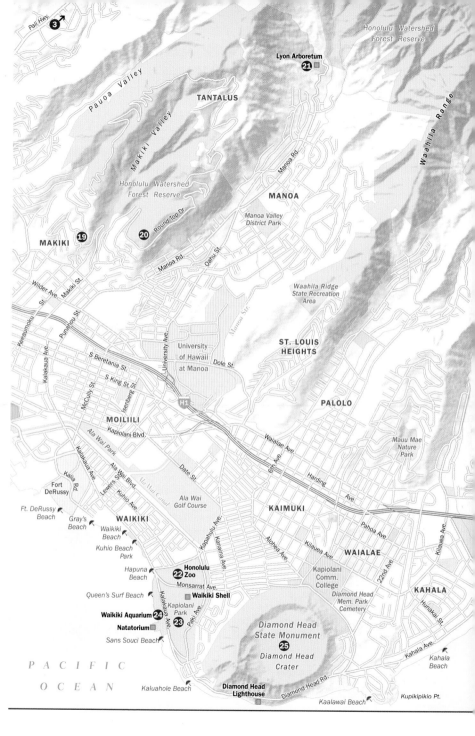

Pali Hwy. **3**↗

Honolulu Watershed Forest Reserve

Lyon Arboretum **21** ◼

TANTALUS

Pauoa Valley

Makiki Valley

Manoa Rd.

MANOA

Honolulu Watershed Forest Reserve

Round Top Dr.

Manoa Valley District Park

MAKIKI **19**

20

Manoa Rd. Oahu St.

Waahila Ridge State Recreation Area

Wilder Ave.

Makiki St.

Keeaumoku St.

Punahou St.

S Beretania St.

University Ave.

Dole St.

University of Hawaii at Manoa

ST. LOUIS HEIGHTS

S King St St.

Isenberg

McCully St.

H1

MOILIILI

Kapiolani Blvd.

PALOLO

Waialae Ave.

6th Ave.

Mauu Mae Nature Park

Ala Wai Park

Ala Wai Blvd.

Kalakaua Ave.

Lewers St.

Kuhio Ave.

Date St.

Ala Wai Canal

Ala Wai Golf Course

Harding Ave.

KAIMUKI

Fort DeRussy

Kalia Rd.

Ft. DeRussy Beach

Gray's Beach

WAIKIKI

Waikiki Beach

Kuhio Beach Park

Pahoa Ave.

Kapahulu Ave.

Kamana Ave.

Alohea Ave.

Kilauea Ave.

22nd Ave.

WAIALAE

Kilauea Ave.

KAHALA

Hapuna Beach

22 Honolulu Zoo

Monsarrat Ave.

■ Waikiki Shell

Kapiolani Comm. College

Kalakaua Ave.

Hunakai St.

Queen's Surf Beach

Kapiolani Park

Paki Ave.

Diamond Head Mem. Park Cemetery

Waikiki Aquarium **24**

23

Natatorium ◼

Kahala Ave.

Sans Souci Beach

Diamond Head State Monument

25

Diamond Head Crater

Kahala Beach

P A C I F I C

O C E A N

Kaluahole Beach

Diamond Head Lighthouse ◼

Diamond Head Rd.

Kaalawai Beach

Kupikipikio Pt.

Waahila Range

ATTRACTIONS IN & AROUND HONOLULU & WAIKIKI

Historic Honolulu

The Waikiki you see today bears no resemblance to the Waikiki of yesteryear, a place of vast taro fields extending from the ocean to deep into Manoa Valley, dotted with numerous fish ponds and gardens tended by thousands of people. This picture of old Waikiki can be recaptured by following the emerging **Waikiki Historic Trail** ★ (www.waikikihistorictrail.com), a meandering 2-mile walk with 20 bronze surfboard markers (standing 6 ft., 5 in. tall—you can't miss 'em), complete with descriptions and archival photos of the historic sites. The markers note everything from Waikiki's ancient fishponds to the history of the Ala Wai Canal. The trail begins at Kuhio Beach and ends at the King Kalakaua statue, at the intersection of Kuhio and Kalakaua avenues.

Bishop Museum ★★★ MUSEUM   This is a museum for adults and kids alike. For the adults: the original **Hawaiian Hall,** built in 1889 to house the collection of Hawaiian artifacts and royal family heirlooms of Princess Bernice Pauahi Bishop, the last descendant of King Kamehameha I. Today, the exhibits, spread out over three floors, give the most complete sense of how ancient native Hawaiians lived. On display are carvings representing Hawaiian gods and the personal effects of Hawaiian royalty, including an intricate feathered cape worn by Kamehameha himself. In the Hawaiian Hall Atrium, traditions come to life with the daily **hula show** (2pm). In 2013, renovations to **Pacific Hall** (previously known as Polynesian Hall) doubled the collection to include artifacts from all the Pacific Islands, including a restored Fijian fishing canoe.

For the kids, there's the 50-foot sperm whale skeleton and the **Richard T. Mamiya Science Adventure Center,** featuring interactive exhibits on how volcanoes, wind, and waves work. Don't miss the planetarium show **"Wayfinders: Waves, Winds, and Stars"** (Wed–Mon 1:30pm), which alternates between scenes shot on the voyaging canoe *Hokulea* and interactive segments that teach the basics on navigating using the stars. It's educational and awe-inspiring to realize that ancient voyagers navigated using just the night sky, the wind, and wave patterns. It's also how the current crew of the *Hokulea,* which set sail in 2014, is finding its way around the world. At the end of the presentation, you'll get an update on the crew's worldwide voyage.

1525 Bernice St., just off Kalihi St./Likelike Hwy. www.bishopmuseum.org. ⓒ **808/847-3511.** Admission $20 adults, $17 seniors, and $15 children 4–12. Wed–Mon 9am–5pm. Bus: 2.

The Bishop Museum.

ESPECIALLY FOR kids

Checking out the Honolulu Museum of Art on Family Sunday (p. 59)   Every third Sunday of the month, the Museum of Art is free, offering a variety of art activities and movies for the kids. Past programs have included sessions making pirate sock puppets and screenings of animated shorts from around the world. You can also take the shuttle to the Spalding House, where the fun continues.

Visiting the Waikiki Aquarium (p. 66) Visit Africa in Hawaii at Waikiki's Kapiolani Park, where the lions, giraffes, zebras, and elephants delight youngsters and parents alike.

Peeking Under the Sea at the Waikiki Aquarium (p. 66)   The aquarium is pretty small, but it has a fascinating collection of alien-like jellyfish and allows for up-close encounters of the endangered Hawaiian monk seal and an octopus that changes color before your eyes. Check the aquarium website for family-friendly activities, which include "Exploring the Reef at Night," an after-dark walk along the ocean reef outside the aquarium, where you'll hunt for crabs and octopuses with flashlights. During the "Behind the Scenes" tour, you'll learn what makes the aquarium run, from habitat creation to fish food.

Flying a Kite at Kapiolani Park   Great open expanses of green and constant trade winds make this urban park one of Hawaii's prime locations for kite-flying. You can watch the pros fly dragon kites and stage kite-fighting contests, or join in the fun after checking out the convenient kite shop across the street in New Otani's arcade.

Eating Shave Ice (p. 123)   No visit to Hawaii is complete without shave ice—powdery soft ice drenched in tropically flavored fruit syrups.

Beating Drums in a Tongan Village (p. 79)   The Polynesian Cultural Center introduces kids to the games played by Polynesian and Melanesian children. The activities, which range from cracking coconuts to Tongan shuffleboard, go on every day from 12:30 to 5:30pm.

Hawaiian Mission Houses Historic Site and Archives HISTORIC SITE Formerly the Mission Houses Museum, centered on the first mission houses built in the 1800s, this site is undergoing a rebranding. Possibly it's because missionaries have been cast as the bad white guys who eradicated Hawaiian culture. Now, instead of just depicting early American missionary life, the focus has expanded to include collaborations between Hawaiians and missionaries, which resulted in successes like the printed Hawaiian language and widespread literacy (by the 1860s, Hawaii had the highest literacy rate of any nation). Through a series of programs, such as the evolution of Hawaiian music, and new exhibits in the cellar of the 1821 Mission House (saloon pilot crackers and 19th-century bone saw reproduction, anyone?), the new plan is to encourage "emotional learning." Missionaries, it turns out, were people, too.

553 S. King St. (at Kawaiahao St.). www.missionhouses.org. © **808/447-3910.** Admission $10 adults, $8 military personnel and seniors, $6 students and children 6 and over, free for children 5 and under. Tues–Sat 10am–4pm. Bus: 2 and 42.

Honolulu Museum of Art ★ MUSEUM   In 2011, the Honolulu Academy of Art merged with the Contemporary Museum and was renamed the (more

Iolani Palace.

apropos) Honolulu Museum of Art. It also recently finished a reinstallation of the European and American art galleries, bringing to light many new pieces from the archives. The museum's Asian collection includes a significant number of items from Japan, China, and Korea.

The Honolulu Museum of Art is also where tours of **Shangri La ★★** start. Shuttles from the museum take visitors to tobacco heiress Doris Duke's private palace on a 5-acre sanctuary in Black Point. It's absolutely stunning, packed with Islamic art and intricate tilework from Iran, Turkey, and Syria; textiles from Egypt and India; and custom-painted ceilings by Moroccan artisans. Outside's not so bad either, with ocean views all the way to Diamond Head. Make sure to book far in advance—the tours fill up quickly, a testament to this unique wonder. Tours take 2½ hours.

Admittedly, I love the **Spalding House** (formerly the Contemporary Museum) more for its views and surrounding gardens than for its art collection. It's in Tantalus, high above the city, and yet only a 10-minute drive from downtown. One of my favorite activities is the "Lauhala and Lunch," where you picnic on the expansive lawn overlooking Honolulu. Call ahead to reserve a picnic basket from the Spalding House Café, which comes complete with tatami mats ($35 lunch for two).

900 S. Beretania St. www.honolulumuseum.org. ✆ **808/532-8700;** 808/532-3853 for Shangri La reservations; 808/237-5225 for the Spalding House Café. $10 adults; $5 students, seniors, and military personnel; free for children under 12. Tues–Sat 10am-4:30pm, Sun 1–5pm. Shangri La tours $25, children under 8 not admitted; advance reservations a must.

Iolani Palace ★ HISTORIC BUILDING   If you want to really "understand" Hawaii, this 45-minute tour is well worth the time. The Iolani Palace was built by King David Kalakaua, who spared no expense. The 4-year project, completed in 1882, cost $360,000—and nearly bankrupted the Hawaiian kingdom. This four-story Italian Renaissance palace was the first electrified building in Honolulu (it had electricity before the White House and Buckingham Palace). Royals lived here for 11 years, until Queen Liliuokalani was deposed and the Hawaiian monarchy fell forever, in a palace coup led by U.S. Marines on January 17, 1893, at the demand of sugar planters and missionary descendants.

Cherished by latter-day royalists, the 10-room palace stands as an architectural statement of the monarchy period. Iolani attracts 60,000 visitors a year in groups of 15; everyone must don booties to scoot across the royal floors. Visitors take either a comprehensive **guided tour ★**, which offers a docent-guided tour of the interior, or a self-led **audio tour.** Finish either tour by exploring the Basement Gallery on your own, where you'll find crown jewels, ancient feathered cloaks, the royal china, and more.

364 S. King St. (at Richards St.). www.iolanipalace.org. © **808/538-1471.** Guided tour $22 adults, $6 children 5–12; not available Mon; reservations required. Audio tour $15 adults, $6 children 5–12. Gallery tour $7 adults, $3 children 5–12. Mon–Sat 9:30am–4pm; closed Sun. Children 4 and under allowed only in the Basement Gallery (in the company of an adult). Extremely limited parking on palace grounds; try metered parking on the street. Bus: 2.

Kawaiahao Church ★ CHURCH   In 1842, Kawaiahao Church stood complete at last, the crowning achievement of missionaries and Hawaiians working together for the first time on a common project. Designed by Rev. Hiram Bingham (grandfather of explorer and politician Hiram Bingham III) and supervised by Kamehameha III, who ordered his people to help build it, the project took 5 years to complete. Workers quarried 14,000 coral blocks weighing 1,000 pounds each from the offshore reefs and cut timber in the forests for the beams. This proud stone church, complete with bell tower and colonial colonnade, was the first permanent Western house of worship in the islands. It became the church of the Hawaiian royalty and remains in use today. Some fine portraits of Hawaiian royalty hang inside. English- and Hawaiian-language services are conducted on Sundays at 9am.

957 Punchbowl St. (at King St.). © **808/522-1333.** Free admission (donations appreciated). Mon–Fri 8am–4:30pm; Sun services 9am. Bus: 2.

Queen Emma Summer Palace PALACE   Hanaiakamalama, the name of the country estate of Kamehameha IV and Queen Emma, was once in the secluded uplands of Nuuanu Valley. These days, it's adjacent to a six-lane highway full of speeding cars. This simple, seven-room New England–style house, built in 1848 and restored by the Daughters of Hawaii, is worth about an hour of your time to see the interesting blend of Victorian furniture and hallmarks of Hawaiian royalty, including feather cloaks and *kahili,* the feathered standards that mark the presence of *alii* (royalty). Other royal treasures include a canoe-shaped cradle for Queen Emma's baby, Prince Albert, who died at the age of 4. (Kauai's ritzy Princeville Resort is named for the little prince.)

2913 Pali Hwy. (at Old Pali Rd.). http://daughtersofhawaii.org. © **808/595-3167.** Admission $8 adults, $1 children 11 and under. Daily 9am–4pm. Bus: E or 57.

Wartime Honolulu

USS *Arizona* Memorial at Pearl Harbor ★★★ HISTORIC SITE   On December 7, 1941, the USS *Arizona,* while moored here in Pearl Harbor, was bombed in a Japanese air raid. The 608-foot battleship sank in 9 minutes without

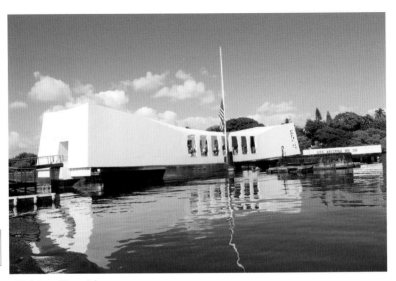

USS *Arizona* Memorial.

firing a shot, taking 1,177 sailors and Marines to their deaths—and catapulting the United States into World War II.

Nobody who visits the memorial will ever forget it. The deck of the ship lies 6 feet below the surface of the sea. Oil still oozes slowly up from the Arizona's engine room and stains the harbor's calm, blue water; some say the ship still weeps for its lost crew. The memorial is a stark white, 184-foot rectangle that spans the sunken hull of the ship; it was designed by Alfred Pries, a German architect interned on Sand Island during the war. It contains the ship's bell, recovered from the wreckage, and a shrine room with the names of the dead carved in stone.

Today, free U.S. Navy launches take visitors to the *Arizona*. You can make an **advance reservation** to visit the memorial at **www.recreation.gov** for an additional $1.50 per-ticket convenience fee. This is highly recommended; if you try to get walk-up tickets directly at the visitor center, you may have to wait a few hours before the tour. While you're waiting for the free shuttle to take you out to the ship, get the **audio tour ★★★**, which will make the trip even more meaningful. The tour (on an MP3 player) is about 2½ hours long, costs $7.50, and is worth every nickel. It's like having your own personal park ranger as your guide. The tape is narrated by the late Ernest Borgnine and features stories told by actual Pearl Harbor survivors—both American and Japanese. Plus, while you're waiting for the launch, the tour will take you step by step through the museum's personal mementos, photographs, and historic documents. You can pause the tour for the moving 20-minute film that precedes your trip to the ship. The tour continues on the launch, describing the shore line and letting you know what's in store at the memorial itself. At the memorial, the tour gives you a mental picture of that fateful day, and the narration continues on your boat ride back. Allow a total of at least 4 hours for your visit.

Due to increased security measures, visitors cannot carry purses, handbags, fanny packs, backpacks, camera bags (though you can carry your camera, cellphone, or video camera with you), diaper bags, or other items that offer concealment on the boat. However, there is a storage facility where you can stash carry-on-size items (no bigger than 30×30×18 in.), for a fee. *A reminder to parents:* Baby strollers, baby carriages, and baby backpacks are not allowed inside the theater, on the boat, or on the USS *Arizona* Memorial. All babies must be carried. *One last note:* Most unfortunately, the USS *Arizona* Memorial is a high-theft area—so leave your valuables at the hotel.

Pearl Harbor. www.nps.gov/usar. © **808/422-3300.** Free admission. $7.50 for the audio guide. **Highly recommended:** Make an advance reservation to visit the memorial at www.recreation. gov. Daily 7am–5pm (programs run 8am–3pm). Children 11 and under should be accompanied by an adult. Wheelchairs gladly accommodated. Drive west on H-1 past the airport; take the USS *Arizona* Memorial exit and follow the green-and-white signs; there's ample free parking. Bus: 40 or 42; or *Arizona* Memorial Shuttle Bus VIP (© **866/836-0317**), which picks up at Waikiki hotels 7am–12pm ($10 per person round-trip).

USS *Bowfin* Submarine Museum & Park ★ HISTORIC SITE   Ever wonder what life on a submarine is like? Then go inside the USS *Bowfin,* aka the "Pearl Harbor Avenger," to experience the claustrophobic quarters where soldiers lived and launched torpedoes. The *Bowfin* Museum details wartime submarine history and gives a sense of the impressive technical challenges that must be overcome for submarines to even exist. The Waterfront Memorial honors submariners lost during World War II.

11 Arizona Memorial Dr. (next to the USS *Arizona* Memorial Visitor Center). www.bowfin.org. © **808/423-1341.** Admission $12 adults, $8 active-duty military personnel and seniors, $5 children 4–12 (children 3 and under not permitted for safety reasons). Daily 7am–5pm (last admission at 4:30pm). See USS *Arizona* Memorial, above, for driving, bus, and shuttle directions.

USS *Missouri* Memorial ★ HISTORIC SITE   In the deck of this 58,000-ton battleship (the last one the navy launched), World War II came to an end with the signing of the Japanese surrender on September 2, 1945. The *Missouri* was part of the force that carried out bombing raids over Tokyo and provided firepower in the battles of Iwo Jima and Okinawa. In 1955, the navy decommissioned the ship and placed it in mothballs at the Puget Sound Naval Shipyard, in Washington State. But the *Missouri* was modernized and called back into action in 1986, eventually being deployed in the Persian Gulf War, before retiring once again in 1992. Here it sat until another battle ensued, this time over who would get the right to keep this living legend. Hawaii won that battle and brought the ship to Pearl Harbor in 1998. The 887-foot ship is now open to visitors as a museum memorial.

Pearl Harbor Visitor Center: Getting Tickets

The **USS *Arizona* Memorial, USS *Bowfin* and Submarine Museum, USS *Missouri* Memorial,** and **Pacific Aviation Museum** are all accessed via the Pearl Harbor Visitor Center. Park here and purchase tickets for all the exhibits. (Entry to the USS *Arizona* Memorial is free, but you still must get a ticket. Better yet, for the USS *Arizona,* reserve your spot at **www.recreation.gov** to avoid a long wait.) Shuttle buses will deliver you to the sites within Pearl Harbor.

You're free to explore on their own or take a guided tour. Highlights of this massive (more than 200-ft. tall) battleship include the forecastle (or "fo'c's'le," in navy talk), where the 30,000-pound anchors are "dropped" on 1,080 feet of anchor chain; the 16-inch guns (each 65 ft. long and weighing 116 tons), which can accurately fire a 2,700-pound shell some 23 miles in 50 seconds; and the spot where the Instrument of Surrender was signed as Douglas MacArthur, Chester Nimitz, and "Bull" Halsey looked on.

Battleship Row, Pearl Harbor. www.ussmissouri.com. © **877/MIGHTY-MO.** Admission $25 adults, $13 children 4–12. Mighty Mo Tour (35 min.); Battle Stations Tour (90 min.) $25 extra. Daily 8am–5pm; guided tours 8:15am–4:15pm. Check in at the USS *Bowfin* Submarine Museum, next to the USS *Arizona* Memorial Visitor Center. See USS *Arizona* Memorial, above, for driving, bus, and shuttle directions.

Pacific Aviation Museum MUSEUM   The Pacific Aviation Museum is the flashiest (and newest) of the Pearl Harbor exhibits, with its propaganda-esque written histories and signs. There are two hangars: Hangar 37 includes planes involved in the 1942 attack, but the best is Hangar 79, the doors still riddled with bullet holes from the Pearl Harbor strafing. It houses military aircraft, old and new; you can even climb into the cockpit of some of them. On the far end is the Restoration Shop, where you can watch vintage aircraft actively being restored. For an additional $10, sit in a Combat Flight Simulator, like an immersive video game in which you fly a plane and shoot down the enemy.

Hanger 39, 319 Lexington Blvd., Ford Island (next to the Red White Control Tower). www.pacific aviationmuseum.org. © **808/441-1000.** Admission $25 adults, $15 children 4–12; guided behind-the-scenes tour $35 adults, $25 children 4–12. Daily 9am–5pm. See USS *Arizona* Memorial, above, for driving, bus, and shuttle directions.

National Memorial Cemetery of the Pacific CEMETERY   The National Memorial Cemetery of the Pacific (also known as the Punchbowl) is an ash-and-lava tuff cone that exploded about 150,000 years ago—like Diamond Head, only smaller. Early Hawaiians called it Puowaina, or "hill of sacrifice." The old crater is a burial ground for 35,000 victims of three American wars in Asia and the Pacific: World War II, Korea, and Vietnam. Among the graves, you'll find many unmarked ones with the date December 7, 1941, carved in stone. Some names will be unknown forever; others are famous, like that of war correspondent Ernie Pyle, killed by a Japanese sniper in April 1945 on Okinawa; still others buried here are remembered only by family and surviving buddies. The white stone tablets known as the Courts of the Missing bear the names of 28,788 Americans missing in action in World War II.

Survivors come here often to reflect on the meaning of war and to remember those, like themselves, who stood in harm's way to win peace a half-century ago. Some fight back tears, remembering lost buddies, lost missions, and the sacrifices of those who died.

Punchbowl Crater, 2177 Puowaina Dr. (at the end of the road). Free admission. Daily 8am–5:30pm (Mar–Sept to 6:30pm). Bus: 2 or 42, with a long walk.

Just Beyond Pearl Harbor

Hawaiian Railway TRAIN   All aboard! This is a train ride back into history. Between 1890 and 1947, the chief mode of transportation for Oahu's sugar mills was the Oahu Railway and Land Co.'s narrow-gauge trains. The line carried not only equipment, raw sugar, and supplies, but also passengers from one side of the island to the other. You can relive those days every Sunday with a 1½-hour narrated ride through Ko Olina Resort and out to Makaha. As an added attraction, on the second Sunday of the month, you can ride on the nearly 100-year-old custom-built parlor-observation car belonging to Benjamin F. Dillingham, founder of the Oahu Railway and Land Co.; the fare is $20 (no kids under 13), and you must reserve in advance.

91-1001 Renton Rd., Ewa. www.hawaiianrailway.com. ✆ **808/681-5461.** Admission $12 adults, $8 seniors and children 2–12; Parlour Car 64 $25. Departures Sun at 1 and 3pm and weekdays by appointment. Take H-1 west to Exit 5A; take Hwy. 76 south for 2½ miles to Tesoro Gas; turn right on Renton Rd. and drive 1½ miles to end of paved section. The station is on the left. Bus: E or 42, with a 1½-mile walk.

Foster Botanical Garden.

Hawaii's Plantation Village HISTORIC SITE   The hour-long tour of this restored 50-acre village offers a glimpse back in time to when sugar planters shaped the land, economy, and culture of Hawaii. From 1852, when the first contract laborers arrived here from China, to 1947, when the plantation era ended, more than 400,000 men, women, and children from China, Japan, Portugal, Puerto Rico, Korea, and the Philippines came to work the sugarcane fields. The "talk story" tour brings the old village alive with 30 faithfully restored camp houses, Chinese and Japanese temples, the Plantation Store, and even a sumo-wrestling ring.

94–695 Waipahu St. (at Waipahu Depot Rd.), Waipahu. www.hawaiiplantationvillage.org. ✆ **808/677-0110.** Admission (including escorted tour) $13 adults, $10 seniors, $7 military personnel, $5 children 4–11. Mon–Sat 10am–2pm. Take H-1 west to Waikele-Waipahu exit (Exit 7); get in the left lane on exit and turn left on Paiwa St.; at the 5th light, turn right onto Waipahu St.; after the 2nd light, turn left. Bus: 40 or 42.

Gardens, Aquariums & Zoos

Foster Botanical Garden ★★ GARDEN   You could spend days in this unique historic garden, a leafy oasis amid the high-rises of downtown Honolulu. Combine a tour of the garden with a trip to Chinatown (just across the street) to maximize your time and double your pleasure. The giant trees that tower over the garden's main terrace were planted in the 1850s by William Hillebrand, a German physician and botanist, on royal land leased from Queen Emma. Today this 14-acre public garden, on the north side of Chinatown, is a living museum of plants, some rare and endangered, collected from the tropical regions of the world. Of special interest are 26 "Exceptional Trees" protected by state law, a large palm collection, a primitive cycad garden, and a hybrid orchid collection.

50 N. Vineyard Blvd. (at Nuuanu Ave.). ✆ **808/522-7066.** Admission $5 adults, $1 children 6–12. Daily 9am–4pm; guided tours Mon–Sat at 1pm (reservations recommended). Bus: 19 or E.

Honolulu Zoo ★ ZOO   Nobody comes to Hawaii to see an Indian elephant or African lions and zebras. Right? Wrong. This 43-acre municipal zoo in Waikiki attracts visitors in droves. If you've got kids, allot at least half a day. The highlight is the African Savanna, a 10-acre exhibit with more than 40 African critters including antelope and giraffes. The zoo also has a rare Hawaiian nene goose, one of the few indigenous animals left in Hawaii.

151 Kapahulu Ave. (between Paki and Kalakaua aves.), at entrance to Kapiolani Park. www. honoluluzoo.org. (✆ **808/971-7171.** Admission $14 adults, $6 children 3–12. Daily 9am–4:30pm. Zoo parking lot (entrance on Kapahulu Ave.) $1 per hour. Bus: 8 and 42.

Lyon Arboretum ★ GARDEN   The Lyon Arboretum dates from 1918, when the Hawaiian Sugar Planters Association wanted to demonstrate the value of watershed for reforestation. In 1953, it became part of the University of Hawaii, where they continued to expand the extensive collection of tropical plants. Six-story-tall breadfruit trees, yellow orchids no bigger than a nickel, ferns with fuzzy buds as big as a human head—these are just a few of the botanical wonders you'll find at the 194-acre arboretum. A whole different world opens up to you along the self-guided, 20-minute hike through the arboretum to Inspiration Point. You'll pass more than 5,000 exotic tropical plants full of singing birds in this cultivated rainforest at the head of Manoa Valley.

3860 Manoa Rd. (near the top of the road). www.hawaii.edu/lyonarboretum. (✆ **808/988-0456.** Suggested donation $5. Mon–Fri 8am–4pm; Sat 9am–3pm. Bus: 5.

Waikiki Aquarium ★★★ AQUARIUM   Do not miss this! Half of Hawaii's beauty is its underwater world. Behold the chambered nautilus, nature's submarine and inspiration for Jules Verne's "20,000 Leagues Under the Sea." You can see this tropical, spiral-shelled cephalopod mollusk—the only living one born in

Waikiki Aquarium.

captivity—any day of the week here. Its natural habitat is the deep waters of Micronesia, but former aquarium director Bruce Carlson not only succeeded in trapping the pearly shelled creature in 1,500 feet of water (by dangling chunks of raw tuna), but also managed to breed this ancient relative of the octopus. There are plenty of other fish to see in this small but first-class aquarium, located on a live coral reef. The Hawaiian reef habitat features sharks, eels, a touch tank, and habitats for the endangered Hawaiian monk seal and green sea turtle. The rotating jellyfish exhibit is otherworldly—it's like watching alien life.

2777 Kalakaua Ave. (across from Kapiolani Park). www.waquarium.org. ⓒ **808/923-9741.** Admission $12 adults, $8 active military, $5 seniors and children 4–12. Daily 9am–4:30pm. Bus: 2 and Waikiki Trolley's Green Line.

Other Natural Wonders & Spectacular Views

In addition to the attractions listed below, check out the hike to **Diamond Head Crater ★★★** (p. 97); almost everybody can handle it, and the 360-degree views from the top are fabulous.

Nuuanu Pali Lookout ★ NATURAL ATTRACTION   Gale-force winds sometimes howl through the mountain pass at this 1,186-foot-high perch guarded by 3,000-foot peaks, so hold on to your hat—and small children. But if you walk up from the parking lot to the precipice, you'll be rewarded with a view that'll blow you away. At the edge, the dizzying panorama of Oahu's windward side is breathtaking: Clouds low enough to pinch scoot by on trade winds; pinnacles of the pali (cliffs), green with ferns, often disappear in the mist. From on high, the tropical palette of green and blue runs down to the sea. Combine this 10-minute stop with a trip over the pali to the windward side.

Near the summit of Pali Hwy. (Hwy. 61); take the Nuuanu Pali Lookout turnoff.

Nuuanu Valley Rainforest NATURAL ATTRACTION   It's not the same as a peaceful nature walk, but if time is short and hiking isn't your thing, Honolulu has a rainforest you can drive through. It's only a few minutes from downtown Honolulu in verdant Nuuanu Valley, where it rains nearly 300 inches a year. And it's easy to reach: As the Pali Highway leaves residential Nuuanu and begins its climb through the forest, the last stoplight is the Nuuanu Pali Road turnoff; turn right for a jungley detour of about 2 miles under a thick canopy strung with liana vines, past giant bamboo that creaks in the wind, Norfolk pines, and wild shell ginger. The road rises and the vegetation clears as you drive, blinking in the bright light of day, past a small mountain reservoir. Soon the road rejoins the Pali Highway. Kailua is to the right and Honolulu to the left—but it can be a hair-raising turn. Instead, turn right, go a half-mile to the Nuuanu Pali Lookout (see above), stop for a panoramic view of Oahu's windward side, and return to the townbound highway on the other side.

Take the Old Nuuanu Pali Rd. exit off Pali Hwy. (Hwy. 61).

Puu Ualakaa State Park ★ STATE PARK/NATURAL ATTRACTION   The best **sunset view** of Honolulu is from a 1,048-foot-high hill named for sweet potatoes. Actually, the poetic Hawaiian name means "rolling sweet potato hill" and was named such because of how early planters used gravity to harvest their crop. The panorama is sweeping and majestic. On a clear day—which is often—you can see from Diamond Head to the Waianae Range, almost the length of

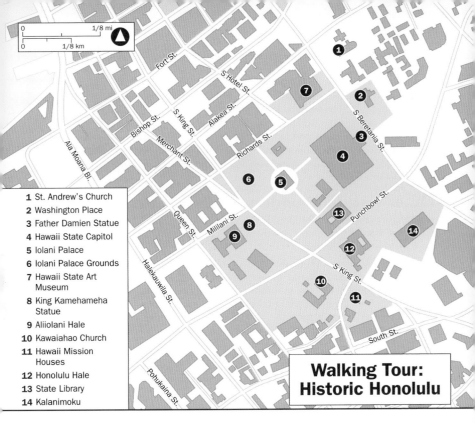

1 St. Andrew's Church
2 Washington Place
3 Father Damien Statue
4 Hawaii State Capitol
5 Iolani Palace
6 Iolani Palace Grounds
7 Hawaii State Art Museum
8 King Kamehameha Statue
9 Aliiolani Hale
10 Kawaiahao Church
11 Hawaii Mission Houses
12 Honolulu Hale
13 State Library
14 Kalanimoku

**Walking Tour:
Historic Honolulu**

Oahu. At night, several scenic overlooks provide romantic spots for young lovers who like to smooch under the stars with the city lights at their feet. It's a top-of-the-world experience—the view, that is.

At the end of Round Hill Dr. Daily 7am–6:45pm (to 7:45pm in summer). From Waikiki, take Ala Wai Blvd. to McCully St., turn right, and drive mauka (inland) beyond the H-1 on-ramps to Wilder St.; turn left and go to Makiki St.; turn right, and continue onward and upward about 3 miles.

WALKING TOUR: **HISTORIC HONOLULU**

GETTING THERE: **From Waikiki, take Ala Moana Boulevard in the Ewa direction. Ala Moana Boulevard ends at Nimitz Highway. Turn right on the next street on your right (Alakea St.). Park in the garage across from St. Andrew's Church after you cross Beretania Street. Bus: 2, 13, 19, or 20.**

START & FINISH: **St. Andrew's Church, Beretania and Alakea streets.**

TIME: **2 to 3 hours, depending on how long you linger in museums.**

BEST TIMES: **Wednesday through Saturday, daytime, when the Iolani Palace has tours.**

The 1800s were a turbulent time in Hawaii. By the end of the 1790s, Kamehameha the Great had united all the islands. Foreigners then began arriving by ship—first explorers, then merchants, and then, in 1820, missionaries. The rulers of Hawaii were hard-pressed to keep up. By 1840, it was clear that the capital had shifted from Lahaina, where the Kingdom of Hawaii was actually centered, to Honolulu, where the majority of commerce and trade was taking place. In 1848, the Great Mahele (division) enabled commoners and, eventually, foreigners to own crown land, and in two generations, more than 80 percent of all private lands had shifted to foreign ownership. With the introduction of sugar as a crop, the foreigners prospered, and in time they put more and more pressures on the government.

By 1872, the monarchy had run through the Kamehameha line and, in 1873, David Kalakaua was elected to the throne. Known as the "Merrie Monarch," Kalakaua redefined the monarchy by going on a world tour, building Iolani Palace, having a European-style coronation, and throwing extravagant parties. By the end of the 1800s, however, the foreign sugar growers and merchants had become extremely powerful in Hawaii. With the assistance of the U.S. Marines, they orchestrated the overthrow of Queen Liliuokalani, Hawaii's last reigning monarch, in 1893. The United States declared Hawaii a territory in 1898.

You can witness the remnants of these turbulent years in just a few short blocks.

Cross the street from the garage and venture back to 1858 when you enter:

1 St. Andrew's Church

The Hawaiian monarchs were greatly influenced by the royals in Europe. When King Kamehameha IV saw the grandeur of the Church of England, he decided to build his own cathedral. He and Queen Emma founded the Anglican Church of Hawaii in 1858. The king didn't live to see the church completed, however; he died on St. Andrew's Day, 4 years before King Kamehameha V oversaw the laying of the cornerstone in 1867. The church was named St. Andrew's in honor of King Kamehameha IV's death. This French-Gothic structure was shipped in pieces from England. Even if you aren't fond of visiting churches, you have to see the floor-to-eaves, hand-blown stained-glass window that faces the setting sun. In the glass is a mural of Rev. Thomas Staley (the first bishop in Hawaii), King Kamehameha IV, and Queen Emma. Services are conducted in English and Hawaiian. On Sundays at 8am the Hawaiian Choir sings Hawaiian hymns, and at 10:30am the Cathedral Choir, in existence for 150 years, performs.

Next, walk down Beretania Street in the Diamond Head direction to the gates of:

2 Washington Place

This was the former home of Queen Liliuokalani, Hawaii's last queen. For 80 years after her death, it served as the governor's house, until a new home was built on the property in 2002 and the historic residence was opened to the public. Tours are held Thursdays at 10am by reservation only. They're free; call © **808/586-0248** (www.iolanipalace.org) at least 2 days in advance to reserve. The Greek Revival–style home, built in 1842 by a U.S. sea captain named John Dominis, got its name from the U.S. ambassador who once stayed here and told so many stories about George Washington that people starting calling the home Washington Place. The sea captain's son married a beautiful Hawaiian princess, Lydia Kapaakea, who later became Queen

Liliuokalani. When the queen was overthrown by U.S. businessmen in 1893, she moved out of Iolani Palace and into Washington Place, where she lived until her death in 1917. On the left side of the building, near the sidewalk, is a plaque inscribed with the words to one of the most popular songs written by Queen Liliuokalani, "Aloha Oe" ("Farewell to Thee").

Cross the street and walk to the front of the Hawaii State Capitol, where you'll find the:

3 Father Damien Statue

The people of Hawaii have never forgotten the sacrifice this Belgian priest made to help the sufferers of leprosy when he volunteered to work with them in exile on the Kalaupapa Peninsula on the island of Molokai. After 16 years of service, Father Damien himself died of leprosy, at the age of 49. The statue is frequently draped in leis in recognition of Father Damien's humanitarian work.

Behind the Father Damien Statue is the:

4 Hawaii State Capitol

Here's where Hawaii's state legislators work from mid-January to the end of April every year. This is not your typical white-domed structure, but rather a building symbolic of Hawaii. Unfortunately, it symbolizes more of Hawaii than the architect and the state legislature probably bargained for. The building's unusual design has palm tree–shaped pillars, two cone-shaped chambers (representing volcanoes) for the legislative bodies, and, in the inner courtyard, a 600,000-tile mosaic of the sea (Aquarius) created by a local artist. A reflecting pool (representing the sea) surrounds the entire structure. Like a lot of things in Hawaii, it was a great idea, but no one considered the logistics. The reflecting pond draws brackish water, which rusts the hardware; when it rains, water pours into the rotunda, dampening government business; and the Aquarius floor mosaic was so damaged by the elements that it became a hazard. In the 1990s, the circa-1969 building underwent renovations. It's open today, and you are welcome to go into the rotunda and see the woven hangings and murals at the entrance; pick up a self-guided-tour brochure at the governor's office on the fourth floor. The public is also welcome to observe the state government in action during legislative sessions (www.capitol.hawaii.gov).

Walk down Richards Street toward the ocean and stop at:

5 Iolani Palace ★

Hawaii is the only state in the U.S. to have not one but two royal

The Iolani Palace.

palaces: one in Kona, where the royals went during the summer, and Iolani Palace (*iolani* means "royal hawk"). Don't miss the opportunity to see this grande dame of historic buildings. Guided tours are $22 adults, $6 children 5 to 12; self-guided audio tours are $15 adults, $6 children 5 to 12; and basement gallery tours are $7 adults, $3 children 5 to 12. It's open Monday to Saturday 9:30am to 4pm and closed Sunday; call © **808/522-0832** (www.iolanipalace.org) to reserve in advance, as spots are limited.

In ancient times, a *heiau* (temple) stood in this area. When it became clear to King Kamehameha III that the capital should be transferred from Lahaina to Honolulu, he moved to a modest building here in 1845. The construction of the palace was begun in 1879 by King David Kalakaua; it was finished 3 years later at a cost of $350,000. The king spared no expense: You can still see the glass and iron work imported from San Francisco, and the palace had all the modern conveniences for its time. Electric lights were installed 4 years before the White House had them, and every bedroom had its own full bathroom with hot and cold running water, copper-lined tub, flush toilet, and bidet. The king had a telephone line from the palace to his boathouse on the water a year after Alexander Graham Bell introduced it to the world.

It was also in this palace that Queen Liliuokalani was overthrown and placed under house arrest for 9 months. Later, the territorial and then the state government used the palace until it outgrew it. When the legislature left in 1968, the palace was in shambles. It has since undergone a $7-million overhaul to restore it to its former glory.

After you visit the palace, spend some time on the:

6   Iolani Palace Grounds

You can wander around the grounds at no charge. The ticket window to the palace and the gift shop are in the former barracks of the Royal Household Guards. The domed pavilion on the grounds was originally built as a Coronation Stand by King Kalakaua (9 years after he took the throne, he decided to have a formal European-style coronation ceremony where he crowned himself and his queen, Kapiolani). Later he used it as a **Royal Bandstand** for concerts (King Kalakaua, along with Henri Berger, the first Royal Hawaiian Bandmaster, wrote "Hawaii Pono'i," the state anthem). Today the Royal Bandstand is still used for concerts by the Royal Hawaiian Band.

From the palace grounds, turn in the Ewa direction, cross Richards Street, and walk to the corner of Richards and Hotel streets to the:

7   Hawaii State Art Museum

Opened in 2002, the Hawaii State Art Museum is housed in the original Royal Hawaiian hotel, built in 1872 during the reign of King Kamehameha V. Most of the art displayed in the 300-piece collection was created by local artists. The pieces were purchased by the state, thanks to a 1967 law that says that 1 percent of the cost of state buildings will be used to acquire works of art. Nearly 5 decades later, the state has amassed almost 6,000 pieces.

Walk makai down Richards Street and turn left (toward Diamond Head) on South King Street to the:

8 King Kamehameha Statue

At the juncture of King, Merchant, and Mililani streets stands a replica of the man who united the Hawaiian Islands. The striking black-and-gold bronze statue is magnificent. Try to see the statue on June 11 (King Kamehameha Day), when it is covered with leis in honor of Hawaii's favorite son.

King Kamehameha Statue.

The statue of Kamehameha I was cast by Thomas Gould in 1880 in Paris. However, it was lost at sea somewhere near the Falkland Islands. Subsequently, the insurance money was used to pay for a second statue, but in the meantime, the original statue was recovered. The original was eventually sent to the town of Kapaau on the Big Island, the birthplace of Kamehameha, and the second statue was placed in Honolulu in 1883, as part of King David Kalakaua's coronation ceremony.

Right behind the King Kamehameha Statue is:

9 Aliiolani Hale

The name translates to "House of Heavenly Kings." This distinctive building, with a clock tower, now houses the Supreme Court of Hawaii and the Judiciary History Center. King Kamehameha V originally wanted to build a palace here and commissioned the Australian architect Thomas Rowe in 1872. However, it ended up as the first major government building for the Hawaiian monarchy. Kamehameha V didn't live to see it completed, and King David Kalakaua dedicated the building in 1874. Ironically, less than 20 years later, on January 17, 1893, Stanford Dole, backed by other prominent sugar planters, stood on the steps to this building and proclaimed the overthrow of the Hawaiian monarchy and the establishment of a provisional government. Self-guided tours are available Monday through Friday from 7:45am to 4:30pm; admission is free.

Walk toward Diamond Head on King Street; at the corner of King and Punchbowl, stop in at the:

10 Kawaiahao Church ★

When the missionaries came to Hawaii, the first thing they did was build churches. Four thatched-grass churches (one measured 54×22 ft. and could seat 300 people on lauhala mats; the last thatched church held 4,500 people) had been built on this site through 1837, before Rev. Hiram Bingham began building what he considered a "real" church: a New England–style congregational structure with Gothic influences. Between 1837 and 1842, the construction of the church required some 14,000 giant coral slabs (some weighing more than 1,000 pounds). Hawaiian divers ravaged the reefs, digging out huge chunks of coral and causing irreparable environmental damage.

Kawaiahao is Hawaii's oldest church and has been the site of numerous historic events, such as a speech made by King Kamehameha III in 1843, an excerpt from which became Hawaii's state motto ("*Ua mau ke ea o ka aina i ka pono*," which translates as "The life of the land is preserved in righteousness").

The church is open Monday through Saturday 8am to 4pm; you'll find it to be very cool in temperature. Don't sit in the back pews marked with kahili feathers and velvet cushions; they are still reserved for the descendants of royalty. Sunday service (in English and Hawaiian) is at 9am.

Cross the street, and you'll see the:

11 Hawaiian Mission Houses

On the corner of King and Kawaiahao streets stand the original buildings of the Sandwich Islands Mission Headquarters: the **Frame House** (built in 1821), the **Chamberlain House** (1831), and the **Printing Office** (1841). The complex is open Tuesday through Saturday from 10am to 4pm; admission is $10 adults, $8 seniors and military personnel, and $6 students and children 6 and older. The tours are often led by descendants of the original missionaries to Hawaii. For information, go to www.missionhouses.org.

Believe it or not, the missionaries brought their own prefab house along with them when they came around Cape Horn from Boston in 1819. The Frame House was designed for New England winters and had small windows (it must have been stiflingly hot inside). Finished in 1821 (the interior frame was left behind and didn't arrive until Christmas 1820), it is Hawaii's oldest wooden structure. The Chamberlain House, built in 1831, was used by the missionaries as a storehouse.

The missionaries believed that the best way to spread the Lord's message to the Hawaiians was to learn their language, and then to print literature for them to read. So it was the missionaries who gave the Hawaiians a written language. The Printing House on the grounds was where the lead-type Ramage press (brought from New England, of course) was used to print the Hawaiian Bible.

Cross King Street and walk in the Ewa direction to the corner of Punchbowl and King to:

12 Honolulu Hale

The **Honolulu City Hall,** built in 1927, was designed by Honolulu's most famous architect, C. W. Dickey. His Spanish Mission–style building has an open-air courtyard, which is used for art exhibits and concerts. It's open Monday through Friday.

13 State Library

Anything you want to know about Hawaii and the Pacific can be found here, the main branch of the state's library system. Located in a restored historic building, it has an open garden courtyard in the middle, great for stopping for a rest on your walk.

Head mauka up Punchbowl to the corner of Punchbowl and Beretania streets, where you'll see:

14 Kalanimoku

A beautiful name, "Ship of Heaven," has been given to this dour state office building. Here you can get information from the Department of Land and Natural Resources on hiking and camping in state parks.

Retrace your steps in the Ewa direction down Beretania to Alakea back to the parking garage.

4

BEYOND HONOLULU: EXPLORING THE ISLAND BY CAR

The moment always arrives—usually after a couple of days at the beach, snorkeling in the warm blue-green waters of Hanauma Bay, enjoying sundown mai tais—when a certain curiosity kicks in about the rest of Oahu. It's time to find the rental car in the hotel garage and set out around the island.

Oahu's Southeast Coast

From the high-rises of Waikiki, venture down Kalakaua Avenue through tree-lined Kapiolani Park to take a look at a different side of Oahu, the arid south shore. The landscape here is more moonscape, with prickly cacti onshore and, in winter, spouting whales cavorting in the water. Some call it the South Shore, others Sandy's (after the mile-long beach here), but Hawaiians call it **Ka Iwi,** which means "the bone"—no doubt because of all the bone-cracking shore breaks along this popular body-boarding coastline. The beaches here are long, wide, and popular with local daredevils.

To get to this coast, follow Kalakaua Avenue past the multi-tiered Dillingham Fountain and around the bend in the road, which now becomes Poni Moi Road. Make a right on Diamond Head Road and begin the climb up the side of the old crater. At the top are several lookout points, so if the official Diamond Head Lookout is jammed with cars, try one of the other lookouts just down the road. The view of the rolling waves is spectacular; take the time to pull over.

Diamond Head Road rolls downhill into the ritzy community of **Kahala.** At the fork in the road at the triangular Fort Ruger Park, veer to your right and continue on the palm tree–lined Kahala Avenue. Make a left on Hunakai Street, and then take a right on Kilauea Avenue and look for the sign H-1 west–Waimanalo. Turn right at the sign, although you won't get on the H-1 freeway; instead, get on the Kalanianaole Highway, a four-lane highway interrupted every few blocks by a stoplight. This is the suburban bedroom community to Honolulu, marked by malls on the left and beach parks on the right.

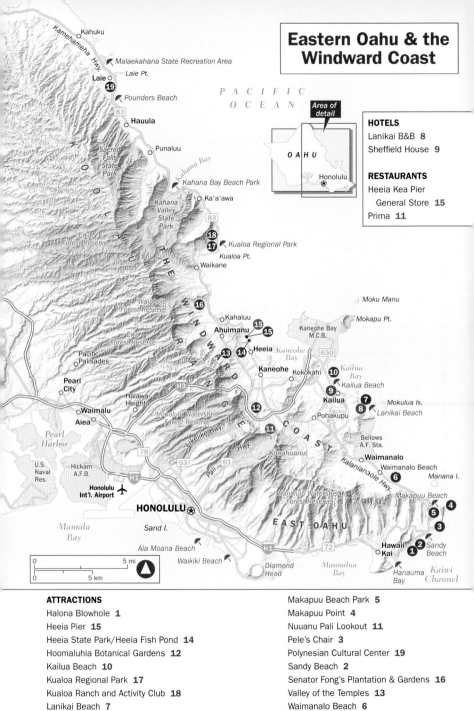

Eastern Oahu & the Windward Coast

Area of detail

P A C I F I C
O C E A N

O A H U

Honolulu

HOTELS
Lanikai B&B **8**
Sheffield House **9**

RESTAURANTS
Heeia Kea Pier
    General Store **15**
Prima **11**

Kahuku

Malaekahana State Recreation Area

Laie Pt.
Laie **19**

Pounders Beach

Hauula

Punaluu

Sacred Falls State Park

Kahana Bay

Kahana Bay Beach Park

Ka'a'awa

Kahana Valley State Park

Ewa Forest Reserve

18
17 Kualoa Regional Park

Kualoa Pt.

Waikane

Waiahole Forest Reserve

Moku Manu

Mokapu Pt.

Ewa Forest Reserve

16

Kahaluu
15
Ahuimanu **15**

Kaneohe Bay M.C.B.

13 **14** **Heeia**
Kaneohe Bay

Kaneohe
Kokokahi

630

Kailua Bay

Pacific Palisades

Pearl City

Halawa Heights

Honolulu Watershed Forest Reserve

H3

10
Kailua Beach

9
Kailua

7
8 Lanikai Beach

Mokulua Is.

Waimalu
Aiea

12

Pohakupu

Likelike Hwy.

11

Konahuanui

Bellows A.F. Sta.

Waimanalo

Waimanalo Beach

Pearl Harbor

U.S. Naval Res.

Hickam A.F.B.

78

63

61

Pali Hwy.

6

Manana I.

Honolulu Int'l. Airport

H1

HONOLULU

Sand I.

Honolulu Watershed Forest Reserve

Makapuu Beach

4
5
Makapuu Beach

E A S T O A H U

3

Mamala Bay

Ala Moana Beach

Waikiki Beach

72

Hawaii Kai

2
1 Sandy Beach

Diamond Head

Maunalua Bay

Hanauma Bay

Kaiwi Channel

0   5 mi
0   5 km

ATTRACTIONS

Halona Blowhole **1**
Heeia Pier **15**
Heeia State Park/Heeia Fish Pond **14**
Hoomaluhia Botanical Gardens **12**
Kailua Beach **10**
Kualoa Regional Park **17**
Kualoa Ranch and Activity Club **18**
Lanikai Beach **7**

Makapuu Beach Park **5**
Makapuu Point **4**
Nuuanu Pali Lookout **11**
Pele's Chair **3**
Polynesian Cultural Center **19**
Sandy Beach **2**
Senator Fong's Plantation & Gardens **16**
Valley of the Temples **13**
Waimanalo Beach **6**

One of these parks is **Hanauma Bay** ★★ (p. 86); you'll see the turnoff on the right when you're about half an hour from Waikiki. This marine preserve is a great place to stop for a swim; you'll find the friendliest fish on the island here. *A reminder:* The beach park is closed on Tuesday.

Around mile marker 11, the jagged lava coast itself spouts sea foam at the **Halona Blowhole.** Look out to sea from Halona over Sandy Beach and across the 26-mile gulf to neighboring Molokai and the faint triangular shadow of Lanai on the far horizon. **Sandy Beach** ★ (p. 86) is one of Oahu's most dangerous beaches. Body boarders just love it.

The coast looks raw and empty along this stretch, but the road weaves past old Hawaiian fish ponds and the famous formation known as **Pele's Chair,** just off Kalanianaole Highway (Hwy. 72) above Queen's Beach. From a distance, the lava-rock outcropping looks like a mighty throne; it's believed to be the fire goddess's last resting place on Oahu before she flew off to continue her work on other islands.

Ahead lies 647-foot-high **Makapuu Point,** with a lighthouse that once signaled safe passage for steamship passengers arriving from San Francisco. The automated light now brightens Oahu's south coast for passing tankers, fishing boats, and sailors. You can take a short hike up the **Makapuu Lighthouse Trail** ★★ (p. 97) for a spectacular vista.

Turn the corner at Makapuu and you're on Oahu's windward side, where cooling trade winds propel windsurfers across turquoise bays; the waves at **Makapuu Beach Park** ★ (p. 88) are perfect for bodysurfing.

Ahead, the coastal vista is a profusion of fluted green mountains and strange peaks, edged by golden beaches and the blue, blue Pacific. The 3,000-foot-high, sheer, green Koolau mountains plunge almost straight down, presenting an irresistible jumping-off spot for paragliders. Most likely, you'll spot their colorful chutes in the sky, looking like balloons released into the wind.

Winding up the coast, Kalanianaole Highway (Hwy. 72) leads through rural **Waimanalo,** a country beach town of nurseries and stables. Nearly 4 miles long, **Waimanalo Beach** is Oahu's longest beach and popular with local families here on weekends. Take a swim here or head on to **Kailua Beach** ★★★ (p. 88), one of Hawaii's best.

If it's still early in the day, you can head up the lush, green Windward Coast by turning right at the Castle Junction, where Hwy. 72 meets Hwy. 61 (which is called Kailua Rd. on the makai, or seaward, side of the junction, and Kalanianaole Hwy. on the mauka, or inland, side of the junction), and continuing down Kailua Road (Hwy. 61). After Kailua Road crosses the Kaelepulu Stream, the name of the road changes to Kuulei Road. When Kuulei Road ends, turn left onto Kalaheo Avenue, which becomes Kaneohe Bay Drive after it crosses the Kawainui Channel. Follow this scenic drive around the peninsula until you get to Kamehameha Highway (Hwy. 83); turn right and continue on Kamehameha Highway for a scenic drive along the ocean.

If you're in a hurry to get back to Waikiki, turn left at Castle Junction and head over the Pali Highway (Hwy. 61), which becomes Bishop Street in Honolulu and ends at Ala Moana. Turn left for Waikiki; it's the second beach on the right.

The Windward Coast

From the **Nuuanu Pali Lookout** ★, near the summit of the Pali Highway (Hwy. 61), you get the first hint of the other side of Oahu, a region so green and lovely that it could be an island sibling of Tahiti. With its many beaches and bays, the scenic 30-mile Windward Coast parallels the corduroy-ridged, nearly perpendicular cliffs of the Koolau Range, which separates the windward side of the island from Honolulu and the rest of Oahu. As you descend on the serpentine Pali Highway beneath often-gushing waterfalls, you'll see the nearly 1,000-foot spike of **Olomana,** a bold pinnacle that beckons intrepid hikers, and, beyond, the Hawaiian village of **Waimanalo.**

From the Pali Highway, to the right is Kailua, Hawaii's biggest beach town, with more than 50,000 residents and two special beaches, **Kailua Beach ★★★** (p. 88) and **Lanikai Beach ★★★** (p. 88). Although the Pali Highway (Hwy. 61) proceeds directly to the coast, it undergoes two name changes, becoming first Kalanianaole Highway—from the intersection of Kamehameha Highway (Hwy. 83)—and then Kailua Road as it heads into Kailua town; but the road remains Hwy. 61 the whole way. Kailua Road ends at the T intersection at Kalaheo Drive, which follows the coast in a northerly and southerly direction. Turn right on South Kalaheo Drive to get to Kailua Beach and Lanikai Beach. No signs point the way, but you can't miss them.

If you spend a day at the beach here, stick around for sunset, when the sun sinks behind the Koolau Range and tints the clouds pink and orange. After a hard day at the beach, you'll work up an appetite, and Kailua has several great inexpensive restaurants (see p. 133 for a few ideas).

If you want to skip the beaches this time, turn left on North Kalaheo Drive, which becomes Kaneohe Bay Drive as it skirts Kaneohe Bay and leads back to Kamehameha Highway (Hwy. 83), which then passes through Kaneohe. The suburban maze of Kaneohe is one giant strip mall of retail excess that mars one of the Pacific's most picturesque bays. After clearing this obstacle, the place begins to look like Hawaii again.

At Heeia State Park is **Heeia Fish Pond,** which ancient Hawaiians built by enclosing natural bays with rocks to trap fish on the incoming tide. The 88-acre fish pond, which is made of lava rock and had four watchtowers to observe fish movement and several sluice gates along the 5,000-foot-long wall, is now in the process of being restored.

Stop by the **Heeia Pier,** which juts onto Kaneohe Bay. You can take a snorkel cruise here or sail out to a sandbar in the middle of the bay for an incredible view of Oahu that most people, even those who live here, never see. Sit down to the fresh catch of the day at **Heeia Kea Pier General Store & Deli ★** (p. 133), serving fishermen, sailors, and kayakers the town's best omelets and plate lunches since 1979.

Incredibly scenic Kaneohe Bay is spiked with islets and lined with gold-sand beach parks like **Kualoa Regional Park ★** (p. 89), a favorite picnic spot. The bay has a barrier reef and four tiny islets, one of which is known as Moku o loe, or Coconut Island. Don't be surprised if it looks familiar—it appeared in *Gilligan's Island.*

Everyone calls the other distinctively shaped island **Chinaman's Hat,** but it's really named **Mokolii.** It's a sacred *puu honua,* or place of refuge, like the restored Puu Honua Honaunau on the Big Island of Hawaii. Excavations have unearthed evidence that this area was the home of ancient *alii* (royalty). Early Hawaiians believed that Mokolii (Fin of the Lizard) is all that remains of a *mo'o,* or lizard, slain by Pele's sister, Hiiaka, and hurled into the sea. At low tide you can swim out to the island, but keep watch on the changing tide, which can sweep you out to sea. The islet has a small sandy beach and is a bird preserve, so don't spook the red-footed boobies.

Little poly-voweled beach towns like **Kahaluu, Kaaawa, Punaluu,** and **Hauula** pop up along the coast, offering passersby shell shops and art galleries to explore. Famed hula photographer **Kim Taylor Reece** lives on this coast; his gallery at 53–866 Kamehameha Hwy., near Sacred Falls (www.kimtaylorreece. com; ✆ **808/293-2000**), is open Monday through Wednesday from noon to 5pm. You'll also see roadside fruit and flower stands vending ice-cold coconuts (to drink) and tree-ripened mangoes, papayas, and apple bananas (short bananas with an apple aftertaste).

Sugar, once the sole industry of this region, is gone. But **Kahuku,** the former sugar-plantation town, has found new life as a small aquaculture community with shrimp farms.

From here, continue along Kamehameha Highway (Hwy. 83) to the North Shore.

Attractions Along the Windward Coast

The attractions below are arranged geographically as you drive up the coast from south to north.

Hoomaluhia Botanical Garden ★ GARDEN   This 400-acre botanical garden at the foot of the steepled Koolau Range is the perfect place for a picnic. Its name means "a peaceful refuge," and that's exactly what the Army Corps of Engineers created when they installed a flood-control project here, which resulted in a 32-acre freshwater lake and garden. Just unfold a beach mat, lie back, and watch the clouds race across the rippled cliffs of the majestic Koolau Mountains. This is one of the few public places on Oahu that provides a close-up view of the steepled cliffs. The park has hiking trails and a lovely, quiet campground (p. 116). If you like hiking and nature, plan to spend at least a half-day here. **Note:** Be prepared for rain, mud, and mosquitoes.

45–680 Luluku Rd., Kaneohe. ✆ **808/233-7323.** Free admission. Daily 9am–4pm. Guided nature hikes Sat 10am and Sun 1pm. Take H-1 to the Pali Hwy. (Hwy. 61); turn left on Kamehameha Hwy. (Hwy. 83); at the 4th light, turn left onto Luluku Rd. Bus: 55 or 56 will stop on Kamehameha Hwy.; it's a 2-mile walk to the visitor center.

Valley of the Temples HISTORIC SITE   This famous cemetery in a cleft of the pali is stalked by wild peacocks and about 700 curious people a day, who pay to see the 9-foot meditation Buddha, acres of ponds full of more than 10,000 Japanese koi carp, and a replica of Japan's 900-year-old Byodo-In Temple of Equality. The original, made of wood, stands in Uji, on the outskirts of Kyoto; the Hawaiian version, made of concrete, was erected in 1968 to commemorate the 100th anniversary of the arrival of the first

Polynesian Cultural Center.

Japanese immigrants to Hawaii. It's not the same as seeing the original, but it's worth a detour.

47–200 Kahekili Hwy. (across the street from Temple Valley Shopping Center), Kaneohe. www. byodo-in.com. ℂ **808/239-8811.** Admission $3 adults, $2 seniors, $1 children 11 and under. Daily 9am–5pm. Take the H-1 to the Likelike Hwy. (Hwy. 63); after the Wilson Tunnel, get in the right lane and take the Kahekili Hwy. (Hwy. 63); at the 6th traffic light is the entrance to the cemetery (on the left). Bus: 65.

Senator Fong's Plantation Gardens GARDEN   Hiram Fong, the first Chinese American elected to the U.S. Senate, served 17 years before retiring to this 725-acre tropical garden years ago. This land originally belonged to King Lunalilo; Senator Fong purchased it in 1950. The landscape you see today is relatively the same as what early Polynesians saw hundreds of years ago, with forests of *kukui, hala, koa,* and *ohia-'ai* (mountain apple). Ti and pili grass still cover the slopes. It's definitely worth an hour—if you haven't already seen enough flora to last a lifetime.

47–285 Pulama Rd., Kaneohe. www.fonggarden.net. ℂ **808/239-6775.** Admission $15 adults, $13 seniors, $9 children 5–12. Daily 10am–2pm; guided walking tours Sun–Fri 10:30am and 1pm. Take the H-1 to the Likelike Hwy. (Hwy. 63); turn left at Kahekili Hwy. (Hwy. 83); continue to Kaneohe and turn left on Pulama Rd. Bus: 55; it's a 1-mile walk uphill from the stop.

Kualoa Ranch and Activity Club RANCH   Kualoa Ranch does raise cattle, but people don't come here to see the cows. They come for various adventure packages covering numerous activities on its 4,000 acres. Options include horseback riding, ATV rides, and movie-site tours (Kualoa Ranch was the backdrop for "Jurassic Park," "Godzilla," and more).

49–560 Kamehameha Hwy., Kaaawa. www.kualoa.com. ℂ **800/231-7321** or 808/237-7321. Reservations required. Various packages available; single activities $23–$95. Daily 8am–3:30pm. Take H-1 to the Likelike Hwy. (Hwy. 63), turn left at Kahekili Hwy. (Hwy. 83), and continue to Kaaawa. Bus: 55.

Polynesian Cultural Center THEME PARK   This is the Disneyland version of Polynesia, operated by the Mormon Church. Which means that some will see it as a tourist trap, while others, especially families, will enjoy the show. (My thoughts: I would never bring friends here when they visit, but I still remember my parents taking me when I was young and how delighted I was by the spectacle.) Here you can see the lifestyles, songs, dance, costumes, and architecture of seven Pacific islands or archipelagos—Fiji, New Zealand, Marquesas, Samoa, Tahiti, Tonga, and Hawaii—in the re-created villages scattered throughout the 42-acre lagoon park.

You "travel" through the theme park on foot or in a canoe on a man-made freshwater lagoon. Native students from Polynesia who attend Hawaii's Brigham Young University are the "inhabitants" of each village. They engage the audience with spear-throwing competitions, coconut tree climbing presentations, and invitations to pound Tongan drums. There's a show and luau every evening, but you'll get better food at the Hawaiian restaurants in town I recommend later in this chapter (see "Where to Eat" on p. 118).

Just beyond the center is the Hawaii Temple of the Church of Jesus Christ of Latter-day Saints, built of volcanic rock and concrete in the form of a Greek cross; it includes reflecting pools, formal gardens, and royal palms. Completed in 1919, it was the first Mormon temple built outside the continental United States.

An optional tour of the Temple Visitors Center, as well as neighboring Brigham Young University Hawaii, is included in the package admission price.

55–370 Kamehameha Hwy., Laie. www.polynesia.com. © **800/367-7060**, 808/293-3333, or 808/923-2911. Various packages available for $50–$229 adults, $36–$179 children 3–11. Mon–Sat noon–9pm. Take H-1 to Pali Hwy. (Hwy. 61) and turn left on Kamehameha Hwy. (Hwy. 83). Parking $8. Bus: 55. Polynesian Cultural Center coach $22 round-trip; call numbers above to book.

Central Oahu & the North Shore

If you can afford the splurge, rent a bright, shiny convertible—the perfect car for Oahu because you can tan as you go—and head for the North Shore and Hawaii's surf city: **Haleiwa ★★**, a quaint sugar-plantation town and a designated historic site. A collection of faded clapboard stores with a picturesque harbor, Haleiwa has evolved into a surfer outpost with a hippie vibe. For more, see "Surf City: Haleiwa," below.

Getting here is half the fun. You have two choices: The first is to meander north along the lush Windward Coast, through country hamlets with roadside stands selling mangoes, bright tropical pareu, fresh corn, and pond-raised prawns. Attractions along that route are discussed in the previous section.

The second choice is to cruise up the H-2 through Oahu's broad and fertile central valley, past Pearl Harbor and the Schofield Barracks of "From Here to Eternity" fame, and on through the red-earthed heart of the island, where pineapple and sugarcane fields stretch from the Koolau to the Waianae mountains, until the sea reappears on the horizon.

Once you're on H-1, stay to the right side; the freeway tends to divide abruptly. Keep following the signs for the H-1 (it separates off to Hwy. 78 at the airport and reunites later on; either way will get you there), and then the H-1/H-2. Leave the H-1 where the two highways divide; take the H-2 up the middle of the island, heading north toward the town of Wahiawa. That's what the sign will say—not North Shore or Haleiwa, but Wahiawa.

The H-2 runs out and becomes a two-lane country road about 18 miles outside downtown Honolulu, near Schofield Barracks. The highway becomes Kamehameha Highway (Hwy. 99 and later Hwy. 83) at Wahiawa. Just past Wahiawa, about a half-hour out of Honolulu, the **Dole Pineapple Plantation,** 64–1550 Kamehameha Hwy. (www.dole-plantation.com; © **808/621-8408;** daily 9:30am–5pm; bus: 52), offers a rest stop with pineapples, pineapple history, pineapple trinkets, and pineapple juice. This agricultural exhibit/retail area features a maze kids will love to wander through, and is open daily from 9:30am to 5pm ($6 adults, $4 children 4–12). The **Pineapple Express** is a single-engine diesel locomotive with four cars that takes a 22-minute tour around 2¼ miles of the plantation's grounds, with an educational spiel on the legacy of the pineapple and agriculture in Hawaii.

"Kam" Highway, as everyone calls it, will be your road for most of the rest of the trip to Haleiwa, on the North Shore.

CENTRAL OAHU ATTRACTIONS

On the central plains of Oahu, tract homes and malls with factory-outlet stores are now spreading across abandoned sugarcane fields, where sandalwood forests used to stand at the foot of Mount Kaala, the mighty summit of Oahu. Hawaiian chiefs once sent commoners into thick sandalwood forests to cut down trees, which were then sold to China traders for small fortunes. The scantily clad natives caught cold in the cool uplands, and many died.

Central & Leeward Oahu

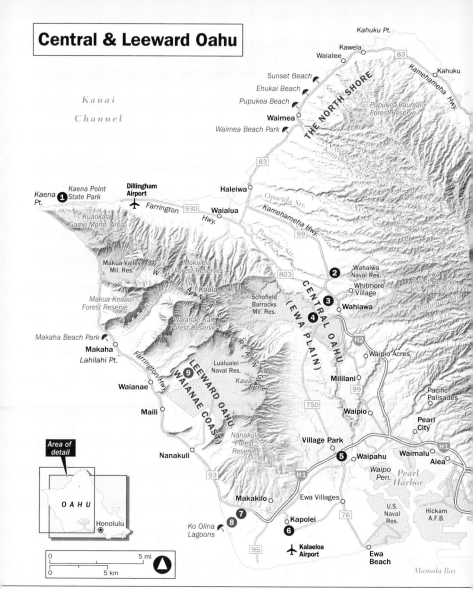

ATTRACTIONS
Dole Pineapple Plantation **2**
Hawaii's Plantation Village **5**
Hawaiian Railway **6**
Kaena Point State Park **1**
Kukaniloko Birthing Stones **3**
U.S. Army Schofield Barracks **4**

HOTELS
Aulani, a Disney Resort & Spa, Ko Olina Hawaii **7**

RESTAURANTS
Kahumana Café **9**
Monkeypod Kitchen **8**

Surfboards in Haleiwa.

On these plains in 1908, the U.S. Army pitched a tent that later became a fort. And on December 7, 1941, Japanese pilots came screaming through Kolekole Pass to shoot up the barracks at Schofield, sending soldiers running for cover, and then flew on to sink ships at Pearl Harbor.

Kukaniloko Birthing Stones HISTORIC SITE   This is the most sacred site in central Oahu. Two rows of 18 lava rocks once flanked a central birthing stone, where women of ancient Hawaii gave birth to potential *alii* (royalty). The rocks, according to Hawaiian belief, held the power to ease the labor pains of childbirth. Birth rituals involved 48 chiefs who pounded drums to announce the arrival of newborns likely to become chiefs. Children born here were taken to the now-destroyed Holonopahu Heiau in the pineapple field, where chiefs ceremoniously cut the umbilical cord.

Used by Oahu's *alii* for generations of births, the *pohaku* (rocks), many in bowl-like shapes, now lie strewn in a grove of trees that stands in a pineapple field here. Some think the site may also have served ancient astronomers—like a Hawaiian Stonehenge. Petroglyphs of human forms and circles appear on some of the stones. The Wahiawa Hawaiian Civic Club recently erected two interpretive signs, one explaining why this was chosen as a birth site and the other telling how the stones were used to aid in the birth process.

Off Kamehameha Hwy., btw. Wahiawa and Haleiwa, on Plantation Rd., opposite the road to Whitmore Village.

NORTH SHORE ATTRACTIONS

Puu o Mahuka Heiau ★ HISTORIC SITE   Go around sundown to feel the *mana* (sacred spirit) of this Hawaiian place. The largest sacrificial temple on Oahu, it's associated with the great Kaopulupulu, who sought peace between Oahu and Kauai. This prescient *kahuna* predicted that the island would be overrun by strangers from a distant land. In 1794, three of Capt. George Vancouver's

SURF CITY: haleiwa

Only 28 miles from Waikiki is Haleiwa, the funky former sugar-plantation town that's now the world capital of big-wave surfing. This beach town really comes alive in winter, when waves rise up, light rain falls, and temperatures dip into the 70s (low to mid-20s Celsius); then, it seems, every surfer in the world is here to see and be seen.

Officially designated a historic cultural and scenic district, Haleiwa was founded by sugar baron Benjamin Dillingham, who built a 30-mile railroad to link his Honolulu and North Shore plantations in 1899. He opened a Victorian hotel overlooking Kaiaka Bay and named it Haleiwa, or "house of the Iwa," the tropical seabird often seen here. The hotel and railroad are gone, but the town of Haleiwa, which was rediscovered in the late 1960s by hippies, manages to hold onto some of its rustic charm. Of course, like other places on Oahu, that is changing; some of the older wooden storefronts are being redeveloped and local chains such as T&C Surf are moving in. Arts and crafts, boutiques, and burger joints line both sides of the town. There's also a busy fishing harbor full of charter boats and captains who hunt the Kauai Channel daily for tuna, mahimahi, and marlin. With a great harbor and sunset view, **Haleiwa Joe's,** 66–011 Kamehameha Hwy. (http://haleiwajoes.com; ℂ 808/637-8005), serves fresh local seafood and fun tropical drinks.

Once in Haleiwa, the hot and thirsty traveler should report directly to the nearest shave-ice stand, like **Matsumoto Shave Ice ★★**, 66–087 Kamehameha Hwy. (ℂ 808/637-4827). For 40 years, this small, humble shop operated by the Matsumoto family has served a popular rendition of the Hawaii-style snow cone flavored with tropical tastes.

Just down the road are some of the fabled shrines of surfing—**Waimea Beach, Banzai Pipeline, Sunset Beach**—where some of the world's largest waves, reaching 20 feet and more, rise up between November and January. November to December is the holding period for the Vans **Triple Crown of Surfing** (http://vanstriplecrownofsurfing.com), one of the world's premier surf competition series, when professional surfers from around the world descend on the 7-mile miracle of waves. Hang around Haleiwa and the North Shore and you're bound to run into a few of the pros and perhaps even get invited to the surf houses for a party. Battle the traffic to come up on competition days (it seems like everyone ditches work and heads north on these days): It's one of Oahu's best shows. For details on North Shore beaches, see p. 89.

men of the *Daedalus* were sacrificed here. In 1819, the year before New England missionaries landed in Hawaii, King Kamehameha II ordered all idols here to be destroyed.

A national historic landmark, this 18th-century *heiau,* known as the "hill of escape," sits on a 300-foot bluff overlooking Waimea Bay and 25 miles of Oahu's wave-lashed north coast—all the way to Kaena Point, where the Waianae Range ends in a spirit leap to the other world. The *heiau* appears as a huge rectangle of rocks twice as big as a football field, with an altar often covered by the flower and fruit offerings left by native Hawaiians.

1 mile past Waimea Bay. Take Pupukea Rd. mauka (inland) off Kamehameha Hwy. at Food-land, and drive 1 mile up a switchback road. Bus: 52, then walk up Pupukea Rd.

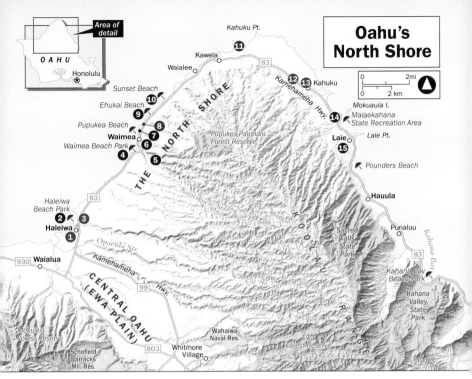

Oahu's North Shore

Kahuku Pt.

Kawela

Waialee

Sunset Beach

Ehukai Beach

Pupukea Beach

Waimea

Waimea Beach Park

Haleiwa
Beach Park

Haleiwa

Waialua

Kahuku

Mokuauia I.

**Malaekahana
State Recreation Area**

Laie

Laie Pt.

Pounders Beach

Hauula

Punaluu

Kahana Bay
Beach Park

Kahana
Valley
State
Park

Pupukea-Paumalu
Forest Reserve

THE NORTH SHORE

Kamehameha Hwy

Kaunala Str.

KOOLAU RANGE

Sacred
Falls
State
Park

CENTRAL OAHU
(EWA PLAIN)

Mokuleia
Forest Reserve

Schofield
Barracks
Mil. Res.

Whitmore
Village

Wahiawa
Naval Res.

Ewa
Forest Reserve

Opaeula Str.

Kamehameha Hwy

Kahana Bay

*Area of
detail*

OAHU

Honolulu

0   2mi
0   2 km

ATTRACTIONS

Banzai Pipeline (Ehukai Beach Park) **9**
Haleiwa Beach Park **2**
Malaekahana Bay State Recreation Area **14**
Polynesian Cultural Center **15**
Puu o Mahuka Heiau **6**
Shark's Cove, Pupukea Beach Park **7**
Sunset Beach **10**
Waimea Beach Park **4**
Waimea Valley **5**

HOTELS

Ke Iki Beach Bungalows **8**
Turtle Bay Resort **11**

RESTAURANTS

Beet Box Café **1**
Haleiwa Joe's **3**
Kahuku Farms **12**
Matsumoto Shave Ice **1**
Opal Thai **1**
Shrimp trucks **13**

Waimea Valley ★ NATURAL ATTRACTION   For nearly 3 decades, this 1,875-acre park has lured visitors with activities from cliff diving and hula performances to kayaking and ATV tours. In 2008, the Office of Hawaiian Affairs took over and formed a new nonprofit corporation, Hiipaka, to run the park, with an emphasis on perpetuating and sharing the "living Hawaiian culture." A visit here offers a lush walk into the past. The valley is packed with archaeological sites, including the 600-year-old Hale O Lono, a heiau dedicated to the Hawaiian god Lono, which you'll find to the left of the entrance. The botanical collection has 35 different gardens, including super-rare Hawaiian species such as the endangered *Kokia cookei* hibiscus. The valley is also home to fauna such as the endangered Hawaiian moorhen; look for a black bird with a red face cruising in the ponds. The 150-acre Arboretum and Botanical Garden contains more than 5,000 species of tropical plants. Walk through the gardens (take the paved paths or dirt trails) and wind up at 45-foot-high Waimea Falls—bring your bathing suit and you can dive into the cold, murky water. The public is invited to hike the trails and spend a day in this quiet oasis. There are several free walking tours all starting at 9am, plus cultural activities like lei making, kappa demonstrations, hula lessons, Hawaiian games and crafts, and music and storytelling.

59–864 Kamehameha Hwy. ✆ **808/638-7766.** Admission $15 adults, $7.50 seniors and children 4–12. Daily 9am–5pm. Bus: 52.

BEACHES
The Waikiki Coast
ALA MOANA BEACH PARK ★★

Gold-sand Ala Moana (meaning "path to the sea," in Hawaiian), on sunny Mamala Bay, stretches for more than a mile along Honolulu's coast between downtown and Waikiki. This 76-acre midtown beach park, with spreading lawns shaded by banyans and palms, is one of the island's most popular playgrounds. It has a man-made beach, created in the 1930s by filling a coral reef with Waianae Coast sand, as well as its own lagoon, yacht harbor, tennis courts, music pavilion, bathhouses, picnic tables, and enough wide-open green spaces to accommodate 4 million visitors a year. The water is calm almost year-round, protected by black-lava rocks set offshore. There's a large parking lot as well as metered street parking.

WAIKIKI BEACH ★★★

No beach anywhere is so widely known or so universally sought after as this narrow, 1½-mile-long crescent of imported sand (from Molokai) at the foot of a string of high-rise hotels. Home to the world's longest-running beach party, Waikiki attracts nearly 5 million visitors a year from every corner of the planet. First-timers are amazed to discover how small Waikiki Beach really is, but there's always a place for them under the tropical sun here.

Waikiki Beach.

Waikiki is actually a string of beaches that extends between **Sans Souci State Recreational Area,** near Diamond Head to the east, and **Duke Kahanamoku Beach,** in front of the Hilton Hawaiian Village to the west. Great stretches along Waikiki include **Kuhio Beach,** next to the Moana Surfrider, which provides the quickest access to the Waikiki shoreline; the stretch in front of the Royal Hawaiian, hotel known as **Grey's Beach,** which is canted so it catches the rays perfectly; and **Sans Souci,** the small, popular beach in front of the New Otani Kaimana Beach Hotel that's locally known as "Dig Me" Beach because of all the gorgeous bods that strut their stuff here.

Waikiki is fabulous for swimming, board surfing, bodysurfing, outrigger canoeing, diving, sailing, snorkeling, and pole fishing. Every imaginable type of watersports equipment is available for rent here. Facilities include showers, lifeguards, restrooms, grills, picnic tables, and pavilions at the **Queen's Surf** end of the beach (at Kapiolani Park, btw. the zoo and the aquarium). The best place to park is at Kapiolani Park, near Sans Souci.

East Oahu

HANAUMA BAY ★★

Oahu's most popular snorkeling spot is this volcanic crater with a broken sea wall; its small, curved, 2,000-foot gold-sand beach is packed elbow-to-elbow with people year-round. The bay's shallow shoreline water and abundant marine life are the main attractions, but this good-looking beach is also popular for sunbathing and people-watching. Serious divers shoot "the slot" (a passage through the reef) to get to Witch's Brew, a turbulent cove, and then brave strong currents in 70-foot depths at the bay mouth to see coral gardens, turtles, and even sharks. (**Divers:** Beware of the Molokai Express, a strong current.) You can snorkel in the safe, shallow (10-ft.) inner bay, which, along with the beach, is almost always crowded. Because Hanauma Bay is a conservation district, you cannot touch or remove any marine life here. Feeding the fish is also prohibited.

The **Marine Education Center** features exhibits and a 7-minute video orienting visitors to this Marine Life Sanctuary. The 10,000-square-foot center includes a training room, gift shop, public restrooms, snack bar, and staging area for the motorized tram, which, for a fee, will take you down the steep road to the beach. Facilities include parking, restrooms, a pavilion, a grass volleyball court, lifeguards, barbecues, picnic tables, and food concessions. Alcohol is prohibited in the park; there is no smoking past the visitor center. Expect to pay $1 per vehicle to park plus an entrance fee of $7.50 per person (free for children 12 and under and Hawaii residents).

If you're driving, take Kalanianaole Highway to Koko Head Regional Park. Avoid the crowds by going early, about 8am, on a weekday morning; once the parking lot's full, you're out of luck. Alternatively, take TheBus to escape the parking problem: The Hanauma Bay Shuttle runs from Waikiki to Hanauma Bay every half-hour from 8:45am to 1pm; you can catch it at the Ala Moana Hotel, the Ilikai Hotel, or other city bus stops. It returns every hour from noon to 4pm. Hanauma Bay is closed every Tuesday so the fish can have a day off. For information, call ✆ **808/396-4229.** Hanauma Bay is open from 6am to 7pm in the summer and 6am to 6pm in the winter.

SANDY BEACH ★

Sandy Beach is one of the best bodysurfing beaches on Oahu; it's also one of the most dangerous. It's better to just stand and watch the daredevils literally risk their

BEACHES

Ala Moana Beach Park **1**
Banzai Pipeline **24**
Haleiwa Beach Park **27**
Hanauma Bay **5**
Kailua Beach **12**
Kualoa Regional Park **17**
Lanikai Beach **10**
Makaha Beach Park **30**
Makapuu Beach Park **9**
Malaekahana Bay State
Recreation Area **20**
Sandy Beach **7**
Sunset Beach **23**
Waikiki Beach **2**
Waimea Beach Park **25**
Yokohama Bay **29**

CABINS & CAMPGROUNDS

Hoomaluhia Botanical
Garden **13**
Kahana Bay Beach Park **18**
Kualoa Regional Park **17**
Malaekahana Bay State
Recreation Area **20**

GOLF COURSES

Ala Wai Municipal
Golf Course **3**
Hawaii Kai Golf Course **6**
Kahuku Golf Course **21**
Ko Olina Golf Club **31**
Olomana Golf Links **11**
Pearl Country Club **16**
Turtle Bay Resort **22**
West Loch Municipal
Golf Course **32**

HIKES

Diamond Head Crater **4**
Hauula Loop Trail **19**
Kaena Point **28**
Makapuu Lighthouse Trail **8**
Manoa Falls Trail **14**
Pali (Maunawili) Trail **15**
Waimea Valley **26**

PACIFIC OCEAN

Kahuku Pt.
Kawela
Waialee
Waimea
Haleiwa
Waialua
Dillingham Airport
Kaena Pt.
Kaena Point State Park
Makua Keaau Forest Reserve
Makua Valley Mil. Res.
Makaha
Waianae
Maili
Nanakuli
Kapolei
Ewa Villages
Ewa Beach
Makakilo
Waipahu
Waimalu
Aiea
Pearl City
Waipio
Mililani
Wahiawa
Whitmore Village
Wahiawa Naval Res.
Schofield Barracks Mil. Res.
Waipio Acres
Pearl Harbor
U.S. Naval Res.
Hickam A.F.B.
Honolulu Int'l Airport
HONOLULU
Diamond Head
Mamala Bay

NORTH SHORE
CENTRAL OAHU (EWA PLAIN)
LEEWARD OAHU (WAIANAE COAST)
WAIANAE RANGE
KOOLAU RANGE
THE WINDWARD COAST
EAST OAHU

Laie Pt.
Hauula
Laie
Punaluu
Ka'a'awa
Kualoa Pt.
Kualoa Pt.
Kahaluu
Waikane
Waiahole
Kaneohe
Heeia
Kaneohe Bay
Kaneohe Bay M.C.B.
Kailua
Kailua Bay
Mokulua Is.
Waimanalo
Waimanalo Beach
Bellows A.F. Sta.
Hawaii Kai
Kaiwi Channel
Moku Manu
Mokapu Pt.
Maunalua Bay
Halawa Heights
Palisades
Pacific
Mahana Valley State Park
Sacred Falls State Park
Pupukea-Paumalu Forest Reserve
Ewa Forest Reserve
Waimano Forest Reserve
Waiahole Forest Reserve
Nuuanu Watershed Forest Reserve

5 mi
5 km

necks at this 1,200-foot-long gold-sand beach that's pounded by wild waves and haunted by a dangerous shore break and strong backwash. Weak swimmers and children should definitely stay out of the water here; Sandy Beach's heroic lifeguards make more rescues in a year than those at any other beach. Visitors, easily fooled by experienced bodysurfers who make it look easy, often fall victim to the bone-crunching waves. Lifeguards post flags to alert beachgoers to the day's surf: Green means safe, yellow means caution, and red indicates very dangerous water conditions.

Facilities include restrooms and parking. Go weekdays to avoid the crowds or weekends to catch the bodysurfers in action. From Waikiki, drive east on the H-1, which becomes Kalanianaole Highway; proceed past Hawaii Kai, up the hill to Hanauma Bay, past the Halona Blowhole, and along the coast. The next big gold beach on the right is Sandy Beach. TheBus no. 22 will also bring you here.

MAKAPUU BEACH PARK ★

Makapuu Beach is a beautiful 1,000-foot-long gold-sand beach cupped in the stark black Koolau cliffs on Oahu's easternmost point. Even if you never venture into the water, it's worth a visit just to enjoy the great natural beauty of this classic Hawaiian beach. (You've probably already seen it in countless TV shows, from "Hawaii Five-O" to "Magnum, P.I.") In summer, the ocean here is as gentle as a Jacuzzi, and swimming and diving are perfect; come winter, however, and Makapuu is a hit with expert bodysurfers, who come for the big, pounding waves that are too dangerous for most regular swimmers.

Facilities include restrooms, lifeguards, barbecue grills, picnic tables, and parking. To get here, follow Kalanianaole Highway toward Waimanalo, or take TheBus no. 22 or 23.

The Windward Coast

LANIKAI BEACH ★★★

One of Hawaii's best spots for swimming, gold-sand Lanikai's crystal-clear lagoon is like a giant saltwater swimming pool that you're lucky enough to be able to share with the resident tropical fish and sea turtles. Too gorgeous to be real, this is one of Hawaii's postcard-perfect beaches: It's a mile long and thin in places, but the sand's as soft as talcum powder. Prevailing onshore trade winds make this an excellent place for sailing and windsurfing. Kayakers often paddle out to the two tiny offshore Mokulua islands, which are seabird sanctuaries. Because Lanikai is in a residential neighborhood, it's less crowded than other Oahu beaches, the perfect place to enjoy a quiet day. Sun worshipers should arrive in the morning, though, as the Koolau Range blocks the afternoon rays.

There are no facilities here, just off-street parking. From Waikiki, take the H-1 to the Pali Highway (Hwy. 61) through the Nuuanu Pali Tunnel to Kailua, where the Pali Highway becomes Kailua Road as it proceeds through town. At Kalaheo Avenue, turn right and follow the coast about 2 miles to Kailua Beach Park; just past it, turn left at the T intersection and drive uphill on Aalapapa Drive, a one-way street that loops back as Mokulua Drive. Park on Mokulua Drive and walk down any of the eight public-access lanes to the shore. Or take TheBus no. 57A or 57 (Kailua), and then transfer to the shuttle bus.

KAILUA BEACH ★★★

Windward Oahu's premier beach is a wide, 2-mile-long golden strand with dunes, palm trees, panoramic views, and offshore islets that are home to seabirds. The swimming is excellent, and the azure waters are usually decorated

Kailua Beach.

with bright sails; this is Oahu's premier windsurfing beach, as well. It's a favorite spot to sail catamarans, bodysurf the gentle waves, or paddle a kayak. Water conditions are quite safe, especially at the mouth of Kaelepulu Stream, where toddlers play in the freshwater shallows at the middle of the beach park. The water is usually about 78°F (26°C), the views are spectacular, and the setting, at the foot of the sheer green Koolau Range, is idyllic. It's gotten more and more crowded over the years—guess the secret's out—but you can usually find a less-occupied stretch of sand the farther you are from the beach park.

Facilities at the beach park include picnic tables, barbecues, restrooms, a volleyball court, a public boat ramp, and free parking. To get here, take Pali Highway (Hwy. 61) to Kailua, drive through town, turn right on Kalaheo Avenue, and go a mile until you see the beach on your left. Or take TheBus no. 57A or 57 into Kailua, and then the no. 70 shuttle.

KUALOA REGIONAL PARK ★

This 150-acre coco palm–fringed peninsula is the biggest beach park on the windward side and one of Hawaii's most scenic. It's located on Kaneohe Bay's north shore, at the foot of the spiky Koolau Ridge. The park has a broad, grassy lawn and a long, narrow, white-sand beach ideal for swimming, walking, beachcombing, kite-flying, or just enjoying the natural beauty of this once-sacred Hawaiian shore, listed on the National Register of Historic Places. The waters are shallow and safe for swimming year-round (lifeguards are on duty). Offshore is Mokolii, the picturesque islet otherwise known as Chinaman's Hat. At low tide, you can swim or wade out to the island, which has a small sandy beach. It's also a bird preserve—so don't spook the red-footed boobies.

> **Impressions**
>
> *The boldness and address with which we saw them perform these difficult and dangerous maneuvers was altogether astonishing.*
> —Capt. James Cook's observations of Hawaiian surfers

The North Shore

MALAEKAHANA BAY STATE RECREATION AREA ★★

This white-sand crescent, almost a mile long, lives up to just about everyone's image of the perfect Hawaii beach. It's excellent for swimming. On a weekday, you may be the only one here; but should some net fisherman—or a kindred soul—intrude upon your delicious privacy, you can swim out to Goat Island (or wade across at low tide), a sanctuary for seabirds and turtles (so don't chase 'em, brah).

Facilities include restrooms, barbecues, picnic tables, outdoor showers, and parking. To get here, take Kamehameha Highway (Hwy. 83) 2 miles north of the Polynesian Cultural Center; as you enter the main gate, you'll come upon the wooded beach park. Or you can take TheBus no. 55.

WAIMEA BEACH PARK ★★★

This deep, sandy bowl has gentle summer waves that are excellent for swimming, snorkeling, and bodysurfing. To one side of the bay is a huge rock that local kids like to climb and dive from. In this placid scene, the only clues of what's to come in winter are those evacuation whistles on poles beside the road. But what a difference a season makes: Winter waves pound the narrow bay, sometimes rising to 50 feet high. When the surf's really up, very strong currents and shore breaks sweep the bay—and it seems like everyone on Oahu drives out to Waimea to get a look at the monster waves and those who ride them. Weekends are great for watching the surfers; to avoid the crowds, go on weekdays.

Facilities include lifeguards, restrooms, showers, parking, and nearby restaurants and shops in Haleiwa town. The beach is located on Kamehameha Highway (Hwy. 83); from Waikiki, you can take TheBus no. 52.

Leeward Oahu: The Waianae Coast

MAKAHA BEACH PARK

When the surf's up here, it's spectacular: Monstrous waves pound the beach. This is the original home of Hawaii's big-wave surfing championship; surfers today know it as the home of **Buffalo's Big Board Surfing Classic** (www.buffalosurfingclassic.com), where surfers ride the waves on 10-foot-long wooden boards in the old Hawaiian style of surfing. Nearly a mile long, this half-moon, gold-sand beach is tucked between 231-foot Lahilahi Point, which locals call Black Rock, and Kepuhi Point, a toe of the Waianae mountain range. Summer is the best time to hit this beach—the waves are small, the sand abundant, and the water safe for swimming. Children hug the shore on the north side of the beach, near the lifeguard stand, while surfers dodge the rocks and divers seek an offshore channel full of big fish. A caveat: This is a "local" beach; you are welcome, of course, but you can expect "stink eye" (mild approbation) if you are not respectful of the beach and the local residents who use the facility all the time.

Facilities include restrooms, lifeguards, and parking. To get here, take the H-1 freeway to the end of the line, where it becomes Farrington Highway (Hwy. 93), and follow it to the beach; or you can take TheBus no. C.

YOKOHAMA BAY ★

Where Farrington Highway (Hwy. 93) ends, the wilderness of Kaena Point State Park begins. It's a remote 853-acre coastline park of empty beaches, sand dunes, cliffs, and deep-blue water. This is the last sandy stretch of shore on the northwest coast of Oahu. Sometimes it's known as Keawalua Beach or Puau Beach, but everybody here calls it Yokohama, after the Japanese immigrants who came from that port city to work the cane fields and fished along this shoreline. When the surf's calm—mainly in summer—this is a good area for snorkeling, diving, swimming, shore fishing, and picnicking. When the surf's up, board surfers and bodysurfers are out in droves; don't go in the water then unless you're an expert.

There are no lifeguards or facilities, except at the park entrance, where there's a restroom and lifeguard stand. There's no bus service, either.

WATERSPORTS

If you want to rent beach toys (snorkeling equipment, boogie boards, surfboards, stand-up paddleboards, kayaks, and more), check out **Snorkel Bob's,** on the way to Hanauma Bay at 700 Kapahulu Ave. (at Date St.), Honolulu (www.snorkel bob.com; ☎ **808/735-7944**), or **Aloha Beach Service,** in the Moana Surfrider, 2365 Kalakaua Ave., in Waikiki (☎ **808/922-3111,** ext. 2341). On Oahu's windward side, try **Kailua Sailboards & Kayaks,** 130 Kailua Rd., a block from Kailua Beach Park (www.kailuasailboards.com; ☎ **808/262-2555**). On the North Shore, get equipment from **Surf-N-Sea,** 62–595 Kamehameha Hwy., Haleiwa (www.surfnsea.com; ☎ **800/899-7873**).

Boating

A funny thing happens to people when they come to Hawaii: Maybe it's the salt air, the warm tropical nights, or the blue Hawaiian moonlight, but otherwise-rational people who have never set foot on a boat in their life suddenly want to go out to sea. You can opt for a "booze cruise"—jammed with loud, rum-soaked strangers—or you can sail on one of these special yachts, all of which will take you out **whale-watching** in season (roughly Jan–Apr). For fishing charters, see "Sport Fishing," below.

Captain Bob's Picnic Sail ★   See the majestic Windward Coast the way it should be seen—from a boat. Captain Bob will take you on a 4-hour lazy-day sail of Kaneohe Bay aboard his 42-foot catamaran, which skims across the almost always calm water above the shallow coral reef, lands at the disappearing sandbar Ahu o Laka, and takes you past two small islands to snorkel spots full of tropical fish and sometimes turtles. The color of the water alone is worth the price. This

Snorkeling the Hawaiian waters.

is an all-day affair: A shuttle will pick you up at your Waikiki hotel between 9 and 9:30am and bring you back at about 4pm.

Kaneohe Bay. www.captainbobspicnicsail.com. © **808/942-5077.** All-day cruise $99 adults, $85 children 3–12. Rates include all-you-can-eat barbecue lunch and transportation from Waikiki hotels. No cruises on Sun and holidays. Bus: 55.

Navatek I ★   You've never been on a boat, you don't want to be on a boat, but here you are being dragged aboard one. Why are you boarding this weird-looking vessel? It guarantees that you'll be "seasick-free," that's why. The 140-foot-long *Navatek I* isn't even a boat; it's actually a SWATH (Small Waterplane Area Twin Hull) vessel. That means the ship's superstructure—the part you ride on—rests on twin torpedo-like hulls that cut through the water so you don't bob like a cork and spill your mai tai. It's the smoothest ride on Mamala Bay. In fact, *Navatek I* is the only dinner cruise ship to receive U.S. Coast Guard certification to travel beyond Diamond Head.

   Sunset dinner cruises leave Pier 6 nightly. If you have your heart set on seeing the city lights, take the Royal Sunset Dinner Cruise, which runs from 5:30 to 7:30pm. The best deal is the **lunch cruise** (which runs during **whale season,** roughly Jan–Apr), with a full buffet and a great view of Oahu offshore—plus you get to see whales, to boot. The lunch cruise lasts from 12:15 to 2:30pm. Both cruises include live Hawaiian music.

Aloha Tower Marketplace, Pier 6, c/o Hawaiian Cruises Ltd. www.atlantisadventures.com/oahu. cfm. © **808/973-1311.** Dinner cruises $99–$144 adults, $57–88 children 2–12; lunch cruises $79 adults, $39 children 2–12. Validated parking is half off. Bus: 20 and E. **Hint:** Check website for Internet deals.

Wild Side Tours ★   Picture this: You're floating in the calm waters off the Waianae coast, where your 42-foot sailing catamaran has just dropped you off. Below, in the reef, are turtles, and suddenly in the distance, you see spinner dolphins. This happens every day on the 4-hour tours operated by the Cullins family, which has swum in these waters for decades. In winter, you may spot humpback whales on the morning cruise, which also includes lunch, snorkel gear, instruction, and a flotation device. The tour lasts from 8am to noon; you'll check in at 7:30am.

Waianae Boat Harbor, 85–471 Farrington Hwy., Waianae. www.sailhawaii.com. © **808/306-7273.** Morning sail/snorkel $195 for age 12 and up (not recommended for younger children). Bus: C.

Body Boarding (Boogie Boarding) & Bodysurfing

Good places to learn to body board are in the small waves of **Waikiki Beach ★★★** and **Kailua Beach ★★★** (both reviewed under "Beaches," earlier in this chapter), and **Bellows Field Beach Park,** off Kalanianaole Highway (Hwy. 72) in Waimanalo, which is open to the public on weekends (from noon Fri to midnight Sun and holidays). To get here, turn toward the ocean on Hughs Road, and then right on Tinker Road, which takes you to the park.

   See the introduction to this section for a list of rental shops where you can get a boogie board.

Ocean Kayaking/Stand-Up Paddling

For a wonderful adventure, rent a kayak or a stand-up paddle (SUP) board, arrive at Lanikai Beach just as the sun is appearing, and paddle across the emerald lagoon to the pyramid-shape islands called Mokulua—it's an experience you won't forget. On the windward side, check out **Kailua Sailboards & Kayaks,**

130 Kailua Rd., a block from Kailua Beach Park (www.kailuasailboards.com; ✆ **808/262-2555**), where single kayaks rent for $59 for a half-day and double kayaks rent for $69 for a half-day. SUP boards rent for $59 for a half-day.

If you're staying on the North Shore, go to **Surf-N-Sea,** 62–595 Kamehameha Hwy., Haleiwa (www.surfnsea.com; ✆ **800/899-7873**), where kayak rentals start at $10 per hour and go to $60 for a full day. SUP board rentals start at $20 per hour and go to $60 for a full day.

Scuba Diving

Oahu is a wonderful place to scuba dive, especially for those interested in wreck diving. One of the more famous wrecks in Hawaii is the *Mahi,* a 185-foot former minesweeper easily accessible just south of Waianae. Abundant marine life makes this a great place to shoot photos—schools of lemon butterfly fish and taape (blue-lined snapper) are so comfortable with divers and photographers that they practically pose. Eagle rays, green sea turtles, manta rays, and white-tipped sharks occasionally cruise by as well, and eels peer out from the wreck.

For non-wreck diving, one of the best dive spots in summer is **Kahuna Canyon.** In Hawaiian, *kahuna* means priest, wise man, or sorcerer; this massive amphitheater, located near Mokuleia, is a perfect example of something a sorcerer might conjure up. Walls rising from the ocean floor create the illusion of an underwater Grand Canyon. Inside the amphitheater, crabs, octopuses, slippers, and spiny lobsters abound (be aware that taking them in summer is illegal), and giant trevally, parrotfish, and unicorn fish congregate as well. Outside the amphitheater, you're likely to see an occasional shark in the distance.

Because Oahu's greatest dives are offshore, your best bet is to book a two-tank dive from a dive boat. Hawaii's oldest and largest outfitter is **Aaron's Dive Shop,** 307 Hahani St., Kailua (www.hawaii-scuba.com; ✆ **808/262-2333**), which offers boat and beach dive excursions off the coast. The two-tank boat dives start at $115 per person if you have all your gear or $129 including gear, and transportation from the Kailua shop is provided. The beach dive off the North Shore in summer or the Waianae Coast in winter is the same price as a boat dive, including all gear and transportation, so Aaron's recommends the boat dive. Price includes pickup in Honolulu.

In Waikiki, **Dive Oahu,** 1085 Ala Moana (www.diveoahu.com; ✆ **808/922-3483**), offers everything from shipwreck dives in Waikiki to exploring the sunken wreck of a World War II Corsair plane for just $129 for a two-tank boat dive (friends or family members can tag along for just $35 each to snorkel). Captain Brian, who has been diving for a couple of decades, loves to help beginners feel comfortable, as well as show experienced scuba divers what the Waikiki coast has to offer.

On the North Shore, **Surf-N-Sea,** 62–595 Kamehameha Hwy., Haleiwa (www.surfnsea.com; ✆ **808/637-9887**), has dive tours from the shore (starting at $75 for one tank) and from a boat ($140 for two tanks). Surf-N-Sea also rents equipment and can point you to the best dive sites in the area.

Snorkeling

Some of the best snorkeling in Oahu is at **Hanauma Bay ★★**. It's crowded—sometimes it seems there are more people than fish—but Hanauma has clear, warm, protected waters and an abundance of friendly reef fish, including Moorish idols, scores of butterfly fish, damselfish, and wrasses. Hanauma Bay has two reefs, an inner and an outer—the first for novices, the other for experts. The

EXPERIENCING jaws: UP CLOSE & PERSONAL

You're 4 miles out from land, surrounded by open ocean. From out of the blue depths, a shape suddenly emerges: the sleek, pale shadow of a 6-foot-long grey reef shark, followed quickly by a couple of 10-foot-long Galapagos sharks. Within moments, you are surrounded by sharks on all sides. Do you panic? No, you paid $96 to be in the midst of these jaws of the deep. And, of course, you have a 6×6×10-foot aluminum shark cage separating you from all those teeth.

It happens every day at **North Shore Shark Adventures** (www.hawaiishark adventures.com; © **808/228-5900**), the dream of Capt. Joe Pavsek, who decided after some 30 years of surfing and diving to share the experience of seeing a shark with visitors. To make sure that the predators of the deep will show up for the viewing, Captain Pavsek heaves "chum," a not very appetizing concoction of fish trimmings and entrails, over the side of his 26-foot boat, *Kailolo*. After a few minutes, the sharks (generally grey reef, Galapagos, and sandbars, ranging 5–15 ft.) show up—sometimes just a few, sometimes a couple dozen. Depending on the sea conditions and the weather, snorkelers can stay in the cage as long as they wish, with the sharks just inches away. The shark cage, connected to the boat with wire line, holds up to four snorkelers (it's comfortable with two but pretty snug at full capacity). You can also stay on the boat and view the sharks from a more respectable distance for just $70. The more adventurous, down in the cage with just thin aluminum separating them from the sharks, are sure to have an experience they won't forget. Transportation from Waikiki and Kahala is an additional $45. Check the website for specials.

inner reef is calm and shallow (less than 10 ft.); in some places, you can just wade and put your face in the water. Go early: It's packed by 10am. And it's closed on Tuesdays. For details, see "Beaches," earlier in this chapter.

Braver snorkelers may want to head to **Shark's Cove ★★**, on the North Shore just off Kamehameha Highway, between Haleiwa and Pupukea. Sounds risky, I know, but I've never seen or heard of any sharks in this cove, and in summer this big, lava-edged pool is one of Oahu's best snorkel spots. Waves splash over the natural lava grotto and cascade like waterfalls into the pool full of tropical fish. To the right of the cove are deep-sea caves and underwater tunnels to explore.

Sport Fishing

Kewalo Basin, located between the Honolulu International Airport and Waikiki, is the main location for charter fishing boats on Oahu. From Waikiki, take Kalakaua Avenue Ewa (west) beyond Ala Moana Center; Kewalo Basin is on the left, across from Ward Centers. Look for charter boats all in a row in their slips; when the fish are biting, the captains display the catch of the day in the afternoon. You can also take TheBus no. 19 or 20 (Airport).

The best sport-fishing booking desk in the state is **Sportfish Hawaii** ★ (www.sportfishhawaii.com; ✆ **877/388-1376** or 808/396-2607), which books boats on all the islands. These fishing vessels have been inspected and must meet rigorous criteria to guarantee that you will have a great time. Prices range from $812 to $1,300 for a full-day exclusive charter (you, plus five friends, get the entire boat to yourself), from $717 for a half-day exclusive, or from $191 for a full-day shared charter (you share the boat with five other people).

Submarine Dives

Here's your chance to play Jules Verne and experience the underwater world from the comfort of a submarine, which will take you on an adventure below the surface in high-tech comfort. The entire trip is narrated as you watch tropical fish and sunken ships just outside the sub; if swimming's not your thing, this is a great way to see Hawaii's spectacular sea life. Shuttle boats to the sub leave from the Hilton Hawaiian Village Pier. Call **Atlantis Submarines** ★ (www.atlantis adventures.com/hawaii.cfm; ✆ **800/548-6262** or 808/973-9811) to reserve. The cost is $109 for adults, $45 for kids 12 and under (children must be at least 36 in. tall). *Tip:* Book online for discount rates of $99 for adults and $35 for kids. *Warning:* Skip this if you suffer from claustrophobia.

Surfing

In summer, when the water's warm and there's a soft breeze in the air, the south swell comes up. It's surf season in Waikiki, the best place on Oahu to learn how to surf. For lessons, go early to **Aloha Beach Service,** next to the Moana Sur-frider, 2365 Kalakaua Ave., Waikiki (✆ **808/922-3111**). The beach boys offer group lessons for $40 an hour in the water; board rentals are $15 for the first hour and $5 for every hour after that (everything is cash only). You must know how to swim.

On the North Shore, there's no excuse not to learn to surf: Hans Hede-mann, a champion surfer for some 34 years, has opened the **Hans Hedemann Surf School** (www.hhsurf.com; ✆ **808/924-7778**) at Turtle Bay Resort. Hede-mann himself gives private lessons—at $150 for an hour. (He has taught celebri-ties such as Cameron Diaz and Adam Sandler.) If the expenditure is beyond your budget, go for a $75 2-hour group lesson (maximum four people). The surf school has another location, in Waikiki at the Park Shore Waikiki.

Surfboards are also available for rent on the North Shore at **Surf-N-Sea,** 62–595 Kamehameha Hwy., Haleiwa (www.surfnsea.com; ✆ **800/899-7873**), for $5 to $7 an hour. Lessons go for $85 for 2 to 3 hours. For the best surf shops, where you can soak in the culture as well as pick up gear, see "Oahu Shopping" (p. 136).

More experienced surfers should drop in on any surf shop around Oahu, or call the **Surf News Network Surfline** (✆ **808/596-SURF**) to get the latest surf conditions. The **Cliffs,** at the base of Diamond Head, is a good spot for advanced surfers; 4- to 6-foot waves churn here, allowing high-performance surfing.

If you're in Hawaii in winter and want to see the serious surfers catch the really big waves, bring your binoculars and grab a front-row seat on the beach at **Waimea Bay, Sunset Beach,** or **Pipeline.**

Hiking Oahu.

Windsurfing

Windward Oahu's **Kailua Beach** ★★★ is the home of pioneer windsurfer Robby Naish; it's also the best place to learn to windsurf. The oldest and most established windsurfing business in Hawaii is **Naish Hawaii/Naish Windsurfing Hawaii,** 155-A Hamakua Dr., Kailua (www.naish.com; ✆ **808/262-6068**). The company offers everything: lessons, sales, rentals, repair, and free advice on where to go when the wind and waves are happening. Private 90-minute lessons start at $100 for one; you'll need about three lessons to be up and happening. Naish also has kitesurfing rentals (boards only) for $30 a day.

NATURE HIKES

People are often surprised to discover that the great outdoors is less than an hour away from downtown Honolulu. The island's 33 major hiking trails traverse razor-thin ridgebacks, deep waterfall valleys, and more. The best source of hiking information on Oahu is the state's **Na Ala Hele (Trails to Go On) Program** (www. hawaiitrails.org; ✆ **808/973-9782**). The website has everything you need: detailed maps and descriptions of 40 trails in the state's Na Ala Hele, a hiking safety brochure, updates on the trails, hyperlinks to weather information, health warnings, info on native plants, how to volunteer for trail upkeep, and more.

The **Hawaiian Trail and Mountain Club** (www.htmclub.org) offers regular hikes on Oahu. Bring a couple of bucks for the donation, your own lunch, and drinking water, and meet up with the club members at the scheduled location to join them on a hike. In addition, the club meets for Saturday and Sunday hikes at the Iolani Palace, at King Street between Richard and Punchbowl streets in downtown Honolulu. Generally club members meet at 8am; look for a group of people dressed in hiking clothes and boots at the left rear of the palace.

Other organizations that offer regularly scheduled hikes are the **Sierra Club** (www.sierraclubhawaii.com) and the **Hawaii Nature Center** (www.hawaiinaturecenter.org; © **888/955-0100**).

Honolulu-Area Hikes

DIAMOND HEAD CRATER ★★★

This is a moderate but steep walk to the summit of Hawaii's most famous landmark. Kids love to look out from the top of the 760-foot volcanic cone, where they have 360-degree views of Oahu up the leeward coast from Waikiki. The 1.5-mile round-trip takes about 1½ hours, and the entry fee is $5 per car load; if you walk in, it's $1 per person.

Diamond Head was created by a volcanic explosion about half a million years ago. The Hawaiians called the crater Leahi (meaning "the brow of the ahi," or tuna, referring to the shape of the crater). Diamond Head was considered a sacred spot; King Kamehameha offered human sacrifices at a *heiau* (temple) on the western slope. It wasn't until the 19th century that Mount Leahi got its current name: A group of sailors found what they thought were diamonds in the crater; it turned out they were just worthless calcite crystals, but the name stuck.

Before you begin your journey to the top of the crater, put on some decent shoes (rubber-soled tennies are fine) and don't forget water (very important), a hat to protect you from the sun, and a camera. You might want to put all your gear in a pack to leave your hands free for the climb.

Go early, preferably just after the 6am opening, before the midday sun starts beating down. The hike to the summit starts at Monsarrat and 18th avenues on the crater's inland (or mauka) side. To get here, take TheBus no. 58 from the Ala Moana Center or drive to the intersection of Diamond Head Road and 18th Avenue. Follow the road through the tunnel (which is closed 6pm–6am) and park in the lot. From the trail head in the parking lot, you'll proceed along a paved walkway (with handrails) as you climb up the slope. You'll pass old World War I and World War II pillboxes, gun emplacements, and tunnels built as part of the Pacific defense network. Several steps take you up to the top observation post on Point Leahi. The views are incredible.

MANOA FALLS TRAIL ★★

This easy .75-mile (one-way) hike is terrific for families; it takes less than an hour to reach idyllic Manoa Falls. The trail head, marked by a footbridge, is at the end of Manoa Road, past Lyon Arboretum. The staff at the arboretum prefers that hikers not park in their lot, so the best place to park is in the residential area below Paradise Park; you can also get to the arboretum via TheBus no. 5. The often-muddy trail follows Waihi Stream and meanders through the forest reserve past guavas, mountain apples, and wild ginger. The forest is moist and humid and inhabited by giant bloodthirsty mosquitoes, so bring repellent. If it has rained recently, stay on the trail and step carefully because it can be very slippery (and it's a long way down if you slide off the side).

East Oahu Hikes

MAKAPUU LIGHTHOUSE TRAIL ★★

You've seen this famous old lighthouse on episodes of "Magnum, P.I." and "Hawaii Five-O." No longer staffed by the Coast Guard (it's fully automated now), the lighthouse sits at the end of a precipitous cliff trail on an airy perch over the Windward Coast, Manana (Rabbit) Island, and the azure Pacific. It's about a 45-minute, 1-mile hike from Kalanianaole Highway (Hwy. 72), along a paved road that begins across from Hawaii Kai Executive Golf Course and winds around the 646-foot-high sea bluff to the lighthouse lookout.

The view of the ocean all the way to Molokai and Lanai is often so clear that, from November to March, if you're lucky, you'll see migrating humpback whales.

To get to the trail head from Waikiki, take Kalanianaole Highway (Hwy. 72) past Hanauma Bay and Sandy Beach to Makapuu Head, the southeastern tip of the island; you can also take TheBus no. 22 or 23.

Blowhole alert: When the south swell is running, usually in summer, there are a couple of blowholes on the south side of Makapuu Head that put the famous Halona Blowhole to shame.

Windward Coast Hikes
HAUULA LOOP TRAIL ★

For one of the best views of the coast and the ocean, follow the Hauula Loop Trail on the windward side of the island. It's an easy 2.5-mile loop on a well-maintained path that passes through a whispering ironwood forest and a grove of tall Norfolk pines. The trip takes about 3 hours and gains some 600 feet in elevation.

To get to the trail, take TheBus no. 55 or follow Hwy. 83 to Hauula Beach Park. Turn toward the mountains on Hauula Homestead Road; when it forks to the left at Maakua Road, park on the side of the road. Walk along Maakua Road to the wide, grassy trail that begins the hike into the mountains. The climb is fairly steep for about 900 feet but turns into easier-on-the-calves switchbacks as you go up the ridge. Look down as you climb: You'll spot wildflowers and mushrooms among the matted needles. The trail continues up, crossing Waipilopilo Gulch, where you'll see several forms of native plant life. Eventually, you reach the top of the ridge, where the views are spectacular.

PALI (MAUNAWILI) TRAIL ★

For a million-dollar view of the Windward Coast, take this 11-mile (one-way) foothill trail. The trail head is about 6 miles from downtown Honolulu, on the windward side of the Nuuanu Pali Tunnel, at the scenic lookout just beyond the hairpin turn of the Pali Highway (Hwy. 61). Just as you begin the turn, look for the scenic overlook sign, slow down, and pull off the highway into the parking lot (sorry, no bus service available).

The mostly flat, well-marked, easy-to-moderate trail goes through the forest on the lower slopes of the 3,000-foot Koolau mountain range and ends up in the backyard of the coastal Hawaiian village of Waimanalo. Go halfway to get the view and then return to your car, or have someone meet you in 'Nalo.

North Shore Hikes
WAIMEA VALLEY ★

For nearly 3 decades, 1,875-acre Waimea Valley, 59–864 Kamehameha Hwy., Haleiwa (www.waimeavalley.net; © **808/638-7766**), has lured visitors with activities from cliff diving and hula performances to kayaking and ATV tours. In 2008, the Office of Hawaiian Affairs took over and formed a nonprofit corporation, Hiipaka, to run the park, with an emphasis on perpetuating and sharing the "living Hawaiian culture."

A visit here offers a lush walk into the past. The valley is packed with archaeological sites, including the 600-year-old Hale O Lono, a *heiau* dedicated to the Hawaiian god Lono, which you'll find to the left of the entrance. The botanical collection has 35 different gardens, including super-rare Hawaiian species such as the endangered *Kokia cookei* hibiscus. The valley is also home to fauna such as the endangered Hawaiian moorhen; look for a black bird with a red face cruising in the ponds. The 150-acre Arboretum and Botanical Garden contains more than 5,000 species of tropical plants. Walk through the gardens (take the paved paths or dirt trails) and wind up at 45-foot-high Waimea Falls—bring your bathing suit and you can dive into the cold, murky water. The public is invited to hike the trails and spend a day in this quiet oasis. There are several guided hikes (ranging from 2 miles to 6-plus miles starting at $80), plus cultural activities such as lei-making, kapa demonstrations, hula lessons, Hawaiian games and crafts and music, and storytelling. Admission to the park is $15 ($7.50 for seniors and children age 4–12). It's open daily 9am to 5pm.

To Land's End: A Leeward Oahu Hike

KAENA POINT ★

At the very western tip of Oahu lie the dry, barren lands of Kaena Point State Park, 853 acres of jagged sea cliffs, deep gulches, sand dunes, endangered plant life, and a remote, wild, wind- and surf-battered coastline. *Kaena* means "red-hot" or "glowing" in Hawaiian; the name refers to the brilliant sunsets visible from the point.

Kaena is steeped in numerous legends. A popular one concerns the demigod Maui: Maui had a famous hook that he used to raise islands from the sea. He decided that he wanted to bring the islands of Oahu and Kauai closer together, so one day he threw his hook across the Kauai Channel and snagged Kauai (which is actually visible from Kaena Point on clear days). Using all his might, Maui was able to pull loose a huge boulder, which fell into the waters very close to the present lighthouse at Kaena. The rock is still called Pohaku o Kauai (the Rock from Kauai). Like Black Rock in Kaanapali on Maui, Kaena is thought of as the point on Oahu from which souls depart.

To hike out to the departing place, take the clearly marked trail from the parking lot of Kaena Point State Park. The moderate 5-mile round-trip hike to the point will take a couple of hours. The trail along the cliff passes tide pools abundant in marine life and rugged protrusions of lava reaching out to the turbulent sea; seabirds circle overhead. Do *not* go off the trail; you might step on buried birds' eggs. There are no sandy beaches, and the water is nearly always turbulent here. In winter, when a big north swell is running, the waves at Kaena are the biggest in the state, averaging heights of 30 to 40 feet. Even when the water appears calm, offshore currents are powerful, so don't plan on taking a swim. Go early in the morning to see the schools of porpoises that frequent the area just offshore.

To get to the trail head from Honolulu or Waikiki, take the H-1 west to its end; continue on Hwy. 93 past Makaha and follow Hwy. 930 to the end of the road. There's no bus service.

OTHER OUTDOOR ACTIVITIES

Biking

Oahu is not bike-friendly. Drivers don't always share the road and the road itself is full of potholes.

Still, it doesn't mean you can't bike; just be careful. If you're in Waikiki, you can rent a bike for as little as $10 for a half-day and $20 for 24 hours at **Big Kahuna Rentals,** 407 Seaside Ave. (www.bigkahunarentals.com; ☏ **888/451-5544** or 808/924-2736).

For a bike-and-hike adventure, contact **Bike Hawaii** (www.bikehawaii.com; ☏ **877/682-7433** or 808/734-4214), which has a variety of group tours, such as its Mountain Biking Kaaawa Valley at Kualoa. This guided mountain-bike tour follows dirt roads and a single track meandering through the 1,000-acre Kaaawa Valley on Oahu's northeast shore, with stops at a reconstructed Hawaiian *hale* (house) and *kalo lo'i* (taro terrace) for some cultural narrative, plus an old military bunker that has been converted into a movie museum for films shot here ("Jurassic Park," "Godzilla," "Mighty Joe Young," "Windtalkers," and more). The 6-mile trip, which takes 2 to 3 hours of riding, includes van transportation from your hotel, bike, helmet, snacks, picnic lunch, water bottle, and guide; it's $120 for adults and $77 for children 13 and under.

Golf

Oahu has nearly 3 dozen golf courses, ranging from bare-bones municipal courses to exclusive country-club courses with membership fees running to six figures a year. Below are the best of a great bunch.

As you get to know Oahu's courses, you'll see that the windward courses play much differently than the leeward courses. On the windward side, the prevailing winds blow from the ocean to shore, and the grain direction of the greens tends to run the same way—from the ocean to the mountains. Leeward golf courses have the opposite tendency: The winds usually blow from the mountains to the ocean, with the grain direction of the greens corresponding.

Tips on beating the crowds and saving money: Oahu's golf courses tend to be crowded, so I suggest that you go midweek, if you can. Also, most island courses have twilight rates that offer substantial discounts if you're willing to tee off in the afternoon; these are included in the listings below, where applicable.

> ### Tee-Time Discounts
>
> For last-minute and discount tee times, call **Stand-by Golf** (www.hawaiistandbygolf.com; ☏ **888/645-BOOK** [2665]), which offers discounted tee times for same-day or next-day golfing. Call between 7am and 10pm for a guaranteed tee time with up to a 30-percent discount on greens fees.

Transportation note: TheBus does not allow golf-club bags onboard, so if you want to use TheBus to get to a course, you're going to have to rent clubs there.

WAIKIKI

Ala Wai Municipal Golf Course   Some 500 rounds a day are played on this 18-hole municipal course within walking distance of Waikiki's hotels. It's something of a challenge to get a tee time at this busy par-70, 6,020-yard course, and the computerized tee reservations system for all of Oahu's municipal courses will allow you to book only 3 days in advance, but keep trying. Ala Wai has a flat layout bordered by the Ala Wai Canal on one side and the Manoa-Palolo Stream on the other. It's less windy than most Oahu courses, but pay attention to the 372-yard, par-4 1st hole, which demands a straight and long shot to the very tiny green. If you miss, you can make it up on the 478-yard, par-5 10th hole—the green is reachable in two, so with a two-putt, a birdie is within reach.

404 Kapahulu Ave., Waikiki. www.co.honolulu.hi.us/des/golf/alawai.htm. © **808/733-7387** for golf course, or 808/296-2000 for tee-time reservations. Greens fees $55; twilight rates $28; cart $20. From Waikiki, turn left on Kapahulu Ave.; the course is on the mauka side of Ala Wai Canal. Bus: 19, 20, or 13.

EAST OAHU

Hawaii Kai Golf Course   This is actually two golf courses in one. The par-72, 6,222-yard **Championship Course** is moderately challenging, with scenic vistas. The course is forgiving to high-handicap golfers, although it does have a few surprises. The par-55 **Executive Course** is fun for beginners and those just getting back in the game after a few years. The course has lots of hills and valleys, with no water hazards and only a few sand traps. Lockers are available.

8902 Kalanianaole Hwy., Honolulu. www.hawaiikaigolf.com. © **808/395-2358.** Greens fees: Championship Course $115, twilight rates $70; Executive Course $39 Mon–Fri, $44 Sat–Sun. Take H-1 east past Hawaii Kai; it's immediately past Sandy Beach on the left. Bus: 22 and 23.

THE WINDWARD COAST

Olomana Golf Links   Low-handicap golfers may not find this gorgeous course difficult, but the striking views of the craggy Koolau mountain ridge alone are worth the fees. The par-72, 6,326-yard course is popular with locals and visitors alike. The course starts off a bit hilly on the front 9 but flattens out by the back 9, where there are some tricky water hazards. The 1st hole, a 384-yard par-4 that tees downhill and approaches uphill, is definitely a warm-up. The next hole is a 160-yard par-3 that starts from an elevated tee to an elevated green over a severely banked V-shaped gully. Shoot long here—it's longer than you think, and short shots tend to roll all the way back down the fairway to the base of the gully. This course is very, very green; the rain gods bless it regularly with brief passing showers. You can spot the regular players here—they all carry umbrellas, wait patiently for the squalls to pass, and then resume play. Reservations are a must. Facilities include a driving range, practice greens, club rental, a pro shop, and a restaurant.

41–1801 Kalanianaole Hwy., Waimanalo. www.olomanagolflinks.com. © **808/259-2484.** Greens fees $95; twilight fees $80. Frequent player discounts. Take H-1 to the Pali Hwy. (Hwy. 61); turn right on Kalanianaole Hwy.; after 5 miles, it will be on the left. Bus: 23/57.

THE NORTH SHORE

Kahuku Golf Course   This 9-hole budget golf course is a bit funky. It has no club rentals, no clubhouse, and no facilities other than a few pull carts that disappear with the first handful of golfers. But a round at this scenic oceanside course amid the tranquillity of the North Shore is quite an experience nonetheless. Duffers will love the ease of this recreational course, and weight watchers will be happy to walk the gently sloping greens. Don't forget to bring your camera for the views (especially at holes 3, 4, 7, and 8, which are right on the ocean). No reservations are taken; tee times are first come, first served, and with plenty of retirees happy to sit and wait, the competition is fierce for early tee times. Bring your own clubs and call ahead to check the weather.

56–501 Kamehameha Hwy., Kahuku. © **808/293-5842.** Greens fees $33. Take H-1 west to H-2; follow H-2 through Wahiawa to Kamehameha Hwy. (Hwy. 99, then Hwy. 83); follow it to Kahuku.

Turtle Bay Resort ★   This North Shore resort is home to two of Hawaii's top golf courses. The 18-hole **Arnold Palmer Course** (formerly the Links at Kuilima) was designed by Arnold Palmer and Ed Seay. Now that the casuarina (ironwood) trees have matured, it's not as windy as it used to be, but this is still a challenging course. The front 9, with rolling terrain, only a few trees, and lots of wind, play like a British Isles course. The back 9 have narrower tree-lined fairways and water. The course circles Punahoolapa Marsh, a protected wetland for endangered Hawaiian waterfowl.

Another option is the par-71, 6,200-yard **George Fazio Course**—the only Fazio course in Hawaii. Larry Keil, pro at Turtle Bay, says that people like it because it's a more forgiving course, without all the water hazards and bunkers of the Palmer course. The 6th hole has two greens, so you can play the hole as a par-3 or a par-4. The toughest hole has to be the par-3, 176-yard 2nd hole, where you tee off across a lake with a mean crosswind. The most scenic hole is the 7th, where the ocean is on your left; in winter, you might get lucky and see some whales.

Facilities include a pro shop, a driving range, putting and chipping greens, and a snack bar. Weekdays are best for tee times.

57–049 Kamehameha Hwy., Kahuku. www.turtlebayresort.com. ✆ **808/293-8574.** Greens fees: Palmer Course $185 before noon, $140 noon–2pm, $105 2–4pm, $85 after 4pm; Fazio Course $115 before noon, $95 noon–2pm, $75 after 2pm (after 3pm you can walk the Fazio course for $25!). Take H-1 west past Pearl City; when the freeway splits, take H-2 and follow the signs to Haleiwa; at Haleiwa, take Hwy. 83 to Turtle Bay Resort. Bus: 52 or 55.

CENTRAL OAHU

Pearl Country Club   Looking for a challenge? You'll find one at this popular public course, located just above Pearl City in Aiea. Sure, the 6,230-yard, par-72 looks harmless enough, and the views of Pearl Harbor and the USS *Arizona* Memorial are gorgeous, but around the 5th hole, you'll start to see what you're in for. That par-5, a blind 472-yard hole, doglegs seriously to the left (with a small margin of error between the tee and the steep out-of-bounds hillside on the entire left side of the fairway). A water hazard and a forest await your next two shots. Suddenly, this nice public course becomes not so nice. Oahu residents can't get enough of it, so don't even try to get a tee time on weekends. Stick to weekdays—Mondays are usually the best bet. Facilities include a driving range, practice greens, club rental, a pro shop, and a restaurant.

98–535 Kaonohi St., Aiea. www.pearlcc.com. ✆ **808/487-3802.** Greens fees $140; after 3:30pm $50. Book at least a week in advance. Take H-1 past Pearl Harbor to Hwy. 78 (Moanalua Fwy.), exit 13A; stay in the left lane where Hwy. 78 becomes Hwy. 99 (Kamehameha Hwy.); turn right on Kaonohi St.; entrance is on the right. Bus: 53 and 54 (stops at Pearlridge Shopping Center at Kaonohi and Moanalua sts.; you'll have to walk about ½-mile uphill from here).

Pearl Country Club.

LEEWARD OAHU

Ko Olina Golf Club ★★★   The Ted Robinson–designed course has rolling fairways and elevated tee and water features. "Golf Digest" once named it one of "America's Top 75 Resort Courses." The signature hole—the 12th, a par-3—has an elevated tee that sits on a rock garden with a cascading waterfall. At the 18th hole, you'll see and hear water all around you—seven pools begin on the right side of the fairway and slope down to a lake. A waterfall is on your left off the elevated green. You'll have no choice but to play the left and approach the green over the water. Book in advance; this course is crowded all the time. Facilities include a driving range, locker rooms, a Jacuzzi, steam rooms, and a restaurant and bar. Lessons are available.

92–1220 Aliinui Dr., Kapolei. www.koolinagolf.com. © **808/676-5300.** Greens fees $199 ($179 for Ihilani Resort guests); twilight rates (after 1pm) $139. Ask about transportation from Waikiki hotels. Collared shirts requested for men and women. Take H-1 west until it becomes Hwy. 93 (Farrington Hwy.); turn off at the Ko Olina exit; take the exit road (Aliinui Dr.) into Ko Olina Resort; turn left into the clubhouse. No bus service.

West Loch Municipal Golf Course   This par-72, 6,615-yard course located just 30 minutes from Waikiki, in Ewa Beach, offers golfers a challenge at bargain rates. The difficulties on this unusual municipal course, designed by Robin Nelson and Rodney Wright, are water (lots of hazards), constant trade winds, and narrow fairways. To help you out, the course features a "water" driving range (with a lake) to practice your drives. In addition to the driving range, West Loch has practice greens, a pro shop, and a restaurant.

91–1126 Okupe St., Ewa Beach. © **808/675-6076.** Greens fees $55; 9 holes after 1pm $28; cart $20. Book 3 days in advance. Take H-1 west to the Hwy. 76 exit; stay in the left lane and turn left at West Loch Estates, just opposite St. Francis Medical Center. To park, take 2 immediate right turns. Bus: E.

Horseback Riding

You can gallop on the beach at the **Turtle Bay Resort ★★**, 57–091 Kamehameha Hwy., Kahuku (www.turtlebayresort.com; © **808/293-6024;** bus: 52 or 55), where 45-minute rides along sandy beaches with spectacular ocean views and through a forest of ironwood trees cost $70 for age 7 and up (riders must be at least 4 ft., 4 in. tall). Romantic evening rides are $105 per person. Private rides for up to four people are $125 per person.

ORGANIZED TOURS
Guided Sightseeing Tours

If your time is limited, you might want to consider a guided tour. These tours are informative, can give you a good overview of Honolulu or Oahu in a limited amount of time, and are surprisingly entertaining.

E Noa Tours, 1141 Waimanu St., Suite 105, Honolulu (www.enoa.com; © **800/824-8804** or 808/591-2561), offers a range of narrated tours, from island loops to explorations of Pearl Harbor, on air-conditioned, 27-passenger minibuses. The Royal Circle Island Tour ($83 for adults, $67 for children 6–11, $58 for children under 5) stops at Diamond Head Crater, Hanauma Bay, Byodo-In Temple, Sunset Beach, Waimea Valley (admission included), and various beach sites along the way. Other tours go to the Pearl Harbor/USS *Arizona* Memorial and the Polynesian Cultural Center.

To understand why Oahu was the island of kings, you need to see it from the air. **Island Seaplane Service ★★★** (www.islandseaplane.com; © **808/836-6273**) operates flights departing from a floating dock in the protected waters of Keehi Lagoon in either a six-passenger DeHavilland Beaver or a four-passenger Cessna 206. There's nothing quite like feeling the slap of the waves as the plane skims across the water and then effortlessly lifts into the air.

The half-hour tour ($179) gives you aerial views of Waikiki Beach, Diamond Head Crater, Kahala's luxury estates, and the sparkling waters of Hanauma and Kaneohe bays; the 1-hour tour ($299) continues on to Chinaman's Hat, the Polynesian Cultural Center, and the rolling surf of the North Shore. The flight returns across the island, over Hawaii's historic wartime sites: Schofield Barracks and the Pearl Harbor memorials.

Waikiki Trolley Tours ★, 1141 Waimanu St., Suite 105, Honolulu (www.waikikitrolley.com; © **800/824-8804** or 808/593-2822), offers four tours of sightseeing, entertainment, dining, and shopping. These are a great way to get the lay of the land. You can get on and off the trolley as needed (trolleys come along every 2–20 min.). An all-day pass (8:30am–11:35pm) is $35 for adults, $19 for children 4 to 11; a 4-day pass is $57 for adults, $25 for children. For the same price, you can experience the 2-hour narrated Ocean Coast Line tour (Green Line) of the southeast side of Oahu, an easy way to see the stunning views.

Specialty Tours

Below is a sampling specialty tours found on Oahu.

ECOTOURS

Oahu isn't just high-rises in Waikiki or urban sprawl in Honolulu, but extinct craters, hidden waterfalls, lush rainforests, forgotten coastlines, and rainbow-filled valleys. To experience the other side of Oahu, contact **Oahu Nature Tours** (www.oahunaturetours.com; © **808/924-2473**). It offers a dozen different ecotours, starting at $30 per person, and provides everything: expert guides (geologists, historians, archaeologists), round-trip transportation, entrance fees, bottled water, and use of day packs, binoculars, flashlights, and rain gear.

FARM/FOOD TOURS

Hawaii Coffee Company ★★, 1555 Kalani St. (www.hawaiicoffeecompany.com; © **808/847-3600**), has an excellent behind-the-scenes tour of its LION and Royal Kona Coffee facility (as well as its Hawaiian Island Tea Company). You are met in the retail/cafe area of the facility and taken through the 55,000-square-foot plant on a step-by-step tour of how Hawaii's oldest and largest coffee company processes and roasts its dozens of different brands and types of coffee. Tea lovers will also get to experience the processing of tea. Allow 30 to 45 minutes for the tour, plus extra time to try the various coffees in the cafe. This is one of the best places in Oahu to stock up on a few bags of coffee or boxes of teas (not to mention the logo retail items). Not only are the prices competitive, but in November and December specialty Christmas coffee can be purchased at this location only.

Free tours are given Monday through Thursday (call for current tour times and reservations). The E Noa Trolley no. 10 also stops here for the tour.

GHOST TOURS

For a really different look at Honolulu and the island, **Oahu Ghost Tours ★★** (www.oahughosttours.com; © **877/597-7325**) offers a look at the supernatural side of this ancient place. Originally started by Glen Grant, who dedicated his life to exploring stories and sightings of the paranormal, the company has continued his investigations of ghosts, unusual sightings, and the unexplainable. The offerings include **Honolulu City Haunts,** a 2-hour walking tour of places where it's rumored that supernatural events are still happening today ($39 for adults, $29 for children 11 and under); **Sacred Spirits,** a 5-hour walking tour of the most sacred native Hawaiian spots on Oahu ($59 adults, $49 children); and the **Orbs of Oahu** driving tour, which circles the island, stopping at some of the "most haunted" locations ($59 adults, $49 children).

WHERE TO STAY ON OAHU

Before you reach for the phone to book a place to stay, consider when you'll be visiting. The high season, when hotels are full and rates are at their peak, is mid-December to March. The secondary high season, when rates are high but rooms are somewhat easier to come by, is June to September. The low seasons—when you can expect fewer tourists and better deals—are April to June and September to mid-December. (For more on Hawaii's travel seasons, see "When to Go" on p. 35.) No matter when you travel, you can often get a good rate at many of Waikiki's hotels by booking a package.

For a description of each neighborhood, see "The Island in Brief" (p. 48). It can help you decide where you'd like to base yourself.

Remember that hotel and room taxes of 13.962 percent will be added to your bill (Oahu has a .546 percent additional tax that the other islands do not have). And don't forget about parking charges—at up to $30 a day in Waikiki, they can add up quickly.

WAIKIKI BY segway

One of my favorite ways to tour Waikiki is on a Segway Personal Transporter, the silly-looking, two-wheeled machine that looks like an old push lawn mower (big wheels and a long handle). Amazingly enough, within just a few minutes, you get the hang of this contraption, which is propelled through twisting the hand throttle and works through a series of high-tech stabilization mechanisms that read the motion of your body to turn or go forward or backward. It's lots of fun—think back to the first time you rode a bicycle, and the incredible freedom of zipping through space without walking. **Segway of Hawaii** (www.segwayof hawaii.com; © **808/941-3151**) will instruct you on the Segway (the staff makes sure that you are fully competent before you leave their training area) and then take you on a 30-minute introduction tour for $71 per person. The 2½-hour tour of Waikiki, Kapiolani Park, and Diamond Head costs $167 per person. All tours start the Hilton Hawaiian Village.

Note that more and more hotels charge a mandatory daily "resort fee" or "amenity fee," usually somewhere between $25 and $30, which can increase the room rates by 20 percent. The hotels say these charges cover amenities, some of which you may not need (such as movie rentals, a welcome drink, a color photograph of you on the property—drinking that welcome drink, perhaps?) and some which are awfully handy (such as Internet access and parking). We have listed resort charges next to the room rates in the reviews below; note that Outrigger and Aqua properties do not charge resort fees, something to take into account when comparing prices.

VACATION RENTALS   Oahu has few true bed-and-breakfast inns. Instead, if you're looking for a non-hotel experience, your best bet is a vacation rental. You can rent direct from owners via **VRBO.com** (Vacation Rentals by Owner) and **airbnb.com**. On these sites, you'll find a range of offerings, from $80-a-night studios to unique, off-the-beaten-path lodgings, like a Portlock cottage near Hanauma Bay on the water (listed on vrbo.com) or a North Shore treehouse (listed on airbnb.com). Make sure to read the reviews before booking so you have a general idea of what you're getting into. Note that for VRBO, unless you purchase VRBO's "Vacation Protection Services," most places won't provide a refund if a rental is not what you expected. Airbnb.com gives renters more peace of mind; it withholds payment until check-in so renters can make sure the listing is as advertised. But I've booked places on both sites, basing my picks on reviews, and I've found the hosts friendly and listings accurate.

Waikiki

EWA WAIKIKI

All the hotels listed below are located between the ocean and Kalakaua Avenue, and between Ala Wai Terrace in the Ewa (western) direction and Olohana Street and Fort DeRussy Park in the Diamond Head (eastern) direction.

Very Expensive

The Modern Honolulu ★   Waikiki's trendiest hotel is hip and modern and not your typical Hawaiian hotel, which means you won't find rattan furniture nor slack key music over the speakers. Instead, you get sleek, all-white, and blond-wood-accented rooms and electronic funk a la Ibiza played in the common areas. Come here to see and be seen, at the clubby lobby bar behind the bookcase or alongside two oceanview pools—each with its own bar and expansive daybeds. Choose this hotel, too, if you're looking to get away from the kids—the top pool is adults only. There's no beach access here, but the pool has its own beachy sand—a blend culled from all the islands—to pretend like there is.

1775 Ala Moana Blvd. (at Hobron Lane), Honolulu. www.themodernhonolulu.com. ℂ **855/970-4161** or 808/943-5800. 353 units. $280–$540 double; from $699 suite. Valet parking only (no self-parking) $28. Bus: 19 or 20. **Amenities:** Restaurant; nightclub; 4 lounges; concierge; fitness center; pool; 24-hr. room service; spa; Wi-Fi (free).

Outrigger Reef on the Beach ★★   You may arrive by car, but the Outrigger reminds you—with the 100-year-old koa wood canoe suspended in the long-house entryway—that long ago, the Polynesians came to Hawaii by boat, navigating their way only by the stars. The Hawaii-based Outrigger chain has a handful of hotels on Oahu, and this one is its most striking, with lovely Hawaiian cultural touches. You'll find the outrigger theme throughout the hotel, such as in

Waikiki Hotels

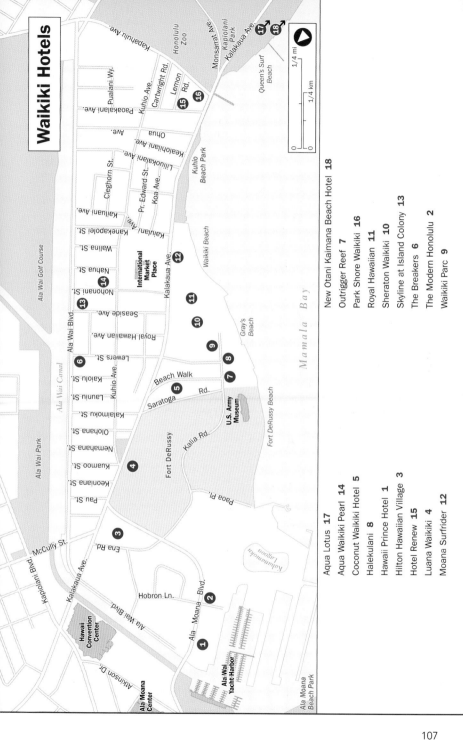

Aqua Lotus **17**
Aqua Waikiki Pearl **14**
Coconut Waikiki Hotel **5**
Halekulani **8**
Hawaii Prince Hotel **1**
Hilton Hawaiian Village **3**
Hotel Renew **15**
Luana Waikiki **4**
Moana Surfrider **12**

New Otani Kaimana Beach Hotel **18**
Outrigger Reef **7**
Park Shore Waikiki **16**
Royal Hawaiian **11**
Sheraton Waikiki **10**
Skyline at Island Colony **13**
The Breakers **6**
The Modern Honolulu **2**
Waikiki Parc **9**

the collection of Polynesian canoe art by Herb Kane, who some call the "father of the Hawaiian Renaissance." (Most notably, he built the double-hulled voyaging canoe the *Hokulea* in 1975, which revived ancient celestial navigation methods. In 2014, the *Hokulea* was set to sail around the world—without a compass, GPS, or any other modern-day navigational equipment.) But don't worry, at Outrigger Reef, you can have your historical culture and modern amenities too, such as free Internet, a large pool, and three restaurants, including the ever-popular beachside **ShoreBird,** serving $3.50 mai tais until 5pm and grill-your-own steaks. Decked out in tasteful Hawaiian decor, rooms are spacious—a recent renovation actually decreased the number of rooms in order to make them bigger.

Note that **Outrigger Waikiki on the Beach** (www.outriggerwaikikihotel. com) has a similar feel and price point to Outrigger Reef on the Beach, but its location in the center of Waikiki and its resident bar—Duke's Waikiki, the area's most happening bar—means it's a little more bustling and noisy.

2169 Kalia Rd. (at Saratoga Rd.), Honolulu. www.outriggerreef.com. ✆ 800/OUTRIGGER (688-7444) or 808/923-3111. 639 units. $249–$429 hotel room double. Extra person (over 2 adults) $75 per person per night. Children 17 and under stay free in parent's room. Valet parking only (no self-parking) $30. Bus: 19 or 20. **Amenities:** 3 restaurants; 2 bars; babysitting; fitness center; spa; outdoor pools; Wi-Fi (free).

Expensive

Hawaii Prince Hotel Waikiki ★   These two towers look like they're from "The Jetsons," especially with the glass-walled elevators zipping up and down the exterior. The rooms are kind of characterless, in shades of beige and gray, but you'll probably spend most of your time looking outward, anyway; every room, even on the lower floors, boasts a yacht harbor view. This hotel is on the quiet side of Waikiki. There's no beach in front, but it's about a 10-minute walk to Ala Moana Beach Park, a more local and less-busy beach than Waikiki. The hotel also has two of Honolulu's favorite buffets: the **Prince Court** and **Hakone.** I prefer the latter for its Japanese fare and all-you-can-eat sashimi and made-to-order sushi.

100 Holomoana St. (just across Ala Wai Canal Bridge, on the ocean side of Ala Moana Blvd.), Honolulu. www.princeresortshawaii.com/hawaii-prince-hotel-waikiki. ✆ 888/977-4623 or 808/956-1111. 548 units. $209–$399 double; from $619 suite. Extra person $60. Children 17 and under stay free in parent's room using existing bedding. Valet parking $27, self-parking $21. Bus: 19 or 20. **Amenities:** 2 restaurants; outdoor bar; babysitting; concierge; 27-hole golf club a 40-min. drive away in Ewa Beach (reached by hotel shuttle); fitness room; outdoor pool; room service; small day spa; Internet ($12 per day).

Hilton Hawaiian Village Beach Resort & Spa ★★   This sprawling resort is like a microcosm of Waikiki—on good days it feels like a lively little beach town with hidden nooks and crannies to discover and great bars in which to make new friends, and on bad days it's just an endless traffic jam, with lines into the parking garage, at the front desk, and in the restaurants. Need an oasis in the middle of it all? Choose the Alii Tower, the most recently renovated of the resort's five towers. It has its own lobby lounge, reception, and concierge, and even its own pool and bar; it's like a hotel within a hotel.

But there's something for everyone at the Hilton Hawaiian—I've seen families settling in for a screening of "The Lorax" on the lawn, winter breakers leaving the Tapa Tower (the largest tower) to hit the bars, and well-heeled (literally) tourists returning to the Alii Tower with their shopping bags. Room views can range from a straight-on view of the tower in front to oceanfront, so close to the water

AFFORDABLE parking IN WAIKIKI

It is possible to find affordable parking in Waikiki if you know where to look. I've divided up the parking in Waikiki into free or metered parking and carry-a-big-wallet parking.

FREE OR METERED PARKING:
- All side streets in Waikiki.
- Ala Wai Boulevard along the Ala Wai Canal.
- Kalakaua Avenue along Kapiolani Park.
- Waikiki Zoo.

BEST OF THE NOT-SO-AFFORDABLE PARKING:
- Aston at the Waikiki Banyan, 201 Ohua Ave. ($12 per day).
- Across from Hale Koa Hotel, 2055 Kalia Rd. (parking lot is across from the hotel; $4 for the first hour, $3.50 per subsequent hour, $18 maximum).
- Hilton Hawaiian Village, 2005 Kalia Rd. (up to 4 hr. free if you eat here, $8 per hour if you don't).
- Ohana East, 150 Kaiulani Ave. ($6 per hour, 5 hr. maximum).
- Waikiki Beach Marriott, 2552 Kalakaua Ave. (entrance on Ohua Ave.; (free if you eat here, $8 per hour if you don't).
- Waikiki Parking Garage, 333 Seaside Ave. ($4 per hour).
- Waikiki Shopping Plaza, 2270 Kalakaua Ave. ($5 per hour, $5 flat-rate all day Sun and Mon–Sat 6pm–midnight).

you can hear waves lapping. Cheaper rooms are in the Kalia, Tapa, and Diamond Head towers (which are farther from the beach), and the more expensive ones in the Rainbow and Alii, which are closest to the water and more recently renovated. I found rooms in all the towers to be spacious, clean, and comfy, so ultimately it comes down to how close you want to be to the beach and how new you want your furnishings.

2005 Kalia Rd. (at Ala Moana Blvd.), Honolulu. www.hiltonhawaiianvillage.com. © **800/HILTONS** or 808/949-4321. 2,860 units. $279–$479 double; from $499 suite. $30 resort charge per day includes Internet access and movie rentals. Extra person (over 2 adults) $50. Children 17 and under stay free in parent's room. Valet parking $33, self-parking $27. Bus: 19 or 20. **Amenities:** 9 restaurants; 4 bars; year-round children's program; concierge; fitness center; 5 outdoor pools; room service; Wi-Fi (included in resort fee).

MID-WAIKIKI, MAKAI

All the hotels listed below are between Kalakaua Avenue and the ocean, and between Fort DeRussy in the Ewa (western) direction and Kaiulani Street in the Diamond Head (eastern) direction.

Very Expensive

Halekulani ★★★ This is one of Waikiki's most luxurious hotels; its name means "house befitting heaven." The history of the Halekulani tracks that of Waikiki itself: At its inception at the turn of the century, it was just a beachfront house and a few bungalows, and Waikiki was an undeveloped stretch of sand and drained marshland. By the 1980s, Waikiki was a different place, and so was the Halekulani, which was relaunched by its new Japanese owners as an oasis of mostly oceanfront hotel rooms, marble foyers, and beautifully landscaped courtyards—and so it remains. It's all very understated—it actually doesn't look like much from the outside. But what it lacks in splashy grandeur, a la Royal Hawaiian, it makes up with a quiet elegance.

The large rooms are done in what the Halekulani calls its signature "seven shades of white." Generously sized tile-and-marble bathrooms and louver shutter doors separating the lanais contribute to the spare-yet-luxe feel. Of all the hotels in Waikiki, this one feels the most peaceful, abetted by lovely, personable service. It's a true escape.

2199 Kalia Rd. (at the ocean end of Lewers St.), Honolulu. www.halekulani.com. © **800/367-2343** or 808/923-2311. 453 units. $520–$565 double; from $1,055 suite. Extra person $125. 1 child 17 and under stays free in parent's room using existing bedding; additional rollaway bed $40. Maximum 3 people per room. Parking $28. Bus: 19 or 20. **Amenities:** 3 restaurants; 3 bars; 24-hr. concierge; fitness center; gorgeous outdoor pool; room service; spa; complimentary tickets to the Honolulu Museum of Art, Bishop Museum, and Doris Duke's Shangri La estate; Wi-Fi (free).

Expensive

Moana Surfrider, a Westin Resort ★★ This is Waikiki's oldest hotel, built in 1901. Even after more than 100 years, multiple renovations, and the construction of two towers in the '50s and '60s, the hotel has managed to retain its original and still-grand Beaux Arts main building. It's so picturesque you're likely to encounter many a Japanese wedding couple trying to get their perfect shot along the staircase and in the lobby. I prefer the rooms in the Banyan Wing for their nostalgic character, but these tend to be small in size. Larger rooms with lanais are in the Tower Wing, and although they are as well appointed as any you'll find at other Westin properties, with granite baths and signature Heavenly beds, they don't feel very Hawaii. Of course, to change that, get a room with a view of Diamond Head, or just step out under the giant banyan tree in the courtyard and enjoy the nightly live Hawaiian music and a mai tai.

2365 Kalakaua Ave. (ocean side of the street, across from Kaiulani St.), Honolulu. www.moana-surfrider.com or www.starwoodhotelshawaii.com. © **800/325-3535** or 808/922-3111. 793 units. $340–$610 double; from $970 suite. $30 resort charge per day (covers self-parking, Internet, and local calls). Extra person $120. Children 17 and under stay free in parent's room using existing bedding. Valet parking $8 additional. Bus: 19 or 20. **Amenities:** 3 restaurants; bar; babysitting; children's program; concierge; nearby fitness room (about a 2-min. walk down the beach at the Sheraton Waikiki); outdoor pool; room service; Wi-Fi (included in resort fee).

Royal Hawaiian ★★★ The "Pink Palace of the Pacific" is as pink as the Halekulani is white. Everytime I step into the Royal Hawaiian, it still takes my breath away. I love its vibrant exoticism—the Spanish-Moorish architecture manifested in graceful stucco arches, the patterned floor tiles, the exquisite, ornate lamps. Who knew that pink could look so good against Hawaii's blue skies and waters? The historic rooms are my favorite, with the pink and gold-embossed wallpaper and dark-wood furniture. Rooms in the Tower wing are larger, the colors more muted (although, don't worry, there are still pink accents) and the bathrooms there have fancy Toto toilets. Here, even your *okole* (rear end) is pampered.

2259 Kalakaua Ave. (at Royal Hawaiian Ave., on the ocean side of the Royal Hawaiian Shopping Center), Honolulu. www.royal-hawaiian.com or www.starwoodhotelshawaii.com. © **800/325-3535** or 808/923-7311. 528 units. $395–$675 double; from $490 suite. $35 resort charge per day (covers valet parking, Internet access, and local and long-distance calls). Extra person $155. Bus: 19 or 20. **Amenities:** 2 restaurants; landmark bar; babysitting; bike rentals; year-round children's program (available next door at the Sheraton Waikiki); concierge; preferential tee times at various golf courses; nearby fitness room (next door at the Sheraton Waikiki); outdoor pool; room service; spa; Wi-Fi (included in resort fee).

Sheraton Waikiki ★   At 30 stories tall, the Sheraton towers over its neighbors. With almost 2,000 rooms and a location right in the middle of the busiest section of Waikiki, this is not the place to book if you're looking for a peaceful getaway. What you do get: views of the ocean (available in most rooms), the Helumoa Playground pool for kids, and an infinity pool for adults. Expect crowds, though. Drinks at **Rumfire** are fun, with great views to match. Dining is expensive (as is expected at most of the Waikiki hotels); for cheap, grab-and-go meals, I like to go to **Lawson Station,** something of a Japanese version of 7-Eleven but with much better food, such as bento boxes, oden, and yummy desserts made by local companies.

2255 Kalakaua Ave. (at Royal Hawaiian Ave., on the ocean side of the Royal Hawaiian Shopping Center and west of the Royal Hawaiian), Honolulu. www.sheraton.com or www.starwood hotelshawaii.com. © **800/325-3535** or 808/922-4422. 1,852 units. $295–$495 double; from $705 suite. $30 resort charge per day for self-parking, Internet, and local and long-distance calls. Extra person $120. Children 17 and under stay free in parent's room. Valet parking $33. Bus: 19 or 20. **Amenities:** 5 restaurants; 2 bars; nightclub; babysitting; bike rentals; children's program (operated by an independent vendor, Poppins Keiki Hawaii); concierge; fitness center; 2 large outdoor pools; room service; Wi-Fi (included in resort fee).

Moderate

Waikiki Parc ★★   This is the Halekulani's younger, hipper sister. It's right across the street and run by the same management company. It has a **Nobu** restaurant, the lobby entrance glows blue to the beat of electronica, and you can rent the flashy Lotus sports cars parked near the valet. The rooms aren't as posh as the rest of the hotel, though—the floors are tile and the walls are plain white. Plus, the rooms are much smaller than the Halekulani and the service isn't as accommodating, but it's also half the price and still close to the beach. Spring for an ocean view; otherwise you might be overlooking the parking lot.

2233 Helumoa Rd. (at Lewers St.), Honolulu. www.waikikiparc.com. © **800/422-0450** or 808/ 921-7272. 297 units. $221–$425 double. Extra person $75. Children 17 and under stay free in parent's room. Bus: 19 or 20. **Amenities:** 2 restaurants; babysitting; concierge; fitness center; 8th-floor pool deck; room service; complimentary admission to the Bishop Museum and Honolulu Museum of Art; Wi-Fi (free).

Inexpensive

The Breakers ★   In the 1950s and '60s, thanks to statehood and the jet age, Waikiki's low-rise skyline gave way to larger and taller hotels. A lot of the more modest hotels are long gone … except for The Breakers. The two-story building, built in 1954, has managed to hold on to its family feel and prime real estate (just a few minutes' walk to the beach and the center of Waikiki). It's like a Hawaii-style motel, built around a pool, with charming touches such as double-pitched roofs, shoji doors to the lanai, and tropical landscaping. All of the rooms come with a kitchenette, though the appliances look like they're from the '70s. Sure, decor is dated (some say vintage), but it's clean.

250 Beach Walk (btw. Kalakaua Ave. and Kalia Rd.), Honolulu. www.breakers-hawaii.com. © **800/ 426-0494** or 808/923-3181. 64 units, all with shower only. $150–$170 double (extra person $20 per day); $220 garden suite double. Limited free parking (just 6 stalls); additional parking across the street $16 per day. Bus: 19 or 20. **Amenities:** Restaurant; grill; outdoor pool; Wi-Fi (free, in lobby).

AFFORDABLE waikiki: AQUA HOTELS

Unfortunately, inexpensive accommodations are few and far between on Oahu, and especially in Waikiki . . . at least places that you'd actually *want* to stay in. But a good bet is the Aqua chain. Its inexpensive to moderately priced properties (from $119 a night) are managed by a Hawaii-based company. Hotels do range in quality (with furnishings from dated tropical to bright and modern), but they are generally clean, well-maintained, and regularly updated. Another plus? Free Wi-Fi! Book directly from the website (www.aquaresorts.com) for the best rates and special deals.

Some of the standout hotels in the Aqua portfolio include the **Aqua Waikiki Pearl,** 415 Nahua St. (© **808/954-7425**), right in the middle of Waikiki and about a 10-minute walk to the beach. It has spacious room options, and I was able to find a 450-square-foot room for $125 online. Staying at the 44-floor **Aqua Skyline at Island Colony,** 445 Seaside Ave. (© **808/954-7411**), feels very urban, with a fresh new green-and-slate color scheme and views of Waikiki's skyline. The rooms have kitchenettes, and a pool and grill area on the sixth floor means you can save even more money making meals instead of going out. Not bad for a place with rates just a little over $100. Going up a tad in price ($150–$250) gets you a room in the **Luana Waikiki,** 2045 Kalakaua Ave. (© **808/955-6000**), which Aqua recently acquired from Outrigger. It offers a pool and suites with a kitchen. Best of the

mid-range Aqua hotels is the **Park Shore Waikiki,** 2586 Kalakaua Ave. (© **808/954-7426**), which was renovated in 2013 and offers views of Diamond Head and the ocean—vistas that are hard to beat, even at pricier hotels.

One of Aqua's most expensive—and nicest—hotels is the **Aqua Lotus Honolulu,** 2885 Kalakaua Ave. (© **808/954-7420**), on the east end of Waikiki, facing Kapiolani Park. It's a former W Hotel property, newly updated with dark hardwood floors, platform beds, granite-tiled bathrooms, and—in the corner units—a lanai and window that frame Diamond Head beautifully. You can sleep with the windows open here; this is the quiet side of Waikiki. Rates start at $250.

The Aqua portfolio continues to expand—it runs about a dozen properties in Honolulu and just added two new Oahu properties in 2013.

MID-WAIKIKI, MAUKA

These mid-Waikiki hotels, on the mountain side of Kalakaua Avenue, are a little farther away from the beach than those listed above. All are between Kalakaua Avenue and Ala Wai Canal, and between Kalaimoku Street in the Ewa (western) direction and Kaiulani Street in the Diamond Head (eastern) direction.

Inexpensive

Coconut Waikiki Hotel ★ The boutique hotel company Joie de Vivre recently took over this former Best Western hotel and renovated it. The result: cheery chic with lime-green accents, reggae-inflected "Jawaiian" music in the lobby, a super-friendly staff, and a chalkboard featuring a Hawaiian "Word of the Day" and "Local Food of the Day." Rooms are spacious and immaculate and come with a wet bar and a microwave. The small pool is kind of wedged between the hotel and a fence—better to grab the free beach towel rental and head to the ocean sands. Note that Joie de Vivre also runs the **Shoreline Hotel Waikiki**

(www.jdvhotels.com/hotels/hawaii/shoreline-hotel-waikiki) a few blocks away, with similar amenities and a midcentury-modern vibe, with maroon pops of color. In my mind, the two properties are equivalent in value, although the Shoreline's rooftop pool feels less claustrophobic.

450 Lewers St. (at Ala Wai Blvd.), Honolulu. www.jdvhotels.com/hotels/hawaii/coconut-waikiki-hotel. *©* **808/923-8828.** 81 units. $139–$219 double; from $249 suite. Valet parking only (no self-parking) $26. Bus: 19 or 20. **Amenities:** Tiny outdoor pool w/sun deck; Wi-Fi (free).

DIAMOND HEAD WAIKIKI

You'll find all these hotels between Ala Wai Boulevard and the ocean, and between Kaiulani Street and world-famous Diamond Head itself.

Moderate

Hotel Renew ★★   This boutique hotel proves that budget can still mean stylish. Like its lobby bar, rooms at Hotel Renew are pretty small but well-edited and well-designed. You get a minimalist, Japanese aesthetic; mood lighting; and plush beds with a down featherbed and down comforter. The crowd that stays here are 20- and 30-somethings who don't need hibiscus and tropical prints to tell them they're vacationing in Hawaii.

129 Paoakalani Ave. (at Lemon Rd.), Honolulu. www.hotelrenew.com. *©* **888/485-7639** or 808/687-7700. 72 units. $156–$275 double. Amenity fee $25 per day. Valet parking $25. Bus: 19 or 20. **Amenities:** Lounge; concierge; Wi-Fi (included in amenity fee).

New Otani Kaimana Beach Hotel ★   On the other side of the park is this hotel, where the tables are Formica and the color palette grandma pastels, at least for the cheaper rooms. But also here, right in front of the New Otani, is my favorite Waikiki beach. About a 15-minute walk from central Waikiki, it tends to be less crowded and the water cleaner than at other spots. In the mornings and right before sunset, you'll see regulars doing laps to the windsock and back. The quiet location, plus the right-on-the-beach **Hau Tree Lanai** restaurant, makes this hotel's lower-end rooms just right for the price. If you want a more updated decor and space, you can opt for the higher-end rooms, some of which were recently renovated—but at those prices, I'd rather head to the new Aqua Lotus Honolulu (p. 112).

2863 Kalakaua Ave. (ocean side of the street just Diamond Head of the Waikiki Aquarium, across from Kapiolani Park), Waikiki. www.kaimana.com. *©* **800/356-8264** or 808/923-1555. 124 units. $157–$255 double; from $165 studio; from $289 1-bedroom; from $508 suite. Extra person $50. Children 12 and under stay free in parent's room using existing bedding. Check website for special packages. Valet parking $23. Bus: 2 or 14. **Amenities:** 2 restaurants; beachfront bar; babysitting; concierge; room service; Wi-Fi (free).

HONOLULU BEYOND WAIKIKI

Manoa Valley

Manoa Valley Inn ★   I'm including this bed-and-breakfast because there's really nothing like it, but it takes a unique traveler to love it. It's like staying at your eccentric great-aunt's house, if she lived in a 100-year-old Victorian and furnished it with ornate antiques, four-poster beds, lace curtains, rose wallpaper, and floral bedspreads, which have all faded over the years. The yard, accessed via an overgrown trellis, is lush and tropical, and dense vegetation surrounds a small saltwater pool. The house itself is quite grand, with three stories and a view over the city all the way to Diamond Head. Some of the rooms on the top floor have an attic-like feel with sloping ceilings and quirky, hidden corners. One of my favorites is the T. C. Davis room (the rooms are named for prominent businessmen in Honolulu's history) for its lovely southern-facing window and smaller side windows that let in Honolulu's cooling trade winds. (Only two of the rooms have A/C; the rest have fans.) A new owner took over a few years ago; the caretaker and assorted family members, three dogs, and one cat live on site. Be aware that this house is in a residential neighborhood near the University of Hawaii; you'll need a car to get around and see the sights.

2001 Vancouver Dr. (at University Ave.), Honolulu. http://manoavalleyinn.com. © **808/947-6019.** 7 units, each with a private bathroom. $155–$195 doubles and triples. Rates include a hot breakfast. Free parking. Bus: 4 or 6. Children 12 and older preferred. **Amenities:** A/C (in some units); small saltwater pool; Wi-Fi (free).

To the East: Kahala

Kahala Hotel & Resort ★★★ Hotel magnate Conrad Hilton opened the Kahala in 1964 as a secluded and exclusive retreat away from Waikiki. Fifty years and a different owner later, it still retains that feeling of peacefulness and exclusivity. Its rooms convey a unique island luxury, aka "Kahala chic." In your private quarters, you'll get a plush bed and enormous bathroom with a soaking tub and separate shower. On the property, you have access to a small beach with a private feel (in Hawaii, all beaches are public, but few people come here). There's a pool, too, but what makes the Kahala unique is the Dolphin Quest, which allows you to get up close and personal with the dolphins in the lagoon. The restaurants on the property offer experiences such as a beachfront brunch buffet, afternoon tea on the veranda, and an upscale Pacific Rim dinner, all of which make the Kahala a worthy escape from the bustle of Waikiki.

5000 Kahala Ave. (next to the Waialae Country Club), Honolulu. www.kahalaresort.com. © **800/367-2525** or 808/739-8888. 343 units. From $423 double; from $1,340 suite. Extra person $175. Children 17 and under stay free in parent's room. Check "Specials & Packages" online discounts. Parking $28. **Amenities:** 5 restaurants; 4 bars; babysitting; year-round children's program (for a fee); concierge; nearby golf course; fitness center; large outdoor pool; room service; watersports equipment rentals, Wi-Fi (free).

THE WINDWARD COAST

Note: Windward Coast accommodations are located on the "Eastern Oahu & the Windward Coast" map (p. 75).

Kailua

Lanikai Bed & Breakfast ★ This is one of the few options for staying in the exclusive Lanikai neighborhood, which still keeps its laidback, beachy vibe— you'll see people heading to the beach on bikes or with kayaks or stand-up paddleboards in tow. You'll feel a part of the neighborhood, staying in this old-style, homey, and comfortable Lanikai house just across the street from the beach. It has two units: the 1,000-square-foot, two-bedroom Tree House and the smaller Garden Studio, decorated in Hawaiiana print and recently updated with rattan furniture. Rick Maxey is the second-generation owner: "I grew up in this house," he says. He and his family live on the first floor, below the Tree House. Each unit has its own private entrance and kitchenette, and the Garden Studio has its own patio. Each is furnished with cooking utensils and beach equipment—all you need to make it home.

1277 Mokulua Dr. (btw. Onekea and Aala drives in Lanikai), Kailua. www.lanikaibeachrentals. com. © **808/261-7895.** 2 units. $170 studio double; $185 apt double or $250 for 3 or 4.

Cleaning fee $50–$100. Rates include breakfast items in fridge left at the beginning of your stay. 5-night minimum. Free parking. Bus: 56. **Amenities:** Wi-Fi (free).

Sheffield House   Kailua is a small beach town, with restaurants, shops, and a business center anchored by Whole Foods. Staying at Sheffield House puts you right in the middle of everything—it's just a few minutes' walk to the beach but also a short stroll to Whole Foods, the Sunday farmer's market, and "town" for groceries and entertainment. (Convenience does have its drawbacks, though—the house is on one of Kailua's busy streets, which means traffic sounds.) There are two vacation rentals here—a one-bedroom and a studio, each with its own private entry and kitchenette.

131 Kuulei Rd. (at Kalaheo Dr.), Kailua. www.hawaiisheffieldhouse.com. *ⓒ* **808/262-0721.** 2 units. $144–$164 double guest room; $164–$184 1-bedroom. Extra person $20. Cleaning fee $65–$75. Rates include 1st day's continental breakfast. Free parking. Bus: 56. **Amenities:** Wi-Fi (free).

THE NORTH SHORE

The North Shore has few accommodations and tourist facilities—some say that's its charm. VRBO.com and airbnb.com (mentioned above in "Vacation Rentals") offer a good range of places to stay, such as a Haleiwa studio on the first floor of a two-story home for $85 a night, a North Shore loft with three beds from $159, and a three-bedroom house steps away from Sunset Beach for $410 a night. Cleaning fees vary.

   Note: North Shore accommodations are located on the "Oahu's North Shore" map (p. 84).

Very Expensive

Turtle Bay Resort ★★   The North Shore's only resort completed property-wide renovations in 2014, updating everything in a beachy, laidback-luxurious style befitting the less-developed, unhurried North Shore. The lobby and gym have been opened up with ocean views, the spa has doubled in size, the restaurants' menus have been revamped to highlight locally grown ingredients, and revamped rooms have a calming, neutral palette and walk-in stone showers. What hasn't changed: Every room still has an ocean view. Turtle Bay has also embraced its role as a surf-scene hub, especially in the wintertime, when the surfing season is in full swing. All the pros come to **Lei Lei's Bar and Grill** for a drink, and the new **Surfer, The Bar,** a collaboration between the resort and "Surfer" magazine, offers Talk Story nights, bringing in pro surfers and watermen to share their stories. All in all, Turtle Bay's renovations really make the resort feel a part of the North Shore landscape. Of all the resorts outside of Waikiki (including Kahala, Aulani, and Ihilani), this would be my pick, for the vibe, the value, and the surroundings.

57–091 Kamehameha Hwy. (Hwy. 83), Kahuku. www.turtlebayresort.com. *ⓒ* **800/203-3650** or 808/293-6000. 477 units. $319–$389 double; from $599 cottage; from $499 suite; from $1,169 villa. Daily $32 resort fee for self-parking, Internet access, and more. Extra person $50. Children 17 and under stay free in parent's room. **Amenities:** 5 restaurants; 2 bars; concierge; 36 holes of golf; stable w/horseback riding; 2 outdoor heated pools (w/80-ft. water slide); room service; spa w/fitness center; 4 tennis courts; watersports equipment rentals; Wi-Fi (included in resort fee).

Inexpensive

Ke Iki Beach Bungalows ★   These bungalows are right on a beautiful, wide, and uncrowded beach, between Sharks Cove (great for snorkeling in the summer) and Pipeline (for the best pro-surfer wave-watching come winter). Ranging from basic studios to two bedrooms, each unit is equipped with bamboo furniture and a full kitchen, plus its own grill. Stock up on groceries at the nearby Foodland (part of the largest locally owned supermarket chain in Hawaii). Be aware that units have no air-conditioning, but ceiling fans and North Shore breezes are usually enough to keep the air cool. Settle into one of the hammocks strung up between the palm trees overlooking the beach—this is island living.

59–579 Ke Iki Rd. (off Kamehameha Hwy.), Haleiwa. www.keikibeach.com. © **866/638-8229** or 808/638-8229. 11 units. $135 double gardenview studio or 1-bedroom; $185–$215 double beachfront 1-bedroom; $155–$185 double gardenview 2-bedroom; $210–$230 double beachfront 2-bedroom. Extra person stays free. Cleaning fee $55–$100 per week or per visit (if less than a week). Free parking. Bus: 52. **Amenities:** Complimentary bikes; CD player; kitchen; TV; complimentary watersports equipment; Wi-Fi (free).

LEEWARD OAHU: THE WAIANAE COAST

Aulani, a Disney Resort & Spa, Ko Olina, Hawaii ★★★ Aulani has plenty of Mickey Mouse and friends to entertain the kids, such as a character breakfast with photo ops, but it's also a celebration of Hawaiian culture. Disney's "imagineers" worked with locals to get many of the details just right, from murals and woodcarvings throughout the property that tell the story of Hawaii, to the **Olelo Room,** one of the resort bars, where you can learn the Hawaiian language from bartenders who are fluent in Hawaiian (everyone learns a new language better when they're drinking, right?). A 900-foot-long lazy river threads the resort, which—along with children's programs like storytelling nights under the stars, Hawaiian crafts classes, and Disney movies on the lawn—makes the Aulani, perhaps unsurprisingly, one of the best lodging choices for families. Even I, by now a cynical adult, am always delighted when I step foot on this property.

92–1185 Ali'inui Dr., Kapolei. http://resorts.disney.go.com/aulani-hawaii-resort. © **714/520-7001** (reservations) or 808/674-6200 (hotel). 359 units in hotel, $399–$549 hotel room, from $1,340 suite. Parking $35. No bus service. Take H-1 west toward Pearl City/Ewa Beach; stay on H-1 until it becomes Hwy. 93 (Farrington Hwy.); look for the exit sign for Ko Olina Resort; turn left on Ali'inui Dr. **Amenities:** 3 restaurants; 3 bars; babysitting; championship 18-hole Ko Olina Golf Course designed by Ted Robinson; numerous outdoor pools and water features; room service; spa; watersports equipment rentals; Wi-Fi (free).

Camping & Wilderness Cabins

If you plan to camp, you must bring your own gear or buy it here—no one on Oahu rents gear. If you are bringing your own equipment, remember that you can't transport fuel (even in a canister) on the plane.

The best places to camp on Oahu are listed below. TheBus's Circle Island route can get you to or near all these sites, but remember: On TheBus, you're allowed only one bag, which has to fit under the seat. If you have more gear, you're going to have to drive or take a cab.

THE WINDWARD COAST

Hoomaluhia Botanical Garden ★

This little-known windward campground outside Kaneohe is a real treasure. It's hard to believe that it's just half an hour from downtown Honolulu. The name Hoomaluhia, or "peace and tranquillity," accurately describes this 400-acre botanical garden at the foot of the jagged Koolau Range. In this lush setting, gardens are devoted to plants specific to tropical America, native Hawaii, Polynesia,

India, Sri Lanka, and Africa. A 32-acre lake sits in the middle of the scenic park (no swimming or boating allowed), and there are numerous hiking trails. The visitor center offers free guided walks Saturday at 10am and Sunday at 1pm (call the number below to register).

Facilities for this tent-camp area include restrooms, cold showers, dishwashing stations, picnic tables, and water. Shopping and gas are available in Kaneohe, 2 miles away. Stays are limited to 3 nights, from 9am Friday to 4pm Monday only. Reserve a campsite up to 2 weeks in advance at **camping. honolulu.gov**. Permits are $32, valid for the entire weekend (Fri–Sun). To get here from Waikiki, take H-1 to the Pali Highway (Hwy. 61); turn left on Kamehameha Highway (Hwy. 83); and at the fourth light, turn left on Luluku Road. TheBus nos. 55 and 65 stop nearby on Kamehameha Highway; from here, you'll have to walk 2 miles to the visitor center.

Kahana Bay Beach Park ★

Lying under Tahiti-like cliffs, with a beautiful gold-sand crescent beach framed by pine-needle casuarina trees, Kahana Bay Beach Park is a place of serene beauty. You can swim, bodysurf, fish, hike, and picnic or just sit and listen to the trade winds whistle through the beach pines (and sometimes, cars—the campsite is along Kamehameha Highway).

Facilities include restrooms, outdoor showers, picnic tables, and drinking water. *Note:* The restrooms are located at the north end of the beach, far away from the camping area.

Permits can be obtained at **camping.ehawaii.gov** for $18 a night. Camping is only allowed from Friday through Wednesday.

Kahana Bay Beach Park is located in the 52–222 block of Kamehameha Highway (Hwy. 83) in Kahana. From Waikiki, take the H-1 west to the Likelike Highway (Hwy. 63). Continue north on the Likelike, through the Wilson Tunnel, turning left on Hwy. 83; Kahana Bay is 13 miles down the road on the right. You can also get here via TheBus no. 55.

Kualoa Regional Park ★★

This park has a spectacular setting on a peninsula on Kaneohe Bay. The gold-sand beach is excellent for snorkeling, and fishing can be rewarding as well (see "Beaches," earlier in this chapter, for details).

There are two campgrounds: Campground A—located in a wooded area with a sandy beach and palm, ironwood, kamani, and monkeypod trees—is mainly used for groups. It does have a few sites for families, except during the summer (June–Aug), when the Department of Parks and Recreation conducts a children's camping program here. Campground B is on the main beach; it has fewer shade trees but a great view of Mokolii Island. Facilities at both sites include restrooms, outdoor showers, picnic tables, and drinking fountains. Campground A also has sinks for washing dishes, a volleyball court, and a kitchen building. Gas and groceries are available in Kaaawa, 2½ miles away. The gate hours at Kualoa Regional Park are 7am to 8pm.

Permits are $32 for the 3-day permit (for Campground A) and $52 for the 5-day permit (for Campground B). No camping allowed in Campground A Monday to Thursday; in Campground B, no camping Wednesday and Thursday. Reserve a campsite up to 2 weeks in advance at **camping.honolulu.gov**.

To get to the park, take the Likelike Highway (Hwy. 63); after the Wilson Tunnel, get in the right lane and turn off on Kahakili Highway (Hwy. 83). Or take TheBus no. 55.

THE NORTH SHORE
Malaekahana Bay State Recreation Area ★★

This is one of the most beautiful beach-camping areas in the state, with a mile-long, gold-sand beach on Oahu's North Shore (see "Beaches," earlier in this chapter, for details). There are two areas for tent camping. Facilities include picnic tables, restrooms, showers, sinks, and drinking water. For your safety, the park gate is closed between 6:45pm and 7am; vehicles cannot enter or exit during those hours. Groceries and gas are available in Laie and Kahuku, each less than a mile away.

Permits are $18 a night and available at **camping.ehawaii.gov**. Camping is limited to Friday through Wednesday.

The recreation area is located on Kamehameha Highway (Hwy. 83) between Laie and Kahuku. Take the H-2 to Hwy. 99 to Hwy. 83 (both roads are called Kamehameha Hwy.); continue on Hwy. 83 just past Kahuku. You can also get here via TheBus no. 55.

WHERE TO EAT ON OAHU

Hawaii offers food experiences that exist nowhere else in the world, from dishes based on foods eaten by ancient Native Hawaiians to plate lunches in which you can see the history of Hawaii, from postwar-era hole-in-the-walls where the only thing that's changed is the prices to fancy dining rooms that spawned the birth of Hawaii Regional Cuisine. Asian food dominates, thanks to the state's demographics (as of 2012, Hawaii is the country's only majority-Asian state, comprising 56.9 percent of the total population). On Oahu, the most promising places to eat are often found in the most unexpected places. For the adventurous, eating here is like a treasure hunt.

Honolulu: Waikiki

Thanks to an influx of Japanese tourists, Waikiki now has some of the best Japanese food outside of Japan. Plus, here are some of Honolulu's most luxurious dining rooms with ocean views—at a price.

VERY EXPENSIVE

La Mer ★★ NEOCLASSICAL FRENCH   La Belle Epoque meets Pacific teak and rattan against heartachingly romantic views of the ocean and Diamond Head. Sometimes, it's all a little over the top, when a red rose the size of your fist is perched on your cocktail, but those into haute French cuisine with a touch of the theatrical will love La Mer. Choose from three- or four-course tasting menus, or the *menu dégustation*, seven courses featuring luxe ingredients such as foie gras tiled with shiitake mushrooms, abalone *meunière*, lobster tail bathed in butter and lobster consommé, and a filet of beef with truffle. Luxe indeed. La Mer is one of the few restaurants on Oahu that requires men to wear a jacket or long-sleeved shirt.

At the Halekulani, 2199 Kalia Rd., Waikiki, Honolulu. www.halekulani.com. ✆ **808/923-2311.** Reservations recommended. Jackets or long-sleeved shirts required for men. Prix-fixe menu $175, $85 for wine pairing. Daily 6–10pm.

MODERATE

Goofy Café and Dine ★ HEALTHY   Named not after the Disney character but the right-foot-forward surfing stance, this charming spot has a cozy, beachy

Waikiki Restaurants

Ginza Bairin **2**
Goofy Café **1**
Hula Grill Waikiki **5**
Jinroku **6**
La Mer **3**
Marukame Udon **4**
Sansei **7**
Tokkuri Tei **9**
Tucker & Bevvy **8**

dining out AT THE HALEKULANI

Sure, dining in Waikiki's high-end hotels is often an overpriced affair, but sometimes the occasion warrants everything that comes with it—including oceanside views and upscale service. My pick for special events is the **Halekulani** ★★★ (p. 109). Here are my favorite ways to soak up the Halekulani's rarefied restaurant experiences.

o The Sunday brunch buffet at **Orchids** is a must—it's the best in Hawaii. It has everything from a roast-suckling-pig carving station to a sashimi and poke bar. Leave room if you can for the ice cream sundae bar, the Halekulani's signature fluffy coconut cake, and lots of pretty, dainty desserts. (**Note:** You'll need to make reservations weeks in advance.) Love afternoon tea? Orchids also serves my favorite afternoon tea service on the island, with a lovely array of sandwiches and sweets and an excellent selection of premium teas.

o Come sunset, head to **House Without a Key** for a mai tai and the lovely hula of former Miss Hawaiis, including the legendary Kanoe Miller. If the grill is fired up at this outdoor gathering spot (Tues and Thurs), I might order some lamb chops or Cajun-spiced *shutome*.

o If the occasion calls for something more romantic and intimate, I go to **L'Aperitif,** the bar inside La Mer, where the drinks are inspired by 19th-century French cocktail culture and you can watch ice formed into a sphere before your very eyes.

vibe, lined with reclaimed wood and decorated with surfboards that, from the looks of it, are waxed and ready to go. (The popular locals' surfing spot, Bowls, is nearby.) It's a surfer's cafe as envisioned by a Japanese company that also runs Aloha Table in Waikiki. Goofy has a breakfast, lunch, and dinner menu, but breakfast (served all day) is the best part: Look for eggs Benedict, French toast drizzled with creamy Big Island honey, green smoothies poured over chia seeds, and huge acai bowls mounded over with fresh fruit. Come later, for dinner or to sit at the bar, and you can get a shochu sour, shaken with Hawaiian Shochu Co.'s unique, Haleiwa-made sweet-potato spirit.

1831 Ala Moana Blvd., Suite 201., Waikiki, Honolulu. ℂ **808/943-0077.** Breakfast $10–$14. Daily 7am–11pm.

Ginza Bairin ★★ JAPANESE   The Japanese take their *tonkatsu*—fried pork cutlets—very, very seriously. Here, a kurobota pork loin katsu can run you $36, but, oh, there's such joy in the crispy, greaseless panko crust and the juicy pork within. Grind some sesame seeds into the plummy tonkatsu sauce, and dip your pork in. The tonkatsu is served on a wire pedestal (to keep the bottom from steaming and going soggy) and a bottomless chiffonade of cabbage salad. *Tip:* Just as good, and only $10, is the pork tenderloin katsu sandwich—a thinner cut of pork, expertly fried, between two slices of white bread with the crusts cut off. 255 Beach Walk, Waikiki, Honolulu. ℂ **808/926-8082.** Main courses $8–$32. Sun–Wed 11am–10:30pm; Thurs–Fri 11am–11:30pm.

Hula Grill Waikiki ★ AMERICAN   The night before, you might be slamming back tiki drinks and making new friends at the ever-popular and rowdy Duke's down below. For the morning after, head to Hula Grill (owned by the same restaurant group as Duke's), where the ocean views, pineapple-coconut pancakes, and sweet potato-chorizo hash will smooth out any hangover. Not so adventurous in the morning? There's standard waffle-and-omelet breakfast fare, too. Breakfast and brunch are the most reasonably priced meals; dinner gets into the $30 range and isn't worth it.

At the Outrigger Waikiki on the Beach, 2335 Kalakaua Ave., Waikiki, Honolulu. www.hulagrill waikiki.com. © **808/923-HULA** [4852]. Reservations recommended for dinner. Breakfast $7–$14; main courses $21–$35. Daily 6:30–11pm, 4–6pm (happy hour with light menu).

Jinroku ★★ JAPANESE   The specialty here is *okonomiyaki*, a cross between an omelet and a savory pancake, topped with fluttering bonito flakes. Try the mochi shiso one, with chewy rice cakes and an herb that's like a mint and basil hybrid, or pork kimchee okonomiyaki. They can take almost 20 minutes to cook on the teppan grill, but it's oh-so-worth-it. The open-air setting—one side opens onto bustling Kuhio Street—is like Osaka meets Waikiki.

2427 Kuhio Ave., Waikiki, Honolulu. www.jinrokupacific.com. © **808/926-8955.** Appetizers $6–$14; main courses $20–$72. Daily 11:30am–2:30pm, 5:30–10:30pm.

Sansei Seafood Restaurant & Sushi Bar ★ SUSHI/PACIFIC RIM   Sushi purists and sticklers for rice/fish ratios need not come. But those looking for creativity in their sushi should make their way to restaurateur D. K. Kodama's most popular restaurant. The best rolls here don't even have rice, like the moi sashimi wrapped around sweet Maui onions in a pool of ponzu, or the panko-crusted ahi in a soy mustard sauce. Don't miss the crab truffle ramen. *Tip:* Sushi is half off from 10pm to 1am Friday and Saturday, although you might have to put up with some very loud karaoke. Just hope your fellow diners are good singers.

At the Waikiki Beach Marriott Resort, 2552 Kalakaua Ave., 3rd floor, Waikiki, Honolulu. www. sanseihawaii.com. © **808/931-6286.** Reservations recommended. Sushi $3–$18; main courses $16–$35. Sat–Wed 5:30–10pm; Thurs–Fri 5:30pm–1am.

Inexpensive

Marukame Udon ★★ JAPANESE   There's always a line out the door at this cafeteria-style noodle joint, but it moves quickly. Pass the time by watching the cooks roll out and cut the dough for udon right in front of you. Bowls of udon, hot or cold, with toppings such as a soft poached egg or Japanese curry, are all under $7.

2310 Kuhio Ave., Waikiki, Honolulu. © **808/931-6000.** Noodles $4–$7. Daily 11am–10pm.

Tucker & Bevvy ★ HEALTHY   Aussie slang for "food and drink" (owner Cecily Ho Sargent was born in Honolulu, but spent 17 years in Australia), this white clapboard cafe with blackboard menus offers food for an instant picnic: grab-and-go sandwiches and salads, like a smoked ahi wrap, sesame chicken salad with beets and almonds, and quinoa tabbouleh. You can get hot sandwiches, too, such as a pastrami Reuben or turkey Brie. Come in the morning, and you'll find surfers rehydrating at the fresh juice and smoothie bar, post dawn patrol.

At the Park Shore Hotel, 2586 Kalakaua Ave., Waikiki, Honolulu. www.tuckerandbevvy.com. © **808/922-0099.** Most items under $10. Daily 7am–7pm.

4

Honolulu Beyond Waikiki

KAPAHULU

Moderate

Side Street Inn on Da Strip ★ LOCAL   The newer and bigger version of Side Street Inn opened in 2010. You can still go to the original one near Ala Moana for the divey, locals-only atmosphere. But I've found that the food is better prepared at this new location, even though it's pretty much the same menu of fried pork chops and kim chee fried rice with bacon, Portuguese sausage, and *char siu.* The portion sizes are still as big as ever.

614 Kapahulu Ave., Honolulu. ✆ **808/739-3939.** Starters $8–$14; main courses $13–$23. Mon–Fri 3–11:30pm; Sat–Sun 1–11:30pm.

Tokkuri Tei ★ LOCAL/JAPANESE/SUSHI   This is a local-style *izakaya,* a Japanese pub with snacks made for sharing. The menu is long and quirky—before diving in to make sense of it all, start with the squid pancake and *Norichos,* strips of nori tempura-battered and fried, topped with nacho cheese, tobiko, and teriyaki sauce. For purists, there are simple nigiri sushi. The truly adventurous can sample ice cream with shiso, honey, and love-it-or-hate-it *natto,* the infamous Japanese slimy, stinky fermented soybeans.

449 Kapahulu Ave., Honolulu. ✆ **808/732-6480.** Sushi $5–$50. Mon–Sat 10:30am–2pm and 5:30pm–midnight; Sun 5:30–10pm.

Inexpensive

Ono Seafood ★★ LOCAL   Not to be confused with Ono Hawaiian Food (though that restaurant, immediately recognizable with its long line of tourists and locals, is also worth going to for its monster-size *laulau* and other more reasonably sized portions of Hawaiian food). This little seafood counter serves some of Honolulu's freshest poke—ruby red ahi (tuna) cut and seasoned to order with soy sauce and onions for the shoyu poke or *limu* (seaweed) and Hawaiian salt for the Hawaiian-style poke.

747 Kapahulu Ave., Apt. 4, Honolulu. ✆ **808/732-4806.** Poke bowls around $8. Mon and Wed–Sat 8am–6pm; Sun 10am–3pm.

Rainbow Drive In ★ LOCAL   Founded in 1961, Rainbow Drive In delivers on the nostalgia with its iconic rainbow neon and school-cafeteria-style seating. Surfers and old-timers make this spot their meeting place, catching up over Hawaii-style plate lunches: two scoops rice, one scoop mac salad, and hearty portions of meat such as shoyu chicken, chili, or the Hawaii original loco moco (a hamburger patty over rice, topped with brown gravy and an egg).

3308 Kanaina Ave., Honolulu. www.rainbowdrivein.com. ✆ **808/737-0177.** Plates under $10. Daily 7am–9pm.

ALA MOANA & KAKAAKO

Expensive

MW ★★ HAWAII REGIONAL   Michelle Karr-Ueoka and Wade Ueoka, the wife-and-husband team in the kitchen, are Alan Wong alums, and here, they give their own take on Hawaii Regional Cuisine. What that means at MW is local comfort food re-envisioned for fine dining. An ahi poke dish turns the familiar staple into something unexpected, with spicy tuna, ikura, ahi, and uni topped with crispy rice crackers. Oxtail soup becomes oxtail, deboned and stuffed with

going local: UNIQUELY HAWAIIAN EATS

Talk to locals who move away from Hawaii, and these are the foods they miss. Everyone's got their own go-to place and go-to dishes—people here could spend hours arguing over the best. Here are some of my favorites:

Poke Ruby red cubes of fresh ahi (tuna), tossed with limu (seaweed), kukui nut, and Hawaiian chili pepper: Ahi poke (pronounced "po-keh") doesn't get better than the Hawaiian-style version at **Ono Seafood ★★** (p. 122).

Saimin An only-in-Hawaii mashup of Chinese-style noodles in a Japanese dashi broth. Join the regulars at the communal table at **Palace Saimin,** 1256 N. King St. (© **808/841-9983**), where the interior is as simple as this bowl of noodles. Palace Saimin has been around since 1946, and it looks like it. (I mean that in the nicest way possible.)

Loco moco Two sunny-side up eggs over a hamburger patty and rice, all doused in brown gravy. I love it at **Liliha Bakery ★★** (p. 130).

Spam musubi Ah yes, Spam. Hawaii eats more Spam per capita than any other state. A dubious distinction to some, but don't knock it before you try it. Spam musubi (think of it as a giant sushi topped with Spam) is so ubiquitous you can find it at 7-Elevens and convenience stores (where it's pretty good). But for an even finer product, **Iyasume Musubi's,** 2410 Koa Ave., #4 (© **808/921-0168**), is the tops.

Hawaiian plate Laulau (pork wrapped in taro leaves), kalua pig (shredded, roasted pork), poi (milled taro), and haupia (like coconut jello): It's Hawaiian luau food, based on what native Hawaiians used to eat. But you can get it without the fuss at **Helena's Hawaiian Food ★★** (p. 130), **Highway Inn ★★** (p. 126), and **Ono Hawaiian Food,** 726 Kapahulu Ave. (© **808/737-2275**). (Sorry, I couldn't pick a favorite for this one!)

Malasadas Hole-less doughnuts, rolled in sugar, by way of Portugal. **Leonard's Bakery,** 933 Kapahulu Ave. (© **808/737-5571**), was started in 1946 by the descendants of Portuguese contract laborers brought to work in Hawaii's sugarcane fields. I love Leonard's malasadas dusted with li hing mui powder (made from sweet-tart plums).

Shave ice Nothing cools better on a hot day than powdery-soft ice drenched in tropical fruit syrups. I go to **Waiola Shave Ice,** 3113 Mokihana St. (© **808/735-8886**), for the nostalgia factor, but since you'll probably need more than one shave ice while you're in town, also hit up **Ailana Shave Ice,** 1430 Kona St. (© **808/955-8881**), which offers a variety of homemade syrups from real fruit (a rarity).

more meat, and set on beef-stew risotto. Desserts outshine the entrees, though, such as a chocolate banana cream pie layered into a jar or a lemon meringue brûlée, full of custard, chewy jellies, and lemon sorbet and sealed with a torched sugar crust. You've never had anything like it.

1538 Kapiolani Blvd., #107, Honolulu. www.mwrestaurant.com. © **808/955-6505.** Reservations recommended. Lunch $14–$26; dinner main courses $24–$36; desserts $9. Mon–Sat 10:30am–10pm; Sun 10:30am–9pm.

Sushi Sasabune ★★ SUSHI This formerly austere restaurant has recently been updated with faux maple trees that reflect the progression of seasons. But

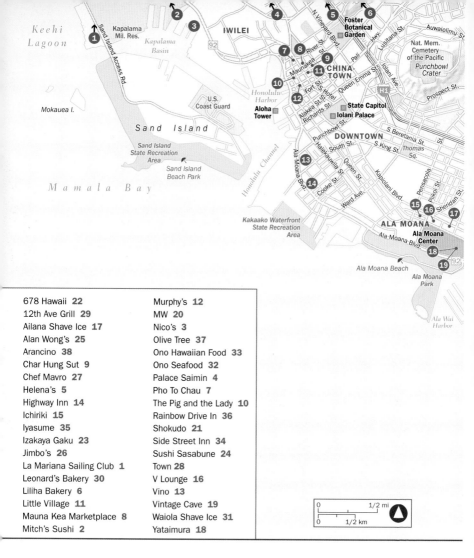

if you think that means that Seiji Kumagawa, aka the "Sushi Nazi," has also softened up, you'd be mistaken. Sitting at his sushi bar and submitting to the *omakase* menu means you'll eat what he decides to feed you, and you've given up all control of your own soy sauce and wasabi dish. Follow his orders (dip gently in soy sauce only when instructed), and your reward is gorgeous orbs of house-cured ikura, scallop dusted with yuzu kosho (a citrusy, peppery condiment), mackerel topped with a translucent sheet of seaweed, and fish you may have never heard of. The rice is just as important—watch how Kumagawa molds it, just so, and then feel it break apart softly in your mouth, melding with the fish. This is sushi art. ***Tip:*** Want to experience the sushi without the stress? Sit at the tables, and you're free to order sushi a la carte.

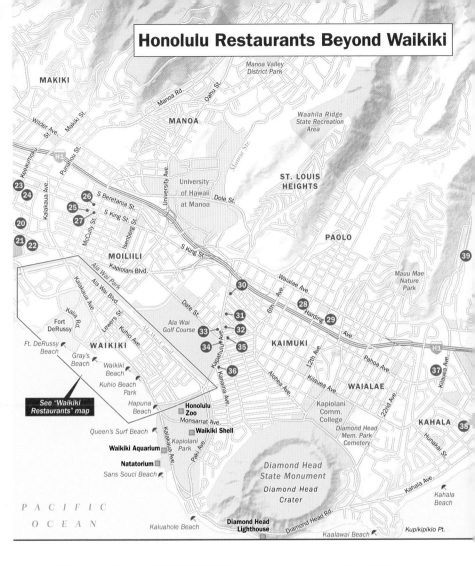

1417 S. King St., Honolulu. ☎ **808/947-3800.** Reservations recommended. Sushi $5–$50; *omakase* $80–$100 per person. Tues–Fri noon–2pm and Tues–Sat 5:30–10pm.

Vintage Cave ★★★ MODERN AMERICAN   An eccentric Japanese billionaire builds "a private society elevating art, culture, and pleasure," in the former storage basement of a Japanese department store (which he also owns), and what do you get? Honolulu's most stunning food (and its priciest). Fresh truffle shavings and a Parmesan cream give way to a silky egg yolk. Caviar glossed with maple gel and set like jewels on crème fraîche and fried brioche. There's only one menu a night, and it's constantly changing. The young chef, Chris Kajioka, insists on the finest ingredients, whether it's baby lettuces grown on the Big Island, or *amadai* (a fish with skin that puffs and crisps up like chips when it hits hot oil) from Japan, and applies impeccable technique to it all. The interior is luxe-man-cave-meets-art-gallery—18 original Picasso drawings hang in the dining room, which is lined with bricks. Vintage Cave was originally envisioned as a members-only club, with membership starting at $5,000 and going up to $500,000, but currently it's still open to the public.

1450 Ala Moana Blvd., #2250, Honolulu. www.vintagecave.com. ✆ **808/441-1744.** Reservations required. $295 tasting menu. Mon–Sat 5:30–8pm.

Moderate

Highway Inn ★★ HAWAIIAN/LOCAL   The original Highway Inn in Waipahu opened in 1947, serving Hawaiian food such as *laulau* (pork wrapped in taro leaves and steamed), kalua pig (smoky, roasted pork), and poi (mashed taro). Also on the menu: classic American fare like beef stew and hamburgers, recipes that founder Seiichi Toguchi picked up in internment-camp mess halls during World War II. For decades, Highway Inn remained a snapshot of food in post-war Hawaii. Then, in 2012, it opened a new location in Honolulu and introduced some return-to-the-land dishes like fish and poi—fried whole akule or opelu served with fresh-milled, sweet Waipio Valley poi, unlike at other Hawaiian food restaurants, which tend toward the bagged poi. Make room for the desserts, where classics meet found-again ingredients, such as poi Twinkies and pineapple-upside-down cake made with kiawe bean flour (ground from the pods of mesquite trees).

680 Ala Moana Blvd., Honolulu. www.myhighwayinn.com. ✆ **808/954-4955.** Plates $10–$14. Mon–Thurs 8:30am–8:30pm; Fri–Sat 8:30am–9pm; Sun 9am–2:30pm.

Ichiriki ★★ JAPANESE/NABE   Okay, so I know it's hot in Hawaii most of the time, but that hasn't stopped dozens of nabe and hotpot restaurants from opening, and it hasn't stopped the locals from going. This place was one of the first to get the trend going. Pick your soup base (I'm partial to the *pirikara*, seasoned with a spicy soy sauce) and choose from thinly sliced chicken, pork, or beef. The server sets your broth on the tabletop gas grill, and as it comes to a boil, you cook your meat in the soup. You'll also get a heaping plate of vegetables to throw in and deep-fried tofu that soaks up the broth like a sponge. My favorite part: the meatballs dispensed from a bamboo sheath. After all that good stuff has enriched the soup, order noodles to throw in and absorb what's left.

510 Piikoi St., Honolulu. www.ichirikinabe.com. ✆ **808/589-2299.** Lunch $12–$20, dinner $19–$32. Sun–Thurs 11am–11pm; Fri–Sat 11am–midnight.

678 Hawaii ★★ KOREAN   This is Honolulu's hippest Korean barbecue restaurant, where different cuts of high-quality pork and beef sizzle on the tabletop grill in front of you. It was started by the Korean celebrity Kang Ho Dong (that's his likeness in the glowing cutout in front), who has also opened other locations in Korea, Los Angeles, and Atlanta. The atmosphere draws young and old alike, with everyone reaching over for bits of meat to dip into the moat of corn cheese and egg custard warmed by the grill. Servers are quick and cheerful—call them by pressing a button on the table—and happy to replenish the *banchan*, or little side dishes, until you can't eat anymore. If only all eating experiences were this fun!

1726 Kapiolani Blvd., Honolulu. ✆ **808/941-6678.** Reservations recommended. Combination meal for 2–3 people $44–$55. Sun–Thurs 11am–1am; Fri–Sat 11am–2am.

KEEAUMOKU ST., AKA koreamoku

There's been a push in recent years to officially designate the Keeaumoku area as Koreatown, to bring attention to the Korean restaurants and culture here, as well as tell the story of Korean immigration to Hawaii since 1902. Whether it happens or not, locals have already nicknamed the stretch of Keeaumoku St. from the mall to King St. "Koreamoku" for the sheer number of Korean eateries.

At **So Gong Dong,** 627 Keeaumoku St. (© **808/946-8200**), the specialty is *soon dubu,* the red and spicy stew brimming with custardy tofu, which arrives at a rolling boil in a blazing-hot clay pot. Crack the raw egg and stir in to thicken. Go down Keeaumoku a few blocks mauka, and find **Sikdorak,** 655 Keeaumoku St. (© **808/949-2890**), tucked away in a cramped strip mall. You'll spot it from the line of people waiting outside. Here, the lure is all-you-can-eat Korean barbecue for $20 and served 24 hours a day. Pick your meats, such as thinly sliced brisket, rib-eye, spicy pork, or even beef tongue, throw it on the tabletop grill, and just keep it coming.

Forget New York: Seoul is the true city that never sleeps. Which explains why there are so many late-night Korean restaurants in Honolulu. The most famous is **Sorabol,** 805 Keeaumoku St.

(© **808/947-3113**), open 24 hours a day, where you'll find Korean ladies who lunch, families having dinner, club kids sobering up in the late night, and Korean cabbies getting off their shift in the wee morning hours. All the Korean staples are here, from *kalbi* (marinated short ribs) to *bi bim bap* (rice topped with marinated beef and vegetables) to a raw ahi rice salad, mixed tableside with plenty of *kochujang,* the singular Korean chili sauce. For dessert, head to **Ireh,** 911 Keeaumoku St. (© **808/943-6000**), a little Korean snack shop, for *pat bing soo,* a Korean sundae of sorts with shave ice, red bean, and roasted sesame powder. Still hungry? Order a plate of the homemade *mandoo* (Korean dumplings) or homey bowls such as the sesame-leaf, hand-shaved noodles or extra elastic chewing noodles.

Inexpensive

Shokudo ★ JAPANESE   What you cannot miss here: the honey toast. As in, you literally won't miss it as servers bring it to the tables around you. Get your own—it's a tower of toast, practically half a loaf of Japanese bread, griddled in butter, cubed, drizzled with honey, and topped with ice cream. It sounds simple, but it's ridiculously enjoyable. As for the rest of the menu, Shokudo recently revamped it. What's new: otoro sashimi from Japan's Tsukiji fish market and a deep-fried California roll topped with spicy ahi. Shokudo is sort of a cross between Denny's and Morimoto—a fun, trendy, stylish, eclectic eatery offering Japanese comfort food and decent (but not the best) sushi. Try the fresh tofu and mochi cheese gratin, too.

At the Ala Moana Pacific Center, 1585 Kapiolani Blvd., Honolulu. www.shokudojapanese.com. © **808/941-3701.** Main courses $7–$25; sushi $6.50–$15. Sun–Thurs 11:30am–1am; Fri–Sat 11:30am–2am.

V Lounge ★★ PIZZA   Behind an unpromising exterior is the best pizza in Honolulu. It's Neopolitan-style, the thin crust blistered in a kiawe-wood fired oven. Pizzas include the Boquerones, topped with Spanish white anchovies cured in vinegar; Diavola, loaded with chili, spicy pepperoni, and peppers; and Prosciutto, with ribbons of the salty meat and arugula. Come in the early evening, and it's families and couples in the divey space; stay past midnight, and it turns clubby as a DJ cranks up the music.

1344 Kona St., Honolulu. www.vloungehawaii.com. ℂ **808/953-0007.** Pizza $16–$18. Mon–Sat 5pm–4am.

Yataimura at Shirokiya ★★ JAPANESE   Yes, it's a food court in a department store, but if you love Japanese food, you have to go. Shirokiya emulates Japan's busy street food scene by devoting its entire top floor to food. It can be overwhelming with the sights and sounds and smells—almost 2 dozen stalls and vendors are packed in here. Here's where to go: **Takoyaki Yama-chan** for *takoyaki*, little doughy pancake balls crisp on the outside and filled with chopped octopus; **Menya Ifu Do** for *tonkotsu* (pork bone) ramen; fresh-from-the-Honolulu-fish-auction sashimi by **Take's Fish Market;** and affordable chirashi bowls at **Maguro Zanmai.**

At the Ala Moana Center, 1450 Ala Moana Blvd., Honolulu. www.shirokiya.com. Plates $5–$15. Daily 10am–9pm.

DOWNTOWN/CHINATOWN

Char Hung Sut ★ LOCAL CHINESE   For locals, this 60-year-old Chinatown institution is synonymous with *manapua,* Hawaii's version of Chinese *char siu bao.* At Char Hung Sut, they're big, fluffy steamed buns stuffed with slightly sweet, shredded pork. Go early and watch them being made right in front of you. It's takeout only here—the shop is more of a factory than a restaurant. Also try the pork hash (also known as *siu mai* on the Mainland)—juicy ground pork steamed in wonton-style wrappers.

64 N. Pauahi St., Honolulu. ℂ **808/538-3335.** Under $10. Cash only. Mon and Wed–Sat 5:30am–2pm; Sun 5:30am–1pm.

Little Village Noodle House ★ CHINESE   For almost every year it's been open, Little Village has been awarded Best Chinese Restaurant by readers of local publications. It's Chinese food geared toward local tastes, but that doesn't mean it's not tasty. Added plus: a clean, charming interior decorated with Christmas lights and bamboo, a nice change from the sometimes harsh spaces of Chinatown's other restaurants. I like the Shanghai mochi stir fry, honey walnut shrimp, dried green beans, and beef chow fun.

1113 Smith St., Honolulu. www.littlevillagehawaii.com. ℂ **808/545-3008.** Most items under $17. Sun–Thurs 10:30am–10pm; Fri–Sat 10:30am–midnight.

Mauna Kea Marketplace Food Court ★ CHINESE/THAI/FILIPINO Tour Chinatown's Mauna Kea Marketplace, where you'll find everything from bok choy to bullfrogs for cooking. And when you get hungry, head to the food court, which feels as if you've been dropped into the streets of Bangkok, Manila, and Hong Kong. All of them, all at once. Grab a seat next to the Filipinos dipping their spoons into pork adobo from **Nestor Filipino Fast Food.** Get a crispy rice salad from **Malee Thai** and follow it up with an egg custard tart from **Rainbow Tea Stop.** It's the best in town, yellow and glossy with a crumbly and buttery crust.

1120 Maunakea St., Honolulu. ℂ 808/524-3409. Most items under $10. Cash only. Daily 5:30am–2pm.

tasty **TOURS**

See Honolulu—one restaurant at a time. Former Honolulu newspaper food critic and chef Matthew Gray has put together **Hawaii Food Tours** to show you a side of Hawaii that you likely would not discover on your own. He offers three different tours, all with transportation from your Waikiki hotel in an air-conditioned van and all with running commentary on Hawaii's history, culture, and architecture. My favorite is the **Hole-in-the-Wall Tour,** a lunch tour from 10am to 2pm, for $99 per person, that includes a visit to at least six different ethnic restaurants (plus a behind-the-scenes walking and tasting tour of Chinatown—yum, yum). For information and booking, go to www.hawaiifoodtours.com or call ℂ **808/926-FOOD.**

Murphy's Bar and Grill ★ IRISH   Maybe you didn't come to Honolulu to hang out in an Irish bar. But if you did, Murphy's is the place to be. At lunch, it's packed with downtown businessmen tucking into Blarney Burgers (a hamburger with Guinness cheese) or open-face turkey sandwiches. After work, this is one of Honolulu's favorite *pau hana* (after-work) spots with great wings, local beers on draft (get anything from Maui Brewing Co.), and some of the friendliest bartenders in town. You would expect nothing less from an Irish bar.

2 Merchant St., Honolulu. http://murphyshawaii.com. ℂ **808/531-0422.** Main courses $12–$23. Lunch daily 11:30am–2:30pm; dinner Sun–Wed 5:30–9pm; Thurs–Sat 5:30–10pm.

The Pig and the Lady ★★ MODERN VIETNAMESE   It's one of Chinatown's most stylish dining rooms, with exposed brick walls, long communal tables hewed from single slabs of mango wood, benches reupholstered with burlap rice bags, and jars of colorful pickles that greet you beside the hostess stand. The Pig and the Lady introduces you to a world of Vietnamese noodle soups beyond pho—such as one with oxtail, another with crab and tomato. But chef Andrew Le also applies creative twists to Southeast Asian food for unique eats like a pho French dip banh mi and a Dutch Baby (baked pancake) with kaya jam, lychee, and basil (Sat brunch only).

83 N. King St., Honolulu. http://thepigandthelady.com. ℂ **808/383-2152.** Reservations recommended. Main courses $11–$30. Tues–Thurs 10:30am–2pm and 5:30–9:30pm; Fri 10:30am–2pm and 5:30–10pm; Sat 10am–2pm and 5:30–10pm.

To Chau ★★ VIETNAMESE PHO   Is there anything on the menu other than pho? I couldn't even tell you. I just walk in, order a medium number 9, meat outside, iced coffee with milk. What arrives: strong, black coffee percolating into a mug and a cup of ice and condensed milk. When the coffee is finished brewing, dump it into the cup and stir. By that time, you'll have a plate mounded with bean sprouts, Thai basil, sawtooth coriander, jalapeños, and lemon wedges. Soon after, the bowl of pho arrives, with flank, tendon, and tripe and slices of rare steak on the side to dip into the hot broth-like fondue. You can also get your pho with all the meat in and just steak if you want; there are 14 different possible combinations. That's the only hard choice in this Chinatown Vietnamese. Getting the pho and Vietnamese coffee shouldn't be one.

1007 River St., Honolulu. ℂ **808/533-4549.** Reservations not accepted. All items under $10. Cash only. Mon–Fri 8:30am–2:30pm.

Vino Italian Tapas & Wine Bar ★ ITALIAN   Master sommelier Chuck Furuya and D. K. Kodama (chef and owner of **Sansei Seafood Restaurant & Sushi Bar** ★ on p. 121) re-create an Italian trattoria where the focus is on the wine. The wine selection—more than 30 varietals—changes almost weekly, and everything is available in tasting-pour portions so you can sample a wide variety. The menu is built to be uber-wine-friendly, with housemade pastas such as Ligurian-style trofie pasta and Dungeness crab linguine with a lobster and uni sauce.

On Restaurant Row, 500 Ala Moana Blvd., Honolulu. http://vinohawaii.com. ✆ **808/524-8466.** Reservations recommended. Shared plates $7–$25. Wed–Thurs 5:30–9:30pm; Fri–Sat 5:30–10:30pm.

KALIHI/LILIHA/SAND ISLAND

Helena's Hawaiian Food ★★ HAWAIIAN   Definitely seek out this humble little restaurant, which was awarded the James Beard Foundation's Regional Classics award in 2000. When first-generation Chinese Helen Chock started Helena's in 1946 (she added an "a" at the end to make it sound more "Hawaiian"), she served Chinese and Hawaiian food. Eventually, she pared down the menu to the most popular items—the Hawaiian food such as laulau, kalua pig, and poi. Sixty years later, her grandson runs the place, and it's still as popular as ever. What makes Helena's stand out among other Hawaiian food restaurants? The *pipikaula:* marinated, bone-in short ribs hung above the stove to dry and fried right before they land on your table.

1240 N. School St., Honolulu. www.helenashawaiianfood.com. ✆ **808/845-8044.** Full meals $9–$20. Cash only.

La Mariana Sailing Club ★ AMERICAN   There is only one authentic vintage tiki bar left in Honolulu, and it's in the industrial wasteland near the airport (which makes it awfully convenient to have your last drink here before getting on the plane). But once you enter, you'll feel as if you've stepped back into 1955, the year La Mariana opened. It's pure kitsch, with glass floats and puffer fish lamps hanging from the ceiling. Come for a mai tai or a zombie and watch the sunset over the docked sailboats. Stay for the live piano entertainment nightly, when regulars croon their favorite Hawaiian and American songs. You're here for the ambience and entertainment, not so much for the forgettable food.

50 Sand Island Rd., Honolulu. www.lamarianasailingclub.com. ✆ **808/848-2800.** Reservations recommended, especially Sat–Sun. Main courses $8–$16 lunch, $15–$29 dinner. Daily 11am–9pm. Turn makai (toward the ocean) on Sand Island Rd. from Nimitz Hwy.; immediately after the first light on Sand Island, take a right and drive toward the ocean; it's not far from the airport.

Liliha Bakery ★★ AMERICAN/LOCAL   It's a bakery, well known for its Coco Puffs (similar to cream puffs), but it's also one of Oahu's favorite old-school diners, beloved by young and old alike. Sit at the Formica counter and watch the ladies expertly man the flattop and grill, turning out light and fluffy pancakes, crispy and seriously buttery waffles, loaded country-style omelets, and satisfying hamburgers and hamburger steaks.

515 N. Kuakini St., Honolulu. www.lilihabakeryhawaii.com. ✆ **808/531-1651.** Most items under $10. Open 24 hr. from Tues at 6am to Sun at 8pm.

Mitch's Sushi ★★ SUSHI   The family that owns Mitch's Sushi also owns a seafood import business, which is why Mitch's has some of the freshest fish around. It's one of Honolulu's most expensive sushi bars, as well as its most casual, a place where slippers (local lingo for flip-flops) and T-shirts are the norm, along with a cooler of beer (Mitch's is BYOB). Here, you'll find New Zealand salmon, as luxurious as fatty tuna belly, and Mitch's famous lobster sashimi, which you inspect as it's brought to your table, alive and kicking, and then sample in the form of sashimi and lobster miso soup.

524 Ohohia St., Honolulu. http://mitchssushi.com. ✆ **808/837-7774.** Reservations recommended. Sushi $4–$30. Daily 11:30am–8:30pm.

Nico's at Pier 38 ★ FRESH FISH The new Nico's has expanded from a hole in the wall to a gleaming, open-air restaurant almost four times its original size. The food isn't quite as good as it used to be, but it's still one of the best places around to get fresh fish plates for under $20. I also love its setting along the industrial waterfront, where Hawaii's commercial fishing fleet resides—this isn't a fake fisherman's wharf but the real deal. Popular dishes here are the furikake pan-seared ahi and the catch-of-the-day special—perhaps opah sauced with tomato beurre blanc, or swordfish topped with crab bisque (the chef, Nico Chaize, is French-born). As part of the expansion, there's also a fish market next door where you can take out fresh poke and smoked swordfish to eat on the tables outside. Renting a place with a kitchen? Pick up fresh fish filets to take home and cook.

Pier 38, 1129 N. Nimitz Hwy., Honolulu. www.nicospier38.com. ✆ **808/540-1377.** Takeout orders accepted by phone. Lunch $8–$13; dinner $14–$26. Mon–Sat 6:30am–9pm; Sun 10am–9pm.

MANOA VALLEY/MOILIILI/MAKIKI
Very Expensive
Alan Wong's Restaurant ★★★ HAWAII REGIONAL Alan Wong was one of the founders of Hawaii Regional Cuisine, which championed Hawaii farmers and local flavors back in the '90s when most Hawaii restaurants were of the Continental variety and flying in frozen seafood and meat. Wong brought uniquely local flavors to the fine-dining table, in dishes such as a ginger-crusted onaga, soy-braised shortrib, and li hing mui tomato salad. To this day, Alan Wong's remains one of Honolulu's best restaurants. Its menu still retains many of the classics—for newer dishes, try the chef's tasting menu, which features the kitchen's latest, creative dishes, like a pan-seared opakapaka on kim chee risotto or Maui Cattle Co. rib steak with a beef and foie gras "burger."

1857 S. King St., 3rd floor, Honolulu. www.alanwongs.com. ✆ **808/949-2526.** Reservations highly recommended. Main courses $28–$55; 5-course sampling menu $105 ($125 with wine); chef's 7-course tasting menu $95 ($135 with wine). Daily 5–10pm.

Chef Mavro Restaurant ★★★ HAWAII REGIONAL James Beard Award–winner George Mavrothalassitis melds his French background with pristine Hawaii ingredients for one of Hawaii's best fine-dining experiences. The menu changes quarterly to reflect the seasons. A recent menu featured onaga baked in a Hawaiian salt crust; lemongrass lobster with a pea puree gnocchi au gratin, and tomato confit; and for dessert, a lilikoi and vanilla "creamsicle" crowned with an anise coconut froth. Four-, six-, and eleven-course menus are offered. Wine is only available as pairings for each course, which elevates the experience to divine.

1969 S. King St., Honolulu. www.chefmavro.com. ✆ **808/944-4714.** Reservations recommended. Prix-fixe menu $85–$175 ($140–$273 with wine pairings). Tues–Sun 6–9pm.

Izakaya Gaku ★★★ JAPANESE There is life beyond maguro and hamachi nigiri, and the best place to experience it is at Izakaya Gaku. The Izakaya restaurants embrace small plates as the best way to eat and drink with friends; while there are many in Honolulu, Izakaya Gaku is the best. Here, you can get uncommon seasonal sushi and seafood, such as wild yellowtail and grilled ray. One of the best dishes here is a hamachi tartare with hamachi scraped off the bones and topped with tobiko and raw quail egg, served with sheets of crisp nori. But you're not likely to be disappointed with any dish.

1329 S. King St., Honolulu. ℂ **808/589-1329.** Reservations highly recommended. Sashimi $12–$40; small plates $4–$13. Mon–Sat 5–11pm.

Inexpensive
Jimbo's Restaurant ★ JAPANESE   Jimbo's offers fresh noodles made by hand—or should we say foot? To give the udon noodles their characteristic chew, Jimbo cooks stomp on the noodle dough (wrapped, of course) before rolling it out. Enjoy it cold with a dipping sauce or hot in a shoyu and dashi-based broth. For sumo-sized appetites, get the nabeyaki udon, brought to the table in a heavy pot and filled with udon, vegetable and shrimp tempura, chicken, and an egg.

1936 S. King St., Honolulu. ℂ **808/947-2211.** Main courses $10–$14. Daily 11am–2:30pm and 5–9:45pm (Fri–Sat until 10:30pm).

KAIMUKI
Moderate
Town ★★ CONTEMPORARY ITALIAN   Town's motto is "Local first, organic whenever possible, with Aloha always." Chef/owner Ed Kenney lovingly showcases local ingredients: in a pork sugo on the lightest gnocchi you may ever have, or as the seasonal produce tossed with hand-cut pasta. Kenney definitely has a way with pork: If you see it on the menu—as charcuterie, porchetta, or roasted shoulder—get it. I also love the mussels in a fennel and Cinzano broth. Order it with a side of fries, and use them to soak up all the goodness.

3435 Waialae Ave. (at 9th St.), Honolulu. www.townkaimuki.com. ℂ **808/735-5900.** Reservations highly recommended for dinner. Main courses $5–$8 breakfast, $9–$16 lunch, $16–$26 dinner. Mon–Sat 7am–2:30pm and 5:30–9:30pm (Fri–Sat until 10pm).

12th Ave Grill ★★ CONTEMPORARY AMERICAN   Outside of Waikiki and the Keeaumoku region, Honolulu lacks dense, walkable neighborhoods—it's more like Los Angeles than San Francisco. But one of the few urban neighborhoods is Kaimuki, which has been up-and-coming for the last 30 years. Recently, it's been living up to its reputation, with an influx of newer, hipper restaurants. Chef/owner Kevin Hanney is betting on the wave of change; he recently moved his tiny neighborhood restaurant down the street (so he gets to keep his restaurant's name) and expanded it to almost four times its original size. It manages to keep its comfortable, neighborhood vibe, though, with banquette seating and a warm-hued interior. The menu leans toward comfort food, like baked mac 'n' cheese and locally raised meat, such as pork chops with potato pancakes and rib-eye on fresh pappardelle. Another reason why I love this place? It's the rare restaurant that serves good food *and* good cocktails. **Tip:** Sit in the bar area during opening or closing hours, when the bar serves a special menu of terrifically satisfying hamburgers and meatloaf sandwiches, and nothing costs more than $10.

1120 12th Ave., Honolulu. http://12thavegrill.com. ℂ **808/732-9469.** Reservations recommended. Small plates $7–$13; large plates $23–$36. Daily 5:30–11pm.

TO THE EAST: KAHALA

Arancino at The Kahala ★★ MODERN ITALIAN   This is Arancino's third location (the other two are in Waikiki), which opened in 2013. Befitting its new digs, this Arancino isn't a casual trattoria; it's meant to be a fine-dining destination, with a prix-fixe dinner menu starting at $85 and a dress code (pants and shoes required for the men). Standouts on the menu include a *bagna cauda,* with the vegetables planted in a pot of cremini mushroom "dirt"; grilled calamari, shrimp, and seafood over housemade squid-ink chitarra; and Okinawan sweet-potato gnocchi with a sage–brown butter sauce, prosciutto, and walnuts. For a town surprisingly short on alfresco dining, Arancino at The Kahala is a breath of fresh air (even if it is facing the Kahala resort's valet).

At the Kahala Hotel Resort, 5000 Kahala Ave., Honolulu. www.kahalaresort.com. ✆ **808/380-4000.** Reservations recommended. Collared shirts and long pants preferred for men. 3-course prix-fixe $56; 4-course $79. Daily 11:30am–2:30pm and 5–10:30pm.

Olive Tree Cafe ★★ GREEK/EASTERN MEDITERRANEAN   With Greek music over the speakers, lively chatter, and clinking glasses, you'd almost believe you were in Santorini rather than a Kahala strip-mall parking lot. But who cares when the food is this good and affordable? Get the souvlaki, either with lamb or fresh local fish. You might want to start with the *taramasalata,* a fish roe spread, and definitely finish with a slice of baklava. Nothing fancy here, but it's always delicious. *Tip:* Olive Tree is BYOB. If you forget to bring a bottle, you can pick up one next door at Oliver.

4614 Kilauea Ave., next to Kahala Mall, Honolulu. ✆ **808/737-0303.** Reservations not accepted. Main courses $10–$15. Cash only. Daily 5–10pm.

East Oahu

Roy's Restaurant ★ HAWAII REGIONAL   This is the original Roy's, the one that launched more than 30 Roy's restaurants around the world (6 of them in Hawaii). One of Hawaii Regional Cuisine's most famous founders, Roy Yamaguchi started fusing local flavors and ingredients with European techniques 20 years ago. The original menu items are still here, such as blackened island ahi with spicy soy mustard and Roy's famous melting-hot chocolate soufflé. Sit on the lanai to watch the sunset over Maunalua Bay.

6600 Kalanianaole Hwy., Hawaii Kai. www.roysrestaurant.com. ✆ **808/396-7697.** Reservations recommended. Main courses $20–$40; 3-course prix-fixe $42. Mon–Thurs 5:30–9pm; Fri 5:30–9:30pm; Sat 5–9:30pm; Sun 5–9pm.

The Windward Coast

Note: The following restaurants are located on the "Eastern Oahu & the Windward Coast" map (p. 75).

Heeia Kea Pier General Store & Deli ★ LOCAL   You can't beat the setting: right on the pier overlooking Kaneohe Bay. This old-school spot serves plate lunches with luau stew and guava chicken, poke bowls, and a catch-of-the-day plate based on what local fishermen bring in. There aren't many places left on Oahu where you can eat fresh fish with this view and at these prices.

46-499 Kamehameha Hwy., at Heeia Pier, Kaneohe. ✆ **808/235-2192.** Most items under $10. Tues–Sun 7:30am–3pm.

Prima ★ CONTEMPORARY ITALIAN   This newcomer to Kailua (by the same owners of V Lounge in town) serves the same style of wood-fired pizzas in a more inviting, industrial-chic atmosphere. Unique to this location are the spicy meatball pizza and "Five-P," with pickled piquillo peppers, pepperoncini, and pepperoni. The appetizers and small plates are inventive, such as butter-roasted maitake mushroom with a smooth and creamy cauliflower puree, grilled local octopus with watermelon and fennel, and the not-very-Italian-at-all tandoori pear accompanied by grapefruit and yogurt. It's BYOB, so pick up a bottle of wine at the R. Fields/Foodland next door.

108 Hekili St., #107, Kailua. www.primahawaii.com. © **808/888-8933.** Reservations recommended. Pizza $16–$19, small plates $9–$19. Lunch Fri–Sun 11am–3pm; dinner daily 5–9pm (Fri and Sun until 10pm).

The North Shore

Note: The following can be located on the "Oahu's North Shore" map (p. 84).

INEXPENSIVE

Beet Box Café ★ VEGETARIAN   For me, a perfect day on the North Shore involves waves and a stop at Beet Box. You'll find this groovy little cafe tucked into the back of the Celestial Natural Foods store. Here, veggies are transformed into tasty, satisfying sandwiches with portobello and feta or avocado and local greens. The breakfast burritos and smoothies are popular, too. Beet Box also has a lunch-wagon parked near Pipeline. The menu is much more limited there, but it's a good option if you're hungry and want to keep hanging at the beach.

Inside Celestial Natural Foods store, 66-443 Kamehameha Hwy., Haleiwa. www.thebeetboxcafe. com. © **808/637-3000.** Items $7–$11. Mon–Sat 9am–5pm; Sun 9am–4pm.

The Shrimp Trucks

Shrimp farming took hold in Kahuku in the '90s, and, before long, the first shrimp truck set up, serving fresh shrimp from a lunchwagon window. Now, you can smell the garlic cooking before you see all the trucks and shrimp shacks—at least five, by last count. **Giovanni's Original White Shrimp Truck,** 56-505 Kamehameha Hwy. (© **808/293-1839**), is the most popular—so popular that a make-shift food court with picnic tables, shade, and a handful of other businesses have sprung up around the beat-up old white truck scrawled with tourists' signatures. It's also so popular now that the shrimp are imported and previously frozen. Still, Giovanni's knows how to cook them perfectly. "Scampi" style is my favorite—shell-on shrimp coated in lots of butter and garlic. Twelve bucks gets you a dozen plus two scoops of rice. Head north from Giovanni's about a mile, and you'll hit **Romy's,** 56-781 Kamehameha Hwy. (© **808/232-2202**), a shrimp shack instead of a truck. Here the shrimp served actually comes from the farm behind it. Romy's is my favorite for the sauce—tons of sautéed and fried garlic over a half-pound of head-on shrimp, plus a container of spicy soy sauce for dipping. The shrimp, however, are inconsistent—sometimes firm and sweet, sometimes mealy.

LUAU!

The sun is setting, the Tiki torches are lit, the pig is taken from the *imu* (an oven in the earth), the drums begin pounding—it's luau time! "Before 'luaus' there were 'aha 'aina'—a feast of food, *mele* (song), and hula," says **Royal Hawaiian** general manager Kelly Hoen about its oceanfront luau. "In ancient times the Hawaiian people came together to celebrate momentous occasions, and these gatherings were called **aha 'aina,**" says Hoen. "We have created a modern, yet timeless *aha 'aina* to honor the land's majestic history through food, song, stories, hula, and culture." The Royal Hawaiian's luau takes place every Monday from 5:30 to 9pm, and costs $188 for adults, $106 for children 5 to 12. It's on the beachfront of the hotel grounds at 2259 Kalakaua Ave. (www.royal-hawaiian.com; ✆ 888/808-4668).

Te Moana Nui is the name of the luau at the **Pacific Beach Hotel,** 2490 Kalakaua Ave., also in Waikiki (www.temoananui.com; ✆ **808/441-4880**), which features an epic journey across the Pacific through song and dance and a lavish Polynesian dinner. It takes place on Monday, Wednesday, and Thursday at 5:30pm; the price for the show and luau is $68 to $115 for adults, $41 to $82 for children 5 to 12.

Outside of Waikiki, there are two large luau companies about an hour's drive to the Leeward Coast: **Germaine's,** 91–119 Olai St., Kapolei (www.germaines luau.com; ✆ **800/367-5655** or 808/949-6626), and **Paradise Cove Luau,** 92–1089 Alii Nui Dr., Kapolei (www.paradisecove hawaii.com; ✆ **808/842-5911**). Waikiki bus pickup and return are included in the package prices: Germaine's luau is nightly at 6pm and costs $80 for adults, $70 for children 14 to 20, $60 for children 6 to 13, and free for children 5 and under. Paradise Cove's luau is nightly at 6pm, and costs $88 to $153 for adults, $78 to $137 for teens 13 to 18, $68 to $124 for children 4 to 12, and free for children 3 and under.

Kahuku Farms SANDWICHES & SNACKS   Not a fan of shrimp? Then stop by Kahuku Farms' Farm Café, where you can get a simple grilled veggie panini, made with veggies all grown right here on the farm, and a smoothie with papaya and banana, also grown here. If I'm driving up this way, I always try to stop for the grilled banana bread topped with caramel and *haupia* (coconut) sauce and a scoop of ice cream. Yup, so decadent and so good.

56-800 Kamehameha Hwy., Kahuku. www.kahukufarms.com. ✆ **808/293-8159.** Items $8–$10. Wed–Mon 11am–4pm.

Opal Thai ★ THAI   Once a popular food truck, now a no-frills, sit-down restaurant in Haleiwa Town Center, Opal Thai serves the best Thai food on the island. My favorites are the crab stir-fried noodles, duck curry, and fried tofu with garlic sauce and fried basil leaves. But it may be hard for you to order; owner Opel Sirichandhra likes you to leave the dishes up to him, asking only for your spice preference and favorite Thai dishes as a guide.

66-197 Kamehameha Hwy., Haleiwa. © **808/381-8091.** Dishes $11–$20. Tues–Sat 11am–3pm and 5–10pm.

Leeward Oahu: The Waianae Coast

Kahumana Café ★ FARM   The fare here is simple but fresh and tasty; the setting is right on an organic farm. Enjoy a veggie-tofu stir-fry or veggie wrap while overlooking the herbs and vegetables grown right there. There aren't a lot of eating options on the west side, which makes Kahumana Café even more welcome.

86-660 Lualualei Homestead Rd., Waianae. http://kahumanafarms.org. © **808/696-2655.** Main courses $10–$15. Tues–Sat 11:30am–2:30pm and 6–7:30pm. Head up Farrington Hwy. and turn right on Mailiilii Rd. Go straight for 2 miles, past Puhawai Rd. Continue until you reach the Kahumana gate. The cafe is the blue building at the end of the driveway.

Monkeypod Kitchen ★ AMERICAN   This is the best dining option at the new Ko Olina Station, a strip mall of casual (and overpriced) eateries servicing Ko Olina Resort. Monkeypod Kitchen is one of the latest ventures from Peter Merriman, who pioneered farm-to-table fine dining on the Big Island in the '80s. This is his larger and more casual restaurant (with another location on Maui). The vibe in this two-story space is welcoming and friendly, with live music on the lanai and a long bar with 36 (!) beers on tap. Expect fresh salads and entrees like fish and chips and burgers. I always go for the saimin, which is nothing like the traditional, local-style version you'll find elsewhere; here, it comes with kalua pork and fresh vegetables. To drink: the bracingly zingy housemade ginger beer. *Tip:* Want a more intimate bar experience? Head upstairs, where the bartenders spend a little more time making your cocktails, which include fresh takes on the mai tai (topped with a honey lilikoi foam) and the Makawao Ave, made with rye and that terrific ginger beer.

At Ko Olina Station, 92-1048 Olani St., Suite 4-107, Kapolei. www.monkeypodkitchen.com. © **808/380-4086.** Reservations recommended. Main courses $12–$35. Daily 11am–11pm.

OAHU SHOPPING

The trend in Honolulu shopping of late has been toward luxury brands, catering to Japanese (and increasingly, Chinese) tourists. Witness the demise, at the end of 2013, of the International Marketplace. Truthfully, this open-air Waikiki marketplace had become a maze of kitschy junk, but it had a 56-year run, long enough for many people to feel sentimental about it. In its place will go the new, high-end **International Marketplace mall** anchored by Saks Fifth Avenue, projected to open in 2015.

You can also find plenty of luxury goods at the new **Ala Moana Center** wing. But just as the luxury market is growing, so is Honolulu's boutique culture and the vitality of the local crafts scene, as artisans endeavor to capture what makes Hawaii so unique.

The section that follows is not about finding cheap souvenirs or tony items from designer fashion chains; you can find these on your own. Rather, I offer a guide to finding those special treasures that lie somewhere in between.

Open-air market in Honolulu.

Shopping in & Around Honolulu & Waikiki

CLOTHING

One of Hawaii's lasting afflictions is the penchant tourists have for wearing loud, matching aloha shirts. I applaud such visitors' good intentions (to act local), but no local resident would be caught dead in such a get-up. Aloha shirts are wonderful, but the real thing is what island folks wear to work and to special parties where the invitation reads "Aloha Attire."

Vintage 1930s to 1950s Hawaiian wear is still beautiful, found in collectibles shops, such as the packed-to-the-rafters **Bailey's Antiques and Aloha Shirts,** 517 Kapahulu Ave. (© 808/734-7628). Of the contemporary aloha-wear designers, one of the best Oahu-based ones is **Tori Richard,** who creates tasteful tropical prints in the form of linen and silk shirts for the men and flowy dresses for women. **Reyn Spooner** is another source of attractive aloha shirts in traditional and contemporary styles; the new Modern Collection appeals to younger tastes, combining more fitted sleeves and a 1960s preppy look with some of Reyn Spooner's classic prints.

The hippest guys and gals go to **Roberta Oaks,** 19 N. Pauahi St. (www. robertaoaks.com; © 808/428-1214), in Chinatown, where a slew of trendy boutiques have opened in recent years. Roberta Oaks ditches the too-big aloha shirt for a more stylish, fitted look, but keeps the vintage designs. Plus, she even has super-cute, tailored aloha shirts for the ladies. Also in Chinatown, **Fighting Eel,** 1133 Bethel St. (www.fightingeel.com; © 808/738-9300), creates bright, easy-to-wear dresses and shirts with island prints that are in every local fashionista's closet. Perfect for Honolulu weather, but chic enough to wear back home.

No modern woman wears a muumuu anymore, unless it's a repurposed one from **Muumuu Heaven,** 767 Kailua Rd. (www.muumuuheaven.com;

SHOPPING IN chinatown

This neighborhood isn't like other Chinatowns you know. But alongside the historical Chinatown, there's a new Chinatown, one with chic boutiques, hip clubs and bars, and Moroccan and French/Latin restaurants, interspersed among the old Chinese and Vietnamese noodle shops. In addition to locally designed clothes by **Roberta Oaks** and **Fighting Eel** (see "Clothing," above, for both) and vintage Hawaiiana at **Tin Can Mailman** (see "Hawaiiana & Gift Items," below), you'll find **Owens & Co.,** 1152 Nuuanu Ave. (✆ **808/531-4300**), with a well-edited selection of home and fashion items, locally designed cards, and gifts. A sampling: Bradley and Lily's locally letterpressed "aloha" cards, By Chari's shark tooth jewelry, and Tiare Style's beach sheets for your next picnic. Also in the area is **The Human Imagination,** 1154 Nuuanu Ave. (✆ **808/538-8898**), a skatewear shop and pop-up art gallery best known for its friendly hi logo T-shirt. Need sweet gifts to bring home? Head to **Madre Chocolate,** 8 N. Pauahi St. (✆ **808/377-6440**), which sells bars produced on Oahu using cacao grown right here on this island. Talk about bean to bar!

✆ **808/263-3366**). This funky shop breathes new life into old muumuu and vintage fabrics, discovered at estate and garage sales around the islands. Pieces of the found fabrics are incorporated into dresses, from short and flirty to floor-length and dramatic. Each dress is literally one of a kind.

EDIBLES

Nisshodo Candy Store Mochi (Japanese rice cake) is so essential to locals' lives that even the drugstores sell it. But for the freshest and widest variety, go straight to the source: Nisshodo, an almost century-old business. Choose among pink-and-white *chichi dango* (or milk mochi), mochi filled with smooth azuki bean, *monaka* (delicate rice wafers sandwiching sweetened lima-bean paste), and much more. 1095 Dillingham Blvd. ✆ 808/847-1244.

Padovani's Chocolates Brothers Philippe and Pierre Padovani are two of Hawaii's best chefs, involved with the Hawaii Regional Cuisine movement. In recent years, they've been devoting their attention to chocolate truffles. Their edible gems come in delightful flavors such as a calamansi (a small Filipino lime) and pirie mango ganache, flavored with fragrant, local mangoes picked at the height of the season. Some of my other favorite

Flower leis.

farmers MARKETS

Farmers markets have proliferated on Oahu—there's now one for every neighborhood for every day of the week. Unfortunately, the number of farmers has not kept up. In fact, some of the markets have vendors that sell repackaged Mainland produce. The best farmers markets are those run by the **Hawaii Farm Bureau Federation** (**HFBF;** www.hfbf.org/markets) and **FarmLovers** (www.haleiwafarmersmarket.com), which mandate locally grown meats, fruits, and veggies. Check their websites for the most up-to-date information. Here are my favorites:

o **Kapiolani Community College:** The original and still the biggest and best. Unfortunately, you're going to have deal with crowds—busloads of tourists get dropped off here. But you'll find items unavailable at any other market— endless varieties of bananas and mangoes, plus tropical fruit you've never seen before, persimmons, baby corn, and local duck eggs. Pick up cut, chilled pineapple or jackfruit to snack on, yogurt from Oahu's only remaining dairy, perhaps some grilled abalone from Kona, and corn from Kahuku. And with a healthy dose of prepared-food vendors serving everything from fresh tomato pizzas to raw and vegan snacks, you definitely won't go hungry (4355 Diamond Head Rd.; ✆ **808/848-2074;** Sat 7:30–11am; TheBus: 23 or 24).

o **Honolulu Farmers Market:** This HFBF market is less crowded and has more locals stopping by to pick up groceries after work. It has some of the same vendors as the Kapiolani Community College market (777 Ward Ave.; ✆ **808/848-2074;** Wed 4–7pm; TheBus: 13).

o **Haleiwa Farmers Market:** This market, operated by FarmLovers, has actually moved to Waimea Valley. Here, you might find avocadoes as big as your head, breadfruit, and lots of other tropical fruit. And don't miss the macnut sticky buns (59-864 Kamehameha Hwy.; ✆ **808/388-9696;** Thurs 3–7pm; TheBus: 55)!

truffles incorporate ginger, Manoa honey, and lilikoi (Hawaiian passionfruit). You might pick up some of these to bring home, but I'm guessing they'll never make it. 650 Iwilei Rd., #280. ✆ 808/536-4567.

FLOWERS & LEIS

At most lei shops, simple leis sell for $12 and up, deluxe leis for $50 and up. For a special-occasion designer bouquet or lei, you can't do better than Michael Miyashiro of **Rainforest at Kilohana Square** (Kilohana Sq., on Kapahulu Ave.; www.rainforesthawaii.com; ✆ **808/738-0999**). He's an ecologically aware, highly gifted lei maker—his leis are pricey but worth it. He custom-designs the lei for the person and occasion. Order by phone or stop by Michael's new larger shop, an oasis of green and beauty. Upon request, Miyashiro's leis will come in ti-leaf bundles called *pu'olo,* custom floral arrangements in woven green coconut baskets. You can even request the card sentiments in Hawaiian, with English translations.

health-food STORES

Honolulu's largest health-food store is **Whole Foods,** 4211 Waialae Ave., in the Kahala Mall (📞 **808/738-0820**), and 641 Kailua Rd., Kailua. The Kailua location has a comfy outdoor seating area, where you can enjoy *pau hana* specials such as a pint and slice of pizza for $5. I also like to hit the self-serve poke bar (dangerous!) and sample one of the local beers on tap. Both Whole Foods locations do a great job of sourcing local, both in produce and in specialty items such as honey, jams, hot sauces, coffee, and chocolate. It's also got one of the best selections of locally made soaps, making this a great one-stop shop to pick up gifts for home. In the university district, **Down to Earth,** 2525 S. King St., Moiliili (📞 **808/947-7678**), sells organic vegetables and vegetarian bulk foods, with good prices, a strong selection of supplements and herbs, and a vegetarian juice-and-sandwich bar. Nearby is **Kokua Market,** 2643 S. King St. (📞 **808/941-1922**), a health-food cooperative. It is small but mighty, beating out all the other supermarkets in its local food sourcing. You'll find locally brewed kombucha on tap; eggs from the North Shore; beef, goat, and lamb from Big Island (all frozen, though); and a nice selection of locally grown, seasonal fruits.

In Chinatown, lei vendors line Beretania and Maunakea streets, and the fragrances of their wares mix with the earthy scents of incense and ethnic foods. My top picks are **Lita's Leis,** 59 N. Beretania St. (📞 **808/521-9065**), which has fresh *puakenikeni,* gardenias that last, and a supply of fresh and reasonable leis; **Lin's Lei Shop,** 1017-A Maunakea St. (📞 **808/537-4112**), with creatively fashioned, unusual leis; and **Cindy's Lei Shoppe,** 1034 Maunakea St. (📞 **808/536-6538**), with terrific sources for unusual leis such as feather dendrobiums, firecracker combinations, and everyday favorites like ginger, tuberose, orchid, and *pikake.* "Curb service" is available with phone orders. Just give them your car's color and model, and you can pick up your lei curbside—a great convenience on this busy street.

HAWAIIANA & GIFT ITEMS

Visit the **Museum Shop** at the Honolulu Museum of Art, 900 S. Beretania St. (📞 **808/532-8703**), for crafts, jewelry, art books, and prints, including some of Georgia O'Keefe's illustrations from her time in Hawaii. You'll find gifts to bring home, such as lauhala clutches, macadamia nut oil soaps, and color-saturated screenprints. In particular, I'm a fan of the local artists' limited-edition T-shirts and collection of beautiful ceramics.

Native Books/Na Mea Hawaii   Recently joined by the Hula Supply Center, the space is now a one-stop shop and resource for all things local and Hawaiian. You'll find hula stones and *ipu* (gourds); Niihau shell lei; prints, crafts, and jewelry from local artists; local jams and coffee; and shelves of Hawaiian history and culture books. Regular classes in lauhala weaving, Hawaiian featherwork, ukulele, the Hawaiian language, and more are also held here. Call for the schedule. At the Ward Warehouse, 1050 Ala Moana Blvd. 📞 **808/596-8885.**

Nohea Gallery   During its 25 years in business, Nohea Gallery has carried the work of more than 2,100 artists, almost all local. Here you'll find original *gyotaku,* or prints using real fish such as ono and opelu, by Naoki Hayashi and woodwork, including beautiful bowls made of mango wood and koa. I love that you can buy everything from trinkets such as koa wood magnets to ki*ele's beachy, delicate jewelry using sea glass and shells to a Russell Lowrey original (painting) of Pounder's Beach for $7,500. At the Ward Warehouse, 1050 Ala Moana Blvd. www.noheagallery.com. ✆ **808/596-0074.**

Tin Can Mailman   What, not looking for a 1950s oil hula lamp? Check out this shop anyway. It's tightly packed with vintage Hawaiiana to emulate old-school general stores. The emphasis is on ephemera, such as pinups, postcards, old sheet music and advertisements, and the elusive Betty Boop hula girl bobble-head. 1026 Nuuanu Ave. ✆ **808/524-3009.**

SHOPPING CENTERS

Ala Moana Center   Hawaii's largest mall, with luxury brands such as **Tiffany, Chanel, St. John,** and **Diane von Furstenburg,** is getting even bigger and even more luxe, with a new 367,000-square-foot wing anchored by Bloomingdale's opening in 2015. You'll find mainstream chains here, too, such as **J. Crew, Gap,** and **Banana Republic.** If you're here for more local items, head to **Tori Richard** ot **Reyn Spooner** (see "Clothing," above, for both); for surf-and-skate wear, check out **Hawaiian Island Creations** or **T&C Surf Designs.** Local boutique **Cinnamon Girl** is a perennial favorite for ultra-feminine dresses and mother-and-daughter matching outfits. For presents to bring home, stop in **Blue Hawaii Lifestyle,** which offers locally made food gifts such as chocolate and honey, as well as Hawaii-made soaps and beauty products. Pick up beautifully packaged, chocolate-dipped macnut shortbread at **Big Island Candies** and only-in-Hawaii treats such as *manju* (resembling a filled cookie) and ume-shiso chocolates. Hungry? Head to the food court at **Shirokiya ★★** (p. 128) or treat yourself to a slice of cake and a plantation iced-tea jelly at the Japanese/French patisserie **Palme D'Or.** The center is open Monday to Saturday 9:30am to 9pm, and Sunday 10am to 7pm. 1450 Ala Moana Blvd. www.alamoanacenter.com. ✆ **808/955-9517.** Bus: 8, 19, or 20. Various shuttle services also stop here. For Waikiki Trolley information, see "Getting Around" (p. 54). Farmers Market Sat 9am–1pm, Level 2 across from Sears.

Ward Centers   Ward Centers has a number of recommended restaurants and shops. **Honolulu Chocolate Co.** offers dark-chocolate macadamia-nut clusters, lacquered apricots dipped in chocolate, and lots more chocolate treats. Find unique gifts at **Red Pineapple,** such as Sumadra clutches printed with silhouettes of the Mokulua Islands off Kailua, and Saffron James' scents, which capture the exoticism of Hawaii's flowers. Don't miss the Everything is Jake! retro-styled travel posters of Oahu's Haleiwa town and other iconic Hawaii landscapes. It's open Monday through Saturday from 10am to 9pm, Sunday from 10am to 6pm. 1200 Ala Moana Blvd. www.wardcenters.com. ✆ **808/591-8411.**

Ward Warehouse   Ewa of Ward Centers is Ward Warehouse, which houses **Native Books/Na Mea Hawaii** and the **Nohea Gallery** (see "Hawaiiana & Gift Items," above, for both), terrific sources for good, locally made arts and crafts. **Kaypee Soh,** a local designer, opened his eponymous store here recently, showcasing colorful, tropical designs on housewares, from pillows to rugs, bowls to plates. Sure, you can pick up 5-buck flip-flops from Long's, but you can also get slippers designed and handmade in Hawaii at **Island Slipper.** It's open Monday through Saturday from 10am to 9pm, Sunday from 10am to 6pm. 1050 Ala Moana Blvd. www.wardcenters.com. ✆ **808/591-8411.**

OAHU NIGHTLIFE

Nightlife in Hawaii begins at sunset, when all eyes turn westward to see how the day will end. Sunset viewers always seem to bond in the mutual enjoyment of a natural spectacle. People in Hawaii are fortunate to have an environment that encourages this cultural ritual.

Enjoy hula dancing and a torch-lighting ceremony on Tuesday, Thursday, Saturday, and Sunday from 6:30 to 7:30pm (6–7pm Nov–Jan), as the sun casts its golden glow on the beach, at the **Kuhio Beach Hula Mound,** close to Duke Kahanamoku's statue (Ulunui and Kalakaua sts.). This is a thoroughly delightful free offering of hula and music by some of the Hawaii's finest performers. Start off early with a picnic basket and walk along the oceanside path fronting Queen's Beach, near the Waikiki Aquarium. (You can park along Kapiolani Park or near the zoo.) There are few more pleasing spots in Waikiki than the benches at water's edge at this Diamond Head end of Kalakaua Avenue. It's a short walk to where the seawall and daring boogie boarders attract hordes of spectators and on to the Wizard Stones. To check the schedule, go to www.waikikiimprovement.com/waikiki-calendar-of-events/kuhio-beach-hula-show and click on the calendar.

The Bar Scene

ON THE BEACH Waikiki's beachfront bars offer many possibilities, from the **Mai Tai Bar** (© 808/923-7311) at the Royal Hawaiian (p. 110), a few feet from the sand, to the unfailingly enchanting **House Without a Key** (© 808/923-2311) at the Halekulani (p. 109), where the breathtaking **Kanoelehua Miller** dances hula to the riffs of Hawaiian steel-pedal guitar under a century-old kiawe tree with the sunset and ocean glowing behind her—a romantic, evocative, nostalgic scene. (It doesn't hurt, either, that the Halekulani happens to make the best mai tais in the world.) The Halekulani has the after-dinner hours covered, too, with light jazz by local artists in the Lewers Lounge from 9pm to 2am nightly (see "Live Blues, R&B, Jazz & Pop," below).

Another great bar for watching the sun sink into the Pacific is **Duke's Waikiki** (www.dukeswaikiki.com; © 808/922-2268), in the Outrigger Waikiki on the Beach resort. The outside Barefoot Bar is perfect for sipping a tropical drink, watching the waves and sunset, and listening to music. It can get crowded, so get here early. Hawaii sunset music is usually from 4 to 6pm daily, and there's live entertainment nightly from 9:30pm to midnight.

Who could resist drinking classic tropical cocktails in the place they were invented? Head to the Hilton Hawaiian Village, where legendary bartender Harry Yee first created now-iconic drinks such as the Blue Hawaii and Tropical Itch (with a backscratcher!) in the 1950s. **Tropics Bar and Grill** (© 808/949-4321) has a "Tribute to Harry Yee" cocktail menu and live music nightly. For a more relaxed and less-crowded atmosphere, go to **Paradise Lounge,** where you can get a Scorpion Bowl to share and other fabulous tiki drinks (four different kinds of mai tais!). Paradise Lounge hosts live music Friday and Saturday.

DOWNTOWN/CHINATOWN **First Fridays,** which originally started as an art gallery walk on the first Friday of the month, has now turned into a club and bar crawl that can sometimes turn Chinatown into a frat party on the streets. Go on a non–First Friday weekend for a mellower scene. The activity is concentrated on Hotel Street, on the block between Smith and Nuuanu. That's where you'll find

get down with **ARTafterDARK**

On the last Friday of every month (except Nov–Dec), the place to be after the sun goes down is **ARTafterDARK,** a *pau hana* (after-work) mixer in the **Honolulu Academy of Arts,** 900 S. Beretania St. (www.artafterdark.org; © **808/532-8700**), that brings residents and visitors together around a theme combining art with food, music, and dancing. In addition to the exhibits in the gallery, ARTafterDARK features visual and live performances. Previous themes have ranged from "Plant Rice"—with rice and sake tastings, rice dishes, Asian beers, live Asian fusion music, and a tour of the "Art of Rice" exhibit—to "'80s Night," "Turkish Delights," "Cool Nights, Hot Jazz and Blues," and "Havana Heat." The entrance fee is $10. The party gets going around 6 and lasts till 9pm. The crowd ranges from 20s to 50s, and the dress is everything from jeans and T-shirts to designer cocktail-party attire.

Smith's Union Bar, 19 N. Hotel St., 538-9145 (© **808/538-9145**), Honolulu's oldest bar (the very definition of a dive), and **Manifest,** 32 N. Hotel St., one of the best craft cocktail bars in town, with a great selection of whiskey and gin. Bartender Justin Park is happy to whip up complex whiskey drinks or simple, classic cocktails. After 10pm, DJs and live music make the laidback bar more clubby. Across the street is **Bar 35,** 35 N. Hotel St. (© **808/537-3535**), whose claim to fame is its 110 beers available, plus wine, cocktails, and even pizza. You must be 21 to enter (strictly enforced).

Hanks Cafe, around the corner on Nuuanu Avenue between Hotel and King streets (www.hankscafehawaii.com; © **808/526-1410**), is a tiny, kitschy, friendly pub with live music nightly, open-mic nights, and special events that attract great talent and a supportive crowd. On some nights, the music spills out into the streets and it's so packed you have to press your nose against the window to see what you're missing. Upstairs at the **Dragon Upstairs,** there's more live music Tuesday through Sunday nights (http://thedragonupstairs.com; © **808/526-1411**). At the makai end of Nuuanu, toward the pier, **Murphy's Bar and Grill ★** (p. 129) is a popular downtown ale house and media haunt that has kept Irish eyes smiling for years.

The Club Scene

The nightclub scene in Waikiki and Honolulu is just as hot as the sun-kissed beaches during the day. It's more laidback than in big cities like New York, dress is casual (though no slippers, tank tops, or athletic wear), and there's no point even showing up until midnight.

The 20-something crowd, visitors, and military personnel head to **Moose's McGillycuddy's,** 310 Lewers St., in Waikiki (www.moosewaikiki.com; © **808/923-0751**). Downstairs is a cafe serving breakfast, lunch, and dinner; upstairs is a happening entertainment and dance club. Cocktails and beer are $3 from 4 to 7pm, $7 cover for the club.

The hot dance club of the moment is **Addiction** (© **808/943-5800**), inside The Modern Honolulu hotel (p. 106). It's a sleek club, the kind with bottle service, a VIP section, and visiting DJs flown in from Los Angeles and Las Vegas.

Slack key guitarists.

Rumours Nightclub, in the lobby of the Ala Moana Hotel, 410 Atkinson Dr. (✆ **808/955-4811**), is the disco of choice for those who remember Paul McCartney as someone other than Stella's father. Friday from 5 to 9pm is retro music (oldies); 9pm to 3am is Top 40. On Saturday (9pm–3am) it's all retro. A spacious dance floor, a good sound system, and Top 40 music draw a mix of generations.

The main live-music venue in town is **The Republik,** 1349 Kapiolani Blvd., #30 (http://jointherepublik.com; ✆ **808/941-7469**), which brings in bands such as Iron and Wine and Jurassic 5.

Nightlife in **Chinatown** is currently in flux, with venues closing and new ones opening. (Chinatown trailblazer Indigo recently closed after 19 years in business, as did the popular bar/art gallery/club 39Hotel. At press time, promising new restaurant Fresh Café was opening in the Indigo space.) Pick up the Friday "Star Advertiser" for the entertainment listings in its TGIF section, or just stroll Chinatown streets to find out where the party's happening. At the moment, for DJ dance parties, head to the sleek newcomer **eleven44,** 1144 Bethel St. (✆ **808/528-1144**), and the recently reopened, brick-and-industrial **Next Door,** 43 N. Hotel St. (✆ **808/852-2243**), which also hosts live indie rock bands.

Hawaiian Music

Oahu has several key spots for Hawaiian music. The **Brothers Cazimero** remain one of Hawaii's most gifted duos (Robert on bass, Roland on 12-string guitar), appearing at **Chef Chai** (www.chefchai.com; ✆ **808/585-0011**) for a monthly full moon dinner show. If you're here in early December, the Brothers Caz do a Christmas show at the **Hawaii Theatre** (www.hawaiitheatre.com) that is not to be missed. Locals dress up in their leis and best aloha shirts, and you can feel the holidays in the air.

House Without a Key (see "The Bar Scene," above) is one of my favorite places to listen to Hawaiian music, both for the quality and the ambience. The

Hilton Hawaiian Village (☏ 808/949-4321) has live music nightly at the Tapa Bar and at the Tropics Bar and Grill. Plus, every Friday night is Rockin' Hawaiian Rainbow revue (a tribute to Duke Kahanamoku) at 7pm with fireworks starting at 7:45 ($20). Its Waikiki Starlight Luau features Hawaiian entertainment with dinner 5 nights a week (Sun–Thurs) for $99 to $125.

Kana ka pila means to make music, so it makes sense then that the **Kana Ka Pila Grille** (☏ 808/924-4994) at the Outrigger Reef on the Beach has one of the city's best Hawaiian-music lineups, including slack key guitarists Cyril Pahinui (son of famed guitarist Gabby Pahinui).

Live Blues, R&B, Jazz & Pop

The blues are alive and well in Hawaii, with quality acts (both local and from the Mainland) drawing enthusiastic crowds. The best-loved Oahu venue, Anna Bannana's, is now **Anna O'Brian's,** 2440 S. Beretania St., between University Avenue and Isenberg Street (☏ 808/946-5190), still rocking after 30 years in the business, with reggae, blues, and rock—plus video games and darts. New owners seem to have done some upgrades but have kept the important stuff the same; look for blues on Sunday.

Tops in taste and ambience is the perennially alluring **Lewers Lounge,** in the Halekulani, 2199 Kalia Rd. (www.halekulani.com; ☏ 808/923-2311). Recent renovations (including comfy intimate seating around the pillars) make this a great spot for contemporary jazz nightly from 8:30pm to midnight.

Outside Waikiki, the **Veranda,** at the Kahala Hotel & Resort, 5000 Kahala Ave. (www.kahalaresort.com; ☏ 808/739-8888), is a popular spot for the over-40 crowd, with nightly jazz music and a dance floor.

Check www.honolulujazzscene.com for daily listings.

Showroom Acts & Revues

Showroom acts that have maintained a following include "**The Magic of Polynesia**" (www.magicofpolynesia.com; ☏ 808/971-4321), a show with illusionist **John Hirokana** nightly at 6:30pm (dinner show $99–$149 adults, $67–$78 children 4–11; show only $55 adults, $35 children 4–11). This was also the home of Hawaiian entertainer Don Ho, who passed away in 2007.

"**Te Moana Nui,**" formerly "Creation—A Polynesian Journey at the Sheraton Princess Kaiulani," is now at the Pacific Beach Hotel. Produced by Tihati, the state's largest entertainment company, the show is a theatrical journey of fire dancing, special effects, illusions, hula, and dances from Hawaii and the South Pacific. Shows are Monday, Wednesday, and Thursday (dinner show starts at $115 adults, $82 children 5–12; cocktail show $68 adults).

The Performing Arts

"Aloha shirt to Armani" is how I describe the night scene in Honolulu—mostly casual, but with ample opportunity to part with your flip-flops and dress up.

Audiences have grooved to the beat of off-Broadway percussion hit "Stomp" and have enjoyed the talent of "Tap Dogs," Momix, the Jim Nabors Christmas show, the Hawaii International Jazz Festival, the American Repertory Dance Company, barbershop quartets, and John Ka'imikaua's *halau*—all at the **Hawaii Theatre,** 1130 Bethel St., downtown (www.hawaiitheatre.com; ☏ 808/528-0506). The theater is still basking in its renaissance as a leading multipurpose center for the performing arts following a 4-year, $22-million renovation. The neoclassical Beaux Arts landmark features a 1922 dome, 1,400 plush seats, a hydraulically elevated organ, breathtaking murals, and gilt galore.

Other smaller theaters on Oahu are the **Manoa Valley Theatre,** 2833 E. Manoa Rd. (www.manoavalleytheatre.com; © **808/988-6131**), Honolulu's equivalent of Off Broadway, with well-known shows performing; **Diamond Head Theatre,** 520 Makapuu Ave. (www.diamondheadtheatre.com; © **808/733-0274**), hosting a variety of performances from musicals to comedies to classical dramas; **Kumu Kahua Theatre,** 46 Merchant St. (www.kumukahua.org; © **808/536-4222**), producing plays dealing with the island experience, often written by residents; and **Leeward Community College Theatre,** 96-045 Ala Ike St. (www.LCCtheatre.hawaii.edu; © **808/455-0385**), featuring an eclectic slate of productions, from visiting performing companies to local students' work.

A new symphony orchestra has formed on the island: the **Hawaii Symphony** (www.hawaiisymphonyorchestra.org; © **808/593-2468**). Meanwhile, the highly successful **Hawaii Opera Theatre** (www.hawaiiopera.org; © **808/596-7372** or 800/836-7372), celebrating more than 50 seasons (past hits have included "La Bohème," "Carmen," and "Aïda"), still draws fans to the Neal Blaisdell Concert Hall (www.blaisdellcenter.com; © **808/591-2211**), as do Hawaii's ballet companies, including **Hawaii Ballet Theatre** (http://hawaiiballettheatre.org) and **Ballet Hawaii** (www.ballethawaii.org). Contemporary performances by **Iona** (www.iona360.com), a strikingly creative group whose dance evolved out of Butoh (a contemporary dance form that originated in Japan), are worth tracking down if you love the avant-garde.

HAWAII, THE BIG ISLAND

Larger than all the other Hawaiian Islands combined, the Big Island truly deserves its nickname. Its 4,028 square miles—a figure that's growing, thanks to an active volcano—contain 10 of the world's 13 climate zones. In less than a day, a visitor can easily traverse tropical rainforest, lava desert, verdant pastures, misty uplands, and chilly tundra, the last near the summit of Mauna Kea, almost 14,000 feet above sea level. The shoreline also boasts diversity, from golden beaches to enchanting coves with black, salt-and-pepper, even olivine sand. Above all, the island home of Kamehameha the Great and Pele, the volcano goddess, is big in *mana:* power and spirituality.

ESSENTIALS

Arriving

The Big Island has two major airports for interisland and trans-Pacific jet traffic: Kona and Hilo.

Most people arrive at **Kona International Airport** (**KOA;** http://hawaii.gov/koa) in Keahole, the island's westernmost point, and can be forgiven for wondering if there's really a runway among all the crinkly black lava and golden fountain grass. Leaving the airport, the ritzy Kohala Coast is to the left (north) and the town of Kailua-Kona—often just called "Kona," as is the airport—is to the right (south).

U.S. carriers offering nonstop service to Kona, in alphabetical order, are **Alaska Airlines** (www.alaskaair.com; ✆ 800/252-7522), with flights from the Pacific Northwest hubs of Seattle, Portland, and Anchorage, and from San Jose and Oakland, California; **American Airlines** (www.aa.com; ✆ 800/433-7300), with flights from Los Angeles; **Delta Air Lines** (www.delta.com; ✆ 800/221-1212), with flights from Salt Lake City (originating in Atlanta); **Hawaiian Airlines** (www.hawaiianairlines.com; ✆ 800/367-5320), with summer flights from Oakland and Los Angeles; **United Airlines** (www.united.com; ✆ 800/241-6522), with year-round flights from Los Angeles, San Francisco, Denver, and seasonal flights from Chicago; and **US Airways** (www.usairways.com; ✆ 800/428-4322), scheduled to merge with American, but at press time still offering nonstop flights from Phoenix.

Air Canada (www.aircanada.com; ✆ 888/247-2267) and **WestJet** (www.westjet.com; ✆ 888/937-8358) also offer nonstop service to Kona, with frequency changing seasonally, from Vancouver.

Only United offers nonstop service to **Hilo International Airport (ITO)** (http://hawaii.gov/ito), via Los Angeles.

For connecting flights or island-hopping, Hawaiian (see above) is the only carrier offering interisland jet service, available from Honolulu and Kahului, Maui, to both Kona and Hilo airports. **Mokulele Airlines** (www.mokulele airlines.com; ✆ 866/260-4040) flies nine-passenger, single-engine turboprops between Kona and Kahului and Kapalua, Maui, and between the Big Island upcountry town of Waimea and Kahului.

Visitor Information

The **Big Island Visitors Bureau** (www.gohawaii.com/big-island) has two offices on the Big Island: one in the Shops at Mauna Lani, 68-1330 Mauna Lani Dr., Suite 109B (𝄐 **808/885-1655**); the other at 101 Aupuni St., No. 238, Hilo (𝄐 **808/961-5797**).

The free tourist publications "This Week" (www.thisweekhawaii.com/big-island) and "101 Things to Do on Hawaii the Big Island" (www.101thingstodo.com/big-island) offer lots of useful information, as well as discount coupons for a variety of island adventures. Copies are easy to find all around the island.

Coast of Kailua-Kona.

Konaweb.com has an extensive event calendar and handy links to sites and services around the island, not just the Kona side. **Gokohala.com** has detailed maps and listings for the North and South Kohala districts.

Those fascinated by the island's active volcanoes should check out the detailed daily reports, maps, photos, videos, and webcams on the U.S. Geological Survey's **Hawaiian Volcano Observatory** website (http://hvo.wr.usgs.gov), which also tracks the island's frequent but usually minor earthquake activity.

Holualoa Village.

The Island in Brief

THE KONA COAST

Kona means "leeward side" in Hawaiian—and that means hot, dry weather virtually every day of the year on the 70-mile stretch of black lava shoreline encompassing the North and South Kona districts.

NORTH KONA With the exception of the sumptuous but serenely low-key Four Seasons Resort Hualalai ★★★ north of the airport, most of what everyone just calls "Kona" is an affordable vacation spot. An ample selection of midpriced condo units, timeshares, and several recently upgraded hotels lie between the bustling commercial district of Kailua-Kona ★★★, a one-time fishing village and royal compound now renowned as the start and finish of the Ironman World Championship, and Keauhou, an equally historic area about 6 miles south that boasts upscale condominiums, a shopping center, and golf-course homes.

The rightly named Alii ("Royalty") Drive begins in Kailua-Kona near King Kamehameha's royal compound at **Kamakahonu Bay,** including the temple complex at **Ahuena Heiau,** and continues past Hulihee Palace ★★★, an elegant retreat for later royals that sits across from the oldest church in the islands. Heading south, the road passes by the snorkelers' haven of Kahaluu Beach and sacred and royal sites on the now-closed Keauhou Beach Resort, before the intersection with King Kamehameha III Road, which leads to that monarch's birthplace by Keauhou Bay. Several kayak excursions and snorkel boats leave from Keauhou, but Kailua Pier sees the most traffic—from cruise-ship tenders to fishing and dive boats, dinner cruises, and other sightseeing excursions.

Beaches between Kailua-Kona and Keauhou tend to be pocket coves, but heading north toward South Kohala (which begins near the entrance to the Waikoloa Resort), beautiful, uncrowded sands lie out of sight from the highway, often reached by unpaved roads across vast lava fields. Among the steep coffee fields in North Kona's cooler upcountry, you'll find the rustic, artsy village of **Holualoa.**

SOUTH KONA The rural, serrated coastline here is indented with numerous bays, from **Kealakekua,** a marine life and cultural preserve that's the island's best diving spot, down to **Honaunau,** where a national historical park recalls the days of old Hawaii. This is a great place to stay, in modest plantation-era inns or bed-and-breakfasts, if you want to get away from the crowds but still be within driving distance of beaches and the sights of Kailua. The higher, cooler elevation of the main road means you'll pass many coffee, macadamia nut, and tropical fruit farms, some with tours or roadside stands.

> ### A Desert Crossing
>
> If you follow Highway 11 counterclockwise from Kona to Kilauea Volcano, you'll get a preview of what lies ahead in the Hawaii Volcanoes National Park: hot, scorched, quake-shaken, rippling new/dead land. This is the great **Kau Desert,** layer upon layer of lava flows, fine ash, and fallout. As you traverse the desert, you cross the Great Crack and the Southwest Rift Zone, a major fault zone that looks like a giant groove in the earth, before you reach Kilauea.

THE KOHALA COAST

Also on the island's "Kona side," sunny and dry Kohala is divided in two distinctively different districts, although the resorts are more glamorous and the rural area that much less developed.

Essentials

HAWAII, THE BIG ISLAND

Keck Observatory.

SOUTH KOHALA   Pleasure domes rise like palaces no Hawaiian king ever imagined along the sandy beaches carved into the craggy shores here, from the more moderately priced **Waikoloa Beach Resort** at Anaehoomalu Bay to the posher **Mauna Lani** and **Mauna Kea** resorts to the north. Mauna Kea is where Laurance Rockefeller opened the area's first resort in 1965, a virtual mirage of opulence and tropical greenery rising from bleak, black lava fields, framed by the white sands of Kaunaoa Beach and views of the eponymous mountain. But you don't have to be a billionaire to enjoy South Kohala's fabulous beaches and historic sites (such as petroglyph fields), all open to the public, with parking and other facilities (including restaurants and shopping) provided by the resorts.

Several of the region's attractions are also located off the resorts, including the white sands of **Spencer Beach ★★**; the massive **Puukohola Heiau ★★★**, a lava rock temple commissioned by King Kamehameha the Great; and the excellent restaurants and handful of stores in **Kawaihae,** the commercial harbor just after the turnoff for upcountry Waimea. **Note:** Despite its name, the golf course community of **Waikoloa Village** is not in the Waikoloa Beach Resort, but instead lies 5½ miles uphill from the coastal highway.

WAIMEA (KAMUELA) & MAUNA KEA   Officially part of South Kohala, the old upcountry cow town of Waimea on the northern road between the coasts is a world unto itself, with rolling green pastures, wide-open spaces dotted by *puu* (cindercone hills), and real cowpokes who work mammoth **Parker Ranch,** Hawaii's largest working ranch. Sometimes called Kamuela, after ranch founder Samuel (Kamuela) Parker, to distinguish it from Kauai's cowboy town with the same name, Waimea is split between a "dry side" (closer to the Kohala Coast) and a "wet side" (closer to the Hamakua Coast), but both sides can be cooler than sea level. It's also headquarters for the **Keck Observatory,** whose twin telescopes atop the nearly 14,000-foot **Mauna Kea ★★★**, some 35 miles away, are the largest and most powerful in the world. Waimea is home to several affordable B&Bs and shopping centers, while **Merriman's ★★★** remains a popular foodie outpost at Opelo Plaza.

NORTH KOHALA   Locals may remember when sugar was king here, but for visitors, little-developed North Kohala is most famous for another king, Kamehameha the Great. His birthplace is a short walk from one of the Hawaiian Islands' largest and most important temples, **Mookini Heiau,** which dates to A.D. 480. A yellow-cloaked bronze statue of the warrior-king stands in front of the community center in **Kapaau,** a small plantation-era town with a side road leading to the picturesque, wooden-framed **Kalahikiola Church,** built in the 1850s and rebuilt after the 2006 earthquake. The road ends at the breathtaking **Polulu Valley Overlook.**

Once the center of the Big Island's sugarcane industry, **Hawi** remains a regional hub, with a 3-block-long strip of sun-faded, false-fronted buildings holding a few shops and restaurants of interest to visitors. Eight miles south, **Lapakahi State Historical Park ★★** merits a stop to explore how less-exalted Hawaiians than Kamehameha lived in a simple village by the sea. Beaches are less appealing here, with the northernmost coves subject to strong winds blowing across the Alenuihaha Channel from Maui, 26 miles away and visible on clear days.

THE HAMAKUA COAST

This emerald coast, a 52-mile stretch from Honokaa to Hilo on the island's windward northeast side, was once plaited with sugarcane; it now blooms with flowers, macadamia nuts, papayas, vanilla, and mushrooms. Resort-free and virtually without beaches, the Hamakua Coast includes the districts of Hamakua and North Hilo, with two unmissable destinations. Picture-perfect **Waipio Valley** has impossibly steep sides, taro patches, a green riot of wild plants, and a winding stream leading to a broad, black-sand beach, while **Akaka Falls State Park ★★★** offers views of two lovely waterfalls amid lush foliage. Also worth checking out: **Laupahoehoe Beach Park,** with its mournful memorial to young victims of a 1946 tsunami; and the lively scene at the Saturday farmers' market in the historic plantation town of **Honokaa.**

HILO

Hawaii's largest metropolis after Honolulu is a quaint, misty, flower-filled city of Victorian houses overlooking a half-moon bay, with a restored historic downtown and a clear view of Mauna Loa, often snowcapped in winter. Hilo catches everyone's eye until it rains—and it rains a lot in Hilo, with 128 inches of rain annually. It's ideal for growing ferns, orchids, and anthuriums, but not for catching constant rays.

Yet there's a lot to see and do in Hilo and the surrounding South Hilo district, both indoors and out—including visiting the bayfront Japanese-style **Liluokalani Gardens ★★**, the **Pacific Tsunami Museum ★**, the **Mokupapapa Discovery Center ★★**, and **Rainbow Falls ★**—so grab your umbrella. The rain is warm (the temperature seldom dips below 70°F/21°C), and there's usually a rainbow afterward.

The town also holds Hawaii's best bargains for budget travelers, with plenty of hotel rooms—most of the year, that is. Hilo's magic moment comes in spring, the week after Easter, when hula *halau* (schools) arrive for the annual **Merrie Monarch Hula Festival** hula competition (www.merriemonarch.com). Plan ahead if you want to go: Tickets are sold out by the first week in January, and hotels within 30 miles are usually booked solid. Hilo is also the gateway to **Hawaii Volcanoes National Park ★★★**, where hula troupes perform chants and dances before the Merrie Monarch festival; the park is 30 miles away, or about an hour's drive up-slope.

PUNA DISTRICT

PAHOA, KAPOHO & KALAPANA Between Hilo and Hawaii Volcanoes National Park is the "Wild Wild East," an emerging visitor destination with geothermal wonders such as the ghostly hollowed trunks of **Lava Tree State Monument ★★**, the volcanically heated waters of **Ahalanui Park ★★** and the **Kapoho tide pools,** and the acres of lava from a 1986 flow that rolled through the Hawaiian hamlet of **Kalapana** and covered a popular black-sand beach. The rough ocean has carved a new beach at Kalapana, where the county opens a site to view lava flowing into the ocean when conditions are right. With or without active lava, Kalapana's Wednesday-night farmers market and live music on Friday nights attract a large local crowd, and you're welcome to join. The part-Hawaiian, part-hippie plantation town of **Pahoa** is the funky gateway here; vacation rentals and the yoga-focused **Kalani Oceanside Retreat ★** are the primary lodging options.

HAWAII VOLCANOES NATIONAL PARK ★★★ This is America's most exciting national park, where a live volcano called Kilauea has been continuously erupting since 1983. Depending on where the flow is, you may not be able to see molten lava—or have to walk across miles of rough lava rock to do so—but there's always something else impressive to see. A towering plume of ash, which at night reflects the glow of the lava lake below it, has been rising from Kilauea's Halemaumau Crater since 2008, while steam vents have been belching sulphurous odors since long before Mark Twain visited in 1866. Ideally, you should plan to spend 3 days at the park exploring its many trails, watching the volcano, visiting the rainforest, and just enjoying this spectacular place. But even if you have only a day, get here—it's worth the trip. Bring your sweats or jacket (honest!); it's cool up here. *Note:* The vast park, most of which straddles the Puna and Kau districts, includes the separate, 116,000-acre Kahuku Unit, 43 miles west of the Kilauea Visitor Center in Kau. The former ranchlands and trails are open three or four weekends a month.

VOLCANO VILLAGE If you're not camping or staying at historic, 33-room **Volcano House ★★** inside the park, you'll want to overnight in this quiet hamlet, just outside the national park entrance. Several cozy inns and B&Bs, some with fireplaces, reside under tree ferns in this cool mountain hideaway. The tiny highland community (elevation 4,000 ft.), first settled by Japanese immigrants, is now inhabited by artists, soul-searchers, and others who like the crisp air of Hawaii's high country.

KAU DISTRICT

Written variously in Hawaiian as *Ka'ū* or *Kā'ū,* and typically pronounced *"kah-oo,"* this windswept, often barren district between Puna and South Kona is one visitors are most likely to just drive through on their way to and from the national park. Nevertheless, it contains several noteworthy sites.

KA LAE (SOUTH POINT) This is the Plymouth Rock of Hawaii. The first Polynesians arrived in seagoing canoes, probably from the Marquesas Islands, around A.D. 500 at this rocky promontory 500 feet above the sea. To the west is the old fishing village of Waiahukini, populated from A.D. 750 until the 1860s; ancient canoe moorings, shelter caves, and *heiau* (temples) poke through windblown pili grass today. The east coast curves inland to reveal the olivine sand of **Papakolea**

Ka Lae.

Beach, a world-famous anomaly that's accessible only by foot or four-wheel-drive. Along the point, the southernmost spot in the 50 states, trees grow sideways due to the relentless gusts that also power wind turbines. It's a slow, nearly 12-mile drive from the highway to the tip of Ka Lae, so many visitors opt just to stop at the marked overlook on Highway 11, west of South Point Road.

NAALEHU, WAIOHINU & PAHALA Nearly every business in Naalehu and Waiohinu, the two wide spots on the main road near South Point, claims to be the southernmost this or that. But except for a monkeypod tree planted by Mark Twain in 1866, and the delicious *malasadas* (doughnuts) and other sweets at the **Naalehu Bakery ★**, there's no reason to linger before heading to **Punaluu Beach,** between Naalehu and Pahala. Protected green sea turtles bask on the fine black-sand beach when they're not bobbing in the clear waters, chilly from the fresh springs bubbling from the ocean floor. An ancient fish pond and temple ruins are among historic sites within the park, well worth a detour on the way to the volcano. Pahala is the center of the burgeoning Kau coffee-growing scene ("industry" would be a bit overstated), so fans of caffeine should also allot at least a half-hour for a side trip to the **Kau Coffee Mill.**

GETTING AROUND

BY TAXI Taxis are readily available at both Kona and Hilo airports, although renting a car (see below) is a more likely option. On the Kona side, call **Kona Airport Taxi** (© 808/324-1111) or **Kona Taxicab** (www.konataxicab.com; © 808/324-4444). In Hilo, call **Ace-1** (© 808/935-8303). Rates start at $3 plus nearly $3 each additional mile—about $25 to $30 from the Kona airport to Kailua-Kona and $50 to $60 to the Waikoloa Beach Resort.

BY CAR You'll need a rental car on the Big Island; not having one will really limit you. All major car-rental agencies have airport pickups; some even offer cars at Kohala and Kona resorts. For tips on insurance and driving rules, see "Getting Around Hawaii" (p. 511).

The Big Island has more than 480 miles of paved road. The highway that circles the island is called the **Hawaii Belt Road.** From North Kona to South Kohala and Waimea, you have two driving choices: the scenic "upper" road, **Mamalahoa Highway** (Hwy. 190), or the speedier "lower" road, **Queen Kaahumanu Highway** (Hwy. 19). South of Kailua-Kona, Hawaii Belt Road continues on Mamalahoa Highway (Hwy. 11) all the way to downtown Hilo, where it becomes Highway 19 again and follows the Hamakua Coast before heading up to Waimea.

North Kohala also has upper and lower highways. In Kawaihae, you can follow **Kawaihae Road** (Hwy. 19) uphill to the left turn on the often-misty **Kohala Mountain Road** (Hwy. 250), which eventually drops down into Hawi. The **Akoni Pule Highway** (Hwy. 270) hugs the coast from Kawaihae to pavement's end at the Pololu Valley Lookout.

Note: **Saddle Road** (Hwy. 200) snakes between Mauna Kea and Mauna Loa en route from Hilo to Mamalahoa Highway (Hwy. 190). Despite recent improvements to its once-rough pavement and narrow shoulders, it's still frequented by large military vehicles and plagued by bad weather; as a result, most rental-car agencies forbid you from driving on it.

BY BUS & SHUTTLE   SpeediShuttle (www.speedishuttle.com; ✆ 808/329-5433) and **Roberts Hawaii** (www.robertshawaii.com; ✆ 866/570-2536 or 808/954-8640) offer door-to-door airport transfers to hotels and other lodgings. Sample shared-ride rates from the Kona airport are $25 to $27 per person to Kailua-Kona, and $55 to $57 per person to the Mauna Lani Resort; Roberts' agents meet you outside security and provide porter service in baggage claim, but be aware there may be up to five stops before your destination.

The islandwide bus system, the **Hele-On Bus** (www.heleonbus.org; ✆ 808/961-8744), offers a great flat rate for riders: $2 general; $1 for students, seniors, and people with disabilities; and free for children under 5. Unfortunately, its routes have limited value for visitors, other than the Intra-Kona line between Kailua-Kona's big-box stores (Wal-Mart, Costco) and the Keauhou Shopping Center; the same bus makes two stops a day at the Kona airport. Longer-distance routes, such as Kona–Hilo, are generally designed for early-morning commuters.

Travelers staying in Kailua-Kona and the Keauhou Resort can hop on the open-air, 44-seat **Keauhou Resort Honu Express Trolley,** running from 9am to 9:15pm daily along Alii Drive. It makes six stops a day at 31 locations from the Sheraton Keauhou Bay Resort and Keauhou Shopping Center to Kahaluu Beach, Kailua Pier, and the shops of downtown Kailua-Kona. The fare is $2, free for those with vouchers from their hotel (such as the Sheraton); you can also ask for a voucher from stores in the Keauhou and Kona Commons shopping centers when spending $25 or more.

BY BIKE   Due to elevation changes, narrow shoulders (with the notable exception of the Queen Kaahumanu Hwy. between Kailua-Kona and Kawaihae), and high traffic speeds, point-to-point bike travel isn't recommended. However, several areas are ideal for recreational cycling and sightseeing. See "Bicycling" under "Other Outdoor Activities" for rental shops and routes.

BY MOTORCYCLE & SCOOTER   The sunny Kohala and Kona coasts are ideal for tooling around on a motorcycle, while those sticking to one resort or Kailua-Kona can easily get around by scooter. **Big Island Motorcycle Co.,** in Kings' Shops in the Waikoloa Beach Resort, 69-250 Waikoloa Beach Rd. (www.thrillseekershawaii. com; ✆ 808/886-2011), rents a variety of motorbikes to those 21 and older with a valid motorcycle license (from $100 a day, including gear, insurance, and unlimited miles). Moped rentals, available to those 18 and up with a standard driver's license, are $20 an hour, $45 half-day, and $60 full day ($75 for 24 hr.). In Kailua-Kona, **Big Island Harley-Davidson,** 75-5633 Palani Rd. (www.bigislandharley. com; ✆ 888/904-3155 or 808/217-8560), rents a variety of Harleys starting at $179 daily ($763 weekly), with gear and unlimited mileage, to qualified drivers, while **Big Island Mopeds** (www.konamopedrentals.com; ✆ 808/443-6625) will deliver mopeds to your door for $50 day ($250 weekly; prices double during Ironman week in mid-Oct).

[FastFACTS] THE BIG ISLAND

ATMs/Banks ATMs are located everywhere on the Big Island, at banks, supermarkets, Long Drugs, and at some shopping malls. The major banks on the Big Island are First Hawaiian, Bank of Hawaii, American Savings, and Central Pacific, all with branches in both Kona and Hilo.

Business Hours Most businesses on the island are open from 8 or 9am to 5 or 6pm.

Dentists In Kohala, contact **Dr. Craig C. Kimura** at Kamuela Office Center, 65-1230 Mamalahoa Hwy. (ℂ **808/885-5947**). In Kailua-Kona, call **Dr. Christopher Bays** at **Kona Coast Dental Care,** 75-5591 Palani Rd., in the Frame 10 Center, above the bowling alley (www.konacoastdental.com; ℂ **808/329-8067**). In Hilo, **Kuhio Dental Group,** in Prince Kuhio Plaza, 111 E. Puainako St. (www.kuhio dentalgroup.net; ℂ **808/ 959-3433**), is open daily from 8am to 5pm, with dental surgeons **Jonathan Mah** and **Grace Chen** on staff.

Doctors For minor emergencies or drop-in appointments on weekdays, visit **Urgent Care of Kona,** 77-311 Sunset Dr., off Highway 11, Kailua-Kona (www.urgentcareofkona.com;

ℂ **808/327-4357**). **Hilo Urgent Care Center** has offices open daily at 45 Mohouli St., Hilo (ℂ **808/ 969-3051**), and Monday to Saturday at 16-612 Old Volcano Rd., Keaau (ℂ **808/ 966-7942**).

Emergencies For ambulance, fire, and rescue services, dial ℂ **911.**

Hospitals Hospitals offering 24-hour, urgent-care facilities include the **Kona Community Hospital,** 79-1019 Haukapila St., off Highway 11, Kealakekua (www.kch.hhsc.org; ℂ **808/ 322-9311**); **Hilo Medical Center,** 1190 Waianuenue Ave., Hilo (www.hilo medicalcenter.org; ℂ **808/ 932-3900**); and **North Hawaii Community Hospital,** 67-1125 Mamalahoa Hwy., Waimea (www.nhch.com; ℂ **808/885-4444**).

Internet Access Pretty much every lodging on the island has Wi-Fi; ask about the charges, which can be exorbitant in rooms but free in public spaces, ahead of time. **Starbucks, McDonald's,** and numerous local coffee shops also offer free Wi-Fi.

Pharmacies There are no 24-hour pharmacies on the Big Island. The pharmacies in **Longs Drugs** (www.cvs.com), which has 10 locations around the island,

open as early as 7am and close as late as 9pm Monday to Saturday, and are open 8am to 6pm Sunday. Kona and Hilo's national chain stores such as **Kmart, Target, Wal-Mart,** and **Costco** (Kailua-Kona only) also have pharmacy hours.

Police Dial ℂ **911** in case of emergency; otherwise, call the **Hawaii Police Department** at ℂ **808/ 935-3311** islandwide.

Post Office The **U.S. Postal Service** (www.usps.com; ℂ **800/275-8777**) has more than 2 dozen branches around the island, including in Kailua-Kona at 74–5577 Palani Rd., in Waimea at 67-1197 Mamalahoa Hwy., and in Hilo at 1299 Kekuanaoa St. All are open weekdays; some are also open Saturday morning.

Volcanic Activity To find out if you can see flowing lava in or near **Hawaii Volcanoes National Park,** including from Hawaii County's free viewing area in Kalapana, visit www.nps.gov/havo/planyourvisit/lava2.htm. The county also has a recorded hot line for the **Kalapana viewing area** (ℂ **808/961-8093**). For daily **air-quality reports,** based on sulfur dioxide and particulates from ongoing eruptions, visit **www. hawaiiso2network.com.**

EXPLORING THE BIG ISLAND
Attractions & Points of Interest

While parks are open year-round, some of the other attractions below may be closed on major holidays such as Christmas, New Year's, or Thanksgiving Day. Admission is often reduced for Hawaii residents (*kama'āina*) with state ID.

NORTH KONA

Hulihee Palace ★★★ HISTORIC SITE   John Adams Kuakini, royal governor of the island, built this stately, two-story New England–style mansion overlooking Kailua Bay in 1838. It later became a summer home for King Kalakaua and Queen Kapiolani and, like Queen Emma's Summer Palace and Iolani Palace on Oahu, is now lovingly maintained by the Daughters of Hawaii as a showcase for royal furnishings and Native Hawaiian artifacts, from hat boxes to a 22-foot spear. You can take a self-guided tour of its six spacious rooms, but guided tours, offered throughout the day, are worth the extra $2 to learn more of the monarchs' history and cultural context; guided tours are also the only ones permitted on the oceanfront lanai. A sign directs you to remove your shoes before entering; free booties are provided upon request.

The palace lawn hosts 12 free events a year honoring a different member of Hawaiian royalty, with performances by local hula *halau* (schools) and musicians. Called **Afternoon at the Palace,** they're generally held at 4pm on the third Sunday of the month (except June and Dec, when the performances are held in conjunction with King Kamehameha Day and Christmas). Check the Daughters of Hawaii website for dates. *Note:* The www.huliheepalace.net website looks official but is unauthorized as well as outdated.

75–5718 Alii Dr., Kailua-Kona. http://daughtersofhawaii.org. ✆ **808/329-1877.** Admission $8 adults, $6 seniors, $1 children 18 and under. $2 more per adult for guided tours. Mon–Sat 9am–4pm (arrive at least 1 hr. before closing for guided tour).

Hulihee Palace.

Kaloko-Honokohau National Historical Park ★★ HISTORIC SITE/ NATURAL ATTRACTION   With no erupting volcano, impressive tikis, or massive temples, this 1,160-acre oceanfront site just north of Honokohhau Harbor tends to get overlooked by visitors in favor of its showier siblings in the national park system. That's a shame for several reasons, among them that it's a microcosm of ancient Hawaii, from fish ponds (one with an 800-ft.-long rock wall), house platforms, petroglyphs, and trails through barren lava to marshlands with native waterfowl, reefs teeming with fish, and a tranquil beach where green sea turtles bask in the shadow of Puuoina Heiua. Plus, it's rarely crowded, and admission is free. Stop by the small visitor center to pick up a brochure and ask about ocean

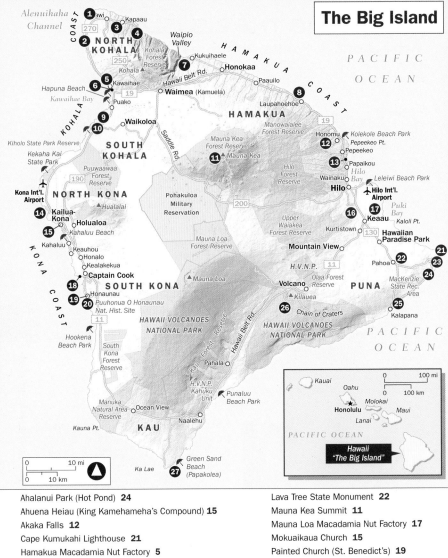

The Big Island

conditions (if you're planning to snorkel), and then backtrack to Honokohau Harbor, a half-mile south, to park closer to the beach.

Ocean side of Hwy. 19, 3 miles south of Kona airport. www.nps.gov/kaho. (℗ **808/326-9057.** Visitor center and parking lot ½-mile north of Honokohau Harbor daily 8:30am–4pm. Kaloko Rd. gate daily 8am–5pm. No time restrictions on parking at Honokohau Harbor; from Hwy. 19, take Kealakehe Pkwy. west into harbor, then take 1st right and follow to parking lot near Kona Sailing Club, a short walk to beach.

Mokuaikaua Church ★ RELIGIOUS/HISTORIC SITE   In 1820, just a few months after King Kamehameha II and Queen Regent Kaahumanu had broken

Mokuaikaua Church.

the kapu system at Ahuena Heiau, the first missionaries to land in Hawaii arrived on the brig *Thaddeus* and received the royals' permission to preach. Within a few years a thatched-roof structure had risen on this site, on land donated by Gov. Kuakini, owner of Hulihee Palace, across the road. But after several fires, Rev. Asa Thurston had this massive, New England–style structure erected, using lava rocks from a nearby *heiau* (temple) held together by coral mortar, with gleaming koa for the lofty interior; the 112-foot steeple is still the tallest structure in Kailua-Kona. Visitors are welcome to view the sanctuary, open daily, and a rear room with a small collection of artifacts, including a model of the *Thaddeus*, a rope star chart used by Pacific Islanders, and a poignant plaque commemorating Henry Opuka-haia. As a teenager, the Big Island native (known then as "Obookiah") boarded a ship to New England in 1807, converted to Christianity, and helped plan the first mission to the islands, but he died of a fever in 1818, the year before the *Thaddeus* sailed. (In 1993 his remains were reinterred at Kahikolu Congregational Church, 16 miles south of Mokuaikaua.) On most Sundays at 12:15pm, following the service, Mokuaikaua Church hosts a free history talk.

75–5713 Alii Dr., Kailua-Kona, ⅕-mile south of Palani Rd., across from Hulihee Palace. www.mokuaikaua.org. (℗ **808/329-0655.** Daily 7:30am–5:30pm.

Ocean Rider Seahorse Farm ★★ AQUACULTURE   On the coastline just behind the Natural Energy Lab (NELHA) lies this 3-acre, conservation-oriented "aqua-farm" that breeds and displays more than half of the world's 36 species of seahorses. The farm began breeding seahorses in 1998 as a way of ending demand for wild-collected seahorses and, once successful, expanded its interests to include similarly threatened sea dragons and reef fish. Although the $40 cost of the biologist-led, 1-hour tour may seem excessive, proceeds benefit the farm's

CRAZY FOR KONA coffee

More than 600 farms grow coffee in the Kona Coffee Belt on the slopes of Hualalai, from Kailua-Kona and Holualoa in North Kona to Captain Cook and Honaunau in South Kona. The prettiest time to visit is between January and May, when the rainy season brings white blossoms known as "Kona snow." Harvesting takes place by hand—one reason Kona coffee is so costly—from late August through early winter. At least 40 farms offer **regular tours with tastings,** and many more provide samples at farmstands. Much of the fun in visiting is simply making impromptu stops along Mamalahoa Highway (Hwy. 11 and Hwy. 180), but you can also search the online listings of the **Kona Coffee Farmers Association** (www.konacoffeefarmers.org) to locate more obscure farms or those that require tour reservations.

Here are some highlights, heading north to south, of coffee growers ready to show around drop-ins and offer free samples:

○ **Mountain Thunder Coffee Plantation,** 73-1944 Hao St. (off Kaloko Dr.), Kailua-Kona (www.mountainthunder.com; ☏ **808/325-2136**): In the hills known as Kaloko Mauka above the airport, Trent Bateman mills award-winning coffee from his own 21-acre organic farm Mountain Thunder, as well as from other Kona growers. Mountain Thunder also grows organic coffee, pineapple, *mamaki* (used for herbal tea), cacao, sugarcane, and green tea at another location: Kainaliu, on Highway 11, just south of mile marker 113. Both farms offer free tours on the hour from 10am to 4pm daily; farmstands open at 9am.

○ **Kona Blue Sky Coffee Company,** 76-973 Hualalai Rd., Holualoa (www.konablueskycoffee.com; ☏ **877/322-1700** or 808/322-1700): The Christian Twigg-Smith family and staff grows and sells its coffee on a scenic, 400-acre estate, with free guided walking tours Monday to Saturday from 9am to 3:30pm.

○ **Holualoa Kona Coffee Company,** 77-6261 Mamalahoa Hwy. (Hwy. 180), Holualoa (www.konalea.com; ☏ **800/334-0348** or 808/322-9937): Owned by Desmond and Lisen Twigg-Smith, this farm and mill sells its own and others' premium, organic Kona coffee. Tour the orchards (mowed and fertilized by a large flock of geese) and witness all phases of processing, weekdays from 8am to 4pm.

○ **Kona Joe Coffee,** 79–7346 Mamalahoa Hwy., Kainaliu (Hwy. 11 between mile markers 113 and 114; www.konajoe.com; ☏ **808/322-2100**): The home of the world's first trellised coffee farm offers a free, self-guided tour with 8-minute video, as well as guided tours by request ($15 adults, free for kids 12 and under) daily from 8am to 5pm. Guided tours of the 20-acre estate include a mug, coffee, and chocolate, with reservations recommended for groups of six or more.

○ **Greenwell Farms,** 81-6581 Mamalahoa Hwy., Kealakekua (www.greenwellfarms.com; ☏ **808/323-2295**): If any farm can claim to be the granddaddy of Kona coffee, this would be it. Englishman Henry Nicholas Greenwell began growing coffee in the region in 1850. Now operated by his great-grandson and agricultural innovator Tom Greenwell, the farm offers free tours daily from 8:30am to 4:30pm.

research and conservation; in any case, people still find their way here in droves, excited to see pregnant male seahorses and their babies, and to have one of the delicate creatures wrap its tail around their fingers.

73–4388 Ilikai Place (behind Natural Energy Lab), Kailua-Kona. From Hwy. 19 (at mile marker 94), follow OTEC Rd. past Wawalaloli Beach Park to 1st left; farm is on the right. www.seahorse.com. ☎ **808/329-6840.** Tour $40 ($38 online). Mon–Fri noon and 2pm; also 10am Thanksgiving week, Dec 19-Apr 30, and June 1–Labor Day. Reservations recommended. Gift shop Mon–Fri 9:30am–3:30pm.

SOUTH KONA

Amy B. H. Greenwell Ethnobotanical Garden ★ GARDEN

You can pick up a brochure to tour this 12-acre garden yourself, home to more than 200 native plants as well as Polynesian introductions, but you'll learn so much more about Hawaiian culture and plants on a guided tour (especially since the lush vegetation can occasionally overgrow pathways and signs). Amy Greenwell, Stanford-educated granddaughter of Kona coffee pioneer Henry Nicholas Greenwell, performed botanical and archaeological surveys in the area and created this "pre-Cook" garden on her estate, which she willed to the Bishop Museum at her death in 1974. Rarities include six varieties of the only native Hawaiian palm tree, loulu, and a highly endangered species of hibiscus. The garden, which has an intriguing gift shop, also hosts a lively farmers market every Sunday from 9am to 2pm.

82-6188 Mamalahoa Hwy. (Hwy. 11, mountain side), Captain Cook, across from the Manago Hotel. www.bishopmuseum.org/greenwell. ☎ **808/323-3222.** $7 adults, $6 seniors 65 and older, free for children 12 and under. Tues–Sun 9am–4pm; guided tours at 1pm.

H. N. Greenwell Store Museum ★ & Portuguese Bread Baking ★★

MUSEUM   This charming museum tells the story of rural Kona through costumed interpreters in a vintage setting—the region's oldest surviving store, built of lava rock in 1870. Coffee grower and rancher Henry Nicholas Greenwell (see "Crazy for Kona Coffee" on p. 160), his wife, and daughter-in-law sold everything from denim and parasols to tobacco and poi, including many items now stocked on the restored shelves. On Thursday, folks line up at its roadside stand to buy hot **Portuguese sweet bread** ($7), baked in the communal stove oven in the pasture below from 10am to 1pm. Museum admission is not required to join the volunteers kneading and shaping the dough; the first loaves emerge around 12:30pm and sell out quickly.

Ocean side of Hwy. 11, btw. mile markers 111 and 112, Kealakekua, just south of Greenwell Farms. www.konahistorical.org. ☎ **808/323-3222.** $7 adults, $5 seniors 60 and older, $3 children 5–12. Mon and Thurs 10am–2pm.

Kealakekua Bay State Historical Park ★ NATURAL ATTRACTION

The island's largest natural sheltered bay, a marine life conservation district, is not only one of the best places to snorkel on the Big Island, but it's also an area of deep cultural and historical significance. On the southern side, now called Napoopoo (*nah-poh-oh-poh-oh*), stands the large stacked-rock platform of **Hikiau Heiau,** a temple once used for human sacrifice and still considered sacred today. A rocky beach park here includes picnic tables, barbecues, and restrooms. On the north side, a steep but relatively broad 2-mile trail leads down to the historic Kaawaloa area, where *alii* (royalty) once lived; when they died, their bodies were taken to **Puhina O Lono Heiau** on the slope above them, prepared for burial, and hidden in caves on the 600-foot-cliff above the central bay. An obelisk known as the **Captain Cook Monument** stands on Kaawaloa Flat, near where the British explorer was slain in 1779, after misunderstandings between Hawaiians and Cook's crew led to armed conflict. The Hawaiians then showed respect by taking Cook's body to Puhina O Lono before returning some of the remains to his crew. Please be careful not to walk on the reef or any cultural sites; to protect the area, only hikers and clients of three guided kayak tour companies have access to Kaawaloa Flat (see "Kayaking" on p. 201).

From Hwy. 11 in Captain Cook heading south, take right fork onto Napoopoo Rd. (Hwy. 160). Kaawaloa trailhead is about 500 ft. on right. By car, continue on Napoopoo Rd. 4¼ miles to left on Puuhonua Rd., go ⅕-mile to right on Manini Beach Rd. www.hawaiistateparks.org. Daily during daylight hours.

Kona Coffee Living History Farm ★ FARM/HISTORIC SITE   With money earned from working the sugar plantations, a number of Japanese immigrants bought small farms and became pioneers in growing coffee. Learn more about their daily lives during the 1920s to 1940s and how their flavorful, hand-picked beans are still produced today on the 5½-acre **Uchida Coffee Farm,** where costumed interpreters demonstrate tasks and "talk story" with visitors. After you explore the vintage farmhouse, stroll through the orchards of coffee and macadamia nut trees, meet the chickens and donkey, and pick up a bag of 100-percent Kona coffee.

Ocean side of Mamalahoa Hwy. at mile marker 110, Captain Cook. www.konahistorical.org. ✆ **808/323-3222.** $15 adults, $13 seniors, $5 children 5–12, free for children under 5. Mon–Fri 10am–2pm.

The Painted Church (St. Benedict's) ★★ RELIGIOUS SITE   Beginning in 1899, Father John Berchman Velghe (a member of the same order as Father

The Painted Church.

Damien of Molokai) painted biblical scenes and images of saints inside quaint St. Benedict's Catholic Church, built in 1842 and restored in 2002. As with stained-glass windows of yore, his pictures, created with simple house paint, were a way of sharing stories with illiterate parishioners. It's a wonderfully trippy experience to look up at arching palm fronds and shiny stars on the ceiling. Health issues forced the priest to return to Belgium in 1904 before finishing all the pictures. The ocean-view church, which also boasts an ornate belfry, is typically open during daylight hours, but keep in mind it's an active parish, with Mass celebrated most days. 84–5140 Painted Church Rd., Captain Cook. www.thepaintedchurch.org. © **808/328-2227.** Turn off Hwy. 11 (toward the ocean) at about the 104 mile marker onto Rte. 160. Go on about a mile to the 1st turnoff on the right, opposite from a King Kamehameha sign. Follow the narrow, winding road about ¼-mile to church sign and turn right. Free admission.

Some of the idols at Puuhonua O Honaunau National Historical Park.

Puuhonua O Honaunau National Historical Park ★★★ HISTORIC SITE

With its fierce, haunting idols (ki'i), this sacred site on the black-lava Kona Coast certainly looks forbidding. To ancient Hawaiians, it served as a 16th-century place of refuge (puuhonua), providing sanctuary for defeated warriors and *kapu* (taboo) violators. A great rock wall—1,000 feet long, 10 feet high, and 17 feet thick—defines the refuge where Hawaiians found safety. On the wall's north end is **Hale O Keawe Heiau,** which holds the bones of 23 Hawaiian chiefs. Other archaeological finds include a royal compound, burial sites, old trails, and a portion of an ancient village. On a self-guided tour of the 420-acre site—much of which has been restored to its pre-contact state—you can see and learn about reconstructed thatched huts, canoes, and idols, and feel the *mana* (power) of old Hawaii, but do try to include one of the free daily ranger talks, held at 10:30am and 2:30pm in a covered amphitheater. A free, 2-day cultural festival, usually held the last weekend in June, allows you to join in games, learn crafts, sample Hawaiian food, see traditional hula, and experience life in pre-contact Hawaii. **Note:** There are no concessions in the park, other than bottled water at the bookstore, but there are picnic tables on the sandy stretch of the park's south side.

Hwy. 160 (off Hwy. 11 at mile marker 104), Honaunau. www.nps.gov/puho. © **808/328-2288.** Admission $5 per vehicle; $3 per person on foot, bicycle, or motorcycle; good for 7 days. Visitor center daily 8:30am–4:30pm; park daily 7am–sunset. From Hwy. 11, it's 3½ miles to the park entrance.

SOUTH KOHALA

Hamakua Macadamia Nut Factory ★★ FACTORY TOUR   The self-guided tour of shelling, roasting, and other processing that results in bountiful varieties of flavored macadamia nuts and confections is not that compelling if production has stopped for the day, so go before 3pm or plan to watch a video to get caught up. But who are we kidding—it's really all about the free tastings here, generous samples of big, fresh nuts in island flavors such as chili "peppah," Spam, and Kona coffee glazed. (Just the plain salted ones are fine by me, thank you.) The affable staff can pack your purchases in flat-rate priority-mail boxes (you just pay postage). Outside the hilltop factory warehouse are picnic tables with an ocean view.

61-3251 Maluokalani St., Kawaihae. www.hawnnut.com. ℰ **888/643-6688** or 808/882-1690. Free admission. Daily 9:30am–5:30pm. From Kawaihae Harbor, take Hwy. 270 north ¾-mile, turn left on Maluokalani St., and drive ⅕-mile uphill; factory is on right.

Puukohola Heiau National Historic Site ★★★ HISTORIC SITE   This seacoast temple, called "the hill of the whale," is the single most imposing and dramatic structure of the early Hawaiians. It was built by Kamehameha I from 1790 to 1791. The *heiau* stands 224 feet long by 100 feet wide, with three narrow terraces on the seaside and an amphitheater to view canoes. Kamehameha built this temple to the war god, Ku, after a prophet told him he would conquer and unite the islands if he did so. He also slayed his cousin on the site, and 4 years later fulfilled his kingly goal. The site includes an interactive visitor center; a smaller *heiau*-turned-fort; the house of John Young (a trusted advisor of Kamehameha); and, offshore, the submerged ruins of what is believed to be **Hale O Kapuni,** a shrine dedicated to the shark gods or guardian spirits, called *'aumakua.* (You can't see the temple, but shark fins are often spotted slicing through the waters.) In mid-August, Puukohola Heiau hosts a 2-day Hawaiian cultural festival, with games and crafts in which visitors are welcome to participate.

Hwy. 270, near Kawaihae Harbor. www.nps.gov/puhe. ℰ **808/882-7218.** Free admission. Daily 8:15am–4:45pm. The visitor center is on Hwy. 270; the *heiau* is a short walk away.

Kalahuipuaa & Anaehoomalu Fish Ponds ★ HISTORIC SITES   Like their Polynesian forebears, Hawaiians were among the first aquaculturists on the planet. Scientists still marvel at the ways they used ponds along the shoreline to stock and harvest fish. There are actually two different types of ancient fish ponds (or *loko i'a*). Closed ponds, located inland in shallow lava pools known as anchialine ponds, were fed by freshwater springs as well as the ocean. Open

Catch a Wave in a Traditional Sailing Canoe

One of most exhilarating programs in all of Hawaii's national parks is called **Catch a WAVE** (*Wa'akaulua* Authentic Voyaging Experience), a free, 45-minute ride on a double-hulled Hawaiian sailing canoe offered six times a day (Tues–Thurs), at Puukohola Heiau National Historic Site. Tickets are issued on a first-come, first-served basis in the visitor center, which opens at 8:15am. Passengers help launch and paddle the canoe from the beach at Pelekane Bay. Be sure to wear clothes and shoes that can get wet; you'll also want to lock anything you don't want to get wet in the trunk of your car, or leave it at your hotel. Children 12 and under must be accompanied by an adult. Since this isn't Disneyland, rides may be canceled in bad weather or during rough ocean conditions.

ponds used rock walls as a barrier to the ocean and sluice gates that connected the ponds to the ocean, leaving just enough room for juvenile fish to swim in at high tide while keeping the bigger, fatter fish from swimming out. Generally, the Hawaiians kept and raised mullet, milkfish, and shrimp in these open ponds; juvenile manini, papio, eels, and barracuda occasionally found their way in, too.

The seven ponds of the **Kalahuipuaa Fish Ponds,** just south of the Mauna Lani Bay Hotel & Bungalows (© **808/885-6622**), include examples of both types of ponds; they're still stocked with mullet and milkfish that are rotated through ponds as they grow. The trail through the ponds is marked with interpretive signs, as are the sprawling **Kuualii** and **Kahapapa Fish Ponds,** just behind the thin crescent of Anaehoomalu Beach in front of the Waikoloa Beach Marriott Resort & Spa (© **808/886-6789**). They're not as actively managed, but you can spot fish of all sizes in them.

Kohala Petroglyph Fields ★★ ROCK CARVINGS The Hawaiian petroglyphs are a great enigma of the Pacific—no one knows who made them or why. They appear at 135 different sites on six inhabited islands, but most are found on the Big Island, including images of dancers and paddlers, fishermen and chiefs, and tools of daily life such as fish hooks and canoes. The most common representations are family groups, while some petroglyphs depict post–European contact objects such as ships, anchors, horses, and guns. Simple circles with dots were used to mark the *puka,* or holes, where parents would place their child's umbilical cord (*piko*).

The largest concentration of these stone symbols in the Pacific lies within the 233-acre **Puako Petroglyph Archaeological Preserve,** near the Mauna Lani Resort. A total of 3,000 designs have been identified. The 1.5-mile **Malama Trail** through a kiawe field to the large, reddish lava field starts north of the Fairmont Orchid Hawaii in the Mauna Lani Resort. Take Highway 19 to the resort turnoff and drive toward the coast on North Kaniku Drive, which ends at the Holoholokai Beach parking lot; the trailhead on your right is marked by a sign and interpretive kiosk. Go in the early morning or late afternoon, when it's cooler, take water, wear shoes with sturdy soles (to avoid kiawe thorns), and stay on the trail.

A free 1-hour tour of the surrounding petroglyphs, led by expert Kalei'ula Kaneau, is offered Thursday and Friday at 9:30am by the **Kings' Shops** (© **808/886-8811**) at the Waikoloa Beach Resort. Just show up at the shopping center's Center Stage by 9:30am. You can also follow the signs to the trail through the petroglyph field on your own, but be aware that the trail is exposed, uneven, and rough; wear closed-toe shoes, a hat, and sunscreen.

Note: The petroglyphs are thousands of years old and easily destroyed. Do not walk on them or take rubbings (the Puako preserve has a replica petroglyph you may use instead). The best way to capture a petroglyph is with a photo in the late afternoon, when the shadows are long.

NORTH KOHALA

King Kamehameha Statue ★★ MONUMENT Here stands King Kame-hameha the Great, right arm outstretched, left arm holding a spear, as if guarding the seniors who have turned a century-old, New England–style courthouse into an airy civic center. It's worth a stop just to meet the town elders, who are quick to point out the local sights, hand you a free "Guide to Historic North Kohala," and give you a brief tour of the former courthouse, whose walls are covered with the faces of innocent-looking local boys killed in World War II, Korea, and Vietnam.

But the statue is the main attraction. There's one just like it in Honolulu, across the street from Iolani Palace, but this is the original: an 8-foot, 6-inch bronze by Thomas R. Gould, a Boston sculptor. Cast in Europe in 1880, it was lost at sea on its way to Hawaii. After a sea captain recovered the statue, it was placed here, near Kamehameha's Kohala birthplace, in 1912. Kamehameha is believed to have been born in 1758 under Halley's Comet and became ruler of Hawaii in 1810. He died in Kailua-Kona in 1819, but his burial site remains a mystery.

In front of North Kohala Civic Center, mountain side of Hwy. 270, Kapaau, just north of Kapaau Rd.

Kohala Historical Sites State Monument ★ HISTORIC SITES It takes some effort to reach this windswept, culturally important site on the northern tip of the island, but for those with 4WD vehicles or the ability to hike 3 miles round-trip, it's well worth it. The 1,500-year-old **Mookini Luakini Heiau,** once used by kings to pray and offer human sacrifices, is among Hawaii's oldest, largest, and most significant shrines. Nearly the size of a football field, with stacked rock walls almost 30 feet high, it was originally dedicated to Ku, the Hawaiian god of war, when it was erected in A.D. 480. Each stone is said to have been passed hand to hand from Pololu Valley, some 13 miles away, by 18,000 men who worked from sunset to sunrise. The latest in an unbroken family line of *kahuna nui* (temple caretakers) rededicated the eerie site in 1978 as a *heiau* (temple) for healing and children's education. A half-mile west lies the Kamehameha I Birth Site, where the great leader was born circa 1758. Later spirited away to Waipio Valley, where he was raised, Kamehameha returned to seek spiritual guidance at Mookini before embarking on his campaign to unite Hawaii. **Note:** Please do not stand on or remove any rocks from the site.

Off coastal dirt road, 1½ miles southwest of Upolu Airport. www.hawaiistateparks.org. Free admission. Thurs–Tues 9am–8pm. From Hwy. 270, take Upolu Airport Rd. north to airport. Park and hike 1½ miles southwest on dirt road; Mookini Luakini Heiau is on the left (mountain side). If road conditions permit (avoid during or after rain), use 4WD vehicle to drive to the *heiau*. Kamehameha I Birth site is another ½-mile southwest, also on the mountain side of the dirt road.

Lapakahi State Historical Park ★★ HISTORIC SITE This 14th-century fishing village, on a hot, dry, dusty stretch of coast, offers a glimpse into the lifestyle of the ancients. Lapakahi is the best-preserved fishing village in Hawaii. Take the self-guided, 1-mile loop trail past stone platforms, fish shrines, rock shelters, salt pans, and restored *hale* (houses) to a coral-sand beach and the deep-blue sea of Koaie Cove, a marine life conservation district with good snorkeling. Wear good walking shoes and a hat, go early in the morning or late in the after-noon to beat the heat, and bring your own water. Facilities include porta-potties and picnic tables.

Hwy. 270, Mahukona, 12 miles north of Kawaihae. www.hawaiistateparks.org. © **808/327-4958.** Free admission. Daily 8am–4pm.

Pololu Valley Lookout ★★★ NATURAL ATTRACTION At this end-of-the-road scenic lookout, you can gaze at the vertical dark-green cliffs of the Hamakua Coast and two islets offshore or peer back into the often-misty uplands. The view may look familiar once you get here—it often appears on travel posters. Linger if you can; adventurous travelers can take a switchback trail (a good 45-min. hike) to a secluded black-sand beach at the mouth of a wild valley once planted in taro; bring water and bug spray and avoid the strong currents in the surf.

At the end of Hwy. 270, 5½ miles east of Kapaau.

Pua Mau Place ★ GARDEN Perched on the sun-kissed western slope of Kohala Mountain and dotted with deep, craggy ravines is one of Hawaii's most unusual botanical gardens, Pua Mau Place, a 45-acre oasis with breathtaking views of both the ocean and the majestic mountains. It's dedicated to plants that are "ever-blooming," an expansive collection of continuously flowering tropical flowers, trees, and shrubs that can handle the arid heat (in other words, don't expect orchids). The gardens also have peacocks and wild turkeys, which children are invited to feed, and a unique hibiscus maze planted with some 200 varieties. Visitors can take the self-guided tour (a booklet is filled with the names and descriptions of all the plants) along mulched pathways, where every plant is clearly marked. The requested "donation" for admission to this nonprofit may seem steep to those who aren't diehard plant lovers, but gardeners will appreciate the setting, which includes a picnic area (snack and drinks are sold in the visitor center).

Pua Mau Place.

10 Ala Kahua Dr., Kawaihae. www.puamau. com. © **808/882-0888.** Admission $15 adults, $13 seniors, $5 students, free for children 9 and under. Daily 9am–4pm. Located off Hwy. 270 on Ala Kahua Dr. (in Kohala Estates), just north of Kawaihae. Turn at mile marker 6, head ½-mile uphill to the gate at lava rock wall.

WAIMEA & MAUNA KEA

Mauna Kea ★★★ The 13,796-foot summit of Mauna Kea, the world's tall-est mountain if measured from its base on the ocean floor, is one of the best

Mauna Kea.

places on earth for astronomical observations, thanks to its location in the tropics, pollution-free skies, and pitch-black nights. It's home to the world's largest telescopes—and more are planned, to the dismay of some Native Hawaiians—but the stargazing is fantastic even with the naked eye.

SAFETY TIPS Always check the weather and Mauna Kea road conditions before you head out (© 808/935-6268). Dress warmly; the temperatures drop into the 30s (around 0°C) after dark. Don't go within 24 hours of scuba diving, to avoid the bends, and stay well-hydrated in advance of your visit. Wear dark sunglasses to avoid snow blindness, use lots of sunscreen and lip balm, and bring a flashlight for night visits. Pregnant women, children under 13, and those with heart or lung conditions should skip this trip. **Note:** Since many rental-car agencies still ban the use of the recently improved Saddle Road, the only access to Summit Road (which requires a four-wheel-drive vehicle), those who can afford a private tour will find it's the safest bet (see "Seeing Stars While Others Drive," below).

VISITOR CENTER The **Onizuka Center for International Astronomy** (www.ifa.hawaii.edu/info/vis; © 808/961-2180), as the visitor center is formally known, lies about an hour from Hilo or Waimea, 6¼ miles up Summit Road and at 9,200 feet of elevation, above which people may start to feel light-headed. Named for Big Island native Ellison Onizuka, a victim of the 1986 *Challenger* explosion, it's open daily from 9am to 10pm (with 24-hr. restrooms), offering displays, interactive exhibits, and a bookstore with food and drink for sale, including hot items to take the chill off.

You can do also some serious **stargazing** from 6 to 10pm, for free. The program begins inside with a screening of "First Light," a documentary about the cultural and astronomical significance of Mauna Kea, and then offers visitors a chance to peer through telescopes at planets and other celestial phenomena, with a guide highlighting where to look. Feel free to bring your own telescope or binoculars, along with a flashlight (with a red filter, to avoid glare).

AT THE SUMMIT It's another 6 miles and 30 to 45 minutes to the summit from the visitor center, which offers **free summit tours** that begin with a caravan drive at 1pm Saturday and Sunday. You must be 16 or older and in good health (and not pregnant), and have a four-wheel-drive vehicle with plenty of fuel and low gears. Reservations are not required, but you must arrive at the visitor center by 1pm.

seeing stars **WHILE OTHERS DRIVE**

Don't want the hassle of driving yourself up Mauna Kea? Several excellent companies offer tour packages that provide cold-weather gear, dinner, hot drinks, guided stargazing, and, best of all, someone else to worry about maneuvering the narrow, unpaved road to the summit. All tours are offered weather permitting, but most nights are clear—that's why the observatories are here, after all. For both of the following tours, be sure to read the fine print on health restrictions before booking, and don't forget to tip your guide ($5–$10 per person).

o **Hawaii Forest & Trail** (www.hawaii-forest.com; ✆ **800/464-1993** or 808/331-8505), the island's premier environmentally and culturally oriented outfitter, operates a daily **Mauna Kea Summit & Stars Adventure,** including a late-afternoon picnic dinner, sunset at the summit, and stargazing at the visitor center, for $199. The company uses two customized off-road buses, with a maximum of 14 passengers each, for the 7- to 8-hour tour, open to ages 16 and older (due to high altitude). Tours depart from Hawaii Forest & Trail's headquarters in Kailua-Kona, Waikoloa Kings' Shops, and the junction of Saddle Road (Hwy. 200)

and Highway 190 south of Waikoloa Village.

o **Monty "Pat" Wright** was the first to run a sunset and stargazing tour on Mauna Kea when he launched **Mauna Kea Summit Adventures** (www.maunakea.com; ✆ **888/322-2366** or 808/322-2366) in 1983. Guests now ride in a large-windowed, 4WD van instead of a Land Cruiser and don hooded parkas instead of old sweaters, but otherwise it's much the same. The 7½- to 8-hour tour costs $204 (check for discounts on the website) and is open to children 14 and older. Pickups are in Kailua-Kona, Waikoloa Queens' MarketPlace, and the Highway 200/190 junction.

Up here, 11 nations have set up peerless infrared telescopes to look into deep space, making this the world's largest astronomical observatory. Two of the thirteen current telescopes are the world's biggest, eight stories high and both part of **Keck Telescope,** developed by the University of California and the California Institute of Technology. The **W. M. Keck Observatory** at the summit does not offer tours, but it does provide a visitor gallery with informational panels, restrooms, and a viewing area (behind a blue door) with partial views of the Keck Telescope and dome. Gallery hours are weekdays 10am to 4pm.

Also at the summit, up a narrow footpath, is a cairn of rocks; from here, you can see across the Pacific Ocean with a 360-degree view that's beyond words and pictures. On cloudy days, the summits of Mauna Loa and Maui's Haleakala appear like ships sailing in the mist. Here is where ancient astronomers and priests came to study the skies, and where modern cultural practitioners still worship today. Some are fighting to prevent even larger telescopes from being built atop Mauna Kea, which could alter these unparalleled view planes and sacred sites, such as **Lake Waiau.** At 13,020 feet above sea level, the lake is one of the highest in the world, and although drastically shrunken in recent years—from 100 yards wide to just 15 yards wide at press time—it has never dried up, even though it gets only 15 inches of rain a year. (Scientists suspect the lake is replenished by snowmelt and permafrost from submerged lava tubes.) You can't see the lake from Summit Road; you must take a brief hike: On the final approach to the summit, on the blacktop road, go about 600 feet to the major switchback and make a hard right turn. Park on the shoulder of the road and look for the obvious .5-mile trail leading down to the small, greenish lake. Follow the base of the big cinder cone on your left; the summit of Mauna Loa is in view directly ahead of you. **Note:** Please respect cultural traditions by not drinking or entering the water, and leave all rocks undisturbed, as well.

THE HAMAKUA COAST

Don't forget the bug spray when exploring this warm, moist environment, beloved by mosquitoes, and be prepared for passing showers. You're in rainbow territory here.

Akaka Falls State Park ★★★ NATURAL ATTRACTION   See one of Hawaii's most scenic waterfalls via a relatively easy .4-mile paved loop through a rainforest, past bamboo and flowering ginger, and down to an observation point. You'll have a perfect view of 442-foot Akaka Falls, plunging down a horseshoe-shape green cliff, and nearby Kahuna Falls, a mere 100-footer. Keep your eyes

Lake Waiau, inside the cinder cone just below the summit of Mauna Kea.

Akaka Falls.

peeled for rainbows. The chirping noise you hear is the sound of coqui frogs (see below). Facilities include restrooms and drinking water.

End of Akaka Falls Rd. (Hwy. 220), Honomu. From Hilo, drive north 8 miles on Hwy. 19 to left at Akaka Falls Rd. Follow 3½ miles to parking lot. $5 per car, $1 per person on foot or bicycle.

Hawaii Tropical Botanical Garden ★★ GARDEN   More than 2,000 species of tropical plants thrive in this little-known Eden by the sea. The 40-acre valley garden, nestled between the crashing surf and a thundering waterfall, includes torch gingers (which tower on 12-ft. stalks), a banyan canyon, an orchid garden, a banana grove, a bromeliad hill, an anthurium corner, and a golden bamboo grove, which rattles like a jungle drum in the trade winds. Some endangered Hawaiian specimens, such as the rare *Gardenia remyi,* flourish in this habitat. The self-guided tour takes about 90 minutes, but you're welcome to linger. Pick up a loaner umbrella in the visitor center, where you register, so that passing showers don't curtail your visit. **Note:** You enter the garden via a 500-foot-long boardwalk that descends along a verdant ravine. Free golf-cart assistance is provided for wheelchair users to reach the wheelchair-accessible path below; for those without wheelchairs but with limited physical ability, the cost to ride the cart there and back is $5.

27-717 Old Mamalahoa Hwy. (4-Mile Scenic Route), Papaikou. www.htbg.com. © **808/964-5233.** Admission $15 adults, $5 children 6–16, free for children 5 and under. Daily 9am–5pm (admissions end promptly at 4pm). From Hilo, take Hwy. 19 north 7 miles to right turn on Scenic Route; visitor center is 2 miles on the left.

Laupahoehoe Point ★ HISTORIC SITE/NATURAL ATTRACTION   This idyllic place holds a grim reminder of nature's fury. On April 1, 1946, a tsunami swept across the schoolhouse that once stood on this lava-leaf (that's what *laupahoehoe* means) peninsula and claimed the lives of 24 students and teachers, who had at first not known what to make of the receding waves that returned each time with more power. Their names are engraved on a stone memorial in this

Co-key, Co-key: What Is That Noise?

That loud, chirping noise you hear after dark, especially on the eastern side of the Big Island, is the cry of the male coqui frog looking for a mate. A native of Puerto Rico, where the frogs are kept in check by snakes, the coqui frog came to Hawaii in some plant material, found no natural enemies, and spread quickly across the Big Island (and a few sites off Oahu, Maui, and Kauai. A few frogs will sound like singing birds; a chorus of thousands—in Hawaii, they can reach densities of up to 10,000 an acre—can be deafening. In some places, like Akaka Falls, there are so many frogs that they are now chirping during daylight hours.

Coqui frogs don't like the cool weather of Waimea and Volcano as much, but anywhere else that's lush and rural is likely to have large populations. Pack earplugs if you're a light sleeper.

pretty little beach park, while a separate display holds newspaper stories on the tragedy. The land here ends in black sea stacks that resemble tombstones; when high surf crashes on them, it's positively spooky (and dangerous if you stand too close). The unprotected shoreline is not a place for swimming, but the views are spectacular. Facilities include restrooms, picnic tables, and drinking water.

Off Hwy. 19, Laupahoehoe Point exit, Laupahoehoe (25 miles north of Hilo, 31 miles south of Waimea).

Umauma Falls ★★ WATERFALL/GARDEN   Formerly accessed through the World Botanical Gardens (see below), the triple-tiered, cascading pools of Umauma Falls are now the exclusive province of visitors to the neighboring Umauma Experience, which offers an array of ziplining, hiking, swimming, and kayaking excursions on its lush 90 acres. The less adventurous can also just pay $10 to drive the paved road to the waterfall lookout, and then take a self-guided garden hike that crosses several bridges over the Umauma River. Pick up a map at the visitor center, which also sells sandwiches, snacks, and drinks. You can enjoy your repast at the river walk's observation area, under guava trees (feel free to sample their fruit when ripe), or on the visitor center's back lanai, which overlooks the river and the last line on the zip course (see "Ziplining" on p. 217).

31-313 Old Mamalahoa Hwy., Hakalau. www.umaumaexperience.com. Ⓒ **808/930-9477.** Admission $10 adults, free for children 11 and under; includes waterfall viewing, garden, and river walk. Daily 8am–5pm. Various times: Zipline tours $189–$239; hike/swim/picnic $125; kayak/swim/picnic $49. From Hilo, take Hwy. 19 north past mile marker 16, turn left on Leopolino Rd., then right on Old Mamalahoa Hwy., and follow ½-mile to entrance.

Waipio Valley ★★★ NATURAL ATTRACTION/HISTORIC SITE   This breathtakingly beautiful valley has long been a source of fascination, inspiring song and story. From the black-sand bay at its mouth, Waipio ("curving water") sweeps 6 miles between sheer, cathedral-like walls some 2,000 feet high. Hawaii's tallest waterfall, Hiilawe, tumbles down 1,300 feet from its rear cliffs. It's called "the valley of kings," in part due to the royal burial caves dotting its

A TASTE OF the hamakua coast

When the Hamakua Sugar Company—the Big Island's last sugar plantation—closed in 1996, it left a huge void in the local economy, transforming already shrinking villages into near ghost towns. But some residents turned to specialty crops that are now sought after by chefs throughout the islands. Hidden in the tall eucalyptus trees outside the old plantation community of Paauilo, the **Hawaiian Vanilla Company** ★★ (www.hawaiian vanilla.com; ℂ **808/776-1771**) is the first U.S. company to grow vanilla. It hosts one of the truly sensuous experiences on the Big Island—the **Hawaiian Vanilla**

Luncheon—plus shorter tastings and a weekly afternoon tea. Before you even enter the huge Vanilla Gallery, you will be embraced by the heavenly scent of vanilla. The four-course Hawaiian Vanilla Luncheon ($39 for age 12 and up; $19 for kids 4–11) takes place weekdays from 12:30 to 2:30pm; the 45-minute **Vanilla Tasting** ($25 for age 4 and up; free for kids 3 and under) is weekdays at 10:30am, and the **Upcountry Tea** ($29), including vanilla-flavored savories and desserts, occurs at 11am on Saturday. Reservations required.

forbiddingly steep walls. Some believe the ancient *ali'i* buried here rise up to become Marchers of the Night, whose chants reverberate through the valley. In a more modern mystery, the mystery thieves who stole the woven caskets of Hawaiian chiefs Liloa and Lonoikamakahiki from the Bishop Museum in 1994 are believed to have secretly reinterred them here.

Between 4,000 and 10,000 Hawaiians—including a young Kamehameha—are said to have lived here before Westerners arrived, growing taro in Waipio's stream-laced plain and catching fish beyond the surging shoreline. Chinese immigrants later joined them, but in 1946, the same tsunami that devastated Hilo and Laupahoehoe swept through the valley, washing away modest homes, shops, and other buildings, though luckily without fatalities. The town was never rebuilt, and later floods also discouraged regrowth. Only about 50 people live in the valley today, most with no electricity or phones, although others live above Waipio and come down on weekends to tend taro patches, camp, and fish.

To get to Waipio Valley, take Highway 19 from Waimea or Hilo to Highway 240 in Honokaa, and follow the highway almost 10 miles to Kukuihaele Road and the **Waipio Valley Lookout** ★★★, a grassy park on the edge of Waipio Valley's sheer cliffs, with splendid views of the wild oasis below. The lookout is a great place for a picnic; you can sit at old redwood tables and watch the white combers race along the black-sand beach at the mouth of the valley.

To explore the valley itself, it's best to go with a guided tour, for reasons of safety and access. The road in is extremely steep—averaging a 25-percent grade, and nearly 40 percent in places—as well as narrow and potholed; by law you must use a 4WD vehicle, and even then rental-car agencies ban drivers from taking it, to avoid very expensive tow jobs. Hiking down the 900-foot-road is hard on the knees going down and on your lungs coming up, while you have to watch out for cars in both directions. Once you're in the valley, most of the land and unpaved roads are privately owned, with trespassing actively discouraged. Those who try to see Hiilawe by walking toward it in streams may fall on slippery rocks or expose themselves to leptospirosis, a serious infection caused by bacteria that

Waipio Valley.

enter through cuts. The black-sand beach, though gorgeous, is not good for swimming or snorkeling and has no facilities. Locals understandably disapprove of people who leave all kinds of waste here, especially since unmarked burial sites lie just behind the beach.

Instead, book a ride on the **Waipio Valley Shuttle ★★** (www.waipiovalley shuttle.com; ✆ **808/775-7121**) for a 90- to 120-minute guided tour that begins with an exciting (and bumpy) drive down in an open-door van. Once on the valley floor, you'll be rewarded with breathtaking views of Hiilawe and its occasional twin falls, Hakalaoa, if conditions permit, plus a narrated tour of the taro patches (*lo'i*) and ruins from the 1946 tsunami. The tour is offered Monday through Saturday at 9 and 11am, and 1 and 3pm; tickets are $55 for adults and $28 for kids 10 and under; reservations are recommended. Check-in is less than a mile from the lookout at **Waipio Valley Artworks** (www.waipiovalleyartworks.com; ✆ **808/ 775-0958**), on Kukuihaele Road, a right turn from Highway 240 about 10 miles west of its intersection with Highway 19 in Honokaa.

Waipio Valley Artworks is also the pickup point for Naalapa Stables' **Waipio Valley Horseback Adventure ★★** (www.naalapastables.com; ✆ **808/755-4419**), offered at 9am and 12:30pm Monday through Saturday. After a van trip to the stables on the valley floor, you'll saddle up for a 2½-hour guided ride ($94) on rainforest trails and through streams on sure-footed horses from the hardy local stock. Wear long pants and covered shoes, and bring bottled water; children must be 8 or older.

All ages may take the mule-drawn surrey ride offered by **Waipio Valley Wagon Tours ★** (www.waipiovalleywagontours.com; ✆ **808/775-9518**), a narrated, 90-minute excursion that also begins with a van ride down to stables. Tours are offered Monday through Saturday at 10:30am and 12:30 and 2:30pm; cost is $60 for adults, $55 for seniors 65 and older, and $30 for children 3 to 12, Reservations are a must because weight distribution is a factor in who can ride when. Check-in is at **Neptune's Gardens Gallery** on Kukuihaele Road, a half-mile east of Waipio Valley Artworks (www.neptunesgarden.net; ✆ **808/775-1343**).

World Botanical Gardens ★ WATERFALL/GARDEN   Just north of Hilo is one of Hawaii's largest botanical gardens, with some 5,000 species. Although it no longer offers a vista of spectacular, triple-stacked Umauma Falls (see above), it still lays claim to a huge children's maze (second in size only to Dole Plantation's on Oahu), a tropical fruit arboretum, ethnobotanical and wellness gardens, and flower-lined walks. Waterfall lovers will be heartened to note that the owners have also created a road and trail leading to viewing areas above and below the previously hidden 100-foot Kamaee Falls, as well as a trail leading past a series of shorter, bubbling cascades in Hanapueo Stream. If that's just too peaceful for you, there are also Segway excursions ranging from 30 minutes to 3 hours ($57–$147) and a zipline tour ($147), which should be reserved in advance; rates include garden admission.

31-240 Old Mamalahoa Hwy., Hakalau. www.wbgi.com. © **888/947-4753** or 808/963-5427. Admission $13 adults, $6 teens 13–17, $3 children 5–12, free for children 4 and under. Guided 2-hr. garden tours $49 adults, $39 teens 13–17, $19 children 5–12, free for children 4 and under; 24-hr. advance reservation required. Daily 9am–5:30pm. From Hilo, take Hwy. 19 north past mile marker 16, turn left on Leopolino Rd., then right on Old Mamalahoa Hwy.; entrance is ⅒-mile on right.

HILO

Download the informative self-guided walking tour of Hilo, which focuses on 21 historic sites dating from the 1870s to the present, from the website of the **Downtown Hilo Improvement Association** (www.downtownhilo.com; © **808/935-8850**), which also has sightseeing guides for the greater area. Or pick up a copy in person at its office, 329 Kamehameha Ave., in the Mooheau Bus Depot.

Hilo Bay ★★★ NATURAL ATTRACTION   Old banyan trees shade **Banyan Drive ★**, the lane that curves along the waterfront from Kamehameha Avenue (Hwy. 19) to the Hilo Bay hotels. Most of the trees were planted in the mid-1930s by visitors like Cecil B. DeMille (here in 1933 filming "Four Frightened People"), Babe Ruth (his tree is in front of the Hilo Hawaiian Hotel), King George V, Amelia Earhart, and other celebrities, whose fleeting fame didn't last as long as the trees themselves.

It's worth a stop along Banyan Drive—especially if the coast is clear and the summit of Mauna Kea is free of clouds—to make the short walk across the concrete-arch bridge in front of the Hilo Naniloa Hotel to **Coconut Island (Moku Ola) ★**, if only to gain a panoramic sense of Hilo Bay and its surroundings.

Continuing on Banyan Drive, just south of Coconut Island, are **Liliuokalani Gardens ★★**, the largest formal Japanese garden this side of Tokyo. This 30-acre park, named for Hawaii's last monarch, Queen Liliuokalani, and dedicated in 1917 to the islands' first Japanese immigrants, is as pretty as a postcard, with stone lanterns, koi ponds, pagodas, rock gardens, bonsai, and a moon-gate bridge. Admission is free; it's open 24 hours.

Lyman Museum & Mission House ★ HISTORIC SITE   Yankee missionaries Rev. David and Sarah Lyman had been married for just 24 days before they set sail for Hawaii in 1832, arriving 6 months later in a beautiful but utterly foreign land. Seven years later, they built this two-story home for their growing family (eventually seven children) in a blend of Hawaiian and New England design, with plastered walls, koa floors, and lanais on both floors. Long a museum of 19th-century missionary life, the **Mission House** was completely restored in 2010, and Rev. Lyman's office in an 1845 annex was opened to the public for the first time. The annex now hosts exhibits on the Hilo Boarding School for young men, which the Lymans founded near their home, and 19th-century trade. Along with the rest of the house, which includes furnishings and other belongings of the Lymans, you can only visit it as part of a guided tour, offered twice daily except Sunday.

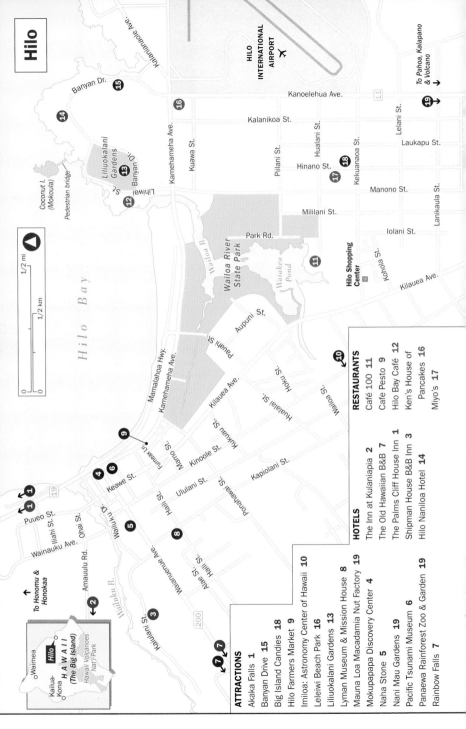

Hilo

Hilo Bay

Coconut I. (Mokuola)

Pedestrian bridge

Liliuokalani Gardens

Banyan Dr.

Kalanianaole Ave.

HILO INTERNATIONAL AIRPORT

Kanoelehua Ave.

Kalanikoa St.

Hualani St.

Lelani St.

Laukapu St.

Piilani St.

Hinano St.

Kekuanaoa St.

Manono St.

Lanikaula St.

Mililani St.

Iolani St.

Kohola St.

Kilauea Ave.

Hilo Shopping Center

Waiakea Pond

Wailoa River State Park

Park Rd.

Wailoa R.

Kamehameha Ave.

Kuawa St.

Lihiwai St.

Banyan Dr.

To Pahoa, Kalapana & Volcano →

1/2 mi
1/2 km

Aupuni St.

Paani St.

Hoku St.

Wailoa St.

Kamehameha Ave.

Mamalahoa Hwy.

Kilauea Ave.

Hualalai St.

Mamo St.

Kukuau St.

Kinoole St.

Kapiolani St.

Ponahawai St.

Kalanikoa St.

Turnea Ln.

Keawe St.

Ululani St.

Haili St.

Wainuku Dr.

To Honomu & Honokaa ↑

Puueo St.

Pauahi St.

Wainaku Illahi St.

Ohai St.

Wainaku Ave.

Amauulu Rd.

Waianuenue Ave.

Kaiulani St.

Akee St.

Haili St.

To Honomu & Honokaa

Waimea

HAWAII
(The Big Island)

Hilo

Kailua-Kona

Hawaii Volcanoes Nat'l Park

Wailuku R.

ATTRACTIONS

Akaka Falls **1**
Banyan Drive **15**
Big Island Candies **18**
Hilo Farmers Market **9**
Imiloa: Astronomy Center of Hawaii **10**
Leleiwi Beach Park **16**
Liliuokalani Gardens **13**
Lyman Museum & Mission House **8**
Mauna Loa Macadamia Nut Factory **19**
Mokupapapa Discovery Center **4**
Naha Stone **5**
Nani Mau Gardens **19**
Pacific Tsunami Museum **6**
Panaewa Rainforest Zoo & Garden **19**
Rainbow Falls **7**

HOTELS

The Inn at Kulaniapia **2**
The Old Hawaiian B&B **7**
The Palms Cliff House Inn **1**
Shipman House B&B Inn **3**
Hilo Naniloa Hotel **14**

RESTAURANTS

Café 100 **11**
Cafe Pesto **9**
Hilo Bay Café **12**
Ken's House of Pancakes **16**
Miyo's **17**

176

The larger **Lyman Museum** complex next door gives a broader perspective of Hawaiian history and culture. Walk through a lava tube and check out life-size displays of sea life in the **Earth Heritage Gallery,** where exhibits include renowned collections of seashells and mineral rocks (the rare orlymanite was named for David and Sarah's great-grandson Orlando Lyman.) The **Island Heritage Gallery** examines the life of early Hawaiians, with artifacts such as stone poi pounders, wooden bowls, and *kapa*, the delicate bark cloth. Another exhibit focuses on the five major immigrant groups from the era of sugar plantations, starting in the late 19th century. Another gallery offers well-organized special exhibits, many featuring the work of island artists, photographers, and artisans.

276 Haili St. (at Kapiolani St.). www.lymanmuseum.org. © **808/935-5021.** Admission $10 adults, $8 seniors 60 and over, $3 children 6–17; $21 per family. Mon–Sat 10am–4:30pm; guided house tours at 11am and 2pm (call to reserve).

Maunaloa Macadamia Nut Factory ★ FACTORY TOUR You'll drive through 3 miles of macadamia nut orchards before you reach the visitor center of this factory, where you can learn how Hawaii's favorite nut is grown and processed. (Try to come Mon–Sat, when the actual husking, drying, roasting, and candy-making takes place.) Of course, you'll want to try a few samples while you're here.

16-701 Macadamia Nut Rd., Keaau (5 miles from Hilo, 20 miles from Hawaii Volcanoes National Park). www.maunaloa.com. © **888/628-6256** or 808/966-8618. Free admission; self-guided

IMILOA: EXPLORING THE unknown

The star attraction, literally and figuratively, of Hilo is **Imiloa: Astronomy Center of Hawaii ★★★**. The 300 exhibits in the 12,000-square-foot gallery make the connection between the Hawaiian culture and its explorers, who "discovered" the Hawaiian Islands, and the astronomers who explore the heavens from the observatories atop Mauna Kea. 'Imiloa, which means "explorer" or "seeker of profound truth," is the perfect name for this architecturally stunning center, overlooking Hilo Bay on the University of Hawaii at Hilo Science and Technology Park campus, 600 Imiloa Place (www.imiloahawaii.org; © **808/969-9700**). Plan to spend at least a couple of hours here; a half-day would be better, to allow time to browse the excellent, family-friendly interactive exhibits on astronomy and Hawaiian culture, and to take in one of the planetarium shows, which boast a state-of-the-art digital projection system. You'll also want to stroll through the native plant garden, and grab a power breakfast or lunch in the **Sky Garden Restaurant** (© **808/969-9753**), open 7am to 4pm Tuesday through Sunday; the restaurant is also open for dinner Thursday through Sunday from 5 to 8:30pm. The center itself is open Tuesday through Sunday from 9am to 5pm; admission is $18 for adults, $16 for seniors, and $10 for children 4 to 12; extra planetarium shows are $5 for adults and $3 for children.

factory tours. Daily 8:30am–5pm (factory closed Sun and holidays). Heading south from Hilo on Hwy. 11, turn left on Macadamia Nut Rd. and head 3 miles to factory.

Mokupapapa Discovery Center ★★ MUSEUM You may never get to the vast coral-reef system that is the Northwest Hawaiian Islands—the protected chain of islets and atolls spanning 1,200 nautical miles is remote (stretching from Nihoa, 155 miles northwest of Kauai, to Kure Atoll, 56 miles west of Midway), and visitation is severely limited. But enough people have been intrigued by the wonders of this Marine National Monument that in spring 2014 its educational center moved into much larger quarters in a handsomely renovated, century-old building on the Hilo waterfront. The new center has 20,000 square feet to reveal the beauties and mysteries of the region's ecosystem and its relationship with Hawaiian culture—a prime reason why the region was named a World Heritage Site in 2010. Exhibits include a 3,500-gallon saltwater aquarium; wall panels and interactive displays; and a giant mural by Hilo artist Layne Luna, who also created the life-size models of giant fish, sharks, and the manta ray. Both the content and the cost of admission—free—are great for families.

76 Kamehameha Ave. (at Waianuenue Ave.). www.papahanaumokuakea.gov/education/center. html. © **808/935-8358.** Free admission. Tues–Sat 9am–4pm.

Naha Stone HISTORIC SITE Tradition holds that this massive stone was brought to Hilo from the sacred valley of Wailua, Kauai, centuries ago, and was later used as a test of royal heritage and strength. If the infant of an *ali'i* was placed on the stone and didn't cry, its chiefly status was confirmed. The ability to lift the 2½-ton boulder was also a sign of royal power. Kamehameha is said to have hoisted the stone in 1789. **Note:** Please don't sit or stand on the stone, which is considered an important cultural resource.

In front of the Hilo Public Library, 300 Waianuenue Ave.

Nani Mau Gardens ★ GARDEN In 1972 Makato Nitahara turned a 20-acre papaya patch just outside Hilo into a tropical garden. Today Nani Mau (Forever Beautiful) holds more than 2,000 varieties of plants, from fragile hibiscus, whose blooms last only a day, to durable red anthuriums imported from South America. It also has rare palms, a fruit orchard, Japanese gardens (with a bell tower built without nails), an orchid walkway, and a ginger garden. The gardens went through a rough patch a few years ago, even closing the doors before Los Angeles tour operator Helen Koo purchased the site in 2012. With the help of four full-time gardeners working around the clock, she reopened the gardens in 2013, along with a restaurant that offers a surprisingly delicious buffet lunch ($15), with a steep discount if you purchase admission and lunch at the same time.

421 Makalika St. www.nanimaugardens.com. © **808/959-3500.** Admission $5 adults, $4 seniors, $3 children 4–10; with lunch, $16 adults, $14 seniors, $13 children 4–10. Daily 10am–4pm. Go 3 miles south of Hilo Airport on Hwy. 11, turn on Makalika St., and continue ¾-mile.

Pacific Tsunami Museum ★ MUSEUM Poignant exhibits on Japan's 2011 tsunami (which also caused significant property damage on the Big Island) and the 2004 Indian Ocean tragedy have broadened the international perspective in this compact museum in a former bank, which also offers displays explaining the science of the deadly phenomenon. Still, the stories and artifacts related to Hilo's two most recent catastrophic tsunamis are impressive, including a parking meter nearly bent in two by the force of the 1960s killer wave, and accounts from survivors of the 1946 tsunami that washed away the school at Laupahoehoe. Many of the volunteers have hair-raising stories of their own to share—but you'll feel better after reading about the warning systems now in place.

130 Kamehameha Ave. (at the corner of Kalakaua Ave.). www.tsunami.org. © **808/935-0926.** Admission $8 adults, $7 seniors, $4 children 6–17, free for children 5 and under. Mon–Sat 9am–4pm.

Panaewa Rainforest Zoo & Gardens ★ ZOO/GARDEN   This 12-acre zoo, in the heart of the Panaewa Forest Reserve south of Hilo, is the only outdoor rainforest zoo in the United States. Some 80 species of animals from rainforests around the globe call Panaewa home—including several endangered Hawaiian birds and "Kona nightingales," the wild donkeys that have been virtually eliminated from Kona, where they once worked on coffee farms and startled motorists after they started running wild. All of the animals are exhibited in a natural setting. Sadly, the zoo's most famous resident, a 15-year-old white Bengal tiger named Namaste, had to be euthanized in 2014, but there are still cute pygmy goats, capuchin monkeys, and giant anteaters, among other critters, to enjoy at this free attraction.

800 Stainback Hwy., Keaau (off Hwy. 11, 5 miles south of its intersection with Hwy. 19 in downtown Hilo). www.hilozoo.com. © **808/959-7224.** Free admission. Daily 9am–4pm. Petting zoo Sat 1:30–2:30pm.

Rainbow Falls (Waianuenue) ★ WATERFALL   Go in the morning, around 9 or 10am, just as the sun comes over the mango trees, to see Rainbow Falls, or Waianuenue, at its best. Part of **Wailuku River State Park,** the 80-foot falls (which can be slender in times of drought) spill into a big round natural pool surrounded by wild ginger. If you're lucky, you'll catch the rainbow created in the falls' mist. According to legend, Hina, the mother of Maui, once lived in the cave behind the falls. Swimming in the pool is not allowed, but you can follow a trail left through the trees to the top of the falls (watch your step). About 2 miles upriver, the Wailuku also passes through a picturesque series of hexagonal pools nicknamed **Boiling Pots,** although the often-bubbling water is actually cool. From the parking lot at Rainbow Falls, take Rainbow Drive to Waianuenue Avenue, and follow it another 1¾ miles west to a right on Peepee Falls Road, named for the falls (pronounced "peh-eh-peh-eh") that feed the Boiling Pots. There's a parking lot at the end of the road. It's a local swimming and diving hole, but both activities are risky—waters can rise quickly after a cloudburst.

Off Rainbow Dr., just past the intersection of Waianuenue Ave. (Hwy. 200) and Puuhina St. www.hawaiistateparks.org. Free admission.

PUNA

Most visitors will understandably want to head straight to **Hawaii Volcanoes National Park** ★★★ (p. 182) when exploring this region, where Pele still consumes the land and creates still more. But the celebrated national park is far from the only place where you can experience Puna's geothermal wonders, or see the destruction the volcano has wrought.

The easiest way to explore the **Pahoa-Kapoho-Kalapana** triangle is to start by taking Highway 130 west from Pahoa about 9 miles to Kalapana. Along the way, you'll pass **steam vents** ★★★ on the ocean side of the two-lane highway in the Keauohana Forest Reserve, near mile marker 15. (Though some have been used as natural saunas, do not enter the caves on your own.) **Star of the Sea Painted Church** ★ will also be on your left, shortly before Highway 130 meets Highway 137. The wooden church was moved here in advance of the 1990 lava flow that destroyed area homes, buried the black-sand beach at Kaimu, and severed the highway link to Chain of Craters Road in the national park. Now whenever glowing lava is visible on the distant *pali* (cliffs), or steam clouds are billowing from lava pouring into the sea, Hawaii County stages an evening **lava viewing area** at the end of Highway 130 (call © **808/961-8093** to check if it's open).

In Kalapana, you'll want to see the **new black-sand beach,** reached by walking carefully along a short red-cinder trail, past fascinating fissures and dramatically craggy rocks. A crafts stand near the start often has sprouting coconuts for you to wedge into the ground, available for a few dollars' donation; no digging is required—like the ohia lehua that have started to reappear here, coconut palms are used to tough conditions. So are the people of Puna, who gather in great numbers at the open-air **Uncle Robert's Awa Club** for the Wednesday night market and Hawaiian music on Fridays. During the day, it's open for snacks and drinks, sold "by donation" for permit purposes (don't worry, they'll let you know exactly how much to donate).

From Kalapana/Kaimu, you'll pick up Highway 137 (the Kapoho-Kalapana Rd.), and follow it east to Kapoho along 15 miles of nearly pristine coastline, past parks, forests, rugged beaches, and tide pools, some geothermally heated. The highway is nicknamed the **Red Road,** for the terra-cotta-hued cinders once used to pave it, although it's now mostly covered by black asphalt.

The adventurous (or exhibitionists) may want to make the tricky hike down to unmarked **Kehena Black Sand Beach,** off Highway 137 about 3½ miles east of Kalapana. Here the law against public nudity is widely ignored, although the view of the ocean is usually more entrancing. (Clothed or not, avoid going into the water—currents are dangerous.) It's easier to take a brief detour to see the waves pounding the base of ironwood-shaded cliffs in the **Makenzie State Recreation Area,** 9 miles northeast of Kalapana, before heading another 3 miles farther to the scenic "hot pond" at **Ahalanui Park ★★** (see below); both have picnic facilities.

From Ahalanui, Highway 137 veers inland; drive 1¾ miles to a right turn on Kapoho Kai Road and follow it for a mile to the small parking area for the **Waiopae Tide Pools ★**, a state marine-life conservation district (state.hi.us/dlnr/dar/mlcd_waiopae.html). Snorkelers will go crazy here, but with proper footwear, you can walk along the edges of numerous tide pools, many very shallow and teeming with coral and fish, while the breakers crash in the distance. (**Note:** The private road and parking lot are maintained by the community, with a volunteer usually on hand to collect a $3 fee.)

Back on Highway 137, head 1 mile north to Kapoho Beach Road. On your left is the **Green Lake Fruit Stand,** named for the unusual, freshwater **Green Lake,** inside nearby **Kapoho Crater ★**. The lake is actually a crater within the 360-foot-tall Kapoho Crater, formed 200 to 400 years ago. If she's not at the stand, call caretaker Smiley Burrows (© **808/965-5500**) to arrange a scenic hike or drive up the crater for $5. (You can also swim in the lake, one of only two on the island, but no one knows its depths, and algae sometimes obscure the water.)

Just past the Green Lake Fruit Stand, Highway 137 intersects Highway 132 (Kapoho Rd.). A right turn onto an unpaved portion leads to Hawaii's easternmost point and the **Cape Kumukahi Lighthouse ★**, which miraculously survived the 1960 lava flow that destroyed the original village of Kapoho. Who cares if its modern steel frame isn't all that quaint? The fact that it's standing at all is impressive—the molten lava parted in two and flowed around it—while its bright-white trusses make a great contrast in photos against the black lava, dotted with a few green trees and framed by a cerulean sea.

A left turn onto Highway 132 takes you back 9 miles to the funky, somewhat ramshackle village of Pahoa, passing eerie **Lava Tree State Monument ★★** (see below) and the towering monkeypod and invasive albizia trees of **Nanawale Forest Reserve** as you go. *Note:* If you're heading to Hilo, take the Highway 130 bypass road all the back to Highway 11, about 14 miles from Pahoa; if you're heading toward Volcano, you'll pick up another bypass in Keaau, about a mile before Highway 130 intersects Highway 11.

Ahalanui Park (Hot Pond) ★★ PARK   Warmed by one of the area's many volcanically heated springs, this balmy, shallow pool lined with lava rocks and shady trees is protected from the surging ocean by a concrete wall, although very high surf can crash over it. It's not a snorkeling site per se, but silver fish use inlets to dart around the pool's usually clear waters, while a few eels hide in the rocks (if you don't bother them, they won't bother you). Shaded by tall palms, it's a pretty setting even if you don't plan to go into the water (which you shouldn't if you have any open cuts, due to possible bacteria, although the county does perform regular tests). Facilities include a lifeguard, picnic tables, and porta-potties—wear your bathing suit under your clothes so you don't have to change in one.

Ocean side of Hwy. 137, between mile markers 10 and 11, Pahoa (9 miles southeast of town). Free admission. Daily 7am–7pm (closed till 1pm 2nd Wed each month for maintenance).

Lava Tree State Monument ★★ NATURAL ATTRACTION   In 1790, a fast-moving lava flow raced through a grove of ohia lehua trees here, cooling quickly and creating lava rock molds of their trunks. Today the ghostly sentinels punctuate a well-shaded, paved .7-mile loop trail through the rich foliage of the 17-acre park. Facilities include restrooms and a few spots for picnicking (or ducking out of the rain during one of the area's frequent showers). Some areas with deep fissures are fenced off, but keep to the trail regardless for safe footing.

Off Hwy. 132 (Pahoa–Pohoiki Rd.), 2¾ miles southeast of Pahoa. Free admission. Daily during daylight hours.

Star of the Sea Painted Church ★ RELIGIOUS/HISTORIC SITE   From the outside, this could be just another quaint wooden church, pale mint green with white trim around its arched windows, entrance, and belfry. But from the inside, it's a wonderful kaleidoscope, starting with the detailed life-size paintings of Bible scenes and Catholic teachings by Father Evarist Gielen, the Belgian priest who built the church in Kaimu in 1928. In the 1940s, American-born artists added vivid *trompe l'oeil* frescoes and painted depictions of Father Damien, who spent 8 years on the island of Hawaii before devoting his life to the sufferers of leprosy (now called Hansen's disease) exiled to Molokai. The story of how this jewel box got here is equally colorful: To save it from being slowly devoured by the 1990 lava flow, locals hoisted it onto a trailer and moved it up the road. They moved the church again in 1996, when it was restored to its present state. Donations are appreciated to help with upkeep. Visitors are welcome, but note that Mass is held at 4pm the first Friday of the month.

Hwy. 130, between mile markers 19 and 20, Kalapana. Free admission. Daily 9am–4pm.

VOG & OTHER volcanic VOCABULARY

Hawaii's volcanoes have their own unique vocabulary. The lava that resembles ropy swirls of brownie batter is called **pāhoehoe** (pa-hoy-hoy); it results from a fast-moving flow that ripples as it moves. The chunky, craggy lava that looks like someone put asphalt in a blender is called **'a'ā** (ah-ah); it's caused by lava that moves slowly, breaking apart as it cools and then overruns itself. Newer words include **vog,** which is smog made of volcanic gases and smoke, and **laze,** which results when sulfuric acid hits the water and vaporizes, and mixes with chlorine to become, as any chemistry student knows, hydrochloric acid. Both vog and laze sting your eyes and can cause respiratory illness; don't expose yourself to either for too long. Since Halemaumau began spewing its dramatic plume of smoke in 2008, vog has been more frequent, particularly on the Kona and Kohala coasts, thanks to wind patterns. The state **Department of Health** (www.hiso2index.info) lists current air-quality advisories for the Big Island, based on sulfur dioxide levels.

HAWAII VOLCANOES NATIONAL PARK ★★★

Before tourism became Hawaii's middle name, the islands' singular attraction for visitors wasn't the beach, but the volcano. From the world over, curious spectators gathered on the rim of Kilauea's Halemaumau crater to see one of the greatest wonders of the globe. Nearly a century after it was named a national park (in 1916), **Hawaii Volcanoes National Park** (www.nps.gov/havo; © **808/985-6000**) remains Hawaii's premier natural attraction, home to an active volcano and one of only two World Heritage Sites in the islands.

There's never a guarantee you'll see flowing lava—none was visible at press time—but it's undeniably spectacular even without liquid rocks (check the website for updates before you go). Still, after driving to the park, off Highway 11, about 100 miles from Kailua-Kona and 29 miles from Hilo, many visitors keep on driving, briefly pausing by the highlights along **Crater Rim Drive ★★★** before heading back to their hotels. To allow the majesty and *mana* (spiritual energy) of this special place to sink in, you should really take at least 3 days—and certainly 1 night—to explore the park, including its miles of trails.

Fortunately, the admission fee ($10 per vehicle, $5 per bicyclist or hiker) is good for 7 days. Be prepared for rain and bring a jacket, especially in winter, when it can be downright chilly at night, in the 40s or 50s (single digits to mid-teens Celsius). *Note:* For details on hiking and camping in the park, see "Hiking" (p. 212) and "Camping" (p. 233).

Crater Rim Drive Tour

Stop by the **Kilauea Visitor Center** (daily 7:45am–5pm) to get the latest updates on lava flows and the day's free ranger-led tours and watch an informative 25-minute film, shown on the hour from 9am to 4pm. Just beyond the center lies vast **Kilauea Caldera ★★★**, a circular depression nearly 2 miles by 3 miles and 540 feet deep. It's easy to imagine Mark Twain marveling over the sights here in 1866, when a wide, molten lava lake bubbled within view in the caldera's **Halemaumau Crater ★★★**, itself 3,000 feet across and 300 feet deep.

Hawaii Volcanoes National Park.

Though different today, the caldera's panorama is still compelling. Since 2008, a towering plume of ash, visible from miles away, has billowed from Halemaumau, the legendary home of Pele. The sulfurous smoke has forced the ongoing closure of nearly half of Crater Rim Drive, now just a 6-mile crescent. The fumes normally drift northwest, where they often create vog (see "Vog & Other Volcanic Vocabulary" on p. 182), to the dismay of Kona residents. (Scientists monitor the park's air quality closely, just in case the plume changes direction, with rangers ready to evacuate the park quickly if needed.) In the evening the pillar of smoke turns a rosy red, reflecting the lava lake that rises and falls deep below. You can also admire Halemaumau's fiery glow over a drink or dinner in **Volcano House ★★** (p. 232), the only inn in the park.

Less than a mile from the visitor center, several **steam vents ★★★** line the rim of the caldera, puffing out moist warm air. Across the road, a boardwalk leads through the stinky, smoking **sulphur banks ★★★**, called Haakulamanu in Hawaiian, and home to hardy ohia lehua trees and unfazed native birds. (As with all trails here, stay on the path to avoid possible serious injury, or worse.)

Shortly before Crater Rim Drive closes to traffic (due to the current eruption), the **observation deck ★★★** at **Thomas A. Jaggar Museum ★★** offers a prime spot for viewing the crater and its plume, especially at night. By day you can also see the vast, barren Kau Desert and the massive sloping flank of Mauna Loa. The museum itself is open daily 8:30am to 7:30pm, with free admission. The museum shows video from days when the volcano was really spewing, explains the cultural significance of Pele, and tracks earthquakes (a precursor of eruptions) on a seismograph. There's also a gift shop here.

Heading southeast from the visitor center, Crater Rim Drive passes by the smaller but still impressive **Kilauea Iki Crater ★★**, which in 1959 was a roiling lava lake spewing lava 1,900 feet into the air. From here, you can walk or drive to **Thurston Lava Tube ★★★**, a 500-year-old lava cave in a pit of giant tree ferns. Known in Hawaiian as Nahuku, it's partly illuminated, but take a flashlight and wear sturdy shoes so you can explore the unlit area for another half-mile or so.

Continuing on Crater Rim Drive leads to the **Puu Puai Overlook ★** of Kilauea Iki, where you find the upper trailhead of the aptly named half-mile **Devastation Trail ★★**, an easy walk through a cinder field that ends where Crater Rim Drive meets **Chain of Craters Road ★★★**.

Pedestrians and cyclists only can continue on Crater Rim Drive for the next .8 mile of road, closed to vehicular traffic since the 2008 eruption began. The little-traveled pavement leads to **Keanakakoi Crater ★★**, scene of several eruptions in the 19th and 20th centuries and yet another dazzling perspective on the Kilauea Caldera. Turn your gaze north for an impressive view of Mauna Loa and Mauna Kea, the world's two highest mountains, when measured from the sea floor.

Chain of Craters Road ★★★

It's natural to drive slowly down the 19-mile **Chain of Craters Road,** which descends 3,700 feet to the sea and ends in a thick black mass of rock from a 2003 lava flow. You feel like you're driving on the moon, if the lunar horizon were a brilliant blue sea. Make sure you have food and water for the journey, since there are officially no concessions after you pass the Volcano House; the nearest fuel lies outside the park, in Volcano Village.

Two miles down, before the road really starts twisting, the one-lane, 8½-mile **Hilina Pali Road ★★** veers off to the west, crossing windy scrublands and old lava flows. The payoff is at the end, where you stand nearly 2,300 feet above the coast along the rugged 12-mile *pali* (cliff). Some of the most challenging trails in the park, across the Kau Desert and down to the coast, start here.

Back on Chain of Craters Road, 9¾ miles below the Crater Rim Drive junction, the picnic shelter at **Kealakomo ★★** provides another sweeping coastal vista. At mile marker 16.5, you'll see the pullout parking lot for **Puu Loa ★★★**, an enormous field of some 23,000 petroglyphs—the largest in the islands. A three-quarter-mile, gently rolling lava trail leads to a boardwalk where you can view the stone carvings, 85 percent of which are holes known as cupules; Hawaiians often placed their infants' umbilical cords in them.

At the end of Chain of Craters Road, a lookout area allows a glimpse of 90-foot **Holei Sea Arch ★★**, one of several striking formations carved in the cliffs by the ocean's fury. Stop by the ranger station before treading carefully across the 21st-century lava, "some of the youngest land on Earth," as the park calls it. In the distance you may spot fumes from the Puu Oo vent, steam clouds in the ocean, or a red glow at night. Bear in mind it's a slow drive back up at night.

KAU

At the end of 11 miles of bad road that peters out at Kaulana Bay, in the lee of a jagged, black-lava point, you'll find *Ka Lae* ("The Point")—the tail end of the United States. From the tip, the nearest continental landfall is Antarctica, 7,500

THE BRUTE FORCE OF THE volcano

Volcanologists refer to Hawaii's volcanic eruptions as "quiet" eruptions because gases escape slowly instead of building up and exploding violently all at once. The Big Island's eruptions produce slow-moving, oozing lava that generally provide excellent, safe viewing when they're not in remote areas.

Even so, Kilauea has still caused its share of destruction. Since the current eruption began on January 3, 1983, lava has covered some 50 square miles of lowland and rainforest, ruining 215 homes and businesses, wiping out the pretty, black-sand beach of Kaimu, and burying other landmarks. Kilauea has also added more than 500 acres of new land on its southeastern shore. (Be aware such land occasionally falls under its own weight and slides into the ocean.)

The most prominent vent of the eruption has been Puu Oo, a 760-foot-high cinder-and-spatter cone 10 miles east of Kilauea's summit, in an off-limits natural reserve. When its lava flows to the sea, about 7 miles away, the county opens a **public viewing area** in Kalapana (*©* **808/961-8093**), and companies such as **Lava Ocean Adventures** (www.seelava.com; *©* **808/966-4200**) offer boat tours that come seemingly perilously close to the lava, hissing where it oozes into the water.

Scientists are also keeping an eye on Mauna Loa, which has been swelling since its last eruption in 1984, and Hualalai, which hovers above Kailua-Kona and last erupted in 1801.

miles away. It's a rugged 2-mile hike down a cliff from South Point to the anomaly known as **Green Sand Beach ★★**, described on p. 195. Beware the big waves that lash the shore there.

Kahuku Unit, Hawaii Volcanoes National Park ★★ NATURAL ATTRACTION   Few visitors (or even residents) are familiar with this 116,000-acre portion of the national park, some 24 miles from the Kilauea Visitor Center and accessible only since 2009. But if your timing is right—it's only open weekends, and closed the first Saturday of each month as well as holidays—you can hike, bike, or drive to see a forested pit crater, cinder cone, and tree molds from an 1866 lava flow, plus ranch-era relics. Admission is free and rangers frequently lead free hikes. *Note:* There are restrooms and picnic tables but no water; bring your own food and drinks.

Mountain side of Hwy. 11, between mile markers 70 and 71, Pahala. www.nps.gov/havo/planyourvisit/kahuku-hikes.htm. *©* **808/985-6000.** Free admission. Sat–Sun 9am–3pm; closed 1st Sat of each month.

Kau Coffee Mill ★ FACTORY TOUR   In the former sugarcane fields on the slopes of Mauna Loa, a number of small farmers are growing coffee beans whose quality equals—some say surpasses—Kona's. More and more tasting competitions seem to agree; in any case, this farm and mill in tiny Pahala provides an excellent excuse to break up the long drive to the main entrance of Hawaii Volcanoes National Park, 23 miles northeast. Free 45-minute guided tours are offered three times daily; enjoy tastings of coffee and macadamia nuts throughout the day in the pleasant visitor center. *Note:* The 10-day **Kau Coffee Festival** (www.kaucoffeefestival.com) in early May includes hikes, music, hula, farm tours, and plenty of coffee samples.

96-2694 Wood Valley Rd., Pahala. www.kaucoffeemill.com. © **808/928-0550.** Free admission. Daily 8:30am–4:30pm. Guided tours 10am, noon, and 2pm, weather permitting. From Kailua-Kona, take Hwy. 11 71 miles to a left on Kamani St., take 3rd right at Pikake St., which becomes Wood Valley Rd., and follow uphill 2½ miles to farm on left.

Kula Kai Caverns & Lava Tubes ★★ NATURAL ATTRACTION   Before you trudge up to Pele's volcanic eruption, take a look at its underground handiwork. Ric Elhard and Rose Herrera have explored and mapped out the labyrinth of lava tubes and caves, carved out over the past 1,000 years or so, that crisscross their property near South Point. Their "expeditions" range from the Lighted Trail tour, an easy, half-hour walk suitable for families, to longer (up to 2 hr.), more adventurous caving trips, where you crawl through tunnels and wind through labyrinthine passages (some restricted to kids 8 and older). Wear sturdy shoes. 92-8864 Lauhala Dr., Ocean View (46 miles south of Kailua-Kona). www.kulakaicaverns.com. © **808/929-9725.** Lighted Trail tour $20 adults, $15 children 6–12, free for children 5 and under; longer tours $60–$95 adults ($60–$65 children 8–12). By reservation only; gate security code provided at booking.

Organized Tours

Farms, gardens, historic houses, and other points of interest that may be open only to guided tours are listed under "Attractions & Points of Interest," above. For boat, kayak, bicycle, and similar tours, see listings under "Outdoor Activities."

HELICOPTER TOURS ★

Don't believe the brochures with pictures of fountains of lava and "liquid hot magma," as Dr. Evil would say. Although there no guarantees you'll see *any* red-hot lava (and for safety reasons, you're not going to fly all that close to it, anyway), a helicopter ride over hundreds of acres of hardened black lava, Kilauea's enormous fuming caldera, and the remote, still-erupting Puu Oo vent in Hawaii Volcanoes National Park nevertheless offers a unique perspective on any given day. And if you're pressed for time, a helicopter ride beats driving to the volcano and back from Kohala and Kona resorts.

Blue Hawaiian Helicopters ★★ (www.bluehawaiian.com; © **800/786-2583** or 808/886-1768), a professionally run, locally based company with comfortable, top-of-the-line copters, and pilots who are extremely knowledgeable about everything from volcanology to Hawaii lore, flies three different tours out of Waikoloa, at Highway 19 and Waikoloa Road. The 2-hour **Big Island Spectacular ★★** stars the volcano, tropical valleys, the Hamakua Coast waterfalls, and the Kohala Mountains, and costs $450 to $563 ($396–$495 online, which requires 5-day advance booking). If time is money for you, and you've got all that money, it's an impressive trip, particularly if you ride in the roomier and quieter Eco-Star. If you just want to admire waterfalls, green mountains, and the deep valleys, including Waipio, of North Kohala and the Hamakua Coast, the 50-minute **Kohala Coast Adventure** is a less exorbitant but reliably picturesque outing, costing $242 to $294 ($213–$259 online).

If you've "done" the volcano and have an adventurous spirit, consider the 2-hour **Big Island–Maui tour ★**, which includes the Kohala Mountains/ Hamakua waterfalls leg and also crosses the Alenuihaha Channel to Maui, where you view Haleakala Crater (a long-dormant volcano) and dozens of waterfalls in the verdant Hana rainforest. It costs $500 to $563 ($440–$495 online, with advance booking). Blue Hawaiian also operates out of the Hilo airport (© **808/961-5600**),

PLANTING A koa legacy tree

One of the most inspiring and memorable experiences I've ever had in Hawaii has been with **Hawaiian Legacy Tours** ★★★ (www.hawaiianlegacytours.com; ℂ **877/707-8733**), which allows visitors to help restore the native koa forest high above the Hamakua Coast. More koa means more native birds and less runoff, which can harm the reefs far below. Over its lifetime, the tree can also offset the carbon impact of a week's vacation on this beautiful island. The freshly baked scones that await in the welcome center are pretty awesome, too.

After you check in at the welcome center, itself a handsomely restored ranch house in the tiny village of Umikoa (at 3,200 ft. elevation), guides in ATVs, or a Pinzgauer six-wheeler for larger groups, drive you even higher up the misty slopes of Mauna Kea, to the former personal forest of King Kamehameha the Great. Later cleared for ranchland, these fields at 5,000 feet bear only a few remaining old-growth trees, from which Hawaiian Legacy Hardwoods (the tours' parent company) extracts seeds to propagate seedlings in its nurseries. Amid the new groves growing on the mountainside, where the *mana* (spiritual power) and beauty of your surroundings are spine-tingling, you'll be shown how to plant a seedling. You can dedicate it to a loved one on a special commemorative certificate, and you'll also receive its GPS coordinates, allowing you to monitor its growth via Google Earth.

The 2-hour **Planters Tour,** including one tree for planting, costs $110 for adults, $55 for kids 5 to 18, while the 3½-hour **Grand Tour,** which spends more time in the nurseries and on the Umikoa Trail, costs $180 for adults, $90 for kids 5 to 18. (Children's rates exclude a tree for planting, but additional trees may be purchased for $60 each.) Private tours and shuttles (from the Kona and Hilo airports, Four Seasons Resort Hualalai, and Hilo cruise terminal) are available for additional fees.

flying the 50-minute **Circle of Fire** ★★ tour, which is significantly cheaper—$223 to $274 ($196–$241 online)—because it's closer to the volcano and waterfalls. On the other hand, if you're willing to drive to Hilo, you really should continue on to the national park. *Tip:* Ask about a AAA discount when booking flights.

The similarly professional **Sunshine Helicopters** ★★ (www.sunshine helicopters.com; ℂ **866/501-7738** or 808/270-3999) offers a **Volcano Deluxe Tour** ★, including Kohala Mountains/Hamakua waterfalls, out of the Hapuna heliport, near the Mauna Kea Resort, but it's even more expensive: $560 to $635 ($510–$585 online) for the 105-minute ride. Less of a splurge—and less dependent on the ooh factor of oozing lava—is Sunshine's 30- to 40-minute **Kohala/Hamakua Coast Tour** ★★, which hovers waterfall-lined sea cliffs and the Pololu, Waimanu, and Waipio valleys, for $199 ($169 online).

Note: On all rides, your weight may determine where you sit in the helicopter. You should also dress in light layers; both cool rain and strong sun can occur.

VAN & BUS TOURS

Many of the outdoor-oriented, but not especially physically taxing, excursions of **Hawaii Forest & Trail** ★★★ (www.hawaii-forest.com; ℂ **800/464-1993** or

808/331-8505) include a significant time in vans heading to and from remote areas, with guides providing narration along the way. Thus, they're also a good way to see large chunks of the island without being behind the wheel yourself.

For those able to depart from Hilo, **Discover Hawaii** ★★ (www.discover hawaiitours.com; ✆ **808/690-9050**) offers the 9-hour **Volcano Eco-Adventure Tour,** covering all the major attractions of Hawaii Volcanoes National Park and scenic sites in Hilo. Led by expert guides, the small-group tours in large-windowed mini-coaches depart at 10:30am Monday to Thursday and Saturday. The cost is $135 for adults, $100 for children 2 and older, excluding lunch (there's a restaurant stop in Hilo where you pay your own way).

Kailua-Kona visitors can also book all-day volcano trips and "circle" tours, which include the black-sand **Punaluu Beach** ★★★ (p. 196), the national park, Hilo, and Waimea. The cheaper tours, such as those offered by **Roberts Hawaii** (www.robertshawaii.com; ✆ **800/831-5541** or 808/539-9400), use large buses, often with fewer stops and less informed narration than those of the smaller companies. I recommend going with a provider such as **KapohoKine Adventures** ★★ (www.kapohokine.com; ✆ **808/964-1000**), which offers a variety of tours from Kona and Hilo.

BEACHES

Too young geologically to have many great beaches, the Big Island instead has more colorful ones: brand-new black-sand beaches, salt-and-pepper beaches, and even a green-sand beach. If you know where to look, you'll also find some gorgeous pockets of golden sand off the main roads here and there, plus a few longer stretches of the soft stuff, often hidden from view by either acres of lava or high-end resorts. Thankfully, by law all beaches are public, so even the toniest hotel must provide access (including free parking) to its sandy shores. *Note:* Never leave valuables in your trunk, particularly in remote areas, and always respect the privacy of residents with homes on the beach. For more information on state beach parks, visit **www.hawaiistateparks.org**.

Note: You'll find relevant sites on the "Big Island" map on p. 158.

North Kona

KAHALUU BEACH ★★

The most popular beach on the Kona Coast has reef-protected lagoons and county park facilities that attract more than 400,000 people a year. Kahaluu is the best all-around beach off Alii Drive, with coconut trees lining a narrow salt-and-pepper-sand shore that gently slopes to turquoise pools. Schools of brilliantly colored tropical fish make this a great place to snorkel. In summer, it's also an ideal spot for children and beginning snorkelers; the water is so shallow you can just stand up if you feel uncomfortable—but please, not on the living coral, which can take years to recover. In winter, there's a rip current when the high surf rolls in; look for any lifeguard warnings. Kahaluu isn't the biggest beach on the island, but it's one of the best equipped, with off-road parking, beach-gear rentals, a covered pavilion, restrooms, barbecue pits, and a food concession. It gets crowded, so come early to stake out a spot. If you have to park on Alii Drive, be sure to poke your head into tiny, blue-roofed **St. Peter's by the Sea,** a Catholic chapel next to an old lava rock *heiau* where surfers once prayed for waves.

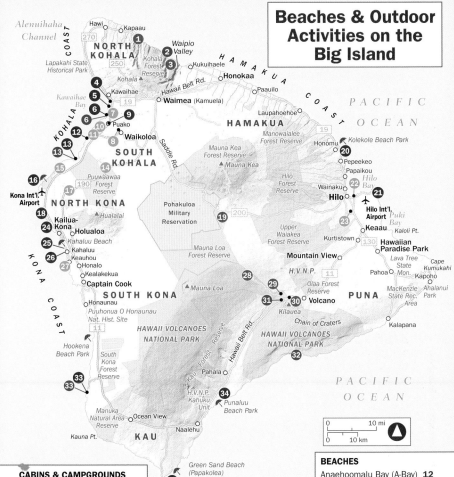

Beaches & Outdoor Activities on the Big Island

Alenuihaha Channel

Hawi ○
Kapaau ○
① Waipio Valley
②
③
Kukuihaele ○
Honokaa
Paauilo ○

NORTH KOHALA
Kohala Forest Reserve
Kohala ▲
Lapakahi State Historical Park
250
270

④
⑤
Kawaihae ○
Waimea (Kamuela)
Kawaihae Bay
19

⑥
⑥
⑦
⑨
Puako ○
⑫
⑩
⑪
⑧
Waikoloa

Laupahoehoe ○
Manowaialee Forest Reserve
Honomu ○
⑳ Kolekole Beach Park

HAMAKUA
HAMAKUA COAST

SOUTH KOHALA
Puuwaawaa Forest Reserve
⑭
190

⑬
⑬
⑮
Saddle Rd.
Mauna Kea Forest Reserve
▲ Mauna Kea

Pepeekeo ○
Papaikou ○
Wainaku ○
Hilo ○
②②
Hilo Bay
②①
Puki Bay

⑯
Kona Int'l. Airport
⑰

NORTH KONA
▲ Hualalai
Pohakuloa Military Reservation

Hilo Forest Reserve

Hilo Int'l. Airport
②③
Keaau ○
Kaloli Pt.

⑱
Kailua-Kona
②④
Holualoa ○
②⑤
Kahaluu Beach
Kahaluu ○
Keauhou ○
②⑥
②⑦
Honalo ○
Kealakekua ○
Captain Cook ○

200
19
⑲
Upper Waiakea Forest Reserve
Kurtistown ○

130
Hawaiian Paradise Park
Lava Tree State Mon.
Pahoa ○
Cape Kumukahi
Kapoho ○

KONA COAST
Honaunau ○
Puuhonua O Honaunau Nat. Hist. Site
11

SOUTH KONA
▲ Mauna Loa
Mauna Loa Forest Reserve

Mountain View ○
H.V.N.P.
28
29
11
⑳①
30
Volcano ○
Kilauea
Chain of Craters

PUNA
Olaa Forest Reserve
MacKenzie State Rec. Area
Ahalanui State Rec. Park
Kalapana ○

Hookena Beach Park
South Kona Forest Reserve
33
33

HAWAII VOLCANOES NATIONAL PARK
Kau Forest Reserve
Hawaii Belt Rd.
HAWAII VOLCANOES NATIONAL PARK
32

Manuka Natural Area Reserve
Ocean View ○
Kauna Pt.
KAU
Naalehu ○
Pahala ○
H.V.N.P. Kahuku Unit
34
Punaluu Beach Park

PACIFIC OCEAN
PACIFIC OCEAN

Green Sand Beach (Papakolea)
35

0 ─── 10 mi
0 ─── 10 km
▲

CABINS & CAMPGROUNDS
Hapuna Beach State Park **6**
Hawaii Volcanoes National Park
  Backcountry Camping **34**
Hookena Beach Park **33**
Kiholo State Park Reserve
Namakanipaio **31**
Waimanu Valley **2**

HIKES
Ala Kahakai National Historic Trail **4**
Kilauea Caldera Trails **29**
Kipuka Puaulu (Bird Park) Trail **29**
Mauna Loa Trail **28**
Muliwai Trail **3**
Puu Huluhulu Trail **19**
Pololu Valley Trail **1**

GOLF COURSES
Big Island Country Club **14**
Hapuna Golf Course **8**
Hilo Municipal Golf Course **23**
Hualalai Golf Course **15**
Kona Country Club **27**
Makalei Golf Club **17**
Mauna Kea Golf Course **7**
Mauna Lani Francis Ii Brown
  Championship Courses **10**
Naniloa Country Club **22**
Waikoloa Beach Resort
  Courses **11**
Waikoloa Village Golf Course **8**

BEACHES
Anaehoomalu Bay (A-Bay) **12**
Green Sand (Papakolea)
  Beach **35**
Hapuna Beach State Park **6**
Hookena Beach Park **33**
Kahuluu Beach Park **26**
Kaunaoa (Mauna Kea) Beach **5**
Kekaha Kai State Park **16**
Kiholo State Park Reserve **13**
Kohanaiki Beach **18**
Kolekole Beach Park **20**
Laaloa (White Sands) Beach **25**
Old Kona Airport State
  Recreation Area **24**
Punaluu Beach Park **34**
Spencer Beach Park **4**
Waialea Bay (Beach 69) **9**

KEKAHA KAI STATE PARK ★★

Formerly known as Kona Coast State Park, this beach park is known for its brilliant white sand offsetting even more brilliant turquoise water. With several sandy bays and coves well-hidden from the highway, the park has two official entrances. About 4½ miles north of the airport off Highway 19 (across from West Hawaii Veterans Cemetery) is the turnoff for Maniniowali Beach, better known as **Kua Bay.** A thankfully paved road crosses acres of craggy lava, leading to the parking lot and a short, paved walkway to an even shorter, sandy scramble down a few rocks to the beach. It has restrooms and showers, but absolutely no shade or drinking water, so come prepared. Locals flock here to sunbathe, swim, bodyboard, and bodysurf, especially on weekends, so go during the week, and in mornings, when it's cooler. If you have a 4WD vehicle, you can take the marked turnoff 2½ miles north of the airport off Highway 19 and drive 1½ bumpy miles over a rough lava road to the parking area for sandy **Mahaiula Beach,** reached by another short trail. Sloping more steeply than Kua Bay, this sandy beach has stronger currents than Kua Bay, although if you're fit you can still swim or snorkel in calm conditions. You can also just laze under the shade—you're likely to see a snoozing green sea turtle or two. A 4.5-mile coastal trail to Kua Bay starts at the north end of Mahaiula; about a mile in you pass white-sand **Makalawena Beach,** not safe for swimming but occasionally attractive to nude sunbathers. Midway on the trail, mostly on lava bed that radiates heat, is the 342-foot-high cinder cone **Puu Kuili,** which you can climb for a sweeping view. The state park is open daily from 9am to 7pm.

KIHOLO STATE PARK RESERVE ★★★

To give yourself a preview of why to come here, pull over at the marked Scenic Overlook on Highway 19 north of Kekaha Kai State Park, between mile markers 82 and 83. You'll see a shimmering pale blue lagoon, created by the remains of an ancient fish pond, and the bright cerulean **Kiholo Bay,** jewels in a crown of

Kekaha Kai State Park.

Kohanaiki Beach.

black lava. Now take the unmarked lava-gravel road (much smoother than Kekaha Kai's road to Mahaiula Beach) just south of the overlook and drive carefully to the end, taking the right fork for one of two parking areas, both a short walk from the shore (and both with portable toilets). The "beach" here is black sand, lava pebbles, and coral, but it's fine for sunbathing or spotting dolphins and seasonal humpback whales. Keep your sturdy-soled shoes on, though, because you'll want to keep walking north to **Keanalele** (also called "Queen's Bath"), a collapsed lava tube found amid kiawe trees with steps leading into its fresh water, great for a cooling dip. Continue on past several mansions to the turquoise waters of the former fishpond, cut off by a lava flow, and the darker bay, clouded by freshwater springs (not great for snorkeling). Green sea turtles love this area—as do scampering wild goats. The park opens at 7am daily year-round, with the access gate off the highway locked promptly at 7pm April to Labor Day (early Sept), and then at 6pm through March 31.

KOHANAIKI BEACH ★

Hidden behind the Kohanaiki golf course development, 2 miles north of the main entrance to Kaloko-Honokohau National Historical Park off Highway 19, the 1½ miles of shoreline here include a white-sand beach on a reef- and rock-lined bay that's home to a popular surf break called Pine Trees. Paddlers, snorkelers, and fishermen also flock to the rugged coastline, which officially became a county park in 2013, after years of negotiations with various stakeholders. The new status means improved access and parking, restrooms, showers, designated campgrounds, and a *halau* (covered pavilion) for cultural practices. From Highway 19 and Palani Road in Kailua-Kona, take the highway 4¾ miles north, turn left at the entrance to Kohanaiki and take the next right for beach access. It's open daily from 5:30am to 9pm (no camping Tues–Wed).

LAALOA BEACH (WHITE SANDS/MAGIC SANDS BEACH) ★★

Don't blink as you cruise Alii Drive, or you'll miss Laaloa, often called White Sands, Magic Sands, or Disappearing Beach. That's because the sand at this small pocket beach, about 4½ miles south of Kailua-Kona's historic center, does occasionally vanish, especially at high tide or during storms. On calm summer days, you can swim here, next to bodyboarders and bodysurfers taking advantage of the gentle shorebreak; you can also snorkel in a little rocky cove just to the south. In winter, though, a dangerous rip develops and waves swell, attracting expert surfers and spectators; stay out of the water then, but enjoy the gawking. The palm-tree-lined county beach park includes restrooms, showers, lifeguard station, and a small parking lot.

OLD KONA AIRPORT STATE RECREATION AREA ★

Yes, this used to be the airport for the Kona side of the island—hence the copious parking on the former runway, at the end of Kuakini Highway, about a half-mile north of Palani Road in Kailua-Kona. It's easy to get distracted by all the other free amenities here you'll pass first: two Olympic-size pools, gym, tennis courts, ball fields. But there's a mile of sandy beach here—not in a swimmable area, true, but fronting tide pools that are great for families with small children. The beach area also has covered picnic tables and grills, restrooms, and showers.

South Kona

HOOKENA BEACH PARK ★

A community group known as **Friends of Hookena** (www.hookena.org) has taken responsibility for upkeep and concessions at this secluded, taupe-colored sandy beach (technically a county park) since 2007. You can rent kayaks and snorkel gear to explore Kauhako Bay's populous reefs (avoid during high surf), or beach and camping gear to enjoy the view—sometimes including wild spinner dolphins—from the shore. Reservations for gear and campgrounds can be made online; the welcome concession stand at this remote spot even accepts credit cards. Facilities include showers, restrooms, water fountains, picnic tables, pavilions, and parking. From Kailua-Kona, take Highway 11 22 miles south to the Hookena Beach Road exit just past Hookena Elementary School, between mile markers 101 and 102. Follow it downhill 2 miles to the end, and turn left on the one-lane road to the parking area.

The Kohala Coast

ANAEHOOMALU BAY ★★

The Big Island makes up for its dearth of beaches with a few spectacular ones, like Anaehoomalu, or A-Bay, as many call it. This popular gold-sand beach, fringed by a grove of palms and backed by royal fishponds still full of mullet, is one of Hawaii's most beautiful. It fronts the Waikoloa Beach Marriott Resort & Spa and is enjoyed by guests and locals alike (it's busier in summer, but doesn't ever get truly crowded). The beach slopes gently from shallow to deep water; swimming, snorkeling, diving, kayaking, and windsurfing are all excellent here. At the far edge of the bay, snorkelers and divers can watch endangered green sea turtles line up and wait their turn to have small fish clean them. Equipment rental and snorkeling, scuba, and windsurfing instruction are available at the north end of the beach. Facilities include restrooms, showers, picnic tables, and plenty of parking.

HAPUNA BEACH ★★★

Just off Queen Kaahumanu Highway, below the Hapuna Beach Prince Hotel, lies this crescent of gold sand—a half-mile long and up to 200 feet wide. In summer, when the beach is widest, the ocean calmest, and the crowds biggest, this is a terrific place for swimming, bodysurfing, and snorkeling. But beware of Hapuna in winter, when its thundering waves and strong rip currents should only be plied by local experts. Facilities at **Hapuna Beach,** part of the Hapuna Beach State Recreation Area, include A-frame cabins (for camping by permit), picnic tables, restrooms, showers, water fountains, lifeguard station, and parking. You can also pick up the coastal **Ala Kahakai National Historic Trail** (p. 212) here to Spencer or Holoholokai beach parks to the north and south, respectively.

KAUNAOA BEACH (MAUNA KEA BEACH) ★★★

Nearly everyone refers to this gold-sand beach at the foot of Mauna Kea Beach Hotel by its hotel nickname, but its real name is Hawaiian for "native dodder," a lacy, yellow-orange vine that once thrived on the shore. A coconut grove sweeps around this golden crescent, where the water is calm and protected by two black-lava points. The sandy bottom slopes gently into the bay, which often fills with tropical fish, sea turtles, and manta rays, especially at night, when the hotel lights flood the shore. Swimming is excellent year-round, except in rare winter storms. Snorkelers prefer the rocky points, where fish thrive in the surge. Facilities include restrooms, showers, and public-access parking (go early), but there are no lifeguards.

SPENCER BEACH ★★

Virtually in the shadow of the massive Puukohola Heiau (p. 164) to the north, this is a great place to stop heading to or from the scenic and historic sites in North Kohala. The county park is named for a prominent local official, Samuel Mahuka Spencer; the name for the gently sloping, white-yellow sand beach is actually Ohaiula, but most just call it Spencer. It's protected by both a long reef

Spencer Beach.

and Kawaihae Harbor, allowing for relatively safe swimming year-round; there's also a lifeguard station. Parking is plentiful, but the park may fill up on weekends and holidays. From the intersection of highways 19 and 270, take Highway 270 (Akoni Pule) north Kailua-Kona, head a half-mile north to a left turn at the sign for the park and Puukohola Heiau, and follow to either of two parking areas at the end of the road. Facilities include picnic tables, restrooms, showers, large grassy lawns, and shade trees; at either end of the beach are campsites, which sometimes serve the area's homeless population. (As long as you're here in the day and avoid walking through their tents, it's perfectly safe.)

WAIALEA BAY (BEACH 69) ★★

Once a hidden oasis, this light-golden sandy beach in Puako, between the Waiko-loa Beach and Mauna Lani resorts, earned its nickname from the number on a former telephone pole off Old Puako Road, which signaled one of the beach's public-access points. Still tucked behind private homes, it's now a proper beach park, with a paved parking lot and trail to the beach, restrooms, and water fountains—but no lifeguards. Waialea Bay is generally very calm in summer, good for swimming and snorkeling; waves can get big in winter, when surfers and body-boarders tend to show up. From Kailua-Kona, take Highway 19 north to a left on Puako Road, then a right on Old Puako Road; the access road to the parking area is on your left, near telephone pole No. 71 (the nickname has not caught up with the times).

Hilo

LELEIWI BEACH PARK ★★

This string of palm-fringed black-lava tide pools fed by freshwater springs and rippled by gentle waves is a photographer's delight—and the perfect place to take

Leleiwi Beach.

a plunge. In winter, big waves can splash these ponds, but the shallow pools are generally free of currents and ideal for families with children, especially in the protected inlets at the center of the park. Leleiwi often attracts endangered sea turtles, making this one of Hawaii's most popular snorkeling spots. Open 7am to 7pm, the beach park is 4 miles east of town on Kalanianaole Avenue. Facilities include a lifeguard station, picnic tables, pavilions, and parking. A second section of the park, known as Richardson's Ocean Park, includes showers, restrooms, and the marine life exhibits of Richardson Ocean Center. *Tip:* If the area is crowded, check out the tide pools and/or small sandy coves in the five other beach parks along Kalanianaole Avenue between Banyan Drive and Leleiwi, especially the protected white sand lagoon of **Carlsmith Beach Park,** just 2 minutes' drive west, which also has a lifeguard.

KOLEKOLE BEACH PARK ★

Not a place to enter the rough water, this streamside park is nonetheless an unusually picturesque spot for a picnic. The lush greenery around you contrasts with the black rock beach, aquamarine sea, and white sea foam where waves meet Kolekole Stream, several miles below **Akaka Falls** (p. 170) in Honomu. You may see local kids jumping from a rope swing into the stream, which also has a small waterfall. Facilities include picnic pavilions, grills, restrooms, and parking. It's open 6am to 11pm. From Hilo, take Highway 19 north 11 miles to a left turn on Old Mamalahoa Highway, and take the first (sharp) right, which descends a quarter mile down to the park.

Puna District

Most of the shoreline in this volcanically active area is craggy, with rough waters and dangerous currents, although the oceanfront thermal pond at **Ahalanui ★★** (p. 181) and the **Waiopae Tide Pools ★** (p. 180) are certainly worth seeking out. The still-forming black-sand beach near **Kalapana,** which has its origins in the 1990 lava flow that buried Kaimu Beach, is best viewed from the cliff above it; if you venture closer, beware of rogue waves that may suddenly break much higher on the beach.

Kau District

GREEN SAND BEACH (PAPAKOLEA BEACH) ★★

Hawaii's famous green-sand beach is located at the base of Puu o Mahana, an old cinder cone spilling into the sea. The place has its problems: It's difficult to reach; the open bay is often rough; there are no facilities, fresh water, or shade from the relentless sun; and howling winds scour the point. Nevertheless, each year the unusual green sands attract thousands of oglers, who follow a well-worn, four-wheel-drive-only road for 2½ miles to the top of a cliff, which you have to climb down to reach the beach. The sand is crushed olivine, a green semiprecious mineral found in eruptive rocks and meteorites. If the surf's up, check out the beach from the cliff's edge; if the water's calm, you can go closer, but keep an eye on the ocean at all times (there are strong rip currents here).

To get to Green Sand Beach from the boat ramp at South Point, follow the four-wheel-drive trail; even if you have a 4WD vehicle, you may want to walk—the wind-blown trail is very, very bad in parts. Make sure to have appropriate closed-toe footwear. After the first 10 to 15 minutes of walking, the trail leaves lava to cross pastureland. After about 30 to 40 minutes more, you'll see an eroded cinder cone by the water; continue to the edge, and there lie the green sands

Green Sand Beach.

below. The best way to reach the beach is to go over the edge from the cinder cone, not around the south side, to the beach trail.

PUNALUU BEACH ★★★

Green sea turtles love to bask on this remote, black-sand beach, beautifully framed by palm trees and easily photographed from the bluff above. The deep-blue waters can be choppy; swim only in very calm conditions, as there's no life-guard present. You're more than welcome to admire the turtles, but at a respectful distance; the law against touching or harassing them is enforced here (if not by authorities, then by locals who also like to congregate in the park). County park facilities include camping, restrooms, showers, picnic tables, pavilions, water fountains, a concession stand, and parking. There are two access roads from Highway 11, at 7¾ and 8 miles northeast of Naalehu. The first, Ninole Loop Road, leads past the somewhat overgrown-looking Sea Mountain golf course to a turnoff for a paved parking lot by the bluff. The second access from Highway 11, Punaluu Road, has a turnoff for a smaller, unpaved parking area.

WATERSPORTS
Boat, Raft & Submarine Tours

The relatively calm waters of the Kona and Kohala coasts are home to inquisitive reef fish, frolicking spinner dolphins, tranquil green sea turtles, spiraling manta rays, and spouting whales and their calves in season (Dec–Mar). A wide variety of vessels offer sightseeing and snorkel/dive tours (gear provided). Cocktail and dinner cruises take advantage of the region's predictably eye-popping sunsets. On the wild Puna side of the island, boat rides may pass lava flowing into the sea or coastal waterfalls. For fishing charters, see p. 205.

KONA COAST

Atlantis Submarines ★   If you have what it takes (namely, no claustropho-bia), you'll enjoy venturing up to 100 feet below the sea in a 65-foot **submarine,** with a large porthole for every passenger. During your 45 minutes underwater, the sub glides slowly through an 18,000-year-old, 25-acre coral reef in **Kailua Bay,** teeming with schools of colorful fish (including, unfortunately, invasive spe-cies such as goatfish and taape) and two shipwrecks encrusted in coral. You'll take a 5-minute boat shuttle from Kailua Pier, across from the ticket office, to the air-conditioned submarine.

75–5669 Alii Dr. (across the street from Kailua Pier), Kailua-Kona. © **800/548-6262.** www.atlantis adventures.com. Trips leave four times a day 10am–2:30pm (check-in 30 min. earlier). $109 age 13 and older, $45 under 13 (must be at least 3 ft. tall). Website booking discount $10.

Body Glove Cruises ★★   Body Glove's Kanoa II, a 65-foot, solar-powered catamaran carrying up to 100 passengers, runs an environmentally friendly, 4½-hour **snorkel/dive** morning cruise, along with shorter lunch and dinner excur-sions for those who just want to enjoy the views, as well as seasonal whale-watching trips; all depart from Kailua Pier. In the morning, you'll be greeted with fresh Kona coffee, fruit, and breakfast pastries before sailing north to **Pawai Bay,** a marine preserve where you can snorkel, scuba dive, swim, or just hang out on the deck. Before chowing down on the deli lunch buffet, take the plunge off the boat's 20-foot water slide or 15-foot-high diving board. The only thing you need to bring is a towel; all gear is provided, along with "reef safe" sunscreen. And if you don't see dolphins, you can do a repeat cruise for free (the same is true if you don't see whales on a whale-watching excursion). Dinner and lunch cruises fea-ture a historian who points out some 50 significant sites on the 12 miles from Kailua Pier to **Kealakekua Bay,** where passengers feast on a buffet spread and enjoy live Hawaiian music by notable entertainer LT Smooth. Parents will appre-ciate that all cruises are free for children 5 and under. *Note:* The boat is wheel-chair accessible, including its restrooms.

Kailua Pier, Kailua-Kona. www.bodyglovehawaii.com. © **800/551-8911** or 808/326-7122. Snor-kel cruises (daily 9am–1:30pm) $128 adults, $78 children 6–17; see website for additional scuba charges. Dinner cruise (Tues–Sat 4pm) $108 adults, $78 children 6–17, free for children 5 and under. Lunch cruise (Wed 1pm) $94 adults, $73 children 6–17. Whale-watching cruises (Dec–Apr only; Tues and Thurs–Sat 1pm, Sun–Mon 2pm) $84 adults, $68 children 6–17.

Captain Dan McSweeney's Whale Watch Learning Adventures ★★★

Hawaii's most impressive visitors—45-foot humpback whales—return to the islands' warm waters, including those on the Big Island's **Kona side,** every win-ter. Capt. Dan McSweeney, who founded the Wild Whale Research Foundation in 1979, works daily with the whales and has no problem finding them. During the 3-hour **whale-watching tours,** offered twice daily in late December through April, he drops a hydrophone (an underwater microphone) into the water so you can listen to their songs, and sometimes uses an underwater video camera to show you what's going on. Cruises are aboard the *Lady Ann,* which has restrooms and a choice of sunny or shaded decks; cold drinks and snacks are provided. Trips depart from Honokohau Harbor, where parking is free and typically easy.

Honokohau Harbor, 74-380 Kealakehe Pkwy. (off Hwy. 19), Kailua-Kona. www.ilovewhales.com. © **888/942-5376** or 808/322-0028. Whale-watching cruises $110 adults, $99 children 11 and under who also weigh under 90 pounds.

Captain Zodiac ★   It's a wild, 14-mile ride to **Kealakekua Bay** aboard one of Captain Zodiac's 16-passenger, 24-foot **rigid-hull inflatable rafts,** or Zodiacs. There you'll spend about an hour snorkeling in the bay, perhaps with spinner dolphins, and enjoy snacks and beverages at the site. The small size of the craft mean no restrooms, but it also means you can explore sea caves on this craggy coast. Four-hour **snorkel trips** take place twice daily, with morning and afternoon departures; the 5-hour midday tour ingeniously arrives at Kealakekua when most other boats have left, with extra time for a second snorkel site, seasonal **whale-watching,** or other experiences at the captain's discretion, plus a deli lunch. Be prepared to get wet (that includes your camera). *Warning:* Pregnant women and those with bad backs should avoid this often bumpy ride.

In Gentry's Kona Marina, Honokohau Harbor, 74-425 Kealakehe Pkwy. (off Hwy. 19), Kailua-Kona. www.captainzodiac.com. ✆ **808/329-3199.** 4-hr. snorkel cruise (Wed–Thurs and Sat–Sun 8:15am and 1pm) $99 adults, $78 children 4–12; 5-hr. snorkel cruise (Mon–Tues and Fri 10am) $112 adults, $87 children 4–12. Whale-watching cruises (Dec–Apr only; Tues and Thurs 9am) $84 adults, $59 children 4–12. Online booking discounts available.

Fair Wind Snorkeling & Diving Adventures ★★★   I love Fair Wind, for several reasons, starting with its home in Keauhou Bay, 8 miles south of Kailua Pier and so that much closer to **Kealakekua Bay,** where its two very different but impressively equipped boats head for **snorkel/dive tours:**

FAIR WIND II   When traveling with kids, I book a cruise on the *Fair Wind II,* a 60-foot catamaran that includes two 15-foot water slides, a high-dive jump, playpens, and child-friendly flotation devices with viewfinders, so even toddlers can take a peek at Kealakekua's glorious sea life. Year-round, the *Fair Wind II* offers a 4½-hour morning snorkel cruise that includes breakfast and a barbecue lunch; most of the year it also sails a 3½-hour afternoon snorkel cruise that provides snacks, which in summer becomes a deluxe 4½-hour excursion with barbecue dinner. Swimmers age 8 and up can also try **SNUBA**—kind of a beginner's version of scuba—for an optional $69, with an in-water guide.

HULA KAI   When traveling with teens or adults, I prefer the *Hula Kai,* the Fair Wind's 55-foot foil-assist catamaran, open only to ages 7 and up. The boat provides a plusher experience (such as comfy seating with headrests) and, on its 5-hour morning snorkel cruise, a faster, smoother ride to two uncrowded Kona Coast snorkeling sites, which vary according to conditions (but not usually Kealakekua Bay). Guests have the option to try **stand-up paddleboarding, SNUBA** (see above), or the propulsive **"Sea Rocket"** ($25 per half-hour) to cover even more ground underwater. The *Hula Kai* also offers a fascinating night snorkel/dive with **manta rays,** a 1½-hour tour that doesn't have to voyage far from **Keauhou Bay** to find them. Although you can see these gentle giants (no stingers!) during the day, at night they're lured closer to the ocean's surface by the plankton that also rise there. Like other tour companies, Fair Wind uses dive lights to attract even more plankton; on the off chance you don't get to see a manta ray, you're welcome back another evening or on afternoon snorkel tour. It's fairly balmy at night, but you'll be tempted to stay in the water with the magnificent rays as long as you can, so wetsuits, warm soup, and hot drinks are provided to ward off chills. One-tank scuba dives are also available on all *Hula Kai* excursions ($31 without gear; $45 with); the manta night trip also charges $45 per "ride-along" (no snorkeling) passenger.

High & Dry: Glass-Bottomed Boats

If you're not a swimmer, you don't have to forgo seeing the intriguing coral formations and multi-hued marine life for which the Kona and Kohala coasts are justly famous. Of the several glass-bottomed boat cruises on the Big Island, **Kailua Bay Charters'** tour on the 36-foot *Marian*, which has comfy benches and shade, is well-suited to families. Departing from Kailua Pier, the trip is just an hour long, with a naturalist on board to explain what you're seeing. When you tire of staring down, head to the bow to scan for dolphins or migratory humpback whales. Tours are $40 for adults, $20 for children under 12 (www.konaglass bottomboat.com; ℂ **808/324-1749**). For even shorter attention spans, take a 30-minute spin on **Ocean Sports'** 26-foot boat, also with benches, shade, and a naturalist, departing from Anaehoomalu Bay at the Waikoloa Resort. Tours are $27 for adults, $14 for children 6 to 12, and free for children under 6 (www.hawaiioceansports.com; ℂ **888/724-5924,** ext. 103, or 808/886-6666, ext. 103).

Note: Many of Fair Wind cruises sell out several days in advance, or as much as 2 to 3 weeks in peak season, so book ahead.

Keauhou Bay Pier, 78-7130 Kaleiopapa St., Kailua-Kona. www.fair-wind.com. ℂ **800/677-9461** or 808/322-2788. *Fair Wind II* morning snorkel cruise (daily 9am) and deluxe afternoon snorkel cruise (daily 2pm in summer only) $129 adults, $75 children 4–12, $29 children 3 and under. Afternoon snack snorkel cruise (daily 2pm fall–spring) $75 adults, $45 children 4–12, free for children 3 and under. *Hula Kai* morning snorkel/dive cruise (daily 9:30am) $149 age 7 and up (under 7 not permitted). Manta ray snorkel/dive (daily 7:15pm) $105 age 7 and up. Parking is on opposite side of Keauhou Bay, at end of King Kamehameha III Rd.

Kamanu Charters ★★   The *Kamanu*, a sleek 38-foot sailing catamaran, provides a laidback **sail-and-snorkel cruise** from Honokohau Harbor to the marine preserve of **Pawai Bay.** The 3½-hour trip includes a tropical lunch (deli sandwiches, chips, fresh fruit, and drinks), snorkeling gear, and personalized instruction for first-time snorkelers; weather permitting, it sails at 9am and 1:30pm. It can hold up to 24 people but often has fewer, making it even more relaxed. Some morning cruises are offered with a **swim with spinner dolphins,** while the adults-only **sunset cocktail cruises** are sometimes paired with snorkeling with **manta rays.** Whale-watching is also offered in season. At press time, Kamanu Charters had announced plans to add *Kamanu Elua*, a Zodiac-style rigid-hull inflatable boat with seating, which will offer **Kealakekua Bay** snorkel tours.

Honokohau Harbor, 74-7380 Kealakehe Pkwy. (off Hwy. 19), Kailua-Kona. www.kamanu.com. ℂ **800/348-3091** or 808/329-2021. Sail-and-snorkel cruises (daily 9am and 1:30pm) $95 adults ($85 for 1:30pm cruise), $50 children 12 and under. Dolphin swim, sail, and snorkel (times/days vary) $139 all ages. Sunset cruises (daily 5pm) $95 adults only. Sunset manta snorkels (times/days vary) $95. Whale-watching (Dec. 15–May 15; times/days vary) $75. Check website for online discounts.

Sea Quest ★   With a head start from Keauhou Bay, Sea Quest's four **rigid-hull inflatable rafts** offer three varieties of **Kealakekua Bay snorkeling**

Watersports

cruises and one excursion to **swim with spinner dolphins,** which may also include a Kealakekua snorkel. The Zodiac-style rafts hold 18 passengers, but Sea Quest takes just 14; rafts on longer tours include shade. Both the 5-hour Expedition South Kona and 4-hour Deluxe Morning Adventure depart in the mornings and include snorkeling among the incredibly diverse marine life of **Honaunau Bay,** within view of the towering wood tikis and restored cultural sites at Puuhonua o Honaunau National Historical Park (p. 163); the Expedition includes a third site and deli lunch. The aptly named 3-hour Captain Cook Express heads straight to Kealakekua; all three tours explore Kona Coast lava tubes and sea caves that larger boats can't. Operating under the name **Blue Ocean Dolphin Encounters** (www.blueoceanhawaii.net), Sea Quest also offers a 5-hour tour that starts by locating a pod of wild spinner dolphins to swim with, under the tutelage of a certified divemaster, before their late-morning sleep (which is why they're often spotted closer to shore that time of day). Afterward, you head to Kealakekua or another Kona Coast reef for snorkel and lunch.

Keauhou Bay Pier, 78-7128 Kaleiopapa St., Kailua-Kona. www.seaquesthawaii.com. ✆ **808/329-7238.** Morning snorkel tour (daily 8am) $96 adults, $78 children 5–12. Afternoon snorkel tour (daily 12:30pm) $76 adults, $65 children 5–12. South Kona snorkel tour (weekdays 8am year-round; also weekends in summer and holiday periods) $114 adults, $92 children 5–12. 3-hr. whale-watching cruise (in season; times vary) $72 adults, $62 children 5–12. Children under 6, pregnant women, and people with bad backs are not allowed. Discounts for booking online. Park in dirt parking lot at end of King Kamehameha III Rd., across from pier.

HILO, THE HAMAKUA COAST & PUNA DISTRICT

Lava Ocean Tours ★ The unpredictability of Pele, at least as evidenced by the on-again, off-again lava flows into the sea from Kilauea, means it's hard to know in advance if you'll be able to take one of the **lava-viewing tours** aboard the *Lava Kai* catamaran (34 ft. long; 24-passenger capacity but limited to 12) or the smaller *Kuewa* (27 ft.; six passengers). The 2-plus-hour Sunset Volcano Boat Tour at press time offered views of lava flowing on the *pali* (cliff) about 6 miles away, along with closer views of volcanic features along the coast—not quite as exhilarating as seeing molten rock pour into a hissing ocean, but still adventurous, given the open waters. The tour departs from Pohoiki (Isaac Hale Beach Park) in Pahoa, as does the 6-hour Castaway Adventure **snorkel/dive tour at Halape,** an extremely secluded sandy beach far below the cliffs of Hawaii Volcanoes National Park; the 2½-hour cruise there includes a narrated guide to the unique geological formations along the way, such as the new black-sand beach at Kalapana. Captain Shane Turpin's fleet also has two less demanding tours offered from Hilo's Wailoa Harbor. The 3-hour **Hilo Waterfall Swim & Wildlife Tour** travels along the **Hamakua Coast** past sea caves, black-sand beaches, abandoned sugar mills, and waterfalls, including one where you can swim in the river below it. Wildlife often include spinner dolphins and, in season, humpback whales; the latter are the focus of a separate 2-hour **whale-watching tour** from Hilo December through April; a hydrophone (underwater microphone) on board lets you listen to the cetaceans' songs.

Departures from Wailoa Harbor, off Hwy. 11, Hilo, and Pohoiki (Isaac Hale Beach Park), Pahoa. www.seelava.com. ✆ **808/966-4200.** Volcano boat tours (daily 3 and 5pm) $150 adults, $125 children 12 and under. Hilo waterfall tour (daily 9am and noon) $150 adults, $125 children 4–12. Whale-watching (Dec–Apr); times vary) $125 adults, $75 children 4–12.

Body Boarding (Boogie Boarding) & Bodysurfing

As with other watersports, it's important to stay out of rough surf in winter or during storms that bring big surf. In normal conditions, the best beaches for body boarding and bodysurfing on the Kona side of the island are **Hapuna Beach** on the Mauna Kea Resort, **Laaloa Beach (White Sand/Magic Sands Beach)** ★★ in Kailua-Kona, and **Kua Bay** (Maniniowali Beach) in **Kekaha Kai State Park,** north of the airport. Experienced bodysurfers may want to check out South Kona's **Hookena Beach Park.** On the Hilo side, try **Leleiwi Beach Park.** See "Beaches" (p. 188) for details.

Hotel beach concessions and most surf shops (see "Surfing" on p. 206) rent body boards, but you can also find inexpensive rentals at **Snorkel Bob's,** in the parking lot of Huggo's restaurant, 75-5831 Kahakai St. at Alii Drive, Kailua-Kona (www.snorkelbob.com; ✆ **808/329-0770**), and on the Kohala Coast in the Shops at Mauna Lani, 68-1330 Mauna Lani Dr., facing the road on the Mauna Lani Resort (✆ **808/885-9499**). Both stores are open 8am to 5pm daily.

Kayaking

Imagine sitting at sea level, eye to eye with a turtle, a dolphin, even a whale—it's possible in an ocean kayak. After a few minutes of instruction and a little practice in a calm area (like **Kamakahonu Cove** in front of the Courtyard King Kamehameha Kona Beach Hotel), you'll be ready to explore. Beginners can practice their skills in **Kailua Bay;** intermediate kayakers might try paddling from **Honokohau Harbor** to **Kekaha Kai State Park;** while the more advanced can tackle the 5 miles from **Keauhou Bay** to **Kealakekua Bay** or the scenic but challenging **Hamakua Coast.** You can also rent kayaks, including a clear "peekaboo" version that allows you to view sea life, at **Hookena Beach Park** (p. 192) for $40 to $50 a day.

KEALAKEKUA BAY GUIDED TOURS & RENTALS Although technically you can rent kayaks for exploring Kealakekua Bay on your own (and even land near the

---

DOING THE ditch

The most unusual kayak tour in Hawaii—maybe anywhere—takes place in the 17 miles of flumes that once irrigated North Kohala's vast sugarcane fields, with **Kohala Ditch Adventures** ★★ (www.kohaladitchadventures.com; ✆ **888/288-7288**). The family-run tours ($139 adults, $75 kids 5–11) begin with a 15-minute, off-road drive up the mountain and a short hike on a flume that crosses over a waterfall. Then you board three-person inflatable kayaks for a gentle cruise/paddle through 2½ miles of flumes,

including 10 earthen tunnels built more than a century ago. This isn't a theme-park ride, with white-water plunges, but a delightful journey during which fifth-generation guides explain local cultural and natural history. At the end, four-person mountain buggies (used by the company's other tour business, **ATV Outfitters**) shuttle you back to the office, on Highway 270, past mile marker 24 in Kapaau. Wear closed-toe shoes and clothing that can get wet, and bring a waterproof camera.

Captain Cook Monument, if you follow the arduous process of snagging one of 10 daily state permits), it's best to go with a guided tour. Only three kayak companies are allowed to offer guided tours in Kealakekua Bay that land at the Cook monument (Kaawaloa), all launching from Napoopoo Wharf. Tours include equipment, snorkeling gear, snacks or lunch, and drinks and should be booked in advance, due to the tight limit on permits. Note that Napoopoo is a residential area, where parking can be difficult if you're not on a tour.

Kona Boys ★★ (www.konaboys.com; ✆ 808/328-1234) was the first outfit to offer kayak rentals in Kona, and is still widely regarded as the best. Its Kealakekua Bay tours, held daily by reservation, meet at the shop at 79-7539 Mamalahoa Hwy. (Hwy. 11), Kealakekua, at 7:15 am, and finish at 1pm. Tours cost $169 for adults $149 for children. You can also rent gear from Kona Boys' **beach shack** at Kamakahonu Bay (✆ 808/329-2345), the only one of its two sites to offer kayaks by the hour, not just by the day or week. Rentals include kayak, paddles, backrests, cooler, life jackets, dry bag, and a soft rack to carry kayaks on top of your car (including convertibles). Hourly rates are $19 single kayak, $29 double, with daily rates $54 and $74, respectively (weekly $174/$279).

Owned by a Native Hawaiian family, **Aloha Kayak ★★** (www.alohakayak. com; ✆ 877/322-1444 or 808/322-2868) offers two tours of different lengths to Kealakekua Bay and Kaawalao Flats, where the memorial to Captain Cook stands. The 3½-hour tour (add an hour for check-in/check-out) departs at 8am and noon daily and costs $99 for adults and $50 for children 11 and under. The 5-hour tour, which allows more time at Kaawaloa and its cultural sites, departs at 7:15am Sunday, Tuesday, and Thursday; it's $129 for adults and $70 for children (check website for $20-off coupon). Half-day rental rates are $25 for a single and $45 for a double; full-day rates are $35 for a single and $60 for a double, with triple kayaks and discounts for longer periods also available. Aloha Kayak's shop is in Honalo, about 8½ miles south of Kailua-Kona, at 79-7248 Mamalahoa Hwy. (Hwy. 11), just south of its intersection with Highway 180.

The environmentally conscious **Adventures in Paradise ★★** (www.big islandkayak.com; ✆ 888/210-5365 or 808/447-0080) has a small office at 82-6020 Mamalahoa Hwy. (Hwy. 11) in Captain Cook, but generally meets clients at Napoopoo for its 3½-hour Kealakekua tours ($90 for ages 5 and up), departing at 7 and 10:45am daily. (*Tip:* Book the early tour for the least crowded snorkeling.) It also offers a **Manta Ray Night Snorkel** with a brief paddle from Keauhou Bay to a spot where lights attract the huge but harmless manta rays, their jaws open wide to let plankton swim in. The 2-hour tours ($80) in tandem kayaks are open to ages 10 and older with at least moderate fitness (no pregnancies or mobility issues), held at 6:45pm Wednesday to Saturday. Manta sightings, though not guaranteed, take place on about 80 to 85 percent of trips.

Parasailing

Get a bird's-eye view of Hawaii's pristine waters with **UFO Parasail** (www.ufo parasail.net; ✆ 800/FLY-4-UFO or 808/325-5836), which offers parasail rides daily between 8am and 5:30pm from Kailua Pier. The cost is $65 for the standard flight of 8 minutes of air time at 800 feet, and $75 for a deluxe 10-minute ride at 1,200 feet. You can go up alone or with a friend (or two); no experience is necessary, but single riders must weigh at least 130 pounds, and groups no more than 450 pounds. The boat may carry up to eight passengers (observers pay just $35), and the total time in the boat, around an hour, varies on the rides they've booked. *Tip:* Save $5 by booking online per ride.

Scuba Diving

The Big Island's leeward coast offers some of the best diving and snorkeling in the world; the water is calm, warm, and clear. Want to swim with fast-moving game fish? Try **Ulua Cave,** at the north end of the Kohala Coast, from 25 to 90 feet deep; dolphins, rays, and the occasional Hawaiian monk seal swim by. And don't forget to book a night dive to see the majestic and mysterious **manta rays,** regularly seen in greater numbers here than anywhere else in Hawaii (or most of the world, for that matter). There are more than 2 dozen dive operators on island, offering everything from scuba-certification courses to guided dives to snorkeling cruises.

Founded in 1984, **Kohala Divers** (www.kohaladivers.com; © **808/882-7774**) has daily two-tank dives ($139–$149) to spectacular sites off North and South Kohala, including a 30-foot-high lava dome covered in plate and knob coral that attracts huge schools of fish, and several spots off Puako frequented by green sea turtles. Snorkelers (gear included) and ride-alongs pay $85 to join these and other charters aboard the 42-foot dive boat, which books just 15 of its 24-passenger capacity. You can also rent scuba and snorkel gear at its shop in Kawaihae Harbor Shopping Center, 61-3665 Akoni Pule Hwy. (Hwy. 270), about a mile north of its intersection with Highway 19. It's open daily 8am to 6pm.

"This is not your mother or father's dive shop," says the owner Simon Key of the **Kona Diving Company,** in the Old Industrial area, 74–5467 Luhia St. (at Eho St.), Kailua-Kona (www.konadivingcompany.com; © **808/331-1858**). "This is a dive shop for today's diver." What sets Kona Diving Company apart, Simon claims, is its willingness to take its 34-foot catamaran (complete with showers, TV, and restrooms) to unusual dive sites, and "not those sites just 2 minutes from the mouth of the harbor." Kona Diving also offers introductory dives ($200), two-tank morning dives ($130), and one- and two-tank manta ray night dives from Honokohau Harbor. Snorkelers and ride-alongs pay $80 to $115, gear included, depending on the trip; scuba gear sets cost $30 a day.

One of Kona's oldest and most eco-friendly dive shops, **Jack's Diving Locker,** in the Coconut Marketplace, 75–5813 Alii Dr., Kailua-Kona (www.jacksdivinglocker.com; © **800/345-4807** or 808/329-7585), boasts an 8,000-square-foot dive center with solar-heated swimming pool (and underwater viewing windows), classrooms, and full-service rentals and sports-diving and

SOME LIKE IT HOT: lava dives

Here's a wonderfully unusual opportunity for advanced divers: diving where the lava flows into the ocean, guided by **Hot-Lava and Hilo-Side Dives,** Hilo's Nautilus Dive Center (www.nautilusdivehilo.com; © **808/935-6939**). "Sometimes you can feel the pressure from the sound waves as the lava explodes," owner Bill De Rooy says. "Sometimes you have perfect visibility to the color show of your life." Call to see whether the lava is flowing and Bill considers it safe enough to conduct the tours; a two-tank dive goes for as much as $500 per person (two-person minimum). The dive shop at 382 Kamehameha Ave. at Nawahi Lane (next to the Shell gas station) also offers two-tank tours in the reefs off Hilo ($85); Pohoiki, between Pahoa and Kalapana ($150); and the black-sand beach at Punaluu ($150); rates include transportation. The shop is open Monday to Saturday 9am to 5pm.

technical-diving facility. It offers the classic two-tank dive for $125 ($65 snorkelers) and a two-tank manta-ray night dive for $145 ($125 snorkelers), on four roomy boats taking 10 to 18 divers (split into groups of six). It also offers a free repeat dive for those who don't see manta rays on those night dives.

Snorkeling

If you come to Hawaii and don't snorkel, you'll miss half the fun. The clear waters along the dry Kona and Kohala coasts, in particular, are home to spectacular marine life, including spinner dolphins by day and giant manta rays by night. You'll want to take an evening **boat tour** (p. 196) or **kayak tour** (p. 201) to see the latter; for the rest, go in the mornings, before the Kona side's typical afternoon clouds and winds lessen visibility. At all snorkeling sites, please be very careful not to stand on, kick, or touch the live coral. *Tip:* Rent your gear the night before you plan to snorkel so you won't be tempted to rush the fitting process.

GEAR RENTALS If you're staying at a Kona or Kohala resort, the hotel concession should have basic gear for hourly rental. If you're thinking of exploring more than the beach outside your room, an inexpensive place to get basic rental equipment ($9 per week) is **Snorkel Bob's,** in the parking lot of Huggo's restaurant, 75-5831 Kahakai St. at Alii Drive, Kailua-Kona (www.snorkelbob.com; © **808/ 329-0770**), and on the Kohala Coast in the Shops at Mauna Lani, 68-1330 Mauna Lani Dr., facing the road on the Mauna Lani Resort (© **808/885-9499**). Higher-quality gear costs $35 a week for adults, $22 for children ($44/$32 for prescription masks). Both stores are open 8am to 5pm daily.

You can also rent high-quality gear from **Jack's Diving Locker,** Coconut Grove Shopping Center (next to Outback Steak House), 75-5813 Alii Dr., Kailua-Kona (www.jacksdivinglocker.com; © **800/345-4807** or 808/329-7585), open 8am to 8pm Monday to Saturday, till 6pm Sunday. Snorkel sets cost $9 a day. On the Kohala Coast, visit **Kohala Divers** (www.kohaladivers.com; © **808/ 882-7774**) in the Kawaihae Shopping Center, 61-3665 Akoni Pule Highway (Hwy. 270), in Kawaihae a mile north of the intersection with Highway 19. It's open 8am to 6pm daily, with snorkel sets starting at $10 a day.

On the island's east side, **Nautilus Dive Center,** 382 Kamehameha Ave. at Nawahi Lane (next to the Shell gas station) in Hilo (www.nautilusdivehilo.com; © **808/935-6939**), has daily snorkel packages for $6.

TOP SNORKEL SITES If you've never snorkeled in your life, **Kahaluu Beach** ★★ (p. 188) is the best place to start. Just wade in on one of the small, sandy paths through the lava-rock tide pools and you'll see colorful fish. Even better, swim out to the center of the shallow, well-protected bay to see schools of surgeon fish, Moorish idols, butterfly fish, and even green sea turtles. The friendly and knowledgeable volunteers of the **Kahaluu Bay Education Center** (**KBEC;** www.kohalacenter.org/kahaluubay; © **808/640-1166**) are on-site daily from 9:30am to 4:30pm to explain reef etiquette—essentially: "Look, but don't touch"—and answer questions about its marine life, including "Lefty," the green sea turtle with only one front flipper. After beachgoers spotted fishing line tightly wrapped around the turtle's right front flipper, which had cut off circulation and caused its tissue to die, KBEC volunteers caught him and had him sent to Oahu, where the state's top sea turtle veterinarian had to amputate the flipper. Lefty returned home 10 days later, and the KBEC crew keeps a careful watch over his favorite waters. The KBEC even rents snorkel gear and boogie boards with viewing windows (so you don't have to put your face underwater); proceeds benefit conservation at this popular spot, visited annually by some 400,000 snorkelers, swimmers, and surfers.

Kealakekua Bay ★★★ may offer the island's best overall snorkeling (coral heads, lava tubes, calm waters, underwater caves and more), but because it's a marine life conservation district and state historical park (p. 161), access is restricted to preserve its treasures. The best way to snorkel here is via permitted **boat tours** (p. 196), generally departing from Kailua Pier or Keauhou Bay, or **kayak tours** (p. 201) with permits to launch from Napoopoo Wharf and land near the Captain Cook Monument. You can paddle a rental kayak, canoe, or stand-up paddleboard from Napoopoo on your own, if the company has acquired a special permit; otherwise, it's about a 10-mile round-trip paddle from Keauhou. Carrying your snorkel gear down and up the steep 5-mile trail from the highway is possible but not recommended. Watch out for spiny urchins as well as fragile coral when entering the water from lava rocks along the shore.

Much more easily accessible snorkeling, with a terrific display of aquatic diversity, can be found at **Honaunau Bay,** nicknamed "Two Step" for the easy entry off flat lava rocks into the crystalline waters just before **Puuhonua O Honaunau National Historical Park** (p. 163). Snorkeling is not permitted within the park itself, but you can pay the entrance fee to park your car there and walk to the bay, if the 25 or so spaces on the bayfront road—look for the coastal access sign off Highway 160—are taken.

North of the Kohala resort, the well-protected waters of **Spencer Beach** (p. 193) are a great site for families to try snorkeling, with convenient facilities (restrooms, showers, picnic tables), not to mention a lifeguard and a reputation for attracting green sea turtles. (Remember to look but don't touch or approach turtles.) It can get windy, so mornings are again your best bet here.

Sport Fishing: The Hunt for Granders ★★

Big-game fish, including gigantic blue marlin and other Pacific billfish, tuna, mahimahi, sailfish, swordfish, ono (also known as wahoo), and giant trevallies (*ulua*), roam the waters of the Kona Coast, known internationally as the marlin capital of the world. When anglers catch marlin that weigh 1,000 pounds or more, they call them "granders"; there's even a "wall of fame" in Kailua-Kona's Waterfront Row shopping mall, honoring those who've nailed more than 20 tons of fighting fish. Nearby photos show Hollywood celebrities such as Sylvester Stallone posing with their slightly less impressive catches. The celebrities of the fishing world descend on Kailua-Kona in late July for the 5-day **Hawaiian International Billfish Tournament** (www.hibtfishing.com), based at Kailua Pier. Note that it's not all carnage out there: Teams that tag and release marlin under 300 pounds get bonus points.

Nearly 100 charter boats with professional captains and crew offer fishing charters out of **Keauhou, Kawaihae, Honokohau,** and **Kailua Bay** harbors. If you're not an expert angler, the best way to arrange a charter is through a booking agency like the **Charter Desk at Honokohau Marina** (www.charterdesk.com; © **888/566-2487** or 808/326-1800), which can sort through the more than 40 different types of vessels, fishing specialties, and personalities to match you with the right boat. Prices range from $750 to $3,500 or so for a full-day exclusive charter (you and up to five friends have an entire boat to yourselves) or $450 to $600 for a half-day. One or two people may be able to book a "share" on boats that hold four to eight anglers, who take turns fishing—generally for smaller catch, to increase everyone's chances of hooking something. Shares start at $95 to $150 per person for half-day trips, $250 for a full day.

Serious sport-fishers should call the boats directly. They include **Anxious** (www.alohazone.com; ✆ **808/326-1229**) and **Marlin Magic** (www.marlinmagic.com; ✆ **808/960-1713**). If you aren't into hooking a 1,000-pound marlin or 200-pound tuna and just want to have fun catching some smaller fish, contact **Reel Action** (www.fishkona.org/reel_action.html; ✆ **808/325-6811**); they also do saltwater fly-fishing. Light-tackle anglers and saltwater fly-fishermen should contact **Sea Genie II ★★** (www.seageniesportfishing.com; ✆ **808/325-5355**), which has helped several anglers set world records. All operate out of Honokohau Harbor.

Most big-game charter boats carry six passengers max, and the boats supply all equipment, bait, tackle, and lures. No license is required. Many captains now tag and release marlins; other fish caught belong to the boat, not to you—that's island style. If you want to eat your catch or have your trophy mounted, arrange it with the captain before you go.

Stand-Up Paddleboarding (SUP)

Anywhere the water is calm is a fine place to learn stand-up paddleboarding (SUP), which takes much less finesse than traditional surfing but offers a fun alternative to kayaking for exploring the coastline. Numerous hotel concessions offer rentals and lessons, as do most traditional surf shops.

Kona Boys ★★ (www.konaboys.com; ✆ **808/328-1234**) has the best locale in Kailua-Kona to try your hand at SUP: **Kamakahonu Cove,** next to Kailua Pier and the King Kamehameha's royal compound. The spring water in the well-protected cove is a little too cool and murky for snorkeling, but just right for getting your bearings. The 90-minute lessons costs $99 in a group setting, $149 private; once you've got the hang of it, you can also join one of Kona Boys' 90-minute tours ($99 group/$149 private) or just pick up a rental ($29 hourly, $74 daily). It also offers lessons and rentals at its Kealakekua location, 79-7539 Mamalahoa Hwy. (Hwy. 11), 1¼ miles south of its intersection with Highway 180.

Another good option in North Kona is at Keauhou Bay, where **Ocean Safaris** (www.oceansafariskayaks.com; ✆ **808/326-4699**) offers 2-hour lessons and tours (each $60) on Tuesday, Thursday, and Saturday. It also offers rentals ($25 hourly, $300 weekly), but paddlers must stay within Keauhou Bay. On the Kohala Coast, the smooth crescents of **Anaehoomalu Bay** and **Puako Bay** are also well-suited to exploring via SUP.

The sport has taken off in Hilo, too, where outrigger canoes also crisscross the usually tranquil bay. **Hulakai** (http://hulakai.com), which rents all kinds of beach gear from two locations, offers 1-hour SUP lessons ($68) and 90-minute "adventures" ($98), plus rentals for $75 a day, $295 a week. It has stores in the Shops at Mauna Lani (✆ **808/896-3141**) on the Mauna Lani Resort, and in downtown Hilo, 1717 Kamehameha Ave. (at Banyan Dr.), near the intersection of highways 11 and 19 (✆ **808/315-7497**).

Surfing

Most surfing off the Big Island is for the experienced only, thanks to rocks, coral reef, and rip currents at many of the reliable breaks. As a general rule, the beaches on the north and west shores of the island get northern swells in winter, while those on the south and east shores get southern swells in summer. You'll also need to radiate courtesy and expertise in the lineup with local surfers, understandably territorial about their challenging breaks.

In Kailua-Kona, experienced surfers should check out the two breaks in **Holualoa Bay,** off Alii Drive between downtown Kailua-Kona and Keauhou:

Banyans near the northern point and **Lyman's** near the southern point, once home to a surfers' temple. If you don't have the chops, don't go in the water; just enjoy the show. Another surfing shrine, its black-lava rock walls still visible today, stands near **Kahaluu Beach ★★** (p. 188), where the waves are manageable most of the year and there's also a lifeguard. Less-experienced surfers can also try **Pine Trees** north of town, at **Kohanaiki Beach ★** (p. 191), where it's best to avoid the busy weekends.

Surf breaks on the east side of the island are also generally best left to skilled surfers. They include **Honolii Point,** north of Hilo; **Richardson's Point** at **Leleiwi Beach Park** (p. 194); **Hilo Bay Front Park;** and **Pohoiki Bay,** home to **Isaac Hale Beach Park.**

PRIVATE & GROUP LESSONS You can have a grand time taking a surf lesson, especially with instructors who know where the breaks are best for beginners and who genuinely enjoy being out in the waves with you. The Native Hawaiian–owned **Hawaii Lifeguard Surf Instructors** (www.surflessonshawaii.com; ✆ 808/324-0442), which gives lessons daily except Sunday at Kahaluu Beach, has an especially good touch with kids and teens. For $110, adults and children as young as 3 can take a 90-minute private lesson (little ones under 55 pounds ride on the same board as their lifeguard/teacher). Lessons for ages 11 and up cost $75 per person for small groups (no more than three students per instructor) and $185 for a group of two. On days when the waves are tame, HLSI offers the same lessons with stand-up paddleboards.

Ocean Eco Tours (www.oceanecotours.com; ✆ 808/324-7873), owned and operated by veteran surfers since 1996, gives lessons in **Kaloko-Honoko-hau National Historical Park ★★** (p. 157). Private lessons cost $150 per person and usually last a minimum of 2 hours; 2½-hour group lessons go for $95, with a maximum of four students, taught at 8:30 and 11:30am daily. Semi-private lessons cost $125 per person. The minimum age is 8.

BOARD RENTALS You're never going to rent a board as good as your own, but you'll enjoy getting to know the local vibe at the appropriately named **Pacific Vibrations,** 75-5702 Likana Lane, tucked off Alii Drive just north of Mokuai-kaua Church (✆ 808/329-4140), founded in 1978 by the McMichaels, a Native Hawaiian family with deep ties to surfing and the Ironman triathlon. It's a trip just to visit the densely stocked surf shop in downtown Kailua-Kona. Surfboards rent for $10 to $20 a day, and body boards for just $5. Stand-up paddleboards go for $15 an hour. The staff is happy to help steer you to waves to match your skills.

Founded in Puako in 1997, surfboard shaper **Hulakai** (http://hulakai.com) also rents surfboards for $40 a day ($150 a week) from two locations: the Shops at Mauna Lani (✆ 808/896-3141) on the Mauna Lani Resort and in downtown Hilo (✆ 808/315-7497), at 1717 Kamehameha Ave. (at Banyan Drive), near the intersection of highways 11 and 19. You can also sign up for 2-hour private and semiprivate surfing lessons ($150 and $125 per person, respectively).

OTHER OUTDOOR ACTIVITIES

Biking

KONA & KOHALA COASTS

When you're planning to spend a fair amount of time in Kailua-Kona, where parking can be at a premium, consider renting a bicycle for easy riding and sightseeing along flat, often oceanview Alii Drive. A cruiser can also be handy if you're staying at a Kohala Coast resort and want an easy way to shuttle around shops, beaches, and condos without having to jump in the car. Experienced cyclists may also want to trace part of the Ironman course (112 miles round-trip) along the wide-shouldered "Queen K" and Akoni Pule highways from Kailua-Kona to Hawi, or join in one of the frequent group rides of the **Hawaii Cycling Club** (www.hawaiicyclingclub.com).

For simple cruisers, head to **Hawaiian Pedals,** Kona Inn Shopping Village, 75-5744 Alii Dr., Kailua-Kona (www.hawaiianpedals.com; ✆ **808/329-2294**), which has 7-speed city and hybrid bikes for $25 a day and just $91 a week; a 24-speed city bike is $30 a day, $112 a week. Pros and amateurs alike flock to its sister store, **Bike Works,** Hale Hana Centre, 74–5583 Luhia St., Kailua-Kona (www.bikeworkskona.com; ✆ **808/326-2453**) for an even bigger selection of bikes: cruisers ($25 a day), mountain bikes ($40 a day), hybrids ($20 a day), and racing bikes and front-suspension mountain bikes ($60 a day), all with discounts for longer bookings. Bike Works also has a shop in Queens' MarketPlace in the **Waikoloa Beach Resort** (www.bikeworkshawaii.com; ✆ **808/886-5000**) with similar offerings; both locations offer weekly group rides open to all.

Also in Kailua-Kona, **Cycle Station** (www.cyclestationhawaii.com; ✆ **808/ 327-0087**) has quality hybrid bikes for as low as $15 a day, with road and triathlon bikes starting at $30, including helmet, pump, and other gear. It's in Hale Kua Plaza in the Kaloko Industrial Area, 73-5619 Kauhola St.; entrance is on Kamanu Street behind Home Depot.

Note: Reserve well in advance for rentals in the first 2 weeks of October, during the leadup to the Ironman World Championship.

HAWAII VOLCANOES NATIONAL PARK

The national park has miles of paved roads and trails open to cyclists, from easy flat rides to challenging ascents, but you'll need to watch out for cars and buses on the often winding, narrow roads, and make sure you carry plenty of water and sunscreen. Download a cycling guide on the park's website (www.nps.gov/havo/ planyourvisit/bike.htm) or pick one up at the Kilauea Visitor Center. The closest bike-rental shops are in Hilo, including **Mid-Pacific Wheels,** 1133 Manono St. (www.midpacificwheelsllc.com; ✆ **808/935-6211**), which has mountain and road bikes for $25 to $45 a day, including a helmet; bike racks are $10 a day.

Or leave the planning to **Volcano Bike Tours** (www.bikevolcano.com; ✆ **888/934-9199** or 808/934-9199), which offers fully supported half- and full-day guided tours ($105–$129) in the national park that include some off-road riding and, on the longer tour, a van trip down to the end of Chain of Craters Road. There's also an all-day tour of Kilauea's East Rift zone outside the park, including visits to Lava Tree State Monument, Star of the Sea Painted Church, and Kalapana ($129). The longer tours include lunch; snacks are offered on the half-day tour.

Golf

If you'd like to improve your game while on the Big Island, **Darrin Gee's Spirit of Golf Academy** ★ (www.spiritofgolfacademy.com; ✆ **866/465-3433** or 808/887-6800) has a unique focus on mental preparation, with clinics held at the Big Island Country Club, Hapuna Golf Course, and Makalei Golf Club. The 2½-hour session costs $200 if booked online (ask for Web discount if booking by phone).

All rates below are for visitors; those with Hawaii state ID (*kamaʻāina*) may receive substantial discounts.

THE KONA COAST

Although the 18-hole Mountain Course of the **Kona Country Club** (www. konagolf.com; ✆ **808/322-3431**) in Keauhou has permanently closed, the club's popular Ocean Course was due to reopen after extensive renovations in late 2014. The fabulous **Hualalai Golf Course ★★★** at the Four Seasons Resort Hualalai (p. 220) is open only to resort guests—but for committed golfers, this Jack Nicklaus–designed championship course is reason enough to book a room and pay the sky-high greens fee of $275 ($150 for kids 13–18, free for children 12 and under with paying guest).

Luckily, upcountry Kona has two literally cooler alternatives to South Kohala's often hot, expensive oceanfront links, both listed below.

Big Island Country Club ★★   Designed by Perry Dye, this par-72, 18-hole course offers sweeping views of towering Mauna Kea and the bright blue coastline from its perch 2,000 feet above sea level. Although it's not on the ocean, water features wind around nine of the holes, including the spectacular par-3 No. 17. Waterfalls, tall palms, and other lush greenery add to the tropical feel; look for native birds such as the nene (Hawaiian goose), hawks, stilts, and black-crowned night herons. The wide fairways and gently rolling terrain make it appropriate for players of every level. Facilities include club rentals, driving range, pro shop, lounge, and snack bar.

71-1420 Mamalahoa Hwy. (Hwy. 190), Kailua-Kona. www.bigislandcountryclub.com. ✆ **808/325-5044.** Greens fees $89 before noon; $65 after noon. 9 holes (after 3pm) $35.

Makalei Golf Club ★   This par-72, 18-hole upcountry course—some 1,800 to 2,850 feet in elevation—goes up and down through native forests, cinder cones, and lava tubes over its championship length of 7,091 yards. The signature hole is the par-3 No. 15, offering a distant view of Maui and the best chance for a hole-in-one. A local favorite, Makalei is also visited by wild peacocks, pheasants, and turkeys. Facilities include a golf shop, driving range, putting greens, club rentals (with drop-off and pickup available), and the **Peacock Grille** restaurant, which serves burgers, salads, and snacks such as spam musubi.

72-3890 Hawaii Belt Rd. (Mamalahoa Hwy./Hwy. 190), Kailua-Kona. www.makalei.com. ✆ **808/325-6625.** Greens fees $89; $69 noon–2pm; $59 after 2pm. From the intersection of Palani Rd. and Hwy. 11 in Kailua-Kona, take Palani Rd. (which becomes Hwy. 190) east 7¼ miles, and look for green gates and small white sign on right.

THE KOHALA COAST

Hapuna Golf Course ★★★   Since its opening in 1992, this 18-hole championship course has been named the most environmentally sensitive course by "Golf" magazine, as well as "Course of the Future" by the U.S. Golf Association. Designed by Arnold Palmer and Ed Seay, this links-style course extends nearly 6,900 yards from the shoreline to 700 feet above sea level, with views of the pastoral Kohala Mountains and the Kohala coastline; look for Maui across the channel from the signature 12th hole. The elevation changes on the course keep it challenging (and windy the higher you go). There are a few elevated tee boxes and only 40 bunkers. Facilities include putting and chipping greens, driving range, practice bunker, lockers, showers, a pro shop, fitness center, and spa.

At the Hapuna Beach Prince Hotel, Mauna Kea Resort, off Hwy. 19 (near mile marker 69). www. princeresortshawaii.com. ☏ **808/880-3000.** Greens fees $125; twilight (after 1pm) $75.

Mauna Kea Golf Course ★★★

This breathtakingly beautiful, par-72, 7,114-yard championship course, designed by Robert Trent Jones, Jr., and recently updated by son Rees Jones, is consistently rated one of the top golf courses in the United States. The signature 3rd hole is 175 yards long; the Pacific Ocean and shoreline cliffs stand between the tee and the green, giving every golfer, from beginner to pro, a real challenge. Another par-3 that confounds duffers is the 11th hole, which drops 100 feet from tee to green and plays down to the ocean, into the steady trade winds. When the trades are blowing, 181 yards might as well be 1,000 yards. Book ahead; the course is very popular, especially for early weekend tee times. Facilities include a pro shop and clubhouse with restaurant, named **No. 3** for the hole Jones, Sr., once called "the most beautiful in the world."

At the Mauna Kea Beach Hotel, Mauna Kea Resort, off Hwy. 19 (near mile marker 68). www. princeresortshawaii.com. ☏ **808/882-5400.** Greens fees $255 ($230 for resort guests); twilight (after 1:30pm) $160.

Mauna Lani Francis H. I'i Brown Championship Courses ★★★

Carefully wrapped around ancient trails, fish ponds, and petroglyphs, the two 18-hole courses here have won "Golf" magazine's Gold Medal Award every year since the honor's inception in 1988. The **South Course,** a 7,029-yard, par-72, has two unforgettable ocean holes: the over-the-water 15th hole and the downhill, 221-yard, par-3 7th, which is bordered by the sea, a salt-and-pepper sand dune, and lush kiawe trees. The **North Course** may not have the drama of the oceanfront holes, but because it was built on older lava flows, the more extensive indigenous vegetation gives the course a Scottish feel. The hole that's cursed the most is the 140-yard, par-3 17th: It's beautiful but plays right into the surrounding lava field. Facilities include two driving ranges, a golf shop (with teaching pros), a restaurant, and putting greens. Mauna Lani also has the island's only *keiki* (children's) course, a 9-hole walking course for juniors, beginners, and families.

At the Mauna Lani Resort, Mauna Lani Dr., off Hwy. 19 (20 miles north of Kona Airport). www. maunalani.com. ☏ **808/885-6655.** Greens fees vary by time and season: Before noon, $165–$225 ($145–$170 for resort guests); after noon, $135–$145 ($125–$130 resort guests).

Waikoloa Beach Resort Courses ★

Two 18-hole courses beckon here. The pristine 18-hole, par-70 Beach Course certainly reflects the motto of designer Robert Trent Jones, Jr.: "Hard par, easy bogey." Most golfers remember the par-5, 505-yard 12th hole, a sharp dogleg left with bunkers in the corner and an elevated tee surrounded by lava. The Kings' Course, designed by Tom Weiskopf and Jay Morrish, is about 500 yards longer. Its links-style tract has a double green at the 3rd and 6th holes, and carefully placed bunkers see a lot of play, courtesy of the ever-present trade winds. Facilities include a golf shop, 15-acre practice range (with complimentary clubs and unlimited balls for just $15), and the affordable, Scottish-themed **Kings' Grille** restaurant; call for a free shuttle within the resort.

At the Waikoloa Beach Resort, 600 Waikoloa Beach Dr., Waikoloa. www.waikoloabeachgolf. com. ☏ **808/886-7888.** Greens fees: Before 11:30am, $145–$180 ($140 for resort guests); after 11:30am, $90–$120; 9 holes (after 8:30am), $69; children 6 to17, $50.

Waikoloa Village Golf Course ★

This semiprivate 18-hole course, with a par-72 for each of the three sets of tees, is hidden in the town of Waikoloa and

Other Outdoor Activities

HAWAII, THE BIG ISLAND

Manua Kea Golf Course.

usually overshadowed by the glamour resort courses along the Kohala Coast. Not only is it a beautiful course with great views, but it also offers some great golfing. The wind can play havoc with your game here (like most Hawaii golf courses). Robert Trent Jones, Jr., in designing this challenging course, inserted his trademark sand traps, slick greens, and great fairways. The par-5, 490-yard 18th hole is a thriller: It doglegs to the left, and the last 75 yards up to the green are water, water, water. Enjoy the fabulous views of Mauna Kea and Mauna Loa, and—on a very clear day—Maui's Haleakala in the distance.

In Waikoloa Village, 68-1793 Melia St., Waikoloa. www.waikoloavillagegolf.com. © **808/883-9621.** Greens fees $84 ($72 Village guests). From the airport, turn left on Hwy. 19, head 18 miles to stoplight at Waikoloa Rd. Turn left, drive uphill 6½ miles to left on Paniolo Ave. Take 1st right onto Lua Kula St. and follow ½-mile to Melia St.

HILO

Hilo Municipal Golf Course This 146-acre course is great for the casual golfer: It's flat, scenic, and often fun. **Warning:** Don't go after a heavy rain (especially in winter), when the fairways can get really soggy and play can slow way down. The rain does keep the course green and beautiful, though. Wonderful trees (monkeypods, coconuts, eucalyptus, banyans) dot the grounds, and the views—of Mauna Kea on one side and Hilo Bay on the other—are breathtaking. There are four sets of tees, with a par-71 from all; the back tees give you 6,325 yards of play. Since it's the only municipal course on the island, and in the state's second largest city, getting a tee time can be a challenge; weekdays are your best bet. Facilities include driving range, pro shop, club rentals, restaurant, and snack bar.

340 Haihai St. (btw. Kinoole and Iwalani sts.), Hilo. © **808/959-7711.** Greens fees $34 Mon–Fri, $45 Sat–Sun and holidays; carts $16.

Naniloa Country Club   At first glance, this semi-private 9-hole course just off Hilo Bay looks pretty flat and short, but once you get beyond the 1st hole—a wide, straightforward 330-yard par-4—things get challenging. The tree-lined fairways require straight drives, and the huge lake on the 2nd and 5th holes is sure to haunt you. This course is very popular with locals and visitors alike. Facilities include driving range, putting green, pro shop, and club rentals.

120 Banyan Dr. (at the intersection of hwys. 11 and 19), Hilo. © **808/935-3000.** Greens fees: 9 holes, $10 adults ($9 seniors 62 and over, $5 children under 18); 18 holes, $15 adults ($12 seniors 62 and over, $9 children under 18). Cart $10 ($15 for 18 holes).

Hiking

Trails on the Big Island wind through fields of coastal lava rock, deserts, rainforests, and mountain tundra, sometimes covered with snow. It's important to wear sturdy shoes, sunscreen, and a hat, and take plenty of water; for longer hikes, particularly in remote areas, it may also be essential to bring food, a flashlight, and a trail map—not one that requires a cellphone signal to access (coverage may be nonexistent). Hunting may be permitted in rural, upcountry, or remote areas, so stay on the trails and wear bright clothing.

The island has 15 trails in the state's **Na Ala Hele Hawaii Trail & Access System** (www.hawaiitrails.org; © **808/974-4382**), highlights of which are included below; see the website for more information. For an even greater number of trails on a variety of public lands, see the detailed descriptions on **www.bigislandhikes.com**.

KONA & KOHALA COASTS

The **Ala Kahakai National Historic Trail** (www.nps.gov/alka; © **808/326-6012,** ext. 101) is the designation for an ancient, 175-mile series of paths through coastal lava rock, from Upolu Point in North Kohala along the island's west coast to Ka Lae (South Point) and east to Puna's Wahaula Heiau, an extensive temple complex. Some were created as long-distance trails, others for fishing and gathering, while a few were reserved for royal or chiefly use. There's unofficial access through the four national park sites—Puukohola Heiau, Kaloko-Honokoau, Puuhonua O Honaunau, and Hawaii Volcanoes (see "Attractions & Points of Interest" on p. 157)—but it's easy, free, and fun to walk a portion of the 15.4-mile stretch between Kawaihae and Anaehoomalu Bay, part of the state's **Na Ala Hele** trails system (www.hawaiitrails.org; © **808/974-4382**). Signs mark only the 8-mile portion of Ala Kahakai between **Spencer Beach** (p. 193), its northern terminus, and Puako, at **Holoholokai Beach Park,** near the petroglyph field on the Mauna Lani Resort, but it's fairly easy to follow farther south by hugging the shoreline, past resort hotels and multimillion-dollar homes, anchialine ponds, and jagged lava formations.

For those not satisfied with the view from the **Pololu Valley Lookout** (p. 167), the steep, 1-mile **Pololu Valley Trail** will lead you just behind the black-sand beach (beware of high surf and riptides). In addition to a 420-foot elevation change, the trail's challenges can include slippery mud and tricky footing over ancient cobblestones. As with all windward (that is, rainy) areas, be prepared for pesky mosquitos and/or cool mist.

If you're willing to venture on Saddle Road (Hwy. 200), which some rental-car companies still forbid, the **Puu Huluhulu Trail** is an easy, .6-mile hike that gradually loops around both crests of this forested cinder cone, with panoramic views of Mauna Kea and Mauna Loa between the trees. There's a parking lot in

Hiking Devastation Trail.

front of the hunter check-in station at the junction of the Mauna Loa observatory access road and Saddle Road.

THE HAMAKUA COAST

The 25-percent grade on the 1-mile "hike" down the road to **Waipio Valley** (p. 172) is a killer on the knees, and no picnic coming back up, but that's just the start of the epic, 18-mile round-trip adventure involving the **Muliwai Trail,** a very strenuous hike to primeval, waterfall-laced **Waimanu Valley.** This trail is the island's closest rival to Kauai's **Kalalau Trail** (p. 467), and so is only worth attempting by very physically fit and well-prepared hikers. Once in Waipio Valley, you must follow the beach to Wailoa Stream, ford it, and cross the dunes to the west side of the valley. There the zigzag Muliwai Trail officially begins, carving its way some 1,300 feet up the cliff; the reward at the third switchback is a wonderful view of Hiilawe Falls. Ahead lie 5 miles of 12 smaller, tree-covered gulches to cross before your first view of pristine Waimanu Valley, which has nine campsites (see "Camping" on p. 233) and two outhouses, but no drinking water. The trail is eroded in places and slippery when wet—which is often, due to the 100-plus inches of rain, which can also flood streams. This explains why the vast majority of those who see Waimanu Valley do so via helicopter (p. 186).

HAWAII VOLCANOES NATIONAL PARK

This magnificent national treasure and Hawaiian cultural icon (p. 182) has more than 150 miles of trails, including many day hikes, most of which are well-maintained and well-marked; a few are paved or have boardwalks, permitting strollers and wheelchairs. **Warning:** If you have heart or respiratory problems or if you're pregnant, don't attempt any hike in the park; the fumes will bother you. Also: Stacked rocks known as *ahu* mark trails crossing lava; please do not disturb or create your own.

GUIDED hikes

A guided day or night hike is a safe but stimulating way for city slickers to explore natural Hawaii. Book one of these excursions before you arrive; trips fill up quickly.

A longtime resident of Hawaii, Dr. Hugh Montgomery of **Hawaiian Walkways** ★ (www.hawaiianwalkways.com; ℂ **800/457-7759** or 808/775-0372), one-time winner of "Tour Operator of the Year" by the Hawaii Ecotourism Association of Hawaii, offers a variety of options, ranging from excursions that skirt the rim of immense valleys to hikes through the clouds on the volcano. Hikes range from $119 to $185 for adults, and $99 to $130 for kids. Custom hikes are available for one to four hikers from $600. Prices include food, beverages, and equipment.

Naturalist and educator Rob Pacheco of **Hawaii Forest & Trail** ★★★ (www. hawaii-forest.com; ℂ **800/464-1993** or 808/331-8505) offers fully outfitted day trips to some of the island's most remote, pristine areas, including lands to which his company has exclusive access. His well-trained guides narrate the entire trip, offering extensive ecological, geological, and cultural commentary (and more than a little humor). Tours are limited to 12 to 14 people and are highly personalized to meet the group's interests and abilities. Options include my personal favorite, the 8-hour **Kohala Waterfalls Adventure** ($169 for adults, $139 for children 12 and under), which you can pair with ziplining (p. 217); exceptionally well-run, all-day **birding tours,** for ages 8 and older ($179–$189); all-day trips to **Hawaii Volcanoes National Park** ★★★, some 300 miles round-trip ($179–$189 for adults, $159 for children) and some shorter (6–7 hr.); and stargazing atop **Mauna Kea** ★★★ ($199; for ages 16 and up only).

Tours often involve the assistance of a 6×6 Pinzgauer Scrambler that allows you to explore hard-to-reach places; the "hiking" is generally 2 to 4 hours of easy-to-moderate walking, over terrain manageable by anyone in average physical condition. Walking sticks, food, and beverages are provided, along with rain ponchos and warm gear, depending on the itinerary. **Note:** The amount of driving and overall length of the birding and volcano tours (11–12 hr.) make them unsuitable for young or restless children.

Plan ahead by downloading maps and brochures on the park website (www. nps.gov/havo), which also lists areas closed due to current eruptions. Always check conditions with the rangers at the Kilauea Visitor Center, where you can pick up detailed trail guides. **Note:** All overnight backcountry hiking and camping requires a free permit, available only the day of or the day before your hike, from the park's **Backcountry Office** (ℂ **808/985-6178**).

In addition to sights described on the **Crater Rim Drive** tour (p. 182) and **Chain of Craters Road** tour (p. 184), here are some of the more accessible highlights for hikers, all demonstrating the power of Pele:

Kilauea Iki Trail   The 4-mile loop trail begins 2 miles from the visitor center on Crater Rim Road, descends through a forest of ferns into still-fuming Kilauea Iki Crater, and then crosses the crater floor past the vent where a 1959 lava blast shot a fountain of fire 1,900 feet into the air for 36 days. Allow 2 hours for this fair-to-moderate hike, and look for white-tailed tropicbirds and Hawaiian hawks above you.

Devastation Trail ★★   Up on the rim of Kilauea Iki Crater, you can see what an erupting volcano did to a once-flourishing ohia forest. The scorched earth with its ghostly tree skeletons stands in sharp contrast to the rest of the lush forest. Everyone can take this 1-mile round-trip hike on a paved path across the eerie bed of black cinders. The trailhead is on Crater Rim Road at Puu Puai Overlook.

Kipuka Puaulu (Bird Park) Trail   This easy 1.2-mile round-trip hike lets you see native Hawaiian flora and fauna in a little oasis of living nature in a field of lava, known as a *kīpuka*. For some reason, the once red-hot lava skirted this mini-forest and let it survive. Go early in the morning or in the evening (or, even better, just after a rain) to see native birds like the *'apapane* (a small, bright-red bird with black wings and tail) and the *'i'iwi* (larger and orange-vermilion colored, with a curved salmon-hued bill). Native trees along the trail include giant ohia, koa, soapberry, kolea, and mamane.

Puu Huluhulu   This moderate 3-mile round-trip hike to the summit of a cinder cone (which shares its name with the one on Saddle Rd., described above) crosses lava flows from 1973 and 1974, lava tree molds, and kipuka. At the top is a panoramic vista of Mauna Loa, Mauna Kea, the coastline, and the often steaming vent of Puu Oo. The trailhead is 8 miles from the visitor center, in the Mauna Ulu parking area on Chain of Craters Road. *Note:* Sulfur fumes can be stronger here than on other trails.

For avid trekkers, several long, steep, unshaded hikes lead to the beaches and rocky bays on the park's remote shoreline; they're all considered overnight backcountry hikes and, thus, require a permit. Only hiking diehards should consider attempting the **Mauna Loa Trail,** perhaps the most challenging hike in all of Hawaii. Many hikers have had to be rescued over the years due to high-altitude sickness or exposure, after becoming lost in snowy or foggy conditions. From the trailhead at the end of Mauna Loa Road, about an hour's drive from the visitor center, it's 7.5 miles to the Puu Ulaula ("Red Hill") cabin at 10,035 feet, and then 12 more miles up to the primitive Mauna Loa summit cabin at 13,250 feet, where the climate is subarctic and overnight temperatures are below freezing year-round. In addition to backcountry permits (see above), this 4-day round-trip requires special gear, great physical condition, and careful planning.

Horseback Riding

Although vast Parker Ranch, the historic center of Hawaiian ranching, no longer offers horseback tours, several other ranches in upcountry Waimea provide opportunities for riding with sweeping views of land and sea. Picturesque Waipio Valley is also another focus of equestrian excursions. *Note:* Most stables require riders to be at least 8 years old and weigh no more than 230 pounds; confirm before booking.

The 11,000-acre Ponoholo Ranch, whose herd of cattle (varying between

Horseback riding at Parker Ranch.

HOME ON THE RANGE: paniolo & pā'ū riders

The Big Island is home to Hawaii's original *paniolo,* Mexican cowboys brought over by King Kamehameha III in the 1830s to round up herds of wild cattle. The unruly live-stock were the descendants of cattle that British Capt. George Vancouver had given to King Kamehameha I in the early 1790s; with no predators, the cattle's numbers bur-geoned wildly after the king placed a *kapu* (ban) on their being hunted or eaten, a restriction that lasted till 1830. Fortunately, an American named Richard Cleveland had also given Kamehameha a mare and a stallion in 1803, so horses were a known quan-tity when the Mexican *vaqueros* arrived on the scene. (The Hawaiian word for cowboy, *paniolo,* is said to derive from their word for the language the cowboys spoke, *español.*)

Although they didn't stay long—apparently, just a year—the Mexican cowboys taught their Hawaiian students well. In 1908, three *paniolo* from the Big Island competed at Frontiers Days in Cheyenne, Wyoming, then the country's premiere rodeo contest, wearing cowboy hats adorned with lei. Ikua Purdy won the steer-roping contest, while his island companions came in second and sixth. Purdy was inducted into the National Rodeo Cowboy Hall of Fame in 1999, and in 2003 the Paniolo Preservation Society erected a statue in Waimea of him roping a steer.

Hawaiian women also quickly adapted to riding horses, but rather than do so sidesaddle, as expected of proper ladies then, they straddled their steeds and cov-ered their hiked-up skirts and petticoats with long, billowing over-skirts called *pā'ū* or pau ("pah-oo"). Pau riders on horses covered with lei are now a staple of parades celebrating King Kamehameha Day (June 11) and other Hawaiian cultural celebrations, particularly on the Big Island.

6,000 and 8,000) is second only to Parker Ranch's, is the scenic home base for **Paniolo Adventures** (www.panioloadventures.com; ℂ **808/889-5354**). Most of its five rides are open-range style and include brief stretches of trotting and cantering, although the gorgeous scenery outweighs the equine excitement—all but the 4-hour Wrangler Ride ($175) are suitable for beginners. The tamest option is the 1-hour City Slicker ride ($69), but the 1½-hour Sunset Ride ($89) appears to be the most popular. Boots, light jackets, Australian dusters, chaps, helmets, hats, drinks, and even sunscreen are provided. Look for Paniolo Adventures' red barn on Kohala Mountain Road (Hwy. 250), just north of mile marker 13.

Naalapa Stables (www.naalapastables.com; ℂ **808/889-0022**) operates rides at Kahua Ranch, which also has an entrance on Kohala Mountain Road, north of mile marker 11. Riding open-range style, you'll pass ancient Hawaiian ruins, through lush pastures with grazing sheep and cows, and along mountain-tops with panoramic coastal views. The horses and various riding areas are suited to everyone from first-timers to experienced equestrians. There are several trips a day: a 2½-hour tour at 9am and 1pm for $94 and a 1½-hour tour at 10am and 1:30pm for $73; check-in is a half-hour earlier.

Naalapa has another stable in Waipio Valley (ℂ **808/775-0419**), which offers the more rugged **Waipio Valley Horseback Adventure ★★**, a 2½-hour ride that starts with a 4WD van ride down to this little-inhabited but widely revered valley (p. 174). The horses are sure-footed in the rocky streams and muddy trails, while the guides, who are well-versed in Hawaiian history, provide running commentary. The cost is $94 for adults, with tours at 9:30am and 12:30pm Monday to Saturday. Don't forget your camera or bug spray; check in a half-hour earlier at **Waipio Valley Artworks,** 48-5415 Kukuihaele Road, off Highway 240, about 8 miles northwest of Honokaa.

Waipio Valley Artworks (see above) is also the check-in point for **Waipio Ridge Stables** (www.waipioridgestables.com; ☎ **877/757-1414** or 808/775-1007), which leads riders on a 2½-hour Valley Rim Ride ($85), including views of the beach below and Hiilawe waterfall at the rear of the deep valley. The 5-hour Hidden Waterfalls Ride ($165) includes the sights along the rim ride, and then follows the stream that feeds Hiilawe through the rainforest to a picnic and swim in a bracingly cool waterfall pool, but it's rather long if you're not into riding. *Note:* Fog sometimes obscures views of Waipio Valley from the rim.

Tennis

While most resorts do not allow nonguests to use their tennis facilities, there are two fine exceptions on the Kohala Coast (both with a stadium court if you really want to strut your stuff). In the Mauna Lani Resort, the **Hawaii Tennis Center** at the Fairmont Orchid Hawaii, 1 North Kaniku Dr., Waimea (www.fairmont. com/orchid; ☎ **808/887-7532**), offers 10 courts, equipment and ball machine rentals, and lessons. Hourly court fees are $30; check in at pro shop first. The **Ocean Sports Tennis Centre** at Hilton Waikoloa Village, 69-425 Waikoloa Beach Dr., Waikoloa (www.hawaiioceansports.com; ☎ **808/886-6666,** ext. 108), provides six cushioned courts, lessons, clinics, and racket rentals. Court fees are $35 per hour, with rackets included.

You can also play for free at any Hawaii County tennis court; the easiest way to find one nearest you is to visit **www.tennisinhawaii.com**.

Ziplining

Ziplining gives Big Island visitors an exhilarating way to view dramatic gulches, thick forests, gushing waterfalls, and other inspiring scenery—without significantly altering the landscape. Typically, the pulley-and-harness systems have redundant safety mechanisms, with lines and gear inspected daily and multiple checks of your equipment during the tour; your biggest worry may be losing your cellphone or anything not in a zipped pocket. Most outfitters also rent GoPro video cameras that attach to your helmets, so you can relive your whizzing rides at home.

Note: For safety reasons, tours have minimum ages (4–10 years, depending on the outfitter) and minimum and maximum weights; read the fine print carefully before booking. Outfitters also go out several times a day, rain or shine, which on the Hilo side is likely to include both on any given day; dress accordingly. Most excursions last 2 to 3 hours, but the exact length of your tour will vary based on number of riders, so don't schedule your day too tightly.

NORTH KOHALA The Australian eucalyptus and native kukui trees on **Kohala Zipline's Canopy Tour ★★** (www.kohalazipline.com; ☎ **800/464-1993** or 808/331-3620) might not provide the most colorful panoramas, but this nine-line adventure ($169 adults, $139 kids 8–12) emphasizes environmental awareness and cultural history in a compelling way—and the extra-quiet ziplines and multiple suspension bridges are a hoot, too. You'll fly from platform to platform in a sylvan setting that includes ancient taro terraces believed to have been farmed by

Kamehameha before he became king. Tours depart from the zip station on Highway 270 between Hawi and Kapaau, but shuttle service is also available from South Kohala and North Kona resorts for the 8:30am and 1pm tours; the package costs $209 for adults and $179 for children, with lunch included. For a very special splurge, take the outfitter's 8-hour **Kohala Zip & Dip ★★★** ($249), which combines the Canopy Tour with Hawaii Forest & Trail's fascinating Kohala Waterfalls Adventure (p. 214), including a waterfall swim and picnic overlooking beautiful Pololu Valley. The Zip & Dip tours depart from Queens' MarketPlace in Waikoloa Beach Resort and Hawaii Forest & Trail headquarters on Highway 19 in Kailua-Kona, 74-5035 Queen Kaahumanu Hwy. (north of Kealakehe Parkway). *Tip:* Book online for 10-percent discount.

KAILUA-KONA The eight-line course of **Kona Eco Adventures ★** (www.kona zip.com; ℂ **808/324-4111**), some 4,000 feet above the Keauhou coastline, is exciting while still being suitable for beginners. Opened in 2013, the tree-to-tree course ($155) includes two suspension bridges and a good look at the livestock and wildlife on Misty Mountain Farm, a working cattle ranch. A shuttle meets participants at the Keauhou Shopping Center to deliver them to the farm, where a rugged six-wheel Pinzgauer van then ferries them to the course. Bring a light jacket, since you're at high elevation,

THE HAMAKUA COAST I don't like the misleading name, but I can't begrudge the thrills involved on the **Akaka Falls Skyline Adventure ★★** (www.zipline hawaii.com; ℂ **888/864-6947**), which actually zips past the nearly 250-foot-tall **Kolekole Falls,** downstream from the taller and more famous **Akaka Falls** (p. 170) in Honomu, about 12 miles north of Hilo. The seven-line course builds in length and speed, while the well-informed guides share insights into local flora and fauna—including banana, taro, and wild pigs—and the area's history as a sugar plantation. The 2½- to 3-hour tour costs $170, with 10 percent off for online bookings.

The **Umauma Falls Zipline Tour ★★** (www.umaumaexperience.com; ℂ **808/930-9477**) lives up to its name, where you see the captivating, three-tiered falls (p. 172) along with 13 other smaller cascades, as you zip along its nine-line course ($189) in Hakalau, about 16 miles north of Hilo. The Zip and Dip option ($239) includes an hour of kayaking and swimming under a waterfall; for a four-line option, contact the company directly.

Just down the road from Umauma Falls, **Zip Isle Zip Line ★** (www.zip isle.com; ℂ **888/947-4753** or 808/963-5427) operates a seven-line course ($147) at **World Botanical Gardens ★** (p. 174) that's a little easier on the legs (less climbing) and nerves, unless suspension bridges bother you. Those who still don't want to zip can watch those who do while strolling through the tropical gardens below.

WHERE TO STAY ON THE BIG ISLAND

For additional information on **bed-and-breakfasts,** visit the website of **Hawaii Island B&B Association** (www.stayhawaii.com), which only allows licensed, inspected properties to become members. **Vacation rentals,** which Hawaii County does not regulate the way it does B&Bs and hotels, are currently less of a hot-button issue here than on other islands. You'll find numerous listings of condos and houses on sites such as VRBO.com and airbnb.com. To help you more easily compare units and complexes, as well as guarantee rapid assistance should issues arise during your stay, though, consider booking vacation rentals through an island-based company, such as those listed for specific regions below.

Remember to add Hawaii's 13.41 percent tax to your final bill. In the listings below, all rooms come with a full private bathroom (with tub and/or shower) and free parking unless otherwise noted. All pools are outdoors.

The Kona Coast

Many of the lodgings in Kailua-Kona and Keauhou are timeshares or individually owned condos; rates, decor, and amenities in the latter may vary widely by unit. For a broad selection of well-managed condos and a smaller selection of homes (most with pools), contact **Kona Rentals** (www.konarentals.com; ⓒ **800/799-5662**) or **Kona Hawaii Vacation Rentals** (www.konahawaii.com; ⓒ **809/244-4752** or 808/329-3333). *Note:* Prices and minimum-stay requirements may be significantly higher during the week before and after the Ironman World Championship (usually the second Sat in Oct), as well as during holidays.

CENTRAL KAILUA-KONA

In addition to the lodgings below, consider booking a condo at the **Royal Sea Cliff ★★**, on the ocean side of Alii Drive about 2 miles south of the Kailua Pier. There's no beach, but it has two oceanfront pools, often the site of free entertainment, and a tennis court. **Outrigger Hotels & Resorts** (www.outrigger.com; ⓒ **800/688-7444** or 808/329-8021) manages 62 large, well-appointed units there, with full kitchens and washer-dryers, out of 148 total (others are timeshares or individually managed rentals.) Outrigger charges $129 to $399, plus cleaning fees of $75 to $115, for accommodations ranging from studios (650 sq. ft.) up to two-bedroom, two-bathroom units (1,100–1,300 sq. ft.).

Moderate

Courtyard King Kamehameha Kona Beach Hotel ★★★   Long a somewhat shabby hotel in a premium setting—in front of King Kamehameha's royal compound on Kailua Bay, Kamakahonu Beach, and Kailua Pier—King Kam is shabby no more. Rooms and public spaces have been revitalized with flatscreen TVs, new bathrooms, and modern furnishings but have also been imbued with a new sense of history and place. Subtle patterns in the stylish guest rooms reflect lava, native plants, and traditional tattoo designs, while colors suggest sand, coffee, and rainforest ferns. The high-ceilinged, bright-toned lobby is home to a gallery of royal portraits and Hawaiian cultural scenes by the late Herb Kawainui Kane, a revered artist. And when the March 2011 tsunami sent saltwater coursing through the pool bar and ground floor, management quickly restored the public areas—including the infinity-edge pool overlooking the bay—yet again. More recently, the hotel restored its two tennis courts and pro shop, and expanded the food offerings and music (including sushi and jazz) at **Honu's on the Beach,** its popular indoor/outdoor restaurant. *Note:* For a week or so in early October, this is Ironman central, full of buff bodies, many belonging to international triathletes, all abuzz about the world championship that starts and ends just outside the "King Kam's" door.

75–5660 Palani Rd., Kailua-Kona. www.konabeachhotel.com. ⓒ **800/367-2111** or 808/329-2911. 460 units. $154–$329 up to 4 people; from $259 suite. Check for online discounts and packages. Parking $14. **Amenities:** 2 restaurants; poolside bar; convenience store; fitness center; coin-operated laundry; luau; infinity pool; Dollar rental-car agency; room service; 2 lighted tennis courts and pro shop; watersports equipment rentals; Wi-Fi (free).

Kona Magic Sands ★ With Kailua-Kona's largest (if somewhat fickle) sandy beach next door, and oceanfront lanais on every unit to soak in the fabulous sunsets and let in the sound of pounding waves, this location is ideal for couples who don't want to spend a bundle at a resort. All the units are studios, with the living/sleeping area bracketed by the lanai on one end and the kitchen on the other; because they're individually owned (and some managed by other companies than the one listed below), furnishings vary greatly unit to unit. Try to book a corner unit, since those have larger lanais, or spring for the luxuriously remodeled No. 302, which comes with granite counters, travertine tile floors, and gorgeous hardwood cabinets, including one that hides a Murphy bed with Tempurpedic mattress. The pool is also right on the ocean. *Note:* The ground-floor restaurant was closed at press time, but units above it can expect to hear noise if it reopens.

77–6452 Alii Dr. (next to Laaloa/Magic Sands Beach Park), Kailua-Kona. Reservations c/o Hawaii Resort Management. www.konahawaii.com. ✆ **800/244-4752** or 808/329-3333. 37 units, all with shower only. Apr 15–Dec 14: $115, $125 corner, $159 No. 302. Dec15–Apr 14: $150, $160 corner, $179 No. 302. Cleaning fee $85 for 3-night or longer stays. **Amenities:** Pool; Wi-Fi (free).

Inexpensive

Kona Tiki Hotel ★★ How close are you to the ocean here? Close enough that waves occasionally break on the seawall, sending seaspray into the oceanfront pool, and close enough that their constant crashing drowns out all or most of the traffic noise from nearby Alii Drive (ask for a unit away from the road if you're a light sleeper). The small, simply furnished rooms (no TV or phones) feature homey decor, such as pastel tropical print bedspreads. All come with oceanfront lanais, mini-fridges, and ceiling fans (you'll need them); upper-story units have kitchenettes so you can make light meals in addition to the basic continental breakfast (bagels, fruit, coffee) served by the pool. The warm, helpful staff members are quick to lend beach gear and give travel tips; they also make every sunset a special occasion, enlisting guests to help light the tiki torches and blow a conch shell. With no fees for parking, Wi-Fi, or "resort" amenities, this is a true bargain.

75–5968 Alii Dr., Kailua-Kona (about a mile from downtown). www.konatikihotel.com. ✆ **808/329-1425.** 15 units. $85–$105 double; $109-$115 double with kitchenette; $159 suite with king bed. Rates include continental breakfast. 3-night minimum. Extra person $15 per adult ($18 in high season), $6 per child 5–12. Futon or crib $5. Credit cards accepted for deposits over $350; PayPal for lesser amounts. **Amenities:** Outdoor pool; Wi-Fi (free).

NORTH KONA

Expensive

Four Seasons Resort Hualalai at Historic Kaupulehu ★★★ Sometimes, you do get what you pay for—and that's just about anything you could desire at this serenely welcoming resort, only a 15-minute drive from the airport but definitely worlds away from anything resembling hustle and bustle. The 18-hole Jack Nicklaus signature golf course, award-winning spa, and multi-room fitness center are open only to hotel guests and members, while a series of renovations before and after the March 2011 tsunami have only increased the sense of quiet luxury in and around the small clusters of two-story guest-room buildings and villas. Rooms start at 635 square feet, with private lanais and large bathrooms outfitted with glass-walled showers and deep soaking tubs; ask for one with an outdoor lava-rock shower. All have views of the ocean or one of seven swimming pools; the newest is the adults-only Palm Grove Pool, with a swim-up bar and daybeds, but snorkeling in Kings' Pond amid rays and tropical fish

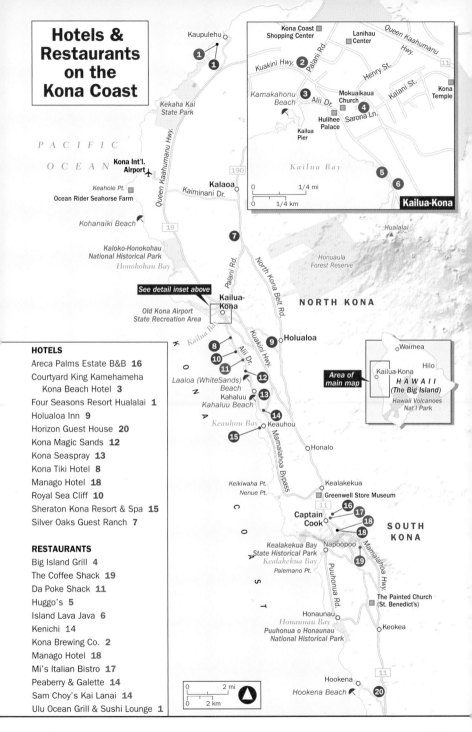

Hotels & Restaurants on the Kona Coast

Kailua-Kona

HOTELS

Areca Palms Estate B&B **16**
Courtyard King Kamehameha Kona Beach Hotel **3**
Four Seasons Resort Hualalai **1**
Holualoa Inn **9**
Horizon Guest House **20**
Kona Magic Sands **12**
Kona Seaspray **13**
Kona Tiki Hotel **8**
Manago Hotel **18**
Royal Sea Cliff **10**
Sheraton Kona Resort & Spa **15**
Silver Oaks Guest Ranch **7**

RESTAURANTS

Big Island Grill **4**
The Coffee Shack **19**
Da Poke Shack **11**
Huggo's **5**
Island Lava Java **6**
Kenichi **14**
Kona Brewing Co. **2**
Manago Hotel **18**
Mi's Italian Bistro **17**
Peaberry & Galette **14**
Sam Choy's Kai Lanai **14**
Ulu Ocean Grill & Sushi Lounge **1**

remains a top draw. Dinner at **Ulu Ocean Grill** or the **Beach Tree** are consistently excellent, if costly; but it can be hard to tear yourself away in search of cheaper options nearly a half-hour away. Kudos to the Four Seasons for continuing to buck the resort-fee trend, for not charging for its children's or cultural programs, and for committing to numerous environmental measures, including the support of the Hawaiian Legacy Hardwoods' koa reforestation (see "Organized Tours," p. 186).

72–100 Kaupulehu Dr., Kailua-Kona. www.fourseasons.com/hualalai. ✆ **888/340-5662** or 808/ 325-8000. 243 units. $545–$1,480 double; from $1,420 suite. Extra person $190. Children 18 and under stay free in parent's room (maximum occupancy in guest rooms is 3 people; couples with more than 1 child must get a suite or 2 rooms). Self-parking free, valet parking $20 per day. **Amenities:** 5 restaurants and lounges; 2 bars (w/nightly entertainment); babysitting; complimentary year-round children's program; concierge; cultural center; fitness center; 18-hole Jack Nicklaus signature golf course, 7 pools, including snorkeling pond; room service; award-winning spa; 8 tennis courts (4 lit for night play); watersports equipment rentals; Wi-Fi (free).

Holualoa Inn ★★   For these rates (starting at $355), you could be staying in one of the lower-priced rooms on the Kohala Coast resort—but then again, the inn on this 30-acre estate with 5,100 coffee trees offers privacy you'd be hard-pressed to match. Off the main road in the art and coffee enclave of Holualoa, the 7,000-square-foot contemporary Hawaiian main building hosts six immaculate suites, all with warm hardwood floors, luxurious baths, and timeless furnishings. Most offer sweeping views of the coastline more than 1,000 feet below; the handsome Coffee Cherry Suite has a lush garden view, as well as a private hot tub. For even more privacy, the one-bedroom Darrell Hill Cottage, a former artist's residence, includes a handsomely appointed kitchen, cozy sitting area, and wraparound lanai, also overlooking the sea. Owner Sandy Hazen's Kona coffee brand, Brazen Hazen, accompanies gourmet breakfasts prepared by a chef, but you can also take a mug up to the rooftop gazebo or enjoy it by the oceanview pool.

76–5932 Mamalahoa Hwy., Holualoa. www.holualoainn.com. ✆ **800/392-1812** or 808/324-1121. 6 units, 1 cottage. $355–$445 double, $595–$695 cottage. Rates include full breakfast. On Mamalahoa Hwy., just after Holualoa post office, look for Paul's Place General Store; the next driveway is the inn. Children must be 13 or older. **Amenities:** Jacuzzi; free laundry facilities; pool; Wi-Fi (free).

Moderate

Silver Oaks Guest Ranch ★   You won't have to worry about sweltering in Kona's afternoon heat here, some 1,300 feet above the coast, where it stays in the 70s (low to middle 20s Celsius) year-round. It's only 5 miles from the historic center of town, but you'll want to leave time to meet the animals on this 10-acre working ranch, including miniature donkeys, Nigerian dwarf goats, and horses, not to mention wild turkeys and other local fowl. Hosts Amy and Rick Decker no longer offer breakfast service, but the 900-square-foot Ranch View and Ranch House cottages, which share a large shaded veranda, each have full kitchens, and the stand-alone Garden Cottage, just 300 square feet, has an ample kitchenette. All have sweeping views that include ocean horizon, but sunsets are particularly special by the hot tub and pool at the main house.

73–4570 Mamalahoa Hwy., Kailua-Kona. www.silveroaksranch.com. ✆ **808/325-2000.** 3 units, plus additional space available for large groups. $120–$195 double. Extra person $20. 5-night minimum. From the airport, take Hwy. 19 ½-mile south to Kaiminani Dr., turn left, drive 3½ miles to Mamalahoa Hwy. (Hwy. 180), turn right. Ranch is 1 mile on your left. **Amenities:** Hot tub; pool; Wi-Fi (free).

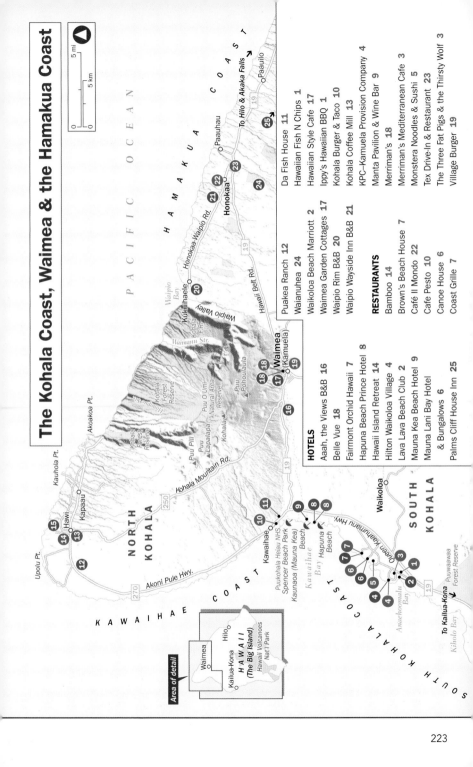

The Kohala Coast, Waimea & the Hamakua Coast

HOTELS

Aaah, the Views B&B **16**
Belle Vue **18**
Fairmont Orchid Hawaii **7**
Hapuna Beach Prince Hotel **8**
Hawaii Island Retreat **14**
Hilton Waikoloa Village **4**
Lava Lava Beach Club **2**
Mauna Kea Beach Hotel **9**
Mauna Lani Bay Hotel
& Bungalows **6**
Palms Cliff House Inn **25**

Puakea Ranch **12**
Waianuhea **24**
Waikoloa Beach Marriott **2**
Waimea Garden Cottages **17**
Waipio Rim B&B **20**
Waipio Wayside Inn B&B **21**

Da Fish House **11**
Hawaiian Fish N Chips **1**
Hawaiian Style Cafe **17**
Ippy's Hawaiian BBQ **1**
Kohala Burger & Taco **10**
Kohala Coffee Mill **13**
KPC–Kamuela Provision Company **4**
Manta Pavilion & Wine Bar **9**
Merriman's **18**
Merriman's Mediterranean Cafe **3**
Monstera Noodles & Sushi **5**
Tex Drive-In & Restaurant **23**
The Three Fat Pigs & the Thirsty Wolf **3**
Village Burger **19**

RESTAURANTS

Bamboo **14**
Brown's Beach House **7**
Café Il Mondo **22**
Cafe Pesto **10**
Canoe House **6**
Coast Grille **7**

223

KEAUHOU

Expensive

Sheraton Kona Resort & Spa at Keauhou Bay ★★ The name and look have changed several times since 2000, but this excellently priced resort overlooking Keauhou Bay and the ocean just keeps getting better. The first dramatic renovation of the former Kona Surf, closed in 2000, came in 2005, when walls were removed to open panoramic views, rooms were modernized to Sheraton standards, and an enormous, multi-level fantasy pool was added to offset the lack of beachfront. Another $20-million makeover, completed in late 2012 and overseen by cultural expert and textile designer Sig Zane (see "Big Island Shopping," p. 244), has added more splashes of bright color, improved landscaping, and highlighted the area's rich cultural history with new signage and tours. In addition to the sandy-bottomed pool, water slide, and kid-pleasing fountain play area, there's a lounge just for teens, with Xbox, Wii, and table tennis. The vast majority of rooms have lanais, at least 80 percent with partial oceanview—all the better to ogle the manta rays that frequent this area. You can also spot rays from the lanai off **Rays on the Bay,** a vivacious restaurant/lounge with firepits and tasty cocktails. Check online for one of the frequent deals with prices at the "moderate" level.

78–128 Ehukai St., Kailua-Kona. www.sheratonkona.com. ✆ **888/488-3535** or 808/930-4900. 509 units. $175–$530 double; from $453 suite. Check for online packages. Daily resort fee $31, includes tax, self-parking (valet $7 additional per day), local calls, Kona Trolley, yoga classes, cultural tours, Wi-Fi, and more. Extra person or rollaway $65. Children 18 and under stay free in parent's room using existing bedding. **Amenities:** 3 restaurants; 1 cafe; 3 bars; babysitting; rental bikes; concierge; fitness center; weekly luau; multilevel pool w/water slide; room service; spa; 2 tennis courts, basketball court, and sand volleyball court; whirlpool; Wi-Fi (included in resort fee).

Moderate

Kona Seaspray ★ Pay close attention to the details when booking a unit here, across Alii Drive from bustling Kahaluu Beach, because the eight, spacious two-bedroom/two-bathroom units in the three-story main building have varying bedding configurations, views, and decor. All offer ocean views (best from the top two floors), full kitchens, and washer-dryers, but some have been recently remodeled with granite counters and stainless-steel sinks in the kitchen and slate tiles on the lanai. Two one-bedroom units in the adjacent, two-story Seaspray building share laundry facilities. A pretty, blue-tiled wall provides privacy for the ground-floor pool, with lounges and a hammock next to the covered grill and dining area.

78–6671 Alii Dr., Kailua-Kona. www.konaseaspray.com. ✆ **808/322-2403.** 10 units. Main building: $155–$195 1-bedroom for 2 (sleeps up to 4); $175–$205 2-bedroom for 4 (sleeps up to 6). Seaspray building: $155–$195 double (sleeps up to 4). 5-percent discount for weekly rentals, 10-percent discount May 1–Dec 1. Extra person $20. Cleaning fee $70–$95, plus $20 per 5th or more person. 3-night minimum. **Amenities:** Barbecue; pool; whirlpool spa; Wi-Fi (free).

SOUTH KONA

This rural region of steeply sloping hills, often dotted with coffee and macadamia nut farms, is home to many unassuming bed-and-breakfasts that may appeal to budget travelers who don't mind being far from the beach.

At the higher end, in every sense, **Horizon Guest House ★★** (www.horizonguesthouse.com; ✆ **808/938-7822**) offers four units ($250–$350) with private entrances and lanais on a 40-acre property, including a spacious pool and whirlpool spa, at 1,100 feet of elevation in Honaunau, 21 miles south of Kailua-Kona. Rates include a gourmet breakfast by host Clem Classen; note that children 13 and under are not allowed. In a more residential area of Captain Cook, 12 miles south of Kailua-Kona, **Areca Palms Estate Bed & Breakfast ★** (www.konabedandbreakfast.com; ✆ 808/323-2276) has four rooms ($135–$145 double, two-night minimum) in a cedar home that backs on to a nature reserve, with a hot tub that's heated on request (some may wish instead for air-conditioning in the rooms). Rates include co-owner Janice Glass's delicious full breakfast.

Inexpensive
Manago Hotel ★   You can't beat the bargain rates at this plantation-era hotel, opened in 1917 and now run by the third generation of the friendly Manago family. Although clean, the original rooms with shared baths ($36) should be considered as just a cut above camping; they're ultra-spartan and subjected to street noise from the Mamalahoa Highway. You'll also find bare walls in rooms ($62–$67) in the newer, three-story wing at the rear. There's no elevator service, but rooms do have private bathrooms and views of the coast; the top floor has the best lookout. Book the third-floor corner Japanese room for a *ryokan* experience, sleeping on a futon and soaking in the *furo* (hot tub). Walls are thin, and sound can carry through jalousie windows used to let cooling breezes in, but neighbors tend to be considerate. If you want to watch TV, head to the lounge next to the **Manago Hotel Restaurant** (p. 237), the latter popular with locals for down-home cooking and affable service.

82-6151 Mamalahoa Hwy., Captain Cook (Hwy. 11, between mile markers 109 and 110, 12 miles south of Kailua-Kona). www.managohotel.com. ✆ **808/323-2642.** 63 units (22 with shared bathrooms). $36 double with shared bathroom; $62–$67 double with private bathroom; $81 double Japanese room with private bathroom. Extra person $3. **Amenities:** Restaurant; bar; Wi-Fi (free).

The Kohala Coast
SOUTH KOHALA
There's no way around it: Hotels are very costly at the three resorts here, but the beaches, weather, amenities, and services are among the best in the state. Although you'll miss out on fabulous resort pools and other facilities, you can shave dining costs by booking a vacation rental. South Kohala Management boasts the most listings (100-plus) of condos and homes in the Mauna Lani, Mauna Kea, and Waikoloa Beach resorts (www.southkohala.com; ✆ **800/822-4252**). Outrigger Hotels & Resorts also manages well-maintained condos and townhomes in five complexes in the Mauna Lani and Waikoloa Beach resorts (www.outrigger.com; ✆ **866/956-4262**).

The lively **Lava Lava Beach Club** restaurant and bar (www.lavalavabeachclub.com; ✆ **808/769-5282**) also offers four adjacent cottages ($450–$550), right on the sand at Anaehoomalu Bay. Opened in 2012, they include king-size beds and kitchenettes; just keep in mind there's live music till 9pm nightly.

Expensive
Fairmont Orchid Hawaii ★★★   The two guest wings at this polished but inviting sanctuary are set off the main lobby like two arms ready to embrace the well-manicured grounds and rugged shoreline; you may feel like hugging it, too, when you have to leave. Tucked among burbling waterfalls and lush greenery are 10 thatched-roof huts in the Spa Without Walls, which has another five

oceanfront cabanas. Beyond the 10,000-square-foot swimming pool lies a cove of soft sand, where the Hui Holokai Beach Ambassadors make guests feel at home in the water and on shore, teaching all kinds of Hawaiiana and sharing their knowledge about the area's cultural treasures, such as the nearby Puako Petro-glyph Archaeological Preserve (p. 165). The elegant, generously proportioned rooms (starting at 510 sq. ft.) with lanais were completely renovated in 2013—the largest redo since the hotel opened in 1990—adding subtle island accents such as rattan and carved wood to marble bathrooms and other luxurious fittings. Golf, tennis, and dining are also exceptional here, as befits the prices.

At the Mauna Lani Resort, 1 N. Kaniku Dr., Waimea. www.fairmont.com/orchid-hawaii. © **800/845-9905** or 808/885-2000. 540 units. $389–$869 double; $689–$779 Gold Floor double; from $759–$1,049 suite. Check for online packages. Extra person $75. Children 17 and under stay free in parent's room. Daily resort fee $25, includes self-parking and Wi-Fi. Valet parking $22. **Amenities:** 6 restaurants; 3 bars; babysitting; bike rentals; year-round children's program; concierge; concierge-level rooms; 2 championship golf courses; fitness center; luau; pool; room service; spa; theater; 10 tennis courts (7 lit for night play); watersports equipment rentals; Wi-Fi (included in resort fee).

Hapuna Beach Prince Hotel ★★★   I'm not sure why more people don't know about this larger, more low-key sibling to the Mauna Kea Beach Hotel, especially since it hovers above the wide, white sands of popular Hapuna Beach. Those who have stayed here relish the fact that rooms start at 600 square feet (the largest standard rooms on the Kohala Coast), all with balconies and an ocean view. Substantial upgrades in 2013 also brought touches of Hawaiiana in subdued colors and improved the area around the long, large pool, great for lap swimming. The sprawling, terraced grounds include an 18-hole championship golf course (p. 209), several open-air restaurants, including the wonderful **Coast Grille** (p. 238), and a small cafe/deli with affordable (for this area) takeout options. The 8,000-square-feet Hapuna Villa, a four-bedroom residence with butler service and pool, is another hidden gem, albeit one that starts at a princely $7,000 a night.

At the Mauna Kea Resort, 62–100 Kaunaoa Dr., Waimea. www.princeresortshawaii.com. © **800/882-6060** or 808/880-1111. 351 units. $440–$800 double; from $1,100 suite. Extra person $60. Children 17 and under stay free in parent's room using existing bedding. Valet parking $20; self-parking $15. **Amenities:** 3 restaurants; 2 bars; babysitting; cafe/gift shop; seasonal children's program; concierge; 18-hole championship golf course (p. 209); fitness center; pool; room service; spa; access to Mauna Kea Beach Hotel tennis center; watersports equipment rentals; Wi-Fi ($12 per day).

Hilton Waikoloa Village ★★   It's up to you how to navigate through this 62-acre oceanfront Disneyesque golf resort, laced with fantasy pools, lagoons, and a profusion of tropical plants in between three low-rise towers. If you're in a hurry, take the Swiss-made air-conditioned tram; for a more leisurely ride, handsome mahogany boats ply canals filled with tropical fish. Or just walk a half-mile or so through galleries of Asian and Pacific art on your way to the ample-sized rooms designed for families. In 2013, the resort unveiled the new Makai section of its Lagoon Tower: 161 rooms and eight suites, all ocean view, with upgraded baths (including dual vanities), roomier closets, and high-end bedding, with a sophisticated palette evoking lava and sand. Kids will want to head straight to the 175-foot water slide and 1-acre pool, and will pester you to pony up for the DolphinQuest encounter with Pacific bottlenose dolphins. The actual beach is skimpy here, hence an enormous swimming and watersports lagoon that's home to green sea turtles and other marine life. There's also a separate lagoon for swimming with two black-tipped reef sharks for a fee; it's free to watch the daily feedings at noon. You won't want for places to eat here, either, although more affordable options are at the two nearby shopping centers.

69–425 Waikoloa Beach Dr., Waikoloa. www.hiltonwaikoloavillage.com. ✆ **800/445-8667** or 808/886-1234. 1,241 units. $199–$409 double; $328–$478 tower deluxe double; from $622 suite; $319–$600 double cabana. Daily resort fee $25, includes Wi-Fi, local/toll-free calls, cultural lessons, in-room PlayStation3 with unlimited movies and games, and more. Extra person $50. Children 18 and under stay free in parent's room. Valet parking $21; self-parking $17. **Amenities:** 9 restaurants; 5 bars; babysitting; bike rentals; children's program; concierge; concierge-level rooms; fitness center; 2 18-hole golf courses (p. 210); luau; 3 pools (including adults-only pool); room service; spa; 6 tennis courts; watersports equipment rentals; Wi-Fi (included in resort fee).

Mauna Kea Beach Hotel ★★   Old-money travelers have long embraced this golf-course resort, which began as a twinkle in Laurance Rockefeller's eye and in 1965 became the first hotel development on the rugged lava fields of the Kohala Coast. The 2006 earthquake provided the literal shakeup behind $150 million in renovations that reduced the number of rooms but expanded their size, with spacious bathrooms and closets, plus iPod docking stations and other tech accouterments. Further renovations in 2013 brightened the family-size rooms and suites in the Beachfront Wing, now with picture windows above the soaking tubs. Although dining, golf, and tennis are all top-notch here, the pool is rather small by today's standards, and I find the orange-accented white room decor a little severe. The true pearls are sandy **Kaunaoa Beach ★★★** (p. 193), where manta rays skim the north point, and the gracious staff members, many of whom know several generations of guests by name.

At the Mauna Kea Resort, 62–100 Mauna Kea Beach Dr., Waimea. www.princeresortshawaii.com. ✆ **866/977-4589** or 808/882-7222. 252 units. $550–$1,150 double; from $1,000 suite. Extra person $75. Valet parking $20; self-parking $15. **Amenities:** 4 restaurants; 3 bars; babysitting; seasonal children's program; concierge; 2 championship golf courses (p. 210); fitness center; Jacuzzi; pool; room service; 11 tennis courts; watersports equipment rentals; Wi-Fi ($15 per day).

Mauna Lani Bay Hotel & Bungalows ★★   After a $30-million renovation that wrapped up in late 2013, the posh guest rooms once again gleam with understated elegance, outfitted in new mahogany cabinets, stone-tiled bathrooms, quilted bedspreads, and ceiling fans behind the signature plantation shutters, also newly refinished. They're still angled for premium ocean views, all with private lanais; some look over the ancient fishponds and historic cottage where the popular "Twilight at Kalahuipua'a" monthly storytelling (p. 249)—one of many free cultural programs—takes place. The pool area has been expanded, but the atrium lobby needs refreshing; koi ponds and evening entertainment help offset its stark decor. Although the opulent two-bedroom bungalows have also been updated, it's less costly to splurge on dining at the **Canoe House** (p. 238) or on a treatment at the thatched-hut spa, with a unique outdoor lava rock sauna. The two beach areas are on the small side but are popular with green sea turtles; some may have been raised by the hotel and released at the annual July 4th celebration. Helping turtles is just one of the hotel's many environmental efforts, which include low-impact care of the two championship golf courses (p. 210).

At the Mauna Lani Resort, 68–1400 Mauna Lani Dr., Puako. www.maunalani.com. ✆ **800/367-2323** or 808/885-6622. 341 units. $450–$850 double; from $1,000 suite; $4,000–$4,500 bungalow (sleeps up to 4). Extra person $75. Daily resort fee $25, includes valet or self-parking, Wi-Fi, local calls, beach cabana, and more. **Amenities:** 3 restaurants; lounge; babysitting; free bike rentals;

concierge; children's program; 2 golf courses; fitness center; Jacuzzi; pool; room service; access to Hawaii Tennis Center's 10 courts at the Fairmont Orchid Hawaii; watersports equipment rentals; Wi-Fi (free).

Waikoloa Beach Marriott Resort & Spa ★★ Of all the lodgings in the Waikoloa Beach Resort, this hotel has the best location on **Anaehoomalu Bay** ★★ (nicknamed "A-Bay"; p. 192), with many rooms offering views of the crescent beach and historic fishponds; others look across the parking lot and gardens toward Mauna Kea. Besides all kinds of watersports at the beach, kids will enjoy the sandy-entrance children's pool, while adults delight in the heated infinity-edge pool, the two-level **Mandara Spa,** and the spacious, well-equipped fitness center. The light-hued rooms (typically 410 sq. ft.) are also enticing, with glass-walled balconies and plush beds with down comforters in crisp white duvets. Families should book one of the spacious corner rooms, which include king-size bed and sofa bed; despite the resort fee ($25 daily), this hotel offers the best value of the Kohala Coast resorts, with access to nearby golf courses.

69–275 Waikoloa Beach Dr., Waikoloa. www.marriotthawaii.com. ✆ **888/236-2427** or 808/886-6789. 555 units. $194–$364 double; from $384 suite. Check for online packages. Daily $25 resort fee includes overnight self-parking, free local and mainland U.S./Canada calls, activity discounts, and Wi-Fi. Extra person $45. Children 17 and under stay free in parent's room. Valet parking $21. **Amenities:** Restaurant; bar; babysitting; concierge; Hawaiian cultural activities; fitness center; Jacuzzi; twice-weekly luau; 3 pools (1 w/water slide); rental-car desk; room service; spa; 2 tennis courts; watersports equipment rentals; Wi-Fi (included in resort fee).

NORTH KOHALA

This rural area, steeped in Hawaiian history and legend, has few overnight visitors, given its distance from swimmable beaches and other attractions. But it does include two luxurious accommodations that reflect its heritage in unique ways. At **Puakea Ranch** ★★ (www.puakearanch.com; ✆ **808/315-0805**), west of Hawi and 400 feet above the coast, three plantation-era bungalows and a former cowboy bunkhouse have been beautifully restored as vacation rentals ($289–$899; three- to seven-night minimum). Sizes vary, as do amenities such as soaking tubs and swimming pools. On the ocean bluff between Hawi and Kapaau, hidden from the road, the "eco-boutique" **Hawaii Island Retreat** ★★ (www.hawaiiislandretreat.com; ✆ **808/889-6336**) offers 10 posh guest rooms with large bathrooms and balconies ($415–$490 double) and, clustered near the excellent spa and saltwater infinity pool, seven spacious yurts (large tent-like structures with vaulted ceilings), with private bathrooms and shared indoor/outdoor showers ($195 double). Rates include a sumptuous organic breakfast of home-grown produce and eggs.

WAIMEA

As an economical alternative to the Kohala resorts, the cowboy town of Waimea offers a few very basic motels (not recommended) and several more comfortable options, all within a 20-minute drive of Hapuna Beach.

The two large suites ($179–$199 double) of **Aaah, the Views Bed & Breakfast** ★★ (www.aaahtheviews.com; ✆ **808/885-3455**) have plenty of windows so you can revel in the majestic views of Mauna Kea, a seasonal stream, ranchlands, or red skies at sunset; breakfast supplies are left in your kitchen or kitchenette to enjoy at your leisure. The two-room Treetop Suite, with four beds, is ideal for families. At the equally tranquil **Waimea Garden Cottages** ★★ (www.waimeagardens.com; ✆ **808/885-8550**), the two well-appointed cottages and attached studio ($155–$185 double, with 3-night minimum; no credit cards) also have lovely views and kitchens or kitchenettes stocked for breakfast, plus private patios with barbecues.

Closer to the center of town, the two-story, two-unit **Belle Vue ★** (www. hawaii-bellevue.com; © **800/772-5044** or 808/885-7732) vacation rental has a penthouse apartment with high ceilings and the best view, from the mountains to the distant sea, and a downstairs studio ($95–$175 double.) Both include kitchenettes with breakfast fixings and private entrances.

The Hamakua Coast

This emerald-green, virtually empty coast is a far drive from resort-worthy beaches and Hawaii Volcanoes National Park, and so is less frequented by overnight visitors (other than coqui frogs). Those who do choose to spend a night or more, though, will appreciate getting away from it all at several elegant bed-and-breakfasts. Off a long, winding road in the hills above Honokaa, **Waianuhea ★★** (www.waianuhea.com; © **888/775-2577** or 808/775-1118) is truly a destination unto itself, with five spacious rooms and suites ($225–$400) boasting hardwood floors, plump bedding, walls of windows, and other tasteful appointments. Being off-grid hasn't prevented the full breakfasts and optional three-course dinners ($58) from being just as sumptuous. Closer to Hilo, but in still very rustic Honomu, the sprawling, Victorian-inspired **Palms Cliff House Inn ★** (www. palmscliffhouse.com; © **866/963-6076** or 808/963-6076) offers eight large oceanview suites ($239–$449), some with air-conditioning and jetted tubs, plus a full breakfast on the lanai overlooking Pohakumanu Bay. Opened in 2001, the inn underwent renovations in 2013.

At the very end of the Honokaa-Waipio Road (Hwy. 240) in Honokaa, you'll find an amazing vista of Waipio Valley and privacy in the single studio ($200) of **Waipio Rim B&B ★★** (www.waipiorim.com; © **808/775-1727**), which has a flatscreen TV, kitchenette, and Wi-Fi for when you tire of the view from the deck. The hot breakfast even comes to you, at 8am. Also off Highway 240 in Honokaa, the **Waipio Wayside Inn Bed & Breakfast ★** (www.waipiowayside.com; © **800/833-8849** or 808/775-0275) doesn't overlook the valley but still has a pretty setting on an ocean bluff. A restored former plantation supervisor's residence, the inn has five rather formal antiques-decorated rooms ($110–$200 double) and a handsome living/dining room, where owner Jackie Horne serves organic breakfasts promptly at 8am.

Note: You'll find these accommodations on the "Kohala Coast, Waimea & the Hamakua Coast" map on p. 223.

Hilo

Although several hotels line scenic Banyan Drive, most fall short of visitors' expectations. However, the new owners of the 12-story, 193-room **Hilo Naniloa ★**, which includes a 9-hole golf course (p. 176) and wonderful views of Hilo Bay and Mauna Kea, began extensive renovations after acquiring the property (formerly the Naniloa Volcanoes Resort) in late 2013. They were expected to relaunch the hotel, already much improved, under a new name by the end of 2014 (doubles $149–$339).

Note: The accommodations in this section are on the "Hilo" map on p. 176.

Shipman House Bed & Breakfast Inn ★★   Built in 1900 as a family home, this grand Victorian mansion on Reed's Island hosted some very distinguished guests in its early years, including Jack London and his wife, who spent a month here in 1907, and Queen Liliuokalani, who is said to have enjoyed playing its Steinway piano. Lovingly restored in 1993 by Barbara Andersen, a descendant of one of its earliest owners, and husband, Gary, the five-room inn now receives guests with modern conveniences tucked among the heirlooms, including mini-fridges and fans. Three rooms are in the main house, one with a bay view; the two-room guest cottage, built in 1907, is a great option for families with older children. Lavish continental breakfasts on the lanai, with tropical fruit from the garden, are a specialty. Guests may join in the Tuesday-night hula classes on the porch.

131 Kaiulani St., Hilo. www.hilo-hawaii.com. ✆ **800/627-8447** or 808/934-80025 units. $219–$249 double. Extra person $35. Rates include continental breakfast. 2-night minimum. From Hwy. 19, take Waianuenue Ave.; turn right on Kaiulani St. and go 1 block over the wooden bridge; look for the large house on the left. **Amenities:** Wi-Fi (free).

MODERATE

The Inn at Kulaniapia Falls ★★   The 120-foot Kulaniapia waterfall provides more than dazzling views at this secluded retreat 4 miles north of Hilo—it generates all the power for the two large guesthouses, private cottage, and spa building. A narrow paved road winds through macadamia and banana orchards up the hill to this 22-acre gem, which includes a 1.5-mile trail to the falls through a bamboo garden and along the Waiau River. Guests in the Asian-themed Harmony House and Hawaiian-themed Residences enjoy made-to-order egg dishes and macadamia-nut waffles with breakfast, while the full kitchen in the Pagoda Cottage is stocked daily with breakfast supplies, including pancake batter. Massages are available by appointment; swimming is allowed in the waterfall pool when deemed safe. Waterfall views (some from balconies) vary by room, so read descriptions carefully when booking online or ask for input by phone.

100 Kulaniapia Dr., Hilo. www.waterfall.net. ✆ **808/966-6373.** 11 units. $179–$199 double; $289 cottage double. Rates include full breakfast. **Amenities:** Hot tub; spa; Wi-Fi (free).

INEXPENSIVE

The Old Hawaiian Bed & Breakfast ★   Breakfast with scones, eggs, and fresh fruit smoothies on the spacious lanai, a garden abloom with flowers, and easy walks to Rainbow Falls and Boiling Pots waterfalls are the highlights of a stay in this quaint 1930s home in a quiet residential neighborhood. Gracious hosts Lory and Stewart Hunter offer three rooms that range vastly in size but have private bathrooms and entrances; the Hawaiian room is the largest (and most private), with a king-size bed, daybed with trundle, sunken bathroom, and two-person shower.

1492 Wailuku Dr., Hilo. www.thebigislandvacation.com. ✆ **877/961-2816** or 808/961-2816. 3 units. $85–$125 double. Extra person $10. 2-night minimum (1-night stays $15 extra). No children under 12. **Amenities:** Wi-Fi (free).

Puna

For choice vacation rentals in **Pahoa** and **Kapoho,** some on the ocean with their own thermal ponds, contact Joanie Lehr of **Hawaii Island Dreams** (www.hawaiiislanddreams.com; ✆ **808/938-2996**). Yoga and nature lovers should investigate the wide variety of funky lodgings and classes at the bohemian **Kalani Oceanside Retreat** ★ on Highway 137 about halfway between Kapoho and Kalapana (www.kalani.com; ✆ **800/800-6886;** 808/965-7828). Be prepared for the noise of coqui frogs.

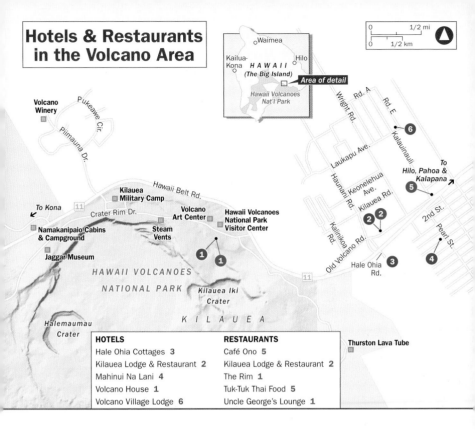

Hotels & Restaurants in the Volcano Area

HOTELS

Hale Ohia Cottages **3**	
Kilauea Lodge & Restaurant **2**	
Mahinui Na Lani **4**	
Volcano House **1**	
Volcano Village Lodge **6**	

RESTAURANTS

Café Ono **5**	
Kilauea Lodge & Restaurant **2**	
The Rim **1**	
Tuk-Tuk Thai Food **5**	
Uncle George's Lounge **1**	

In **Volcano Village,** the frogs don't like the misty, cool nights as much— the village is at 3,700 feet—but ask about heating when booking a rental. Joey Gutierrez of **Hawaii Volcano Vacations** (www.hawaiivolcanovacations.com; ℂ **800/709-0907** or 808/967-7178) manages a great selection of cottages, cabins, and houses ranging from $95 to $200 a night. For those able to climb its ship-style ladder to the sleeping area, **Mahinui Na Lani** (www.mahinui.com; ℂ **510/965-7367**), a rainforest treehouse studio ($235), is a romantic, eco-friendly alternative, with a kitchenette and cedar hot tub for two.

Note: You'll find the following accommodations on the "Hotels & Restaurants in the Volcano Area" map on p. 231.

VOLCANO VILLAGE

Expensive

Volcano Village Lodge ★★ Built as an artists' retreat in 2004, the five romantic cottages in this leafy, 2-acre oasis offer gleaming hardwood floors and paneled walls, vaulted ceilings, fireplaces, kitchenettes, and walls of windows— the lush rainforest envelopes the lodge in privacy. Fixings for a full breakfast— fruit, baked goods, coffee, tea, and an entree to reheat in your microwave—are left in your room each night. Enjoy the communal hot tub in the gardens after a day of hiking in the national park.

19-4183 Road E., Volcano. www.volcanovillagelodge.com. ℂ **808/985-9500.** 5 units. $280–$340 double (up to 4 guests). Hot breakfast. **Amenities:** Hot tub; library w/DVD player; trails; Wi-Fi (free).

Moderate

Kilauea Lodge ★ This former YMCA camp, built in 1938, has served as a gracious inn since 1986. The 10-acre main campus has 12 units in two wings and one cottage; most have gas fireplaces, along with European-Hawaiian decor and thoughtful touches such as heated towel racks. Another four cottages lie within a walk or short drive of the lodge; my favorites are the two-bedroom, two-bathroom Pii Mauna, overlooking the Volcano Golf Course, and the two-bedroom, one-bathroom Olaa Plantation House, an elegantly restored 1935 home with a huge kitchen, breakfast room, and window seats. All rates include gourmet breakfast in the superb **Kilauea Lodge Restaurant** (p. 242).

19-3948 Old Volcano Rd., Volcano. www.kilaualodge.com. © **808/967-7366.** 12 units on main property, 4 cottages nearby. $190–$205 double room; $220–$295 cottage. Extra person $20 (ages 2 and up). Rates include full breakfast. **Amenities:** Restaurant; gift shop; hot tub. Wi-Fi (free).

Inexpensive

Hale Ohia Cottages ★ Kentucky native Michael Tuttle, a former chef and historic building renovator, came across this secluded garden estate in the early 1990s and happily made this "old Volcano home." The main lodge has six units, but I recommend one of the four guest cottages, each with one to three bedrooms and greater privacy. The Ihilani Cottage, which dates from the 1920s, and Cottage 44, a transformed 1930s redwood water tank, have charming turret-shaped bedrooms and inviting nooks. Continental breakfast is included, except at two newer cottages off the main site.

11-3968 Hale Ohia Rd., Volcano. www.haleohia.com. © **800/455-3803** or 808/967-7986. 10 units. $129–$220 double. Extra person $20. 3-percent surcharge for credit cards. Most rates include continental breakfast. 2-night minimum during peak periods. **Amenities:** Wi-Fi (main property; free).

HAWAII VOLCANOES NATIONAL PARK

Expensive

Volcano House ★★ Reopened in 2013 after extensive infrastructure and safety renovations, this historic two-story wooden inn is rather modest for its price, especially compared with Yosemite's Ahwahnee and the grand lodges of other national parks. Still, its location on the very rim of the Kilauea Caldera is nothing short of spectacular—to wake up to that view is very special indeed. Rooms are on the small and plain side and the vintage bathrooms downright tiny, so explore your surroundings during the day and then enjoy dinner and drinks at the **Rim** ★★★ (p. 243) or **Uncle George's Lounge** downstairs, before falling into the comfy beds. *Note:* Only the crater-view rooms ($218–$347) justify the expense. The hotel also manages 10 recently restored cabins and 16 campsites in the park; see "Camping," below.

1 Crater Rim Dr., Hawaii Volcanoes National Park. www.volcanohousehotel.com. © **866/536-7972** or 808/756-9625. 33 units. $185–$347 double. Extra person $30. 1-time $10 park entrance fee. Check for online packages. **Amenities:** Restaurant; bar; bicycles; gift shop; Wi-Fi (free).

Kau

As with the Hamakua Coast, few visitors spend the night in this virtually undeveloped area, about halfway between Kailua-Kona and Hawaii Volcanoes National Park, but there's something about the surroundings that inspires unusual lodgings.

Tiny Waiohinu has three such properties: **Hobbit House** ★ (www.hi-hobbit. com; ☎ **808/929-9755**) is a curvy, cozy retreat, with one bedroom, one bathroom, a full kitchen, and beautiful woodwork and stained glass by owners Bill and Darlene Whaling. High on a hill off a private road, the Tolkien-esque cottage rents for $170 a night, with a three-night minimum.

Also unusual—for having such luxurious furnishings and amenities in a remote, rural area—is **Kalaekilohana** ★★ (www.kau-hawaii.com; ☎ **808/939-8052**), a modern plantation-style home with four large guest suites ($289) in a tranquil setting above the road to South Point. It may sound pricey, but after one night in a plush bed, with a beautifully presented breakfast on the lanai, and true Hawaiian hospitality from hosts Kenny Joyce and Kilohano Domingo, many guests kick themselves for not having booked a second night or more—and multi-night discounts start at $40 off a two-night stay. Kenny's delicious dinners ($25–$35 per person) are also an option on Friday and Saturday nights.

Camping

Camping is available at 10 county beach parks, eight state parks and reserves, a few private campgrounds, and Hawaii Volcanoes National Park.

I don't recommend the county parks, due to noise at popular sites (such as **Spencer Beach,** p. 193) and security concerns at more remote ones (such as **Punaluu Beach,** p. 196). All county campsites require permits, which must be purchased in advance, and cost $20 per night per person for nonresidents (http:// hawaiicounty.ehawaii.gov; ☎ **808/961-8311**).

The most desirable state campsites are at **Hapuna Beach** (p. 192), which has six A-frame screened shelters with wooden sleeping platforms and a picnic table, plus communal restrooms and cold showers. Nonresidents pay $50 per shelter per night for permits; purchase at least a week in advance. **Kiholo State Park Reserve** (p. 190) offers tent camping in a kiawe grove on a pebbly beach, with portable toilets; nonresidents pay $18 per campsite per night (http://camping.ehawaii.gov; ☎ **808/961-9540**).

Now that a local "Aloha Patrol" provides security, the privately run campground at **Hookena Beach Park** (p. 192) in South Kona is one more option for those really wanting to pitch a tent by the waves. Reservations, though recommended, are not required; campsites cost $21 per person per night for ages 13 and older and $20 for younger campers (www.hookena.org; ☎ **808/328-7321**). You can also rent camping stoves, tables, and chairs.

In **Hawaii Volcanoes National Park** (p. 182), the only campground accessible by car is **Namakanipaio,** which has 10 cabins and 16 campsites managed by **Volcano House** (www.hawaiivolcanohouse.com, ☎ **866/536-7972** or 808/441-7750). The recently refurbished one-room cabins sleep four apiece, with bed linens and towels provided, grills, and a community restroom with hot showers; the cost is $80 a night. Tent campers have access to restrooms but not showers; sites cost $15 a night, on a first-come, first-served basis, with a seven-night maximum stay. Backpack camping is allowed at seven remote areas, some with shelters and cabins, but you must register first at the **Backcountry Office** (www.nps.gov/havo; ☎ **808/985-6178**), no more than one day in advance.

Note: There are no places to rent camping gear on the island, but you can buy some at the **Hilo Surplus Store,** 148 Mamo St., Hilo (www.hilosurplus store.com; ☎ **808/935-6398**), or in one of the island's big-box stores such as **Kmart,** 74-5456 Kamaka Eha Ave., Kailua-Kona (☎ **808/326-2331**).

Island RV & Safari Activities (www.islandrv.com; ✆ 800/406-4555 or 808/334-0464) offers weekly rentals of a 22-foot, class-C motor home, which sleeps up to four, for $2,400. Included in the package are airport pickup, all linens, barbecue grill, county park permits, a last night in a hotel, and help with itinerary planning; vehicle-only weekly rentals for a 20-foot, class-B motorhome are $1,400. *Note:* Hawaii state and national parks do not allow RV camping.

WHERE TO EAT ON THE BIG ISLAND

Thanks to its deep waters, green pastures, and fertile fields, the Big Island provides local chefs with a cornucopia of fresh ingredients. The challenge for visitors is finding restaurants to match their budgets. Don't be afraid to nosh at a roadside stand or create a meal from a farmers market (see "Big Island Shopping," p. 244), as locals do, but indulge at least once on an oceanfront dinner at sunset for the best of what the Big Island has to offer.

The Kona Coast

CENTRAL KAILUA-KONA

With few exceptions, this is a no-man's-land for memorable, sensibly priced dining; chains abound, and service is often inordinately slow. One newer bright spot is **Honu's on the Beach ★**, the indoor/outdoor restaurant at the Courtyard King Kamehameha Kona Beach Hotel (p. 219), open daily for breakfast from 6 to 10:30am and dinner from 5:30 to 10pm. Live jazz and sushi Tuesday to Thursday from 5:30 to 8:30pm attract locals and visitors, with well-prepared farm-to-table Hawaii Regional Cuisine available nightly ($15–$28).

Expensive

Huggo's ★★ PACIFIC RIM/SEAFOOD   The setting doesn't get any better in Kailua-Kona than this, a covered wooden deck overlooking tide pools and the sweep of Kailua Bay. But executive chef Ken Schloss isn't content to rest on the visual laurels, frequently introducing new preparations, such as "mangospacho"—chilled mango with avocado, cucumber, and onions—stacked with fresh crab; native pohole ferns might appear in a salad, or kabocha pumpkin in risotto. Mounds of housemade pasta come dressed with local produce, while fresh catch with lemongrass haupia sauce is a must. Next door and even closer to the shore is the more casual and moderately priced **Huggo's on the Rocks ★**, helmed by chef de cuisine Carlos Nava; it's a pulsating nightclub after sunset. **Java on the Rocks ★** occupies the same space from 6 to 11am, serving Kona coffee, toast-your-own bagels, papaya, and a few egg dishes on paper plates, all under the watchful eye of birds just waiting for you to be distracted by the ocean view.

75–5828 Kahakai Rd., Kailua-Kona. www.huggos.com. ✆ **808/329-1493.** Reservations recommended. Main courses $23–$38. Sun–Thurs 5–9pm, Fri–Sat 5–10pm. Huggo's on the Rocks: Main courses $10–$18. Daily 11:30am–midnight, happy hour 3–6pm. Java on the Rocks: Main courses $8–$12. Daily 6–11am.

Moderate

Da Poke Shack ★★★ SEAFOOD   Nestled in an out-of-sight corner of an unassuming stretch of vacation rental condos, with just two outdoor picnic tables for seating, Da Poke Shack has nevertheless put itself on the culinary map with a lineup of eight or so *poke*—diced raw seafood with different marinades and seasonings—that are so fresh you may see fishermen delivering their latest catch while you're in line. Go early for the best selection, since it often sells out; the spicy Pele's Kiss and creamy avocado versions are first-rate. Prices vary daily and are on the high side for lunch plates and bowls with quinoa, rice, or potato salad; it's the seafood that's the star here, so spend your money on that above all.

At the Kona Bali Kai, 75–5702 Kuakini Hwy., Kailua-Kona. www.dapokeshack.com. © **808/326-1153.** Reservations not accepted. Market price, averaging $20 per pound, plates $21, bowls $11. Daily 10am–6pm.

Island Lava Java ★ AMERICAN   Residents of upcountry Waikoloa Village were thrilled when this perennial favorite opened a branch there in 2012, but there's no competing with the lively ambience and oceanview setting of the Kailua-Kona original. Founded in 1994, the former espresso bar has long since blossomed into a full-service cafe for breakfast, lunch, and dinner, with most tables on a patio overlooking the breakers across Alii Drive and a low seawall. Pluses: The coffee is 100-percent Kona; breads, pastries, and desserts are made in house; and organic salads, sandwiches (available in half-orders), and pizzas feature mostly local ingredients. Minuses: With the exception of the Big Island grass-fed beef burger ($15) or pizzas to share ($21–$24), dinner plates are expensive, and service can be leisurely. Enjoy the people- and surf-watching while you wait, and bring your own beer or wine—there's no corkage fee.

75–5799 Alii Dr., Kailua-Kona. www.islandlavajava.com. © **808/327-2161.** Main courses $5–$15 breakfast; $10–$20 lunch; $15–$27 dinner. Daily 6:30am–9:30pm. Also in the Waikoloa Highlands Shopping Center, 68-1845 Waikoloa Rd., Waikoloa. © **808/217-7661**. Weekdays 5:30am–9pm; weekends 6:30am–9pm.

Inexpensive

Big Island Grill ★★ LOCAL/AMERICAN   A welcome blast of true island style, this diner in a small strip mall (with parking!) caters to a primarily local crowd and visitors seeking financial relief from Kona markups. The tile floors are clean and bright, tables uncramped, and portions of everything but fresh vegetables are enormous. If you start with breakfast here, particularly one of the many varieties of loco moco (eggs, meat, rice, gravy) or massive French toast with Portuguese sausage, you may well skip lunch. The American-style sandwich list is unexceptional, except for the broiled fresh fish, a half-pound serving best accompanied by pineapple coleslaw; otherwise go for local favorites such as kalua pork and cabbage or chicken katsu. Be prepared to split the hefty but delicious desserts, such as sweet potato haupia cheesecake, but don't arrive starving—there's often a wait for seats and service.

75–5702 Kuakini Hwy. (south of Henry St.), Kailua-Kona. © **808/326-1153.** Reservations not accepted. Main courses breakfast $5–$17, lunch $8–$20, dinner $9–$24. Mon–Sat 7am–9pm (lunch 10:45am–5pm).

NORTH KONA

Ulu Ocean Grill & Sushi Lounge ★★★ ISLAND FARM/SEAFOOD   The tranquil beachfront setting contrasts nicely with the bold style of chef de cuisine Ricardo Jarquin, who relies on more than 160 local fishermen and farmers for refined yet approachable dishes such as roasted pineapple mahi in a Thai chili black bean sauce, Kona coffee–crusted New York steak with kiawe smoked potatoes, or a Big Island wild boar in a poha berry chutney. Jewel-like sashimi and artful sushi rolls can be ordered in the oceanview lounge (with firepits) or the open-air dining room, behind roe-like curtains of glass balls. Browse the extensive wine list on an iPad, or simply ask the expert waitstaff for advice. On Saturday, sign up for the four-course, prix-fixe Farm-to-Table dinner ($95), limited to

TAPPING INTO kona brewing co.

Father and son Cameron Healy and Spoon Khalsa opened microbrewery and pub **Kona Brewing Co. ★★** (www.konabrewingco.com; ✆ **808/334-2739**) in an obscure warehouse in Kailua-Kona in 1998; now they also run two restaurants on Oahu (one at the Honolulu airport) and enjoy widespread Mainland distribution of their most popular brews, including Fire Rock Pale Ale and Longboard Lager. The Kona brewpub, 75-5629 Kuakini Hwy., still offers affordable lunch specials (pizzas, fish tacos), a palm-fringed patio, and short free tours daily at 10:30am and 3pm.

40 guests, who meet with Jarquin and a local provider before dining on a private lanai.

At the Four Seasons Resort Hualalai, 72–100 Kaupulehu Dr., Kailua-Kona (off Hwy. 19, 6 miles north of Kona airport). ✆ **808/325-8000.** www.uluoceangrill.com. Reservations recommended. Breakfast buffet $30–$44; dinner main courses $32–$55. Daily 6:30–11am (buffet 6:30–10:30am) and 5:30–9pm (sushi till 9:30pm).

KEAUHOU

High above Alii Drive, Keauhou Shopping Center has several more affordable options than Sam Choy's Kai Lanai (below) and **Kenichi ★★** (www.kenichipacific.com; ✆ **808/322-6400**), a stylish but high-priced Asian fusion/sushi dinner spot, open daily 5 to 9:30pm. The best is **Peaberry & Galette ★** (www.peaberryandgalette.com; ✆ **808/322-6020**), which has a wide selection of savory and sweet crepes, plus good coffee, although service can be slow; it's open 7am to 7pm Monday to Thursday, till 8pm Friday to Saturday, and 8am to 6pm Sunday.

Sam Choy's Kai Lanai ★★ HAWAII REGIONAL   The miles-long coastal views from this former Wendy's are reliably spectacular—if only the service and food were as consistent. When they're both in top form, this inviting aerie run by renowned Honolulu chef Sam Choy is hard to beat. Lunch is a true bargain, with expert presentations of local dishes such as saimin (noodle soup), Portuguese bean soup, and beef stew omelet; the copious breakfast buffet ($15) is also a good value and features a changing lineup of American classics and Pacific Islander treats such as Samoan *pani popo* pancakes. Appetizers and dinner courses veer into the expensive category, but the fried poke ($12) and seafood *laulau* (fish and seafood in steamed ti leaves, $28) are worth the expense. Go early to nab a happy hour seat by the firepits, and enjoy the extensive beer and cocktail menu.

In Keauhou Shopping Center, 78-6831 Alii Dr., Kailua-Kona. www.samchoy.com. ✆ **808-333-3434.** Reservations recommended for dinner. Lunch main courses $7–$14; dinner main courses $17–$36. Daily 11am–9pm (happy hour 3–5pm), breakfast buffet ($15) Sat–Sun 8–11am.

SOUTH KONA
Expensive
Mi's Italian Bistro ★★★ ITALIAN   There's no fabulous view here, only superbly executed, thoughtfully created Italian dishes using fresh ingredients such as fruits and vegetables from chef Morgan Starr's own garden, local beef, handmade pasta, and off-the-hook ahi. Starr, formerly at Four Seasons Resort

Hualalai, and wife Ingrid Chan opened their homey, dark-toned restaurant in a drab shopping strip in late 2007 to rave reviews. They've maintained their commitment to top-notch, well-priced cuisine while raising two small children, often at their mother's side. The ahi Bolognese ($17) is a revelation, meaty without a hint of fishiness; porcini-crusted pork tenderloin ($24) with gnocchi comes with a velvety *pioppini* mushroom sauce. Grilled rack of lamb ($35) is worth the splurge, but save some calories for dessert, such as Meyer lemon crème brûlée or white pineapple sorbet. The select wine list is also well-priced.

81-6372 Mamalahoa Hwy. (Hwy. 11), Kealakekua, mountain side; look for flags and park in lot next to Captain Cook Mini Market. www.misitalianbistro.com. © **808/323-3880.** Main courses $14–$35 (most under $25). Daily 4:30–8:30pm.

Moderate

The Coffee Shack ★ COFFEEHOUSE/DELI   It's hard to ignore the charm of watching colorful geckos nibble from packets of guava jam, or the view of Kealakekua Bay from 1,400 feet elevation, but there are, in fact, other reasons to stop by the shack. Pick up a plump sandwich ($11) on your choice of freshly baked bread, such as the savory Greek Isle, made with olives, feta cheese, and cucumbers, or the sweet Luau, made with mac nuts, carrots, pineapple, and coconut. Banana bread ($3) and a Kona café latte ($5) also serve as quick but tasty breakfast if you're on the road.

83-5799 Mamalahoa Hwy. (Hwy. 11), Captain Cook, between mile markers 108 and 109, ocean side. www.coffeeshack.com. © **808/328-9555.** Most items under $10; pizzas $11–$14. Daily 7:30am–3pm.

Inexpensive

Manago Hotel Restaurant ★★ AMERICAN   Like its clean but plainspun hotel, the family-run dining room with Formica tabletops and vinyl-backed chairs has changed little over the years. Service is friendly and fairly swift, with family-style servings of rice, potato salad, and fresh vegetables accompanying the generous portions of pork chops, teri chicken, and sautéed mahimahi, among other popular choices. Breakfast is a steal: papaya or juice, toast or rice, two eggs, breakfast meat, and coffee for $6.

At the Manago Hotel, 82-6151 Mamalahoa Hwy. (Hwy. 11), Captain Cook, between mile markers 109 and 110, ocean side. www.managohotel.com/rest.html. © **808/323-2642.** Reservations recommended for dinner. Breakfast $5–$6, lunch and dinner $6–$17. Tues–Sun 7–9am, 11am–2pm, and 5–7:30pm.

The Kohala Coast

Note: You'll find the following restaurants on the "Kohala Coast, Waimea & the Hamukua Coast" map on p. 223.

SOUTH KOHALA

For a cheaper but still convenient alternative to pricey hotel dining, don't snub the island-style outlets in the food court at Queens' MarketPlace, 69-201 Waikoloa Beach Dr., in Waikola Beach Resort. **Hawaiian Fish N Chips** ★ (© **808/886-1595**) smokes its own fish and serves local delicacies such oxtail soup, while **Ippy's Hawaiian BBQ** ★ (© **808/886-8600**) prepares well-seasoned plate lunches with ribs, chicken, and fish, under the aegis of "Food Network Star" Philip "Ippy" Aiona.

The commercial port of Kawaihae also harbors several inexpensive, homespun eateries, including **Kohala Burger and Taco** ★ , above Café Pesto (see below)

SORTING OUT THE resorts

There's no getting around the sticker shock visitors encounter when dining at the South Kohala resort hotels, especially at breakfast and lunch. Dazzling sunsets help soften the blow at dinner, when chefs at least show more ambition. Here's a quick guide to help you distinguish between the top dinner-only resort restaurants, all offering excellent but costly variations on locally sourced Hawaii Regional Cuisine:

○ **Mauna Lani Resorts: Brown's Beach House** ★★ at the Fairmont Orchid Hawaii (p. 225) offers attentive service at tables on a lawn just a stone's throw from the water; at **Canoe House** ★★ in the Mauna Lani Bay Hotel & Bungalows (p. 227), chef Allen Hess personally presents each dish of his "Captain's Table" Blind Tasting Menu ($100), offered Thursday to Saturday by 24-hour reservation.

○ **Mauna Kea Resorts: Manta & Pavilion Wine Bar** ★★ at the Mauna Kea Beach Hotel (p. 227) offers firepits and a sweeping ocean view, plus 48 high-end wines by the glass from the nifty Enomatic dispenser. The less

elegant but more intriguing **Coast Grille** ★★ at the Hapuna Beach Prince Hotel (p. 226) also provides an expansive view, plus the best value of all the resorts: the $50 four-course Locavore Series menu, each month showcasing a different Big Island ingredient.

○ **Waikoloa Beach Resorts:** Only **KPC–Kamuela Provision Company** ★ at the Hilton Waikoloa Village (p. 226) has the oceanfront views and culinary skills, primarily with steak and seafood, to rival other resorts' restaurants; be sure to book an outdoor table for at least a half-hour before sunset.

in the Kawaihae Shopping Center (www.kohalaburgerandtaco.com; © **808/880-1923**); burgers are made with local grass-fed beef, while buns and tortillas (used for fresh fish tacos, burritos, and quesadillas) are housemade. It's open daily, but hours vary widely by season, closing as early as 4:30pm Saturday to Monday. The lunch wagon next to **Da Fish House** fish market (p. 248) naturally has very fresh fish plates ($9), though little seating; it's open weekdays 10:30am to 3:30pm and takes cash only.

Expensive

Monstera Noodles & Sushi ★★ JAPANESE   Master sushi chef Norio Yamamoto left his namesake restaurant (still called Norio's) at the Fairmont Orchid Hawaii to open this less formal but still handsome, clubby dining room in the Shops at Mauna Lani. No worries if you're not a fan of raw fish: His "sizzling plates" menu includes New York strip steak in a choice of sauces, boneless fried chicken in spicy garlic-sesame sauce, and pork loin stir-fried with kimchee. But it would be a shame to skip seafood specialties like his poke roll (made with seasonal fish and fresh wasabi) or volcano roll (a combination of spicy tuna and shrimp tempura with local avocado), or ultra-fresh, silken sashimi such as Hawaiian fatty tuna (*chu toro*). Individual dishes are moderately priced but add up quickly, especially if ordering from the gourmet sake or tropical cocktail menu has stimulated your appetite.

In the Shops at Mauna Lani, 68-1330 Mauna Lani Dr., Waimea. www.monterasushi.com. © **808/887-2711.** Reservations recommended. Main courses $18–$30; sushi (3 pieces) $7–$16; sashimi $16–$20. Daily 5:30–9:30pm.

Moderate

Café Pesto ★★ PIZZA/PACIFIC RIM   Locals may dart in and out for wood-fired pizzas to go, but there's something to be said for enjoying the capable service and cozy yet uncluttered atmosphere of the original Café Pesto, which opened in 1988, 4 years before the Hilo branch (p. 241). More local produce and proteins appear on the menu now, but otherwise the pizzas, meal-size salads, hearty pastas, and "creative island cuisine" (such as zesty wok-fired shrimp and scallops in a red coconut curry) continue to impress year after year. The playful children's menu ($8) also brims with healthful but enticing choices, including pasta and kalua turkey over rice.

In the Kawaihae Shopping Center, 61-3665 Akoni Pule Hwy. (Hwy. 270), Kawaihae. www.cafe pesto.com. ℂ **808/882-1071.** Main courses $11–$17 lunch; $15–$37 dinner; $10–$21 pizza. Sun–Thurs 11am–9pm; Fri–Sat 11am–10pm.

Merriman's Mediterranean Cafe ★ MEDITERRANEAN   A more casual offshoot of the original (and outstanding) Merriman's in Waimea (p. 240), this pleasant indoor/outdoor cafe in the Kings' Shops open-air mall seems almost reasonably priced compared with the nearby hotel options. It's also had to step up its game in recent years, thanks to the advent of more choices at Kings' Shops and the nearby Queens' MarketPlace. The best bets are among the least expensive items, too: Greek-style fish tacos with an avocado-tzatzki sauce ($16), thin-crust pizzas ($12–$15), and the hearty meatball sandwich ($12).

At Kings' Shops in Waikoloa Beach Resort, 69–250 Waikoloa Beach Dr., Waikoloa. www. merrimanshawaii.com. ℂ **808/886-1700.** Main courses $10–$29. Daily 11:30am–9pm.

NORTH KOHALA

For a light breakfast, lunch, or snack, **Kohala Coffee Mill ★**, 55-3412 Akoni Pule Hwy. (Hwy. 270, across from Bamboo, below; ℂ **808/889-5577**), offers pastries, tasty sandwiches and seasonal hot entrees, Tropical Dreams ice cream (p. 240), and well-crafted coffee drinks. It's open weekdays 6am to 6pm, weekends 7am to 6pm.

Moderate

Bamboo ★★ PACIFIC RIM   Dining here is a trip, literally and figuratively. A half-hour away from the nearest resort, Bamboo adds an element of time travel, with vintage decor behind the screen doors of its plantation-era, pale-blue building; an art gallery and quirky gift shop provide great browsing if you have to wait for a table. And in these parts, the food is well worth the wait, from local lunch faves such as barbecued baby back ribs or kalua pork and cabbage to veggie stir-fry of soba noodles or grilled chicken, shrimp, fish, or tofu with a kicky Thai-style coconut sauce. Dinner adds more fresh-catch preparations, including a grilled filet with a tangy *lilikoi* mustard sauce balanced by crispy goat cheese polenta. If you're dining on Friday or Saturday night, you may luck into live music; in case you want to re-create the hang-loose vibe at home, Bamboo's yummy *lilikoi* cocktails have inspired its line of drink mixes for sale.

55-3415 Akoni Pule Hwy. (Hwy. 270, just west of Hwy. 250/Hawi Rd.), Hawi. www.bamboorestaurant. info. ℂ **808/889-5555.** Dinner reservations recommended. Main courses $10–$20 lunch; $15–$35 dinner (full- and half-size portions available at dinner). Tues–Sat 11:30am–2:30pm and 6–8pm; Sun brunch 11:30am–2:30pm.

WAIMEA

Daunted by high-priced hotel breakfasts? Visit the inexpensive **Hawaiian Style Café ★**, 65-1290 Kawaihae Rd. (Hwy. 19, 1 block east of Opelo Rd.; ℂ **808/885-4925**), which serves pancakes bigger than your head (try them with warm haupia, coconut pudding), kalua pork hash, Portuguese blood sausage, and other local favorites. It's cash only, and very crowded on weekends (Mon–Sat 7am–1:30pm; till noon Sun).

Expensive

Merriman's ★★★ HAWAII REGIONAL   This is where it all began in 1988 for chef Peter Merriman, one of the founders of Hawaii Regional Cuisine and an early adopter of the farm-to-table trend. Now head of a statewide culinary empire that includes various Merriman's and Monkeypod Kitchen incarnations on the four major islands, the busy Merriman has entrusted exciting young chef Zach Sato with maintaining his high standards and inventive flair. Lunch offers terrific values, such as the grilled fresh fish ($15), while weekend brunch, introduced in 2014 (along with a bar), includes a luscious eggs Benedict with ham and jalapeño hollandaise, and a less guilt-inducing kale and beet salad with chèvre and smoke-marinated grape tomatoes. At dinner, you can still order Merriman's famed wok-charred ahi, ponzu-marinated mahimahi, or local grass-fed filet mignon—plus his de rigueur dessert, a molten chocolate purse with vanilla bean ice cream—but you'll also want to consider Sato's fresh-catch preparation, often inspired by his herb garden, or his three-course "chef's choice" dinner ($69).

At the Opelo Plaza, 65-1227 Opelo Rd., off Hwy. 19, Waimea. www.merrimanshawaii.com. ℂ **808/885-6822.** Reservations recommended. Main courses $11–$15 lunch, $29–$49 dinner (half-portions $25–$38). Mon–Fri 11:30am–1:30pm; daily 5:30–9pm; Sat–Sun brunch 10am–1pm.

Tropical Dreams: Ice Cream Reveries

Founded in North Kohala in 1983, ultra-rich **Tropical Dreams** ★★★ ice cream is sold all over the island now, but you'll find the most flavors at the retail store next to its Waimea factory, 66-1250 Lalamilo Farm Rd. (off Hwy. 19; www.tropicaldreamsicecream.com; ℂ **888/888-8031**). For a truly tropical sensation, try ice creams such as Tahitian vanilla, lychee, or poha, or sorbets like dragonfruit, passion-guava, or white pineapple ($3.50 a cup). It's open weekdays 9:30am to 4:30pm.

Moderate

Village Burger ★★ BURGERS   Tucked into a cowboy-themed shopping center with a drafty food court (bring a jacket or sit by the fireplace), this burger stand run by former Four Seasons Lanai and Mauna Lani Bay chef Edwin Goto has a compact menu: plump burgers made with local grass-fed beef or "red veal," grilled ahi, or taro (when available); thick, sumptuous shakes made from Tropical Dreams ice cream (p. 240); and hand-cut, twice-cooked fries, with or without Parmesan "goop" (consider your salt intake first). Other than that, there's just an ahi Niçoise salad ($12) featuring island greens—but it's also delicious. Try the mamaki tea, if on offer; it's brewed from native plants grown by local school kids.

In the Parker Ranch Center, 67–1185 Mamalahoa Hwy., Waimea. www.villageburgerwaimea. com. ℂ **808/885-7319.** Burgers $8–$12. Mon–Sat 10:30am–8pm; Sun 10:30am–6pm.

The Hamakua Coast

This lovely but little-populated area holds few dinner options, and those tend to close early, so plan ahead. *Note:* You'll find these restaurants on the "The Kohala Coast, Waimea & the Hamakua Coast" map on p. 223.

Café Il Mondo ★ PIZZA/ESPRESSO BAR   If you want to order a medium or large version of the pleasantly crusty, stone-oven-baked pizzas, you'll have to get it to go. But if you can find a space in this very cozy bistro, pick your own pie ($12–$15), or consider one of the calzones with the cafe's signature pesto sauce, made with macadamia nuts in lieu of pine nuts. The best values may be the Mama Mia dinners ($13): roast chicken with twice-baked potatoes or beef lasagna with focaccia, both with a garden salad and served at lunch as well. Arrive before 5pm to order one of the sandwiches in freshly baked bread or focaccia buns. *Note:* Bring your own beer and wine (**Malama Market** is just around the corner); the pizzeria charges $2 to $5 for corkage, depending on how many are imbibing.

45-3626 Mamane St. (Hwy. 240, at Lehua St.), Honokaa. www.cafeilmondo.com. ☏ **808/775-7711.** Main courses $7–$15 lunch, $11–$15 dinner. No credit cards. Daily 11am–8pm.

Tex Drive-In & Restaurant ★★ AMERICAN/LOCAL   The two stars here are only for the *malasadas,* Portuguese sweetbread doughnut holes ($1) fried to order, dusted in sugar, and available (for 45¢ more) with a filling, such as Bavarian cream, tropical jellies—guava, mango, pineapple—and chocolate. The Tex malasada is square, larger, and a little chewier than the traditional version sold at church fairs or the Honolulu landmark, Leonard's, and sometimes Tex runs out of certain fillings, but the plain are quite satisfying. The rest of the vast menu—burgers, hot dogs, sandwiches, Hawaiian plate lunches—is modestly priced but adequate at best; you're better off continuing on to Waimea or central Honokaa for a full meal.

45-690 Pakalana St., off Hwy. 19, Honokaa. www.texdriveinhawaii.com. ☏ **808/775-0598.** Malasadas $1 each, fillings 45¢. Main courses $5–$7 breakfast, $4–$9 lunch and dinner. Daily 6:30am–8pm.

Hilo

Hawaii's second largest city hosts a raft of unpretentious eateries serving plate lunches and Japanese cuisine, reflecting East Hawaii's plantation heritage and largest ethnic group. A prime example of the former is **Ken's House of Pancakes** ★, 1730 Kamehameha Ave. (Hwy. 19, just west of Hwy. 11; www.kenshouseofpancakes.com; ☏ **808/935-8711**), which serves large helpings of local dishes and American fare 24 hours a day. The ambience is even more basic (plastic trays and paper plates) at the venerable **Café 100** (www.cafe100.com; ☏ **808/935-8683**), 969 Kilauea Ave., but the price is right, with hefty plate lunches for $7, burgers $2 and up, and more than 30 varieties of loco moco—meat, eggs, rice, and gravy—starting around $3; opt for brown rice to lessen the guilt. It's open daily at 6:45am, closing at 8:30pm Monday to Thursday, 9pm Friday, and 7:30pm Saturday.

Across the street from **Big Island Candies** (p. 247), **Miyo's** ★, 564 Hinano St. (www.miyosrestaurant.com; ☏ **808/935-8825**), prides itself on "home-style" Japanese cooking, with locally sourced ingredients and a few welcome surprises, such as decadent pumpkin flan and a fluffy cheesecake. It's open 11am to 2pm for lunch and 5:30 to 8:30pm for dinner daily except Sunday.

Note: You'll find the following restaurants on the "Hilo" map on p. 176.

Café Pesto ★★ PIZZA/PACIFIC RIM   The menu of wood-fired pizzas, pastas, risottos, fresh local seafood, and artfully prepared "creative island cuisine" such as mango-glazed chicken is much the same as at the original Kawaihae location (p. 239), and that's a good thing. Even better: the airy dining room in a restored 1912 building, with black-and-white tile floors and huge glass windows overlooking the vintage wooden buildings and palm trees of downtown Hilo. Service is attentive and swift, especially by island standards, but don't shy away from the two counters with high-backed chairs if the tables are full.

At the S. Hata Bldg., 308 Kamehameha Ave., Hilo. www.cafepesto.com. ℂ **808/969-6640.** Pizzas $10–$21; main courses $11–$17 lunch, $18–$27 dinner. Sun–Thurs 11am–9pm; Fri–Sat 11am–10pm.

Hilo Bay Café ★★ PACIFIC RIM   Hidden in a strip mall for years, this ambitious restaurant now lives up to its name—it moved in late 2013 to an elevated perch overlooking Hilo Bay, next to Suisan Fish Market and the lovely Liliuokalani Gardens. Fittingly, sushi and seafood dishes are the most reliable pleasers, including horseradish panko-crusted ono and grilled asparagus salad with pan-roasted salmon, but fresh produce from the Hilo Farmers Market also inspires several dishes. Vegetarians will appreciate thoughtful options such as grilled herb eggplant with piquant chimichurri sauce, Hamakua mushroom curry pot pie (one can add chicken or shrimp), or sweet potato gnocchi with broccolini and Gorgonzola. Service can be inconsistent; stay relaxed by sitting on the outdoors deck or at a table with a view, and order one of the creative cocktails.

123 Lihiwai St., just north of Banyan Dr., Hilo. www.hilobaycafe.com. ℂ **808/935-4939.** Reservations recommended for dinner. Main courses $11–$17 lunch, $11–$20 dinner. Mon–Thurs 11am–9pm; Fri–Sat 11am–9:30pm; Sun 5–9pm.

Puna District

Options are limited and frankly often disappointing here, so plan mealtimes carefully and stock up on picnic supplies in Kailua-Kona or Hilo. ***Note:*** You'll find the following restaurants on the "Hotels & Restaurants in the Volcano Area" map (p. 231).

VOLCANO VILLAGE

In addition to the listings below, look for the **Tuk-Tuk Thai Food ★** truck in front of the Volcano Inn, 19-3820 Old Volcano Rd. (www.tuk-tukthaifood.com; ℂ **808/747-3041**), from 11am to 6pm Tuesday to Saturday. You can even call ahead for its hearty curries and noodle dishes ($8–$10), about half the price of the Thai restaurant down the road.

Expensive

Kilauea Lodge Restaurant ★★ CONTINENTAL   Like his inn, owner-chef Albert Jeyte's woodsy restaurant radiates *Gemütlichkeit,* that ineffable German sense of warmth and cheer, symbolized by the "International Fireplace of Friendship" studded with stones from around the world. Although starters such as mushroom caps and baked Brie are ho-hum, the European-style main courses showcase unique proteins such as rabbit, antelope, buffalo, and duck, along with local grass-fed beef and lamb, plus the fresh catch (recommended). The wine list is well-priced, although *lilikoi* margaritas can quickly take the edge off a long day of exploring the nearby national park. Dinner prices are steep (perhaps due in part to the lack of competition), but lunch offers good values, including Kuahiwi Ranch grass-fed beef, buffalo and antelope burgers and a curried chicken bowl. Breakfast is another winner, especially the all-too-tempting French toast made with Punaluu Bake Shop's guava, taro, and white Portuguese sweetbread.

19–3948 Old Volcano Rd., Volcano. www.kilaualodge.com. ℂ **808/967-7366.** Reservations recommended. Main courses $10–$13 breakfast, $9–$13 lunch, $22–$49 dinner. Daily 7:30am–2pm and 5–9pm; Sun brunch 10am–2pm.

Moderate

Café Ono ★ VEGETARIAN   When burgers, plate lunches, and deli sandwiches start to pall, this cafe and tearoom hidden in a quirky art studio/gallery provides a delectably light alternative. The all-vegetarian menu is concise: a soup or two, chili, lasagna, quiche (highly recommended), and sandwiches, most accompanied by a garden salad. Don't pass up the peanut butter and pumpkin soup if available, and ask if you can give Ernest the goat a bite to eat before you explore the lush gardens outside.

In Volcano Garden Arts, 19–3834 Old Volcano Rd., Volcano. www.volcanogardenarts.com. ✆ **808/985-8979.** Main courses $10–$15. Tues–Sun 11am–3pm.

HAWAII VOLCANOES NATIONAL PARK

The Rim ★★★ ISLAND FARM/SEAFOOD   By no means is this your typical national park concession, as some hot dog–seeking visitors are discouraged to find. Since its debut in summer 2013, as part of the reopening of the restored Volcano House hotel, the Rim and the adjacent **Uncle George's Lounge** have tried to match their three-star views of Kilauea Caldera with a menu that's both artful and hyper-local: 95 percent of the ingredients come from the Big Island. The bountiful breakfast buffet includes made-to-order eggs, tropical fruit smoothies, wild turkey hash, local bacon, and freshly baked pastries, among other items. Bento lunch boxes include a choice of kalua pork, chicken braised with lemongrass and kaffir lime, an organic veggie/tofu stir-fry, or macadamia-nut fresh catch, plus four tasty sides and a *lilikoi* cream puff. Make reservations well in advance for a window table at dinner, when lights are periodically dimmed to showcase the glow from Halemaumau Crater. Culinary highlights include *opakapaka* (pink snapper) wrapped in white pineapple, the rare-seared Kona *kampachi*, and the Kuahiwi Ranch steak of the day, served with local wilted kale, mashed Okinawan sweet potatoes, pineapple-rum butter, and crispy onions. The lounge serves excellent pupus ($12–$17) such as chicken satay, Kona cold mussels, and avocado dip that can combine for a meal. ***Note:*** You must pay park admission ($10 a vehicle, good for 7 days) to dine here.

In Volcano House, 1 Crater Rim Dr., Volcano. www.hawaiivolcanohouse.com/dining. ✆ **808/756-9625.** Reservations recommended. Breakfast buffet $18 adults, $9 children; lunch bentos $19 adults, $11 children; dinner main courses $19–$39. Daily breakfast buffet 7–10am, lunch 11am–2pm, dinner 5–9pm. Uncle George's Lounge daily 11am–9pm.

PAHOA

Kaleo's Bar & Grill ★★ ECLECTIC/LOCAL   The best restaurant for miles around has a wide-ranging menu, perfect for multiple visits if you're staying in

---

A TASTE of volcano wines

Volcano Winery (www.volcanowinery.com; ✆ **877/967-7772**) has made a unique pit stop near Hawaii Volcanoes National Park since 1993, when it first started selling traditional grape wines, honey wines, and grape wines blended with tropical fruits. Del and Marie Bothof have owned the winery since 1999, planting Pinot Noir and Cayuga White grapes in 2000 and expanding into tea in 2006. Their latest wine is called Infusion, a macadamia-nut honey wine infused with estate-grown black tea. Wine tastings, for ages 21 and up, are $5 to $8; there's also a picnic area under cork and koa trees. The tasting room and store, 35 Pii Mauna Dr. in Volcano (just off Hwy. 11 near the 30-mile marker), are open 10am to 5:30pm daily.

the greater Pahoa/Kapoho area, and a welcoming, homey atmosphere. Local staples such as chicken katsu and spicy Korean kalbi ribs won't disappoint, but look for dishes with slight twists, such as tempura ahi roll with spicy *lilikoi* sauce or the blackened-ahi BLT with avocado and mango mayo, served with organic greens or fries. The Mediterranean appetizer platter ($15) makes a great vegetarian meal with pesto tomatoes, hummus, grilled veggies, and other goodies. Kids can find pasta and burger choices to their liking, while adults should sample one of the many sweet and spicy pairings, such as volcano-spiced fresh catch with pineapple salsa. Save room for the *lilikoi* cheesecake or banana spring rolls with ice cream.

15–2969 Pahoa Village Rd., Pahoa. www.kaleoshawaii.com. ✆ **808/965-5600.** Main courses $7–$16 lunch, $12–$27 dinner. Daily 11am–9pm.

Kau District

When you're driving between Kailua-Kona and Hawaii Volcanoes National Park in Naalehu, it's good to know about two places on Highway 11 in Naalehu for a quick pick-me-up. The **Punaluu Bake Shop ★** (www.bakeshophawaii.com; ✆ **866/366-3501** or 808/929-7343) is the busier tourist attraction, famed for its varieties of Portuguese sweetbread (including taro, mango, and guava), now also available in stores across the islands; clean restrooms, a deli counter, and gift shop are also part of the appeal. It's open 9am to 5pm daily. Across the highway off a small lane lies **Hana Hou Restaurant ★** (www.hanahourestaurant.com; ✆ **808/929-9717**), which boasts a bakery counter with equally tempting sweets (try the macnut pie or *lilikoi* bar) and a small dining room serving simple but fresh plate lunches ($8–$17), burgers, sandwiches, and quesadillas; look for the large sign saying eat. Open Sunday to Thursday 8am to 7pm, till 8pm Friday to Saturday.

BIG ISLAND SHOPPING

This island is fertile ground, not just for the coffee, tea, chocolate, macadamia nuts, and honey that make tasty souvenirs, but also for artists inspired by the volcanic cycle of destruction and creation, the boundless energy of the ocean, and the timeless beauty of native crafts. You'll find the most galleries in the upcountry art enclaves of **Holualoa** and **Volcano Village,** but even the kitschy shopping complexes along Kailua-Kona's **Alii Drive** hold a few gems. Meanwhile, the **Kohala Coast** resort shopping malls provide a showcase for Hawaiian entertainment and boutiques featuring island designers, along with luxury brands and ubiquitous surf shops. With a few notable exceptions, **Hilo** and **Waimea** shops are primarily geared to residents; you'll also find necessities across the island, except in the more remote areas of the Hamakua Coast, and the Kau and Puna districts. For those cooking meals or packing a picnic, see the "Edibles" listings.

The Kona Coast

KAILUA-KONA

For bargain shopping with an island flair, bypass the T-shirt and trinket shops and head 2 miles south from Kailua Pier to **Alii Gardens Marketplace,** 75–6129 Alii Dr., a friendly, low-key combination farmers market, flea market, and crafts fair, with plenty of parking. The tent-covered stalls don't have quite as many vendors as before the 2008 economic crash, but you'll find fun items handmade in Hawaii as well as China's factories. On Tuesday, Wednesday, and Saturday, visit the **Kona Natural Soap Company** stand (www.konanaturalsoapcompany.com) and let Greg Colden explain the all-natural ingredients and fragrances he uses, many grown at his farm and solar-powered factory in Keauhou.

In Kailua-Kona's historic district, pop into **Lava Light Galleries,** 75-5707 Alii Dr. (www.lavalightgalleries.com; © **808/756-0778**), to admire C. J. Kale and Nick Selway's breathtaking nature photography, which includes sunsets, rainbows, and forests, as well as molten rock. Nearby, the funky, family-run **Pacific Vibrations** (© **808/329-4140**) has colorful surfwear, in 75-5702 Likana Lane, an alley off Alii Drive just north of Mokuaikaua Church. Across the street, the nonprofit **Hulihee Palace Gift Shop** (www.daughtersofhawaii.org; © **808/329-6558**) stocks arts and crafts by local artists, including gorgeous feather lei, silk scarves, art cards, aprons, and woven lauhala hats. Like the palace, it's closed Sunday.

Keauhou Shopping Center, above Alii Drive at King Kamehameha III Road (www.keauhouvillageshops.com), has more restaurants and services than shops, but do check out **Kona Stories** (www.konastories.com; © **808/324-0350**) for thousands of books, especially Hawaiiana and children's titles. Also in the mall, **Jams World** (www.jamsworld.com; © **808/322-9361**) has kicky, comfortable resort wear for men and women, from a Hawaii company founded in 1964.

HOLUALOA

Charmingly rustic Holualoa, 1,400 feet and 10 minutes above Kailua-Kona at the top of Hualalai Road, is the perfect spot for visiting coffee farms (p. 160) and tasteful galleries, with a half-dozen or more within a short distance of each other on Mamalahoa Highway (Hwy. 180). Highlights of the latter include **Dovetail Gallery** (www.dovetailgallery.net; © **808/322-4046**), featuring the wood sculptures and furniture of Gerald Ben and contemporary art curated by wife Renee Fukumoto-Ben; and **Studio 7 Fine Arts** (www.studio7hawaii.com; © **808/324-1335**), a virtual Zen garden with pottery, wall hangings, and paper collages by Setsuko Morinoue and paintings and prints by husband Hiroki. *Note:* Most galleries are closed Sunday and Monday; see www.holualoahawaii.com for more listings.

Lovers of lauhala, the Hawaiian art of weaving leaves (*lau*) from the pandanus tree (*hala),* revel in **Kimura's Lauhala Shop,** farther south at 77-996 Mamalahoa Hwy. Founded in 1914, the store brims with locally woven mats, hats (you can get one custom-made), handbags, and slippers, plus Kona coffee, koa wood bowls, art cards, and feather hatbands. It's closed Sunday.

SOUTH KONA

Many stores along Highway 11, the main road, are roadside fruit and/or coffee stands, well worth pulling over for, if only to "talk story" and pick up a snack. One exception is the wonderfully eclectic **Antiques and Orchids,** 81-6224 Mamalahoa Hwy., Captain Cook, in a green building of 1906 vintage (© **808/323-9851**). Owner Beverly Napolitan's orchids grace Hawaiiana, Victorian, and other antiques and collectibles; an antiques mall sells fellow vendors' "mantiques": vintage tools, fishing gear, and sports memorabilia. Fabric aficionados must stop at **Kimura Store,** a quaint general store and textile emporium with more than 10,000 bolts of aloha prints and other colorful cloth, at 79-7408 Mamalahoa Hwy. (ocean side), Kainaliu (© **808/322-3771**). Both stores are closed Sunday.

The Kohala Coast

SOUTH KOHALA

Three open-air shopping malls claim the bulk of stores here, with a few island-only boutiques amid state and national chains. The real plus is the malls' free entertainment (check their websites for current calendars) and prices somewhat lower than those of shops in resort hotels.

The Waikoloa Beach Resort has two malls, both off its main drag, Waikoloa Beach Road. **Kings' Shops** (www.kingsshops.com) has a *keiki* (children's) hula performance at 6pm Friday and music by Kahalanui, a Hawaiian swing band, at 7pm Wednesday. Along with luxury stores (**Tiffany, Louis Vuitton, Coach**), find a great selection of affordable swimwear at **Making Waves** (© 808/886-1814) and batik-print fashions at **Noa** (© 808/886-5449). **Queens' Market-Place** (http://queensmarketplace.net) includes two fun places for families: **Local Lizard & Friends** (© 808/886-8900), with gecko-themed clothes, toys and tchotchkes, and **Giggles** (© 808/886-0014). Its free shows include hula and Polynesian dance Monday, Wednesday, and Friday at 6pm.

The **Shops at Mauna Lani** (www.shopsatmaunalani.com), on the main road of the Mauna Lani Resort, presents hula and Polynesian fire dancing Monday and Thursday at 7pm. As for its stores, **Hawaiian Island Creations** (www.hicsurf.com; © 808/881-1400) stands out for its diverse lineup of local, state, and national surfwear brands.

In **Kawaihae,** an unassuming shopping strip on Highway 270, just north of the Highway 19 intersection, hosts **Harbor Gallery** (www.harborgallery.biz; © 808/882-1510), displaying the works of more than 150 Big Island artists, and specializing in koa and other wood furniture, bowls, and sculpture. Stock up on savory souvenirs at **Hamakua Macadamia Nut Company,** 61-3251 Maluokalani St., an uphill detour off Highway 270 (www.hawnnut.com; © 808/882-1690).

NORTH KOHALA

When making the trek to the Pololu Valley Lookout, you'll pass a few stores of note along Akoni Pule Highway (Hwy. 270). **As Hawi Turns,** 2 miles west of the Kohala Mountain Road (Hwy. 250), includes eclectic women's clothing, locally made jewelry, shoes, home decor, and a bargain consignment area cheekily called As Hawi Returns (© 808/889-5203). In the center of town, at the highways' junction, look on the ocean side for **Elements** (www.elementsjewelryandcrafts.com; © 808/889-0760), where jeweler John Flynn displays his designs and works by other artists, including pottery, wood bowls, and dyed scarves. Across from the King Kamehameha Statue in Kapaau, near Kapaau Road, **Ackerman Gallery** (www.ackermangalleries.com; © 808/889-5971) also features lovely arts and crafts from the Big Island, including paintings by owner Gary Ackerman.

WAIMEA

The barn-red buildings of **Parker Square,** on Highway 19 east of Opelo Road, hold several pleasant surprises. The **Gallery of Great Things** (www.galleryofgreatthingshawaii.com; © 808/885-7706) has high-quality Hawaiian artwork, including quilts and Niihau shell leis, as well as pieces from throughout the Pacific. Sticking closer to home, literally, **Bentley's Home & Garden Collection** (www.bentleyshomecollection.com; © 808/885-5565) is chock-a-block with Western and country-inspired clothes, accessories, and cottage decor.

East Hawaii

HAMUKUA COAST

Park on Mamane Street (Hwy. 240) in "downtown" **Honokaa** and stroll through a huge selection of antiques and collectibles at the warehouse-sized **Honokaa Trading Company** (© 808/775-0808) and the mini-mall of **Vera's Treasures**

Hilo Farmers Market.

(© 808/775-0244). If you'd like something newer, head to **Big Island Grown,** selling edibles such as coffee, tea, and honey, plus locally made gifts and clothing (© 808/775-9777), or **Taro Patch Gifts** (www.taropatchgifts.com; © 808/ 775-7228), which adds books to the mix. **Waipio Valley Artworks** (www. waipiovalleyartworks.com; © 808/775-0958), on Kukuihaele Road near the overlook, has many handsome wood items plus a cafe serving Hawi's Tropical Dreams ice cream.

HILO

As Hawaii's second largest city, Hilo has both mom-and-pop shops and big-box stores (though locals gripe that the only Costco is in Kona). The **Hilo Farmers Market** is the prime attraction (see "A Feast for the Senses," below), but you should also visit residents' favorite places for *omiyage* (a kind of edible souvenir): **Big Island Candies,** 585 Hinano St. (www.bigislandcandies.com; © 808/935-5510) and **Two Ladies Kitchen,** 274 Kilauea Ave. (© 808/961-4766). The former is a factory store and huge tourist attraction that cranks out addictive macadamia-nut shortbread cookies, while the other is a cash-only hole-in-the-wall selling delicious handmade *mochi,* a pounded-rice treat (try the one with a Waimea strawberry inside), and *manju,* a kind of mini-turnover.

Visit **Sig Zane Designs,** 122 Kamehameha Ave. (www.sigzane.com; © 808/ 935-7077), for apparel and home items with Zane's fabric designs, inspired by native Hawaiian plants and culture, including wife Nalani Kanakaole's hula lineage. **Basically Books,** 160 Kamehameha Ave. (www.basicallybooks.com; © 808/ 961-0144), is also happy to educate you with a stunning assortment of maps and books emphasizing Hawaii and the Pacific.

PUNA DISTRICT

One of the prettiest places to visit in **Volcano Village** is **Volcano Garden Arts,** 19-3834 Old Volcano Rd. (www.volcanogardenarts.com; © 808/985-8979), offering beautiful gardens with sculptures and open studios, delicious **Café Ono** (p. 242), and an airy gallery of artworks (some by owner Ira Ono), jewelry, and

Feast for the Senses: Hilo Farmers Market

You can't beat the **Hilo Farmers Market** (www.hilofarmersmarket.com), considered by many the best in the state, from its dazzling display of tropical fruits and flowers (especially orchids) to savory prepared foods such as pad Thai and bento boxes, plus locally made crafts and baked goods, all in stalls pleasantly crammed around the corner of Kamehameha Avenue and Mamo Street. The full version takes place 6am to 4pm Wednesday and Saturday; go early for the best selection and fewest crowds. (Some vendors set up at 7am–4pm the rest of the week, except Friday, but it's not the same experience.)

home decor by local artists; it's closed Monday. Look for Hawaiian quilts and fabrics, as well as island-made soaps, candles, and cards at **Kilauea Kreations,** 19-3972 Old Volcano Rd. (www.kilaueakreations. com; ✆ **808/967-8090**).

In Hawaii Volcanoes National Park, the **gift shop** at Volcano House (p. 232) has surprisingly tasteful gifts, many of them made on the Big Island, as well as attractive jackets for chilly nights. The original 1877 Volcano House, a short walk from the Kilauea Visitor Center, is home to the nonprofit **Volcano Art Center** (www.volcano artcenter.org; ✆ **808/967-7565**), which sells prints, paintings, photos, and sculptures by local artists, including the intricate, iconic prints of Dietrich Varez, who worked at the newer Volcano House in his youth.

Edibles

Since most visitors stay on the island's west side, the Hilo Farmers Market isn't really an option to stock their larders. If you're in Kailua-Kona, visit the **Keauhou Farmers Market** (www.keauhoufarmersmarket.com) Saturday from 8am to noon at the **Keauhou Shopping Center** (near Ace Hardware), for locally grown produce, fresh eggs, baked goods, coffee, and flowers. Pick up the rest of what you need at the center's **KTA Super Stores** (www.ktasuperstores.com; ✆ **808/323-2311**), a Big Island grocery chain founded in 1916 at which you can find island-made specialties (poke, mochi) as well as national brands. Another **KTA** is in the Kona Coast Shopping Center, 74–5588 Palani Rd. (✆ **808/329-1677**), open daily till 11pm. Wine aficionados will be amazed at the large and well-priced selection in **Kona Wine Market,** in the Kona Commons Shopping Center, 74–5450 Makala Blvd. (www.konawinemarket.com; ✆ **808/329-9400**). If you have a **Costco** membership, its only Big Island warehouse is at 73-4800 Maiau St., near Highway 19 and Hina Lani Street (✆ **808/331-4800**).

On the Kohala Coast, the best prices are in **Waimea,** home to a **KTA** in Waimea Center, Highway 19 at Pulalani Road (✆ **808/885-8866**). Buy smoked meat and fish, hot *malasadas* (doughnut holes), baked goods, and ethnic foods along with a cornucopia of produce at the **Waimea Homestead Farmers Market,** Saturday 7am to noon at Kuhio Hale, 64-759 Kahilu Rd., near Hwy. 19's mile marker 55 (www.waimeafarmersmarket.com). The best deals for fresh fish are at **Da Fish House,** 61-3665 Akoni Pule Hwy. (Hwy. 270) in Kawaihae (✆ **808/882-1052**; closed Sun). Among the options in the resorts, **Foodland Farms** in the Shops at Mauna Lani (www.foodland.com; ✆ **808/887-61010**), has top-quality local produce and seafood, while the Kings' Shops hosts a decent **farmers market** Wednesday 8:30am to 3pm. In the Queens' MarketPlace, **Island Gourmet Markets** (www.islandgourmethawaii.com; ✆ **808/886-3577**) has an almost overwhelming array, including 200-plus kinds of cheese.

BIG ISLAND NIGHTLIFE

With the exception of a few bars in Kailua-Kona and Hilo, the Big Island tucks in early, all the better to rise at daybreak, when the weather is cool and the roads (and waves) are open. But live Hawaiian music is everywhere these days, and it's easy to catch free, engaging hula shows, too, thanks to the courtyard stages at resort malls (see "Shopping," p. 244).

Kailua-Kona

When the sun goes down, the scene heats up in and around Alii Drive. Among the hot spots: **On the Rocks,** next to Huggo's restaurant, at 75-5824 Kahakai Rd. (www.huggosontherocks.com; © 808/329-1493), has Hawaiian music and hula nightly, till 11pm Friday and Saturday and 10pm Sunday. Across the way in the Coconut Grove Market Place, **Laverne's Sports Bar** (formerly Lulu's; www.laverneskona.com; © 808/331-2633) draws a 20-something crowd with happy-hour specials, theme nights, and late-night DJs on weekends. An eclectic mix of musicians—including jazz, country, and rock bands—perform at **Bongo Ben's,** 75-5819 Alii Dr. (www.bongobens.com; © 808/329-9203), open till 10pm nightly. **Rays on the Bay,** inside the **Sheraton Kona Resort & Spa** (p. 224), lures locals and visitors to Keauhou with firepits, a great happy hour, nightly live music, and perhaps best of all, free valet parking.

The Kohala Coast

All the resort hotels have at least one lounge with nightly live music, usually traditional or contemporary Hawaiian, often with hula. Members of the renowned **Lim Family** perform at varying times and venues in the **Mauna Lani Bay Hotel & Bungalows** (p. 227), while award-winning singer **Darlene Ahuna** sings from 7 to 10pm Tuesday to Thursday in the **Reef Lounge** of the Hapuna Beach Prince Hotel (p. 226). **Lava Lava Beach Club** (p. 225) has created a lively scene at the Waikoloa Beach Resort with nightly music and hula overlooking "A-Bay".

Just beyond the resorts lies a great open-air music spot—the **Blue Dragon,** 61–3616 Kawaihae Rd., Kawaihae (www.bluedragonhawaii.com; © 808/882-7771), where you can enjoy music—jazz, rock, Hawaiian swing—often with dancing, Thursday through Sunday.

Sharing Stories & Aloha Under the Stars

If your timing is right, your visit will include the best free entertainment on the island: **Twilight at Kalahuipua'a,** a monthly Hawaiian-style celebration that includes storytelling, singing, and dancing on the oceanside lawn in front of the Eva Parker Woods Cottage on the Mauna Lani Resort (www.maunalani.com/about/big-island-hawaii-events; © 808/881-7911). Held the Saturday closest to the full moon, these events are beloved by visitors and residents alike. Performers include entertainers revered throughout Hawaii as well as local *kupuna* (elders), who gather to "talk story," accompanied by music and hula. The show starts at 5:30pm, but the audience starts arriving an hour earlier, with picnic fare and beach mats. Bring yours, and plan to share food as well as the fun. Parking for the event is free, too.

luaus' new taste **OF OLD HAWAII**

Let's face it, you will probably never have a truly great meal at a luau, thanks to the numbers served, but on the Big Island you can have a very good meal, with a highly enjoyable—and educational—show to boot. That's because buffets now offer more intriguing (and tasty) items such as pohole ferns, warabi shoots, and Molokai sweet potatoes, while the shows feature more local history, from the first voyagers to *paniolo* days, plus the usual fire knife dance and Polynesian revue. Especially if it's your first time in Hawaii, I recommend one of these oceanfront luaus:

o **Haleo** (www.haleoluau.com) at the **Sheraton Kona Resort & Spa** (p. 224) is simply the best in Kailua-Kona and Keauhou (Mon 4:30pm; also Fri in summer; $88 adults, $55 children 6–12).

o **Gathering of the Kings** (www.gatheringofthekings.com) at the **Fairmont Orchid Hawaii** (p. 225), has the best selection of island-style food, including seafood *lū'au*, the taro leaf-coconut stew that gave these feasts their name (Sat 4:30pm; $109 adults, $75 children 5–12).

o **Legends of Hawaii** (www.hilton waikoloavillage.com/resort-experiences/ legends-of-hawaii-luau) at **Hilton Waikoloa Village** (p. 226) is the most family-friendly, with pillow seating upfront for kids, plus a show-only price of $60 (Tues, Fri, and Sun 5:30pm; $112 adults, $102 seniors and teens 13–17, $57 children 5–12; free for children 4 and under).

For a uniquely Big Island alternative to a luau, experience **An Evening at Kahua Ranch** (www.kahuaranch.com), which includes a barbecue with open bar, line dancing, rope tricks, a campfire singalong, and stargazing, on the North Kohala ranch 3,200 feet above the coast. The 3-hour event costs $119 for adults and $60 for kids 6 to 11 (free for kids under 6) with hotel shuttle; drive yourself and it's $95 and $48, respectively. Festivities start at 6pm Wednesday in summer, 5:30pm in winter.

Hilo

Opened in 1925, the neoclassical **Palace Theater,** 38 Haili St. (www.hilopalace. com; © **808/934-7010**), screens first-run independent movies and hosts concerts, festivals, hula, and theater to support its ongoing restoration. **Hilo Town Tavern,** 168 Keawe St. (© **808/935-2171**), is a Cajun restaurant and dive bar open till 2am daily, with a nice pool room and live music. It also supports downtown Hilo's **First Friday Art Walk,** the first Friday of each month, when local shops and galleries offer music and refreshments till 8pm.

Puna District

The bustling Wednesday-night marketplace (5–10pm) at the family compound of **Uncle Robert's Awa Club,** at the end of the road in Kalapana (© **808/443-6913**), typically includes live music from 6 to 9pm. You can try some of the mildly intoxicating *awa* (the Hawaiian word for kava) at the tiki bar then, or come back Friday night for more live music, starting at 6.

MAUI

by Shannon Wianecki

For many, Maui inhabits the sweet spot. It's a tangle of lovely contradictions, with a Gucci heel on one foot and a *puka*-shell anklet on the other. Culturally, it's a mix of farmers, *paniolo* (Hawaiian cowboys), aspiring chefs, artists, New Age healers, and big wave riders. The landscape runs the gamut from sun-kissed golden beaches and fragrant rainforests to the frigid, wind-swept summit of Haleakala. Sure, more traffic lights sprout up around the island every year and spurts of development have turned cherished landmarks into mere memories. But even as Maui transforms, its allure remains.

ESSENTIALS

Arriving

BY PLANE If you think of the island of Maui as the shape of a person's head and shoulders, you'll probably arrive near its neck, at **Kahului Airport** (OGG). Many airlines offer direct flights to Maui from the mainland U.S., including **Hawaiian Airlines** (www.hawaiianair.com; ✆ 800/367-5320), **Alaska Airlines** (www.alaskaair.com; ✆ 800/252/7522), **United Airlines** (www.united.com; ✆ 800/241-6522), **American Airlines** (www.aa.com; ✆ 800/433-7300), **Delta Air Lines** (www.delta.com; ✆ 800/221-1212), and **U.S. Airways** (www.usairways.com; ✆ 800/428-4322). The only international flights to Maui originate in Canada, via **Air Canada** (www.aircanada.com; ✆ 888/247-2262) and **West Jet** (www.westjet.com; ✆ 888/937-8538), which both fly from Vancouver.

Other major carriers stop in Honolulu, where you'll catch an interisland flight to Maui on **Hawaiian Airlines.** (At present it's the only airline offering inter-island flights on jet aircraft.)

A small commuter service, **Mokulele Airlines** (www.mokuleleairlines.com; ✆ 866/260-7070), recently expanded its routes to include flights from Honolulu to Kahului Airport and to Maui's two other airstrips. If you're staying in Lahaina or Kaanapali, you might consider flying in or out of **Kapalua–West Maui Airport** (JHM). From this tiny, one-pony airfield, it's only a 10- to 15-minute drive to most hotels in West Maui, as opposed to an hour or more from Kahului. Same story with **Hana Airport** (HNM): Flying directly here will save you a 3-hour drive.

Mokulele also flies between Maui and Lanai, Molokai, and the Big Island. Check-in is a breeze: no security lines (unless leaving from Honolulu). You'll be weighed, ushered onto the tarmac, and welcomed aboard a nine-seat Cessna. The plane flies low, and the views between the islands are outstanding.

LANDING AT KAHULUI If you're renting a car, proceed to the car-rental desks just beyond baggage claim. All of the major rental companies have branches at Kahului. Each rental agency has a shuttle that will deliver you to the car lot a half-mile away. For tips on insurance and driving rules in Hawaii, see "Getting Around Hawaii" in chapter 10.

Previous page: Windsurfing in Paia.

If you're not renting a car, the cheapest way to exit the airport is the **Maui Bus** (www.mauicounty.gov/bus; ℃ 808/871-4838). For $2 it will deposit you at any one of the island's major towns. Simply cross the street at baggage claim and wait under the awning. The next cheapest option is **Roberts Hawaii Maui Airport Shuttle** (www.airportmauishuttle.com; ℃ 808/877-0907), which operates an on-demand airport shuttle. You can call upon arrival, but you'll get better rates and a written confirmation if you book online. Plan to pay $18 (one-way) to Kahului, $38 to Wailea, $53 to Kaanapali, and $73 to Kapalua—but know that prices drop significantly if you share the shuttle with other riders. **SpeediShuttle** (www.speedishuttle.com; ℃ 877/242-5777) also services Kahului Airport, between 6am and 11pm daily. Rates are $39 (one-way) to Wailea, $54 to Kaanapali, and $74 to Kapalua. You'll need to book in advance.

Taxis are also available, but cost 30 to 40 percent more than the shuttles.

Visitor Information

The website of the **Hawaii Tourism Authority** (www.gohawaii.com/maui) is chock-full of helpful facts and tips. Visit the state-run **Visitor Information Center** at the Kahului Airport baggage claim for brochures and the latest issue of "This Week Maui," which features great regional maps.

The Island in Brief

This medium-sized island lies in the center of the Hawaiian archipelago.

CENTRAL MAUI

Maui, the Valley Isle, is so named for the large isthmus between the island's two towering volcanoes: Haleakala and the West Maui Mountains. The flat landscape in between, Central Maui, is the heart of the island's business community and local government.

KAHULUI Most Maui visitors fly over waving sugarcane fields to land at Kahului Airport, just yards away from rolling surf. Sadly, your first sight out of the airport will likely be a Costco—hardly an icon of Hawaiiana but always bustling with islanders and visitors alike. Beyond that, Kahului is a grid of shops and no-non-sense neighborhoods that you'll pass through en route to your destination.

Wailuku.

WAILUKU   Nestled up against the West Maui Mountains, Wailuku is a time capsule of faded wooden storefronts, old churches, and plantation homes. While most people zip through on their way to see the natural beauty of **Iao Valley,** this quaint little town is worth a brief visit, if only to see a real place where real people actually appear to be working at something other than a suntan. This is the county seat, so you'll see folks in suits (or at least aloha shirts and long pants) on important missions in the tropical heat. The town has some great budget restaurants, interesting bungalow architecture, a wonderful historic B&B, and the intriguing **Bailey House Museum.**

WEST MAUI

Jagged peaks, velvety green valleys, a wilderness full of native species: The majestic West Maui Mountains are the epitome of earthly paradise. The beaches below are crowded with condos and resorts, but still achingly beautiful. This stretch of coastline along Maui's "forehead," from Kapalua to the historic port of Lahaina, is the island's busiest resort area (with South Maui close behind). Expect slow-moving traffic on the two main thoroughfares: Honoapiilani Highway and Front Street.

Vacationers on this coast can choose from several beachside neighborhoods, each with its own identity and microclimate. The West Side tends to be hot, humid, and sunny year-round. As you travel north, the weather grows cooler and mistier. Starting at the southern end of West Maui and moving northward, the coastal communities look like this:

LAHAINA   In days past, Lahaina was the seat of Hawaiian royalty. Legend has it that a powerful *mo'o* (lizard goddess) dwelt in a moat surrounding a palace here. Later, this hot and sunny seaport was where raucous whalers swaggered ashore in search of women and grog. Modern Lahaina is a tame version of its former self. Today Front Street teems with restaurants, T-shirt shops, and galleries. Action revolves around the town's giant, century-old banyan tree and busy recreational harbor. Parts of Lahaina are downright tacky, but you can still find plenty of authentic history here. It's also a great place to stay; accommodations include a few old hotels (such as the 1901 Pioneer Inn on the harbor), quaint bed-and-breakfasts, and a handful of oceanfront condos.

KAANAPALI   Farther north along the West Maui coast is Hawaii's first master-planned destination resort. Along nearly 3 miles of sun-kissed golden beach, pricey midrise hotels are linked by a landscaped parkway and a beachfront walking path. Golf greens wrap around the slope between beachfront and hillside properties. Convenience is a factor here: **Whalers Village** shopping mall and numerous restaurants are easy to reach on foot or by resort shuttle. Shuttles serves the small West Maui airport just to the north and also go to Lahaina (see above), 3 miles to the south, for shopping, dining, entertainment, and boat tours. Kaanapali is popular with groups and families—and especially teenagers, who like all the action.

HONOKOWAI, KAHANA   In the building binge of the 1970s, condominiums sprouted along this gorgeous coastline like mushrooms after a rain. Today, these older oceanside units offer excellent bargains for astute travelers. The great location—along sandy beaches, within minutes of both the Kapalua and Kaanapali resort areas, and close enough to the goings-on in Lahaina town—makes this area a haven for the budget-minded.

In **Honokowai** and **Mahinahina,** you'll find mostly older, cheaper units. There's not much shopping here (mostly convenience stores), but you'll have easy access to the shops and restaurants of Kaanapali. **Kahana** is a little more upscale than Honokowai and Mahinahina, and most of its condos are big high-rise types, newer than those immediately to the south.

NAPILI A quiet, tucked-away gem, with temperatures at least 5 degrees cooler than in Lahaina, this tiny neighborhood feels like a world unto itself. Wrapped around deliciously calm Napili Bay, Napili offers convenient activity desks and decent eateries and is close to the gourmet restaurants of Kapalua. Lodging is generally more expensive here—although I've found a few hidden jewels at affordable prices.

KAPALUA Beyond the activity of Kaanapali and Kahana, the road starts to climb and the vista opens up to include unfettered views of Molokai across the channel. A country lane lined with Cook pines brings you to Kapalua. It's the exclusive domain of the luxurious Ritz-Carlton resort and expensive condos and villas, set above two sandy beaches. Just north are two jeweled bays: marine-life preserves and world-class surf spot in winter. Although rain is frequent here, it doesn't dampen the enjoyment of this wilder stretch of coast.

Anyone is welcome to visit Kapalua, guest of the resort or not. The Ritz-Carlton provides free public parking and beach access. The resort has swank restaurants, spas, golf courses, and hiking trails—all open to the general public.

SOUTH MAUI

The hot, sunny South Maui coastline is popular with families and sun worshippers. Rain rarely falls here, and temperatures hover around 85°F (29°C) year-round. Cows once grazed and cacti grew wild on this former scrubland from Maalaea to Makena, now home to four distinct areas—**Maalaea, Kihei, Wailea,** and **Makena.** Maalaea is off on its own, at the mouth of an active small boat harbor, Kihei is the working-class, feeder community for well-heeled Wailea, and Makena is a luxurious wilderness at the road's end.

MAALAEA If West Maui is the island's head, Maalaea is just under the chin. This windy, oceanfront village centers on a small-boat harbor (with a general store and a handful of restaurants) and the **Maui Ocean Center,** an aquarium/ocean complex. Visitors should be aware that tradewinds are near constant here, so a stroll on the beach often comes with a free sandblasting.

KIHEI Kihei is less a proper town than a nearly continuous series of condos and mini-malls lining South Kihei Road. This is Maui's best vacation bargain. Budget travelers swarm like sun-seeking geckos over the eight sandy beaches along this scalloped, 7-mile stretch of coast. Kihei is neither charming nor quaint; what it lacks in aesthetics, though, it more than makes up for in sunshine, affordability, and convenience. If you want the beach in the morning, shopping in the afternoon, and Hawaii Regional Cuisine in the evening—all at bargain prices—head to Kihei.

WAILEA Just 4 decades ago, the road south of Kihei was a barely paved path through a tangle of kiawe trees. Now Wailea is a manicured oasis of multimillion-dollar resorts along 2 miles of palm-fringed gold coast. Wailea has warm, clear water full of tropical fish; year-round sunshine and clear blue skies; and hedonistic pleasure palaces on 1,500 acres of black-lava shore indented by five beautiful beaches, each one prettier than the next.

This is the playground of the stretch-limo set. The planned resort development has a shopping village, a plethora of award-winning restaurants, several prized golf courses, and a tennis complex. A growing number of large homes

La Pérouse Bay, Makena.

sprawl over the upper hillside, some offering excellent B&Bs at reasonable prices. The resorts along this fantasy coast are spectacular. Next door to the Four Seasons Resort Maui at Wailea, the most elegant, is the Grand Wailea, built by Tokyo developer Takeshi Sekiguchi, who dropped $500 million in 1991 to create the most opulent Hawaiian resort to date. Stop in and take a look—sculptures by Botero and Leger populate its open-air art gallery and gardens. Stones imported from Mount Fuji line the Japanese garden fronting the resort's Amasia restaurant.

MAKENA Suddenly, the road enters raw wilderness. After Wailea's overdone density, the thorny landscape is a welcome relief. Although beautiful, this is an end-of-the-road kind of place: It's a long drive from Makena to anywhere on Maui. If you're looking for an activity-filled vacation, stay elsewhere, or you'll spend most of your vacation in the car. But if you want a quiet, relaxing respite, where the biggest trip of the day is from your bed to the beach, Makena is the place.

Puu Olai stands like Maui's Diamond Head near the southern tip of the island. The red cinder cone shelters tropical fish and **Makena State Beach Park,** a vast stretch of golden sand spanked by feisty swells. Beyond Makena, you'll discover Haleakala's most recent lava flow; the bay named for French explorer La Pérouse; and a sunbaked lava-rock trail known as the King's Highway, which threads around Maui's southernmost shore through the ruins of bygone fishing villages.

UPCOUNTRY MAUI

After a few days at the beach, you'll probably notice the 10,023-foot mountain towering over Maui. The leeward slopes of Haleakala (House of the Sun) are home to cowboys, farmers, and other rural folks who wave as you drive by. They're all up here enjoying the crisp air, emerald pastures, eucalyptus, and flower farms of this tropical Olympus. The neighborhoods here are called "upcountry" because they're halfway up the mountain. You can see a thousand tropical sunsets reflected in the windows of houses old and new, strung along a road that runs like a loose hound from Makawao to Kula, leading up to the summit and **Haleakala National Park.** If you head south on Kula Highway, beyond the tiny outpost of Keokea, the road turns feral, undulating out towards **Tedeschi Winery,** where grapes, cattle, and elk flourish on Ulupalakua Ranch. A stay upcountry is usually affordable and a nice contrast to the sizzling beaches and busy resorts below.

MAKAWAO This small, two-street town has plenty of charm. It wasn't long ago that Hawaiian *paniolo* (cowboys) tied up their horses to the hitching posts outside the storefronts here; working ranchers still stroll through to pick up coffee and packages from the post office. The eclectic shops, galleries, and restaurants

Haleakala.

have a little something for everyone—from blocked Stetsons to wind chimes. Nearby, the **Hui No'eau Visual Arts Center,** Hawaii's premier arts collective, is definitely worth a detour. Makawao's only accommodations are reasonably priced bed-and-breakfasts, perfect for those who love great views and don't mind slightly chilly nights.

KULA A feeling of pastoral remoteness prevails in this upcountry community of old flower farms, humble cottages, and new suburban ranch houses with million-dollar views that take in the ocean, the isthmus, the West Maui Mountains, and, at night, the lights that run along the gold coast like a string of pearls from Maalaea to Puu Olai. Everything flourishes at a cool 3,000 feet (bring a jacket), just below the cloud line, along a winding road on the way up to Haleakala National Park. Everyone here grows something—Maui onions, lavender, orchids, and proteas—and B&Bs cater to guests seeking cool tropical nights, panoramic views, and a rural upland escape. Here you'll find the true peace and quiet that only rural farming country can offer—yet you're still just 30 to 40 minutes away from the beach and an hour's drive from Lahaina.

ON THE ROAD TO HANA On Maui's north shore, **Paia** was once a busy sugar plantation town, with a railroad, two movie theaters, and a double-decker mercantile. As the sugar industry began to wane, the tuned-in, dropped-out hippies of the 1970s moved in, followed shortly by a cosmopolitan collection of windsurfers. When the international wave riders discovered **Hookipa Beach Park** just outside of town, their minds were blown; it's one of the best places on the planet to catch air. Today, high-tech windsurf shops, trendy restaurants, bikini boutiques, and modern art galleries inhabit Paia's rainbow-colored vintage buildings. The Dalai Lama himself blessed the beautiful Tibetan stupa in the center of town. **Mama's Fish House** is located east of Paia, in the tiny community of **Kuau.**

Ten minutes farther east is **Haiku.** Once a pineapple plantation village, complete with two canneries (both now shopping complexes), Haiku offers vacation rentals and B&Bs in a pastoral setting. It's the perfect base for those who want to get off the beaten path and experience the quieter side of Maui.

HANA Set between an emerald rainforest and the blue Pacific is a Hawaiian village blissfully lacking in golf courses, shopping malls, and fast-food joints. Hana is more of a sensory overload than a destination; here you'll discover the simple joys of rain-misted flowers, the sweet taste of backyard bananas and papayas, and the easy calm and unabashed aloha spirit of old Hawaii. What saved "Heavenly" Hana from the inevitable march of progress? The 52-mile **Hana Highway,** which winds around 600 curves and crosses more than 50 one-lane bridges on its way from Kahului. You can go to Hana for the day—it's 3 hours (and a half-century) from Kihei and Lahaina—but 3 days are better.

GETTING AROUND

BY CAR The simplest way to see Maui is by rental car; public transit is still in its infancy here. All of the major car-rental firms—including Alamo, Avis, Budget, Dollar, Enterprise, Hertz, National, and Thrifty—have agencies on Maui. If you're on a budget or traveling with sports gear, you can rent an older vehicle by the week from **Kimo's Rent-a-Car** (www.kimosrentacar.com; ✆ **808/280-6327,** ext. 5). For tips on insurance and driving rules in Hawaii, see "Getting Around Hawaii" (p. 511).

Maui has only a handful of major roads, and you can expect a traffic jam or two heading into Kihei, Lahaina, or Paia. In general, the roads hug the coastlines; one zigzags up to Haleakala's summit. When asking locals for directions, don't bother using highway numbers; residents know the routes by name only.

Traffic advisory: Be alert on the Honoapiilani Highway (Hwy. 30) en route to Lahaina. Drivers ogling whales in the channel between Maui and Lanai often slam on the brakes and cause major tie-ups and accidents. Because this is the only main road connecting the west side to the rest of the island, if there is an accident, flooding, a rock slide, or any other road hazard, traffic can back up for 1 to 8 hours (no joke). So before you set off, check with Maui County for road closure advisories (www.co.maui.hi.us; ✆ **808/986-1200**). The most up-to-date info can be found on its Twitter feed (@CountyofMaui) or that of a local news agency (@MauiNow).

BY MOTORCYCLE Feel the wind on your face and smell the salt air as you tour the island on a Harley, available for rent from **Cycle City Maui,** 150 Dairy Rd., Kahului (www.cyclecitymaui.com; ✆ **808/831-2698**). Rentals start at $99 a day.

BY TAXI Because Maui's various destinations are so spread out, taxi service can be quite expensive and should be limited to travel within a neighborhood. **Alii Taxi** (✆ **808/661-3688**) offers 24-hour service island-wide. Call **Kihei Wailea Taxi** (✆ **808/879-3000**) if you need a ride in South Maui. Metered rate is $3 per mile.

BY BUS The **Maui Bus** (www.mauicounty.gov/bus; ✆ **808/871-4838**) is a public/private partnership that provides convenient and affordable public transit to various communities across the island. Air-conditioned buses service 13 routes, including several that stop at the airport. All routes operate daily, including holidays. Fares are $2. Suitcases (one per passenger) and bikes are allowed; surfboards and sandboards are not.

[FastFACTS] MAUI

Dentists Emergency dental care is available at **Hawaii Family Dental,** 1847 S. Kihei Rd., Kihei (© **808/874-8401**), or at **Aloha Lahaina Dentists,** 134 Luakini St. (in the Maui Medical Group Bldg.), Lahaina (© **808/661-4005**).

Doctors Urgent Care West Maui, Whalers Village, 2435 Kaanapali Pkwy., Suite H-7 (next to the Westin), Kaanapali (www.westmaui doctors.com; © **808/667-9721**), is open 365 days a year; no appointment is necessary. In Kihei, call **Urgent Care Maui,** 1325 S. Kihei Rd., Suite 103 (at Lipoa St., across from Star Market), Kihei (© **808/879-7781**), which is open daily from 7am to 9pm.

Emergencies Call © **911** for police, fire, and ambulance service. District stations are located in Lahaina (© **808/661-4441**) and in Hana (© **808/248-8311**).

Hospitals In Central Maui, **Maui Memorial Hospital** is at 221 Mahalani, Wailuku (© **808/244-9056**). East Maui's **Hana Community Health Center** is at 4590 Hana Hwy. (www.hanahealth.org; © **808/248-8294**). In Upcountry Maui, **Kula Hospital** is at 204 Kula Hwy., Kula (© **808/878-1221**).

Internet Access Many places offer free Wi-Fi. **Starbucks** (www.starbucks.com/store-locator) provides Internet service in its stores

in Kahului, Pukalani, Lahaina, and Kihei.

Post Office To find the nearest post office, call © **800/ASK-USPS.** In Lahaina, there are branches at the Lahaina Civic Center, 1760 Honoapiilani Hwy., and at the Lahaina Shopping Center, 132 Papalaua St. In Kahului, there's a branch at 138 S. Puunene Ave., and in Kihei, there's one at 1254 S. Kihei Rd.

Weather For the current weather, the Haleakala National Park weather, or the marine and surf conditions, call the National Weather Service's **Maui forecast** (© **866/944-5025**) or visit **www.prh.noaa.gov/hnl** and click on the island of Maui.

EXPLORING MAUI
Attractions & Points of Interest
CENTRAL MAUI
Kahului

Under the airport flight path, next to Maui's busiest intersection and across from Costco and Kmart in Kahului's business park, is a most unlikely place: the **Kanaha Wildlife Sanctuary,** Haleakala Highway Extension and Hana Highway (© **808/984-8100**). Look for the parking area off Haleakala Highway Extension (behind the mall, across the Hana Hwy. from Cutter Automotive), and you'll find a 50-foot trail that meanders along the shore to a shade shelter and lookout. A sign proclaims that this is the permanent home of the endangered black-neck Hawaiian stilt, whose population is now down to about 1,000. Naturalists say this is also a good place to see endangered Hawaiian koloa ducks, stilts, coots, and other migrating shorebirds. For a quieter, more natural-looking wildlife preserve, head to the **Kealia Pond National Wildlife Preserve** in Kihei (p. 264).

Maui Nui Botanical Garden GARDEN This garden is a living treasure box of native Hawaiian coastal species and plants brought here by Polynesian voyagers in their seafaring canoes. Stroll beneath the shade of the hala and breadfruit trees. Learn how the first Hawaiians made everything from medicine to musical instruments out of the plants they found growing in these islands. Ask to see the *hapai* (pregnant) banana tree—a variety with fruits that grow inside the trunk! Take a self-guided audio tour or come between Tuesday and Thursday at 10am, when docents lead tours ($10 per person). If the garden happens to be hosting a lei-making or kapa-dyeing workshop while you're on the island, don't miss it.

150 Kanaloa Ave., Kahului. www.mnbg.org. ② **808/249-2798.** Admission $5 adults, free for seniors and children 12 and under. Free admission on Sat.

Wailuku

Wailuku, the historic gateway to Iao Valley, is worth a visit for a little shopping and a stop at the small but fascinating Bailey House.

Bailey House Museum ★ HISTORIC SITE   Since 1957, the Maui Historical Society has welcomed visitors to the charming former home of Edward Bailey, a missionary, teacher, and accomplished artist. The 1833 building—a hybrid of Hawaiian stonework and Yankee-style architecture—is a treasure trove of Hawaiiana. Inside you'll find pre-contact artifacts: precious feather lei, kapa (barkcloth) samples, a wooden spear so large it defies believability, and a collection of gem-like Hawaiian tree-snail shells. Bailey's exquisite landscapes decorate the rock walls, capturing on canvas a Maui that exists only in memory.

2375-A Main St., Wailuku. www.mauimuseum.org. ② **808/244-3326.** Admission $7 adults, $5 seniors/military, $2 children 7–12. Mon–Sat 10am–4pm.

Maui Tropical Plantation GARDEN   About 3 miles south of Wailuku lies the tiny village of Waikapu, which has an attraction that's worth exploring. Relive Maui's past by taking a 40-minute narrated tram ride around fields of pineapple, sugarcane, and papaya trees at a working plantation. A shop sells fresh and dried fruit, a restaurant serves lunch, and a zipline zooms over the plantation's lush landscape. Tram tours start at 10am and leave about every 45 minutes.

1670 Honoapiilani Hwy. www.mauitropicalplantation.com. ② **800/451-6805** or 808/244-7643. Free admission. Tram tours $16 adults, $6 children 3–12. Daily 9am–5pm.

Iao Valley ★

A couple of miles north of Wailuku, where the little plantation houses stop and the road climbs ever higher, Maui's true nature begins to reveal itself. The transition from suburban sprawl to raw nature is so abrupt that most people who drive up into the valley don't realize they're suddenly in a rainforest. This is Iao Valley, a beautiful 6¼-acre state park whose verdant nature, waterfalls, swimming holes, and hiking trails have been enjoyed by millions of people from around the world for more than a century. The head of the valley is a broad circular amphitheater where four major streams converge into Iao Stream. At the back of the amphitheater is rain-drenched Puu Kukui, the West Maui Mountains' highest point. No other Hawaiian valley lets you go from seacoast to rainforest so easily.

To get here from Wailuku, take Main Street to Iao Valley Road to the entrance to the state park. Two paved walkways loop into the massive green amphitheater, across the bridge of Iao Valley Stream, and along the stream itself. This paved .35-mile loop is Maui's easiest hike—you can take your grandmother on this one. The leisurely walk will allow you to enjoy lovely views of Iao Needle and the lush vegetation.

The feature known as **Iao Needle** is an erosional remnant consisting of basalt dikes. This phallic rock juts an impressive 2,250 feet above sea level. Youngsters play in **Iao Stream,** a peaceful brook that belies its bloody history. In 1790, King Kamehameha the Great and his men engaged in the battle of Iao

Iao Needle.

Valley to gain control of Maui. When the battle ended, so many bodies blocked Iao Stream that the battle site was named Kepaniwai, or "Damming of the Waters." An architectural heritage park of Hawaiian, Japanese, Chinese, Filipino, Korean, Portuguese, and New England–style houses stands in harmony by Iao Stream at **Kepaniwai Heritage Garden.** This is a good picnic spot, with plenty of tables and benches. You can see ferns, banana trees, and other native and exotic plants in the **Iao Valley Botanic Garden** along the stream.

WHEN TO GO   The park is open daily 7am to 7pm; the entrance fee is $5 per car. Go early in the morning or late in the afternoon, when the sun's rays slant into the valley and create a mystical mood. You can bring a picnic and spend the day, but be prepared at any time for one of the frequent tropical cloudbursts that soak the valley and swell both waterfalls and streams.

INFORMATION   Contact **Iao Valley State Park,** State Parks and Recreation, 54 S. High St., Room 101, Wailuku, HI 96793 (✆ **808/984-8100**).

The Scenic Route to West Maui: The Kahekili Highway

The main route to West Maui is the Honoapiilani Highway, which sidles around the southern coastline along the *pali* (cliffs) to Lahaina. But those who relish adventures should consider exploring the backside of the West Maui Mountains.

From Wailuku, head north on the **Kahekili Highway** (Hwy. 340)—though "highway" is a bit of a misnomer for this paved and sometimes precarious road. It's named after a fierce Maui king who built houses out of the skulls of his enemies. The narrow and sometimes white-knuckle road weaves for 20 miles along an ancient Hawaiian coastal footpath to Honokohau Bay, at the island's northernmost tip, past blowholes, sea stacks, seabird rookeries, and the imposing 636-foot Kahakaloa headland. On the *mauka* (mountain) side, you'll pass high cliffs, deep valleys dotted with plantation houses, cattle grazing on green plateaus, old wooden churches, taro fields, and houses hung with fishing nets. It's slow going (you often have to inch past oncoming traffic on what feels like a one-lane track) but a spectacular drive. Check for road closures before heading out, especially if it's been raining heavily.

At Honokohau, pick up Hwy. 30 and continue on to the West Maui resorts; the first one you'll reach is Kapalua (see below).

WEST MAUI

For a map of attractions in Lahaina and Kaanapali, see p. 301.

Baldwin Home Museum ★ HISTORIC SITE   Climb the steps up to this coral-and-rock house on Lahaina's Front Street and step back in time. Built in 1835, it belonged to Rev. Dwight Baldwin, a missionary, naturalist, and self-trained physician who saved many Native Hawaiians from devastating influenza and small pox epidemics. Baldwin's rudimentary medical tools (on display here) bear witness to the steep odds he faced. He was rewarded with 2,600 acres in

Kapalua, where he grew pineapple—then an experimental crop. His children later became some of Hawaii's most powerful landholders and business owners. Tour the Baldwin family home and pick up a walking-tour map to Lahaina's most historic sites on your way out. On Friday night, docents dressed in period attire offer candlelit tours and serve free refreshments on the lanai.

120 Dickenson St. (at Front St.). www.lahainarestoration.org. (C) **808/661-3262.** Admission $7 adults, $5 seniors/military, free for children 12 and under (admission also grants entry to Wo Hing Museum). Sat–Thurs 10am–4pm, Fri 10am–8:30pm.

Banyan Tree NATURAL ATTRACTION Of all the Indian banyan trees in Hawaii, this is the greatest—so big that you can't fit it in your camera's view-finder. It was 8 feet tall when planted in 1873. Today the arboreal octopus rises more than 50 feet high, has 12 major trunks, and shades artists and crafters selling their wares in Courthouse Square.

Courthouse Sq.

Wo Hing Museum & Cookhouse ★ HISTORIC SITE Sandwiched between souvenir shops and restaurants on Front Street, this ornate building once served as a fraternal and social meeting hall for Lahaina's Chinese immigrants. Today it houses fascinating Asian artifacts, artwork, and a lovely shrine in the altar room upstairs. Beside the temple is a rustic cookhouse where you can watch some of Thomas Edison's first movies, filmed here in Hawaii. The footage of *paniolo* (cowboys) wrangling steer onto ships offshore and Honolulu circa 1898 is mesmerizing. Wo Hing hosts Lunar New Year festivals and other celebrations that are catnip for kids.

858 Front St. www.lahainarestoration.org. (C) **808/661-3262.** Admission $7 adults, $5 seniors/ military, free for children 12 and under (admission also grants entry to Baldwin House Museum; see above). Daily 10am–4pm.

The banyan tree at the courthouse.

Maui Ocean Center.

Kaanapali

Whalers Village Museum ★ MUSEUM   As you enter Kaanapali's posh shopping center, you're greeted by the almost life-size metal sculpture of a mother whale and two nursing calves. A few steps in is the impressive, bleached-white skeleton of a 40-foot sperm whale. On the mall's second floor, a small interactive museum illuminates the "Golden Era of Whaling" from 1825 to 1860. Follow the self-guided audio tour, check out the harpoons and scrimshaw collection, and experience the cramped quarters of a whaleboat's forecastle. The videos of whale-hunting carnage may be a bit much for youngsters, but the free talks by marine biologists every Monday, Wednesday, and Friday at 11am are terrific. *Tip:* You can get 3 hours' free parking validated here.

In Whalers Village Shopping Mall, 2435 Kaanapali Pkwy. www.whalersmuseum.com. © **808/661-5992.** Admission $3 adults, $2 seniors/students/military, $1 children 6–18, free for children under 6. Daily 10am–4pm.

SOUTH MAUI

Maalaea

Maui Ocean Center ★★★ AQUARIUM   This 5-acre facility houses the largest aquarium in the state and features one of Hawaii's largest predators: the tiger shark. As you walk past the 3 dozen or so tanks and countless exhibits, you'll slowly descend from the tide pools to the pelagic zone—without ever getting wet. Start at the outdoor surge pool, where you'll see shallow-water spiny urchins and cauliflower coral; and move on to the turtle pool and eagle-ray pools before heading indoors for the star of the show: a 100-foot-long, 600,000-gallon main tank featuring tiger, gray, and white-tip sharks, as well as feisty ulua, colorful surgeonfish, and numerous others. The walkway tunnels right through the tank, so you're surrounded on three sides by marine creatures. Check out the hammerhead exhibit where juvenile scalloped hammerhead sharks are on display, and the Shark Dive Maui Program, where scuba divers plunge into the tank with sharks, stingrays, and tropical fish. You, too, can sign up to dive with sharks, and fish-loving kids can book a sleepover in the aquarium, staying up into the wee hours to watch glowing jellyfish and other nocturnal animals.

At the Maalaea Harbor Village, 192 Maalaea Rd. (the triangle btw. Honoapiilani Hwy. and Maalaea Rd.). www.mauioceancenter.com. *☎* **808/270-7000.** Admission $26 adults, $23 seniors, $19 children 3–12 (book online for a week pass upgrade). Daily 9am–5pm (until 6pm July–Aug).

Kihei

West of the junction of Piilani Highway (Hwy. 31) and Mokulele Highway (Hwy. 350) is **Kealia Pond National Wildlife Preserve** (www.fws.gov/kealiapond; *☎* **808/875-1582**), a 700-acre U.S. Fish and Wildlife wetland preserve where endangered Hawaiian stilts, coots, and ducks splash about. These ponds work both as bird preserves and as sedimentation basins that keep the coral reefs from silting from runoff. You can take a self-guided tour along a boardwalk dotted with interpretive signs and shade shelters, through sand dunes, and around ponds to Maalaea Harbor. The boardwalk starts at the outlet of Kealia Pond on the ocean side of North Kihei Road (near mile marker 2 on Piilani Hwy.). Among the Hawaiian water birds seen here are the black-crowned high heron, Hawaiian coot, Hawaiian duck, and Hawaiian stilt. From July to December, the hawksbill turtle comes ashore here to lay its eggs.

Wailea

The best way to explore this golden resort coast is to head for Wailea's 1.5-mile **coastal nature trail ★**, stretching between the Fairmont Kea Lani Maui and the kiawe thicket just beyond the Marriott Wailea Beach Resort. The serpentine path meanders past an abundance of native plants (on the *makai,* or ocean side), old Hawaiian habitats, and a billion dollars' worth of luxury hotels. You can pick up the trail at any of the resorts or from clearly marked shoreline access points along the coast. As the path crosses several bold black-lava points, it affords new vistas of islands and ocean; benches allow you to pause and contemplate the view across Alalakeiki Channel, where you may see jumping whales in season. It's nice in the cool hours of the morning (though often clogged with joggers) and at sunset, when you can watch the burning sun sink into the Pacific.

Makena

A few miles south of Wailea, the manicured coast returns to wilderness; now you're in Makena. At one time cattle were driven down the slope from upland ranches, lashed to rafts, and sent into the water to swim to boats that waited to take them to market. Now **Makena Landing ★** is a great spot to launch kayaks and dive trips.

From the landing, go south on Makena Road; on the right is **Keawalai Congregational Church** (*☎* **808/879-5557**), built in 1855, with walls 3 feet thick. Surrounded by ti leaves, which by Hawaiian custom provide protection, and built of lava rock with coral used as mortar, this church sits on its own cove with a gold-sand beach. It always attracts a Sunday crowd for its 7:30 and 10am Hawaiian-language services.

Farther south on the coast is **La Pérouse Monument,** a pyramid of lava rocks that marks the spot where French explorer Adm. Comte de la Pérouse set foot on Maui in 1789. He described the "burning climate" of the leeward coast, observed several fishing villages near Kihei, and sailed on into oblivion, never to be seen again. To get here, drive south to Ahihi Bay, where the road turns to gravel. Just beyond this is **Ahihi-Kinau Natural Preserve,** 1,238 acres of rare anchialine ponds and sunbaked lava fields from the last eruption of Haleakala, between 200 and 500 years ago. The state closed the preserve to all traffic—both land and sea—hoping to give the fragile ecosystem a chance to rebound.

Continue another 2 miles past Ahihi-Kinau to La Pérouse Bay; the monument sits amid a clearing in black lava at the end of the dirt road. If you've got plenty of water, sunblock, and sturdy shoes, you can embark on foot on the **King's Trail,** a rugged path built by ancient Hawaiian royals.

UPCOUNTRY MAUI

Makawao

Makawao is Hawaiian cowboy country—yup, the islands have a longstanding tradition of ranchers and rodeo masters and this cool, misty upcountry town is its Maui epicenter. Modern day *paniolo* come here to fuel up on cream puffs and stick donuts from **Komoda Store & Bakery,** 3674 Baldwin Ave. (**© 808/572-7261**), a 100-year-old family grocery that seems frozen in time. Neighboring shops offer Tibetan jewelry, shabby-chic housewares, and marvelous paintings by local artists. A handful of decent restaurants crowd the intersection of Baldwin and Makawao avenues; take your pick of sushi, Maui cattle rib-eye, or Italian pasta.

Five minutes down Baldwin Avenue, the **Hui No'eau Visual Arts Center,** 2841 Baldwin Ave. (www.huinoeau.com; **© 808/572-6560**), occupies a two-story, Mediterranean-style stucco home designed in 1917 by C. W. Dickey, one of Hawaii's most prominent architects. The sprawling 9-acre estate, known as **Kaluanui,** hosts visiting artists for lectures and classes in basketry, jewelry making, ceramics, painting, and other media, all at reasonable prices. Call for details. The gallery's rotating exhibits include work by established and emerging artists, and the gift shop features many one-of-a-kind works, including ceramic seconds at a steal. Hours are Monday through Saturday 10am to 4pm.

Kula

While in the upcountry Kula region, visit one of the area's many farms (see "Maui Farms: Stop & Smell the Lavender," p. 276).

Kula Botanical Garden ★ GARDEN   You can take a self-guided, informative, leisurely stroll through this collection of more than 700 native and exotic plants—including three unique assemblages of orchids, proteas, and bromeliads—at this 5-acre garden. It offers a good overview of Hawaii's exotic flora in one small, cool place.

Hwy. 377, south of Haleakala Crater Rd. (Hwy. 378), ½-mile from Hwy. 37. www.kulabotanical garden.com. **© 808/878-1715.** Admission $10 adults, $3 children 6–12. Daily 9am–4pm.

Tedeschi Vineyards and Winery ★ VINEYARD/WINERY   On the southern shoulder of Haleakala is **Ulupalakua Ranch,** a 20,000-acre spread once owned by the legendary sea captain James Makee, celebrated in the Hawaiian song and dance "Hula O Makee." Wounded in a Honolulu waterfront brawl in 1843, Makee moved to Maui and bought Ulupalakua. He renamed it Rose Ranch, planted sugar as a cash crop, and grew rich. Still in operation, the ranch is now home to Maui's only winery, established in 1974 by Napa vintner Emil Tedeschi, who began growing California and European grapes here and produces serious still and sparkling wines, plus a silly wine made of pineapple juice. The rustic grounds are the perfect place for a picnic. Settle in under the sprawling camphor tree, pop the cork on a blanc de blanc, and toast your good fortune in being here.

Off Hwy. 37 (Kula Hwy.). www.mauiwine.com. **© 808/878-6058.** Free tastings daily 10am–5pm. Free tours at 10:30am and 1:30pm.

House of the Sun: Haleakala National Park ★★★

The summit of Haleakala, the House of the Sun, is a spectacular natural phenomenon. More than 1.3 million people a year ascend the 10,023-foot-high mountain to peer into the world's largest dormant volcano. Haleakala has not rumbled for at least 100 years, but it's still officially considered active. The lunar-like volcanic landscape is a national park, home to numerous rare and endangered plants, birds, and insects. Hardy adventurers hike and camp inside the crater's wilderness (see "Hiking," p. 293, and "Camping," p. 329). Those bound for the interior should bring survival gear, for the terrain is raw and rugged—not unlike the moon. Note that the Haleakala Crater is one of the world's quietest places—so silent that it exceeds the technical capacity of microphones.

Haleakala National Park extends from the volcano's summit down its southeast flank to Maui's eastern coast, beyond Hana. There are actually two separate districts within the park: **Haleakala Summit** and **Kipahulu** (see "Tropical Haleakala: Oheo Gulch at Kipahulu," p. 274). No roads link the summit and the coast; you have to approach them separately, and you need at least a day to see each place.

WHEN TO GO   Many drive up to the summit in predawn darkness to watch the **sunrise over Haleakala ★★**, though sunset here can be equally beautiful—and warmer! Weather is extreme at the summit, ranging from blazing sun to sudden snow flurries. Go on full-moon nights for an ethereal experience. But remember, glorious views aren't guaranteed; the summit may be misty or overcast at any time of day. Before you go, get current weather conditions from the park (✆ 808/572-4400) or the **National Weather Service** (✆ 866/944-5025, option 4).

Leleiwi Overlook.

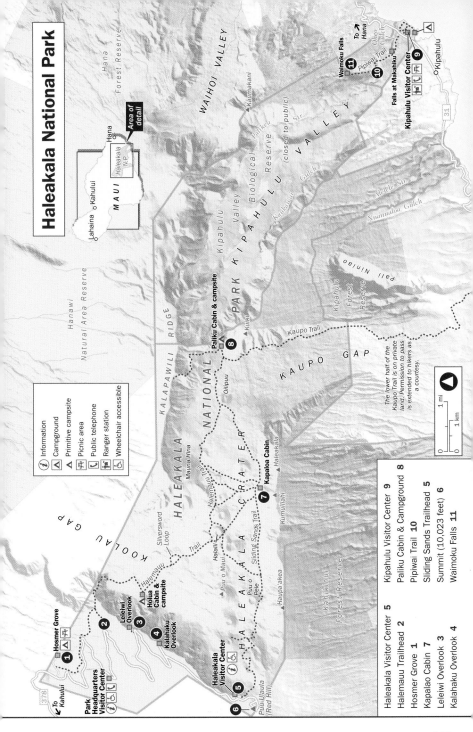

Haleakala National Park

Legend:
- ℹ️ Information
- 🏕️ Campground
- ⛺ Primitive campsite
- 🌲 Picnic area
- 📞 Public telephone
- 🏛️ Ranger station
- ♿ Wheelchair accessible

Haleakala Visitor Center **5**
Halemauu Trailhead **2**
Hosmer Grove **1**
Kapalao Cabin **7**
Leleiwi Overlook **3**
Kalahaku Overlook **4**
Kipahulu Visitor Center **9**
Paliku Cabin & Campground **8**
Pipiwai Trail **10**
Sliding Sands Trailhead **5**
Summit (10,023 feet) **6**
Waimoku Falls **11**

The lower half of the Kaupo Trail is on private land. Permission to pass is extended to hikers as a courtesy.

THE DRIVE TO THE SUMMIT

Just driving up the mountain is an experience. **Haleakala Crater Road (Hwy. 378)** is one of the fastest-ascending roads in the world. Its 33 switchbacks travel through numerous climate zones, passing in and out of clouds to finally deliver a view that extends for more than 100 miles. The trip takes 1½ to 2 hours from Kahului. No matter where you start out, follow Highway 37 (Haleakala Hwy.) to Pukalani, where you'll pick up Highway 377 (also called Haleakala Hwy.), which you take to Highway 378. Fill up your gas tank before you go—Pukalani is the last stop for fuel. Along the way, expect fog, rain, and wind. Be on the lookout for downhill bicyclists, stray cattle, and naïve **nene,** the native Hawaiian geese.

Remember, you're entering a high-altitude wilderness area; some people get dizzy from lack of oxygen. Bring water, a jacket, and, if you go up for sunrise, every scrap of warmth you can find. There are no concessions in the park—not even a coffee urn in sight. If you plan to hike, bring extra water and snacks.

At the **park entrance,** you'll pay an entrance fee of $10 per car or $5 per bicycle. It's good for 3 days of unlimited entry. (This includes the Kipahulu district.) One mile from the park entrance, at 7,000 feet, is **Haleakala National Park Headquarters** (© **808/572-4400**), open daily from 7am to 3:45pm. Restrooms, a pay phone, and drinking water are available. Stop here to pick up information on park programs and activities, get camping permits, and, occasionally, see a native Hawaiian goose. With its black face, buff cheeks, and partially webbed feet, the gray-brown nene looks like a small Canada goose with zebra stripes; it doesn't migrate, and prefers lava beds to lakes. Nene once flourished throughout Hawaii, but habitat destruction and predators (hunters, pigs, feral cats and dogs, and mongooses) nearly caused their extinction. By 1951, there were only 30 left. Now protected as Hawaii's state bird, the wild nene on Haleakala number fewer than 400—the species remains endangered.

Beyond headquarters are **two scenic overlooks** on the way to the summit; stop at Leleiwi on the way up and Kalahaku on the way back down, if only to get out, stretch, and get accustomed to the heights. Take a deep breath, look around, and pop your ears. If you feel dizzy, or get a sudden headache, consider turning around and going back down.

The **Leleiwi Overlook** ★ is just beyond mile marker 17. From the parking area, a short trail leads to a spectacular view of the colorful volcanic crater. When the clouds are low and the sun is in the right place (usually around sunset), you may witness the "Brocken Specter"—a reflection of your shadow, ringed by a rainbow, in the clouds below. This optical illusion—caused by a rare combination of sun, shadow, and fog—occurs in only three places: Haleakala, Scotland, and Germany.

Continue on to the **Haleakala Visitor Center,** open daily at sunrise (5:45am–3pm). It offers panoramic views, with photos identifying the various features, and exhibits that explain the area's history, ecology, geology, and volcanology. Park staff members are often on hand to answer questions. Restrooms and water are available. The actual summit is a little farther on, at **Puu Ulaula Overlook** (also known as Red Hill), the volcano's highest point, where you'll see Haleakala Observatories' cluster of buildings—known unofficially as **Science City.** If you go up for sunrise, the building at Puu Ulaula Overlook, a triangle of glass that serves as a windbreak, is a prime viewing spot. It's also the best place to see a rare **silversword.** This botanical wonder is the punk of the plant world— like a spacey artichoke with attitude. Silverswords grow only in Hawaii, take from

4 to 50 years to bloom, and then, usually between May and October, send up a 1- to 6-foot stalk covered in multitudes of reddish, sunflower-like blooms. They proved highly vulnerable to the goats and cattle that rampaged through the crater before it became a national park and was fenced. Don't walk too close to one, as footfalls can damage their roots.

On your way back down, stop at the **Kalahaku Overlook ★**. On a clear day you can see all the way across Alenuihaha Channel to the often snowcapped summit of Mauna Kea on the Big Island. *Tip:* Put your car in low gear when driving down the Haleakala Crater Road, so you don't destroy your brakes by riding them the whole way down.

Silversword.

East Maui & Heavenly Hana

Hana is about as close to paradise as you can get to it on Earth. In and around Hana, you'll find a lush tropical rainforest dotted with cascading waterfalls, trees spilling ripe fruits onto the grass, and the sparkling blue Pacific, skirted by red- and black-sand beaches.

THE ROAD TO HANA ★★★

Top down, sunscreen on, Hawaiian music playing on a breezy morning—it's time to head out along the Hana Highway (Hwy. 36), a wiggle of a road that runs along Maui's northeastern shore. The drive takes at least 3 hours from Lahaina or Kihei, but don't shortchange yourself—take all day. Going to Hana is about the journey, not the destination.

There are wilder roads, steeper roads, and more dangerous roads, but in all of Hawaii, no road is more celebrated than this one. It winds 50 miles past taro

The road to Hana.

patches, magnificent seascapes, waterfall pools, botanical gardens, and verdant rainforests, and ends at one of Hawaii's most beautiful tropical places.

The outside world discovered the little village of Hana in 1926, when the narrow coastal road, carved by pickax-wielding convicts, opened. The mud-and-gravel track, often subject to landslides and washouts, was paved in 1962, when tourist traffic began to increase; it now sees around 1,000 cars and dozens of vans a day. That translates into half a million people a year, which is way too many. Go at the wrong time, and you'll be stuck in a bumper-to-bumper rental-car parade—peak traffic hours are midmorning and midafternoon year-round, especially on weekends.

In the rush to "do" Hana in a day, most visitors spin around town in 10 minutes and wonder what all the fuss is about. It takes time to soak up the serene magic of Hana, play in the waterfalls, sniff the rain-misted gingers, hike through clattering bamboo forests, and merge with the tension-dissolving scenery. Stay overnight if you can, and meander back in a day or two. If you really must do the Hana Highway in a day, go just before sunrise and return after sunset.

Tips: Practice aloha. Yield at one-lane bridges, wave at oncoming motorists, let the big guys in 4×4s have the right of way—you're not in a hurry, after all! If the guy behind you blinks his lights, let him pass. And don't honk your horn—in Hawaii, it's considered rude.

THE JOURNEY BEGINS IN PAIA Before you start out, fill up on fuel. Paia is the last place for gas until you get to Hana, some 50-plus bridges and 600-plus hairpin turns down the road. (It's fun to make a game out of counting the bridges.)

Paia ★★ was once a thriving sugar-mill town. The skeletal mill is still here, but in the 1950s the bulk of the population (10,000 in its heyday) shifted to

Windsurfers at Hookipa Beach Park.

Kahului. Like so many former plantation towns, Paia nearly foundered, but its beachfront charm lured hippies, followed by adrenaline-seeking windsurfers and, most recently, young families. The town has proven its adaptability. Now chic eateries and trendy shops occupy the old ma-and-pa establishments. Plan to get here early, around 7am, when **Charley's ★**, 142 Hana Hwy. (© **808/579-8085**), opens. Enjoy a big, hearty breakfast for a reasonable price.

WINDSURFING MECCA Just before mile marker 9 is **Hookipa Beach Park ★**, where top-ranked windsurfers come to test themselves against thunderous surf and forceful wind. On nearly every windy day after noon (the board surfers have the waves in the morning), you can watch dozens of windsurfers twirling and dancing in the wind like colored butterflies. To watch them, do not stop on the highway, but go past the park and turn left at the entrance on the far side of the beach. You can either park on the high grassy bluff or drive down to the sandy beach and park alongside the pavilion. Facilities include restrooms, a shower, picnic tables, and a barbecue area.

INTO THE COUNTRY Past Hookipa Beach, the road winds down into **Maliko Gulch.** In the 1940s, Maliko had a thriving community at the mouth of the bay, but its residents rebuilt farther inland after a tidal wave wiped it out. Today, big-wave surfers use the boat ramp here to launch jet skis and head out to **"Jaws,"** one of the world's biggest surf breaks a few coves over.

Back on the Hana Highway, for the next few miles, you'll pass through the rural area of **Haiku,** where you'll see banana patches and guava trees littering their sweet fruit onto the street. Just before mile marker 15 is the **Maui Grown Market and Deli** (© **808/572-1693**), a good stop for drinks or snacks.

At mile marker 16, the curves begin, one right after another. Slow down and enjoy the view of fern-covered hills and plunging valleys punctuated by mango and *kukui* trees. After mile marker 16, the road is still called the Hana Highway, but the number changes from Highway 36 to Highway 360, and the mile markers go back to 0.

HIDDEN HUELO Just before mile marker 4 on a blind curve, look for a double row of mailboxes on the left side by the pay phone. (Incidentally, this is right around the spot where cellphone service evaporates.) Down the road lies a hidden Hawaii from an earlier time, where an indescribable sense of serenity prevails. Gorgeous Waipio and Hoalua bays hem in the remote community of **Huelo** and its historic **Kaulanapueo Church.** This coral-and-cement church, topped with a plantation-green steeple and a gray tin roof, is still in use, although services are only held once or twice a month now. It still has the same austere interior of 1853: straight-backed benches, a no-nonsense platform for the minister, and no distractions on the walls to tempt you from paying attention to the sermon. Next to the church is a small graveyard, a personal history of this village in concrete and stone.

KOOLAU FOREST RESERVE The vegetation grows even more lush after Huelo. This is the edge of the **Koolau Forest Reserve.** *Koolau* means "windward," and this certainly is one of the greatest examples of a verdant windward area: The coastline here gets about 60 to 80 inches of rain a year, as well as runoff from the 200 to 300 inches that falls farther up the mountain. You'll see trees laden with guavas, mangoes, java plums, and avocados the size of softballs. The spiny, long-leafed plants are hala trees, which Hawaiians use for weaving baskets and mats.

From here on out, there's a waterfall (and one-lane bridge) around nearly every turn in the road, so drive slowly and be prepared to stop and yield to oncoming cars.

WILD CURVES   About a half-mile after mile marker 6, there's a sharp U-curve in the road, going uphill. The road is practically a bike lane here, with a brick wall on one side and virtually no maneuvering room. Sound your horn at the start of the U-curve to let approaching cars know you're coming. Take the curve slowly.

Just before mile marker 7, a forest of waving **bamboo** takes over the right-hand side of the road. To the left, you'll see a stand of **rainbow eucalyptus trees,** recognizable by their multicolored trunks. Drivers are often tempted to pull over here, but there isn't any shoulder. Continue on; you'll find many more beautiful trees to gawk at down the road.

A GREAT FAMILY HIKE   At mile marker 9, a small state wayside area has restrooms, picnic tables, and a barbecue area. The sign says koolau forest reserve, but the real attraction here is the **Waikamoi Ridge Trail ★**, an easy .75-mile loop. The start of the trail is just behind the quiet: trees at work sign. The well-marked trail meanders through eucalyptus, ferns, and hala trees.

CAN'T-MISS PHOTO OPS   Just past mile marker 12 is the **Kaumahina State Wayside Park ★**. This is not only a good pit stop and a wonderful place for a picnic (with restrooms, tables, and a barbecue area), but it's also a great vista point. You can see all the way down the rugged coastline to the jutting Keanae Peninsula.

Another mile and a couple of bends in the road, and you'll enter the Honomanu Valley, with its beautiful bay. To get to the **Honomanu Bay County Beach Park,** look for the turnoff on your left, just after mile marker 14, as you begin your ascent up the other side of the valley. The rutted dirt-and-cinder road takes you down to the rocky black-sand beach. There are no facilities here. Because of the strong rip currents offshore, swimming is best in the stream inland from the ocean. You'll consider the detour worthwhile as you stand on the beach, well away from the ocean, and turn to look back on the steep cliffs covered with vegetation.

A church built in 1860 in Keanae.

KEANAE PENINSULA & ARBORETUM   At mile marker 17, the vintage Hawaiian village of **Keanae** ★★ stands out against the Pacific like a place time forgot. Here, on an old lava flow graced by an 1860 stone church and swaying palms, is one of the last coastal enclaves of native Hawaiians. They still grow taro in patches and pound it into poi, the staple of the old Hawaiian diet; and they still pluck *opihi* (limpet) from tide pools along the jagged coast and cast throw-nets for fish. Pick up a loaf of still-warm banana bread from **Aunty Sandy's** (10 Keanae Rd.; ✆ **808/344-1885**).

At nearby **Keanae Arboretum,** Hawaii's botanical world is divided into three parts: native forest, introduced forest, and traditional Hawaiian plants, food, and medicine. You can swim in the pools of Piinaau Stream or press on along a mile-long trail into Keanae Valley, where a lovely tropical rainforest waits at the end.

WAIANAPANAPA STATE PARK ★★   On the outskirts of Hana, the shiny black-sand beach appears like a vivid dream, with bright-green jungle foliage on three sides and cobalt-blue water lapping at its feet. The 120-acre state park on an ancient lava flow includes sea cliffs, lava tubes, arches, and that beach—plus a dozen rustic cabins. See p. 331 for a review of the cabins. Also see "Beaches" and "Camping," below.

HANA ★★★

Green, tropical Hana, which some call heavenly, is a destination all its own, a small coastal village in a rainforest inhabited by 2,500 people, many part-Hawaiian. Beautiful Hana enjoys more than 90 inches of rain a year—more than enough to keep the scenery lush. Banyans, bamboo, breadfruit trees—everything seems larger than life, especially the flowers, like wild ginger and plumeria. Several roadside stands offer exotic blooms for $3 a bunch. Just put money in box. It's the Hana honor system.

The last unspoiled Hawaiian town on Maui is, oddly enough, the home of Maui's first resort, which opened in 1946 by Paul Fagan, then owner of the San Francisco Seals baseball team. Fagan bought an old inn and turned it into the **Hotel Hana-Maui** (now the **Travaasa Hana**), which gave Hana its first and, as it turns out, last taste of tourism. Others have tried to open hotels and golf courses and resorts, but Hana, which is interested in remaining Hana, always politely refuses. Hana does have a few B&Bs, though; see p. 327 for reviews.

A wood-frame 1871 building that served as the old Hana District Police Station now holds the **Hana Cultural Center & Museum,** 4974 Uakea Rd. (www.hanaculturalcenter.org; ✆ **808/248-8622**). The center tells the history of the area, with some excellent artifacts, memorabilia, and photographs. Also stop in at **Hasegawa General Store,** a Maui institution.

On the green hills above Hana stands a 30-foot-high white cross made of lava rock. The cross was erected by citizens in memory of Paul Fagan, who helped keep the town alive. The 3-mile hike up to **Fagan's Cross** provides a gorgeous view of the Hana coast, especially at sunset, when Fagan himself liked to climb this hill (see p. 297 for details).

Most day-trippers to Hana miss the most unusual natural attraction of all: **Red Sand Beach** ★, officially named Kaihalulu Beach (*kaihalulu* means "roaring sea") and truly a sight to see. It's on the ocean side of Kauiki Hill, just south of Hana Bay, in a wild, natural setting in a pocket cove. Kauiki, a 390-foot-high volcanic cinder cone, lost its seaward wall to erosion and spilled red cinders everywhere, creating the red sands. To get here, walk south on Uakea Road, past the Travaasa Hana to the end of the parking lot for Sea Ranch Cottages. Turn left, cross an open field past an old cemetery, and follow a well-worn path down a narrow cliff trail. Stick close to the shoreline; the hillside path has eroded and isn't safe. Some beachgoers shed their clothes in this private setting.

Tropical Haleakala: Oheo Gulch at Kipahulu

If you're thinking about heading out to the so-called Seven Sacred Pools, past Hana in the Kipahulu, let's clear this up right now: There are more than seven pools—and *all* water in Hawaii is considered sacred. **Oheo Gulch ★★★** (the rightful name of the pools) is in the Kipahulu district of Haleakala National Park (though you can't drive here from the summit). It's about 30 minutes beyond Hana town, along Highway 31. Expect rain showers on the Kipahulu coast.

The **Kipahulu Ranger Station** (© **808/248-7375**) is staffed from 8:30am to 5pm daily. Here you'll find park-safety information, exhibits, and books. Rangers offer a variety of walks and hikes year-round; check at the station for current activities. The fee to enter is $5 per person or $10 per car. The Highway 31 bridge passes over some of the pools near the ocean; the others, plus magnificent 400-foot **Waimoku Falls,** are uphill, via an often muddy but always rewarding hour-long hike. Restrooms are available, but there's no drinking water. Tent camping is permitted in the park; see "Camping" (p. 329) for details.

From the ranger station, it's just a short hike above the famous Oheo Gulch to two spectacular **waterfalls.** Check with park rangers before hiking up to or swimming in the pools, and always keep an eye on the water in the streams. The sky can be sunny near the coast, but floodwaters travel 6 miles down from the Kipahulu Valley, and the water level can rise 4 feet in less than 10 minutes. It's not a good idea to swim in the pools in winter.

Red Sand (Kaihalulu) Beach.

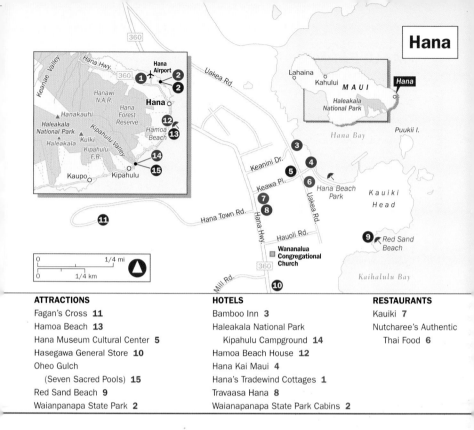

MAUI

Lahaina Kahului

Haleakala
National Park

Hana

Hana Airport

Hana Hwy.

Keanae Valley

Hanawi N.A.R.

Hana Forest Reserve

Hanakauhi

Haleakala National Park

Kuiki

Haleakala

Kipahulu F.R.

Kaupo

Kipahulu Valley

Kipahulu

Hamoa Beach

Uakea Rd.

Keanini Dr.

Keawa Pl.

Hana Town Rd.

Hana Hwy.

Hauoli Rd.

Mill Rd.

Wananalua Congregational Church

Hana Bay

Puukii I.

Hana Beach Park

Kauiki Head

Red Sand Beach

Kaihalulu Bay

0   1/4 mi
0   1/4 km

ATTRACTIONS	HOTELS	RESTAURANTS
Fagan's Cross **11**	Bamboo Inn **3**	Kauiki **7**
Hamoa Beach **13**	Haleakala National Park	Nutcharee's Authentic
Hana Museum Cultural Center **5**	Kipahulu Campground **14**	Thai Food **6**
Hasegawa General Store **10**	Hamoa Beach House **12**	
Oheo Gulch	Hana Kai Maui **4**	
(Seven Sacred Pools) **15**	Hana's Tradewind Cottages **1**	
Red Sand Beach **9**	Travaasa Hana **8**	
Waianpanapa State Park **2**	Waianapanapa State Park Cabins **2**	

Makahiku Falls is easily reached from the central parking area; the trail head begins near the ranger station. **Pipiwai Trail** leads up to the road and beyond for .5 mile to the overlook. If you hike another 1.5 miles up the trail across two bridges and through a magical bamboo forest, you reach **Waimoku Falls.** It's a hard uphill hike, but worth every step.

Beyond Oheo Gulch

A mile past Oheo Gulch on the ocean side of the road is **Lindbergh's Grave.** First to fly across the Atlantic Ocean, Charles A. Lindbergh found peace in the Pacific; he settled in Hana, where he died of cancer in 1974. The famous aviator is buried under river stones in a seaside graveyard behind the 1857 **Palapala Hoomau Congregational Church.**

Adventurers can continue on around Haleakala, back towards civilization in Kula. Be warned that the route, Old Piilani Highway (Hwy. 31), is full of potholes and unpaved in parts. But it threads through ruggedly beautiful territory. If it's open, stop in for ice cream at **Kaupo General Store** (34793 Piilani Hwy.). This remote outpost has a wonderful antique camera collection and many tempting souvenirs. Most rental-car companies warn you against traveling down this road, but it's really not so bad—just check to make sure a rockslide hasn't closed it before you go.

MAUI FARMS: stop & smell the lavender

Idyllic farms abound in upcountry Maui. Many open their doors to visitors and have terrific Maui-made products for purchase.

ALII KULA LAVENDER Stop and smell the lavender when you visit these gorgeous grounds, set high up on the leeward slope of Haleakala, scented by multiple varieties of lavender, tropical flowers, and fruit trees. On the 30-minute walking tour (daily at 9:30, 10:30am, and 11:30am, and 1 and 2:30pm; $12 per person, $10 with advance reservation), you can sniff lavender cuttings and leave with a fragrant bouquet. The store is chock-full of great culinary products (lavender seasonings, honey, jelly, and teas) and bath and body goodies (the salve is a lifesaver). General admission is $3; lunches and treasure hunts for the kids can be arranged with 24-hour notice. 1100 Waipoli Rd., Kula (www.aliikula lavender.com; © **808/878-3004**).

MAUI COUNTRY FARM TOURS This tour operator visits the above farms and many more. Marilyn Jansen Lopes and her husband, Rick, are sweet, knowledgeable guides offering a gorgeous overview of agriculture on the Valley Isle and regaling guests with plenty of anecdotes and extra treats along the way. They share their love of Maui along with the historic background of the island's sugar mills, coffee plantations, family farms, and vineyards. Tours in eight-seat, air-conditioned buses start at $125 (http://mauicountryfarmtours.com; © **808/283-9131**).

MAUI OCEAN VODKA Never heard of a vodka farm? Neither had I until Maui Ocean Vodka opened for business just below Surfing Goat Dairy on Omaopio Road. Sustainably harvested organic sugarcane is blended with deep ocean mineral water to make fine-quality liquor. See how it's done at this solar-powered distillery halfway up the leeward slope of Haleakala. (The views alone are worth the price of admission.) Fun and informative tours are $10 a person (12 years and up). Lunch can be added for $25 with 24-hour advance notice. Those 21 and over get to sample various spirits (and vodka-filled truffles!) and take home a souvenir shot glass. 4051 Omaopio Rd., Kula (www.oceanvodka.com; © **808/877-0009**; daily 9:30am–5pm).

SURFING GOAT DAIRY When heading upcountry, take a detour on wild Omaopio Road to meet the frisky kids at this sweet, off-the-beaten-path destination for those who love goats and/or cheese. When you spot the surfboard nailed to the tree, you'll know you're close. Daily farm tours are $7 for kids and $10 adults. Book in advance if you want to help with evening chores: milking mama goats (Mon–Sat 3:15pm; $15 adults, $10 children). Cheese aficionados will appreciate the Grand Dairy Tours: 2 hours of cheesemaking and sampling the farm's award-winning chèvre, quarks, and truffles. 3651 Omaopio Rd., Kula (www.surfinggoatdairy.com; © **808/878-2870**; Mon–Sat 9am–5pm, Sun 9am–2pm).

Organized Tours

Atlantis Submarine TOUR   Descend more than 100 feet below the ocean's surface in air-conditioned comfort aboard this 48-passenger submarine. You'll see colorful fish, corals, and other marine creatures populating the waters off of Lahaina. Occasionally eagle rays, white tip sharks, or a rare monk seal will swim past the submerged ship's windows. Whales have even been known to cruise alongside—filling the cabin with their otherworldly song. One guaranteed highlight is the sunken *Carthaginian*, a 19th-century replica supply boat that was scuttled to become an artificial reef.

At Pioneer Inn Hotel, 658 Wharf St., Lahaina. www.atlantisadventures.com/maui. © **808/667-2224.** 1-hr. and 45-min. tours offered daily at 9 and 10am, noon, and 1 and 2pm. Admission $109 adults, $45 children 12 and under.

Blue Hawaiian Helicopters ★★ TOUR   Some of Maui's most spectacular scenery—3,000-foot-tall waterfalls thundering away in the chiseled heart of the West Maui Mountains, say, or **Piilanihale,** an impressive 3-acre *heiau* (temple) hidden away in Hana—can only be seen from the air. Blue Hawaiian can escort you there on one of their two types of helicopters: A-star or Eco-Star. Both are good, but the latter is worth the extra cash for its bucket seats (raised in the rear) and wraparound windows. Tours range from 30-minute fly-overs to 2-hour excursions exploring Maui and Molokai or the Big Island. Be aware that if you visit another island, a good portion of the tour will be over ocean—not much to see. The 65-minute Complete Island Tour is the best value, especially if it's been raining and the waterfalls are gushing. After exploring West Maui, your pilot will flirt at the edges of Haleakala National Park so you can peer into the crater's paintbox colors, and then zip over Oprah's organic farm in Kula. *Tip:* Book on the website for substantial savings.

1 Kahului Airport Rd., Kahului. www.bluehawaiian.com. © **800/745-2583** or 808/871-8844. Flight times range 45–90 min. and cost $149–$385. Parking and video of flight are extra.

Temptation Tours TOUR   If you'd rather leave the driving to someone else, this tour company will chauffeur you to Maui's top sites in a comfy deluxe van—much more luxurious than the large, crowded buses used by other agencies. Book a pre-dawn trip to the summit of Haleakala to witness the sunrise (followed by tasting tours at Surfing Goat Dairy and Maui Ocean Vodka; see below) or a picnic out in Hana. You'll pass numerous waterfalls and stop often, but don't expect to swim or get muddy hiking. The Hana Sky-Trek is actually a pretty great value; the half-day adventure starts with a drive along the lush East Maui coast to Hana, where you board a helicopter for a scenic flight back home over hidden waterfalls and Haleakala National Park. The eight-person vans are safe and roomy, tour guides are generally knowledgeable, and the chicken wraps, seared ono, and brownies for lunch are tasty.

www.temptationtours.com. © **808/878-1715.** All-day tours $225–$344. Free hotel pickup.

BEACHES

For beach toys and equipment, head to **Snorkel Bob's** (www.snorkelbob.com), which rents snorkel gear, boogie boards, and other ocean toys at four locations: 1217 Front St., in Lahaina (© **808/661-4421**); Napili Village, 5425-C Lower Honoapiilani Hwy., in Napili (© **808/669-9603**); Azeka Place II, 1279 S. Kihei Rd. #310, in North Kihei (© **808/875-6188**); and Kamaole Beach Center, 2411 S. Kihei Rd., in South Kihei/Wailea (© **808/879-7449**). All locations are open daily from 8am to 5pm. If you're island-hopping, you can rent from a Snorkel Bob's location on one island and return to a branch on another.

West Maui

KAANAPALI BEACH ★

Four-mile-long Kaanapali is one of Maui's best beaches, with sugary golden sand as far as the eye can see. A paved walkway links hotels and condos, open-air restaurants, and the Whalers Village shopping center. Because Kaanapali is so long and broad, and most hotels have adjacent swimming pools, the beach is crowded only in pockets; there's plenty of room to find seclusion. Summertime swimming is excellent. The best snorkeling is around Black Rock, in front of the Sheraton, where the water is clear, calm, and populated with clouds of tropical fish.

Facilities include outdoor showers; you can also use the restrooms at the hotel pools. Various beach-activities vendors line up in front of the hotels. Turn off Honoapiilani Highway into the Kaanapali Resort. Parking can be a problem—the free lots that have been reserved for public access are small and hard to find. Look for the blue shoreline access signs at the Hyatt's southernmost lot, between Whalers Village and the Westin, and just before the Sheraton. Otherwise, you can park (for top dollar) at the mall or any of the resorts.

KAPALUA BEACH ★★

The beach cove that fronts the Coconut Grove Villas is the stuff of dreams: a golden crescent bordered by two palm-studded points. The sandy bottom slopes gently to deep water at the bay mouth; the water's so clear that you can see it turn to green and then deep blue. Protected from strong winds and currents by the lava-rock promontories, Kapalua's calm waters are ideal for swimmers of all ages and abilities, and the bay is big enough to paddle a kayak around in without

Kaanapali Beach.

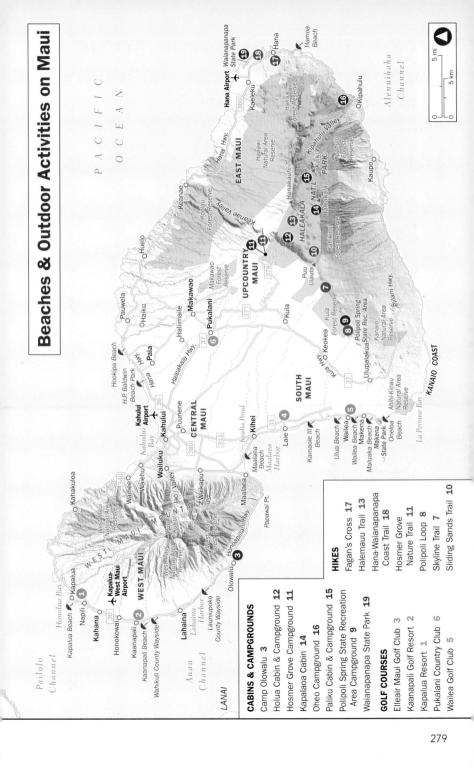

Beaches & Outdoor Activities on Maui

CABINS & CAMPGROUNDS

Camp Olowalu **3**
Holua Cabin & Campground **12**
Hosmer Grove Campground **11**
Kapalaoa Cabin **14**
Oheo Campground **16**
Paliku Cabin & Campground **15**
Polipoli Spring State Recreation
   Area Campground **9**
Waianapanapa State Park **19**

GOLF COURSES

Elleair Maui Golf Club **3**
Kaanapali Golf Resort **2**
Kapalua Resort **1**
Pukalani Country Club **6**
Wailea Golf Club **5**

HIKES

Fagan's Cross **17**
Halemauu Trail **13**
Hana-Waianapanapa
   Coast Trail **18**
Hosmer Grove
   Nature Trail **11**
Polipoli Loop **8**
Skyline Trail **7**
Sliding Sands Trail **10**

Turtle off Ulua Beach.

getting into the more challenging channel that separates Maui from Molokai. Waves come in just right for riding, and fish hang out by the rocks, making it great for snorkeling.

The beach is accessible from the hotel on one end, which provides shaded sun chairs and a beach-activities center for its guests, and a public access way—a small tunnel—on the other. It isn't so wide that you burn your feet getting in or out of the water, and the inland side is edged by a shady path and cool lawns. Parking is limited to about 30 spaces in a small lot off Lower Honoapiilani Road, by Napili Kai Beach Resort, so arrive early. Facilities include showers, restrooms, lifeguards, a rental shack, and plenty of shade.

South Maui

Wailea's beaches may seem off limits, hidden from plain view as they are by an intimidating wall of luxury resorts, but all are public. Look for the shoreline access signs along Wailea Alanui Drive, the resort's main boulevard.

KAMAOLE III BEACH PARK ★

Three beach parks—Kamaole I, II, and III—stand like golden jewels in the front yard of suburban Kihei. This trio is popular with local residents and visitors alike because each is easily accessible and all three have shady lawns. On weekends, they're jam-packed with picnickers, swimmers, and snorkelers. The most popular is Kamaole III, or "Kam-3." It's the biggest of the three beaches, with wide pockets of gold sand, a huge grassy lawn, and a children's playground. Swimming is safe here, but scattered lava rocks are toe-stubbers at the water line. Both the north and south shores are rocky fingers with a surge big enough to attract fish and snorkelers; the winter waves appeal to bodysurfers. Kam-3 is also a wonderful place to watch the sunset. Facilities include restrooms, showers, picnic tables, barbecue grills, and lifeguards. There's plenty of parking on South Kihei Road across from the Maui Parkshore condos.

ULUA BEACH ★

Ulua is a golden stretch of sand that's popular with sunbathers, snorkelers, and scuba divers alike. Some of Wailea's best snorkeling is found on the adjoining reef. The ocean bottom is shallow and gently slopes down to deeper waters, making swimming generally safe. In high season (Christmas–Mar and June–Aug), it's carpeted with beach towels and packed with sunbathers like sardines in cocoa butter. Facilities include showers and restrooms. Beach equipment is available for rent at the nearby Wailea Ocean Activity Center. Look for the blue shoreline access sign on Wailea Alanui Drive, near the Wailea Beach Marriott Resort & Spa.

WAILEA BEACH ★

One of five beaches within Wailea Resort, Wailea might be the prettiest. It's big, wide, and protected on both sides by black-lava points. It's the front yard of the Four Seasons Resort Maui and the Grand Wailea, and hotel staff populates the sand with umbrellas and beach chairs. The view out to sea is magnificent, framed by neighboring Kahoolawe and Lanai and the tiny crescent of Molokini, probably the most popular snorkel spot in these parts. The clear waters tumble to shore in waves just the right size for gentle riding, with or without a board. From shore, you can see Pacific humpback whales in season (Dec–Mar) and unreal sunsets nightly. Facilities include restrooms, outdoor showers, and limited free parking at the blue shoreline access sign, just south of the Grand Wailea on Wailea Alanui Drive.

MALUAKA BEACH ★★★

On the southern end of Maui's resort coast, development falls off dramatically, leaving a wild, dry countryside of green kiawe trees. The Makena Beach & Golf Resort sits in isolated splendor, sharing the resort's 1,800 acres with only a private

Makena Beach.

golf course and a necklace of perfect beaches. The strand nearest the hotel is Maluaka Beach, notable for its uncrowded beauty and its views of Molokini Crater, the offshore islet, and Kahoolawe, the so-called "target" island (it was used as a bombing target from 1945 until the early 1990s). This sun-kissed sandy crescent is bound on one end by a grassy knoll and has little shade, so bring your own umbrella. Swimming is idyllic here, where the water is calm and sea turtles paddle by. Facilities include restrooms, showers, picnic tables, and parking. Along Makena Alanui, look for the shoreline access sign near the hotel, turn right, and head down to the shore.

MAKENA STATE BEACH PARK (BIG BEACH) ★★★

One of the most popular beaches on Maui, Makena is so vast it never feels crowded. Locals call it "Big Beach"—it's more than 100 feet wide and stretches out 3,300 feet from Puu Olai, the 360-foot cinder cone on its north end to its southern rocky point. The golden sand is luxuriant, deep, and soft, but the shorebreak is steep and powerful. Many a visitor has broken an arm in the surf here. If you're an inexperienced swimmer, it's better to watch the pros shred waves on skimboards. Facilities are limited to portable toilets, but there's plenty of parking and lifeguards at the first two entrances. Dolphins often frequent these waters, and nearly every afternoon a heavy cloud rolls in, providing welcome relief from the sun.

If you clamber up the Puu Olai, you'll find **Little Beach** on the other side, a small crescent of sand where assorted nudists work on their all-over tans in defiance of the law. The shoreline doesn't drop off quite so steeply here, and bodysurfing is terrific—no pun intended.

Upcountry & East Maui
HOOKIPA BEACH PARK ★★★

Hookipa means "hospitality," and the wild north shore beach of the same name is certainly hospitable to wave riders. Two miles past Paia on the Hana Highway, it's

Hookipa Beach Park.

among the world's top spots for windsurfing and kiting—thanks to tradewinds that kick up whitecaps offshore. Hookipa offers no less than five surf breaks, and daring watermen and women paddle out to carve waves up to 25 feet tall. Voyeurs are welcome as well; the cliff-top parking lot claims a bird's-eye view. On flat days, snorkelers explore the reef's treasure trove of marine life: Gentle garden eels wave below the surface, and turtles hunt for jellyfish or haul out on the sand to nap. More than once, a rare Hawaiian monk seal has popped ashore during a surf contest. Facilities include restrooms, showers, pavilions, picnic tables, barbecue grills, and parking.

WAIANAPANAPA STATE PARK ★★★

Four miles before Hana, off the Hana Highway, is this beach park, which takes its name from the legend of the Waianapanapa Cave, where Chief Kaakea, a jealous and cruel man, suspected his wife, Popoalaea, of having an affair. Popoalaea left her husband and hid herself in a chamber of the Waianapanapa Cave. She and her attendant ventured out only at night for food. Nevertheless, a few days later, Kaakea was passing by the area and saw the shadow of the servant. Knowing he had found his wife's hiding place, Kaakea entered the cave and killed her. During certain times of the year, the water in the tide pool turns red, commemorating Popoalaea's death. (Scientists claim, less imaginatively, that the water turns red due to the presence of small red shrimp.)

Waianapanapa State Park's 120 acres contain 12 cabins (p. 331), a caretaker's residence, a beach park, picnic tables, barbecue grills, restrooms, showers, a parking lot, a shoreline hiking trail, and a black-sand beach (actually, small black pebbles). This is a wonderful area for shoreline hikes (bring insect repellent—the mosquitoes are plentiful) and picnicking. Swimming is generally unsafe, though, due to strong waves and rip currents. Because Waianapanapa is crowded on weekends with local residents and their families, as well as tourists, weekdays are generally a better bet.

HAMOA BEACH ★★

James Michener called it "a beach so perfectly formed that I wonder at its comparative obscurity." This half-moon-shape, gray-sand beach (a mix of coral and lava) in a truly tropical setting is a favorite of sunbathers seeking rest and refuge. The Travaasa Hana resort maintains the beach and acts as though it's private, which it isn't—so just march down the lava-rock steps and grab a spot on the sand. The wide beach is three football fields long and sits below 30-foot black-lava sea cliffs. Surf on this unprotected beach breaks offshore and rolls in, making it a popular surfing and bodysurfing area. Hamoa is often swept by powerful rip currents, so be careful. The calm left side is best for snorkeling in summer. The hotel has numerous facilities for guests plus outdoor showers and restrooms for non-guests. Parking is limited. Look for the Hamoa Beach turnoff from Hana Highway.

WATERSPORTS

The range of watersports on Maui is mind-boggling—this is one prime watery playground.

It's easy to find rental gear and ocean toys all over the island. Most seaside hotels and resorts are stocked with watersports equipment (complimentary and rentals), from snorkels to kayaks to Hobies. **Snorkel Bob's** (www.snorkelbob. com) rents snorkel gear, boogie boards, wetsuits, and more at numerous locations:

5425 C Lower Honoapiilani Hwy., Lahaina (✆ **808/669-9603**); 1217 Front St., Lahaina (✆ **808/661-4421**); 3350 Lower Honoapiilani Hwy., Lahaina (✆ **808/ 667-9999**); 1279 S. Kihei Rd., Kihei (✆ **808/875-6188**); 2411 S. Kihei Rd., Kihei (✆ **808/879-7449**); and 100 Wailea Ike Dr., Wailea (✆ **808-874-0011**). All locations are open daily from 8am to 5pm. If you're island-hopping, you can rent from a Snorkel Bob's location on one island and return to a branch on another.

Boss Frog's Dive, Surf, and Bike Shops (www.bossfrog.com) has eight locations for snorkel, boogie board, longboard, and stand-up paddleboard rentals and other gear, including: 150 Lahainaluna Rd., in Lahaina (✆ **808/661-3333**); 3636 Lower Honoapiilani Rd., in Kaanapali (✆ **808/665-1200**); Napili Plaza, Napilihau Rd., in Napili (✆ **808/669-4949**); and 1215 S. Kihei Rd. (✆ **808/ 891-0077**), 1770 S. Kihei Rd. (✆ **808/874-8225**), and Dolphin Plaza, 2395 S. Kihei Rd. (✆ **808/875-4477**), in Kihei.

Boating

You'll need a boat to visit the crescent-shape islet called **Molokini,** one of the best snorkel and scuba spots in Hawaii. Trips to the island of **Lanai** (see chapter 8) are also popular for a day of snorkeling. Remember to bring a towel, a swimsuit, sunscreen, and a hat on a snorkel cruise; everything else is usually included. If you'd like to go a little deeper than snorkeling allows, consider trying **SNUBA,** a shallow-water diving system in which you are connected by a 20-foot air hose to an air tank that floats on a raft at the water's surface. Most of these snorkel boats offer it for an additional cost; it's usually around $60 for a half-hour or so. No certification is required for SNUBA. For fishing charters, see "Sport Fishing," later in this section.

Maui Classic Charters ★★ TOUR   Maui Classic Charters offers morning and afternoon **snorkel-sail cruises to Molokini** on *Four Winds II,* a 55-foot glass-bottom catamaran. Rates for the morning sail are $88 for adults and $58 for children 3 to 12, and include continental breakfast and barbecue lunch (afternoon sail $39 adults, $29 children 3–12; optional barbecue lunch $7.50 per person). All *Four Winds* trips include complimentary beer, wine, and soda; snorkeling gear and instruction; and sport fishing along the way. Those looking for speed should book a trip on the state-of-the-art catamaran *Maui Magic.* A 5-hour snorkel journey to both Molokini and La Pérouse costs $110 for adults and $80 for children 5 to 12, including continental breakfast; barbecue lunch; beer, wine, and soda; snorkel gear; and instruction.

Maalaea Harbor, slip 55 and slip 80. www.mauicharters.com. ✆ **800/736-5740** or 808/879-8188. Prices vary depending on cruise; check website for discounts.

Pacific Whale Foundation TOUR   This not-for-profit foundation supports its whale research, public education, and conservation programs by offering **whale-watch cruises, wild dolphin encounters,** and **snorkel tours,** some to Molokini and Lanai. Numerous daily trips are offered from December through May, out of both Lahaina and Maalaea harbors.

300 Maalaea Rd., Suite 211, Wailuku. (Also: Lahaina Ocean Store, 612 Front St., Lahaina.) www. pacificwhale.org. ✆ **800/942-5311** or 808/249-8811. Trips from $25 adults, $18 children 7–12, free for 1 child 6 and under per adult; snorkeling cruises from $80 adults, $35 children. Book online for a 10-percent discount.

Scotch Mist Sailing Charters TOUR   This 50-foot Santa Cruz sailboat offers 4-hour **snorkel cruises;** the cost is $109 for ages 13 and up, $55 for children 5

Hawaiian reef.

to 12. Rates includes a fruit platter and beverages, gear, and instruction. Other options include an afternoon sail or whale-watch ($60 age 13 and up; $30 children 5–12), and an evening champagne sunset cruise ($70 age 13 and up; $35 children 5–12). *Note:* Children under 5 are not allowed unless you charter the whole boat.

Lahaina Harbor, slip 2. www.scotchmistsailingcharters.com. © **808/661-0386.** Prices vary depending on cruise.

Trilogy ★★★ TOUR Trilogy offers my favorite **snorkel-sail trips.** Hop aboard one of Trilogy's fleet of custom-built catamarans, from 54 to 64 feet long, for a 9-mile sail from Lahaina Harbor to **Lanai's Hulopoe Beach,** a terrific marine preserve, for a fun-filled day of sailing, snorkeling, swimming, and **whale-watching** (in season, of course). This is the only cruise that offers a personalized ground tour of the island and the only one with rights to take you to Hulopoe Beach. The full-day trip costs $199 for adults, $149 for teens (ages 13–18), and $100 for children 3 to 12. Ask about overnighters to Lanai, too.

Trilogy also offers **snorkel-sail trips to Molokini,** one of Hawaii's best snorkel spots. This half-day trip leaves from Maalaea Harbor and costs $119 for adults, $89 for teens, and $60 for kids 3 to 12, including breakfast and a barbecue lunch. Other options include a late-morning half-day snorkel-sail off Kaanapali Beach for the same price, plus a host of other trips.

These are the most expensive sail-snorkel cruises on Maui, but they're worth every penny. The crews are fun and knowledgeable, and the boats are comfortable and well equipped. All trips include breakfast (Mom's homemade cinnamon buns) and a very good barbecue lunch (onboard on the half-day trip; on land on the Lanai trip). Note, however, that you will be required to wear a flotation device no matter how good your swimming skills are; if this bothers you, go with another outfitter.

www.sailtrilogy.com. © **888/225-MAUI** or 808/874-5649. Prices and departure points vary depending on cruise.

DAY CRUISES TO MOLOKAI

You can travel across the seas by ferry from Maui's Lahaina Harbor to Molokai's Kaunakakai Wharf on the Hawaiian Ocean Project's **Molokai Princess** (www. hawaiioceanproject.com; © **877/500-6284** or 808/667-6165). Twice daily the 100-foot ferry makes the 2-hour journey from Lahaina to Kaunakakai; the round-trip cost is $142 for adults and $71 for children 3 to 12. I recommend spending 2 or more days on Molokai, but if you can't swing that, try one of the following single day trips. The guided Alii Tour hits Molokai's major sites in an air-conditioned van ($260 per adult and $160 per child, including round-trip passage, breakfast, and lunch). For more independent travelers, the Cruise-Drive package is a good deal. Hop on the ferry and pick up your rental car on arrival ($260 for the driver, $125 per additional adult passenger, and $63 per child). Breakfast is included, and car upgrades are negotiable. Load up on ginger cookies before you go; the ferry can be a bumpy ride, especially during winter.

DAY CRUISES TO LANAI

You can also get to the island of Lanai by booking a trip with **Trilogy** (see above).

Expeditions Lahaina/Lanai Passenger Ferry ★ TOUR The cheapest way to reach Lanai is the ferry, which runs five times a day, 365 days a year. It leaves Lahaina at 6:45 and 9:15am, and 12:45, 3:15, and 5:45pm; the return ferry from Lanai's Manele Bay leaves at 8 and 10:30am, and 2, 4:30, and 6:45pm. The 9-mile channel crossing takes between 45 minutes and an hour, depending on sea conditions. Reservations are strongly recommended. Baggage is limited to two checked bags and one carry-on. Call **Dollar Rent A Car** (© **800/800-4000**) or **Lanai City Service** (© **808/565-7227**) to arrange a car rental or bus ride when you arrive.

Ferries depart from Lahaina Harbor; office: 658 Front St., Suite 127, Lahaina. www.go-lanai.com. © **800/695-2624** or 808/661-3756. Round-trip fares from Maui to Lanai $60 adults, $40 children 2–11.

Ocean Kayaking

For beginners, **Makena Kayak and Tours ★** (© **808/879-8426**) is an excellent choice. Professional guide Dino Ventura leads a 2½-hour trip from Makena Landing and loves taking first-timers over the secluded coral reefs and into remote coves. His wonderful tour will be a highlight of your vacation. This outfitter has kept its low price of $65, which includes refreshments and snorkel and kayak equipment; the 4-hour tour costs $95, including lunch.

South Pacific Kayaks (www.mauikayak.com; © **800/776-2326** or 808/875-4848) is another terrific kayak-tour company. Its experts lead ocean-kayak trips that include lessons, a guided tour, and snorkeling. Tours run from 3 to 5 hours and range in price from $65 to $145.

Outrigger Canoe

Outrigger canoes are much revered in the Hawaiian culture, and several hotels—among them, the Fairmont Kea Lani Maui and Makena Beach & Golf Resort—offer this wonderful cultural activity right off the beach. If you want to give paddling a try, expect to work as a team with five other paddlers. Your guide and steersman will show you how to haul the sleek boat into the water, properly enter and exit the boat, and paddle for maximum efficiency.

Hawaiian Paddle Sports ★★★ CANOE TOUR   For an intimate adventure on the great blue, book an outrigger canoe trip with Hawaiian Paddle Sports. Learn how to paddle in sync with your family or friends, just as the ancient Polynesians did when colonizing these islands. You'll visit some of Maui's very best snorkel spots: Makena Landing or the outer reef at Olowalu. The owner, Tim Lara, is one of the best in the business, brimming with knowledge about the island's culture, history, and marine life. When turtles surface alongside your canoe—or whales, during winter—you'll feel like a "National Geographic" explorer. And you'll have the pictures to prove it. Lara is a whiz with a Go-Pro camera; after the trip he'll send you under- and above-water shots guaranteed to dazzle your friends.

Departs from various locations. www.hawaiianpaddlesports.com. *©* **808/660-4228.** $149–$199 per person.

Ocean Rafting

If you're semi-adventurous and looking for a more intimate experience with the sea, try ocean rafting. The inflatable rafts hold 6 to 24 passengers. Tours usually include snorkeling and coastal cruising. One of the best (and most reasonable) outfitters is **Hawaii Ocean Rafting** (www.hawaiioceanrafting.com; *©* **888/ 677-RAFT** or 808/661-7238), which operates out of Lahaina Harbor. The best deal is the 5-hour morning tour ($74 adults, $53 children 5–12); it includes three snorkeling stops and time spent watching for dolphins, plus continental breakfast and mid-morning snacks. Check the website for discounts.

Scuba Diving

Everyone dives in **Molokini,** one of Hawaii's top dive spots. This crescent-shape crater has three tiers of diving: a 35-foot plateau inside the crater basin (used by beginning divers and snorkelers), a wall sloping to 70 feet just beyond the inside plateau, and a sheer wall on the outside and backside of the crater that plunges 350 feet. This offshore site is very popular, thanks to astounding visibility (you can often peer down 100 ft.) and an abundance of marine life, from manta rays to clouds of yellow butterflyfish.

Ed Robinson's Diving Adventures ★★ DIVE COMPANY   Ed, a widely published underwater photographer, offers specialized charters for small groups. Two-tank dives are $130 ($150 with all the gear). The check-in for the dive is at 165 Halekuai St., in Kihei, and the boat departs from Kihei Boat Ramp.

165 Halekuai St., Kihei. www.mauiscuba.com. *©* **808/879-3584.**

Maui Dreams Dive Company ★★★ DIVE COMPANY   Run by the husband-and-wife team of Rachel and Don Domingo, this is the best full-service dive operation on the island. Stop into their South Maui shop, and you might just end up scuba certified ($420 for 3-day course). The skilled dive masters and instructors are so fun, they make every aspect of getting geared up to go underwater enjoyable. You don't need certification for an intro shore dive at Ulua Beach ($89), but you do for a two-tank adventure to Molokini aboard the *Maui Diamond II* ($144). Captain Don regales his passengers with jokes, snacks, and local trivia. Rachel has a knack for finding camouflaged frogfish on the reef. Even experienced divers will be dazzled by the guided scooter dives ($99–$129). The rideable rockets allow you to zip along the ocean's floor and visit sunken World

War II wrecks, caves, and turtle-cleaning stations. The community-minded Domingos host regular reef cleanups, pirate- and princess-themed dives, and underwater Easter egg hunts.

1993 S. Kihei Rd. www.mauidreamsdiveco.com. ✆ **808/874-5332.**

Mike Severns Diving ★★★ DIVE COMPANY For personalized diving tours on a 38-foot Munson/Hammerhead boat (with a freshwater shower), call Pauline Fiene at Mike Severns Diving. She and her fellow dive masters lead trips for a maximum of 12 people, divided into two groups of six. Exploring the underwater world is educational and fun with Fiene, a biologist who has authored several spectacular marine-photography books and leads dives during coral spawning events. She's particularly knowledgeable about nudibranchs, two of which have been named for her, *Hallaxa paulinae* and *Hypselodoris paulinae*. Two-tank dives are $145, including equipment rental, or $139 if you bring all your own equipment. Trips depart from Kihei Boat Ramp.

www.mikesevernsdiving.com. ✆ **808/879-6596.**

Snorkeling

When the whales aren't around, **Captain Steve's Rafting Excursions** (www.captainsteves.com; ✆ **808/667-5565**) offers 7-hour snorkel trips from Mala Wharf in Lahaina to the waters around **Lanai** (you don't actually land on the island). Discounted online rates of $125 for adults and $85 for children 5 to 12 include breakfast, lunch, snorkel gear, and wetsuits.

Two **truly terrific snorkel spots** are difficult to get to but worth the effort—they're home to Hawaii's tropical marine life at its best:

Molokini ★★ A sunken crater that sits like a crescent moon fallen from the sky, almost midway between Maui and the uninhabited island of Kahoolawe, Molokini stands like a scoop against the tide. On its concave side, Molokini serves as a natural sanctuary and marine-life preserve for tropical fish. Snorkelers commute here daily in a fleet of dive boats. Molokini is accessible only by boat; see "Boating," above, for outfitters that can take you here. Expect crowds in high season.

Ahihi-Kinau Natural Preserve ★★ In Ahihi Bay, you can't miss this 2,000-acre state natural area reserve in the lee of Cape Kinau, on Maui's rugged south coast. It was here, in 1790, that Haleakala spilled red-hot lava that ran to the sea. Fishing is strictly forbidden here, and the fish know it; they're everywhere in this series of rocky coves and black-lava tide pools.

To get here, drive south of Makena past Puu Olai to Ahihi Bay, where the road turns to gravel (and sometimes seems like it will disappear under the waves). At Cape Kinau, three four-wheel-drive trails lead across the lava flow; take the shortest one, nearest La Pérouse Bay. If you have a standard car, drive as far as you can, park, and walk the remainder of the way. **Note:** The Hawaii State Department of Land and Natural Resources has temporarily restricted access to portions of the popular and heavily used preserve. Visit www.hawaii.gov/dlnr/dofaw/nars for details and a downloadable brochure.

Sport Fishing

The best way to book a sport-fishing charter is through the experts; the top booking desk in the state is **Sportfish Hawaii ★** (www.sportfishhawaii.com; ✆ **877/388-1376**), which books boats on all the islands. These fishing vessels have been inspected and must meet rigorous criteria to guarantee that you'll have

Snorkeling with sea turtle.

a great time. Prices range from $1099 to $1,199 for a full-day exclusive charter (meaning you, plus five friends, get the entire boat to yourself); it's $599 to $850 for a half-day exclusive.

Surfing

If you want to learn to surf, the best beginners' spots are **Charley Young Cove** in Kihei (the far north end of Kalama Beach Park), the break in front of **505 Front Street** in Lahaina, and several breaks along Honoapiilani Highway, including **Ukumehame.** The first two are the most convenient, with surf schools nearby. The breaks along Honoapiilani Highway tend to be longer, wider, and less crowded—perfect if you're confident enough to go solo.

During summer, gentle swells roll in long and slow along the south shore. It's the best time to practice your stance on a longboard. During winter, the north shore becomes the playground for adrenaline junkies who drop in on thundering waves 30 feet tall and higher. If you want to watch, head to **Hookipa** or **Honolua Bay,** where you can view the action from a cliff above.

Nancy Emerson School of Surfing ★ SURF INSTRUCTION   Nancy has been surfing since 1961 and has even been a stunt performer for various movies such as "Waterworld." She's pioneered a new instructional technique called "Learn to Surf in One Lesson." It's $78 per person for a 2-hour group lesson; private 2-hour classes are $165. All instructors are lifeguard certified.

505 Front St., Suite 224B, Lahaina. www.mauisurfclinics.com. © **808/244-SURF** [7873].

Zack Howard Surf ★★ SURF INSTRUCTION   Zack is a lifelong waterman who will help you stand up and surf—even on your very first wave. While most surf schools take newbies out into the crowded breaks at Charley Young in Kihei or the Lahaina Breakwall, Zack steers beginning students into the surf at Ukumehame, a gentle, consistent rolling break alongside Honoapiilani Highway. He also helps intermediate surfers sharpen their skills at world-famous Hookipa. In between swells, Zack offers tips on how to improve your stance and technique. Lessons start at $90 per person for 1½ hours.

www.zackhowardsurf.com. © **808/214-7766.**

Whale-Watching

The humpback is the star of the annual whale-watching season, which usually runs from about January to April (though it can begin as early as Dec and last until May).

WHALE-WATCHING FROM SHORE   The best time to whale-watch is between mid-December and April: Just look out to sea. There's no best time of day, but it seems that when the sea is glassy and there's no wind, the whales appear. Once you see one, keep watching in the same vicinity; they may stay down for 20 minutes. Bring a book. And binoculars, if you can.

Some good whale-watching spots on Maui include:

MCGREGOR POINT   On the way to Lahaina, there's a scenic lookout at mile marker 9 (just before you get to the Lahaina Tunnel); it's a good viewpoint to scan for whales.

OLOWALU REEF   Along the straight part of Honoapiilani Highway, between McGregor Point and Olowalu, you'll sometimes see whales leap out of the water. Their appearance can bring traffic to a screeching halt: People abandon their cars and run down to the sea to watch, causing a major traffic jam. If you stop, pull off the road so others can pass.

WAILEA BEACH MARRIOTT RESORT & SPA   In the Wailea coastal walk, stop at this resort to look for whales through the telescope installed as a public service by the Hawaii Island Humpback Whale National Marine Sanctuary.

PUU OLAI   It's a tough climb up this coastal landmark near the Maui Beach & Golf Resort, but you're likely to be well rewarded: This is the island's best spot for offshore whale-watching. On the 360-foot cinder cone overlooking Makena Beach, you'll be at the right elevation to see Pacific humpbacks as they dodge Molokini and cruise up Alalakeiki Channel between Maui and Kahoolawe.

WHALE-WATCHING CRUISES   For a closer look, take a whale-watching cruise. Just about all of Hawaii's snorkel and dive boats become whale-watching boats in season; some of them even carry professional naturalists onboard so you'll know what you're seeing. For the best options, see "Boating," earlier in this section.

WHALE-WATCHING BY KAYAK & RAFT   Seeing a humpback whale from an ocean kayak or raft is awesome. **Capt. Steve's Rafting Excursions** (www.captain steves.com; © **808/667-5565**) offers 2-hour whale-watching excursions out of Lahaina Harbor (from $49 adults, $35 children 5–12). *Tip:* Save $10 by booking the early-bird adventure, which leaves at 7:30am.

Windsurfing

Maui has Hawaii's best windsurfing beaches. In winter, windsurfers from around the world flock to the town of **Paia** to ride the waves; **Hookipa Beach,** known all over the globe for its brisk winds and excellent waves, is the site of several world championship contests. **Kanaha Beach,** west of Kahului Airport, also has dependable winds. When the winds turn northerly, **North Kihei** is the place to be (some days, you can even spot whales in the distance behind the windsurfers). **Ohukai Park,** the first beach as you enter South Kihei Road from the northern end, has good winds plus parking, a long strip of grass to assemble your gear, and easy access to the water.

EQUIPMENT RENTALS & LESSONS **Hawaiian Island Surf & Sport,** 415 Dairy Rd., Kahului (www.hawaiianisland.com; ℂ **800/231-6958** or 808/871-4981), offers lessons (from $89), rentals, and repairs. **Hawaiian Sailboarding Techniques,** 425 Koloa St., Kahului (www.hstwindsurfing.com; ℂ **800/968-5423** or 808/871-5423), offers rentals and 2½-hour lessons from $89. **Maui Windsurf Company,** 22 Hana Hwy., Kahului (www.mauiwindsurfcompany.com; ℂ **800/872-0999** or 808/877-4816), offers complete equipment rental (board, sail, rig harness, and roof rack) from $57, plus 2½-hour group lessons from $89.

DAILY WIND & SURF CONDITIONS For daily reports on wind and surf conditions, call the **Wind & Surf Report** at ℂ **808/877-3611.**

OTHER OUTDOOR ACTIVITIES
Biking

Maui County produced a full-color map of the island with various cycling routes, information on road suitability, climate, mileage, elevation changes, bike shops, and safety tips. It's available at most bike shops. You can also download it at **www. southmauibicycles.com**.

CRUISING HALEAKALA ★

Cruising down Haleakala, from the lunar-like landscape at the top past flower farms, pineapple fields, and eucalyptus groves, can be quite a thrilling experience—but one that should be approached with caution. You'll be riding on steep and curvy public roads without designated bike lanes and little to no shoulder. Despite what various companies claim about their safety record, people have been injured and killed participating in this activity. During winter and the rainy season, conditions can be particularly harsh. At the summit, temperatures drop below freezing and 40-mph winds howl. If you do choose to go, pay close attention to the safety briefing.

Maui's oldest downhill company is **Maui Downhill ★** (www.mauidownhill. com; ℂ **800/535-BIKE** or 808/871-2155), which offers a sunrise safari bike tour, including continental breakfast and a stop for lunch (not hosted), starting at $169 ($149 if booked online). **Mountain Riders Bike Tours** (www.mountain-riders.com; ℂ **800/706-7700** or 808/242-9739) offers sunrise rides for $150 ($120 if booked online) and midday trips for $130 ($104 online). All rates include hotel pickup, transport to the top, coffee and pastries, bicycle, safety equipment, and a meal stop, not hosted. Wear layers of warm clothing—there may be a 30° change in temperature from the top of the mountain to the ocean. Children under 12 and pregnant women can ride along in the van that accompanies the groups.

If you want to avoid the crowds and go down the mountain at your own pace (rather than in a choo-choo train of other bikers), call **Haleakala Bike Company** (www.bikemaui.com; ℂ **888/922-2453**). After assessing your skill, they'll outfit you with the latest gear and shuttle you up Haleakala.

Golf

Golfers have many outstanding greens to choose from on Maui, from world championship courses to municipal parks with oceanfront views. Greens fees are pricy, but twilight tee times can be a giant deal. Be forewarned; the tradewinds pick up in the afternoon and can seriously alter your game. **Stand-by Golf** (www.hawaiistandbygolf.com; © 888/645-2665) offers savings off greens fees at Kaanapali, Wailea Gold and Emerald, and Pukalani golf courses. **Golf Club Rentals** (www.mauiclubrentals.com; © 808/665-0800) has custom-built clubs for men, women, and juniors (both right- and left-handed), which can be delivered island-wide; the rates are $25 a day for steel clubs, and a full graphite set is $30 a day.

WEST MAUI

Kaanapali Golf Resort ★   Both courses at Kaanapali will challenge golfers, from high-handicappers to near-pros. The par-72, 6,305-yard **Royal (North) Course** is a true Robert Trent Jones, Sr., design: It has an abundance of wide bunkers; several long, stretched-out tees; and the largest, most contoured greens on Maui. The tricky 18th hole (par-4, 435-yard) has a water hazard on the approach to the green. The par-72, 6,250-yard **Kai (South) Course** is an Arthur Jack Snyder design; although shorter than the North Course, it requires more accuracy on the narrow, hilly fairways. It also has a water hazard on its final hole, so don't tally up your scorecard until you sink the final putt. Facilities include a driving range and putting course. The clubhouse restaurant is run by celebrated chef Roy Yamaguchi.

Off Kaanapali Pkwy., Kaanapali (1st building on right). www.kaanapali-golf.com. © **808/661-3691.** Greens fees: Royal Course $249 ($179 for Kaanapali guests), twilight rates (starting at 1pm) $139, super twilight rates (starting at 3pm) $89; Kai Course $205 ($139 for Kaanapali guests), twilight rates (starting at 1pm) $119, super twilight rates (starting at 3pm) $69.

Kapalua Resort ★★★   The views from these two championship courses are worth the greens fees alone. The par-72, 6,761-yard **Bay Course** was designed by Arnold Palmer and Ed Seay. This course is a bit forgiving, with its wide fairways; the greens, however, are difficult to read. The often photographed 5th overlooks a small ocean cove; even the pros have trouble with this rocky par-3, 205-yard hole. The **Plantation Course** (© 808/669-8877), site of the PGA Hyundai Tournament of Champions, is a Ben Crenshaw/Bill Coore design. The 6,547-yard, par-73 course, set on a rolling hillside, is excellent for developing your low shots and precise chipping. Facilities for both courses include locker rooms, a driving range, and excellent dining. Sharpen your skills at the attached golf academy, which offers half-day golf school, private lessons, club fittings, and special clinics for beginners. Weekends are your best bet for tee times.

Off Hwy. 30, Kapalua. www.kapaluamaui.com/golf. © **877/KAPALUA.** Greens fees: Bay Course $208 ($178 for resort guests), twilight rates $148; Plantation Course $278 ($228 for guests), twilight rates $178.

SOUTH MAUI

Elleair Maui Golf Club   Hitting in the foothills of Haleakala, just high enough to afford spectacular ocean vistas from every hole, Elleair (formerly Silversword Golf Club) is a course for golfers who love the views as much as the fairways and greens. It's very forgiving. *One caveat:* Go in the morning. Not only is it cooler, but (more important) it's also less windy. In the afternoon, the winds bluster down Haleakala with gusto. It's a fun course to play, with some challenging holes;

the par-5 2nd hole is a virtual minefield of bunkers, and the par-5 8th hole shoots over a swale and then uphill. Premium clubs rent for $50, and slightly older irons for just $25.

1345 Piilani Hwy. (near Lipoa St. turnoff), Kihei. www.elleairmauigolfclub.com. © **808/874-0777.** Greens fees: $120 Dec–Apr, $89 May–Nov, $49 year-round after 1pm.

Wailea Golf Club ★★ There are three courses to choose from at Wailea. The **Blue Course,** a par-72, 6,758-yard course designed by Arthur Jack Snyder and dotted with bunkers and water hazards, is for duffers and pros alike. The wide fairways appeal to beginners, while the undulating terrain makes it a course everyone can enjoy. More challenging is the par-72, 7,078-yard championship **Gold Course,** designed by Robert Trent Jones, Jr., with narrow fairways and several tricky dogleg holes, not to mention such natural hazards as lava-rock walls. The **Emerald Course,** also designed by Robert Trent Jones, Jr., is Wailea's most scenic, with tropical landscaping and a player-friendly design. Sunday mornings are the least crowded times. Facilities include a complete golf training facility, two pro shops, locker rooms, and two restaurants: **Gannon's** by celebrity chef Bev Gannon and **Mulligan's,** a popular Irish pub.

Wailea Alanui Dr. (off Wailea Iki Dr.), Wailea. www.waileagolf.com. © **888/328-MAUI** or 808/875-7450. Greens fees: Blue Course $180 ($170 for resort guests), twilight rates $140 after noon, $115 after 2pm; Gold Course and Emerald Course $215 ($195 for resort guests). Check website for summer rates and early bird specials.

UPCOUNTRY MAUI

Pukalani Country Club This cool par-72, 6,962-yard course at 1,100 feet offers a break from the resorts' high greens fees, and it's really fun to play. The 3rd hole offers golfers two different options: a tough (especially into the wind) iron shot from the tee, across a gully (yuck!) to the green, or a shot down the side of the gully across a second green into sand traps below. (Most people choose to shoot down the side of the gully; it's actually easier than shooting across a ravine.) High handicappers will love this course, and more experienced players can make it more challenging by playing from the back tees. Facilities include club and shoe rentals, practice areas, lockers, a pro shop, and a restaurant.

360 Pukalani St., Pukalani. www.pukalanigolf.com. © **808/572-1314.** Greens fees for 18 holes (including cart) $89, $63 noon–2:30pm, $35 after 2:30pm. Take the Hana Hwy. (Hwy. 36) to Haleakala Hwy. (Hwy. 37) to the Pukalani exit; turn right onto Pukalani St. and go 2 blocks.

Hiking

Over a few brief decades, Maui transformed from a rural island to a fast-paced resort destination, but its natural beauty has remained largely inviolate. Many pristine places can be explored only on foot. Those interested in seeing the backcountry—complete with virgin waterfalls, remote wilderness trails, and quiet, meditative settings—should head to Haleakala or the tropical Hana Coast.

For details on Maui hiking trails and free maps, contact **Haleakala National Park** (www.nps.gov/hale; © **808/572-4400**) or the **State Division of Forestry and Wildlife** (www.hawaii.gov/dlnr/dofaw; © **808/984-8100**).

For information on trails, hikes, camping, and permits for state parks, contact the **Hawaii State Department of Land and Natural Resources** (www.hawaiistateparks.org/camping/fees.cfm; © **808/984-8109**); you can reserve and purchase electronic permits online as well. For Maui County Parks, contact the **Department of Parks and Recreation** (www.co.maui.hi.us; © **808/270-7389** or 808/270-7230).

GUIDED HIKES   If you'd like a knowledgeable guide to accompany you on a hike, call **Maui Hiking Safaris ★** (www.mauihikingsafaris.com; © **888/445-3963** or 808/573-0168). Owner Randy Warner takes visitors on half- and full-day hikes into valleys, rainforests, and coastal areas. Randy's been hiking around Maui for more than 30 years and is wise in the ways of Hawaiian history, native flora and fauna, and volcanology. His rates are $69 for a half-day and $169 for a full day, which include daypacks, rain parkas, snacks, water, and, on full-day hikes, sandwiches. Private half-day tours are $150 per person ($75 per additional person).

Maui's oldest hiking-guide company is **Hike Maui ★** (www.hikemaui.com; © **866/324-6284** or 808/879-5270), headed by Ken Schmitt, who pioneered guided hikes on the Valley Isle. Hike Maui offers numerous treks island-wide, ranging from an easy 1-mile, 3-hour hike to a waterfall ($85) to a strenuous full-day hike in Haleakala Crater ($165). On the popular East Maui waterfall trips, you can swim and jump from the rocks into rainforest pools. All prices include equipment and transportation. Hotel pickup costs an extra $25 per person.

For information on hikes given by the **Hawaii Sierra Club** on Maui, call © **808/573-4147** or go to http://mauisierraclub.org.

HALEAKALA NATIONAL PARK ★★★

For complete coverage of the national park, see p. 266.

Hiking into the Wilderness Area: Sliding Sands & Halemauu Trails

Hiking into Maui's dormant volcano is the best way to see it. The terrain inside the wilderness area of the volcano, which ranges from burnt-red cinder cones to ebony-black lava flows, is astonishing. There are some 27 miles of hiking trails, two camping sites, and three cabins.

Entrance to Haleakala National Park is $10 per car. The rangers offer free guided hikes (usually Mon and Thurs), a great way to learn about the unusual flora and geological formations here. Wear sturdy shoes and be prepared for wind, rain, and intense sun. Bring water, snacks, and a hat. Additional options

Sliding Sands Trail.

include full-moon hikes and star-program hikes. The hikes and briefing sessions may be canceled, so check first. Call ✆ **808/572-4400** or visit www.nps.gov/hale.

Try to arrange to stay at least 1 night in the park; 2 or 3 nights will allow you more time to explore the fascinating interior of the volcano (see below for details on the cabins and campgrounds in the wilderness area of the valley). If you want to venture out on your own, the best route takes in two trails: into the crater along **Sliding Sands Trail,** which begins on the rim at 9,800 feet and descends to the valley floor at 6,600 feet, and back out along **Halemauu Trail.** Before you set out, stop at park headquarters to get trail updates.

The trail head for Sliding Sands is well marked and the trail easy to follow over lava flows and cinders. As you descend, look around: The view is breathtaking. In the afternoon, waves of clouds flow into the Kaupo and Koolau gaps. Vegetation is spare to nonexistent at the top, but the closer you get to the valley floor, the more growth you'll see: bracken ferns, pili grass, shrubs, even flowers. On the floor, the trail travels across rough lava flows, passing by rare silversword plants, volcanic vents, and multicolored cinder cones.

The Halemauu Trail goes over red and black lava and past native ohelo berries and ohia trees as it ascends up the valley wall. Occasionally, riders on horseback use this trail. The proper etiquette is to step aside and stand quietly next to the trail as the horses pass.

Some shorter and easier hiking options include the .5-mile walk down the **Hosmer Grove Nature Trail,** or just the first mile or two down **Sliding Sands Trail.** (Even this short hike is exhausting at the high altitude.) A good day hike is **Halemauu Trail** to Holua Cabin and back, an 8-mile, half-day trip.

Kipahulu

One section of Haleakala National Park is not accessible from the summit: Lush and rainy Kipahulu is all the way out in Hana. From the ranger station just off of Hana Highway, it's a short hike above the famous **Oheo Gulch** (aka the Seven Sacred Pools) to two spectacular waterfalls. The first, **Makahiku Falls,** is easily

Oheo Gulch.

reached from the central parking area; the trail head begins near the ranger station. Pipiwai Trail leads you up to the road and beyond for .5 miles to the overlook. Continue on another 1.5 miles across two bridges and through a magical bamboo forest to **Waimoku Falls.** It's a challenging uphill hike, but mostly shaded and sweetened by the sounds of clattering bamboo canes. In times of hard rain, streams swell quickly. Never attempt to cross flooding waters.

POLIPOLI SPRINGS AREA ★

At this state recreation area, part of the 21,000-acre Kula and Kahikinui forest reserves on the slope of Haleakala, it's hard to believe that you're in Hawaii. First of all, it's cold, even in summer, because the elevation is 5,300 to 6,200 feet. Second, this former forest of native koa, ohia, and mamane, which was overlogged in the 1800s, was reforested in the 1930s with introduced species: pine, Monterey cypress, ash, sugi, red alder, redwood, and several varieties of eucalyptus. The result is a cool area, with muted sunlight filtered by towering trees. There's a campground at the recreation area at 6,300 feet. See p. 331 for details.

Skyline Trail

This is some hike—strenuous but worth every step if you like seeing the big picture. It's 8 miles, all downhill, with a dazzling 100-mile view of the islands dotting the blue Pacific, plus the West Maui Mountains, which seem like a separate island.

The trail is just outside Haleakala National Park at Polipoli Spring State Recreation Area; however, you access it by going through the national park to the summit. It starts just beyond the Puu Ulaula summit building on the south side of Science City and follows the southwest rift zone of Haleakala from its lunar-like cinder cones to a cool redwood grove. The trail drops 3,800 feet on a 4-hour hike to the recreation area in the 12,000-acre Kahikinui Forest Reserve. If you'd rather drive, you'll need a four-wheel-drive vehicle.

Polipoli Loop

One of the most unusual hiking experiences in the state is this easy 3.5-mile hike, which takes about 3 hours; dress warmly for it. Take the Haleakala Highway (Hwy. 37) to Keokea and turn right onto Hwy. 337; after less than a half-mile, turn on Waipoli Road, which climbs swiftly. After 10 miles, Waipoli Road ends at the Polipoli Spring State Recreation Area campgrounds. The well-marked trail head is next to the parking lot near a stand of Monterey cypress; the tree-lined trail offers the best view of the island.

Polipoli Loop is really a network of three trails: **Haleakala Ridge, Plum Trail,** and **Redwood Trail.** After .5 mile of meandering through groves of eucalyptus, blackwood, swamp mahogany, and hybrid cypress, you'll join the Haleakala Ridge Trail, which, about a mile in, joins with the Plum Trail (named for the plums that ripen in June–July). This trail passes through massive redwoods and by an old Conservation Corps bunkhouse before joining up with the Redwood Trail, which climbs through Mexican pine, tropical ash, Port Orford cedar, and, of course, redwood.

WAIANAPANAPA STATE PARK ★★

Tucked in a tropical jungle on the outskirts of the little coastal town of Hana is this state park, a black-sand beach set in an emerald forest.

The **Hana-Waianapanapa Coast Trail** is an easy 6-mile hike that takes you back in time. Allow 4 hours to walk along this relatively flat trail, which parallels the sea, along lava cliffs and a forest of lauhala trees. The best time to take the hike is either early morning or late afternoon, when the light on the lava and surf makes for great photos. Midday is the worst time; not only is it hot (lava intensifies the heat), but there's also no shade or potable water available.

There's no formal trail head; join the route at any point along the Waianapanapa Campground and go in either direction. Along the trail, you'll see remains of an ancient *heiau* (temple), stands of lauhala trees, caves, a blowhole, and a remarkable plant, naupaka, which flourishes along the beach. Upon close inspection, you'll see that the naupaka have only half-blossoms; according to Hawaiian legend, a similar plant living in the mountains has the other half of the blossoms. One ancient explanation is that the two plants represent never-to-be-reunited lovers: The couple bickered so much that the gods, fed up with their incessant quarreling, banished one lover to the mountain and the other to the sea.

Hana: The Hike to Fagan's Cross

This 3-mile hike to the cross erected in memory of Paul Fagan, the founder of Hana Ranch and the former Hotel Hana-Maui (now the Travaasa Hana), offers spectacular views of the Hana Coast, particularly at sunset. The uphill trail starts across Hana Highway from the Hotel Hana-Maui. Enter the pastures at your own risk; they're often occupied by glaring bulls with sharp horns and cows with new calves. Watch your step as you ascend this steep hill on a jeep trail across open pastures to the cross and breathtaking views.

Horseback Riding

Maui offers spectacular adventure rides through rugged ranchlands, into tropical forests, and to remote swimming holes. I recommend riding with **Mendes Ranch Trail Rides** ★, 3530 Kahekili Hwy., 6¼ miles past Wailuku (www. mendesranch.com; ✆ 808/871-5222). The 3,000-acre Mendes Ranch is a real-life working cowboy ranch with all the essential elements of an earthly paradise: rainbows, waterfalls, palm trees, coral-sand beaches, lagoons, tide pools, a rainforest, and its own volcanic peak (more than a mile high). Allan Mendes, a third-generation wrangler, will take you from the edge of the rainforest out to the sea. Allan keeps close watch, turning often in his saddle to make sure everyone is happy. He points out flora and fauna and fields questions, but generally just lets you soak up Maui's natural splendor in golden silence. A 1½-hour morning or afternoon ride costs $99; add a barbecue lunch at the corral for an additional $15.

Another one of my favorites is **Piiholo Ranch,** in Makawao (www.piiholo. com; ✆ **808/270-8750**). A working cattle ranch, owned by the *kamaaina* (long-time resident) Baldwin family, it offers horseback-riding adventures with a variety of different options to suit your ability, from 2-hour morning rides through the misty slopes of the upcountry ($120) to 2- to 3-hour private rides with stops for picnic lunches ($199 plus $20 for lunch). The ranch also has a zipline. Check "Ziplining," p. 299, for more details. Book via the website for a 10-percent discount.

Pony Express Tours (www.ponyexpresstours.com; ✆ **808/667-2200** or 808/878-6698) offers 1½- and 2-hour rides at Haleakala Ranch, located on the beautiful lower slopes of the volcano ($95–$110; book via the website for a 10-percent discount). Pony Express provides well-trained horses and experienced guides, and accommodates all riding levels. You must be at least 10 years old, weigh no more than 235 pounds, and wear long pants and closed-toe shoes.

No horse aficionado should pass up Frank Levinson's magical **Maui Horse Whisperer Experience** (www.mauihorses.com; ✆ **808/572-6211**), which

ESPECIALLY FOR kids

Taking a Submarine Ride The **Atlantis Submarine** (p. 277) takes you and the kids down into the shallow coastal waters off Lahaina in a real sub, where you'll see plenty of fish (and maybe even a shark!). They'll love it, and you'll all stay dry the entire time. Allow about 2 hours for the trip.

Riding the Sugarcane Train Small kids love this ride, as do train buffs of all ages. A steam engine pulls open-passenger cars of the Lahaina/Kaanapali and Pacific Railroad on a 30-minute, 12-mile round-trip through sugarcane fields between Lahaina and Kaanapali while the conductor sings and calls out the landmarks. Along the way, you can see the hidden parts of Kaanapali and the islands of Molokai and Lanai beyond. Tickets are $23 for adults, $16 for kids 3 to 12; call *C* **808/661-0080** or visit www.sugar canetrain.com for details.

Tour the Stars After sunset, the stars over Kaanapali shine big and bright: That's because the tropical sky is almost pollutant-free and no big-city lights interfere with the cosmic view. Amateur astronomers can probe the Milky Way, see the rings of Saturn and Jupiter's moons, and scan the Sea of Tranquillity in a 60-minute star search on the world's first recreational computer-driven telescope. It all takes place nightly at the **Hyatt Regency Maui Resort,** 200 Nohea Kai Dr. (*C* **808/661-1234**), at 8, 9, and 10pm. The cost for hotel guests is $25 for adults and $15 for children 12 and under; nonguests pay $30 for adults and $20 for children 12 and under. Reservations are a must.

includes a seminar on the language of the horse. Prices are $200 for half-day and $300 for full-day workshops.

Tennis

Maui has excellent public tennis courts; all are free and available from daylight to sunset (a few are even lit until 10pm for night play). For a complete list of public courts, call **Maui County Parks and Recreation** (www.co.maui.hi.us/facilities.aspx; *C* **808/270-7383**). The courts are available on a first-come, first-served basis; when someone's waiting, limit your play to 45 minutes. Most public courts do require a wait and are not conveniently located near the major resort areas, so most visitors are likely to play at their own hotels for a fee. The exceptions to this are in Kihei (which has courts in Kalama Park on South Kihei Rd., and in Waipualani Park on West Waipualani Rd., behind the Maui Sunset condo), in Lahaina (which has courts in Malu'uou o lele Park, at Front and Shaw sts.), and in Hana (which has courts in Hana Park, on the Hana Hwy.).

Private tennis courts are available at most resorts and hotels on the island. The **Kapalua Tennis Garden and Village Tennis Center,** Kapalua Resort (www.kapaluamaui.com; *C* **808/662-7730**), is home to the Kapalua Open, which features the largest purse in the state, held on Labor Day weekend. Court rentals are $10 per person ($8 after noon). The staff will match you up with a partner if you need one. In Wailea, try the **Wailea Tennis Club,** 131 Wailea Iki Place (www.waileatennis.com; ✆ **808/879-1958**), with 11 Plexipave courts. Court fees are $15 per player.

Ziplining

Skyline EcoAdventures ★ ZIPLINE TOUR   Go on, let out a wild holler as you soar above a rainforested gulch in Kaanapali or down the slope of Haleakala. The Skyline owners are pioneers of this increasingly popular activity; they brought the first ziplines to the U.S. and launched them from their home, here on Maui. They now have two locations, one on the west side and the other halfway up Haleakala. Both courses are fast and fun, the guides are savvy and safety-conscious, and the scenery is breathtaking. On top of that, this eco-conscious company is carbon-neutral and donates thousands of dollars to local environmental agencies.

2½ miles up Haleakala Hwy., Makawao. www.zipline.com. ✆ **808/878-8400.** Skyline EcoAdventures Kaanapali: 2580 Kekaa Dr. #122 (meet at Fairway Shops), Lahaina (✆ **808/662-1500**).

WHERE TO STAY ON MAUI

Maui has accommodations to fit every kind of vacation, from deluxe oceanfront resorts to reasonably priced condos to historic bed-and-breakfasts. Be sure to reference "The Island in Brief," earlier in this chapter, to help you settle on a location.

Remember that Hawaii's 13.416-percent accommodations tax will be tacked on to your final bill. Also, if you're staying at an upscale hotel or resort, expect to pay a daily "resort fee" ($12–$26 a day) in addition to your room rate. Parking is free unless otherwise noted. All hotels are nonsmoking.

Central Maui

KAHULUI

Moderate

Marriot Courtyard ★   Business travelers and vacationers looking to save on airport drive time will find a comfortable night's sleep here. Built in 2012, the hotel has soundproofed walls that adequately muffle noise from the neighboring airport. Spacious rooms are attractively furnished, featuring contemporary, island-inspired artwork. Suites come with full kitchens—super convenient considering the lobby has a 24-hour market, and several grocery stores are a 5-minute drive away. The palm-fringed pool deck is especially nice at night, when it's lit by the glow of the firepit.

532 Keolani Place, Kahului. ✆ **808/871-1800.** www.marriott.com. 138 units. $199–$249 double; $299 suite; $359 1-bedroom; $568 2-bedroom. Parking $10. Free airport shuttle. **Amenities:** Deli-style restaurant; fitness center; Jacuzzi; coin-operated laundry; 24-hr. market; pool; Wi-Fi (free).

WAILUKU

Old Wailuku Inn at Ulupono ★★   Innkeepers Janice and Thomas Fairbanks and their daughter Shelly offer genuine Hawaiian hospitality at this lovingly restored 1928 estate hidden down a sleepy side street in old Wailuku town.

The nostalgic decor pays homage to Don Blanding, Hawaii's bygone poet laureate. Rooms in both the inn and the three-bedroom Vagabond House are lavishly decorated with native ohia-wood or marble floors, high ceilings, and traditional Hawaiian quilts—most with king-size beds. Each room has a private, ultra-luxurious bathroom stocked with plush towels and Aveda toiletries and either a claw-foot tub, a whirlpool tub, or a deluxe multi-head shower. You'll want to linger in the fragrant gardens and curl up with a book on the enclosed lanai. Your hosts pull out all the stops at breakfast, serving tropical fruits and pastries to early birds and Belgian waffles, five-cheese frittatas, and Molokai sweet potato pancakes after 8am. The inn is located in Wailuku's historic center, just 5 minutes' walk from the Bailey House Museum, Market Street's antique shops, and several good restaurants. Iao Valley is a 5-minute drive away.

2199 Kahookele St. (at High St., across from the Wailuku School), Wailuku. www.mauiinn.com. ✆ **800/305-4899** or 808/244-5897. 10 units. $165–$195 double. Check website for specials. Rates include full breakfast. 2-night minimum. **Amenities:** Jacuzzi; Wi-Fi (free).

Inexpensive

Maui Seaside　As if frozen in time, this harborside hotel looks much the same as it did in the 1970s: rattan furniture, aloha print bedspreads, and faux-leather booth seating in Tante's, the attached restaurant. Rooms in the two-story building face the pool and Kahului Harbor with its sandy beach, where canoe clubs launch their paddling practice.

100 W. Kaahumanu Ave., Kahului. ✆ **800/560-5552** or 808/877-3311. www.mauiseasidehotel. com. 180 units. $110–145 double. Children under 12 stay free in parent's room using existing bedding. Extra person $15. Parking $5. **Amenities:** Restaurant; laundry room; pool; Wi-Fi (free).

West Maui

LAHAINA

Expensive

Outrigger Aina Nalu ★　This lushly landscaped condo complex sprawls over 9 acres on a relatively quiet side street—a rarity in downtown Lahaina. The good-size units are tastefully decorated with modern tropical accents; all have kitchens or kitchenettes, laundry facilities, air-conditioning (a must in Lahaina), and bathrooms with large granite showers (but no tubs). Both pools are appealing places to retreat during the midday heat—particularly the infinity pool deck with its bright red cabanas and pavilion for poolside picnics. All of the historic whaling town's excitement—restaurants, shops, galleries, marine activities, and the small sandy cove at 505 Front St.—is within a 10-minute stroll.

660 Wainee St. (btw. Dickenson and Prison sts.), Lahaina. www.outrigger.com. ✆ **800/OUTRIG-GER** or 808/667-9766. 197 units. $145–$175 studio with kitchenette; $175–$315 1-bedroom with kitchen (sleeps up to 4); $189–$365 2-bedroom with 1 bathroom and kitchen (sleeps 6); $199–$395 2-bedroom with 2 bathrooms and kitchen (sleeps 6). 2-night minimum. Parking $20. **Amenities:** Concierge; grills; Jacuzzi; 2 pools; Wi-Fi (free).

The Plantation Inn ★★　Tucked away behind **Gerard's** (Maui's award-winning French restaurant), this romantic inn was built in 1987 but looks as if it has been here since the days of Hawaiian royalty—an artful deception. Rooms are tastefully furnished with vintage touches: four-poster beds, hardwood floors, French doors, and Hawaiian quilts. All units are blissfully soundproofed, and some have lanais overlooking Lahaina Town. Three extras seal this inn's appeal:

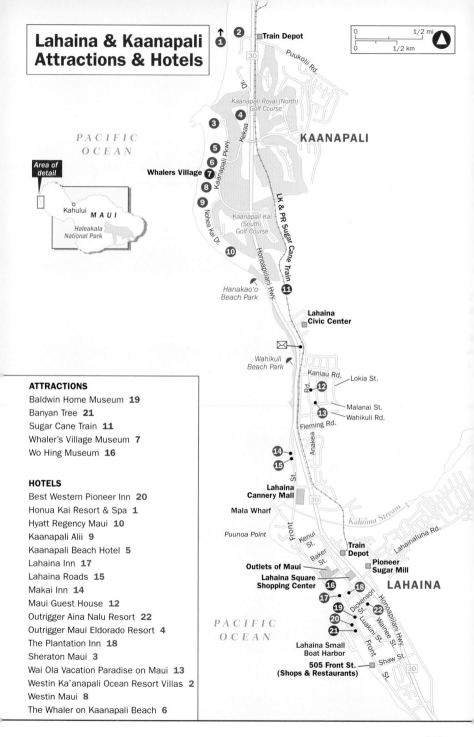

Lahaina & Kaanapali
Attractions & Hotels

Train Depot

Puukolii Rd.

Kaanapali Royal (North) Golf Course

KAANAPALI

PACIFIC OCEAN

Area of detail

Kahului MAUI

Haleakala National Park

Whalers Village

Kaanapali Pkwy.

Kekaa

Nohea Kai Dr.

Kaanapali Kai (South) Golf Course

LK & PR Sugar Cane Train

Honoapiilani Hwy.

Hanakao'o Beach Park

Lahaina Civic Center

Wahikuli Beach Park

Kaniau Rd.

Lokia St.

Malanai St.

Wahikuli Rd.

Fleming Rd.

Rd.

Anakea St.

Lahaina Cannery Mall

Mala Wharf

Puunoa Point

Kūhoma Stream

Lahainaluna Rd.

Front St.

Kenui St.

Baker St.

Train Depot

Pioneer Sugar Mill

Outlets of Maui

Lahaina Square Shopping Center

LAHAINA

Dickenson St.

Honoapiilani Hwy.

Wainee St.

Luakini St.

Front St.

PACIFIC OCEAN

Lahaina Small Boat Harbor

505 Front St. (Shops & Restaurants)

Shaw St.

ATTRACTIONS
Baldwin Home Museum **19**
Banyan Tree **21**
Sugar Cane Train **11**
Whaler's Village Museum **7**
Wo Hing Museum **16**

HOTELS
Best Western Pioneer Inn **20**
Honua Kai Resort & Spa **1**
Hyatt Regency Maui **10**
Kaanapali Alii **9**
Kaanapali Beach Hotel **5**
Lahaina Inn **17**
Lahaina Roads **15**
Makai Inn **14**
Maui Guest House **12**
Outrigger Aina Nalu Resort **22**
Outrigger Maui Eldorado Resort **4**
The Plantation Inn **18**
Sheraton Maui **3**
Wai Ola Vacation Paradise on Maui **13**
Westin Ka'anapali Ocean Resort Villas **2**
Westin Maui **8**
The Whaler on Kaanapali Beach **6**

Guests receive a $50 gift certificate to Gerard's upon check-in; each morning, a complimentary gourmet breakfast (also courtesy of Gerard's) is served poolside; and the super-convenient location—in the heart of Lahaina—makes driving unnecessary.

174 Lahainaluna Rd. (btw. Wainee and Luakini sts., 1 block from Hwy. 30), Lahaina. www.theplantationinn.com. ✆ 800/433-6815 or 808/667-9225. 18 units, some with shower only. $158–$230 double; $248–272 suite. Extra person $30. Check website for deals. Rates include full breakfast and $50 credit at Gerard's; free self-parking. **Amenities:** Restaurant and bar; concierge; Jacuzzi; coin-operated laundry; large outdoor pool; Wi-Fi (free).

Moderate

Best Western Pioneer Inn   Steps from active Lahaina Harbor, this 100-year-old hotel offers a taste of the whaling town's historic past. Simply furnished rooms have smallish bathrooms, mounted air-conditioners (they aren't silent, but they do muffle the outdoor noise), and private balconies. The quietest units face the garden courtyard—an outdoor dining area shaded by an enormous hala tree—but for people-watching off your veranda, pick a room that overlooks Front Street. The restaurant downstairs serves good breakfast and great, cheap drinks at happy hour.

658 Wharf St. (in front of Lahaina Pier), Lahaina. www.pioneerinnmaui.com. ✆ **800/457-5457** or 808/661-3636. 34 units. $145–$205 double; from $185 suite. Free parking (across the street). **Amenities:** Restaurant; bar w/live music; outdoor pool; Wi-Fi (free).

Lahaina Inn ★   A ship's figurehead announces this historic inn smack in the center of Maui's old whaling town. Each tiny, antiques-stuffed room has a private bathroom, air-conditioning, and two rocking chairs on a lanai overlooking Lahaina's action. Rooms 7 and 8 have a view of the glittering Pacific. Right downstairs is **Lahaina Grill,** one of the island's most celebrated restaurants. You won't need a car while staying here—shopping, restaurants, and marine activities are immediately outside your door—but you will need earplugs; this is an urban area, and garbage trucks rumble past in the early morning. The front desk closes at 7pm, so make sure you have everything you need before they leave for the day.

127 Lahainaluna Rd. (near Front St.), Lahaina. www.lahainainn.net. ✆ **800/669-3444** or 808/661-0577. 12 units, most with shower only. $112–$221 double; from $195 suite. Next-door parking $15 per day. **Amenities:** Restaurant; Wi-Fi ($10 per day).

Lahaina Roads ★   Named for the Mala Wharf roadstead where a string of pretty boats anchor offshore, this older condominium complex offers compact, individually owned units. It's located on the northern end of Lahaina, away from crowded downtown, but just down the street from Lahaina Cannery Mall, Old Lahaina Luau, and several terrific restaurants. One- and two-bedroom units benefit from full kitchens, oceanfront lanais, and a seaside pool. The drawbacks: no air-conditioning (it can be boiling hot in Lahaina) and bedrooms face the road, which can make nights noisy. I've listed one property manager, but a quick Internet search will turn up others.

1403 Front St. (1 block north of Lahaina Cannery Mall), Lahaina. Book with Chase'N Rainbows: www.westmauicondos.com/resorts/lahaina-roads. ✆ **877/661-6022** or 808/359-2636. 17 units. $150–$250 1-bedroom (sleeps up to 4), $175–$250 2-bedroom (sleeps up to 6). 5-night minimum. **Amenities:** Oceanside outdoor pool; Internet /Wi-Fi (free) in some units.

Maui Guest House ★★   Tanna Swanson offers guests many extras at her charming bed-and-breakfast, tucked away in a residential Lahaina neighborhood.

For starters, each private room has a full-size Jacuzzi (seriously!), noiseless air-conditioning, and gorgeous, custom stained-glass windows depicting reef fish, flowers, and other Hawaiian scenes. Guests also have access to the saltwater pool; large, fully stocked kitchen; and brand-new 30-foot sundeck for sunbathing, stargazing, and whale-watching. Tanna is a wealth of local information and an experienced scuba diver who takes good care of fellow aqua-holics. She also operates Trinity Tours, a discount activity agency. Her home is 1½ miles from Lahaina's shopping and restaurants and the same distance from Kaanapali's beaches.

1620 Ainakea Rd. (off Fleming Rd.), north of Lahaina town. www.mauiguesthouse.com. ✆ **800/621-8942** or 808/661-8085. 5 rooms. $129–$189 double. Rates include continental breakfast. Take Fleming Rd. off Hwy. 30; turn left on Ainakea; it's 2 blocks down. **Amenities:** Concierge; saltwater pool; watersports equipment; Wi-Fi (free).

Wai Ola Vacation Paradise ★   When you hear the cockatoo squawk hello, you'll know you've found this lovely retreat located in a quiet residential neighborhood halfway between Lahaina and Kaanapali. You can book a studio, suite, one-bedroom apartment, cottage, or the entire 5,000-square-foot house. The Kuuipo suite is the snazziest, with crisp black-and-white decor and a prime view of the Pacific. The honeymoon cottage is the most private, with a giant walk-in shower and Jacuzzi. Guests have access to the full kitchen and living room, the 8-foot-deep pool, and custom barbecue stations. Host Jim Wicker will go to extra lengths to make your vacation fabulous; he's been known to hunt down gluten-free pastries at a guest's request. *Note:* This is an adults-only property, unless booked as a whole.

1565 Kuuipo St., Lahaina. www.waiola.com. ✆ **800/492-4652** or 808/661-7901. 4 units. $169 double; $179 suite; $209 1-bedroom; $995–$1,400 entire house. **Amenities:** Outdoor pool; watersports equipment; Wi-Fi (free).

Inexpensive

Makai Inn ★   At the north end of Lahaina, right on the water, is this turquoise-blue, two-story apartment complex. You can't miss the mermaid fountain decorating the parking lot. Each of the eclectically furnished units is small (averaging 400 sq. ft.) but clean, with a full kitchen with a gas stove. Rooms don't have phones or TVs, but most have views of the ocean with Molokai in the distance. This funky, U-shape "inn" surrounds a tropical garden frequented by colorful Java sparrows. The largish Paradise Found unit on the southern corner has a private lanai that overlooks the Pacific on two sides. There's no beach access here, but the Lahaina Cannery Mall and several great restaurants are a short walk away.

1415 Front St., Lahaina. www.makaiinn.net. ✆ **808/662-3200.** 18 units. $115–$190 double. Extra person $15.

KAANAPALI

Starwood's Maui properties (Sheraton Maui Resort and Spa, Westin Maui Resort & Spa, or the Westin Ka'anapali Ocean Resort Villas) provide complimentary shuttle service to Lahaina and back.

Note: You'll find Kaanapali hotels on the "Lahaina & Kaanapali Attractions & Hotels" map (p. 301).

Expensive

Honua Kai Resort & Spa ★★   Since opening in 2009, this North Kaanapali Beach resort has quickly become a favorite with residents and locals alike. The property sits on Kahekili Beach, immediately north of busier, flashier Kaanapali Beach, and boasting a much better reef for snorkeling. The Honua Kai's upscale-relaxed atmosphere takes a cue from its natural surroundings. The island-inspired artwork in the lobby gives way to colorful koi ponds, artfully landscaped grounds, and meandering swimming pools. Indoors, the luxury accommodations range from huge 590-square-foot studios to even bigger 2,800-square-foot three-bedroom units, with top-of-the-line appliances, private lanais, and ocean views. The resort's sociable restaurant, **Duke's Maui Beach House,** offers an "ono-licious" breakfast and live music during "aloha hour" from 3 to 5pm. Stock up on organic snacks, gelato, and local coffee at **Aina Gourmet Market** in the lobby. The new **Hoola Spa** has the island's only therapeutic Himalayan salt room and incorporates organic, made-in-Hawaii products in its treatments.

130 Kai Malina Pkwy., North Kaanapali Beach. www.honuakaimaui.com. © **888/718-5789** or 808/662-2800. 628 units. $225–$275 studio double; $225–$300 1-bedroom (sleeps up to 4); $325–$425 2-bedroom (sleeps up to 6); $725–$1,550 3-bedroom (sleeps up to 8). Daily $25 resort fee. Free parking. **Amenities:** Restaurant; deli; bar; fitness center; nearby 36-hole golf course; 5 Jacuzzis; 5 outdoor pools; spa w/therapeutic salt room; nearby tennis courts; watersports equipment rentals; Wi-Fi (free).

Hyatt Regency Maui Resort & Spa ★★   You can't help but feel like royalty when walking into this palatial resort with exotic parrots and South African penguins in the lobby. The southernmost property on Kaanapali Beach, it covers some 40 acres with nine man-made waterfalls, abundant Asian and Pacific artwork, and a pool that resembles a water park with a swim-up grotto bar, rope bridge, kids-only adventure pool, and 150-foot lava-tube slide that keeps teens occupied for hours. Spread out among three towers, the resort's ample rooms have huge marble bathrooms and private lanais with eye-popping views of the Pacific or the West Maui Mountains. You will drift into dreams on the feather-soft platform beds. Two Regency Club floors offer a private concierge, complimentary breakfast, sunset cocktails, and snacks—not a bad choice for families looking to save on meals. This is an excellent destination for travelers who want a bevy of activities without having to stray far. Daily activities range from sushi-making classes at **Japengo,** the resort's superb Japanese restaurant, to scuba clinics in the pool and stargazing on the rooftop. Camp Hyatt offers pint-size guests weekly scavenger hunts, penguin-feeding opportunities, and access to a game room. The oceanfront **Spa Moana,** a 20,000-square-foot wellness retreat, boasts 15 treatment rooms, sauna and steam rooms, and a huge menu of island-inspired body treatments.

200 Nohea Kai Dr., Lahaina. www.maui.hyatt.com. © **808/661-1234.** 806 rooms; 31 suites. $349–$534 double; $439–$609 Regency Club double; from $849 suite. Daily $25 resort fee for access to Moana Athletic Club, local newspaper delivery, local and toll-free calls, Internet access, and 1-hr. tennis-court time per day. Extra person $75 ($125 in Regency Club rooms). Children 18 and under stay free in parent's room using existing bedding. Packages available. Valet parking $20; free self-parking. **Amenities:** 5 restaurants; 3 bars; on-site luau; babysitting; children's program ($80 per child full-day, $45 half-day; night camp from 6–10pm $25 per hour); concierge; concierge-level rooms; 36-hole golf course; health club w/weight room; Jacuzzi; half-acre outdoor pool; room service; state-of-the-art spa; 6 tennis courts; watersports equipment rentals; Wi-Fi (included in resort fee).

Kaanapali Alii ★   This luxurious oceanfront condo complex sits on 8 landscaped acres in the center of Kaanapali Beach. Units are individually owned and decorated—which means some are considerably fancier than others. Both one- (1,500 sq. ft.) and two-bedroom (1,900 sq. ft.) units come with all the comforts of home: spacious living areas, gourmet kitchens, washer/dryers, lanais, and two full bathrooms. Resort-like extras include bell service, daily housekeeping, and a complimentary kids' club (summer only). Views from each unit vary dramatically; if watching the sun sink into the ocean is important to you, request a central unit on floor six or higher. Mountain View units shouldn't be disregarded, though. They're cooler throughout the day, and the West Maui Mountains are arrestingly beautiful—particularly on full moon nights. It's got a swimming pool, a separate children's pool, gas barbecue grills and picnic areas, and tennis courts. You can even take yoga classes on the lawn.

50 Nohea Kai Dr., Lahaina. www.kaanapalialii.com. © **866/844-3651.** 264 units. $460–$645 1-bedroom for 4; $650–$975 2-bedroom for 6. Check for Internet specials or call. Free parking **Amenities:** Babysitting; concierge; fitness center; fitness and yoga classes; 36-hole golf course; kids' club (June–Aug); 2 outdoor pools; 3 lighted tennis courts; watersports equipment; Wi-Fi (free).

Sheraton Maui Resort and Spa ★★★   The Sheraton occupies the nicest spot on Kaanapali Beach, built into the side of Puu Kekaa, the dramatic lava rock point at the beach's north end. The stretch of golden sand fronting the resort is widest here and the snorkeling is best around the base of the point, also known as Black Rock. Every night at sunset, cliff divers swan-dive into the sea from the torch-lit cliff—a magical sight to behold. The resort's prime location, ample amenities, and typically great service make it an all-around great place to stay. Rooms feature Hawaiian-inspired decor, private lanais, and trademark Sweet Sleeper beds, which live up to their name. The *ohana* (family) suites accommodate all ages with two double beds plus a *punee* (sleeping chaise). The lagoon-like pool is refreshing, but it can't beat the sea full of real live fish and turtles just steps away. A full roster of activities ranging from outrigger canoe to hula and ukulele lessons will immerse you in Hawaiian culture; at night the Maui Nui Luau has an exciting fire-knife dance finale. The elegant **Spa at Black Rock** lacks the steam rooms and saunas of other resort spas, but treatments here—especially those catering to couples—are exquisite.

2605 Kaanapali Pkwy., Lahaina. www.sheraton-maui.com. © **866/716-8109** or 808/661-0031. 508 units. $369–$569 double; from $699 suite. Daily $30 resort fee. Extra person $89. Children 17 and under stay free in parent's room using existing bedding. Valet parking $5; free self-parking. **Amenities:** 3 restaurants; 1 poolside bar; weekly luau; indoor lounge; babysitting; children's program (at the Westin); lobby and poolside concierge; 36-hole golf course; fitness center; Jacuzzi; lagoon-style pool; room service; shuttle service; day spa; 3 tennis courts; watersports equipment/rentals; Wi-Fi (free).

The Westin Ka'anapali Ocean Resort Villas ★★   In contrast to the hotel-style Westin (see below), this elegant condo complex is so enormous it has two separate lobbies. The 26 acres fronting serene Kahekili Beach function as a small town with two grocery stores (stock up on marinated meats, local eggs, and Maui-grown coffee), three pools (yes, that's a life-size pirate ship in the kids' pool), three restaurants (hit **Pailolo Sports Bar** during a game), a Hawaiian cultural advisor, a luxury spa (the 80-min. Polynesian ritual is unforgettable), and a high-energy gym with its own steam rooms, saunas, and lockers. Managed by Westin, the individually owned units (ranging from studios to two-bedrooms) are uniformly outfitted with trademark Heavenly beds, huge soaking tubs with jets, and upscale kitchen appliances. Despite its seemingly massive footprint, the resort has accrued numerous awards for its eco-friendly practices. One fun example: on July 4th, the resort declines the usual fireworks display (which spreads ash on the fragile coral reefs) and opts instead to celebrate with "flower-works," dropping 60,000 orchids on the property. The lucky guest who finds the rose amid the orchids gets a free spa treatment or snorkel cruise.

6 Kai Ala Dr., Kaanapali Resort. www.westinkaanapali.com. © **866/716-8112** or 808/667-3200. 1021 units. $370–$770 studio; $830–$1,040 1-bedroom; $1,390–$1,810 2-bedroom. Extra person $89. Self-parking $10. **Amenities:** 3 restaurants; 2 bars; babysitting; children's program; concierge; 36-hole golf course; gym; 3 outdoor pools; children's pool w/pirate ship; room service; complimentary shuttle service; spa; tennis courts; Wi-Fi (free).

Westin Maui Resort & Spa ★★   The fantasy begins in the lobby, where waterfalls spill into pools stocked with flamingos and black swans. The lavishly landscaped grounds wind around an 87,000-square-foot water wonderland with five pools and an extra-speedy 128-foot-long water slide. (I screamed the first time I flew down it.) After enjoying the pool amenities (waterfalls, aquatic basketball, volleyball), hit the beach for snorkeling, stand-up paddling, kayaking, or parasailing . . . the sky truly is the limit. Recharge at **Relish,** the poolside restaurant, but save your appetite for **Wailele,** the resort's wonderful 3-hour luau experience. Take a stroll two doors down to shop till you drop at Whalers Village. After you've thoroughly exhausted yourself, return to your room to sink into your fabulous Heavenly Bed, a Westin trademark with no fewer than five different pillows. If you need further refreshment, hit the **Heavenly** spa for a Hualani fruit scrub and lomi lomi massage—I highly recommend it. There's also a "mind and body" studio for yoga and meditation classes and a 2,000-square-foot fitness center. Forgot your workout clothes? No problem. You can borrow a set provided by New Balance.

2365 Kaanapali Pkwy., Lahaina. www.westinmaui.com. © **866/716-8112** or 808/667-2525. 759 units. $339–$939 double; from $759 suite. Children 18 and under stay free in parent's room. Extra person $89. Packages available. Daily $30 resort fee. Valet parking $15. **Amenities:** 3 restaurants; 3 bars; babysitting; bike rental; children's program; concierge; fitness center/yoga studio; 36-hole golf course; 5 free-form outdoor pools; room service; complimentary shuttle service; salon; complimentary logo shopping bag; spa w/steam rooms, saunas, and co-ed lounge; tennis courts; watersports equipment rentals; Wi-Fi (free).

The Whaler on Kaanapali Beach ★   Situated in the center of Kaanapali Beach, next door to Whalers Village, this collection of condos feels more formal and sedate than its high-octane neighbors. Maybe it's the koi turning circles in the meditative lily pond, the manicured lawn between the two 12-story towers, or the lack of a water slide populated by stampeding kids. Decor in the individually owned units varies widely, but most boast full kitchens, upscale bathrooms, private lanais with views of Kaanapali's gentle waves or the emerald peaks of the West Maui Mountains. Unit no. 723, in the back corner of the north tower, is exquisite. The beachfront barbecue area is the envy of passersby on the Kaanapali Beach walkway.

2481 Kaanapali Pkwy. (next to Whalers Village), Lahaina. www.astonhotels.com. © **877/997-6667** or 808/661-4861. 360 units. $260–$345 studio double; $334–$430 1-bedroom (up to 4 people); $575–$899 2-bedroom (up to 6 people). Check website for specials. Parking $12 per day. **Amenities:** Concierge; fitness center; outdoor pool; salon & spa; tennis courts; Wi-Fi (free).

Moderate

Kaanapali Beach Hotel ★   A relic from a bygone era, Kaanapali Beach Hotel has a humble charm and authentic Hawaiian warmth that's missing from many of its upscale neighbors. Depending on your taste, you'll find this property's giant carved tikis, whale-shape pool, and somewhat dated decor either kitschy or refreshingly unpretentious. Instead of African parrots and Asian artwork, the lobby is adorned with traditional Hawaiian hula implements and weapons—many created by the staff during their annual Makahiki celebration. Three low-rise buildings border fabulous Kaanapali Beach; the beachfront units are mere steps from the water. The large-ish, motel-like rooms are decorated with wicker and rattan furniture, historic photos or renderings of native flora and fauna, and Hawaiian-style bedspreads. Tiki torches, hula, and live music create a festive atmosphere every night in the courtyard. During the day, you can snorkel out front, give stand-up paddling a try, or even learn to speak a little *olelo* Hawaii—the islands' lyrical native language. Hawaiian values and customs are honored here, and the service is some of the friendliest around. The staff serenades you during a morning welcome reception and a farewell lei ceremony. Even if you don't stay here, pay a visit to the grassy lawn where a giant checkerboard has red-and-black painted coconuts for game pieces.

2525 Kaanapali Pkwy., Lahaina. www.kbhmaui.com. © **800/262-8450** or 808/661-0011. 430 units. $174–$331 double; from $311–$544 suite. Extra person $40. Packages available, as well as senior discounts. Valet parking $12; self-parking $10. **Amenities:** 2 restaurants; poolside bar; babysitting; children's program (not supervised); concierge; 36-hole golf course nearby; outdoor pool; spa and salon services; access to tennis courts; watersports equipment rentals; Wi-Fi ($10 per day).

Outrigger Maui Eldorado ★   It may have been one of Kaanapali's first properties in the late 1960s, but this 10-acre condo complex still manages to feel new. Developed in an era when real estate was abundant and contractors built to last, each spacious, individually owned unit has a full kitchen, washer/dryer, central air-conditioning, and outstanding ocean and mountain views. This is a great choice for active families. It's set on Kaanapali Golf Course, not on the beach, but guests have exclusive use of a beachfront pavilion on North Kaanapali, aka Kahekili Beach. You're also within walking distance of the Fairway Shops' excellent and affordable restaurants—a real bonus in otherwise pricey Kaanapali. *Note:* It's a two-level walkup without elevators. Grocery service and daily housekeeping are optional.

2661 Kekaa Dr., Lahaina. www.outrigger.com. © **888/339-8585** or 808/661-0021. 204 units, 87 managed by Outrigger. $179–$199 studio double; $205–$345 1-bedroom (up to 4); $365–$509 2-bedroom (up to 6). 2-night minimum. Numerous packages available. Daily $12 resort fee; $115 mandatory cleaning charge. Free parking. **Amenities:** Beach pavilion; concierge; 36-hole golf course; 3 outdoor pools; Wi-Fi (free).

HONOKOWAI, KAHANA & NAPILI

Expensive

Kahana Sunset ★   Set in the crook of a sharp bend on Lower Honoapiilani Road is a series of three-story wooden condos, stair-stepping down a hill to a private Keonenui beach—a strip of golden sand all but unknown, even to locals. Decor varies dramatically in the individually owned units, many of which feature master and children's bedrooms up a short flight of stairs. All units have full kitchens with dishwashers, washer/dryers, cable TV, and expansive lanais with marvelous views. Some rooms have air-conditioning, while most rely on ceiling fans—suitable on this cooler end of the coastline. The center of the property features a small heated pool, Jacuzzi, and barbecue grills. This complex is ideal for families: The units are roomy and the adjoining beach is safe for swimming.

4909 Lower Honoapiilani Hwy. (at the northern end of Kahana), Lahaina. www.kahanasunset. com. (C) **800/669-1488** or 808/669-8700. 79 units. $170–$300 1-bedroom (sleeps up to 4); $295–$550 2-bedroom (sleeps up to 6). 3- 5-night minimum. **Amenities:** Concierge; 2 outdoor pools (1 for children); high-speed Internet (free).

The Mauian Hotel ★★ This vintage property perched above beautiful Napili Bay offers a blend of old-time hospitality and contemporary flair. The verdant grounds burst with tropical color; the pool deck is shaded by umbrellas by day and lit with tiki torches at night; and the beach is among the island's prettiest. Rooms feature full kitchens, Indonesian-style furniture, and ample lanais overlooking the grassy lawn and glittering Pacific. What it doesn't have is phones or TVs—encouraging you to really get away from it all. If you crave electronic entertainment, the *ohana* (family) room has a TV and an extensive DVD library. Each morning guests gather there for coffee, fresh fruit, and pastries before heading out to snorkel or try their luck at stand-up paddling in the supremely calm bay. Live music and free mai tais attract guests to the weekly "aloha party" by the pool, where they share *pupu* (appetizers) and travel tales. Nightly sunsets off the beach are spectacular—particularly during winter when they're punctuated by whale spouts on the horizon.

5441 Lower Honoapiilani Rd. (in Napili), Lahaina. www.mauian.com. (C) **800/367-5034** or 808/669-6205. 44 units. $203 double hotel room; $223–$325 double studio (sleeps up to 4). Extra person $13. Children 4 and under stay free in parent's room; free parking. **Amenities:** Coin-operated laundry; outdoor pool; oceanfront shuffleboard courts; Wi-Fi (free).

Napili Kai Beach Resort ★★★ This small resort nestled on Napili's white sandy cove feels like a well-kept secret. For more than 50 years, the staff at this intimate property has been welcoming return guests for a taste of unspoiled paradise. The weekly mai tai and golf putting parties are blasts from the past, but the modern conveniences in each unit and startling ocean views will focus you on the splendid here and now. From the three buildings on the point (Puna, Puna 2, and Lani), you can gaze at the ocean from your bed; it looks like an infinity pool starting at the edge of your lanai. All units (aside from eight hotel rooms) have full kitchens, washer/dryers, flatscreen TVs, ultra-comfortable king-size beds, and private lanais separated by attractive shoji screens. The resort's emphasis on Hawaiian culture manifests in poi pounding and lauhala weaving workshops, authentic *keiki* (children's) hula shows, and twice-weekly slack key guitar concerts led by Grammy award–winning musician George Kahumoku. Kids 12 and under eat for free at the resort's **Sea House** restaurant, where you can dine in or take food back to your room. As cozy as the accommodations are, you'll probably spend all of your time on the beach or in the protected bay paddling past lazy sea turtles. *An added bonus:* no resort fee.

5900 Honoapiilani Rd. (at north end of Napili, next to Kapalua), Lahaina. www.napilikai.com. (C) **800/367-5030** or 808/669-6271. 162 units. $290–$325 hotel room double; $360–$545 studio double (sleeps 3–4); $575–$750 1-bedroom suite (sleeps up to 5); $650–$1,115 2-bedroom suite (sleeps up to 7); 3-bedroom suite (sleeps up to 7) $940–$1,380. Packages available. **Amenities:**

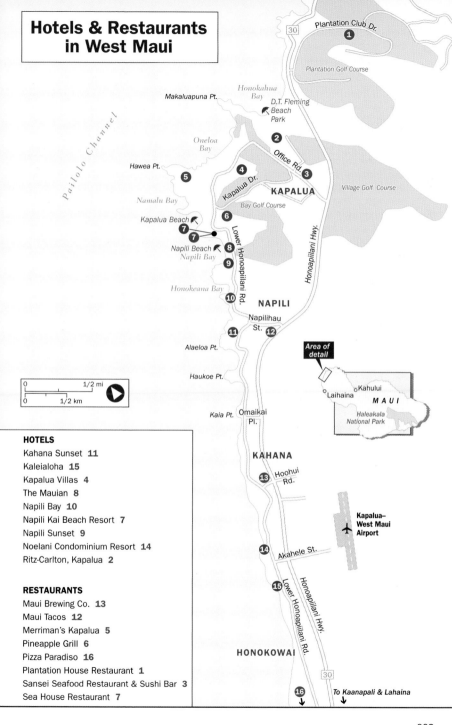

Hotels & Restaurants in West Maui

Plantation Club Dr.

30

1

Plantation Golf Course

Honokahua Bay

Makaluapuna Pt.

D.T. Fleming Beach Park

2

Oneloa Bay

Office Rd.

4

3

Hawea Pt.

5

Kapalua Dr.

KAPALUA

Village Golf Course

Pailolo Channel

Namalu Bay

Bay Golf Course

6

Kapalua Beach

7

7

Napili Beach

8

Honoapiilani Hwy.

Napili Bay

9

Lower Honoapiilani Rd.

Honokeana Bay

10

NAPILI

Napilihau St.

11

12

Alaeloa Pt.

Haukoe Pt.

Area of detail

Kahului

Laihaina

MAUI

Kaia Pt. Omaikai Pl.

Haleakala National Park

0 ————— 1/2 mi
0 ————— 1/2 km

KAHANA

13 Hoohui Rd.

Kapalua– West Maui Airport

14 Akahele St.

15

Lower Honoapiilani Rd.

Honoapiilani Hwy.

HONOKOWAI

16

30

To Kaanapali & Lahaina

HOTELS

Kahana Sunset **11**
Kaleialoha **15**
Kapalua Villas **4**
The Mauian **8**
Napili Bay **10**
Napili Kai Beach Resort **7**
Napili Sunset **9**
Noelani Condominium Resort **14**
Ritz-Carlton, Kapalua **2**

RESTAURANTS

Maui Brewing Co. **13**
Maui Tacos **12**
Merriman's Kapalua **5**
Pineapple Grill **6**
Pizza Paradiso **16**
Plantation House Restaurant **1**
Sansei Seafood Restaurant & Sushi Bar **3**
Sea House Restaurant **7**

Restaurant; bar; babysitting; free children's activities at holidays; concierge; 24-hr. fitness room; 2 18-hole putting greens (w/free use of golf putters); discounted rates at nearby Kapalua golf courses; 4 outdoor pools; free Kapalua shuttle; tennis courts nearby (and complimentary use of tennis rackets); watersports equipment (complimentary); Internet (free).

Napili Sunset ★   This humble property hidden down a small side street consists of three buildings, two facing spectacular Napili Bay and one across the street. At first glance, they don't look like much, but the prime location, low prices, and friendly staff make up for the plain exterior. The one- and two-bedroom units are beachfront. Upstairs units have bathtubs, while those downstairs have direct access to the sand. Across the street, overlooking a kidney-shape pool and gardens, the economical studios feature expansive showers and Murphy beds. All units benefit from daily maid service, full kitchens (with dishwashers), and ceiling fans (no air-conditioning). Unfortunately, bedrooms in the beachfront buildings face the road, but the ocean views from the lanais are outstanding. The strip of grassy lawn adjoining the beach is an added perk—especially when the sandy real estate is crowded. Several good restaurants are within walking distance, along with Kapalua's tennis courts and golf courses, but the resort also has on-site barbecue grills.

46 Hui Rd. (in Napili), Lahaina. www.napilisunset.com. ✆ **800/447-9229.** 43 units. $170 studio double; $255–$350 1-bedroom double (sleeps 5–6); $420-499 2-bedroom (sleeps up to 7). **Amenities:** Coin-operated laundry; small outdoor pool; Wi-Fi (free).

Noelani Condominium Resort ★★   This Kahana condo is a real gem. Whether you book a studio or a three-bedroom unit, everything from the furnishings to the oceanfront pool is first class for budget prices. The only caveat: There's no sandy beach attached. But right next door is a Pohaku Beach Park (good for surfing, not as great for swimming), and better beaches are less than 10 minutes away. All units feature full kitchens, daily maid service, panoramic views of passing whales during winter, and spectacular sunsets year-round; one-, two-, and three-bedrooms have washer-dryers. My favorites are the Orchid building's deluxe studios, where you can see the ocean from your bed. Units in the Anthurium Building boast oceanfront lanais just 20 feet from the water (the nicest are on the ground floor), but the bedrooms face the road. Guests are invited to lei-making and mai tai parties in the poolside cabana and have access to a teeny-tiny gym with a million-dollar view. It doesn't have air-conditioning, but the ceiling fans and ocean breezes are adequate.

4095 Lower Honoapiilani Rd. (in Kahana), Lahaina. www.noelani-condo-resort.com. ✆ **800/367-6030** or 808/669-8374. 40 units. $135–$203 studio double; $185–$237 1-bedroom (sleeps up to 4); $290–$329 2-bedroom (sleeps up to 6); $345–$403 3-bedroom (sleeps up to 8). Extra person $20. Children under 18 stay free in parent's room. Packages available. Rates include continental breakfast on 1st morning. 3-night minimum. **Amenities:** Concierge; fitness center; oceanfront Jacuzzi; laundry center (for studios); 2 freshwater pools (1 heated for night swimming); Wi-Fi (free).

Inexpensive

In addition to the choices below, consider **Hale Maui Apartment Hotel** (www.halemaui.com; ✆ **808/669-6312**), a wonderful, tiny place run by Hans and Eva Zimmerman and their daughter, Marika, whose spirit is 100-percent aloha. The one-bedroom suites, which were remodeled with new furniture in 2008, start at around $115 for a double and come with ceiling fans, private lanais, and complete kitchens. There's no pool, but a private path leads to a great swimming beach.

Kaleialoha ★ This four-story condo complex is conveniently located near Honokowai's grocery shopping, budget restaurants, and public beach park. Each one-bedroom unit comes with a fully equipped kitchen with marble countertops and dishwashers; a sofa bed in the living room; stacked washer/dryers; outdoor barbecues; and a view of Lanai and Molokai across the turquoise expanse of the Pacific. Top-floor units have the best views; bottom-floor units open onto the lawn and oceanfront pool. There's decent snorkeling beyond the rock retaining wall, but you'll have to walk a block down the road for a sandy beach.

3785 Lower Honoapiilani Rd. (in Honokowai), Lahaina. www.mauicondosoceanfront.com. © **800/222-8688** or 808/669-8197. 18 units. $149–$235 1-bedroom double. Extra person $10. Children 3 and under stay free in parent's room. Cleaning fee $95 for less than 7-night stay. **Amenities:** Concierge; Wi-Fi (free).

Napili Bay ★ This small two-story condo complex sits on the southern edge of picturesque Napili Bay. Fall asleep to the sound of the surf and wake to birdsong. The individually owned studio apartments are compact, with king- or queen-size beds in the oceanfront living room (rather than facing the road like so many on this strip). You'll find everything you need to feel at home, including a stocked kitchen, beach and snorkeling equipment, and a lanai with front-row seats for the nightly entertainment: the sun's fiery ball sinking into the Pacific. You won't find a pool on the property or air-conditioning in the rooms, but louvered windows and ceiling fans keep the units fairly cool—and why waste time in a pool when you're steps away from one of the island's calmest, prettiest bays? I've listed contact info below for unit no. 208, owned by Chuck Buser, who has been known to welcome guests with a beach bag stuffed with goodies. A quick Internet search will turn up others.

33 Hui Dr. (off Lower Honoapiilani Hwy., in Napili), Lahaina. www.alohacondos.com. © **877/877-5758.** 28 units. $129–$279 double. Cleaning fees and minimum stays may apply. **Amenities:** Wi-Fi (free).

KAPALUA

Note: You'll find the following hotels on the "Hotels & Restaurants in West Maui" map (p. 309).

Expensive

Kapalua Villas ★★★ The palatial townhouses populating the oceanfront cliffs and fairways of this idyllic coast are a (relative) bargain, particularly if you're traveling with a group. As guests of Kapalua Resort, you're granted signing privileges at its championship golf courses and free access to the resort's deluxe tennis complex, golf academy, and luxurious 5-acre Spa Montage, with its rainwater showers and co-ed saltwater infinity pool—a dreamy place to spend an afternoon. Several of the island's best restaurants (Sansei, Pineapple Grill, and Merriman's) are within walking distance or a quick shuttle trip. Outrigger manages the individually owned one-, two-, and three-bedroom units, which feature upscale furnishings, full kitchens, queen-size sofa beds, and large private lanais. You'll feel like royalty—even the one bedrooms exceed 1,200 square feet. Of the three complexes (Golf, Ridge, and Bay Villas), the Bay units are the nicest, positioned on the windswept bluff overlooking the Pacific with Molokai on the horizon. In the winter you can whale-watch without leaving your living room.

200 Village Rd., Kapalua. www.kapaluavillas.com. © **800/545-0018** or 808/665-9170. $199–$349 1-bedroom; $339–$574 2-bedroom; $599–$1,099 3-bedroom. Daily $25 resort fee; $130–$200 mandatory cleaning fee. Free parking. **Amenities:** Access to Kapalua Resort's 12 dining options; close to 3 excellent beaches; concierge; 9 outdoor pools; complimentary resort shuttle; Wi-Fi (free).

Ritz-Carlton, Kapalua ★★★   Perched majestically on a knoll above D. T. Fleming Beach, this resort is a complete universe, where you can while away whole weeks without leaving the grounds. The property's intimate relationship to Hawaiian culture began during construction: When the remains of hundreds of ancient Hawaiians were unearthed, the owners agreed to shift the hotel inland to avoid disrupting the graves. Today, Native Hawaiian cultural advisor Clifford Naeole helps guide resort developments and hosts the Ritz's exceptional signature events, such as the Celebration of the Arts—a weeklong, complimentary indigenous arts and cultural festival. (The annual Wine & Food Festival is another, worth planning your vacation around.) The resplendent accommodations feature dark wood floors, plush beds and couches, marble bathrooms, and private lanais overlooking the landscaped grounds and mostly undeveloped coast. The Ritz's Club Level offers one of the best lounges in the state, serving gourmet coffee and pastries in the morning, a buffet at lunch, cookies in the afternoon, and hot appetizers and drinks at sunset. Additional amenities include several superior dining options; a 10,000-square-foot, three-tiered pool; Jean-Michel Cousteau's Ambassadors of the Environment center and kids' program; a fitness center; and the 17,500-square-foot **Waihua Spa,** with steam rooms, saunas, whirlpools surrounded by lava-rock walls. A bit of a hike from the resort proper, D. T. Fleming Beach is beautiful but tends to be windier and rougher than the bays immediately south; a 5-minute shuttle ride delivers you to Oneloa or Kapalua. The forest and coastal hiking trails offer superlative views and opportunities to see native flora and fauna.

1 Ritz-Carlton Dr., Kapalua. www.ritzcarlton.com. © **800/262-8440** or 808/669-6200. 463 units. $299–$719 double; $549–$969 Club Level double; from $599 suite; from $899 Club Level suite; residential suites from $595 1-bedroom, $975 2-bedroom. Extra person $50. Daily $30 resort fee; wedding/honeymoon, golf, and other packages available. Valet parking $18; self-parking $18. **Amenities:** 4 restaurants; 4 bars; babysitting; basketball and bocce ball courts; bike rentals; children's program; club floor; concierge; cultural-history tours; 24-hour oceanview fitness room; fitness classes; 2 championship golf courses (each w/its own pro shop) and golf academy; hiking trails; outdoor 3-tiered pool; room service; shuttle service; luxury spa w/steam rooms, saunas, and whirlpools; deluxe tennis complex; watersports equipment rentals; Wi-Fi (free).

South Maui

Two recommended booking agencies rent a host of condominiums and vacation homes throughout South Maui. **Condominium Rentals Hawaii** (www.crh maui.com; © **866/975-1864** or 808/879-2778) offers affordable, quality properties primarily in Kihei, with a few in Wailea. **Destination Resorts Hawaii,** 34 Wailea Gateway Place, #A102, Wailea (www.drhmaui.com; © **866/384-1366** or 808/891-6200) is the more upscale option, offering a wide selection of luxury rentals in Wailea and Makena. One-bedroom units start at $259 and include many extras: a hospitality desk to assist with activity planning, $40 in dining credits at nearby restaurants, a discount grocery card, free Wi-Fi and parking, and in some cases, a free rental car!

Hotels & Restaurants in South Maui

KIHEI

Piilani Hwy.

Kihei Beach

Kulanihakoi St.

Kulanihakoi Gulch

Keonoulu Beach

Waipuilani Rd.

Lipoa St.

LAIE

Halama St.

Kihei Rd.

Lahaina · Kahului

MAUI

Area of detail

Haleakala National Park

Kalama Beach Park

Kamaole Beach Park I

KAMAOLE

Kamaole Beach Park II

Kamaole Beach Park III

Kilohana Dr.

Keawakapu Beach

WAILEA

MAUI MEADOWS

Piilani Hwy.

Mokapu Beach

Ulua Beach

The Shops at Wailea

Wailea Beach

Polo Beach

Palauea Beach

Makena Rd.

Poolenalena Beach

MAKENA

Maluaka Beach

Makena State Park

Makena Rd.

0   1 mi
0   1 km

KIHEI

Expensive

Aston Maui Hill ★ This stately condo complex with Mediterranean-style stucco buildings, red-tile roofs, and three-stories-tall arches marks the border between Kihei and Wailea—an excellent spot to launch your vacation from. Managed by the respected Aston chain, Maui Hill combines the amenities of a hotel—24-hour front desk, concierge, pool, hot tub, tennis courts, putting green, and more—with the convenience of a condo. Units are spacious, with ample kitchens, air-conditioning (welcome in this climate), washer/dryers, queen-size sofa beds, and roomy lanais—most with ocean views. (For prime views, seek out unit nos. 35 and 36.) Two of South Maui's best beaches are immediately across the street; restaurants, shops, and golf courses are nearby. The management goes to lengths to make sure your stay is perfect—right up to the moment you print your boarding pass for free in the lobby. Check the website for significant discounts.

2881 S. Kihei Rd. (across from Kamaole Park III, btw. Keonekai St. and Kilohana Dr.), Kihei. www.astonhotels.com. © **877/997-6667** or 808/879-6321. 140 units. $325–$425 1-bedroom; $379–$499 2-bedroom; $479–$695 3-bedroom. **Amenities:** Concierge; putting green; outdoor pool; tennis courts; Wi-Fi (free).

Maalaea Surf Resort ★ Despite its name, this little-known beachfront retreat isn't in Maalaea, nor is it a proper resort. Rather, it's a collection of charming condos spread out across 5 acres at the far north end of Kihei. The four-unit townhouses with double-hipped roofs all have ocean views, big kitchens (with dishwashers), cable TV, and central air conditioning—a necessity in summer. Sugar Beach, the adjacent salt-and-pepper stretch of sand, extends 3-plus miles to Maalaea. Often windy, it's not the best for swimming, but it's unmatched for sunsets (and whale-watching in winter). This is a decent headquarters for adventurers who want to explore the entire island.

12 S. Kihei Rd. (at N. Kihei Rd. and Mokulele Hwy. 311), Kihei. www.maalaeasurfresort.com. © **800/423-7953** or 808/879-1267. 34 units. $220–$350 1-bedroom (sleeps up to 4); $315–$550 2-bedroom (sleeps up to 6). 5-night minimum. **Amenities:** Concierge; housekeeping 3 days a week; 2 outdoor pools; 2 tennis courts; Wi-Fi (free).

Maui Coast Hotel ★ The chief advantage of Kihei's sole hotel is location, location, location. It's less than a block from sandy, sun-kissed Kamaole Beach Park I and within walking distance of South Kihei Road's bars, restaurants, and shopping. Another plus: nightly entertainment at the popular pool bar. Guest rooms are smallish, with sitting areas, huge flatscreen TVs, central air, and private garden lanais—no ocean views, though. Throughout the hotel, you'll find wonderful paintings by local artist Avi Kiriaty. Book the less-expensive "deluxe room" over the somewhat cramped "one-bedroom suite," unless you absolutely need the extra privacy.

2259 S. Kihei Rd. (across from Kamaole Beach Park I), Kihei. www.mauicoasthotel.com. © **800/895-6284** or 808/874-6284. 265 units. $129 double; $235 suite; $289 1-bedroom (sleeps up to 4). Children 17 and under stay free in parent's room using existing bedding. Daily resort fee $18. Extra person charge $20. Packages available. **Amenities:** Restaurant; pool bar w/nightly entertainment; complimentary bicycles; concierge; fitness room; outdoor pool (plus children's wading pool); room service; 2 lighted tennis courts; Wi-Fi (free).

Moderate

Eva Villa ★★　At the top of the Maui Meadows neighborhood above Wailea, Rick and Dale Pounds have done much to make their affordable bed-and-breakfast one of Maui's classiest. The hillside location offers respite from the shoreline's heat—and yet it's just a few minutes' drive to the beaches, shopping, and restaurants of both Kihei and Wailea. The tastefully designed cottage has a decent-size kitchen and living room, smallish bedroom, washer/dryer, and a sweet outdoor shower. The poolside studio is a single long room with a huge kitchen and barstool seating. The suite next door has two bedrooms and a kitchenette. You aren't forced to be social here; continental breakfast (fresh fruit, juice, muffins, coffee) comes stocked in your kitchen. And with just three units, the luxurious pool deck is rarely ever crowded.

815 Kumulani Dr., Kihei. www.mauibnb.com. © **800/884-1845** or 808/874-6407. 3 units. $155–$210 double. Extra person $20. 5-night minimum. No credit cards. **Amenities:** Heated outdoor pool; Wi-Fi (free).

Mana Kai Maui Resort ★　Even the views outside the elevator are astounding at this eight-story hotel/condo, which practically has its toes in the sand of beautiful Keawakapu Beach. Every unit in the 1973 building is oceanfront. Most, if not all, have been renovated with contemporary, island-inspired furnishings. The north-facing hotel rooms, which account for half of the units, have king-size beds and kitchenettes, but no lanais. The one- and two-bedroom condos have full kitchens, sitting areas, and small lanais that overlook the glittering Pacific and several islands on the horizon. There's a surf shack on site, along with a gourmet grocery and deli, oceanfront restaurant, and yoga studio. *Fun fact:* The lobby's iconic turtle mural appears in the film "Just Go With It."

2960 S. Kihei Rd. (btw. Kilohana and Keonekai rds., at the south end of Kihei), Kihei. www.mana kaimaui.com. © **800/525-2025** or 808/879-1561. 98 units. Rates for booking direct from hotel: $175 hotel room double; $335 1-bedroom (sleeps up to 4); $445 2-bedroom (up to 6). Booking fee $35. Free parking. **Amenities:** Restaurant; bar; barbecues; concierge; coin-operated laundry; daily maid service; outdoor pool; watersports equipment rentals; Wi-Fi (free).

Maui Kamaole　Directly across from Kamaole Beach Park III's sandy beach, enormous lawn, and playground, this comfortable condo complex is ideal for families. Convenience is key here in the center of Kihei's beach and shopping zone. Each roomy, privately owned and furnished unit comes with an all-electric kitchen, central air, two bathrooms (even in the one-bedroom units), and two private lanais. The one-bedroom units—which can easily accommodate four—are a terrific deal, especially during low season. Ground-floor units open onto a grassy lawn. The attractively landscaped property runs perpendicular to the shoreline, and some buildings (indicated by room numbers that start with E, F, K, L, and M) are quite a trek from the beach. Families with small children should seek out units beginning with A, B, G, or H, which are nearest to the beach but off the road. C units are close to beach and pool.

2777 S. Kihei Rd. (btw. Keonekai and Kilohana rds., at the Wailea end of Kihei), Kihei. www.maui kamaole.com (Maui Condo and Home management site). © **800/822-4409** or 808/879-5445. 316 units (not all in rental pool). $190–$339 1-bedroom (sleeps up to 4); $268–$426 2-bedroom (sleeps up to 6). $40 booking fee. **Amenities:** 2 outdoor pools; 2 tennis courts; Wi-Fi (free).

Maui Sunseeker LGBT Resort ★　Across the street from wind-swept Sugar Beach in North Kihei, this cheery, adults-only boutique property welcomes all, but caters especially to gay and lesbian travelers. In 2012, Maui Sunseeker received a snazzy renovation after appearing on the reality TV show "Hotel Impossible." Now when you book a standard room, studio, or suite, expect a bright decor, comfy California king–size beds, air-conditioning (wall mount), and spacious ocean- or mountain-view lanais. Studios and suites have full kitchens or kitchenettes. The two penthouse suites are fabulous—particularly no. 421 with its exposed beam ceiling, loft bedroom, and floating island cooktop. Chat with fellow guests by the pool or in the rooftop hot tub, where you can take in the panoramic view of Maalaea Bay and the West Maui Mountains. Maui's best beaches are a short drive away; the owners supply beach chairs and coolers. This is a great spot to launch an adventurous vacation.

551 S. Kihei Rd., Kihei. www.mauisunseeker.com. ✆ **800/532-6284** or 808/879-1261. 25 units. $144–$239 hotel room or studio double; $180–$289 junior suite double; $219–$349 1-bedroom double; $289–$519 penthouse apt. Extra person $45. No children allowed. **Amenities:** Concierge; 2 Jacuzzis (rooftop hot tub is clothing optional); pool; Wi-Fi (free).

Inexpensive

Dreams Come True on Maui ★   After several years of vacationing on Maui, Tom Croly and Denise McKinnon moved here to open this bed-and-breakfast—a dream come true for both them and their guests. They offer a stand-alone cottage and two private suites in their house, which is centrally located in the Maui Meadows neighborhood, just a 5- to 10-minute drive from the shopping, restaurants, golf courses, and white-sand beaches of Kihei and Wailea. Each of the colorfully decorated suites has a private entrance and lanai, kitchenette, 42-inch TV, air-conditioning, and use of laundry facilities. Continental breakfasts are offered room-service style: Choose from the menu of freshly baked pastries, tropical fruits (mangoes right off of the tree), yogurts, and pop tarts. Hang your order on your door, and in the morning, it'll be delivered at your chosen time. Rooms are a bit tight, but you're free to use the oceanview deck, main living room, and outdoor cooking area. The cozy one-bedroom cottage has ocean views from several rooms, vaulted ceilings in the living room, wraparound decks, marble in the kitchen and bathroom, a private washer/dryer, and a computer with high-speed Internet. Tom is always on duty as a personal concierge, doling out beach equipment and suggestions for where to snorkel, shop, or eat dinner.

3259 Akala Dr., Kihei. www.dreamscometrueonmaui.com. ✆ **877/782-9628** or 808/879-7099. 3 units. $89–$139 double (4-night minimum); $139–$189 cottage double (6-night minimum; extra person $15). Room rates include continental breakfast for the B&B guest rooms. **Amenities:** Concierge; Wi-Fi (free).

Kealia Resort ★   This oceanfront property at the northernmost end of Kihei isn't a resort, but it *is* worth a second look. From the outside, the older building might seem shabby, but on the inside the privately owned units shine—and rates are excellent. Avoid the lower-priced studios facing noisy Kihei Road. Instead, go for one of the oceanfront units (such as no. 203, which hangs over the pool). All have full kitchens, washer/dryers, and private lanais with truly spectacular views of 3-plus-mile-long Sugar Beach. Twice a week the management hosts social events for guests to mingle: Wednesday pupu parties and Friday morning coffee-and-doughnut get-togethers.

191 N. Kihei Rd. (north of Hwy. 31, at the Maalaea end of Kihei), Kihei. www.kealiaresort.com. ✆ **800/265-0686** or 808/280-1192. 51 units. $115–$130 studio double; $150–$190 1-bedroom double; $215–$250 2-bedroom (sleeps up to 4). Children 12 and under stay free in parent's

room. Extra person $10. Cleaning fee $65–$95. 4- to 10-night minimum. **Amenities:** Outdoor pool; Wi-Fi (free).

Nona Lani Cottages ★   Family-owned since the 1970s, this oceanside retreat is one of North Kihei's sweetest deals. Eight tiny, vintage cottages are tucked among the coconut palms and plumeria trees, a stone's throw from Sugar Beach. Inside is everything you'll need: a compact kitchen, a separate bedroom with a queen-size bed, air-conditioning, and a cozy lanai—not to mention new travertine tile floors and cabinetry. The three suites in the main house are a little stuffy; stick to the cottages. The charming grounds include a barbecue area and outdoor hale for weddings or parties—but no pool or spa. Your hosts, the Kong family, don't offer daily maid service, but they do make fresh flower lei—buy one and fill your entire cottage with its fragrance. *Note for business travelers:* Internet is spotty here; it can only be accessed from the hale.

455 S. Kihei Rd. (just south of Hwy. 31), Kihei. www.nonalanicottages.com. © **800/733-2688** or 808/879-2497. 11 units. $150–$195 double. Extra person $15. 4- to 7-night minimum depending on season. Free parking. **Amenities:** High-speed Internet ($10 per day).

Pineapple Inn Maui ★★   Enjoy a resort vacation at a fraction of the price here. This oasis in residential Maui Meadows is luxuriously landscaped with tall coconut palms, dinner-plate-size pink hibiscus, red gingers, a lily pond, and—best of all—a saltwater pool that's lit at night. The four guest rooms in the two-story "inn" are equally immaculate: Each has upscale furnishings, a private lanai with a serene ocean view, and a small kitchenette that your hosts, Mark and Steve, stock with pastries, bagels, oatmeal, juice, and coffee upon arrival. The bright and airy cottage (two bedrooms, one bathroom) is one of the island's best deals. It has a full kitchen (including a dishwasher), dark wood floors, central air, beautiful artwork, and a private barbecue area. It's landscaped for maximum privacy. Guests are invited to stargaze from the communal hot tub and make use of the outdoor kitchen, fully equipped with barbecue utensils. Before you head out on an adventure (shopping, beaches, restaurants, and golf are mere minutes away), you can load up your car with snorkeling equipment, beach chairs, umbrellas, boogie boards, and a cooler.

3170 Akala Dr., Kihei. www.pineappleinnmaui.com. © **877/212-MAUI** (6284) or 808/298-4403. 5 units. $139–$169 double; $215–$255 cottage for 4. 3-night minimum for rooms, 6-night minimum for cottage. Rates include breakfast. No credit cards. **Amenities:** Saltwater pool; watersports equipment; Wi-Fi (free).

Punahoa Beach Condominiums ★   This oceanfront condo complex sits on a large grassy lawn between the Charley Young surf break and Kamaole I Beach—an ideal location for active, sun-seeking travelers. Each unit in the small four-story building boasts a lanai with a marvelous view of the Pacific and islands on the horizon. All are individually owned and decorated, so the aesthetic varies widely. Studios feature queen-size Murphy beds, full bathrooms, and compact, full-service kitchens. The three one-bedroom penthouses—the only units with A/C—are the sweetest option. Kihei's shopping and restaurants are all within walking distance.

2142 Iliili Rd. (off S. Kihei Rd., 300 ft. from Kamaole Beach I), Kihei. www.punahoabeach.com. © **800/564-4380** or 808/879-2720. 15 units. $149–$206 studio double; $189–$279 1-bedroom double; $229–$309 2-bedroom double; $224–$304 1-bedroom penthouse. $90–$120 cleaning fee. Extra person $15. 5-night minimum ($100 fee added for 3- or 4-night stays when available). **Amenities:** Wi-Fi (free).

Tutu Mermaids on Maui B&B (aka the Two Mermaids) ★ Your mermaid hosts, Juddee and Miranda, are both avid scuba divers, and the colorful decor throughout their charming B&B reflects their love of the sea. In the large, one-bedroom Ocean Ohana, the marine theme continues from the turquoise walls and dark stranded bamboo floors all the way to the kitchenette's fish-shape cabinet knobs. This breezy, clean unit has air-conditioning, its own hot tub, and an adjoining "Surf Room" with bunk beds that's available for families. The equally stylish two-bedroom Poolside Suite opens up to the refreshing rock-lined pool. Every morning, Juddee places a deluxe continental breakfast (Greek yogurt, tropical fruits, and homemade banana bread) at your doorstep. Other amenities include flatscreen TVs, barbecues, beach gear, and a tuned guitar in each unit for strumming island serenades. The house sits in a quiet residential cul-de-sac just a 3-minute drive (or 20-min. walk) from Kamaole III Beach. Juddee is a licensed minister and can perform weddings. She'll also help you book massages or childcare.

2840 Umalu Place, Kihei. www.twomermaids.com. © **800/598-9550** or 808/874-8687. 2 units. $150–$230 studio double. Rates include continental breakfast. 3-night minimum. Credit cards through PayPal only. **Amenities:** Babysitting; outdoor pool; Wi-Fi (free).

What a Wonderful World B&B ★ Repeat guests here adore hostess Eva Tantillo, whose years of experience in the travel industry shows in thoughtful touches around her lovely property. Every unit is lovingly furnished with hardwood floors, Hawaiian quilts, and luxurious slate showers. The Guava Suite is smallest and a little dark for my taste. The lovely Papaya Suite, with its spacious living room and bathroom and separate bedroom, is just right. Eva serves continental breakfast on the lanai, which boasts views of the ocean, West Maui Mountains, and Haleakala. You're also welcome to use the full kitchen or barbecue. For movie nights, the common area has a gigantic flatscreen TV and fancy popcorn maker. This elegant B&B is centrally located in a residential Kihei neighborhood—next door to "Tutu Mermaids," above—about a half-mile from Kamaole III Beach Park and 5 minutes from Wailea's golf courses, shopping, and restaurants.

2828 Umalu Place (off Keonakai St., near Hwy. 31), Kihei. www.amauibedandbreakfast.com. © **800/943-5804** or 808/879-9103. 4 units. $99–$195 double. Children 11 and under stay free in parent's room. Rates include breakfast. **Amenities:** Wi-Fi (free).

WAILEA

Golfers should note that all Wailea resorts enjoy special privileges at the Wailea Golf Club's three 18-hole championship courses: Blue, Gold, and Emerald.

Note: You'll find the following hotels on the "Hotels & Restaurants in South Maui" map (p. 313).

Expensive

Andaz ★★★ The newest resort in Wailea opened to rave reviews—small wonder, considering its prime beachfront locale, chic decor, apothecary-style spa, and two phenomenal restaurants, including one by superstar chef Masaharu Morimoto. Foodies should look no further: Not only is Morimoto Maui's sushi bar a must, but the resort's other restaurant, **Ka'ana Kitchen,** might be *even better*. Before you eat, though, you'll want to freshen up in your room. Accommodations here aren't the island's largest, but they ramp up the style quotient a notch with crisp white linens, warm wood furniture, and midcentury accents. Wrap yourself in a plush robe and nosh on the complimentary minibar snacks from the sanctuary of your private lanai. Wander past the tiered infinity pools (which look best at night, when lit in a shifting palette of colors). Then hit gorgeous Mokapu Beach out front to snorkel, kayak, or paddle outrigger canoe. This resort is a dynamic blend of modern and ancient values. Visit with Kainoa Horcajo, the resort's Native Hawaiian cultural advisor, who leads ceremonial cleansings in the shorebreak at dawn and can teach you traditional arts such as braiding ti leaf lei and making coconut fiber cordage. Whatever you do, don't miss the **Awili Spa,** where you can mix your own massage oil and body scrubs. Yoga and fitness classes are complimentary. If you've got cash to spare, consider renting one of the resort's two-, three-, or four-bedroom villas—you'll have an entire wall that opens to the Pacific, a private plunge pool, and a Viking range to call your own. Andaz guests have golf privileges at Wailea Golf Club's three 18-hole championship golf courses nearby, as well as at the courses at Makena and Elleair.

3550 Wailea Alanui Dr., Wailea. www.maui.andaz.hyatt.com. ℂ **808/573-1234.** 198 units. $459–$599 double; $1,074–$1,149 1-bedroom suite; call for villa prices. Valet parking only $30. Complimentary welcome cocktail and snacks. **Amenities:** 3 restaurants, plus 24-hr. market; 3 bars; concierge; 24-hr. fitness center; use of Wailea Golf Club's 3 18-hole championship golf courses; 4 outdoor cascading infinity pools; 24-hr. room service; shuttle service; luxury spa w/steam rooms, lounge, and spa pool; watersports equipment rentals; Wi-Fi (free).

The Fairmont Kea Lani Maui ★★★ At first blush, this blinding-white complex of Arabian turrets and arches may look a tad out of place—but once you enter the orchid-filled lobby and see the big blue Pacific outside, there's no doubt you're in Hawaii. For the price of a regular room at the neighboring luxury resorts, you get an entire suite here—plus some extras. Each unit in the all-suite hotel has a kitchenette with granite countertop, living room with sofa bed (great for kids), spacious bedroom, marble bathroom fit for royalty (head immediately for the deep soaking tub), and large lanai with views of the pools, lawns, and Pacific Ocean. The two- and three-bedroom beachfront villas are perfect for families or couples traveling together. Each two-story unit has its own gourmet kitchen, washer/dryer, and private plunge pool just steps away from the white sand. Polo Beach is public, but feels private and secluded. Huge murals and artifacts decorate the resort's manicured property, which is home to several good restaurants, an excellent bakery and deli, and the brand-new Willow **Stream Spa.** Escape into this heavenly retreat to experience the rain showers, steam rooms, and warm lava-stone foot beds. Youngsters will enjoy building volcanoes in the 1,500-square-foot kids' club, while the entire family can get into rhythm paddling a Hawaiian outrigger canoe.

4100 Wailea Alanui Dr., Wailea. www.fairmont.com/kealani. ℂ **866/540-4456** or 808/875-4100. 450 units. $459–$1,049 suite (sleeps up to 4); from $1,750 villa. $30 resort fee. Valet parking $20; free self-parking. **Amenities:** 4 restaurants, plus gourmet bakery and deli; 3 bars; babysitting; children's program; year-round concierge; 24-hr. fitness center; use of Wailea Golf Club's 3 18-hole championship golf courses; 2 large swimming lagoons connected by a 140-ft. water slide and swim-up bar, plus an adults-only pool; 24-hr. room service; luxury spa and salon; use of Wailea Tennis Center's 11 courts (3 lit for night play) for special rates and pro shop; watersports equipment rentals and 1-hr. complimentary use of snorkel equipment; Wi-Fi (free).

Four Seasons Resort Maui at Wailea ★★★ This resort was perfect even *before* the management built the adults-only infinity pool with its underwater music system and swim-up bar. Now there aren't words to describe how luxurious you'll feel rubbing elbows with celebrities in this uber-elegant yet relaxed atmosphere. Perched above Wailea Beach's golden sand, the Four Seasons Resort Maui inhabits its own world, where poolside attendants anticipate your needs: cucumber slices for your eyes? Mango smoothie sampler? Or perhaps your sunglasses need polishing? The service for which this hotel chain is famous follows you throughout your stay. The spacious (roughly 600-sq.-ft.) guest rooms feature dream-inducing beds, deep marble bathtubs, walk-in showers big enough for two, and furnished lanais, most with superlative ocean views. (If you get stuck with a North Tower room over the parking lot, ask politely to be moved.) The sublime spa offers Kate Somerville facials and an incredible array of body treatments ranging from traditional Hawaiian to craniosacral and Ayurvedic massage. (As nice as the spa facility is, treatments in the oceanside thatched *hale* are even more idyllic). The resort's restaurants are some of island's best; room service here is a must. Finally, this might be the island's most kid-friendly resort: Perks include milk and cookies on arrival, toddler-proofing for your room (everything from furniture bumpers to toilet-seat locks), *keiki* menus in all restaurants, a high-tech game room, and the unmatched Kids for all Seasons program from 9am to 5pm—complimentary, of course.

3900 Wailea Alanui Dr., Wailea. www.fourseasons.com/maui. © **800/311-0630** or 808/874-8000. 380 units. $485–$985 double; $1,195–$1,295 Club Floor double; from $1,295 suite. Extra person $150 in Club Floor rooms. Children 17 and under stay free in parent's room. Packages available. Valet parking $25. **Amenities:** 3 restaurants, 3 bars (w/nightly entertainment); babysitting; free use of bicycles; complimentary children's program; concierge; concierge-level rooms; putting green; use of Wailea Golf Club's 3 18-hole championship golf courses; health club featuring outdoor cardiovascular equipment (w/individual TV/VCRs); 3 outdoor pools; room service; luxury spa and salon; 2 on-site tennis courts (lit for night play); use of Wailea Tennis Center's 11 courts (3 lit for night play); watersports equipment rentals and 1-hr. free use of snorkel equipment; Wi-Fi (free; $20 for premium).

Grand Wailea ★★★ Built by a Japanese multi-millionaire at the pinnacle of Hawaii's fling with fantasy megaresorts, the Grand Wailea is wildly popular with families and corporate groups. It's the grand prize in Hawaii vacation contests and the dream of many honeymooners. No expense was spared during construction: Some $30 million worth of original artwork decorates the grounds, much of it created expressly for the hotel by Hawaii artists and sculptors. More than 10,000 tropical plants beautify the lobby alone, and rocks hewn from the base of Mount Fuji adorn the Japanese garden. A Hawaiian-themed restaurant floats atop a man-made lagoon, and light filters majestically through the stained-glass walls of the wedding chapel. Guest rooms, too, come with lavish accouterments, like oversize bathrooms and plush bedding. But for kids, all that really matters is the resort's unrivaled pool: an aquatic playground with nine separate swimming pools connected by slides, waterfalls, caves, rapids, a Tarzan swing, a swim-up bar, a baby beach, and a water elevator that shuttles swimmers back to the top. If this doesn't sate them, an actual beach made of real golden sand awaits just past the resort hammocks. The Grand is also home to Hawaii's largest and most resplendent spa: a 50,000-square-foot marble paradise with mineral soaking tubs, thundering waterfall showers, Japanese furo baths, Swiss jet showers, and many other luxurious features. Dining options include **Amasia,** by celebrity chef Alan Wong, and **Humuhumunukunukuapuaa,** the aforementioned floating restaurant where you can fish for your lobster straight from the lagoon.

Minimalists may scoff, but the Grand Wailea's extravagance is worth experiencing even if you don't stay here.

3850 Wailea Alanui Dr., Wailea. www.grandwailea.com. ✆ **800/888-6100** or 808/875-1234. 780 units. $399–$1,130 double; from $1,030 suite; from $599 Napua Club Room (in Napua Tower); from $1,036 Hoolei Villas. Extra person $50 ($100 in Napua Tower). $25 daily resort fee. Valet parking only $30. **Amenities:** 7 restaurants; 4 bars; art and garden tours; babysitting; children's program; concierge; concierge-level rooms; use of Wailea Golf Club's 3 18-hole championship golf courses; fitness center; fitness classes; 5 Jacuzzis (including one atop a man-made volcano); adults-only outdoor pool; 2,000-ft.-long Activity Pool, featuring a swim/ride through grottoes; room service; scuba-diving clinics; shuttle service to Wailea area; Hawaii's largest luxury spa and salon; racquetball court; use of Wailea Tennis Center's 11 courts (3 lit for night play) and pro shop; watersports equipment rentals; Wi-Fi (free).

Hotel Wailea ★★   Built in 1990 for Japanese businessmen, this stylish boutique hotel is one of a kind in Wailea. Compared with the flashier resorts at the coastline, it's small, secluded, and serene—a perfect choice for honeymooners. The verdant grounds, fruit orchard, and koi ponds have been transformed into a modern oasis. Suites are spare but outfitted with modern luxuries: wide-planked wood floors, Hawaiian kapa-inspired prints on plush king-size platform beds, super-deep soaking tubs, and daybeds on the lanai. The tidy kitchenette features a two-burner Wolf stove and Sub-Zero pull-out-drawer refrigerator. Breakfast is provided by the excellent on-site restaurant, as is room service. The property sits above Wailea proper—giving it access to even more magnificent views. It's a 3-minute shuttle ride to the beach, and the hotel maintains a kiosk at Wailea Beach to supply you with umbrellas and chairs. Hotel staff will even load up your complimentary tote bag with towels and water and chauffeur you anywhere throughout Wailea and Makena in the resort Mercedes SUV. This isn't a place that nickel-and-dimes guests, and employees come to know you on a first-name basis. As this book went to press, the pool and spa were under renovation—but we expect great things. **Brides- and grooms-to-be, take note:** The lawn and gazebo at the hotel's entrance is a fairy-tale venue for weddings and receptions.

555 Kaukahi St., Wailea. www.hotelwailea.com. ✆ **808/954-7416.** 72 units. $211–$325 double; from $485 suite. Daily $25 resort fee. Extra person $40. Packages available. Valet parking $30. Rates include complimentary breakfast. **Amenities:** Restaurant; 2 bars; concierge; fitness center; outdoor pool; room service; complimentary shuttle service throughout Wailea; signing privileges at nearby Grand Wailea; spa; Wi-Fi (free).

Wailea Beach Marriott Resort & Spa ★★   Airy and comfortable, with touches of Hawaiian art throughout, this hotel fits into its sublime environment without overwhelming it. Eight buildings, all low-rise except for an eight-story tower, unfold along 22 luxurious acres of lawns and gardens punctuated by coconut palms and an exquisite infinity pool—you'll want to spend your entire vacation beneath the cabanas here. Positioned on a grassy slope between Wailea and Ulua beaches, the resort has plenty of sandy expanse to explore. Rooms have tile or wood floors, rattan furnishings, and lanais with views of the picturesque coastline. The small **Mandara Spa** offers an array of treatments, from massages to body wraps and rejuvenating facials in a very Zen atmosphere. Two things distinguish this property. First, it's probably the most affordable resort on the Wailea coast. Second, guests benefit from two fantastic restaurants, including the latest delicious venture by Sheldon Simeon, Hawaii's "Top Chef" finalist.

3700 Wailea Alanui Dr., Wailea. www.waileamarriott.com. ☎ **808/879-1922.** 554 units. $249–$825 double; from $485 suite. Packages available. Extra person $40. Daily $30 resort fee for local and long-distance calls, Internet access, self-parking, discounts on spa services, luau and snorkel-gear rental, and free kids' meals with purchase of adult entree. Valet parking $30. **Amenities:** 3 restaurants; 2 bars; babysitting; concierge; use of Wailea Golf Club's 3 18-hole championship golf courses; fitness center; outdoor pools (including adults-only and 1 for kids only); room service; full-service Mandara Spa w/steam rooms and whirlpools; use of Wailea Tennis Center's 11 courts (3 lit for night play) and pro shop; watersports equipment rentals; Wi-Fi ($15–$19).

MAKENA

Makena Beach & Golf Resort ★★ Located on stunning Maluaka Beach, this quiet resort is ideal for couples or families who want a genuine getaway. It's just a 5-minute drive from busy South Kihei, but feels worlds away. Two five-story wings surround lush gardens and meandering koi ponds. Nearly every room has a view of the Pacific Ocean with the island of Kahoolawe and tiny Molokini crater glittering on the horizon. Accommodations are spacious, with simple but elegant furnishings: granite countertops in the bathrooms and new carpeting in every room. The resort has a weekly calendar full of great activities—stargazing, s'mores and storytelling, sushi-making demos, ukulele lessons, oceanfront yoga, and even hour-long intro scuba lessons—all for free. (There's no daily resort fee, either.) Make sure to book your stay over a Sunday, when the resort's famous brunch is served at the Molokini Bar & Grille. (You won't need to eat for the rest of the day!) Outrigger-canoe trips launch from the golden sandy beach out front, as does the Kai Kanani sailboat. The reef here is good for snorkeling and frequented by sea turtles.

5400 Makena Alanui, Makena. www.makenaresortmaui.com. ☎ **800/321-6284** or 808/874-1111. 310 units. $239–$659 double; from $575 suite. Extra person $15. Packages available. **Amenities:** 4 restaurants; 2 bars; babysitting; free bike rental; concierge; fitness room; private golf course; 2 outdoor pools (1 for adults, 1 for children); room service; complimentary shuttle service throughout Wailea and Makena; day spa; 6 Plexipave tennis courts (2 lit for night play); watersports equipment rentals; Wi-Fi (free).

Upcountry Maui

MAKAWAO

Here you'll be (relatively) close to Haleakala National Park; Makawao is approximately 90 minutes from the entrance to the park at the 7,000-foot level (from there it's another 3,000 ft. and 45 min. to get to the top). Temperatures are 5° to 10° cooler than at the coast, and misty rain is common.

Aloha Cottage ★★ If getting away from it all is your goal, this exotic retreat in the eucalyptus forest above Makawao might be your place. On 5 luxuriously landscaped acres sits an octagonal cottage reminiscent of something you'd see in Southeast Asia. The interior is lavishly furnished with vaulted ceilings, teak floors, Oriental rugs, and intricate Balinese carvings. (Whenever you glance at your reflection in the magnificent bathroom mirror, you'll feel like royalty.) The kitchen's granite counters, gas stove, and teak cabinetry make cooking a pleasure. Olinda Road is a winding, narrow track that ascends through the trees above Makawao—coming and going from here is an adventure unto itself. After a day of exploring Maui, it's a sweet relief to enjoy a home-cooked dinner on the lanai, soak in the outdoor tub (built for two), and retire to the king-size cherrywood bed where you can stare through the skylight at the stars.

1879 Olinda Rd., Makawao. www.alohacottage.com. © **888/328-3330** or 808/573-8555. 1 cottage. $299 double. $100 cleaning fee. Not suitable for children under 10. **Amenities:** Wi-Fi (free).

Banyan Bed & Breakfast Retreat ★

Shaded by huge monkeypod trees, this upcountry estate on meandering Baldwin Avenue has a quaint old-Hawaii ambience. Accommodations include three suites within a beautifully restored 1927 plantation manager's house and four individual cottages. Each suite has a queen-size and a twin bed (perfect for families traveling with youngsters), a marble shower, a private entrance, a modest kitchenette, rich hardwood floors, and lovely antique furniture. The cottages feature similar amenities; some (such as Gardenia) have full kitchens and bathtubs. Each morning, Marty, the retreat's proprietor, delivers a continental breakfast to your door. Fruit trees and flowers decorate the property; hammocks and swings hang from the branches of the massive shade trees. Guests have the use of a 50-foot-long saltwater swimming pool, Jacuzzi, and 700-square-foot yoga and meditation studio equipped with yoga props and a sophisticated audio/video system. This fully handicapped-accessible retreat is ideal for groups, and the house, lavishly decorated with vintage Hawaiian furniture, can be rented as a whole. Makawao's restaurants and shops are just minutes away, and Paia's beaches are less than a 15-minute drive from here.

3265 Baldwin Ave. (less than a mile below Makawao), Makawao. www.banyantreehouse.com. © **808/572-9021.** 7 units. $175–$195 double room in house; $165–$190 cottage for 2. Extra person $30, children 12 and under $15. Cleaning fee $30–$40. Rates include breakfast. **Amenities:** Babysitting; Jacuzzi; outdoor pool; Wi-Fi (free).

Hale Ho'okipa Inn Makawao ★★

Cherie Attix restored this historic 1924 plantation-style home to its original charm, filling it with Hawaiian artwork, antique furniture (a giant oak armoire, wrought-iron bed frame, and vintage shutters repurposed as a headboard), and a generous dose of love. It's a 5-minute walk from the shops and restaurants of Makawao, 15 minutes from beaches, and an hour's drive from the top of Haleakala. The pretty guest rooms have separate outside entrances and private bathrooms—one with a claw-foot tub. The Kona Wing is a two-bedroom suite with use of the kitchen. In addition to a daily continental breakfast, Cherie offers guests fresh eggs from her hens. Unlike many B&B operators, she allows 1-night stays—perfect for hikers wanting a head start on Haleakala in the morning. Best of all: She sponsors a terrific "volunteer on vacation" program. Lend a hand at one of the dozen local organizations listed on her website and she'll knock 5 percent off of your stay at Hale Ho'okipa. (And the experience will undoubtedly be the highlight of your vacation.)

32 Pakani Place, Makawao. www.maui-bed-and-breakfast.com. © **877/572-6698** or 808/572-6698. 4 units. $140–$198 double. $15 surcharge for 1-night stays. Rates include continental breakfast. No children 9 or under allowed. **Amenities:** Wi-Fi (free).

Lumeria ★★

On Maui's scenic north shore, halfway between Paia and Makawao, a historic women's college has been lovingly restored as a boutique resort. Nestled into 6 lavishly landscaped acres are 2 dozen guest rooms, a resplendent lobby, yoga studio, meditation garden, and farm-to-table restaurant. A small but dazzling pool overlooks a valley full of waving sugarcane as hammocks sway in the ironwood trees. The crystals, sacred artwork, and objets d'art tucked into every corner contribute to the charmed ambience of this serene retreat. Rooms are smallish—nearly filled by their plush four-poster beds—but luxuriously appointed with Italian linens, Japanese tansu cabinets, and showers with river-rock floors. A stay includes access to daily yoga, meditation, horticulture, and aromatherapy classes, and breakfast for two at the chic, semi-private restaurant. Baldwin Beach is only 2½ miles away; the staff will set you up with stand-up paddleboard equipment or pack a picnic for an excursion to Hana.

1813 Baldwin Ave., Makawao. www.lumeriamaui.com. © **855/579-8877.** 25 units. $299–$349 double; $449 suite. Resort fee $25. **Amenities:** Restaurant; concierge; 2 Jacuzzis (1 saltwater); outdoor pool; watersports equipment rentals; Wi-Fi (free).

Peace of Maui ★ In tiny Haliimaile, the blink-and-you'll-miss-it-town in between Paia and Makawao, you'll find this casual and extremely convenient place to stay. Choose between one of seven rooms in the main house and a modest two-bedroom cottage with a full kitchen, day bed, and a large lanai that overlooks sugarcane and pineapple fields. Rooms in the "lodge" are fairly spartan, with shared bathroom and kitchen privileges, but if you're looking for an affordable upcountry headquarters, this is a prime spot. If you happen to be traveling during a full moon, keep your eyes open at night: I've seen moonbows more than once here.

1290 Haliimaile Rd., Makawao. www.peaceofmaui.com. © **808/572-5045.** 1 unit. $75–$105 double; $185 cottage. 7-night minimum. $10 per extra person. $75 cleaning fee. **Amenities:** Barbecue; outdoor Jacuzzi; Wi Fi (free).

Ginger Falls Vacation Rental ★★ Hidden amid the sweet-smelling ginger, rustling bamboo, and banana trees in Maliko Gulch, this romantic cottage is perfect for honeymooners and Hawaiian art fans. The moment you step into this artistically decorated retreat, you will be delighted by the extra touches throughout: high-thread-count sheets on the queen-size bed, gallery-quality artwork, and river-rock accents in the large walk-in shower. The kitchen is stocked with everything you could possibly want. The large screened porch has an inviting daybed—perfect for curling up with a good book—and the outdoor Jacuzzi will keep you toasty, even on misty evenings. At the juncture of country roads that connect Paia, Makawao, and Haiku, this secluded spot is 15 minutes from the beach and 5 minutes from multiple restaurants. Your hosts, Bob Flint and his wife, Sonny, are extra-friendly and grow and roast their own coffee on the property.

355 Kaluanui Rd., Makawao. www.wildgingerfalls.com. © **808/573-1173.** 1 unit. $155–$170 double. 3-night minimum. Payment through PayPal. **Amenities:** Barbecue; outdoor Jacuzzi; watersports equipment; Wi-Fi (free).

East Maui: On the Road to Hana

Note: You'll find the accommodations in this section on the "Upcountry & East Maui" map (p. 325).

PAIA

Paia Inn ★★ Embedded in colorful Paia town, this vibrant boutique inn offers a stylish introduction to Maui's north shore. The inn is comprised of several vintage buildings that get progressively closer to the turquoise waters of Paia Bay. The nine rooms in the main building hang right over Hana Highway's restaurants, surf shops, and cafes. After a day of mingling with big-wave surfers, yoga teachers, and other north-shore dwellers, slip up to your soundproofed room and

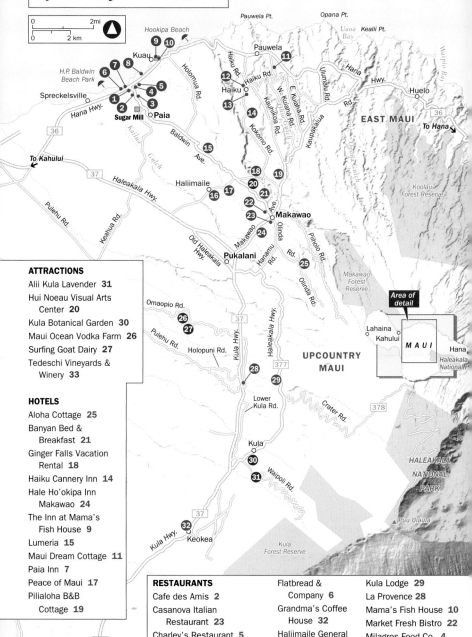

Upcountry & East Maui

PACIFIC OCEAN

Pauwela Pt.   Opana Pt.

Hookipa Beach

Kuau

H.P. Baldwin
Beach Park

Spreckelsville

Hana Hwy.

Sugar Mill Paia

Pauwela Pt.

Uaoa Bay   Kealii Pt.

Pauwela

Hana Hwy.

Huelo

EAST MAUI

To Hana →

Haiku Rd.   Haiku Rd.

Haiku

Ulumalu Rd.

W. Kuiaha Rd.

E. Kuiaha Rd.

Kauhikoa Rd.

Kaupakalua Rd.

To Kahului

Haleakala Hwy.

Baldwin Ave.

Haliimaile

Pulehu Rd.

Keahua Rd.

Kokomo Rd.

Makawao

Olinda Rd.

Piiholo Rd.

Koolau Forest Reserve

Old Haleakala Hwy.

Makawao Ave.

Pukalani

Hanamu Rd.

Olinda Rd.

Makawao Forest Reserve

Area of detail

Lahaina   Kahului   *M A U I*   Hana

Haleakala National P.

Omaopio Rd.

Pulehu Rd.   Holopuni Rd.

Kula Hwy.

Haleakala Hwy.

UPCOUNTRY MAUI

Lower Kula Rd.

Kula

Waipoli Rd.

Crater Rd.

HALEAKALA NATIONAL PARK

▲ Puu Ulaula

Kula Hwy.   Keokea

Kula Forest Reserve

Ulupalakua

sink into the 500-thread-count sheets. The owner's impeccable style seeps into every corner of the inn, from the organic Malie bath products in the travertine-tiled showers to the antique Balinese drawers repurposed as sink cabinets. The one- and two-bedroom suites in the next buildings are spacious, secluded retreats where you'll feel immediately at home. My favorite, no. 10, has a private outdoor shower and four-poster daybed. But it can't rival the three-bedroom beach house nestled up against the golden, sandy beach. Idyllic in every way, this miniature mansion is outfitted with a Viking stove, Jacuzzi, gorgeous artwork, and huge outdoor living room. It's exclusive enough to attract celebrities, who've made it their Maui headquarters. And there's more: At press time, a tapas restaurant and rooftop bar was under construction.

93 Hana Hwy., Paia. www.paiainn.com. © **800/721-4000** or 808/579-6000. 17 units. $199–$259 double; $359–$450 1-bedroom suite; $499 2-bedroom suite, $999 3-bedroom beach house. **Amenities:** Restaurant; watersports equipment and access; Wi-Fi (free).

KUAU

The Inn at Mama's Fish House ★★   The Gaudí-esque architect responsible for Mama's Fish House also works his magic on a handful of private suites and cottages next door. In a coconut grove on a secluded north-shore beach, the Inn at Mama's features gracious accommodations with plenty of extras: daily maid service; large private lanais with barbecues; imaginative Hawaiian artwork; fresh flowers tucked into large, fluffy bath towels; terrific toiletries; free laundry; and a 15-percent discount at what many consider to be the finest restaurant on Maui. Each unit is unique; the luxury junior suites are especially classy, with deep soaking tubs and travertine showers. One- and two-bedroom cottages sit amid the tropical garden's red ginger, while a few two-bedroom units face the ocean. Restaurant guests can stroll about the property until 10pm, but privacy is assured in your cottage's large enclosed lanai. In the morning, you'll be greeted with a tray of fresh fruit and banana bread. The inn sits on a small, sandy beach known simply as Mama's. It's better for exploring tide pools than for swimming—though swimmable Baldwin Beach is a short drive away and the thrills of Hookipa are right next door. Keep in mind that this is the windward side of the island—and it's often windy and rainy. You'll be perfectly situated here for a trip to Hana.

799 Poho Place (off the Hana Hwy. in Kuau), Paia. www.mamasfishhouse.com. © **800/860-HULA** or 808/579-9764. 12 units. $175 garden studio double; $250 1-bedroom (sleeps up to 4); $325 junior suites double; $275–$575 2-bedroom (up to 6). **Amenities:** Free laundry; restaurant discount; Wi-Fi (free).

HAIKU

Haiku Cannery Inn ★★   This is one of my favorite B&Bs, located in the most convenient (and sunny) section of Haiku's rainforest. Built in 1921 for the manager of the bygone pineapple cannery, this charming estate has been converted into a pastoral inn. Tropical fruit trees abound on the 3-acre property, alongside sweet-smelling plumeria and gingers. Guests are welcome to help themselves to papayas, avocados, bananas, and citruses. In the main house are two large, attractively furnished guest rooms and a modest suite with a small kitchenette. The two-bedroom cottage across the lawn has a nicely stocked kitchen and a two-car garage—perfect for families or travelers needing to stow windsurfing or scuba equipment. Much of the inn's handcrafted furniture and flooring was made from eucalyptus and mango trees milled on the property. Local artists contributed the exceptional paintings decorating nearly every wall. Rates include a breakfast of fresh fruits and pastries from the local bakery, lovingly prepared by the resident innkeeper, Benni Denbeau. The long-time Maui resident has marvelous suggestions for where to go and what to do. She raised her family here; the entire property is child-friendly. The inn is just uphill from Haiku's great restaurants, grocery store, and day spa.

1061 Kokomo Rd., Haiku. www.haikucanneryinn.com. 🕿 **808/283-1274.** 4 units. $115–$135 double; $145 suite; $200 cottage. $25 cleaning fee for stays under 3 nights. **Amenities:** Day spa; Wi-Fi (free).

Maui Dream Cottage ★   Danielle Chomel and her husband rent out a piece of their hidden paradise in Haiku. She's an expert orchid grower, and her blooms and bromeliads cover every inch of the property, from the entrance gate onwards. He's a classic car buff, and if you ask nicely he might show you his immaculate antique Porsche and Devins. Tucked in a corner of their fecund fruit orchard and garden, the two-bedroom cottage is comfortably furnished with a smallish kitchen, washer/dryer, pull-out futon bed in the living room, and a California king–size bed with Tempurpedic mattress in each of the cozy bedrooms. The off-the-beaten-path location is quiet and restful, offering a window into how real islanders live. It's a 3-minute walk to a great breakfast spot, but you'll have to drive 20 to 25 minutes to access Paia's restaurants, shopping, and beaches.

265 W. Kuiaha Rd., Haiku. www.mauidreamcottage.com. 🕿 **808/575-9079.** 1 unit, with shower only. $130 double. Extra person $10. 7-night minimum. **Amenities:** Wi-Fi (free).

Pilialoha B&B Cottage ★   In the heart of Haiku, this country cottage is set on a large lot with towering eucalyptus trees and some 200 varieties of roses blooming in the garden. Tastefully appointed in green and white, the cottage has warm wood floors and is private, clean, and spacious. The kitchen and closets are extremely well equipped—you'll find everything you need here, from a rice cooker to beach towels, coolers, yoga mats, and fleece jackets for Haleakala sunrise trips. Your hosts, Machiko and Bill, live on-site and are happy to offer sightseeing suggestions. If you mention you're heading up the mountain to Machiko, she'll likely send you off with a thermos of coffee and her homemade bread. The cottage is minutes from the restaurants and shopping of Haiku and Makawao and a short drive from Paia's beaches. In the winter months when Haiku weather can be cool and rainy, the gas fireplace is a welcome amenity.

2512 Kaupakalua Rd. (½-mile from Kokomo intersection), Haiku. www.pilialoha.com.🕿 **808/572-1440.** 1 unit. $145 double. Suitable for a couple only. 3-night minimum. No credit cards. **Amenities:** Watersports equipment; Wi-Fi (free).

At the End of the Road in East Maui: Hana

Note: You'll find Hana accommodations on the map on p. 275.

EXPENSIVE

Travaasa Hana ★★★   Ahhh . . . arriving at Travaasa (formerly the Hotel Hana Maui) is like letting out a deep sigh. The atmosphere is so immediately relaxing you'll forget everything beyond this remote seaside sanctuary. Nestled in the center of quaint Hana town, the 66-acre resort wraps around Kauiki Head, the dramatic point where Queen Kaahumanu was born. All of the accommodations here are wonderful, but the Sea Ranch Cottages (adults-only, except over the holidays) are downright heavenly. These duplex bungalows face the craggy shoreline, where horses graze above the rolling surf. Floor-to-ceiling sliding doors open to spacious lanais, some with private hot tubs. Book your stay here a la carte or all-inclusive; the latter includes three meals, snacks, and a treatment in one of the planet's nicest spas. Whichever you choose, your room will be stocked with luxurious necessities: plush beds with organic linens, gorgeous Hawaiian artwork, bamboo floors, giant soaking tubs, complimentary bottled water, Fair Trade coffee, homemade banana bread, and irresistibly scented bath products. You'll be far from shopping malls and sports bars, but exotic red-, black-, and white-sand beaches are just a short walk or shuttle ride away. The genuinely hospitable staff will set you up with numerous activities, many at no charge. Ride horseback past waterfalls, try stand-up paddling in the bay, practice your archer's aim, take a tour of a nearby tropical fruit farm, or learn to throw a traditional Hawaiian fishing net. Rooms have no TVs (the Club Room has a giant one), but there are nightly talk-story sessions by around the fire. This is luxury in its purest form.

5031 Hana Hwy., Hana. www.travaasa.com/hana. © **888/820-1043.** 66 units. $350 single a la carte; $600 single inclusive; $400 double a la carte; $925 double inclusive. **Amenities:** 2 restaurants (w/Hawaiian entertainment Sun evenings); 2 bars (entertainment nightly); concierge; fitness center/fitness classes; complimentary use of the 3-hole practice golf courses (complimentary use of clubs); 2 outdoor pools; limited room service; luxury spa; tennis courts; Wi-Fi (free).

MODERATE

Bamboo Inn ★　This oceanfront "inn" is really just three exquisite suites, all with private lanais overlooking Waikaloa Beach's jet-black sand. The sumptuous accommodations include beds with ocean views, separate living rooms, and either a full kitchen or kitchenette. Naia, the largest unit, sleeps four and has a deep soaking tub on the lanai. The rooms and grounds are decorated with artifacts that your friendly and knowledgeable host, John Romain, collected during travels across Asia and Polynesia. Carved Balinese doors, Samoan tapa cloths, coconut wood floors, and a thatched-roof gazebo (where breakfast is served) add a rich and authentic elegance to a naturally lovely location. Waikaloa isn't great for swimming, but it's an incredible spot to watch the sunrise. All of Hana is within easy walking distance.

Uakea Rd. (between Waikaloa and Keanini rds.; look for sign), Hana. www.bambooinn.com. © **808/248-7718.** 3 units. $195–$265 double. Extra person $15. Rates include continental breakfast. 2-night minimum. **Amenities:** Beach equipment; Wi-Fi (free, but only available in outdoor gazebo).

Hamoa Beach House　Just around the bend from famed Hamoa Beach, this enormous three-bedroom, two-bathroom house is a great option for families or big parties. The rich woods, earthy tones, and rattan furnishings imbue the spacious interior of this '70s-era house with a cozy, nostalgic feeling. The living room has cathedral ceilings and two-story-tall windows that open up to the ocean. The upstairs bedrooms have vaulted ceilings, outdoor lanais, and a total of four king-size beds. A sweet little library is stocked with beach reading. Beneath the coconut palms outside, you'll find hammocks, a stone barbecue grill, a Jacuzzi, and an outdoor shower—essentially everything you need to enjoy Hana to the fullest.

487 Haneoo Rd., Hana. www.vrbo.com/242599. © **808/248-8277.** 1 unit. $525 house (sleeps up to 6). 3-night minimum. **Amenities:** Beach equipment; Wi-Fi (free).

Hana Kai Maui Resort ★ "Condo complex" might not mesh with your idea of getting away from it all in Hana, but Hana Kai is truly special. Set on Hana Bay, the individually owned units are dotingly furnished and feature many hotel-like extras, such as organic bath products and fresh tropical bouquets. Studios and one- and two-bedroom units have kitchens and private lanais—but the corner units with wraparound ocean views are worth angling for. Gorgeously appointed Kaahumanu (no. 5) has a daybed on the lanai that you may never want to leave. For couples, Popolana (no. 2) is small but sweet, with woven bamboo walls and a Murphy bed that no one ever puts up. And why would you? You can lie in it and stare out to sea or, at daybreak, watch the sun rise straight out of the ocean.

1533 Uakea Rd., Hana. www.hanakaimaui.com. © **800/346-2772** or 808/248-8426. 18 units. $185–$245 studio double; $210–$260 1-bedroom (sleeps up to 4); $425 2-bedroom. Extra person $15. 2-night minimum. Children 6 and under stay free in parent's room. **Amenities:** Wi-Fi (free).

INEXPENSIVE

Hana's Tradewind Cottages ★ On a 5-acre flower farm, nestled amid pink gingers and scarlet heliconias, you have a choice of two rentals: the Hana Cabana or the Tradewinds Cottage. Each is sequestered in its own private corner of the farm and has a full kitchen, private hot tub, carport, and barbecue. Best for couples, the Cabana is a studio with vaulted ceilings and coconut palm–themed decor. The two-bedroom Tradewinds Cottage has a queen-size bed in one room and two twins in the other, one bathroom (with shower only), and a sizable living room and front porch. Days here are indescribably serene, and stars fill the sky at night. Guests are welcome to pick fruit from the surrounding banana and avocado trees, and you'll almost certainly want to take a box of tropical flowers home with you.

135 Alalele Place (the airport road), Hana. www.hanamaui.net. © **800/327-8097** or 808/248-8980. 2 units. $175 studio double; $175 2-bedroom double. Extra person $25. 2-night minimum. **Amenities:** Wi-Fi (free, but service not consistent).

Camping

Camping on Maui can be extreme (inside a volcano) or laidback (by the sea in Hana). It can be wet, cold, and rainy; or hot, dry, and windy—often all on the same day. If you're heading for Haleakala, remember that U.S. astronauts trained for the moon inside the volcano; pack survival gear. You'll need both a swimsuit and raincoat if you're bound for Waianapanapa. Bring your own equipment—Maui has no place to rent camping gear.

Camp Olowalu Halfway to Lahaina on the Honoapiilani Highway, this cozy campground is nestled right up to one of the island's best coral reefs. It's perfect for avid snorkelers and, during the winter months, whale-watchers. (You can hear them slap their fins against the sea's surface at night—a magical experience.) Tent sites sit beneath shady kiawe trees—watch out for thorns—on flat, relatively soft ground. The porta-potties and outdoor showers are rustic; the campground is next to the highway and can be a tad noisy—but for $15, you'll have the gently lapping Pacific outside your tent's door. Six A-frame cabins with bathrooms, showers, and a kitchen are available for group rentals. You can also rent kayaks on-site.

800 Olowalu Village Rd., Lahaina (off Honoapiilani Hwy.). www.campolowalu.com. © **808/661-4303.** 6 cabins, 36 tent sites. Cabins: $600 for all 6 (sleeps 36); contact camp for individual rates. Tent sites: $15 per night adults ($5 per night children 6–12). No credit cards.

Haleakala National Park ★★   This stunning national park offers a variety of options for campers throughout its diverse landscape: **car camping** at Hosmer's Grove halfway up the summit or at Oheo Gulch in Kipahulu; **pitching a tent** in central Haleakala wilderness; or cozying up in one of the crater's **historic cabins.** The first three are free (aside from the $10 park entrance fee). No permit is required, but there's a 3-night limit. The cabins cost a flat $75, whether you rent them for one or twelve people.

Hosmer Grove, located at 6,800 feet, is a small, open grassy area surrounded by forest and frequented by native Hawaiian honeycreepers. Trees protect campers from the winds, but nights still get very cold; sometimes there's even ice on the ground up here. This is an ideal spot to spend the night if you want to see the Haleakala sunrise. Come up the day before, enjoy the park, take a day hike, and then turn in early. Facilities include a covered pavilion with picnic tables and grills, chemical toilets, and drinking water.

On the other side of the island, **Oheo Campground** is in the Kipahulu section of Haleakala National Park. You can set up your temporary home at a first-come, first-served drive-in campground with tent sites for 100 near the ocean. It has a few tables, barbecue grills, and chemical toilets. No food or drinking water is available, so bring your own. Bring a tent as well—it rains 75 inches a year here. Call the **Kipahulu Ranger Station** (© **808/248-7375**) for local weather.

Inside the volcano are two **wilderness tent-camping** areas: **Holua,** just off the Halemauu Trail and **Paliku,** 10 miles away, near the Kaupo Gap at the eastern end of the valley. Both are well over 6,000 feet in elevation and chilly at night. Facilities are limited to pit toilets and nonpotable catchment water. Water at Holua is limited, especially in summer. No open fires are allowed inside the volcano, so bring a stove if you plan to cook. Tent camping is restricted to the signed area, and is not allowed in the horse pasture or the inviting grassy lawn in front of the cabins. Permits are issued at park headquarters daily from 8am to 3pm, on a first-come, first-served basis on the day you plan to camp. Occupancy is limited to 25 people in each campground.

Also inside the volcano are three **wilderness cabins,** built in 1937 by the Civilian Conservation Corps. Each has 12 padded bunks (bring your own bedding), a table, chairs, cooking utensils, a two-burner propane stove, and a wood-burning stove with firewood. The cabins are spaced so that each one is a nice hike from the next: **Holua** cabin is 3.7 miles down the zigzagging Halemauu Trail; **Kapalaoa** cabin is 5.5 miles down the Sliding Sands Trail; and **Paliku** cabin is the farthest, at 9.3 miles down Sliding Sands and across the moonscape to the crater's eastern end. In spring and summer, the endangered *'ua'u* (Hawaiian dark-rumped petrel) can be heard soaring back home to its burrows in the high cliffs. Some campers and hikers exit through the Kaupo Gap—8.6 miles to the remote Piilani Hwy. You can reserve cabins up to 6 months in advance on the park's new reservation website (www.recreation.gov; © **877/444-6777**). You're limited to 2 nights in one cabin and 3 nights total in the wilderness each month.

Note: All wilderness campers must watch a 10-minute orientation video at the park's visitor center.

Haleakala National Park, at top of Crater Rd., and at Kipahulu Visitor Center, 12 miles past Hana on Hana Hwy. www.nps.gov/hale. © **808/572-4400.** 3 cabins, 100-plus tent sites. $75 flat rate for cabins; tent campers free (aside from $10 park entrance fee). Cabins by reservation only.

Polipoli State Park   High up on the slope of Haleakala, at 6,200 feet in elevation, this state park has extensive trails that wind through conifer forests reminiscent of the Pacific Northwest. It's frequently cold and foggy here—be prepared for extra-chilly nights! One eight-bunk cabin is available for $99; it has a cold shower and a gas stove but no electricity or drinking water (bring your own). Tent-campers can pitch on the grass nearby. Reserve on the website (or in person at the Wailuku office) and print out your permit, which must be displayed. **Note:** This park is only accessible by four-wheel-drive vehicle.

9¾ miles up Waipoli Rd., off Kekaulike (Hwy 377); 4-wheel drive vehicle recommended. By reservation only c/o State Parks Division, 54 S. High St., Room 101, Wailuku. www.hawaiistateparks. org/camping. © **808/984-8109.** 4 units. $99 per cabin per night (sleeps up to 6). $18 for 1st tent-camper, $3 for additional campers. 5-night maximum.

Waianapanapa State Park ★   The 12 rustic cabins tucked in the *hala* (pandanus) groves of Waianapanapa State Park were once the best lodging deal on Maui—but years of use have taken their toll. At press time, the state was planning renovations; call before you book to check the status. In the meantime, you can still pitch a tent above the black-sand beach on Pailoa Bay. Watch the sun rise out of the ocean and beat the crowds to the freshwater cave pool. There's an on-site caretaker, along with restrooms, showers, picnic tables, shoreline hiking trails, and historic sites. Bring rain gear and mosquito protection—this is the rainforest, after all.

End of Wai'anapanapa Rd., off Hana Hwy. By reservation only c/o State Parks Division, 54 S. High St., Room 101, Wailuku. www.hawaiistateparks.org/camping. © **808/984-8109.** 10 units. $90 per cabin per night (sleeps up to 6). $18 for 1st tent-camper, $3 for additional campers. 5-night maximum.

WHERE TO EAT ON MAUI

When it comes to dining in Maui, all I can say is: Come hungry and bring your wallet. Dining has never been better on the Valley Isle, which is presently producing numerous enterprising and imaginative chefs. The farm-to-table concept has finally taken root on this bountiful island where, in past years, up to 90 percent of the food has been imported. Today, chefs and farmers collaborate on menus, filling plates with tender micro-greens and heirloom tomatoes picked that morning. Fishers reel in glistening *opakapaka* (pink snapper), and ranchers offer up flavorful cuts of Maui-grown beef.

A new crop of inspired chefs is taking these ripe ingredients to new heights. At **Ka'ana Kitchen,** chef Isaac Bancaco is outshining his celebrity neighbor, "Iron Chef" Masaharu **Morimoto** (who recently brought his high-octane Japanese fusion cuisine to Wailea). Both are outstanding; make time for each. Next door at **Migrant,** "Top Chef" finalist Sheldon Simeon is showcasing gourmet local-style dishes with Filipino accents. Up the street, chefs Brian Etheredge and Chris Kulis are making traditional Italian seem brand-new again at **Capische.**

The pioneers of Hawaii Regional Cuisine are still stirring things up in the kitchen as well. Alan Wong recently opened **Amasia** at the Grand Wailea; Peter Merriman opened a location in Kapalua with gasp-inducing views; and Mark Ellman of **Mala Ocean Tavern,** added **Honu** and **Migrant** to his empire.

Stellar dining experiences all, but expect to pay for them. Still, you don't *have* to spend a fortune to eat well on Maui. Although the old-fashioned, multi-generational mom-and-pop diners are disappearing, eclipsed by the sophisticated newcomers, Maui does have a few budget eateries, noted below. But if you want to feast, there's never been a better time to do so on Maui.

Central Maui

The **Queen Kaahumanu Center,** the structure that looks like a white "Star Wars" umbrella in the center of Kahului, at 275 Kaahumanu Ave. (10 min. from Kahului Airport on Hwy. 32), has a popular food court. Eateries include **Ramen Ya,** for a steaming bowl of noodles, and **Maui Tacos.** Outside the food court, but still in the shopping center, is **Ruby's,** a kid-friendly '50s-style diner dishing out burgers, fries, and shakes. When you leave Kaahumanu Center, take a moment to gaze at the West Maui Mountains to your left from the parking lot.

MODERATE

Bistro Casanova ★ MEDITERRANEAN   For a casual but classy meal in Kahului, head to this Mediterranean bistro for sweet and savory crepes, duck salad, tasty osso buco, traditional Italian pastas, or a giant bowl of paella. Packed with a business crowd at lunch, and a more relaxed atmosphere at dinner (unless there's a big show at the nearby Maui Arts & Cultural Center—then it will be hopping), this attractive restaurant has a private room for big parties and a full bar for *pau hana* (after work) drinks.

33 Lono Ave., Kahului. www.casanovamaui.com. © **808/873-3650.** Lunch main courses $9–$18; dinner main courses $14–$38. Mon–Sat 11am–9:30pm.

Marco's Grill & Deli ITALIAN   Located just outside the airport, where the roads to Upcountry, West Maui, and South Maui converge, Marco's offers decent Italian fare in an upscale diner with black-and-white booths and white linens on the tables. Portions tend to be huge, and everything is made in house, from the meatballs, sausages, and burgers to the sauces and salad dressing. Favorites include chicken Parmesan and vodka rigatoni with imported prosciutto. Hot and cold sandwiches and entrees are served all day; classic breakfasts are offered in the morning.

395 Dairy Rd., Kahului. © **808/877-4446.** Breakfast $6–14; lunch and dinner main courses $12–$39. Daily 7:30am–10pm (Sat–Sun till 1am).

A Saigon Cafe ★★ VIETNAMESE   It's hard to say which is better at this beloved neighborhood restaurant—the delicious, fresh Vietnamese cuisine or the hilarious waiters who make wisecracks while taking your order. For years, owner Jennifer Nguyen didn't have a sign above her restaurant, which is tucked beneath Wailuku's Main Street bridge. She didn't need advertising; her food speaks for itself. Whatever you order—the steamed *opakapaka* with ginger and garlic, one of a dozen soups, the catfish simmering in a clay pot, or the fragrant lemongrass curry—you'll notice the freshness of the flavors. Nguyen grows many of her own vegetables and herbs and even sprouts her own mung beans. My favorites are the Buddha rolls dunked in spicy peanut sauce and the Vietnamese "burritos," with grilled meat or tofu, vermicelli noodles, pickled carrots, and fresh herbs wrapped in rice paper. You make the latter tableside—it's tricky at first, but fun.

1792 Main St., Wailuku. © **808/243-9560.** Main courses $9–$27. Daily 10am–9:30pm (Sun till 8:30pm). Heading into Wailuku from Kahului, go over the bridge and take the 1st right onto

Central Ave.; then take the 1st right on Nani St. At the next stop sign, look for the building with the neon sign that says open.

INEXPENSIVE

Down to Earth ORGANIC HEALTH FOOD   Stop in here for a healthful vegetarian snack or a bag full of local organic produce. During mango season, this full-service natural-foods store carries as many as three different locally grown varieties of the golden-fleshed fruit—worth their weight in gold. The deli includes a do-it-yourself noodle bar, inventive salad options, lasagna, chili, curries, and dozens of tasty dishes, presented at hot and cold stations. Deli attendants can whip up a faux Reuben sandwich or tasty meatless burger for you. The upstairs dining area is convenient and comfortable. It also sells gluten-free and vegan products.

305 Dairy Rd., Kahului. www.downtoearth.org. ✆ **808/877-2661.** Self-serve hot buffet and salad bar and deli, food sold by the pound, average $7–$12 for a plate; sandwiches $6–$11. Store hours Mon–Sat 7am–9pm, Sun 8am–8pm.

Sam Sato's NOODLES/PLATE LUNCHES   To make a Maui local's mouth water, all you have to do is mention Sam Sato's dry mein. The al dente noodle dish, served with slices of char siu pork, bean sprouts, green onions, and broth on the side, epitomizes simple, Hawaii-style comfort food. Hidden away in Wailuku's industrial area, this humble, family-owned eatery dates back to 1933. It's one of Maui's last ma-and-pa establishments, and everything on the menu is under $10. Sit at the cafeteria-like counter and strike up a conversation with your neighbor. Try your dry mein with a side order of grilled teriyaki meat sticks. On the way out, stock up on Sam Sato's other famous specialty: baked *manju*, flaky pastries filled with sweetened lima or adzuki beans.

At the Millyard, 1750 Wili Pa Loop, Wailuku. ✆ **808/244-7124.** Plate lunches $7.50–$9. No credit cards. Mon–Sat 7am–2pm; 7am–4pm bakery and preordered takeout items.

West Maui

LAHAINA

Expensive

The Feast at Lele ★★ POLYNESIAN   This memorable evening begins with resonant Hawaiian chants and trumpeting conch shells. A canoe lands on the beach in front of your dinner table, delivering dancers who will regale you with stories of Polynesia while you dine on culinary specialties from each island nation. The Feast at Lele stands out from other luaus as the choice for gourmands. Award-winning chef James McDonald partnered with performers from the Old Lahaina Luau (see "Luau, Maui Style" on p. 364) to create this culinary and cultural immersion. While most luau seating is en masse, guests here sit at intimate, elegantly set tables. The Pacific Ocean serves a backdrop for brilliantly costumed dancers performing the traditional dances of Hawaii, New Zealand, Tahiti, and Samoa. As the evening unfolds, you progress from island to island. During the opening hula, you'll sample Hawaiian fish with mango sauce and *imu*-roasted kalua pig. While watching the exciting Maori *haka*, you'll dine on New Zealand sea bean and duck salad. Pace yourself; each of the four savory courses includes three dishes—and then there's dessert! The swish of ti-leaf skirts and beat of the drums enhances the meal's exquisite flavors; it's a sensory experience even for the most jaded luau-goer.

505 Front St., Lahaina. www.feastatlele.com. ☎ **866/244-5353** or 808/667-5353. Reservations required. Set 5-course menu (includes all beverages) $120 adults, $90 children 2–12. Apr 1–Sept 30 daily 6:30–9:30pm; Oct 1–Mar 31 daily 5:30–8:30pm.

Gerard's ★★★ FRENCH Chef Gerard Reversade has called Hawaii home for nearly 4 decades, but his French accent hasn't lost one cédille. The cuisine at his charming residence-turned-restaurant beneath the Plantation Inn in Lahaina is equally authentic, applying impeccable French technique to ripe Maui ingredients. I never would've imagined that a simple chilled cucumber soup could be transcendent—but this one is, its delicacy amplified by goat cheese and fresh dill. The roasted *opakapaka* served with fennel fondue and spiked with hints of orange and ginger is stellar, as is the grilled Hawaiian filet with salsify au gratin. Reversade is every bit as much of a baker as a chef, and the savory dishes that incorporate pastry—such as the Hamakua mushroom appetizer—are delights. The dessert menu has no fewer than 10 excellent offerings, including a Valrhona chocolate mousse with pistachio ice cream and an aristocratic *millefeuille*—pastry leaves layered with fresh berries and lemon curd.

At the Plantation Inn, 174 Lahainaluna Rd., Lahaina. www.gerardsmaui.com. ☎ **808/661-8939.** Reservations recommended. Main courses $39–$60. Daily 6–9pm.

Lahaina Grill ★★★ NEW AMERICAN For more than 2 decades, this classy restaurant has been collecting awards and accolades for its perfectly executed island cuisine, gracious service, and great wine list. The striking decor—splashy artwork by local painter Jan Kasprzycki, pressed-tin ceilings, and warm lighting—creates an appealing atmosphere. The bar, despite lacking an ocean view, is among the busiest in town and often features special pricing. The menu hasn't strayed much over the years; fans will still find their favorites: the zesty "toy box" heirloom-tomato salad served in a martini glass, the aromatic Kona coffee–roasted rack of lamb, and the divinely rich seared ahi with foie gras, truffle oil, and fig compote. If you're planning a special event or a large party, you can book one of two private rooms and design your own menu with the chef.

127 Lahainaluna Rd., Lahaina. http://lahainagrill.com. ☎ **808/667-5117.** Reservations required. Main courses $39–$86. Daily 5:30–9 or 10pm. Bar daily 6–10pm (closing earlier on slow nights).

Pacific'O Restaurant ★★ CONTEMPORARY PACIFIC RIM You can't get any closer to the ocean than these tables overlooking the beach at 505 Front Street. Chef Anton Haines rose from the kitchen ranks to take the helm at this award-winning restaurant; his enthusiasm shines through in a new menu featuring ripe produce from the restaurant's very own O'o Farms. Start with rich lobster ravioli mascarpone and sea urchin emulsion or a bright, citrus-y ceviche with plantain and sweet potato chips. Paired with watercress, the pulled smoked pork draws from island and Southern sensibilities, and the seared scallops unite east and west with coconut carrot dashi, edamame, pea tendrils, and *inamona* (Hawaiian kukui nut relish). Vegetarians will delight in the quinoa mixed with miso, hearts of palm, heirloom carrots, and the prettiest beets you've ever seen. This is a superb and relatively affordable lunch spot: indulge in ginger-crusted fish or Kalbi beef tacos and glass of spicy Syrah while watching the ships sail by.

505 Front St., Lahaina. www.pacificomaui.com. ☎ **808/667-4341.** Reservations recommended. Main courses $13–$16 lunch, $30–$45 dinner. Daily 11:30am–4pm and 5:30–9:30pm.

Restaurants in Lahaina & Kaanapali

PACIFIC OCEAN

KAANAPALI

Kahekili Beach
■ Train Depot
Puukolii Rd.

Kaanapali Royal (North) Golf Course
Kekaa Dr.
Kaanapali Pkwy.

Whalers Village 4

Ka'anapali Beach
Nohea Kai Dr.
Kaanapali Kai (South) Golf Course

LK & PR Sugar Cane Train

Honoapiilani Hwy.

Hanakao'o Beach Park

Lahaina Civic Center

Wahikuli Beach Park

Kaniau Rd.
Lokia St.
Malanai St.
Wahikuli Rd.
Fleming Rd.

Anakea Rd.

Kapunakea St.

Lahaina Cannery Mall

Mala Wharf

Puunoa Point

Keawe St.
Ulupono St.
Kupuohi St.
Kahoma Stream
Lahainaluna Rd.
Lahaina Bypass

Front St.
Kenui St.
Baker St.
Papalaua St.

Train Depot
Pioneer Sugar Mill

Lahaina Center

LAHAINA

Dickenson St.
Luakini St.
Wainee St.
Front St.
Shaw St.

Lahaina Small Boat Harbor

505 Front St. (Shops & Restaurants)

PACIFIC OCEAN

Area of detail

Kahului
MAUI
Haleakala National Park

Scale: 1/2 mi, 1/2 km

Aloha Mixed Plate 10
Choice Health Bar 13
CJ's Deli & Diner 2
Duke's Beach House 1
The Feast at Lele 23
Fleetwoods on Front Street 15
Gerard's 16
Honu 9
Japengo 6
Lahaina Coolers 18
Lahaina Grill 17
Leilani's on the Beach 4
Leoda's 24
Mala Ocean Tavern 8
Maui Sunrise Café 21
Maui Swiss Cafe 20
Maui Taco 14
Old Lahaina Luau 11
Pacific'O 22
Penne Pasta Café 19
Roy's 5
Sangrita Grill & Cantina 3
Son'z Steakhouse 7
Star Noodle 12

Moderate

Fleetwood's on Front Street ★ AMERICAN   Rock and Roll Hall of Famer Mick Fleetwood ventured into the restaurant business in 2012 with commendable results. His snazzy eatery occupies the top two floors of a lovingly restored three-story building on Front Street. For lunch, try a lobster salad sandwich on a sweet brioche bun or French dip made with lamb. For dinner, choose from locally grown salads (including a decent chicken kale salad with apple-fig vinaigrette), fresh fish entrees, or a Harley-Davidson Hog burger—hold the Harley. In truth, the food can be a little lackluster, but the atmosphere is outstanding. The dining room's cozy booths and wraparound bar evoke an older, more sophisticated era. But the real draw is the rooftop dining—plus the live entertainment. Head here at sunset for fried calamari and a "lime and the coconut" cocktail. *Tips:* Nightly at 6pm, local musicians offer a short free performance, ranging from bagpipes to Hawaiian chanting. Mick and his celebrity friends often pop in to play a set. When it's raining, however, the upstairs seating is closed.

744 Front St., Lahaina. www.fleetwoodsonfrontst.com. © **808/669-6425.** Reservations recommended. Main courses $18–$45. Daily 11am–10pm.

Honu ★★★ PIZZA/SEAFOOD   If you can, snag one of the oceanfront tables where the gentle tide nearly tickles your toes and you can spy on the green sea turtles for whom this restaurant is named. In 2011, renowned local chef Mark Ellman opened this restaurant right beside his popular Mala Ocean Tavern, and it's equally as delightful as (if not more than) its neighbor. Each item on Honu's diverse menu is guaranteed to please someone in your party, from the fried oyster sandwiches and authentic Neapolitan pizzas to the wok-fried Dungeness crab. Ingredients are tantalizingly fresh and flavors sing. The Middle Eastern kale salad will turn doubters into believers: Finely chopped kale is massaged with preserved lemon vinaigrette and tossed with bittersweet walnuts, rich and salty pecorino shavings, sweet slivers of chewy dates, and pomegranate seeds that burst on the tongue. Ellman aims to win everyone's heart, with an entire gluten-free menu, a

---

Ululani's Shave Ice

David and Ululani Yamashiro are near-religious about shave ice. At their multiple shops around Maui, these shave-ice wizards take the uniquely Hawaiian dessert to new heights. It starts with the water: Pure, filtered water is frozen, shaved to feather-lightness, and patted into shape. This mini snowdrift is then doused with your choice of syrup—any three flavors from calamansi lime to lychee to red velvet cake. David makes his own gourmet syrups with local fruit purees and a dash of cane sugar. The passionfruit is perfectly tangy, the coconut is free of cloying artificial sweetness, and the electric green kiwi is studded with real seeds. Add a "snowcap" of sweetened condensed milk, and the resulting confection tastes like the fluffiest, most flavorful ice cream ever. Locals order theirs with chewy mochi morsels, sweet adzuki beans at the bottom, or tart li hing mui powder sprinkled on top (Lahaina: 819 Front St. and 790 Front St.; Kahului: 333 Dairy Rd.; Kihei: 61 S. Kihei Rd.; and Maalaea: Maalaea General Store, 132 Maalaea Rd.; www.ululanis shaveice.com; © **360/606-2745;** daily 10:30am–6:30pm [10:30am–10pm in Lahaina]).

keiki menu, and an extensive offering of draft beers, single malt scotches, and handcrafted cocktails.

1295 Front St., Lahaina. www.honumaui.com. ✆ **808/667-89390.** Reservations recommended. Main courses $34–$44. Daily 11am–9:30pm.

Lahaina Coolers ★ AMERICAN/INTERNATIONAL The huge marlin hanging above the bar and persimmon-colored walls set a cheery tone at this casual indoor/outdoor restaurant. Breakfasts are satisfying here; the huevos rancheros come in a sizzling cast-iron skillet heaped with kalua pork, and you have your choice of eggs Benedict: classic; Cajun, with seared fish and salsa; and the "Local" with kalua pork and sweetbreads. On Sunday, breakfast is served until 1pm. Spicy entrees dominate the lunch menu, such as Evil Jungle Pasta spiked with peppery Thai peanut sauce or whaler's stew—a poor man's cioppino. Prices increase at dinner, but are still a fraction of what you'd pay at most Front Street establishments. Dinner is served until midnight.

180 Dickenson St., Lahaina. www.lahainacoolers.com. ✆ **808/661-7082.** Main courses $10–$15 breakfast, $10–$16 lunch, $15–$27 dinner. Daily 8am–midnight.

Mala Ocean Tavern ★★★ AMERICAN/INTERNATIONAL I hope Mark Ellman, one of the 12 pioneers who launched the Hawaii Regional Cuisine movement in the 1980s, never stops making restaurants. His tiny tavern overlooking Mala Wharf in Lahaina is as perfect as can be. Mala Ocean Tavern is much brighter and classier than the name "tavern" suggests, and the oceanfront seating lets diners peers down on sea turtles foraging in the surf break. The bartenders know their business, and the complimentary edamame guacamole alerts your taste buds that something delicious is about to happen. The menu offers both health-conscious and hedonistic options, from the gado gado (a vegan Indonesian rice dish heaped with sugar-snap peas and coconut peanut sauce) to the adult mac and cheese (an insanely rich and delicious oven-baked medley of three cheeses and Hamakua mushrooms). From the oyster shooters to the whole wok-fried fish, you can't go wrong. The weekend brunch is one of the island's tastiest, with local organic eggs served in Benedicts, chilaquiles, and huevos rancheros.

1307 Front St. (across from the Lahaina Cannery Mall's Safeway grocery store), Lahaina. www.malaoceantavern.com. ✆ **808/667-9394.** Main courses $12–$27 lunch, $18–$42 dinner; brunch $8–$15. Mon–Fri 11am–9:30pm; Sat–Sun 9am–9:30pm.

Star Noodle ★★ NOODLES/FUSION This hip noodle house at the top of Lahaina's industrial park burst like a comet across Maui's dining scene. Judging by the hour-long wait for a seat at dinner, the fireworks haven't faded yet. The menu of noodles and share plates is deceivingly simple. The hapa ramen, with its smoky pork and spicy miso broth, is guaranteed to be unlike any you've had before. Each dish is a gourmet twist on a local favorite; the Lahaina fried soup isn't soup at all but thick and chewy house-made noodles tossed with ground pork and bean sprouts. The *ahi avo* is a divine mix of fresh red tuna and buttery avocado swimming in a pool of lemon-pressed olive oil and spiked with sambal. With its stylish bar, long communal table, Shepard Fairey artwork, and glamorous washrooms, this casual eatery has an urban feel. From the window seats you can catch a hint of an ocean view—just enough to remind you that you're still in Hawaii.

286 Kupuohi St., Lahaina. www.starnoodle.com. ✆ **808/667-5400.** Main courses $7–$30. Daily 10:30am–10pm.

Inexpensive

Aloha Mixed Plate ★ PLATE LUNCHES/BEACHSIDE GRILL   Right on the ocean, in the midst of tourist-heavy Lahaina, this local favorite dishes out budget-friendly breakfasts and island-style plate lunches: fresh-made chow mein, teriyaki chicken, and Korean kalbi ribs with the proverbial two-scoops-rice and macaroni salad. If you have a hankering for a loco moco (hamburger, rice, and an egg ladled with gravy), this is your spot. It's also a sweet hideaway at happy hour (3–6pm). Toss out your dietary restrictions, order the furikake garlic fries, coconut prawns, and a few Maui microbrews. The banana caramel cheesecake lumpia is out of this world.

1285 Front St., Lahaina. www.alohamixedplate.com. © **808/661-3322.** Main courses $6–$14. Daily 8am–10pm.

Choice Health Bar ★★ GOURMET DELI/CAFE   This health-conscious juice bar and cafe is where the beautiful people in Lahaina come to fuel up. After a taxing morning of sunbathing or paddling past sea turtles, re-energize here with a sunrise acai bowl drizzled in honey or a "macca-chino"—a frothy blend of banana, cacao, and shijilat. What, you've never heard of shijilat? Don't worry; the friendly chefs behind the counter will give you the lowdown on this Ayurvedic superfood and all of the other exotic treats on the menu. Daily lunch specials include wholesome, creamy soups and savory raw-violis—a colorful raw reinvention of the Italian pasta. The plate lunches are an edible rainbow of scrumptious kale salad, coconut-garlic quinoa, and ruby red beet soup, with a bonus tiny but delicious dessert square on the side.

1087 Limahana Place (off of Honoapiilani Hwy.), Lahaina. www.choicehealthbar.com. © **808/661-7711.** Breakfast and lunch main courses $6–$12. Mon–Sat 8am–4pm.

Leoda's ★★ SANDWICHES/BAKERY   Who would have thought? A pie place in tiny Olowalu, an apostrophe of a town halfway to Lahaina? As you approach the counter, you'll see the reason the line stretches to the door: a glass case full of banana and coconut pies slathered in fresh whipped cream. The sweet pies—especially the chocolate macadamia nut praline—are intergalactic, but the savory pies are good, too. For breakfast, Leoda's serves an outstanding seared ahi Benedict with pesto, watercress, avocado, and eggs raised nearby. Ingredients are locally sourced and sinfully delicious; for lunch, the Ham'n sandwich is hot and juicy mess of duroc ham, island pesto, melted Jarlsberg cheese, and apricot-tomato jam on buttered rye bread. The seasonal fried Brussels-sprout salad is mouth-wateringly delicious. Leoda's belongs to the Star Noodle, Old Lahaina Luau, and Aloha Mixed Plate restaurant family—a crew that knows its business. The eatery's bright, welcoming decor pays homage to Maui's bygone plantation days.

820 Olowalu Village Rd. (off of Honoapiilani Hwy), Lahaina. www.leodas.com. © **808/662-3600.** Breakfast items $3–$19; lunch and dinner items $4–$16. Daily 7am–8pm.

Maui Sunrise Café ★ GOURMET DELI/CAFE   For a bargain lunch or breakfast, follow the surfers to this hole-in-the-wall cafe located just off Front Street. (The address says Front St., but it's really off of Market, across from the library.) The kitchen turns out tasty breakfast burritos, a lox Benedict with home-fried potatoes, and decent sandwiches. Service can be slow, but the prices can't be beat in this neighborhood. Eat in the covered patio out back or take your lunch to go and sit in the adjoining park.

693A Front St., Lahaina. ✆ **808/661-8558.** Breakfast items under $11; lunch items $7–$12. No credit cards. Daily 6am–3pm.

Maui Swiss Cafe SANDWICHES   This cafe boldly announces itself with flamingo-pink fringed umbrellas over its sidewalk seating. Inside is a selection of crepes, sandwiches, and ice creams, along with 12 Internet stations—perfect for printing out your flight's boarding pass. The affordable and tasty crepes all come with side salads and sour cream. The signature melted sandwiches—such as the barbecue roast beef—come with Dijon mustard and cream cheese.

640 Front St., Lahaina. www.swisscafe.net. ✆ **808/661-6776.** Sandwiches and crepes $8–$12. Daily 8am–8pm.

Penne Pasta Café ITALIAN/MEDITERRANEAN   With outdoor seating on a Lahaina side street, this casual spot features delicious Italian and Mediterranean cuisine. Order at the counter, and the manager delivers your pasta, pizza, or salad Niçoise to your table. You'll get a sit-down meal at takeout prices. The penne puttanesca, baked penne with braised beef, and lamb osso buco (Wed night special) are wonderful. Also try the oven-roasted butternut squash simmered in almonds and sage.

180 Dickenson St., Lahaina. www.pennepastacafe.com. ✆ **808/661-6633.** Main courses $9–$18. Daily 11am–9:30pm.

KAANAPALI
Expensive
Japengo ★★ SUSHI/PACIFIC RIM   Meander into this beautiful restaurant for superb Japanese-influenced entrees and inspired sushi, sashimi, and hand rolls. The open-air dining room hanging over the Hyatt pool is divided into multiple private nooks, evoking the feel of a Japanese teahouse. Look around for signs of *tengu,* the long-nosed mythological trickster who serves as the restaurant's mascot. The *moriawase,* or "chef's selection," is a masterpiece. Depending on what the fishermen reeled in that day, the sashimi platter may include achingly red tuna, translucent slivers of Big Island *hirame* (flounder), poached local abalone, creamy wedges of *uni* (sea urchin), or raw New Caledonia prawn. Jay Ledee, the skilled sushi chef, garnishes this bounty with nests of peppery daikon, aromatic shiso leaves, and—a rare treat—fresh wasabi from the Big Island. For a few extra dollars, you can grate the watery, spicy root with an elegant sharkskin grater. Far superior to the usual powdered variety, it's worth a trip to Japengo just to try it.

At the Hyatt Regency Maui Resort, 200 Nohea Kai Dr., Kaanapali. www.maui.hyatt.com. ✆ **808/ 661-1234.** Main courses $24–$50. Daily 5–10pm.

Roy's ★★ HAWAII REGIONAL CUISINE   Roy Yamaguchi, the James Beard award–winning chef and one of the pioneers of Hawaii Regional Cuisine, now owns eponymous restaurants all over the world. His Maui dining room—recently relocated from Kahana—suffered somewhat in the move, and the new location, overlooking the Kaanapali golf course, lacks the flair of the old spot. But chef Joey Macadangdang is still in the kitchen sending out perfect braised ribs with Dijon crust, crab-stuffed mahimahi, and rich misoyaki butterfish. His flexes his creativity with nightly specials, such as thyme-seared ono sprinkled with microgreens atop parsnip puree. The restaurant now serves lunch from 11am to 2pm and a bar menu from 2 to 5pm, which features the "canoe for two," an appetizer platter of ahi poke, pork lumpia, chicken potstickers, Szechuan short ribs, and skewered shrimp. Hallelujah for the bartender who created the "Skinny Colada," a cocktail that delivers the flavor of a piña colada without the overwhelming milky cream.

Tip: Two words: chocolate soufflé. This signature dessert is so tantalizing I sometimes call in an order to eat at the bar. It takes 20 minutes to prepare, so let your waiter know you want it in advance. And when it arrives, wait a moment for it to cool—don't burn your tongue on the hot lava chocolate!

2290 Kaanapali Pkwy., Kaanapali. www.roysrestaurant.com. © **808/669-6999.** Lunch main courses $18–$32; dinner main courses $27–$50. Daily 11am–10pm.

Son'z Steakhouse ★ STEAKHOUSE   Descend a palatial staircase for dinner at Son'z, where tables overlook a lagoon with white and black swans swimming by. The culinary team here recently rebranded this restaurant as a steakhouse; imagine Ruth's Chris with twice the flavor plus a fairy-tale atmosphere. Chef Geno Sarmiento knows how to prepare protein; his filet is on point with "Mauishire" sauce, as is the New Zealand rack of lamb with fig sauce and kohlrabi potato puree. Sides are generally sold separately; choose from grilled asparagus, truffle mac and cheese, or the loaded baked potato: a decadent spud cooked low and slow (200° for 4 hr.) and sinfully stuffed with mascarpone, bacon bits, truffle butter, chives, and Parmesan. Finish with Portuguese sweet bread French toast, vanilla gelato, and sweetly tart local bananas set aflame, Foster's style.

At the Hyatt Regency Maui Resort, 200 Nohea Kai Dr., Kaanapali. www.sonzrestaurant.com. © **808/667-4506.** Main courses $29–$55. Daily 5:30–10pm.

Moderate

Duke's Beach House ★ PACIFIC RIM   There are few more beautiful places to enjoy breakfast than here, facing Kahekili Beach. This restaurant mimics an open-air plantation home and is decorated with memorabilia chronicling the life of Duke Kahanamoku, the famous Hawaiian surfer, Olympic swimmer, movie star, and unofficial Ambassador of Aloha. It's part of the TS Restaurants family, which includes Kimo's, Hula Grill, and Leilani's on Maui, Keoki's on Kauai, and Duke's in Waikiki—among others. The menu reflects much of what you'll find at the other locales: "onolicious" French toast made with Molokai sweet bread, various omelets, and steel-cut oats for breakfast; coconut shrimp and "beach boy" burgers for lunch; macadamia-nut-crusted fish and steak for dinner; and the signature hula pie for dessert. What sets this restaurant apart is its gracious sea-breeze-kissed locale, the "sleepy head" breakfast items served through lunch, and the kitchen's commitment to serving locally raised beef, eggs, and vegetables. Add to that live music during the "aloha hour" daily from 3 to 5pm.

At Honua Kai Resort & Spa, 130 Kai Malina Pkwy., North Kaanapali Beach. www.dukesmaui.com. © **808/662-2900.** Breakfast items $5–$15; lunch main courses $10–$15; dinner main courses $20–$33. Daily 7:30am–9:30pm.

Leilani's on the Beach ★★ STEAK/SEAFOOD   Chef Ryan Luckey now heads the kitchen at Leilani's, which means that everything on the menu just rose three or four points in deliciousness. He's amped up the offerings from generic surf-and-turf to include miso-glazed snapper on black forbidden rice and Jidori chicken with crispy gnocchi, Waipoli watercress, and upcountry ratatouille. The appetizers are miniature meals: poached scallops sprinkled with black Hawaiian salt, braised Duroc pork belly with pickled heirloom carrots, and exquisite ravioli stuffed with ricotta and dressed in Meyer lemon vinaigrette. The **Beachside Grill**—the tables underneath the colorful umbrellas that bank right up to Kaanapali Beach—features a separate, more casual menu. Here you can people-watch while snacking on Cajun-rubbed fish tacos or a kalua pork Cuban and tossing back a Kaanapali cosmo. *Tip:* Ask for the Olala menu, which includes some of the best entrees for just $20.

At Whalers Village, 2435 Kaanapali Pkwy., Kaanapali. www.leilanis.com. ✆ **808/661-4495.** Reservations suggested for dinner. Beachside Grill lunch and dinner main courses $12–$18; Leilani's dinner main courses $23–$33. Beachside Grill daily 11am–11pm. Leilani's daily 5–9:30pm.

Sangrita Grill & Cantina ★★ MEXICAN   This popular new cantina pays homage to Mexico's most inventive gourmet cuisine. The owner, Paris Nabavi, imports *chapulines* (tiny grasshoppers) straight from Oaxaca and serves chorizo with house-made cheese. The rotisserie chicken is mouthwateringly delicious, as are the duck *carnitas* spiced with fig mole. I could eat the jicama slaw by the bucketful—luckily a deli case by the door is stocked with take-away salsas, slaws, and other savory items. The a la carte entree portions are somewhat small, but everything on the menu is fresh, from the house-made corn-and-flour tortilla chips to the trio of guacamoles. Chunks of ripe local avocado are mixed with pomegranate seeds, pico de gallo, and chipotle-spiced pineapple. The bar features a tequila shrine with 30 premium tequila and mescal varieties—perfect for mixing with the restaurant's namesake, sangrita.

At the Fairway Shops at Kaanapali, 2580 Kekaa Dr. (just off the Honoapiilani Hwy.), Kaanapali. www.sangritagrill.com. ✆ **808/662-6000.** Main courses $15–$19. Daily 11am–10pm.

Inexpensive

CJ's Deli & Diner ★ AMERICAN/DELI   Need a break from resort prices? Head to this happening eatery just off of Honoapiilani Highway in Kaanapali. Prices are so low you won't believe you're still on Maui. The atmosphere is colorful and slightly chaotic, with a huge billboard menu that spans the back wall, shelves stuffed with souvenirs and brochures, and a . . . basketball hoop? Practice your free throw while debating over which huge, delicious breakfast to order: a spinach-stuffed omelet, smoked salmon bagel, or French toast made with Hawaiian sweet bread. Lunch ranges from grilled panini sandwiches to fish and chips, mochiko chicken, and barbecue ribs. Kids have their own clever menu with happy-face pancakes and squid-eyes soup—just joking. If you're heading out to Hana or up to Haleakala, stop by for a box lunch. Toppings are packed separately so sandwiches don't get soggy. You can even order online for to-go pickup.

At the Fairway Shops at Kaanapali, 2580 Kekaa Dr. (just off the Honoapiilani Hwy.), Kaanapali. www.cjsmaui.com. ✆ **808/667-0968.** Breakfast items $5–$10; lunch items $8–$19; Hana Lunch Box and Air Travel Lunch Box $12 each. Daily 7am–8pm.

HONOKOWAI, KAHANA & NAPILI

Note: You'll find the restaurants in this section on the "Hotels & Restaurants in West Maui" map (p. 309).

Moderate

Maui Brewing Co. BREWPUB   The island's only microbrewery offers beer flights at the bar, excellent pub fare—much of it beer-battered—and ice cream floats made with coconut porter instead of root beer! (The brewery makes a fine root beer, too.) You can try limited-release brews here, along with the company's standards: Bikini Blonde Ale, Big Swell IPA, Mana Wheat, and the aforementioned rich and chocolatey coconut porter. Note the cute lamps made from miniature kegs. This eco-friendly, community-minded business regularly donates a portion of its sales to the Maui Forest Bird Recovery Project.

At the Kahana Gateway Shopping Center, 4405 Honoapiilani Hwy. www.mauibrewingco.com. ✆ **808/669-3474.** Main courses $12–$25. Daily 11am–9:30pm; late-night menu 9:30pm–midnight; Sun brunch 7am–3pm during football season (Sept–Jan).

Sea House Restaurant PACIFIC RIM Old-fashioned and a bit dated, this oceanfront restaurant at the Napili Kai Beach Resort is a throwback to earlier days. But the view here can't be beat. Breakfast is lovely under the umbrellas outside, overlooking serene Napili Bay. The oven-baked Crater pancake is a special treat, made with custard batter and sprinkled with powdered sugar and lemon. Sunset is a good time to come, too. Sit at the Whale Watcher's Bar and order classic cocktails and crispy tempura artichokes.

At the Napili Kai Beach Resort, 5900 Honoapiilani Hwy. www.napilikai.com. ✆ **808/669-1500.** Main courses $7–$12 breakfast, $10–$16 lunch, $24–$38 dinner; appetizer menu $3–$6 served 2–5pm. Daily 7am–9pm.

Inexpensive

Maui Tacos MEXICAN Many years ago, Mark Ellman launched this restaurant chain, dedicated to Mexican food with "Mauitude." Now it has locations as far away as Minnesota. Ellman has since moved on, but his healthful take on fast food is still worth a try. Menu choices include fish tacos, chimichangas, and "surf burritos," loaded with charbroiled chicken or slow-cooked Hawaiian pork, black beans, rice, and salsa. Other locations are at Lahaina Square, Lahaina (✆ **808/661-8883**); Kamaole Beach Center, Kihei (✆ **808/879-5005**); Piilani Village, Kihei (✆ **808/875-9340**); and Kaahumanu Center, Kahului (✆ **808/871-7726**).

At Napili Plaza, 5095 Napili Hau St., Lahaina. www.mauitacos.com. ✆ **808/665-0222.** All items $5–$12. Mon–Sat 9am–9pm; Sun 9am–8pm.

Pizza Paradiso Mediterranean Grill ITALIAN/MEDITERRANEAN The pledge on the wall at Pizza Paradiso—to use organic, local ingredients wherever possible and to treat employees like family—gives a hint to the quality of food served at this Honokowai hot spot. The large-ish menu includes gourmet and gluten-free pizzas with terrific toppings (such as barbecue chicken, smoked Gouda, and cilantro), chicken schawarma with tahini, lamb gyros, tasty kabobs, pastas, and more. The kitchen makes its own meatballs, out of grass-fed Maui Cattle Company beef, and its own sauces and dressings. Whatever you order, save room for dessert! The tiramisu is an award-winner, and the locally made coconut gelato should be.

At the Honokowai Marketplace, 3350 Lower Honoapiilani Rd., Kaanapali. www.pizzaparadiso. com. ✆ **808/667-2929.** Pastas $9–$11; pizzas $16–$27. Daily 10am–9pm.

KAPALUA

Note: You'll find the restaurants in this section on the "Hotels & Restaurants in West Maui" map (p. 309).

Expensive

Merriman's Kapalua ★★ PACIFIC RIM   This may be most beautiful restaurant location in the state. Merriman's Kapalua sits on a rocky point jutting out into the Pacific, overlooking picturesque Kapalua Bay and the island of Molokai in the distance. As you might have guessed, it belongs to Peter Merriman, a James Beard award–winning chef who helped launch the Hawaii Regional Cuisine movement in the 1990s and has eponymous restaurants on the Big Island and Kauai. He continues to champion the "farm-to-table" concept here, serving Keahole lobster with roasted upcountry vegetables and Lehua taro cakes with plump and meaty Hamakua mushrooms and Hirabura Swiss chard. Fans swear by his wok-charred ahi, dressed in wasabi cilantro and served with curried hearts of palm, a tangle of pohole ferns, and a sultry pyramid of black forbidden rice. For the full Merriman's experience, order the "Mix Plate," an entree sampler that includes the aforementioned ahi, crispy mahimahi with beet ponzu, and filet mignon with whole-grain mustard atop creamed Kula corn. The Waialua molten chocolate purse is a highlight, particularly when paired with the Smith Woodhouse port, which counteracts the phyllo pastry's dryness. To really experience the sensational scenery, book a reservation just before sunset. If twilight tables are booked, come anyway and enjoy a handcrafted Mai Tai with lilikoi foam on the large patio out on the point. The seats around the cozy fire pit are a stone's throw from the water. It's an exceedingly romantic spot; don't be surprised if you see a "Just Maui'd" couple stroll by or witness a neighboring diner propose.

One Bay Club Place, Kapalua Resort, Lahaina. www.merrimanshawaii.com. ✆ **808/669-6400.** Reservations recommended. Dinner main courses $29–$65. Daily 5:30–9pm. Point Bar menu daily 3–9pm.

Moderate

Pineapple Grill ★★ PACIFIC RIM   It's hard to go wrong in Kapalua: Every restaurant, it seems, has arresting views and menus to match. Pineapple Grill is no exception—in fact, for years it has led the pack. This gracious dining room on the Bay golf course offers views of the azure Pacific in one direction and the misty West Maui Mountains in the other. The menu has some real winners; my favorites are the Asian braised short ribs served with house-made kim chee, and the pistachio-encrusted ahi with coconut-scented forbidden black rice. The wine program is inspired; the glass-enclosed cellar is huge, and on Wednesday select bottles are 50 percent off and glasses are discounted 25 percent. The signature dessert is irresistible: moist pineapple upside-down cake with Hana Bay dark-rum sauce and macadamia nut ice cream. For late risers (or those who simply crave Belgian waffles or huevos "carne asada" rancheros with spiced filet mignon), breakfast is served until 2:30pm.

At the Kapalua Golf Club Bay Course, 200 Kapalua Dr., Kapalua. www.pineapplekapalua.com. ✆ **808/669-9600.** Reservations recommended for dinner. Main courses $8–$16 breakfast and lunch, $25–$50 dinner. Daily 8am–9pm.

Plantation House Restaurant ★★ PACIFIC RIM   Now part of the Cohn Restaurant group (which also owns Pineapple Grill and two dozen other dining rooms in California) this gracious clubhouse is a dramatic destination for breakfast, lunch, or dinner. Amid lush golf greens, tables benefit from panoramic ocean views—so make sure to arrive early enough to enjoy them. Chef Jojo

Vasquez's menu features simple yet inventive preparations. Look for delicious accents inspired by molecular gastronomy: basil pearls, lobster foam, compressed pineapple. Vasquez spent time in Europe studying with some of the most innovative culinary minds of our time and knows how to weave innovation into traditional comfort foods. His *kampachi* tartare, lightly dressed in dashi-soy and decorated with a spicy nasturtium flower, is bright and fresh. The *monchong* (pomfret), served in tamarind-coriander broth, is a perfect balance of sweet, sour, and salty flavors. At breakfast, enjoy a bowl of flawlessly ripe tropical fruit or choose from "Six Degrees of Benediction," a half-dozen Benedicts made with such delicacies as lox, roasted Maui vegetables (superb), or seared ahi and wasabi hollandaise.

At the Kapalua Golf Club Plantation Course, 2000 Plantation Club Dr., Kapalua. www.cohn restaurants.com/plantationhouse. ✆ **808/669-6299.** Reservations recommended. Main courses $8–$17 breakfast, $12–$18 lunch, $27–$42 dinner. Daily 8am–9pm.

Sansei Seafood Restaurant & Sushi Bar ★★ PACIFIC RIM/SUSHI   D. K. Kodama collects accolade after accolade for his extensive menu of Japanese and East-meets-West delicacies. With its creative take on sushi (think foie gras nigiri and "Pink Cadillac" rolls with eel, shrimp, *tamago,* and veggies wrapped in light pink rice paper), the menu scores higher with adventurous diners than with purists. But expertly sliced sashimi platters and straightforward gobo rolls will accommodate even the pickiest sushi snobs. Both the small and big plates are meant for sharing: The lobster and blue crab ravioli, misoyaki butterfish, and agedashi tofu are each so rich and savory you'll fight over the last bites. The Dungeness crab ramen ranks as my favorite dish—I like to inhale the fragrant truffle broth flecked with cilantro, Thai basil, and jalapeños. For dessert, I stick to simple green tea ice cream, though most people go for tempura-fried ice cream or the Granny Smith apple tart with homemade caramel sauce. ***Tip:*** On Thursday and Friday nights, a rousing karaoke session erupts at the bar from 10pm to 1am and sushi is 50 percent off. At the second location in Kihei Town Center, Kihei (✆ **808/879-0004**), sushi is 50 percent off on Sunday and Monday from 5 to 6:30pm.

600 Office Rd., Kapalua Resort, Kapalua. www.sanseihawaii.com. ✆ **808/669-6286.** Reservations recommended. Main courses $16–$43. Daily 5:30–10pm.

South Maui

KIHEI/MAALAEA

Note: You'll find the Kihei restaurants in this section on the "Hotels & Restaurants in South Maui" map (p. 313).

Moderate

Cafe O'Lei Kihei ★★ STEAK/SEAFOOD   Over the years, chefs Michael and Dana Pastula have opened multiple Cafe O'Lei restaurants throughout Maui (in Makawao, Lahaina, Wailuku, Maalaea, and Napili), and every one of them has been a winner. This one is the nicest of all. The open, airy dining room is casual and inviting, with tables separated by sheer curtains, hardwood floors, a big circular bar in the center of the restaurant, and a sushi bar and brick oven in back. The food is delicious and a bargain to boot. You can't beat quinoa salad or curry chicken salad for $10 or the daily plate lunch for $8—especially in such an elegant, sit-down atmosphere. (Call ahead for a midday table—locals flood this place during their lunch break.) For dinner, the Maui onion soup (baked in the wood-burning oven) is a savory treat with fresh thyme and brandy. The *togarashi* (chili) and sesame-seared ahi with ginger butter sauce and wasabi aioli over steamed rice is as good as you'll find at fancier restaurants, here for nearly half the price. This is a great place to bring a group—the diverse menu offers something for everyone, from prime rib to sushi and even pizza with gluten-free crust.

2439 S. Kihei Rd., Kihei. http://cafeoleirestaurants.com. ℰ **808/891-1368.** Reservations recommended. Main courses $7–$13 lunch, $15–$27 dinner. Daily 10:30am–3:30pm and 4:30–9:30pm.

Monsoon India ★ INDIAN   If there's one thing Maui could use more of, it's Indian flavors. Thank goodness for Monsoon India, a humble restaurant at the north edge of Kihei—without it, we'd have to board a plane to enjoy piping-hot naan bread and crisp papadum. The chicken korma here is creamy and fragrant, the chana masala spicy and satisfying. Even the simple dal curry is delightful. With tables that overlook Maalaea Bay, this serene spot is lovely just before sunset—particularly during winter when whales are jumping. *Note:* The open-air dining room is closed when it rains.

In the Menehune Shores Bldg., 760 S. Kihei Rd., Kihei. ℰ **808/875-6666.** Main courses $15–$24. Daily 5–9pm; Wed–Sun 11:30am–2pm.

Pita Paradise ★ GREEK/MEDITERRANEAN   If you're craving a gyro or kabob, this is your place. Fresh, flavorful Greek food is cooked to order, served with creamy *ziziki* sauce and rice pilaf. Owner Johnny Arabatzis, Jr., catches his own fish, which he prepares with dill scallionaise and roasted red peppers. The Kihei location serves casual, order-at-the-counter fare, while the upscale Wailea location is a sit-down restaurant with courtyard tables serenaded by a trickling fountain. The baklava ice cream cake is exquisite—though definitely enough to share. Prices are higher in Wailea (where there's live music and sometimes belly dancing), but both locations offer great value.

1913 S. Kihei Rd. (in Kihei Kalama Village, enter on Keala Place), Kihei. www.pitaparadisehawaii. com. ℰ **808/875-7679.** Wailea location: 34 Wailea Gateway Center (ℰ **808/879-7177**). Lunch main courses $8–$15; dinner main courses $16–$30. Daily 11am–9:30pm.

Inexpensive

Joy's Place ★ HEALTHY DELI   Nourish yourself with nutritious, delicious meals at this small cafe, where the emphasis is on healthful living. For breakfast, rev your engine with an acai bowl or a still-warm spelt muffin. Soups are made daily, and the sandwiches are huge, with thick slices of nitrate-free turkey piled onto sprouted grain bread—or, if you prefer, packed into a collard-green wrap. (In fact, most ingredients are organic.) You'll see Joy behind the counter, her bright smile convincing evidence that her diet works. She also makes high-quality live/raw/vegan products that are available in the cooler (and at Whole Foods in Kahului). The cacao shake and Mayan Spice truffles? Well worth the $6 price tag.

In the Island Surf Bldg., 1993 S. Kihei Rd. (entrance on Auhana St.), Kihei. www.joysplacemaui. com. ℰ **808/879-9258.** All items under $12. Mon–Sat 8am–4pm.

WAILEA

Note: You'll find the restaurants in this section on the "Hotels & Restaurants in South Maui" map (p. 313).

Expensive

Amasia ★★★ JAPANESE/FUSION   Chef Alan Wong, one of the state's most beloved restaurateurs, ate his way through Singapore and South America before opening Amasia, his newest restaurant, at the opulent Grand Wailea. The result: a dizzying and decadent international experience. A river runs through the cool, cavernous dining room, which retains the mysterious aura of a traditional Japanese teahouse. Rocks imported from Mount Fuji in Japan stand sentry around the koi pond at the entrance. The menu is exhaustive but dishes are small, in the tradition of Spanish tapas bars and Japanese *izakayas.* Order several plates to share. Don't be shy; try the spicy, crispy whole Dungeness crab, the Kona kampachi sashimi with jalapeño discs, and the uni shot—a tantalizing sliver of sea urchin doused in *leche de tigre,* a Peruvian aphrodisiac. Do not miss dessert. The pineapple shave ice (borrowed from Wong's Honolulu restaurant) is a delectable combination of panna cotta, coconut tapioca, and frozen pineapple shavings that melt on your tongue. It's heavenly, as is haupia sorbet: ice cream shaped like a coconut and ensconced in a chocolate shell.

3850 Wailea Alanui Dr. (at the Grand Wailea), Wailea. www.alanwongs.com/corporate/amasia. © **808/891-3954.** All items under $12. Daily 5–10pm.

Capische? ★★★ FRENCH/ITALIAN   One of Maui's most romantic restaurants is hidden away up on a hill, in the dramatic lobby of the Hotel Wailea. Capische is an intimate, sensual destination, whether you dine in the torch-lit garden surrounded by fresh herbs, or up on the lanai soaking in the sunset. Chef/owner Brian Etheredge and his top knife, Chris Kulis, harvest much of their produce from an on-site garden and orchard and offer a 100-percent-organic tasting menu. They cure their charcuterie from locally raised Berkshire pigs, just as Italian chefs have done for generations. The Caesar crudo, an inventive take on tradition, tops a few seared romaine leaves with Kona kampachi dressed in abalone vinaigrette, garlic aioli, and a sprinkling of black salt. It's phenomenal, and it's just the start. Hand-cut pasta, risotto, and gnocchi are paired with such rich and expertly prepared entrees as aromatic braised lamb shank or aged rib-eye. The cioppino is a revelatory mix of lobster, shrimp, and clams steeped in a saffron broth so tantalizing you'll want to drink it straight from the bowl. *Tip:* Serious gourmands should consider booking a seat at **Il Teatro,** the chef's demonstration kitchen downstairs. Etheredge or Kulis will prepare seven-plus courses a la minute, just for you, discussing each delectable creation as it simmers. It's a cooking class and feast wrapped up into one unforgettable evening.

At the Hotel Wailea, 555 Kaukahi St., Wailea. www.capische.com. © **808/879-2224.** Reservations recommended. Main courses $35–$55. Mon–Sat 5:30–9:30pm.

Ferraro's Bar e Ristorante ★★ ITALIAN   The stunning location—overlooking Wailea Beach with an unobstructed view of the West Maui Mountains—sets the stage for a romantic (if pricey) repast, whether you dine beneath sun-splashed umbrellas by day or the starry sky at night. For lunch, indulge your inner celebrity: Sip a Prosecco or blueberry mojito and snack on a lobster sandwich or roasted pear and Gorgonzola pizza pulled from the wood-burning oven. As the sun sinks into the Pacific, the atmosphere transforms. Live classical music casts a spell around the terraced outdoor tables. The breadbaskets are sumptuous, freshly baked with flecks of olive. You even have your choice of two sea salts to season your meal, should you so desire. The entrees are not particularly adventurous—traditional veal with pappardelle Bolognese and Pacific seabass with roasted potatoes in a slightly peppery watercress sauce—but they are well-executed and delivered in flawless fashion by the waitstaff. The desserts, which change often, are creative and worth every calorie.

At the Four Seasons Resort Maui at Wailea, 3900 Wailea Alanui Dr., Wailea. www.fourseasons. com/maui. © **808/874-8000.** Reservations recommended. Main courses $19–$28 lunch, $34–$52 dinner. Daily 11:30am–9pm (beverages served from 11am).

Ka'ana Kitchen ★★★ HAWAII REGIONAL CUISINE Despite steep competition, Chef Isaac Bancaco scooped the 2014 Chef of the Year prize from "Maui No Ka Oi" magazine for his work at Ka'ana Kitchen. Catch this rising star while you can—he's on fire. You can hardly tell where the dining room ends and the kitchen begins in this bright, open restaurant. Ask to sit ringside where you can watch the action. Start off with a hand-mixed cocktail and the grilled octopus: fat chunks of tender meat tossed with frisée, watercress, and goat cheese. The ahi tataki is edible artwork: ruby-red tuna, heirloom tomato, and fresh burratta decorated with black salt and nasturtium petals. Don't be thrown off by Bancaco's grid menu. Treat it like a gourmet bingo card; every combo is a winner. Breakfasts here are among the island's best, with local poached eggs, Molokai sweet potatoes, and creative bento boxes packed with fried rice and pickled vegetables. The $45 buffet grants you access to the kitchen's novel chilled countertops, which are stocked with every delicacy and fresh juice you could imagine.

At the Andaz Maui, 3550 Wailea Alanui Dr., Wailea. www.maui.andaz.hyatt.com. © **808/573-1234.** Main courses $22–$45 breakfast, $18–$54 dinner. Daily 6:30–11am and 5:30–9pm.

Ko ★★ GOURMET PLANTATION CUISINE *Ko* is Hawaiian for sugarcane, and this restaurant revives the true melting pot of Maui's bygone plantation days. Chef Tylun Pang takes the ethnic foods of the islands' Japanese, Filipino, Chinese, Portuguese, and Korean immigrants and presents them in gourmet fashion, in a spectacularly renovated restaurant. The "ahi on the rock" appetizer is my favorite: large squares of seasoned ruby-red tuna delivered with a hot *ishiyaki* stone. Sear the ahi on the rock to your desired temperature, and then submerge it in orange-ginger miso sauce. The Zarzuela, fat chunks of lobster, shrimp, scallops, and chorizo simmered in rich saffron broth, is also fantastic. If dishes sound unfamiliar, let your waiter guide you. On Sunday, a special Hawaiian *laulau* is served: Fresh fish, shellfish, and bok choy are wrapped in ti leaves and steamed. Served with jasmine rice, it's a marvelous re-creation of a traditional island meal. Monthly winemakers' dinners here are special treats; check the website for dates. At lunchtime, you can order small portions of many of the dinner entrees, as well as ahi sandwiches and *paniolo* burgers.

Fairmont Kea Lani Maui, 4100 Wailea Alanui Dr., Wailea http://korestaurant.com. © **808/875-4100.** Reservations recommended. Main courses $14–$32 lunch, $21–$50 dinner. Daily 11am–9pm.

Longhi's ★ ITALIAN After a tough day sunbathing or shopping, head to the bar at Longhi's for an elegant *pau hana* (finish work) martini. The breezy restaurant with its trademark black-and-white-checkered floor is a great backdrop for breakfast, too. Luxurious lobster eggs Benedict is certainly worth waking up for, served on thick slices of grilled Italian bread. If an omelet is more your style, you can get that with lobster too, along with spinach and fresh mozzarella. At lunch and dinner, standard Italian fare is served: eggplant Parmesan, pasta Bolognese, and fresh fish. Surprisingly, the restaurant's most coveted item isn't even on the menu: the cheesy jalapeño pizza bread. It's served free with dinner, but you should ask for a few slices, even at breakfast.

At the Shops at Wailea, 3750 Wailea Alanui Dr., Wailea. www.longhis.com. © **808/891-8883.** Breakfast items $10–$21; lunch items $11–$38; dinner main courses $17–$120. Mon–Fri 8am–10pm; Sat–Sun 7:30am–10pm.

Mala Wailea ★★ HAWAII REGIONAL CUISINE/SEAFOOD   This Wailea resort restaurant doesn't have the chic intimacy of its cousin, Mala Ocean Tavern in Lahaina (p. 337), but it's still a delicious destination with a nearly identical menu. Beloved chef and restaurateur Mark Ellman knows how to craft locally sourced dishes that are both health-conscious and full of flavor. (One of the pioneers of Hawaii Regional Cuisine, he also owns Migrant [p. 349] and Honu [p. 336], and launched the "Practice Aloha" movement.) Specials include the wonderful fried Tamashiro tofu with coconut peanut sauce and Thai basil, and a perfectly moist panko-crusted snapper with Molokai sweet potato mash. There's an entire menu of gluten-free and vegan items. If that doesn't apply to you, I highly recommend the insanely rich mac and cheese. For breakfast, indulge in the sumptuous buffet or order from an a la carte menu. Don't miss the killer French toast drizzled with house-made caramel sauce and tropical fruit—it's the breakfast version of Ellman's legendary Caramel Miranda dessert.

Wailea Beach Marriott Resort & Spa, 3700 Wailea Alanui Dr., Wailea. www.malawailea.com. © **808/875-9394.** Reservations recommended. Breakfast buffet $29 or main courses $14–$25; dinner main courses $26–$45; tavern plates $15–$20. Daily 6:30–11am and 5:30–9:30pm; bar until 10pm.

Morimoto Maui ★★★ JAPANESE/PERUVIAN   Iron Chef Masaharu Morimoto is a culinary force to be reckoned with. His new Maui restaurant sits beside the pool at Andaz. Decor is sedate and spare, directing all of the attention to the culinary fireworks. Inside Morimoto's immaculate kitchen is a space-age freezer that seals in the flavors of the fish he buys at auction, as well as a rice polisher, there to ensure that every grain is perfect. If you can afford it, go for the *omakase*—the chef's tasting menu. It starts with his signature appetizer, the toro tartare. Balanced on ice, it's edible artwork. A tilted rectangle offers up a delectable smear of minced Kindai bluefin tuna, accented by colorful stripes of condiments: black nori paste, creamy green avocado, wasabi, crème fraîche, Maui onion, and tiny yellow rice crackers. A chilled Japanese mountain peach serves as a palate cleanser. The chef's tribute to Maui features locally caught *opakapaka* (pink snapper) in Thai curry with pohole fern, plump mussels, and sushi rice, topped with grilled bananas that balance the curry's heat. Everything is indulgent here: A *chawanmushi* (Japanese custard) is flavored with foie gras and topped with slivered duck breast; spicy Spanish octopus comes in Morimoto's angry sauce; and an amazing crispy, salty, fatty seared pork is amplified by sweet poha berry and applesauce. For dessert, the resourceful pastry chef uses leftover rice shavings to create an earthy panna cotta paired with miso butterscotch ice cream and crowned with a wee wasabi sprout. The incredibly decadent lunch features flatbreads, sushi, Asian-inspired sandwiches, and many of the items served at dinner.

At the Andaz Maui, 3550 Wailea Alanui Dr., Wailea. www.maui.andaz.hyatt.com. © **808/573-1234.** Main courses $18–$39 lunch, $14–$54 dinner. Daily 11:30am–9pm.

Spago ★★★ ASIAN FUSION/NEW AMERICAN   Wolfgang Puck is Spago's celebrity chef/owner, but the magic in this kitchen belongs to Cameron Lewark. At this gorgeous restaurant tucked into the posh lobby of the Four Seasons Resort Maui at Wailea, Lewark dazzles diners with inventive dishes that are flavorful but light and not overwhelmed by heavy sauces. If he tried to remove the ahi sesame-miso cones from the menu, fans would probably riot. This appetizer is perfection: bright-red spicy ahi spooned into a crunchy, sweet, and nutty cones and topped with flying fish roe. (One is never enough.) His Thai seafood curry with kaffir lime and green papaya salad is a gourmet version of the traditional staple—and it excels on every level. The Chinois lamb chops are worth the steep price tag, though even I balk at the $88 Wagyu sirloin—devotees swear it's sublime, but there are just as many detractors. During truffle season, fragrant shavings of black or white truffles can be added to your dish. If you're a vegetarian, this is heaven. Chef Lewark is masterful at preparing vegetables in unexpected and wonderful ways—consider his foamy tomato "cappuccino," or the sesame-miso cones with hearts of palm standing in for ahi. Seating hangs over the elegant pool with Pacific views, and the bartenders pour handcrafted libations with clever names: Pavlov's Dog, Tainted Love, and Rolling Fog Over Mount Fuji.

At the Four Seasons Resort Maui at Wailea, 3900 Wailea Alanui Dr., Wailea. www.fourseasons. com/maui. © **808/879-2999**. Reservations required. Main courses $39–$135. Daily 6–9:30pm. Bar with pupu daily 6–11pm.

Moderate

Gannon's ★ HAWAII REGIONAL CUISINE/AMERICAN   Set up above the Makena and Wailea coastline, this clubhouse on the Wailea Gold golf course has spectacular views in every direction. Award-winning chef Bev Gannon—the culinary force behind Haliimaile General Store (p. 350) and Lanai City Grille (p. 410)—has brought her gourmet-style comfort food to Wailea. The restaurant opens at 8:30am for continental breakfast, but the kitchen doesn't get cranking until 10am, when you can dine on crab-cake eggs Benedict or a fancy loco moco with Kobe beef, kimchi, and crispy Maui onions. At night, when the view isn't a lure, it's fun to sit at the sparkly Red Bar. Dig into guava barbecue ribs or a trio of crabcake sliders, both served with Bev's Asian slaw. Handcrafted cocktails include the refreshing Wailea Spritz: Aperol and prosecco with a dash of passion-fruit puree or the Laven-Berry: Tanqueray 10 with lavender syrup and fresh blueberries.

At the Wailea Gold Golf Course, 100 Wailea Golf Club Dr., Wailea. www.gannonsrestaurant. com. © **808/875-8080**. Reservations recommended for dinner. Main courses $9–$14 breakfast, $9–$18 lunch, $24–$46 dinner. Daily 8:30am–9pm.

Fabiani's ★ ITALIAN   At the top of tony Wailea, this little bistro serves the most affordable breakfast, lunch, and dinner in the neighborhood. Come here early in your stay because you'll want to return. The Italian-born chef turns out tasty pastas and pizzas for literally half the price of spots down the road. Sate your hunger with chef Lorenzo's meat lasagna—a rich medley of Italian sausage, ground beef, pork, marinara, and béchamel sauce. Make your own thin-crust Italian-style pizza with an array of gourmet toppings—a selection you won't find elsewhere on island—like mascarpone, Kalamata olives, shrimp, and pancetta. The bakery creates French macaroons in tempting flavors like pistachio and caramel sea salt. A second location is in Kihei (95 E. Lipoa St., #101; © **808/874-0888**).

In the Wailea Gateway Plaza, 34 Wailea Gateway Place, #A101, Wailea. © **808/874-1234**. All items under $12. Daily 8am–9pm.

Migrant ★★★ HAWAII REGIONAL CUISINE/FILIPINO   Chef Sheldon Simeon won the nation's heart when he appeared on "Top Chef: Seattle" wearing a red wool cap and an indefatigable smile. He didn't win that contest, but he's won just about every other accolade—including, most recently, the title of Best New Chef in the Pacific/Northwest region by "Food & Wine." For all the hype, Simeon is remarkably humble, and his cuisine reflects his homespun roots. At

Migrant, which he opened with partners Mark Ellman and Shep Gordon, Simeon spotlights Filipino flavors and local-style cooking. Spiced with house-made sambal and calamansi lime, his Hood Canal oyster shooters are the best I've ever had. I'm still fantasizing about the kale salad with miso dressing, pickled cucumbers, and chunks of fig. The hibachi hanger steak lights up the entire tongue, dressed in *nouc cham* (a simultaneously sweet, sour, salty, and spicy Vietnamese fish sauce) and tender watercress leaves. For dessert, Migrant's fun petit fours are composed of extra-light butter mochi puto and a mini rice cake with peanut sauce. In the lobby of the Wailea Marriott, this intimate gastropub is decorated with luminous paintings that echo the Simeon's plantation-inspired cuisine. Come before the waitlist doubles.

Wailea Beach Marriott Resort & Spa, 3700 Wailea Alanui Dr., Wailea. www.migrantmaui.com. ✆ **808/875-9394.** Reservations recommended. Dinner main courses $14–$32. Daily 5–10pm (lounge open till 11pm).

Upcountry Maui

Note: You'll find the restaurants in this section on the "Upcountry & East Maui" map (p. 325).

HALIIMAILE (ON THE WAY TO UPCOUNTRY MAUI)
Moderate
Haliimaile General Store ★ HAWAII REGIONAL/AMERICAN   Twenty-five years ago Bev Gannon, one of the pioneering chefs of Hawaii Regional Cuisine, brought her gourmet comfort food to this renovated plantation store in rural Haliimaile. It was a gamble then; now it's one of the island's most beloved restaurants. Menu items reflect island cuisine with hints of Texas, from which Gannon hails. The Asian duck tostada, for example, pairs shredded duck with ginger chili dressing, jicama, carrot slaw, cranberries, and toasted macadamia nuts in a crispy lumpia shell. Another delicious appetizer is the warm goat cheese tart with slivered poached pears, fennel, and pine nuts. Sauces can be rich (and too many at one time hard to digest), so it's best to stick to one or two items rather than ordering a bunch to share. That rule does not apply to the sashimi Napoleon, however. The creamy wasabi vinaigrette that the waiter pours atop your stack of ahi tartare, smoked salmon, and wonton chips *is* rich, but it's worth the indulgence. Sound ricochets in this vintage camp store, with its polished wooden floors, high ceilings, and open kitchen. It's quieter in the back room, which is worth exploring anyway for its rotating exhibit of paintings by top local artists.

900 Haliimaile Rd., Haliimaile. http://bevgannonrestaurants.com. ✆ **808/572-2666.** Reservations recommended. Main courses $14–$24 lunch, $26–$42 dinner. Mon–Fri 11am–2:30pm; daily 5:30–9pm.

MAKAWAO & PUKALANI
Moderate
Market Fresh Bistro ★ HAWAIIAN/MEDITERRAN   At this off-the-beaten-path bistro, Chef Justin Pardo steadfastly adheres to the locavore ethic: Nearly everything he serves is grown within a few miles of the kitchen. Because of this, the menu changes daily. Salads are exceptional here, with slivered rainbow radishes, heirloom carrots, and greens picked literally that morning. Past entrees have included Kupaa Farm taro-crusted fish with asparagus in fennel-saffron tomato jus, and lamb ragout atop 2-inch-wide pasta ribbons. Breakfasts in the

shaded courtyard will transport you to the French countryside: Thick slices of wheat toast slathered in house-made *lilikoi* (passionfruit) jam accompany omelets stuffed with goat cheese, mushroom, and pesto. The high-quality ingredients are fresh off the farm, and you can taste it. The front of the house is managed by Pardo's sister and brother-in-law, who are alternately gracious and aloof—stay on their good side if you can. On Thursday night, the team serves prix-fixe farm dinners, seven courses for $60 (more with wine pairing).

3620 Baldwin Ave., Makawao. http://marketfreshbistro.com. © **808/572-4877.** Reservations recommended for dinner. Breakfast $10–$13; lunch $10–$15; dinner $28–$34. Tues–Sat 9–11am; Sun 9am–2pm; Tues–Wed 11:30am–4pm; Thurs–Sat 11:30am–3pm; Thurs–Sat prix-fixe 6–8:30pm.

Inexpensive
Casanova Italian Restaurant & Deli ★ ITALIAN   On the corner of Baldwin and Makawao avenues, this upcountry institution serves wonderful Italian fare at a sit-down restaurant and an attached cozy deli. The deli serves simple breakfasts (omelets with fresh mozzarella, and buttermilk muffins and bagels loaded with lox and capers) and terrific sandwiches for lunch. Try the New York meatball on a baguette, or the goat cheese and eggplant on focaccia. The deli's outdoor barstool seating makes a great perch for observing the Makawao traffic—always entertaining. The restaurant proper opens for lunch and serves a range of pastas and pizzas baked in the brick oven, on tables set with white linens. At dinner, snack on freshly baked focaccia with olive oil and balsamic vinegar while waiting for your entree; the truffle ravioli with sage sauce is a favorite of mine. Pizza is served until at least 10pm, and on many nights of the week the dance floor erupts to the sounds of live salsa or reggae music or visiting DJs—dinner earns you free admission. Check the website for the entertainment calendar.

1188 Makawao Ave., Makawao. www.casanovamaui.com. © **808/572-0220.** Reservations recommended for dinner. Lunch items $9–$18; dinner main courses $24–$36; 12-in. pizzas $12–$20; pastas $12–$18. Mon–Sat 11:30am–2pm; daily 5:30–9pm. Dancing Wed and Fri–Sat 10pm–1:30am. Lounge daily 5:30pm–1 or 1:30am. Deli Mon–Sat 7:30am–5:30pm; Sun 8:30am–5:30pm.

KULA
Moderate
Kula Lodge HAWAII REGIONAL/AMERICAN   The Kula Lodge's restaurant is best at breakfast, when the prices are lower and the views through the picture windows have an eye-popping intensity. The million-dollar vista spans the flanks of Haleakala, all of Central Maui, the emerald-green West Maui Mountains, and the Pacific Ocean on two coasts. The kitchen turns out decent eggs Benedicts, including one topped with fresh fish and a veggie version crowned with spinach, tomatoes, and feta cheese. The buttermilk pancakes with macadamia nuts are tasty, but avoid the bland loco moco (hamburger, rice, and a fried egg slathered in listless brown gravy). For dinner, you best bet is pizza baked in the brick oven outdoors. Try the upcountry vegetable pie with San Marzano tomato sauce, smoked mozzarella, and herb-roasted veggies.

15200 Haleakala Hwy. (Hwy. 377), Kula. www.kulalodge.com. © **808/878-2517.** Main courses $10–$18 breakfast, $12–$26 lunch, $12–$35 dinner. Daily 7am–9pm.

Inexpensive
Grandma's Coffee House COFFEEHOUSE/AMERICAN   A coffee plant grows through the deck at this friendly coffeehouse in remote and charming Keokea. Alfred Franco's grandmother started growing and roasting coffee in

1918. Five generations later, this family-run cafe is still fueled by homegrown Haleakala beans and frequented by local *paniolo* (cowboys). Line up at the busy counter for espresso, home-baked pastries, hot oatmeal, scrambled eggs, or, on Sundays, eggs Benedict served on a cornmeal waffle. Rotating lunch specials include spinach lasagna, teriyaki chicken, and beef stew. Sit out on the scenic lanai where the air is always the perfect temperature and listen to a Hawaiian guitarist serenade his bygone sweethearts. Pick up a few lemon squares and a slice of pumpkin bread to go.

At the end of Hwy. 37, Keokea (about 6 miles before the Tedeschi Vineyards in Ulupalakua). www.grandmascoffee.com. ℂ **808/878-2140.** Most items under $10. Daily 7am–5pm.

La Provence ★ BAKERY   Hidden away up in Kula is a family-owned French bakery that's worth driving across the island for. Every item on the brief menu and stashed in the bakery case is exquisite. Get there early (well before noon) or risk arriving as the last almond croissants and mango blueberry scones walk out the door. Chef Thierry Michelier's daughter will ring you up and you'll dine in the garden courtyard beside cyclists who've worked up appetites circumnavigating the island. The crepes, filled with Kula vegetables and goat cheese or salmon and spinach, have a secret addictive ingredient: béchamel sauce. On Sunday, eggs Benedict is served with perfect roasted potatoes and wild greens drizzled in a transcendent *lilikoi* balsamic dressing. For lunch, try the marvelous duck confit salad or roast chicken sandwich with melted Brie cheese.

3158 Lower Kula Hwy., Kula. www.laprovencekula.com. ℂ **808/878-1313.** Breakfast $12–$13; lunch $11–$14. Cash or check only. Wed–Sun 7am–2pm (till 9pm in summer).

East Maui

Note: You'll find the restaurants in this section on the "Upcountry & East Maui" map (p. 325).

PAIA
Moderate
Charley's Restaurant ★ AMERICAN/MEXICAN   Named after a Great Dane named Charley P. Woofer, this north shore institution serves three meals a day, but breakfast is really the time to come. This downtown Paia hangout does double duty as a power-breakfast fuel station for windsurfers and an after-dark saloon with live music and DJs. It's a decent place to grab a bite before heading out to Hana. Lunch is half-pound burgers (made from locally raised beef), fish and chicken sandwiches, Philly cheesesteaks, salads, and pizza. Dinner is grilled fish and steak—hearty, but nothing exciting.

142 Hana Hwy., Paia. http://charleysmaui.com. ℂ **808/579-8085.** Breakfast items $10–$16; lunch items $11–$12; dinner main courses $11–$22. Daily 7am–10pm; food served at the bar until 10pm.

Dazoo ★ AMERICAN/KOREAN   This kitchen turns out delicious, inventive dishes that span multiple cultures: The Kula corn gnocchi hails from Italy via upcountry Maui, while the primavera pasta took a side trip through Asia, collecting a sultry sake and miso sauce along the way. The best bites are Korean mash-ups: the do-it-yourself lettuce wraps with bulgogi steak and the crazy delicious kimchi ba burger, a Maui cattle beef patty topped with kimchi and bacon on a homemade bun. The rainbow chopped salad is a feast for the eyes—ruby tomatoes, roasted golden beets, purple cabbage, creamy goat cheese, and organic spinach tossed in tahini dressing. Plates are small, designed for sharing. The bakery case is filled with sweet treats; the chocolate tartlets are wonderful (the French macaroons a bit too sugary). At press time, management was planning to expand into a full bakery next door. *Tip:* Hit happy hour (3–6pm); it's the only time the burgers and bibimbap are served.

71 Baldwin Ave., Paia. www.dazoomaui.com. © **808/579-9999.** Main courses $7–$17 lunch, $10–$30 dinner. Daily 11am–9pm.

Flatbread & Company ★ PIZZA   This family-friendly Paia outpost embraces a locavore philosophy. The hand-colored menus highlight the best Maui farmers have to offer, particularly where the inventive daily *carne* and veggie specials are concerned. You can watch the chefs hand-toss organic dough, dress it with high-quality toppings—local goat cheese, macadamia-nut pesto, slow-roasted kalua pork, or homemade, nitrate-free sausage—and shovel it into the wood-burning furnace that serves as the restaurant's magical hearth. Salads come sprinkled with grated green papaya and dressing so delicious that everyone clamors for the recipe. Tuesdays are charity night: $3.50 of each flatbread sold benefits a local cause.

71 Baldwin Ave., Paia. www.moanacafe.com. © **808/579-9999.** Reservations recommended for dinner. Breakfast $6–$15; lunch $7–$17; dinner $10–$30. Tues–Sun 8am–9pm; Mon 8am–3pm.

Milagros Food Company SOUTHWESTERN/SEAFOOD   You'll have a prime view of the Paia action from the lanai of this corner restaurant. The kitchen turns out Tex-Mex dishes with Maui flair, such as blackened ahi or mahimahi tacos with salsa, cheese, fresh guacamole, and sweet chili sauce (sounds strange, perhaps, but tastes great). You can also order Anaheim chili enchiladas, fajitas with sautéed vegetables finished in achiote glaze, a variety of burgers, and giant salads. The bar pours an assortment of fine tequilas, offering several flights so that you can compare flavors and no fewer than 10 different margaritas. Don Julio Reposado in a classic margarita on the rocks, please!

3 Baldwin Ave., Paia. www.milagrosfoodcompany.com. © **808/579-8755.** Lunch items $8–$13; dinner main courses $13–$19. Daily 8am–10pm.

Inexpensive

Cafe des Amis ★ CREPES/MEDITERRANEAN/INDIAN   This sweet, eclectic restaurant serves crepes, curries, and Mediterranean platters that are fresh, tasty, and easy on the wallet. Crepes come with organic local greens and a dollop of sour cream. The breakfast crepe with Gruyère and ham is perfect any time of day, as is the Italian lentil crepe with pesto and mozzarella. The curries aren't exactly Indian, but they are delicious and can be ordered as wraps or bowls. Wraps come with cucumber raita; bowls with mango and tomato chutneys. Ask for the extra-hot habañero chutney on the side. The coconut shrimp curry is a fragrant blend of ginger, garlic, cinnamon, cilantro, and Bengal spices; the slow-cooked organic chicken curry has a creamy, tomato-y base. For dessert, sweet crepes are stuffed with melted Nutella or bananas and chocolate. The best espresso in Paia is found here, along with some stiff *lilikoi* margaritas. Musicians often play beneath the twinkling lights in the courtyard seating area.

42 Baldwin Ave., Paia. www.cdamaui.com. © **808/579-6323.** All-day menu items: crepes $9–$12; main courses $15–$20. Daily 8:30am–8:30pm.

Paia Fish Market SEAFOOD   At the corner of Baldwin Avenue and Hana Highway in Paia, this busy fish market must maintain its own fleet of fishing boats. How else to explain how the cooks can dish out filet after giant fresh filet for little more than it would cost to buy the same at the grocery? There's only one thing to order here: a fish sandwich. A giant slab of perfectly grilled ahi, opah, or *opakapaka* laid out on a bun with coleslaw and grated cheese is extra satisfying after a briny day at the beach.

110 Hana Hwy., Paia. www.paiafishmarket.com. © **808/579-8030.** Lunch and dinner plates $11–$16. Daily 11am–9:30pm.

HAIKU
Moderate
Colleen's at the Cannery ★ ECLECTIC   This go-to spot for Haiku residents serves an excellent breakfast, lunch, and dinner in a classy setting. Slide into a booth beside world-famous surfers, yoga teachers, and inspirational speakers: Maui's local celebrities. Wake up with an omelet stuffed with portobello mushroom and goat cheese, accompanied by organic chai or a spicy Bloody Mary, depending on your mood. For lunch, the tasty roasted eggplant sandwich is served warm, with sun-dried tomatoes, carrots, and melted Muenster cheese. Hearty burgers are made from Maui Cattle Company beef, and pizzas are loaded with creative toppings. For dinner, the local fish specials are spot-on, rivaling some of the island's pricier restaurants—but service can be frustratingly inattentive here. The dessert case contains some treasures, like extra-rich espresso brownies and sweetly tart *lilikoi* (passionfruit) bars.

At the Haiku Cannery Marketplace, 810 Haiku Rd., Haiku. www.colleensinhaiku.com. © **808/575-9211.** Reservations not accepted. Breakfast $7.50–$15; lunch $8–15; dinner main courses $9–$30. Daily 6am–10pm.

Nuka ★★ SUSHI   Sushi chef Hiro Takanashi smiles from behind the bar as he turns out beautiful specialty rolls loaded with sprouts, pea shoots, avocado, and glistening red tuna. The garden-fresh ingredients served at this compact sushi restaurant reflect its rural Haiku address, but its stylish decor suggests somewhere more cosmopolitan. Start with a side of house pickles or *kinpira gobo*—a salty, sweet, and sour mix of slivered burdock root. Then proceed to the sushi menu for excellent nigiri, sashimi, and rolls. Not up for sushi? The wonderful Nuka bowls—your choice of protein piled atop fresh herbs, crushed peanuts, sesame lime dressing, rice, and veggies—are deeply nourishing. For dessert, try the house-made black sesame ice cream. *Tip:* Nuka doesn't take reservations and is often packed; plan to eat early (before 6pm) or late (after 7:30pm) to avoid crowds.

780 Haiku Rd., Haiku. www.nukamaui.com. © **808/575-2939.** Reservations not accepted. Dinner $8–$38. Daily 4:30–10pm.

ON THE ROAD TO HANA
Expensive
Mama's Fish House ★★★ SEAFOOD   Overlooking idyllic Kuau Cove on Maui's north shore, this island institution is the realization of a South Pacific fantasy. Though pricey, a meal at Mama's is a complete experience. Recapture the grace of early Hawaii, when feasts lasted for days beneath the swaying palms. The magic begins with complimentary valet parking. Wander through the landscaped grounds down to the restaurant, where smiling servers wear Polynesian prints and flowers behind their ears. The dining room features curved

lauhala-lined ceilings, lavish arrangements of tropical flowers, and windows open wide to let the ocean breeze in. Every nook and cranny is decorated with some fanciful artifact of salt-kissed adventure. Start your repast with the coconut ceviche or the marvelous beef Polynesian—a garlicky mix of seared steak morsels, tomatoes, and onion served in a papaya half. The menu lists the names of the anglers who reeled in the day's catch; you can order ono "caught by Keith Nakamura along the 40-fathom ledge near Hana" or deepwater ahi seared with coconut and lime. As a finale, the Tahitian Pearl dessert is almost too stunning to eat: a shiny chocolate ganache sphere filled with *lilikoi* crème, set in an edible pastry clamshell. Everything is perfect, from the refreshing, umbrella-topped cocktails to the almond-scented hand towels passed out before dessert. As a parting shot, squares of creamy coconut haupia are delivered with your bill.

799 Poho Place, just off the Hana Hwy., Kuau. www.mamasfishhouse.com. © **808/579-8488.** Reservations recommended for lunch, required for dinner. Main courses $26–$48 lunch, $28–$58 dinner. Daily 11am–3pm and 4:15–9pm (last seating).

Inexpensive

Kuau Store ★ DELI   This is my new favorite spot on the north shore for breakfast or lunch to go. The handsome convenience store and deli offers gourmet breakfast paninis, smoothies with all kinds of extras, fresh juices, kombucha on tap, shoyu chicken plate lunches, and pulled pork sandwiches. Inside the deli case you'll find quinoa salads and four types of poke (raw fish seasoned with seaweed and chili pepper). The store's aesthetic is uber-cute, decorated with vintage maps of Maui and bright colors. The espresso counter is built out of repurposed wood from the mart that was here before. For an easy entrance and exit, park on the side street, under the fantastic mural featuring surfers, sharks, and owls.

701 Hana Hwy., Paia. © **808/579-8844.** Deli items $5–$10. Daily 6:30am–7pm.

HANA

Expensive

Kauiki ★   For years, the signature restaurant at Hana's sole resort languished under ineffectual kitchen management. That has changed with the arrival of Derek Watanabe, formerly the chef de cuisine for Alan Wong's Pineapple Room. Watanabe's menu showcases Hana-grown ingredients: The earthy taste of organic pohole fern enlivens salads, while mahimahi caught just offshore is dressed in a savory curry shiitake cream and topped with a pair of caramelized apple bananas. Sweet and starchy breadfruit is the basis of my absolute favorite side dish, *ulu* croquettes. Breakfasts are elegant affairs here, where you can sip coffee and lazily watch *iwa* (frigate birds) circle above Kauiki Hill, for which the restaurant is named. Service is friendly but unhurried. Prices are high, even for Maui. But when you're in Hana, is anything really worth complaining about? The dining room and the lounge next door feature live Hawaiian music and hula dancing throughout the week.

At Travaasa Hana, 5031 Hana Hwy., Hana. www.travaasa.com/hana. © **808/248-8211.** Breakfast $12–28; lunch $17–$32; dinner main courses $30–$50. Daily 7:30am–9pm.

Inexpensive

Nutcharee's Authentic Thai Food ★ THAI   Thank goodness for this hole-in-the-forest Thai restaurant! Hana has few dining options, and even fewer that are both health-conscious and affordable. In fact, this semi-permanent tent across from the ballpark might be the only one. Snag a seat at one of the colorful picnic tables and start off your feast with green papaya salad or spring rolls. The crispy *opakapaka* (pink snapper) entree is spicy, with an ample serving of fried fish (which still tastes fresh) and slivers of scrumptious green mango salad piled on top. Try the Thai iced tea with coconut milk. It's all wonderful—except for the mosquitos, which come here for dinner, too.

5050 Uakea Rd., Hana. Lunch plates $10–$12. Mon–Fri 10:30am–4pm.

MAUI SHOPPING

Maui's best shopping is found in the small, independent boutiques and galleries scattered around the island—particularly in Makawao and Paia. (If you're in the market for a bikini, there's no better spot than the intersection of Baldwin Ave. and Hana Hwy. on Maui's north shore.) The two upscale resort shopping malls, the **Shops at Wailea** in South Maui and **Whalers Village** in Kaanapali, have everything from Louis Vuitton and Coach to Gap—plus a handful of local designers to boot. If you're looking for that perfect souvenir, consider visiting one of Maui's farms (or farmers' markets), most of which offer fantastic value-added products. Take home Kaanapali coffee, Kula lavender spice rub, Maui Ocean vodka (p. 276), Maui Gold pineapple, and other tasty treats that can be shipped worldwide.

Central Maui
KAHULUI

Kahului's shopping is concentrated in two malls. The **Maui Mall,** 70 E. Kaahumanu Ave. (www.mauimall.com; ✆ 808/877-8952), is the place of everyday retail, from **Longs Drugs** and **Whole Foods** to **Tasaka Guri Guri** (the decades-old purveyor of inimitable icy treats that are neither ice cream nor shave ice, but something in between) and Kahului's largest movie theater, a 12-screen megaplex that features mainly current releases.

Queen Kaahumanu Center, 275 Kaahumanu Ave. (www.queenkaahumanu center.com; ✆ 808/877-3369), a 10-minute drive from the Kahului Airport, offers two levels of shops, restaurants, and theaters. It covers the bases, from arts and crafts to a **Foodland** and everything in between: a thriving food court; the island's best beauty supply, **Lisa's Beauty Supply & Salon** (✆ 808/877-6463) and its sister store for cosmetics, **Madison Avenue Day Spa and Boutique** (✆ 808/873-0880); mall standards like **Macy's, Sears, Sunglass Hut,** and **Local Motion** (surf and beach wear).

Maui Swap Meet For just 50¢ you're granted admission to a colorful maze of booths and tables occupying the Maui Community College's parking lot every Saturday from 7am to 1pm. Vendors come from across the island to lay out their treasures: fresh fruits and vegetables from Kula and Keanae, orchids, jewelry, ceramics, clothing, household items, homemade jams, and baked goods. It's fun to stroll around and talk story with the farmers, artists, and crafters. At Maui Community College, in an area bounded by Kahului Beach Rd. and Wahine Pio Ave. (access via Wahine Pio Ave.). ✆ **808/244-3100.**

WAILUKU

Wailuku's vintage architecture, antiques shops, and mom-and-pop eateries imbue the town with charm. You won't find any plastic aloha in Wailuku; in fact, this is the best place to buy authentic Hawaiian souvenirs.

Bailey House Museum Shop   The small gift shop at the entrance of this wonderful museum offers a treasure trove of authoritative Hawaiiana, from hand-sewn feather hatbands to traditional Hawaiian games, music, and limited-edition books. Make sure to stroll through the gracious gardens and view Edward Bailey's paintings of early Maui. At the very least, take time to appreciate the massive koa outrigger canoe displayed outside. At the Bailey House Museum, 2375-A Main St. www.mauimuseum.org. ☎ **808/244-3326.**

Bird of Paradise Unique Antiques   Come here for old Matson liner menus, vintage aloha shirts, silk kimonos, and anything nostalgic that happens to be Hawaiian. Owner Joe Myhand collects everything from 1940s rattan furniture to Depression-era glass, California pottery, and lilting Hawaiian music on vinyl or cassette. 56 N. Market St. ☎ **808/242-7699.**

Native Intelligence ★★★   This wonderful shop feels like a museum or gallery—only you can take the marvelous artifacts home with you. From the rich monkeypod wood floors to the collection of finely woven *lauhala* hats, shopping here is a feast for the senses. The store's owners are committed to supporting indigenous Hawaiian cultural practitioners, who come here both to shop and to stock the shelves with artwork of the highest craftsmanship. Browse the clothing racks and glass cases for truly Hawaiian keepsakes and gifts: locally designed Kealopiko clothing silkscreened with Hawaiian proverbs, *kukui* nut-spinning tops, soaps scented with native herbs, and *lei o manu*—fierce war clubs fringed with shark teeth. You can also buy bags of fresh poi and the island's most precious leis, made of feather, shell, or fragrant flowers. 1980 Market St., #2. www.native-intel.com. ☎ **808/242-2421.**

Central Maui Edibles

Maui's produce has long been a source of pride for islanders. You'll find a selection of fresh Maui-grown fruit, vegetables, flowers, and plants at the **Ohana Farmers Market,** at Queen Kaahumanu Shopping Center (☎ **808/877-3369**), every Tuesday, Wednesday, and Friday from 8am to 4pm.

In the northern section of Wailuku, **Takamiya Market,** 359 N. Market St. (☎ **808/244-3404**), is much loved by local folks and visitors with adventurous palates, who often drive all the way from Kihei to stock up on picnic fare and mouthwatering ethnic foods for sunset gatherings. Unpretentious home-cooked foods from East and West are prepared daily and served on plastic-foam plates. The chilled-fish counter has fresh sashimi and poke, and prepared foods include mounds of shoyu chicken, fried squid, kalua pork, Chinese noodles, fiddlehead ferns, and Western comfort foods such as cornbread and potato salad.

West Maui

LAHAINA

Lahaina's merchants and art galleries go all out from 7 to 10pm every Friday, when **Art Night ★** brings an extra measure of hospitality and community spirit. The Art Night openings are usually marked with live entertainment and refreshments, plus a livelier-than-usual street scene. If you're in Lahaina on the second or last Thursday of the month, stroll by the front lawn of the **Baldwin Home Museum,** 120 Dickenson St. (at Front St.), for a splendid look at the craft of lei-making (you can even buy the results).

Across from the seawall on Front Street, you'll find the **Outlets of Maui,** 900 Front St. (www.theoutletsofmaui.com; ☎ **808/667-9216**). There's plenty

Leis at the Baldwin Home Museum.

of free validated parking and easy access to more than 2 dozen outlet shops including **Calvin Klein, Coach, Banana Republic, Adidas, Kay Jewelers,** and more. **Ruth's Chris Steak House** serves its famed cuts of beef here, and the **Hard Rock Cafe** serves lunch and dinner with live music most nights.

At the northern end of Lahaina town, what was formerly a big, belching pineapple cannery is now a maze of shops and restaurants known as the **Lahaina Cannery Mall,** 1221 Honoapiilani Hwy. (www.lahainacannerymall.com; *⦿* **808/661-5304**). Inside the air-conditioned building there's a **Longs Drugs** and a 24-hour **Safeway** for groceries. **Footprints Maui** may surprise you with its shoe selection—everything from Cole Haan sophisticates to inexpensive sandals. In the food court, try **Ba-Le French Sandwich and Bakery** for great banh mi and croissant sandwiches, while **L & L Drive-Inn** sells plate lunches. At **Lulu's Lahaina Surf Club & Grill,** you can get a frosty beer and watch big-wave surfers on the multiple flatscreen TVs.

Lahaina Arts Society Galleries   Since 1967, the Lahaina Arts Society has been promoting the excellent work of local artists. The society's two galleries inhabit the Old Lahaina Courthouse, the historic building that sits between Lahaina harbor and the giant banyan tree in the center of town. Changing monthly exhibits spotlight individual artists' work. In addition, the both galleries are jam-packed with paintings, photography, fiber art, ceramics, sculpture, jewelry, and more. The artists host "Art in the Park" fairs several times each month in the shade of the sprawling banyan tree (check the website for dates). 648 Wharf St. www.lahaina-arts.com. *⦿* **808/661-3228.**

Le Ru Atelier   Celebrity stylist and fashion designer Larissa Williams left Hollywood for Lahaina; now she glams up islanders with her romantic, approachable fashions. Her charming atelier is part boutique, part workshop. It's filled with gorgeous original designs and handpicked vintage pieces. The tiny upstairs shop is somewhat tricky to find at first; keep poking around until you locate it. 505 Front St. (upstairs). www.loveleru.com. (C) **808/661-2741.**

Lahaina Galleries Sea creatures sculpted from bronze and wood greet you at the entrance of this Front Street haven for art. Whether you fancy Robert Bissell's whimsical portraits of elephants swarmed by monarch butterflies, Guy Buffet's Parisian cafe scenes, or Dario Campanile's provocative still lifes, this gallery has an artist and aesthetic for you. The knowledgeable staff is helpful and not prone to the high-pressured sales pitches of some nearby galleries. Also at the **Shops at Wailea** (3750 Wailea Alanui; (C) **808/874-8583**). 828 Front St. www.lahainagalleries.com. (C) **808/661-6284.**

KAANAPALI

Whalers Village This Kaanapali Beach landmark offers everything from **Louis Vuitton** to **Tommy Bahama** and **Sephora,** with a few local designers in the mix. Of the latter, **Maggie Coulombe** (www.maggiecoulombe.com; (C) **808/344-6672**) is **fashion-forward, with body-hugging** haute couture **silks and pretty baubles.** The wonderful **Lahaina Printsellers** ((C) **808/661-4294**) has stacks of antique prints, maps, paintings, and engravings, including 18th- to 20th-century cartography, which are great fun to browse. You can find classy aloha wear at **Tory Richard** ((C) **808/667-7762**) and matching mother-daughter batik clothing at **Blue Ginger** ((C) **808/667-5793**). The **Sandal Tree** ((C) **808/667-5330**) has one of the best shoe selections on the island—featuring fashionable Olukai sandals with arch support, Charles Jourdan pumps, and even five-fingered shoes by Vibram. The **Totally Hawaiian Gift Gallery** (www.totallyhawaiian.com; (C) **808/667-4070**) carries a selection of Niihau shell jewelry, Hawaiian CDs, Norfolk pine bowls, and Hawaiian quilt kits. In contrast to most Maui shops, stores here remain open until 10pm. The complex is also home to the **Whalers Village Museum** (p. 263), with its interactive exhibits, 40-foot sperm-whale skeleton, and sandcastles on perpetual display. Parking at Whalers Village is unfortunately expensive; be sure to get validation. 2435 Kaanapali Pkwy. www.whalersvillage.com. (C) **808/661-4567.**

HONOKOWAI, KAHANA & NAPILI

Those driving north of Kaanapali toward Kapalua will notice the **Honokowai Marketplace,** on Lower Honoapiilani Road, only minutes before the Kapalua Airport. It houses restaurants and coffee shops, a dry cleaner, the flagship **Times Supermarket,** and a few clothing stores.

KAPALUA

Village Galleries This well-regarded gallery showcases the finest regional artists in a small space within the Ritz-Carlton's lobby. View Pegge Hopper's iconic Hawaiian women, George Allan's luminous oil landscapes, and Betty Hay Freeland's colorful local scenes. Three-dimensional pieces include gemstone-quality Niihau shell leis, hand-blown glass sculptures, and delicately turned bowls of Norfolk pine that gleam in the light. The Ritz-Carlton's monthly artist-in-residence program features the gallery's artists in special hands-on workshops (free, including materials). There are two additional locations in Lahaina, one at 120 Dickenson St. ((C) **808/661-4402**), and another at 180 Dickenson St. ((C) **808/661-5559**). At the Ritz-Carlton Kapalua, 1 Ritz-Carlton Dr. www.villagegalleriesmaui.com. (C) **808/669-1800.**

South Maui

KIHEI

Kihei is one long strip of strip malls. Most of the shopping here is concentrated in the **Azeka Place Shopping Center** on South Kihei Road. Across the street, **Azeka Place II** houses several prominent attractions, including a cluster of specialty shops with everything from children's clothes to shoes, sunglasses, and swimwear.

WAILEA

Shops at Wailea   This elegant high-end mall mainly features luxury brands (**Louis Vuitton, Coach, Tiffany & Co., Gucci**), but some unique gems are hidden amid the complex's 50-odd shops. **Martin & MacArthur** (✆ 808/891-8844) sells luminous curly koa bowls and keepsake boxes. **CY Maui** (✆ 808/891-0782) offers flowing, hand-painted clothing in washable silks and other natural fibers. When Paris Hilton shops for bling on Maui, she heads to **Maui Enchantress** (www.mauienchantress.com; ✆ 808/891-6360), a pinker-than-thou boutique brimming with Swarovski crystal–studded slippers, glitter powder, fringed tank tops, and shell-encrusted silver mirrors. If sparkles aren't your thing, you can always hit up **Gap** or **Banana Republic.** The mall is home to several good restaurants, and the Whalers General Store on the lower level sells Bubbies mochi ice cream (made on Oahu and coveted by locals) by the piece. 3750 Wailea Alanui. www.theshopsatwailea.com. ✆ 808/891-6770.

Upcountry Maui

Hot Island Glassblowing Studio & Gallery   Watch glass blowers transform molten glass into artworks in this Makawao Courtyard studio. If you didn't witness it happening, you might not believe that the kaleidoscopic vases and charismatic marine animals were truly made out of the fragile, fiery-hot medium. Several artists show their work here; prices range from under $20 for pretty plumeria dishes to over $4,000 for stunning sculptural pieces. In the middle range are luminescent jellyfish floating in glass. 3620 Baldwin Ave. www.hotislandglass.com. ✆ 808/572-4527.

The Mercantile   Every texture in this boutique is sumptuous, from the cashmere sweaters to tooled leather belts. In addition to upscale men and women's clothing, you'll find Kiehl's cosmetics, Jurlique organic body products, eye-catching jewelry, and an assortment of French soaps and luxurious linens. 3673 Baldwin Ave. ✆ 808/572-1407.

Viewpoints Gallery ★★   This handsome gallery located in Makawao Courtyard features the museum-quality work of 40 established Maui artists. The front half is dedicated to revolving solo shows and invitational exhibits—including the annual Malama Wao Akua show, which is sponsored by the East Maui Watershed Partnership and celebrates native Hawaiian flora and fauna. The back half of the gallery features pieces by collective artists: luminous oils by George Allan, breathtakingly realistic pastels by Kit Gentry, and ceramic tea sets brimming with personality by Christina Cowan. 3620 Baldwin Ave. www.viewpointsgallerymaui.com. ✆ 808/572-5979.

FRESH FLOWERS IN KULA

Like anthuriums on the Big Island, proteas are a Maui trademark and an abundant crop on Haleakala's rich volcanic slopes. They also travel well, dry beautifully, and can be shipped worldwide with ease. **Proteas of Hawaii,** 15200 Haleakala Hwy., Kula (www.proteasof hawaii.com; ℭ **808/878-2533,** ext. 210), located next door to the Kula Lodge, is a reliable source of this exotic flower.

UPCOUNTRY EDIBLES

Working folks in Makawao pick up spaghetti and lasagna, sandwiches, salads, and changing specials from the **Rodeo General Store,** 3661 Baldwin Ave. (ℭ **808/572-1868**). At the back of the store, a superior wine selection is housed in its own temperature-controlled cave.

For just shy of a century, the hardworking Komoda family has been satisfying Maui's sweet tooth. Untold numbers have creaked over the wooden floors to pick up a box of famous cream puffs at **T. Komoda Store and Bakery,** 3674 Baldwin Ave. (ℭ **808/572-7261**). The coveted pastries (filled with vanilla or mocha cream) are just the beginning; stick donuts encrusted with macadamia nuts, Chantilly cakes, fruit pies, and butter rolls keep loyal customers coming to this nostalgic piece of Maui history. Old-timers know to arrive before noon or miss out. Bring cash and be aware of the odd business hours: It's open 7am to 5pm on Monday, Tuesday, Thursday, and Friday, and 7am to 2pm on Saturday.

King protea.

East Maui

PAIA

Mana Foods ★★   The state's best health-food store hides behind an unimposing dark-green facade. Shopping at Mana Foods is an adventure to be sure—parking can be a nuisance, and the narrow aisles inside are crammed with *nuevo* hippies, yoga instructors, and the wild-haired children of both. Don't let this dissuade you. Though compact, this store has a better natural-foods selection than you'll find in most big cities—at great prices, too. The deli is a cornucopia of deliciousness, with fresh-made sushi, soups, salads, hot entrees, and raw desserts. The produce shelves are worthy of worship: pyramids of ripe avocados, local asparagus, and more tropical fruits than you have names for. Ask the stocker for a sample of rambutan or rolinia. Hit up the health and beauty room for locally made soaps and hard-to-find essential oils. 49 Baldwin Ave. www.manafoodsmaui.com. ℭ **808/579-8078.**

Maui Crafts Guild ★★   On the corner of Hana Highway and Baldwin Avenue, this artists' collective features distinctive, high-quality crafts. For over 3 decades, the guild's dozen or so artists have been fashioning exquisite works out of ceramic, glass, wood, mixed media, and natural fibers. The fluid, evocative stained-glass pieces by Joshua Lee Cox, the unique banana-bark sculptures by Mathew Westcott, and free-spirited mosaics by Monica Morakis are particularly wonderful—and well worth the trouble of shipping home. 120 Hana Hwy. www.maui craftsguild.com. ✆ **808/579-9697.**

Maui Hands ★★ This consignment shop/gallery teems with handcrafted treasures produced by local artisans. You'll find Niihau shell necklaces, vivid paintings of local beaches and tropical flowers, carved koa bowls and rocking chairs, screen-printed textiles, whimsical ceramics, and one-of-a-kind souvenirs for every budget. Get to know the artists, who are on hand and happy to discuss their work. A second location at 1169 Makawao Ave. in Makawao carries a slightly different selection by many of same artists (✆ **808/572-2008**). 84 Hana Hwy. www.mauihands.com. ✆ **808/579-9245.**

Pearl ★ This chic housewares shop supplies everything necessary for beach cottage living: Turkish spa towels, vintage hardware, embroidered cover-ups, and Indonesian furnishings. Stylish shop owner Malia Vandervoort collects treasures from around the globe that match her soulful, simple aesthetic. Among her best-selling items, Annie Fischer's hand-painted, made-in-Maui pillows capture the hypnotic colors of Baldwin Beach just down the road. 285 Hana Hwy. www.pearl butik.com. ✆ **808/579-8899.**

Tamara Catz ★★★ Visiting fashionistas, take note: A stop at local designer Tamara Catz's flagship store is de rigueur. The adorable boutique is small but stocked with wardrobe essentials. Designed on Maui, the filmy cotton slips, silk maxi-dresses, and pantsuits hand-embroidered with birds and flowers capture the relaxed elegance and heat of the tropics. One half of the shop is devoted to Catz's dreamy bridal collection, with ultra-romantic, no-fuss gowns that can easily transition from barefoot vows on the beach to dancing the night away. The jewelry case has tempting pieces studded with crystals, shells, and coral. 83 Hana Hwy. www.tamaracatz.com. ✆ **808/579-9184.**

HANA

Hana Coast Gallery ★★★ Hidden away in the posh Travaasa Hana resort, this critically acclaimed, 3000-square-foot gallery is an aesthetic and cultural experience to savor. You won't find pandering sunsets or jumping dolphins here.

Maui's North Shore Is Bikini Central

Paia has no fewer than five boutiques dedicated to Maui's sun-kissed beach uniform, the bikini. And that's not all; many of the other shops lining Baldwin Avenue and Hana Highway also sell swimwear. Head to this north-shore beach town for everything from skimpy Brazilian bikinis to full-figured, mix-and-match-your-own suits. The best of the bunch are **Maui Girl,** 12 Baldwin Ave. (www.maui-girl.com; ✆ **808/579-9266;** daily 9am–6pm), a cheery beach shack that has outfitted more than one "Sports Illustrated" cover model; and **Le Tarte,** 24 Baldwin Ave. (www.letarteswimwear. com; ✆ **808/579-6022;** daily 10am–6pm), an ultra-chic boutique with embroidered beach cover-ups so pretty you'll want to wear them out and about. Maui Girl and Le Tarte are both owned by local designers, as are two other great spots to shop for suits: **Wings Hawaii,** 69 Hana Hwy. (www.wingshawaii.com; ✆ **808/579-3110), and Tamara Catz,** 83 Hana Hwy. (www.tamaracatz.com; ✆ **808/579-9184).**

Known for its quality curatorship and commitment to Hawaiian culture, this off-the-beaten-path art haven is almost entirely devoted to Hawaii artists. Among the stellar Maui artists represented are *plein air* painter Michael Clements, master carver Keola Sequeria, and Melissa Chimera, whose massive botanical canvases feature endemic Hawaiian flowers. If you're considering purchasing a koa wood bowl or piece of furniture, look here first. You'll be hard-pressed to find a better selection under one roof. At the Travaasa Hana. www.hanacoast.com. *©* **808/248-8636.**

Hasegawa General Store   For more than a century, this family-run mercantile has been serving the Hana community. Established in 1910, this humble, tin-roofed grocery store has just about anything you might need. Harkening back to the days when stores like these were islanders' sole shopping outlet, the aisles are packed with Hawaiian books and music, fishing poles, Hana-grown coffee, diapers, fridge magnets, garden tools, fresh vegetables, dry goods, and ice cream. Don't leave without a Hasegawa T-shirt or baseball cap to prove you were here. Hana Hwy. *©* **808/248-8231.**

MAUI NIGHTLIFE

Maui tends to turn out the lights at 10pm; nightlife options on this island are limited, but you'll find a few gems listed below.

The island's most prestigious entertainment venue is the $32-million **Maui Arts & Cultural Center,** in Kahului (www.mauiarts.org; *©* **808/242-7469**). The center is as precious to Maui as the Met is to New York, with a visual-arts gallery, an outdoor amphitheater, offices, rehearsal space, a 300-seat theater for experimental performances, and a 1,200-seat main theater. Check the website for schedules and buy your tickets in advance.

HAWAIIAN MUSIC   The best of Hawaiian music can be heard every Wednesday night at the Napili Kai Beach Resort's indoor amphitheater, thanks to the **Masters of Hawaiian Slack Key Guitar Series** (www.slackkey.com; *©* **888/669-3858**). The weekly shows present a side of Hawaii that few visitors ever get to see. Host George Kahumoku, Jr., introduces a new slack key master every week. Not only is there incredible Hawaiian music and singing, but George and his guest also "talk story" about old Hawaii, music, and Hawaiian culture. Not to be missed.

The major hotels generally have lobby lounges offering Hawaiian music, soft jazz, or hula shows beginning at sunset. If **Hapa, Amy Hanaialii,** or **Keali'i Reichel** are playing anywhere on their native island, don't miss them; they're among the finest Hawaiian musicians around today. **Willie K** (Maui's answer to Jimi Hendrix) performs weekly at **Mulligan's on the Blue,** 100 Kaukahi St., Wailea (www.mulligansontheblue.com; *©* **808/874-1131**).

West Maui

Make time to see **'Ulalena ★**, Maui Theatre, 878 Front St., Lahaina (www.ulalena.com; *©* **808/856-7900**), a "Cirque du Soleil"–style entertainment that weaves Hawaiian mythology with drama, dance, and state-of-the-art multimedia capabilities in a multimillion-dollar theater. It's interactive; dancers stream down the aisles and musicians play from surprising corners. The story unfolds seamlessly; at the end, you'll be shocked to realize that not a single word of dialogue was spoken. Performances are given Tuesday through Saturday. Tickets are $60 to $80 for adults, $30 to $50 for children 6 to 12.

luau, **MAUI-STYLE**

Most of the larger hotels in Maui's major resorts offer luau on a regular basis. You'll pay about $80 to $120 to attend one, but don't expect it to be a homegrown affair prepared in the traditional Hawaiian way. There are, however, commercial luau that capture the romance and spirit of the luau with quality food and entertainment.

Maui's best choice is indisputably the nightly **Old Lahaina Luau** ★★ (www.oldlahainaluau.com; ✆ **800/248-5828** or 808/667-1998). Located just ocean-side of the Lahaina Cannery, the Old Lahaina Luau maintains its high standards in food and entertainment—and enjoys an oceanfront setting that is peerless. Local craftspeople display their wares only a few feet from the ocean. Seating is provided on lauhala mats for those who wish to dine as the traditional Hawaiians did, but there are tables for everyone else. There's no fire dancing in the program, but you won't miss it (for that, go to the Feast at Lele; p. 333). This luau offers a

healthy balance of entertainment, showmanship, authentic high-quality food, educational value, and sheer romantic beauty. (No watered-down mai tais, either; these are the real thing.)

The luau begins at sunset and features Tahitian and Hawaiian entertainment, including ancient hula, hula from the missionary era, modern hula, and an intelligent narrative on the dance's rocky course of survival into modern times. The food, served from an open-air thatched structure, is as much Pacific Rim as authentically Hawaiian: imu-roasted kalua pig, baked mahimahi in Maui onion cream sauce, guava chicken, teriyaki sirloin steak, lomi salmon, poi, dried fish, poke, Hawaiian sweet potato, sautéed vegetables, seafood salad, and taro leaves with coconut milk. The cost is $109 for adults, $78 for children 12 and under.

For information on all of Maui's luaus, go to **www.mauihawaiiluau.com**.

A very different type of live entertainment, **Warren & Annabelle's,** 900 Front St., Lahaina (www.warrenandannabelles.com; ✆ **808/667-6244**), is a magic/comedy cocktail show with illusionist Warren Gibson and "Annabelle," a ghost from the 1800s who plays the grand piano (even taking requests from the audience) as Warren dazzles you with his sleight-of-hand magic. Appetizers, desserts, and cocktails are available (either as a package or a la carte). Check-in is at 5 and 7:30pm. The show-only price is $64; the show plus gourmet appetizers and dessert costs $105. You must be 21 to attend.

You won't have to ask what's going on at **Cheeseburger in Paradise,** 811 Front St., Lahaina (www.cheeseburgerland.com; ✆ **808/661-4855**), the two-story green-and-white building at the corner of Front and Lahainaluna streets. Just go outside and you'll hear it. Loud, live, and lively tropical rock blasts into the streets and out to sea nightly from 4:30 to 10pm.

Other venues for music in west Maui include the following:

- **Hula Grill,** in Whalers Village, Kaanapali (✆ 808/667-6636), has live music (usually Hawaiian) every day from 11am to 9pm.

- **Kimo's,** 845 Front St., Lahaina (✆ 808/661-4811), has live musicians every night at various times; call for details.

- **Pioneer Inn,** 658 Wharf St., Lahaina (✆ 808/661-3636), offers a variety of live music Tuesday through Thursday nights 5:30 to 8pm.

- **Sansei Seafood Restaurant & Sushi Bar,** 600 Office Rd., Kapalua (© **808/ 669-6286**), has karaoke on Thursday through Saturday from 10pm to 1am.

- **Sea House Restaurant,** at the Napili Kai Beach Resort, Napili (© **808/669- 1500**), has live music nightly from 7 to 9pm.

South Maui

The Kihei, Wailea, and Maalaea areas in south Maui also feature music in a variety of locations:

- **Kahale's Beach Club,** 36 Keala Place, Kihei (© **808/875-7711**), is a bit of a dive bar, but has a potpourri of rock music nightly.

- **Life's a Beach,** 1913 S. Kihei Rd., Kihei (www.mauibars.com; © **808/891- 8010**), has live music nightly and karaoke; call for times.

- **Mulligan's on the Blue,** 100 Kaukahi St., Wailea (www.mulligansontheblue. com; © **808/874-1131**), offers rollicking Irish music on Sunday, a Wednesday dinner show with local legend Willie K, and other entertainers during the week.

- **Sansei Seafood Restaurant & Sushi Bar,** in Kihei Town Center, 1881 South Kihei Rd., Kihei (www.sanseihawaii.com; © **808/879-0004**), has karaoke Thursday through Saturday from 10pm to 1am.

- **South Shore Tiki Lounge,** 1913 S. Kihei Rd., Kihei (www.southshoretiki lounge.com; © **808/874-6444**), has dancing nightly from 10pm to 1:30am.

Upcountry Maui

Upcountry in Makawao, the party never ends at Casanova, 1188 Makawao Ave. (www.casanovamakawao.com; © 808/572-0220), the popular Italian ristorante. If a big-name Mainland band is resting up on Maui following a sold-out concert on Oahu, you may find its members setting up for an impromptu night here. DJs take over on Wednesday (ladies' night); on Friday and Saturday, live music starts between 9 and 10pm and continues to 1:30am. Expect blues, rock 'n' roll, reggae, jazz, and Hawaiian. Elvin Bishop, the local duo Hapa, Los Lobos, and others have taken Casanova's stage. The cover is usually $10 to $20.

Paia & Central Maui

In Central Maui, The **Kahului Ale House,** 355 E. Kamehameha Ave., Kahului (www.alehouse.net; © **808/877-9001**), features live music or a DJ most nights; call for schedule.

In Paia, **Charley's Restaurant,** 142 Hana Hwy. (www.charleysmaui.com; © **808/579-8085**), features an eclectic selection of music, from country-western to reggae to rock 'n' roll Thursday through Saturday.

7

MOLOKAI

by Jeanne Cooper

"**D**on't try to change Molokai; let Molokai change you" is the mantra on this least developed of the major Hawaiian islands. No luxury hotels, no stoplights, and "no hurry" are points of pride for locals, nearly half of whom are of Native Hawaiian descent. The island welcomes adventure travelers, spiritual pilgrims, and others who show appreciation for its untrammeled beauty and unrushed ways.

Known as "the child of the moon" in Native Hawaiian lore, Molokai remains a place apart, luminous yet largely inaccessible to the casual visitor. Tourism, and modern conveniences in general, has only a small footprint here, and although the island is just 38 miles long by 10 miles wide, it takes time to see what it has to offer. As the sign at the airport reads: aloha slow down, this is molokai.

Patience and planning do reward travelers with a compass of superlatives. The world's tallest sea cliffs stand on the North Shore; on the South Shore, historic fish ponds line the state's longest fringing reef. The island's most ancient settlement sits within gorgeous Halawa Valley, on the East End, while the West End offers one of Hawaii's most impressive sandy beaches, nearly 3-mile-long (and often empty) Papohaku.

The percentage of people with Native Hawaiian blood is also higher on Molokai than on the other major islands. Many have maintained or revived Hawaiian traditions such as growing taro, managing fish ponds, and staging games for Makahiki, the winter festival. "Sustainability" isn't a buzzword but a centuries-old way of life that eyes modern innovations with caution—and many on island are fierce in opposition to growth.

Residents and visitors alike take inspiration from the stories of Father Damien and others who cared for the suffering exiles of Kalaupapa. Once a natural prison for those diagnosed with leprosy, the remote North Shore peninsula is now a national historical park with very limited access but profound appeal—much like Molokai itself.

ESSENTIALS
Arriving

BY PLANE   Unless you're flying to the island as part of a Kalaupapa charter tour, you'll arrive in **Hoolehua** (airport code: MKK), which many just call the Molokai Airport. It's about 7½ miles from the center of Kaunakakai town.

'**Ohana by Hawaiian** (www.hawaiianairlines.com/ohana; ✆ **800/367-5320**), a Hawaiian Airlines subsidiary launched in spring 2014, flies three times a day between Hoolehua and Honolulu on 48-passenger, twin-engine turbo-props. *Note:* If you're hoping to connect from a flight from the Mainland, current schedules require several hours' layover in Honolulu—which means landing on Molokai just before nightfall. If you can, spend a night (or more) on Oahu first and catch a morning or midday flight here later. You'll appreciate the aerial sight-seeing as well as the easier navigation once on land.

Facing page: Molokai coastline.

The visuals are even more impressive from the single-engine, nine-seat aircraft of **Mokulele Airlines** (www.mokuleleairlines.com; ✆ **866/260-7070** or 808/270-8767 outside the U.S.), which provides service 10 times a day between Honolulu and Hoolehua, with a bonus evening flight on Friday and Sunday. Mokulele also flies seven times a day (six on Sun) between Kahului (Maui) and Hoolehua, often flying over Lanai en route. *Note:* The Maui flights fill up quickly because they're the only air link for Molokai residents with family or business matters on the Valley Isle. Also, at check-in, you'll be asked to stand on a scale with any carry-on luggage. Only the agent is able to see the results, but customers who weigh more than 350 pounds are not allowed to board. On the upside, you don't have to go through any security screenings (hello, liquids and gels!)

Makani Kai Air (www.makanikaiair.com; ✆ **808/834-1111**) also flies nine-seaters to Molokai, departing from its private terminal on the perimeter of the Honolulu airport ('Ohana by Hawaiian, Island, and Mokulele operate from the more centrally located commuter terminal.) Makani Kai currently flies six times a day between Honolulu and Hoolehua, with additional scheduled service to Kalaupapa from Honolulu and "topside" Molokai (that is, anywhere but Kalaupapa); chartered flights to both Molokai airports from elsewhere in the islands are also available. Flights to and from Kalaupapa must be packaged with a tour from **Damien Tours,** which includes the necessary permit to visit the national historical park (ages 16 and older only).

BY BOAT   Although the ferry generally costs more and takes at least twice as long as a flight from Kahului, day-trippers often choose to travel between Maui's Lahaina Harbor and Molokai's Kaunakakai Wharf on the *Molokai Princess* (www.molokaiferry.com; ✆ **877/500-6284** or 808/667-9266). The 100-foot, 149-passenger yacht is fitted with advanced gyroscopic stabilizers, but note that strong winds and rough waters in the 15-mile Pailolo Channel—particularly in winter—can still induce queasiness. In

calmer conditions, the open-air observation deck provides a great venue for spotting spinner dolphins and whales (Dec–Apr for the latter.) The ferry makes the 90-minute run between Lahaina and Kaunakakai twice daily (once on Sun); the round-trip costs $141 for adults and $71 for children 4 to 12. Most day-trippers opt for one of the ferry's tour packages: **Cruise/Car,** which includes round-trip passage and a rental car for $260 for the driver (age 25 or older), $125 per additional adult passenger, and $62.50 per child age 4 to 12; or the **Alii Tour,** a 6½-hour guided tour in an air-conditioned van for $260 per adult and $160 per child, including a stop for lunch. Both must be booked in advance, with a 10-percent discount for reservations made through the ferry's website.

Coastline of Molokai.

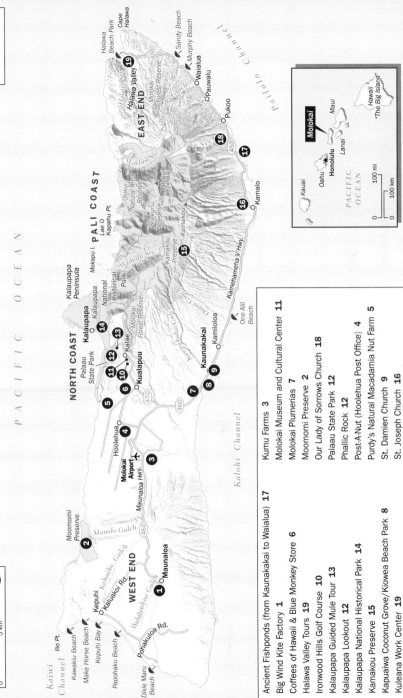

Molokai

Visitor Information

Destination Molokai Visitors Bureau (www.gohawaii.com/molokai; ✆ **800/ 800-6367** from the U.S. mainland and Canada, or 808/553-3876) offers a wealth of practical tips and cultural insights on its website, and encourages first-time visitors in particular to stop by its office in Kaunakakai for sightseeing advice tailored to current conditions as well as personal preferences. Open weekdays from 9am till noon, the bureau is in the Moore Center, 2 Kamoi St. (just off Hwy. 450), next to the office of the island's weekly newspaper, the **"Molokai Dispatch"** (www. themolokaidispatch.com). Browse the latter online before you go to familiarize yourself with local issues and special events, and pick up a free copy, published Wednesdays, on island for current dining specials and entertainment. **Visit-Molokai.com** has not updated all the practical information on its website (slogan: "Everything About Molokai, By Folks Who Live on Molokai"), but still has useful sightseeing tips, photos, and insights. All maintain Facebook pages, too.

The Island in Brief

KAUNAKAKAI ★

If any place on Molokai can be described as "bustling," this centrally located, usually sunny town on the south side would be it. Nearly every restaurant, store, and community facility on the island lies within a few blocks of one another, with a sprinkling of modern edifices to spoil the illusion that you're in the Old West; the state's longest pier serves the ferry, fishing boats, outrigger canoes, and kids enjoying a dip in the ocean. Other than Saturday mornings, when it seems as if the entire town (pop. 3,500) turns out for a street market, it's easy to find a parking space among the local pickup trucks.

CENTRAL UPLANDS & NORTH SHORE ★★

Upland from Kaunakakai, Hawaiian homesteaders in **Hoolehua** tend small plots near the state's largest producer of organic papaya and the main airport. In the nearby plantation town of **Kualapuu,** the espresso bar at Coffees of Hawaii perks up hikers and mule riders returning from **Kalaupapa National Historical Park ★★★** on the North Shore's isolated peninsula, where generations of people diagnosed with leprosy (now called Hansen's disease) were exiled. The forest grows denser and the air cooler as Highway 470 (Kalae Hwy.) passes the island's lone golf course and ends at **Palaau State Park ★★**, known for its phallic rock and dramatic overlook of Kalaupapa, some 1,700 feet below. To the east stand the world's tallest sea cliffs, 3,600 to 3,900 feet, which bracket the North Shore's secluded beaches, waterfalls, and lush valleys, all virtually inaccessible. Fishing charters, helicopter tours from Maui, and, in summer, a strenuous kayak trip can bring them within closer view.

THE WEST END ★

Molokai Ranch owns most of the rugged, often arid west end of the island, famous for the nearly 3-mile-long **Papohaku Beach**—and not much else since the ranch infamously shut down in 2008, closing its lodge, beach camp, movie theater, and golf course, among other facilities. In 2012, the ranch reintroduced cattle and announced intentions to "revitalize" its hospitality operations, but in the meantime, the plantation-era village of **Maunaloa** at the end of the Maunaloa Highway (Hwy. 460) remains a virtual ghost town, and the decaying buildings of Kaluakoi Hotel (closed in 2001), above Kepuhi Beach, look like a set from "Lost." Summer is the best time to explore the shoreline here, although the crash

Halawa Valley.

of winter waves provides a convenient sleep aid for inhabitants of the three still-open condo developments on the overgrown **Kaluakoi** resort. Look out for axis deer when driving here at night; wild turkeys rule the roost by day.

THE EAST END ★★★

From Kaunakakai, the two-lane King Kamehameha V Highway (Hwy. 450) heads 27 miles east through lush greenery to **Halawa Valley,** a culturally significant as well as beautiful enclave, open only for guided tours except for a beach park. Before you arrive, though, you'll pass pocket beaches, historic fish ponds, two churches built by Father Damien, and the entrance to Puu O Hoku, a working cattle ranch that also serves as a reserve for nene, the endangered state bird. Blink along the way and you'll miss the region's one condo resort and single gro-cery/dining outlet. All the greenery indicates you're on the rainier half of the island, with more frequent showers January through March, but be careful: The sun still blazes here, too.

GETTING AROUND

Getting around Molokai isn't easy without a rental car, which you need to reserve as early as possible. During special events and holiday weekends (see "When to Go," in chapter 3), rental agencies simply run out of vehicles.

BY CAR   The international chain **Alamo Rent a Car** (www.alamo.com; ✆ 888/826-6893) has both an office and cars at the airport in Hoolehua. The office of **Molokai Car Rental** (www.molokaicars.com; ✆ 808/336-0670) may be in Kaunakakai, where owner Amanda Schonely also sells her unique shell-deco-rated caps and island jewelry, but she's happy to leave a car (or minivan) for you at the airport or ferry dock, with the keys inside.

BY TAXI   Per state law, taxis charge $3 a mile plus a "drop charge" of $3.50, or about $32 from the airport to the Hotel Molokai in Kaunakakai and $42 to a West End condo. Try to arrange rides a day or two in advance, either with

Midnight Taxi (© 808/658-1410) or **Hele Mai Taxi** (www.molokaitaxi.com; © 808/336-0967).

BY BUS The nonprofit **Maui Economic Opportunity, Inc.** (http://meoinc. charityfinders.org; © 808/877-7651) provides free daytime shuttle bus service on weekdays between Kaunakakai and the East End, Hoolehua/Kualapuu, and Maunaloa/Kaluakoi. It's designed for rural residents but open to all; if you're feeling adventurous, check out the online schedule (click the bus icon at the top of the website).

[FastFACTS] MOLOKAI

Note: All addresses are in Kaunakakai unless otherwise noted.

ATMs/Banks Both **Bank of Hawaii,** 20 Ala Malama St. (www.boh.com; © 808/553-3273), and **American Savings Bank,** 40 Ala Malama St. (www. asbhawaii.com; © 808/553-8391), have 24-hour ATMs.

Cellphones The island has a few cellphone towers, but the signal can be weak, especially outside of Kaunakakai and Hoolehua.

Dentists/Doctors The **Molokai Community Health Center,** 30 Oki Place (www.molokaichc.org; © 808/553-5038), provides dental and medical services

from 8am to 5pm weekdays.

Emergencies Call © **911** in life-threatening circumstances. Otherwise, contact the **police** at © **808/553-5355** or the **fire department** at © **808/553-5601.**

Hospital **Molokai General Hospital,** 280 Homeolu Place (www.molokaigeneralhospital.org; © **808/553-5331**), has 15 beds and an outpatient clinic and is open most weekdays.

Internet Access The **Aqua Hotel Molokai,** most vacation rentals, and a handful of restaurants offer free, if not necessarily

reliable, Wi-Fi. See listings under "Where to Stay" and "Where to Eat," below.

Pharmacy The only pharmacy, **Molokai Drugs,** 28 Kamoi St. (at the rear of the shopping strip; © **808/553-5790**), is open 8:45am to 5:45pm Monday to Friday and 8am to 2pm Saturday.

Post Office The **central office** at 120 Ala Malama is open Monday to Friday 9am to 3:30pm and Saturday 9 to 11am. The **Hoolehua branch,** just off Highway 460 on Puupeelua Avenue, offers the popular "Post-a-Nut" service (p. 373); it's open weekdays 8:30am to noon and 12:30 to 4pm.

EXPLORING MOLOKAI

Note: You'll find the following attractions on the "Molokai" map, on p. 369.

Attractions & Points of Interest

Most of Molokai's attractions are of the natural variety, but a few manmade sights are worth adding to your itinerary.

CENTRAL UPLANDS & NORTH SHORE

Molokai Museum and Cultural Center MUSEUM/HISTORIC SITE Halfway between Coffees of Hawaii and the Kalaupapa Overlook, this small museum on the site of a restored sugar mill has a large gift shop of local arts and crafts and eclectic, minimally labeled exhibits from petroglyphs to plantation-era

Post-a-Nut sign.

furnishings. The most intriguing may be the photos and stone *kii* (tiki) from Kalaupapa, whose historic buildings are the subject of one of two 10-minute videos running continuously. The other focuses on the ingenuity of Rudolph W. Meyer, a German surveyor who married a Hawaiian chiefess and founded the compact mill in 1878. Walk a few yards uphill from the museum (the Meyers' former home) to see the barnlike mill and outdoor pit where circling mules powered cane-crushing machinery.

West side of Kalae Hwy. (Hwy. 470), near mile marker 4 (just after the turnoff for the Ironwood Hills Golf Course), Kalae. Admission $5 adults, $1 children and students. Mon–Sat 10am–2pm.

Post-a-Nut ★ ICON   Molokai's postmaster, Gary Lam, will help you say "Aloha" with a Molokai coconut. Just write a message on the coconut with a felt-tip pen, and he'll send it via U.S. mail. Coconuts are free, but postage averages $10 to $15 for a smaller, Mainland-bound coconut. Gary mails out about 3,000 per year, usually decorated with colorful stamps.

Hoolehua Post Office, Puupeelua Ave. (Hwy. 480), near Maunaloa Hwy. (Hwy. 460). © **808/567-6144.** Mon–Fri 8:30am–noon and 12:30–4:30pm.

EAST END

Ancient Fish Ponds ★ HISTORIC SITE   The rock walls of dozens of ancient fish ponds—a pinnacle of Pacific aquaculture—can be seen for miles along the shoreline from the highway between Kaunakakai and the East End. The U-shaped lava rock and coral walls contain sluices that allowed smaller fish to enter and trapped them as they grew larger. Some are still in use today; join volunteers with **Ka Honua Momona** (www.kahonuamomona.org, © **808/553-8353**) in restoring the 15th-century **Alii Fish Pond,** a half-mile west of One Alii Beach Park (p. 379) and once reserved for kings, and **Kalokoeli Pond,** another 3½ miles east, on the third Saturday of each month.

A HIKE BACK IN history

"There are things on Molokai, sacred things, that you may not be able to see or hear, but they are there," says Pilipo Solatorio, who was born and raised in Halawa Valley and survived the 1946 tsunami that barreled into the ancient settlement. "As Hawaiians, we respect these things."

Solatorio and his family are among the few who allow visitors into emerald **Halawa Valley,** offering daily tours Monday to Saturday by reservation only. After welcoming visitors with traditional chants and the sharing of inhaled breath, foreheads pressed together, Solatorio (or his son Greg) relates the history of the area before guiding the group along the rocky trail, which crosses two shallow streams. He also notes ancient sites, taro terraces, and native and invasive species along the path (1.7 miles each way). Once at the pool below Moaula Falls (which can also be seen from the beach or highway), visitors may swim in the cool water, if conditions permit.

The 70-year-old Solatorio feels that learning about the history and culture of Molokai is part of the secret to appreciating the island. "To see the real Molokai, you need to understand and know things so that you are *pono,* you are right with the land and don't disrespect the culture," says Solatorio.

Book online through **Molokai Outdoors** (www.molokai-outdoors.com; ℂ **877/553-4477** or 808/553-4477; $75 adults, $45 children 6–12) or leave a phone message with the Solatorios (www.halawavalleymolokai.com; ℂ **808/551-5538** or 808/551-1055), giving your name, telephone number, the number of people in your party, and requested date to visit. Wear shoes that can get wet and your swimsuit under your clothes; bring a backpack with insect repellent, sunscreen, water, a poncho, refreshments, a towel, and a camera.

Farms

KAUNAKAKAI

Hundreds of plumeria trees produce fragrant yellow and pink blooms virtually year-round at **Molokai Plumerias** ★, 1342 Maunaloa Hwy., 2½ miles west of Kaunakakai (www.molokaiplumerias.com; ℂ **808/553-3391**). Genial co-owner, artist, and former pro surfer Jaia Waits will lead you on an informative blossom-gathering tour ($25; weekdays by appointment) before showing you how to string your own lei.

CENTRAL UPLANDS

A prolonged drought forced **Coffees of Hawaii,** 1630 Farrington Ave., off Highway 470, Kualapuu (www.coffeesofhawaii.com; ℂ **877/322-FARM** or 808/567-9490), to sell most of its former pineapple land, discontinue tours, and lease its espresso bar/cafe to operators of the nearby mule ride. Yet visitors can still enjoy a cup of joe, hearty lunch, or weekly Hawaiian music jam (Tues 10am–noon) within view of 115 acres of coffee trees producing four estate roasts.

In Hoolehua, Kammy and Tuddie Purdy of **Purdy's All-Natural Macadamia Nut Farm** ★, Lihi Pali Avenue, behind Molokai High School (www.molokai-aloha.com/macnuts; ℂ **808/567-6601**), offer free tours of their homestead orchard, first planted in the 1920s, with samples of raw nuts and macadamia blossom honey. The farm is open weekdays 9:30am to 3:30pm and Saturday

10am to 2pm (Sun and holidays by appointment).

Just south of the airport, **Kumu Farms,** Hua Ai Road, 1 mile south of Highway 460 (*©* **808/351-3326**), has a large stand selling organic produce, herbs, pesto, and other farm products. It's open Tuesday to Friday 9am to 4pm.

EAST END

The Pruet family grows a brilliantly hued mosaic of organic heliconia and ginger at its **Kuleana Work Center** (www.molokaiflowers.com) in Halawa Valley. It's free to drop in (Tues–Sat 10am–4pm; Sun by appointment), but contact Kalani Pruet at kuleanawork-center@yahoo.com for directions and the possibility of a waterfall tour ($40 adults, $20 children).

Coffees of Hawaii.

Parks & Preserves
KAUNAKAKAI

Kapuaiwa Coconut Grove ★ HISTORIC SITE   Planted in the 1860s by King Kamehameha V (born Prince Lot Kapuaiwa), this royal grove of 1,000 coconut trees on 10 oceanfront acres is a major roadside attraction. It's particularly attractive at sunset, but heed the sign warning danger: falling coconuts to avoid a potentially fatal mishap. (**Note:** At press time, the adjacent Kiowea Beach Park and picnic area with restrooms was closed for remodeling.) Across the highway stands Church Row: seven churches, each of a different denomination—clear evidence of the missionary impact on Hawaii.

Ocean side of Maunaloa Hwy. (Hwy. 460), 1 mile west of Kaunakakai. Free admission.

St. Joseph Catholic Church.

THE saints OF MOLOKAI

Tiny Molokai can claim two saints canonized by the Roman Catholic church in recent years, both revered for years of devotion to the outcasts of Kalaupapa (see "Kalaupapa National Historical Park," below). Born in Belgium as Joseph de Veuster, **Father Damien** moved to Hawaii in 1864, building churches around the islands until 1873, when he answered a call to serve in the infamous leper colony (a now-discouraged term). He tended the sick, rebuilt St. Philomena's church, and pleaded with church and state officials for better care for the exiles, the earliest of whom had been thrown overboard and left to fend for themselves. Damien ultimately died of Hansen's disease, as leprosy is now known, in Kalaupapa in 1889. Caring for him at the end was **Mother Marianne,** who came to Hawaii with a group of nuns from New York in 1883. She spent 30 years serving the Kalaupapa community, before dying in 1918 at age 80, without contracting Hansen's disease. (It's only communicable to a small percentage of people.)

You'll see many images of both saints in Kalaupapa as well as "topside," which has three churches worth peeking into. Under the angled red roofs of Kaunakakai's concrete **St. Damien Church** (115 Ala Malama St.) stands a life-size wooden sculpture of the eponymous saint, canonized in 2009. Turn around to see the large banners bearing photographs of Damien and Marianne, canonized in 2012. Ten miles east of Kaunakakai, on the ocean side of Highway 450, **St. Joseph ★** is a diminutive wood-frame church built by Damien in 1876. A lava rock statue of the sainted Belgian priest stands in the little cemetery by the newer, 7-foot marble sculpture of Brother Dutton, a Civil War veteran and former alcoholic inspired by Damien to serve at Kalaupapa for 45 years, until his death in 1931. Four miles east, set back from the large cross on the mountain side of the highway, is the larger but still picturesque **Our Lady of Sorrows ★**, the first church Damien built outside Kalaupapa. Inside both churches hang colorful iconic portraits of the saints by local artist Linda Johnston.

CENTRAL UPLANDS & NORTH SHORE

Kalaupapa National Historical Park ★★★ HISTORIC SITE   Only 100 people a day, age 16 and older, may visit this isolated peninsula below the North Shore's soaring sea cliffs, and then only by reservation with Damien Tours (see "Organized Tours" on p. 378). Visitors must arrive on foot, by mule, or by plane—there's no road, and access by boat is not allowed—but the trek is well worth the effort. After King Kamehameha V signed the "Act to Prevent the Spread of Leprosy" in 1865, some 8,000 people with the dreaded disease were ultimately exiled here, displacing a centuries-old Native Hawaiian fishing village. The exiles' suffering was particularly acute before the arrival of now-canonized Father Damien (see "The Saints of Molokai," above) in 1873, who worked tirelessly on their behalf until his death from the disease in 1889. Only a handful of elderly patients, free to come and go since the 1960s, still live on site, but many buildings and ruins remain from more populous times; the park service is kept busy restoring many of them. Intrepid visitors can take the **Kalaupapa Guided Mule Ride ★★★**, a once-in-a-lifetime ride down and around the 26 switchbacks on the narrow, 2.9-mile **Kalaupapa Trail ★★★**. By the time the mules get to No. 4, riders may start to enjoy the views. Hikers must watch their footing on the knee-pounding descent, which takes 60 to 90 minutes (90–120 min. back up). The Damien

Tours bus picks up passengers at the tiny airport, near the Pacific's tallest lighthouse, before retrieving riders and hikers near the beach at the trail's end. Kalaupapa. www.nps.gov/kala. © **808/567-6802.** Access via **Kalaupapa Guided Mule Tour** (www.muleride.com; © **800/567-7550** or 808/567-6088). Tours start at mule barn near mile marker 5 on Kalae Hwy. (Hwy. 470), Kalae, at 8am Mon–Sat. Riders must be age 16 or older and weigh under 250 pounds with "good height to weight distribution." $199, includes lunch, tour, and certificate. Reservations required; accepted up to 4 months in advance (a year for groups of 6 or more). **Kalaupapa Trail** starts just north of mule barn, on east side of Kalae Hwy.; advance tour booking required. $50 from Damien Tours (© **808/567-6171)** or Molokai Outdoors (www.molokai-outdoors.com; © **877/553-4477** or 808/553-4477). Mule Tours hiking package with tour and lunch, $69. **Makani Kai** (www.makanikaiair.com; © **808/834-1111**) offers air/tour/lunch packages from Hoolehua; $197 round-trip, $143 hike in/fly out; flights also available from Kapalua and Hana, Maui, and Honolulu.

Palaau State Park ★★ PARK   This 234-acre forest park literally puts visitors between a rock and a hard place. From the parking lot, go left on the short but steep dirt trail through an ironwood grove to the **Phallic Rock ★**; go right on the paved path, and the **Kalaupapa Lookout ★★★** offers a panoramic view of the peninsula that was once a place of exile (see "Kalaupapa National Historical Park," above). Interpretive signs identify the sights some 1,700 feet below and briefly relate the tragic history that also spawned inspirational stories. As for that unmistakably shaped, 6-foot boulder, legend holds that it's the fertility demigod Nanahoa, turned to stone after he threw his wife over a cliff during an argument about his roving eye. It's also believed that a woman wishing to become pregnant need only spend the night nearby. (Despite the risqué nature, please treat this cultural site with respect, as signs urge.) *Note:* There are restrooms near the overlook and at a small pavilion on the left before the parking lot, but no potable water.

At the end of Kalae Hwy. (Hwy. 470), Palaau. www.hawaiistateparks.org. © **808/567-6923.** Free admission.

Molokai mules at the ready for guided tours.

Organized Tours

Although Molokai attracts (and rewards) independent travelers, a few group tours are absolute musts for those who are able—they're the only way to see the island's most awe-inspiring sights up close.

DAMIEN TOURS   Run by the family of a former Kalaupapa resident with Hansen's disease (aka leprosy), **Damien Tours ★★★** (📞 808/567-6171) provides the required permit to explore the haunting and inspiring sights of Kalaupapa National Historical Park (p. 376) as part of its guided bus tour. Those able to descend the treacherous sea cliffs by foot, mule, or air are met at 10am (Mon–Sat) for the approximately 4-hour tour, which protects the privacy of the few remaining residents while visiting numerous sites. Stops include the original graves of Father Damien and Mother Marianne (see "The Saints of Molokai," above); St. Philomena Church, where the Belgian priest carved holes in the floor so patients could discreetly spit during services; and a small museum with heart-rending photos and artifacts, such as a spoon reshaped for a disfigured hand. Lunch is an oceanside picnic on the cooler Kalawao side of the peninsula. Restricted to ages 16 and older, the tour costs $50, with limited seating. *Note:* All tours must be booked in advance, which is easier to do through "topside" outfitters. Hikers should contact **Molokai Outdoors** (www.molokai-outdoors.com; 📞 877/553-4477). **Makani Kai Air** (www.makanikaiair.com; 📞 877/255-8532) packages the tour and lunch with flights on its single-engine planes from Hoolehua ($197 round-trip; $143 hike down and fly out). The **Kalaupapa Guided Mule Tour ★★★** (www.muleride.com; 📞 800/567-7550 or 808/567-6088), an epic experience in and of itself (see "Kalaupapa National Historical Park" on p. 376), also includes the Damien tour and lunch in its $199 price.

HALAWA VALLEY TOURS   On the East End, a guided tour or authorized escort is required to go beyond Halawa Beach Park into breathtakingly beautiful Halawa Valley, home to the island's earliest settlement and 250-foot Moaula Falls. **Pilipo Solatorio**'s 4-hour, culturally focused tours are the most renowned (see "A Hike Back in History" on p. 374; $75 adults, $45 children). *Note:* The valley is privately owned, and trespassers may be prosecuted. **Molokai Fish & Dive** (www.molokaifishanddive.com; 📞 808/553-5926) can also arrange cultural tours ($75 adults, $45 children). **Kalani Pruet** will pair Halaway Valley tours ($40 adults, $20 children) with a visit to his flower farm (www.molokaiflowers.com; Tues–Sat 10am–4pm, Sun by appointment; e-mail him first at kuleanaworkcenter@yahoo.com).

WHALE-WATCHING TOURS   If you're on island December through March, don't miss the chance to watch humpback whales from Alaska frolic in island waters, often with their calves. Though you may spot whales spouting or breaching from the shore, a whale-watching

Halawa Falls in Halawa Valley.

cruise from Kaunakakai provides front-row seats. **Molokai Fish & Dive** (www. molokaifishanddive.com; ☎ **808/553-5926**) and **Molokai Ocean Tours** (www. molokaioceantours.com; ☎ **808/553-8391**) offer 2-hour tours for $79 and $75, respectively.

VAN TOURS   If your time on the island is tight—as on a day trip from Maui—I also recommend one of the well-planned **van tours** with a friendly local guide offered by **Molokai Outdoors** (www.molokai-outdoors.com; ☎ **877/553-4477** or 808/553-4477). The Alii Tour ($260) includes round-trip ferry passage from Maui (90 min. each way, departing Lahaina at 7:15am and returning at 5:30pm). The Island Tour ($151) covers more ground but is timed for an overnight stay.

BEACHES

Molokai's beaches, including the county-maintained beach parks, do not have lifeguards; on weekdays, you may even be the sole person there. Enter the water only in calm conditions, and even then be cautious: If you get into trouble, help may take longer to arrive than you need. *Note:* You'll find relevant sites on the "Molokai" map on p. 369.

East End

Protected by miles of fringing reef, the best swimming spots are tucked among the fish ponds heading east of Kaunakakai along the Kamehameha V Highway. Pronounced *"o-nay ah-lee-ee,"* **One Alii Beach Park,** 3 miles east of Kaunakakai, has a thin strip of *one* (sand) once reserved for the *alii* (high chiefs.) It's often crowded with families on weekends, but may be all yours on weekdays. Facilities include outdoor showers and restrooms; tent camping is allowed with a permit (see "Camping" on p. 386)

At mile marker 20, palm-fringed **Murphy Beach ★** offers a small, shaded park with picnic tables, white sand, and good swimming, snorkeling, and diving in calm conditions. Look for **Sandy Beach ★** between mile markers 21 and 22— the last beach before you head uphill en route to lush Halawa Valley. It has no facilities, just winsome views of Maui and Lanai, and generally safe swimming.

At the narrow end of the winding highway, 28 miles east of Kaunakakai, lie the twin coves of **Halawa Beach Park ★★**, one with gray sand and the other

Murphy Beach.

379

more rocky. Neither is safe for swimming—avoid in winter or after heavy rains—but both destination and journey are memorable. Look back into Halawa Valley (accessible only via cultural tours; see p. 374) for distant waterfall views. A picnic pavilion has restrooms but no drinking water; it's 100 yards from the shore, across the road from picturesque Ka Jerusalema Hou, a tiny church built in 1948.

West End

Much of the shoreline here is for sightseeing only, due to dangerous currents and fierce surf, especially in winter, but solitude, sunsets, and clear-day vistas of Oahu's Diamond Head across the 26-mile Kaiwi Channel make it worth the trek. From Kaunakakai, take Maunaloa Highway (Hwy. 460) almost 15 miles west, turn right on Kaluakoi Road and drive 4½ miles till you see the sign on your right pointing to Ke Nani Kai; turn right for public beach access parking at the end of the road. Walk past the eerily decaying hotel to the gold-sand **Kepuhi Beach ★** , and watch surfers navigate the rocky break. A 15-minute walk north along the bluff leads to the Pohaku Mauliuli cinder cone, which shares its name with two sandy coves better known as **Make Horse Beach,** pronounced *"mah-kay"* and meaning "dead horse" (don't ask.) You can snorkel and explore the tide pools in calm conditions, but do keep an eye on the waves. Hiking several miles north on a rugged dirt road leads to the white crescent of **Kawakiu Beach.** The relatively safe summer seas can be quite dangerous in winter and when the surf is up.

Continue on Kaluakoi Road 2 miles south from the resort to the parking lot for **Papohaku Beach Park ★★**, where the light-blond sand is nearly 3 miles long and 300 feet wide. Enjoy strolling the broad expanse, but beware the water's voracious rip currents. County facilities—restrooms, water, picnic, and campsites (see "Camping" on p. 386)—are at the northern end, a third of a mile past the intersection with Pa Loa Loop Road (a shortcut back to upper Kaluakoi Rd.). Don't miss cozy **Dixie Maru Beach ★** (originally Kapukahehu Beach), which offers the most-protected waters and is popular with families in summer. From the Papohaku parking lot, follow Kaluakoi Road 1¾ miles south to the T at Pohakuloa Road; turn right and head another 1¾ miles till the road ends at a small unpaved parking lot, with a short downhill path to the beach.

WATERSPORTS

It would be a mistake not to explore the calm waters along Molokai's miles-long South Shore reef—home to curious turtles and Hawaiian monk seals, billowing eagle and manta rays, and giant bouquets of colorful fish. Surfers, stand-up paddleboarders, kitesurfers, and boogie boarders can also find waves to entertain themselves, but because conditions are variable by day as well as by season, consult one of the Kaunakakai-based outfitters below before venturing out.

Molokai Fish & Dive, 61 Ala Malama St. (www.molokaifishanddive.com; ✆ **808/553-5926**), offers **snorkel tours** ($79) and two-tank **scuba dives** ($145) on a twin-hulled, 31-foot power catamaran, as well as three-tank dives ($295) of the North Shore, when conditions permit. South Shore **kayak tours** ($69) include snorkeling gear, which can be rented separately, along with other equipment. Half-day **deep-sea fishing charters** start at $695.

Molokai Outdoors, 9 Hio Place, by Malama Park (www.molokai-outdoors. com; ✆ **877/553-4477** or 808/553-4477), leads **kayak reef tours** ($68) and rents kayaks ($42), snorkel sets and boogie boards ($7), surfboards ($17–$22),

Kitesurfing.

and stand-up paddleboards ($27–$42). Owner Clare Mawae can also help you arrange a North Shore kayak excursion in summer with drop-off in Halawa Valley and pickup (by boat).

You don't need scuba certification to go deeper in the reef on one of the 2-hour **SNUBA and snorkeling tours** ($75) offered by **Molokai Ocean Tours,** 40 Ala Malama St., above American Savings Bank (www.molokaiocean tours.com; ✆ **808/553-8391**). Its six-passenger, 40-foot power catamaran comes with 30-foot "SNUBA" hoses that connect to a special mouthpiece. Let your killer instinct come out on 2-hour **spearfishing tours** ($125), designed to help rid the reef of invasive (but edible) fish, or on evening **torch fishing expeditions** ($30). Families often enjoy the latter, in which participants don headlamps, carry torches, and throw nets to catch (and often release) prey such as octopus, crabs, eels, and more.

The ancient sport of **outrigger canoe paddling** is available to anyone age 10 and up at 7:15am every Thursday morning (except major holidays or in bad weather) at Kaunakakai Wharf. The $25 cash donation helps buy canoes for the youth teams of community-based **Waakapae Mua Canoe Club** (✆ **808/553-3999**).

For **whale-watching tours** (Dec–Mar), see "Organized Tours" on p. 378.

OTHER OUTDOOR ACTIVITIES
Biking

Molokai is a great place to see by bicycle, with lightly used roads and, on the East End, inviting places to pull over for a quick dip. **Molokai Bicycle,** 80 Mohala St., Kaunakakai (www.mauimolokaibicycle.com; ✆ **808/553-3931**), offers mountain, road, and hybrid bike rentals for $25 to $32 a day, or $95 to $130 a week, including helmet and lock. Because owner Phillip Kikukawa is a schoolteacher,

FRAGILE BEAUTIES: HIKING MOLOKAI'S
nature reserves

For spectacularly unique views of Molokai's natural history, the Nature Conservancy of Hawaii offers monthly guided hikes into two of the island's most fragile landscapes: the windswept dunes in the 920-acre **Moomomi Preserve ★**, on Molokai's northwest shore; and the cloud-ringed forest of its highest mountain in the 2,774-acre **Kamakou Preserve ★★**, on the island's East End.

Just 8½ miles northwest of Hoolehua, Moomomi is the most intact beach and sand dune area in the main Hawaiian islands, harboring rare native plants, nesting green sea turtles, and fossils of now-extinct flightless birds.

Towering over the island's eastern half, 4,970-foot Kamakou provides 60 percent of Molokai's fresh water and shelter for endangered or threatened native species. The Pepeopae Trail boardwalk (3 miles round-trip) meanders through a bog with miniature trees and other delicate greenery that evolved over millennia; it leads to a view of Pelekunu Valley on the North Shore.

It's easy to do both hikes in the same week. Offered March through October, each hike is limited to eight people ($25 per person), so book well in advance;

dates are listed on the conservancy website (www.nature.org/hawaii). Call the Nature Conservancy field office just north of Kaunakakai in Molokai Industrial Park, 23 Pueo Place, off Ulili Street near Highway 460 (✆ **808/553-5236**), or e-mail hike_molokai@tnc.org to check availability.

It's also possible to access either reserve on your own, but you'll need a 4WD vehicle and good road conditions. The field office requests that you first stop by (weekdays 8am–3pm) for directions and an update on road conditions; please clean your shoes and gear before visiting preserves to avoid bringing in invasive species. In the case of Moomomi, you'll need to get a pass for the locked gate from the office.

---

the store is open only Wednesday 3 to 6pm and Saturday 9am to 2pm; call to set up an appointment for other hours.

Golf

Golfing on Molokai can be an aerobic workout, but tee times are open, and the rates are far lower than your score will be. **Ironwood Hills Golf Course** (✆ **808/ 567-6000**) is off Highway 470 in Kualapuu, on the left just before the Molokai Mule Ride Barn. Built in 1929 by the Del Monte Plantation for its executives, it's lovingly maintained by PGA pro Darrell Rego. The high elevation will help cool you as you walk up and down fairways, including the steep, 420-yard 8th hole, with spectacular views of the rest of the island. Greens fees are $27 ($21 twilight) for 9 holes, including cart.

Hiking

Molokai's parks and preserves offer a number of hiking opportunities (see "Parks & Preserves" on p. 375).

WHERE TO STAY ON MOLOKAI

With only one hotel (offering just 40 rooms for the general public) on island, the majority of Molokai's approximately 58,000 annual visitors tend to stay in a very mixed bag of five condo developments. All have individually owned and decorated units that vary widely in taste and quality, leaning heavy on the rattan. (Don't expect air-conditioning or elevators in the two- and three-story buildings, either.)

Molokai also offers a similar patchwork of mostly unassuming vacation rental cottages and basic B&Bs. Unfortunately, nearly all of these are unlicensed. Maui County doesn't make it easy—or inexpensive—to get permits, but out of respect for guest welfare as well as local concerns, the recommendations below include only licensed accommodations. (A licensed property lists the permit number on its website; rental cottages must also have a sign with the number.)

Offering the most choices on the island, as well as excellent customer service, **Molokai Vacation Properties** (www.molokai-vacation-rental.net; ✆ **800/367-2984** or 808/553-8334) represents only licensed homes and condos. While you can book online, it's best to contact the office directly to find the most suitable unit for your needs. For additional, but not necessarily licensed properties, **Molokai Resorts Vacation Rental Center** (www.molokairesorts. com; ✆ **800/600-4158** or 808/553-3666) is another on-island resource, with further options on VRBO.com and other rental websites; price ranges and cleaning fees will vary.

Note: Taxes of 13.416 percent are added to hotel and vacation rental bills. Parking is free.

Kaunakakai

MODERATE

Aqua Hotel Molokai ★   The free earplugs on the nightstands give away the downside of this retro collection of Polynesian-style A-frames and single-story wing: Some rooms suffer from highway and/or parking-lot noise, while the buzz at the popular Hula Shores bar (open till 10pm) may disturb guests in others. Also, as with most lodgings on the South Side, the beach in front isn't good for swimming. The upside: You can easily enjoy views of Lanai from the pool or hammocks, the staff is friendly, and the remodeled rooms are literally cooler than before, thanks to big ceiling fans (a few even have A/C units). All have microwaves, mini-fridges, and coffeemakers, but since most are a petite 228 square feet, it's better to spring for one of the deluxe second-floor rooms (432 sq. ft.) with kitchenette, including a two-burner stove and dishes. Families can take advantage of suites with a king-size bed downstairs and twin beds in a loft. A basic breakfast (pastry, coffee, and fruit) is free while remodeling of the Hula Shores restaurant (burned down in 2012) remains on hold—it's hoped that it will reopen by 2015.

1300 Kamehameha V Hwy. (Hwy. 450), Kaunakakai. www.hotelmolokai.com or www.aquaresorts. com. ✆ **877/553-5347** or 808/553-5347. 40 units (14 timeshares). $169–$310 double. Daily resort fee $5 (includes free Wi-Fi and snorkel gear, beach chair, and cooler rental). Rollaway $25 (not permitted in all rooms); crib free. **Amenities:** Restaurant (closed for restoration at press time); bar; gift shop; outdoor pool; Wi-Fi (free).

West End

MODERATE

Kaluakoi Resort ★ Although developed and managed separately, these three condo complexes have much in common. Negatives include a remote location, varying quality of furnishings and decor, and the slightly haunted ambience of an area gone to seed. Positives: easy access to Kepuhi and other West End beaches (see "Beaches" on p. 379), large lanais, and serene silence—I didn't even hear the crow of wild roosters on my last visit. Built in 1983, the 120-unit, two-story **Ke Nani Kai ★** (50 Kepuhi Place, Maunaloa) is set back farthest from Kepuhi Beach but boasts the nicest pool and the only hot tub and tennis courts of the bunch; units are two-bedroom, two-bathroom (880–990 sq. ft.) or one-bedroom, one-bathroom (680 ft.). The diverse condos of **Kepuhi Beach Villas** (255 Kepuhi Beach, Maunaloa) are closest to the sand, with a generous, ocean-view pool on the grounds of the abandoned Kaluakoi Hotel. Built in 1978, its 148 units are spread among two-story buildings with shared laundry facilities (and thin walls), and eight duplex cottages with individual washer-dryers; the largest units have a ground floor (642 sq. ft.) with master bedroom and bathroom, plus a small loft with a second bedroom and bathroom. Nearly hidden in tropical foliage, 78-unit **Paniolo Hale** (100 Lio Place, Maunaloa) means "cowboy house," and the large screened lanais and wooden floors give it a hint of the Old West. Built in 1980, the 21 two-story buildings also come in a host of floor plans, from studios (548 sq. ft.) to two-bedroom, two-bathroom units (1,398 sq. ft.), some with lofts and sleeping quarters in the living room.

Kaluakoi Resort, Maunaloa. 346 units. Reservations for select units c/o Molokai Vacation Properties: www.molokai-vacation-rental.com. ℂ **800/367-2984** or 808/553-8334. $125–$250 condo; 10-percent discount for stays of a week or more. $75–$100 cleaning fee. 3- to 7-night minimum. **Amenities:** Barbecues; Jacuzzi; outdoor pools; tennis courts (Ke Nani Kai only); Wi-Fi (varies by unit).

East End

MODERATE

Dunbar Beachfront Cottages ★★★ These two attractive, green-and-white, plantation-style cottages sit on their own hidden beaches, where swimming and snorkeling are possible year-round. Recently refreshed, each has two bedrooms (one with twin beds), one bathroom, a full kitchen (with new counters), washer and dryer, and a flatscreen TV with cable TV and DVD player. *Note:* The slightly pricier Puunana cottage has a king-size bed in its master bedroom and sits one flight of stairs above the beach; the family-friendly Pauwalu cottage is at ocean level, with a queen-size bed in the master.

9750 Kamehameha V Hwy. (Hwy. 450), past mile marker 18, Kaunakakai. www.molokai-beachfront-cottages.com. ℂ **800/673-0520** or 808/558-8153. 2 cottages (each sleeps up to 4). $175–$190. $85 cleaning fee. 3-night minimum. No credit cards. **Amenities:** Free Wi-Fi.

Puu O Hoku Ranch ★★★ Its name means "hill of stars," which accurately describes this 14,000-acre retreat on a cloudless night. You'll stay in one of three 1930s-era **cottages,** thoughtfully decorated with Hawaiian and Balinese furnishings. Sitting well above the ocean, the four-bedroom, three-bathroom Grove Cottage is in a field closer to the cattle ranch operations, while the two-bedroom, two-bathroom Sunrise Cottage has a more secluded feel. The one-bedroom, one-bathroom Sugar Mill Cottage, named for the nearby remains of a mill, hides just

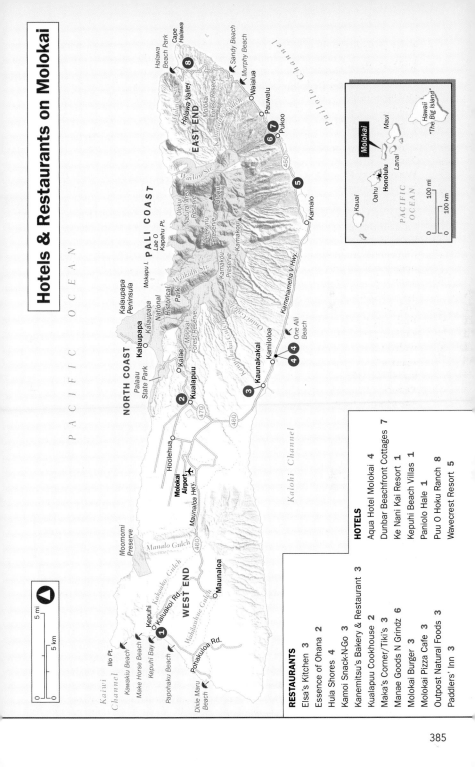

Hotels & Restaurants on Molokai

RESTAURANTS

Elsa's Kitchen **3**
Essence of Ohana **2**
Hula Shores **4**
Kamoi Snack-N-Go **3**
Kanemitsu's Bakery & Restaurant **3**
Kualapuu Cookhouse **2**
Maka's Corner/Tiki's **3**
Manae Goods N Grindz **6**
Molokai Burger **3**
Molokai Pizza Cafe **3**
Outpost Natural Foods **3**
Paddlers' Inn **3**

HOTELS

Aqua Hotel Molokai **4**
Dunbar Beachfront Cottages **7**
Ke Nani Kai Resort **1**
Kepuhi Beach Villas **1**
Paniolo Hale **1**
Puu O Hoku Ranch **8**
Wavecrest Resort **5**

above **Murphy Beach ★** (p. 379). Only ranch guests have access to hiking or riding horses on its numerous trails, which pass ocean bluffs, ancient groves, and a nene nursery. ***Note:*** Groups (minimum 14 people) can also book the handsome 11-room hunting-style **lodge,** which comes with a pool, yoga deck, and fireplace, as well as three meals a day featuring the ranch's organic meat and produce.

Main entrance off Kamehameha V Hwy., at mile marker 25, Kaunakakai. www.puuohoku.com. ✆ **808/558-8109.** 3 units. $200–$300 double. Extra person $30. $100–$175 refundable cleaning fee (charged at check-in). 2-night minimum. **Amenities:** Store (9am–5pm weekdays); Wi-Fi (free at select hotspots).

Wavecrest Resort ★   Your best lodging bet in this complex of three three-story buildings on 6 green acres halfway to Halawa Valley from Kaunakakai: Building A, the closest to the ocean. Top floors offer the best views of Maui, Lanai, and uninhabited Kahoolawe, but keep in mind that the resort has no elevators (or air-conditioning). Bedroom windows face walkways above the parking lot, so you may hear conversations as well as crowing roosters. As with other West End condos, units are individually owned and decorated; you'll want to scrutinize photos and amenity lists closely. The gated pool and cabana with barbecues are well-maintained, and the front desk has free tennis equipment.

7148 Kamehameha V Hwy. (Hwy. 450), 13 miles east of Kaunakakai. 128 total units. Reservations for select units c/o Molokai Vacation Properties: www.molokai-vacation-rental.com. ✆ **800/367-2984** or 808/553-8334. $125–$165 condo; 10 percent discount for stays of a week or more. $75–$100 cleaning fee. 3- to 7-night minimum. **Amenities:** Barbecues; coin laundry; outdoor pool; tennis courts; Wi-Fi (varies by unit).

Camping

All campgrounds are for tents only, and permits must be purchased in advance. You'll have to bring your own equipment or plan to buy it on the island, as there are no rentals.

County Campgrounds ★   The family-friendly **One Alii Beach Park** (p. 379) provides restrooms, barbecues, outdoor showers, drinking water, picnic tables, and electricity, as does the more remote **Papohaku Beach Park ★★** (p. 377), minus the electricity. ***Note:*** The no camping signs near the Papohaku parking lot apply only to the lawn to the right of the restrooms.

Permits $5 adults, $2 minors Mon–Thurs, $8 adults, $3 minors Fri–Sun and holidays. 3-night maximum. Available in person 8am–1pm and 2:30–4pm weekdays at the Maui County parks office, Mitchell Pauole Community Center, 90 Ainoa St., Kaunakakai, 96748 (✆ **808/553-3204**). To purchase by mail, download the form at www.co.maui.hi.us/index.aspx?NID=409 and mail to the parks office with check and self-addressed, stamped envelope.

State Campgrounds ★   The state manages two campgrounds at high, often misty elevations: **Palaau State Park ★★** (p. 377) and the remote **Waikolu Overlook** in the Molokai Forest Reserve. Both have restroom and picnic facilities but no drinking water or barbecues. Waikolu also requires a 4WD to drive 10 miles up mostly unpaved Maunahui Road starting from its unmarked intersection with Maunaloa Highway (Hwy. 460), near mile marker 4; do not attempt in muddy or rainy conditions. If the area is not covered in clouds, you'll be rewarded with views of the pristine Waikolu Valley and the Pacific, and be that much closer to the **Kamakou Preserve ★★** (p. 382).

Permits $18 per campsite (up to 6 persons), $3 per additional person (kids 2 and under free). 5-night maximum. Available online at camping.ehawaii.gov.

WHERE TO EAT ON MOLOKAI

Note: You'll find the restaurants noted below on the "Hotels & Restaurants on Molokai" map on p. 385.

Kaunakakai

Those looking for fine dining on Molokai will be disappointed, but if you just want something fresh and hearty to eat, Kaunakakai has more than a week's worth of options, all inexpensive. For lunch, try **Maka's Corner,** 35 Mohala St. (*C* **808/553-8058**), which has a handful of outdoor tables and serves rib-sticking, local-style plate lunches (try the mahi) and satisfying burgers. Two doors down, at the same address, is **Tiki's Coffee Shack Corner ★** (*C* **808/553-5488**), which provides free Wi-Fi along with tasty panini, baked goodies, espresso drinks, and fresh-squeezed juices; order the kale smoothie if available. The lunch counter at **Outpost Natural Foods,** 70 Makaena Place, behind Kalama's Service Station (*C* **808/553-3377**), also serves juices, plus vegetarian and vegan sandwiches and burritos.

Consider balancing all that healthful fare with an ice cream cone from **Kamoi Snack-N-Go ★,** 28 Kamoi St. (*C* **808/553-3742**); it serves more than 31 flavors of Dave's Hawaiian Ice Cream from Honolulu, including local favorites such as *kulolo* (taro-coconut custard), *haupia* (coconut pudding), and *ube* (purple yam). Or wait till after dinner to go on a "hot bread run" (p. 388) to **Kanemitsu's Bakery,** 79 Ala Malama St. (*C* **808/553-5585**). The newly remodeled bakery churns out pies, pastries, and cookies as well as sweet and savory breads. Kanemitsu's in-house restaurant also serves basic breakfast and lunch items, with local touches such as kim chee fried rice with eggs ($8.75) and a half of local organic papaya (a steal at just $1).

Locals often suggest the cash-only **Molokai Pizza Cafe,** 15 Kaunakakai Place, off Wharf Road (*C* **808/553-3288**), perhaps because it's the only place to get a pizza, plus it's open late (till 11pm Fri–Sat; till 10pm otherwise). We prefer nearby **Molokai Burger ★,** Highway 460 at Kaunakakai Place (*C* **808/553-3533**), which prepares its burgers with island-raised beef; order the Kapakahi burger if you're a meatloaf fan. It also offers dinner plates ($14) such as salmon, fried chicken, or kalbi ribs. Closed Sunday, the bright-white dining room is open till 9pm the rest of the week. At **Elsa's Kitchen,** 17 Ala Malama (*C* **808/553-9068**), home-style Filipino and local fare are the draw three meals a day (closed Sun); check out the *pancit* (noodle) specials.

Note: **Paddler's Inn** (see "Nightlife," below) is the only restaurant that serves alcohol (including draft beer) while the Hotel Molokai's Hula Shores restaurant awaits remodeling, although you can order basic grilled fare with your cocktails from the popular Hula Shores bar from 4 to 8pm.

Elsewhere on the Island

Outside of Kaunakakai, the **Kualapuu Cookhouse ★,** Farrington Road and Uwao Street, Kualapuu (*C* **808/567-9655**), serves a near-gourmet dinner, with entrees like prime rib or sautéed ono in *lilikoi* butter ($11–$30; cash only); still, service is leisurely, even for Molokai, with plastic chairs inside and picnic tables outside. (Note that the restaurant was up for sale at press time.) The **Essence of Ohana** espresso bar at Coffees of Hawaii, 1630 Farrington Ave., Kualapuu (*C* **808/567-9499**), serves a decent breakfast and lunch 7am to 4:30pm (closed

THE hot bread RUN

When people on Molokai mention "hot bread," they're talking about the signature item of **Kanemitsu's Bakery** (p. 387), an iconic island experience. First you have to find the bakery's back door: Head up the Hotel Street alley past the bakery and turn left at the white awning; walk 10 yards past a few benches and turn left again; the window counter is just ahead. You can order loaves of hot (or warm) white bread and a few select pastries from 8 to about 11pm. Ask for butter, jelly, cinnamon, or cream cheese ($7 for two fillings, $8 for the works), and the bakers will cut the hot loaves down the middle and slather on fillings so they

melt in the bread—perfect for dessert, breakfast, and several snacks, if you don't mind the carbs.

Sun), with daily sandwich or plate specials. On the East End, the takeout counter at **Manae Goodz N Grindz,** 8615 Kamehameha V Hwy., Pukoo, near mile marker 16 (✆ **808/558-8498**), is the area's lone dining option, which may make its burgers and lunch plates taste a little better than they really are.

MOLOKAI SHOPPING
Edibles

Kaunakakai has an impressive (for its size) array of family-run general stores, groceries, and convenience shops. Sunday and evening hours are limited, though, with one exception: The surprisingly gourmet **Molokai Minimart,** 35 Mohala St. (✆ **808/553-4447**), is open till 11pm daily.

The island's other regions each have one compact option for groceries. On the West End, it's the **Maunaloa General Store,** 523 Maunaloa Hwy., Maunaloa (✆ **808/552-2346;** Mon–Sat 9am–6pm, Sun 9am–noon). On the East End, the "Goodz" (convenience store) half of **Manae Goodz n Grindz,** 8615 Kamehameha V Hwy., Pukoo, near mile marker 16 (✆ **808/558-8498**), is open weekdays 8am to 6pm (till 5pm weekends). In the central uplands, **Kualapuu Market,** 311 Farrington Rd. at Uwao Street, Kualapuu (✆ **808/567-6243**), is handy for picking up ready-to-grill seafood or a bottle of wine for the BYOB restaurant across the street (Mon–Sat 8:30am–6pm; closed Sun).

Gifts & Souvenirs
KAUNAKAKAI

Shoppers of every stripe will want to schedule a trip to the bustling **Saturday morning farmer's market** (8am–noon) in downtown Kaunakakai; among the couple of aunties sitting on the sidewalk with fresh papaya and other produce, you'll find a dozen or more vendors of island arts and crafts, vintage and new clothing, handmade soaps, and specialty foods such as local vanilla extract.

Other Kaunakakai shopping troves are less visible: Follow the lane between the Imports Gift Shop and Friendly Market on Ala Malama to the **Warehouse** (www.molokaiartgallery.com; ✆ **808/553-5734**), which has the best selection of oil paintings, giclee prints, watercolors, and carvings by Molokai artists, among other pieces. **Molokai Fish & Dive** (www.molokaifishanddive.com; ✆ **808/553-5926**) sells locally designed T-shirts and souvenirs (as well as diving gear, sandwiches, ice cream, and gas) at its new location, the green-and-white gas station next to its old store at 53 Ala Malama. Across the street and above American Savings Bank, **Molokai Ocean Tours**, 40 Ala Malama St. (www.molokaioceantours.com; ✆ **808/553-8391**), sells Tula Hawaii's sterling silver and 14-karat gold jewelry, created by two Molokai sisters with shells and sea glass they've found on the island. An expansion of the island's copy and print shop, **iCandie**, 109 Ala Malama St. (www.facebook.com/Molokai.iCandie; ✆ **808/553-5020**), carries cute children's and women's clothing and accessories, some locally made; it's in the cottage complex behind Home Town Groceries.

Several gift shops are destinations in their own right. In Kaunakakai, the delightfully eclectic **Kalele Bookstore & Divine Expressions,** 64 Ala Malama (www.molokaispirit.com; ✆ **808/553-5112**), offers a wide selection of Molokai-made arts and crafts, including wooden bowls, feather lei, earrings made with *kapa* (traditional bark fabric), and watercolors tinted with red dirt; owner Teri Waros also dispenses free coffee and sightseeing advice. On the outskirts of town, look for the sign on the east side of Highway 460 for **Kamakana Country Store,** 12A Kahanu St. (www.molokaicountrystore.com; ✆ **808/553-5725**), specializing in Hawaii-themed cookbooks, jams, and other locally made treats.

ELSEWHERE ON THE ISLAND

Among the traditional souvenirs at Zach Socher's **Blue Monkey** gift shop at the Coffees of Hawaii plantation, 1630 Farrington Ave. at Highway 470, Kualapuu (www.bigwindkites.com/bluemonkey; ✆ **808/567-6776**), are Molokai-grown coffees and teas, island-made *lauhala* (woven) hats, cutting boards and pens of native woods, and jewelry fashioned from tiny, delicate *kahelelani* shells. Socher's parents, Jonathan and Daphne, own the equally intriguing **Big Wind Kite Factory & Plantation Gallery,** 120 Maunaloa Hwy., Maunaloa (www.bigwindkites.com; ✆ **808/552-2364**), chock full of Balinese furnishings, stone jewelry, Kalaupapa memoirs, and other books on Molokai. Test-fly one of their handmade kites at the nearby park.

The Perfect Molokai Souvenir

Found in nearly every Molokai store, the 11 varieties of local sea salts from **Pacifica Hawaii** (www.pacificahawaii.com) make ideal gifts. Salt master Nancy Gove evaporates seawater in elevated pans at the front of her home in Kaunakakai, and then infuses colors and flavors via ingredients such as local clay (*alae*), Kauai-made rum, Maui sugar, and activated charcoal and cayenne (for the Hot Black Lava). She's happy to show you how it's done; call ✆ **808/553-8484** to set up a tour ($13), which lasts an hour or so, depending on your interest.

MOLOKAI NIGHTLIFE

For those not gazing on a moonlit ocean, most evening entertainment takes place in Kaunakakai. A mile east on Highway 450, the parking lot at the **Aqua Hotel Molokai** (www.hotelmolokai.com; © **808/553-5347**) starts filling up by 3:30pm for Aloha Friday. From 4 to 6pm, "old-style" recording artist Lono plays slack key guitar and leads a group of uke-strumming aunties and uncles known as Na Kupuna (the elders) in American and Hawaiian standards, often with impromptu hula. Until the hotel completes the renovation of the fire-damaged Hula Shores restaurant, patrons can order grilled fare (hot dogs, burgers) and drinks from the bar from 4 till 8pm.

Lono also plays Tuesdays at the closest thing Molokai has to a hot spot, **Paddlers' Inn,** at the intersection of Highway 450 and Mohala Street in the center of Kaunakakai (http://molokaipaddlers.inn; © **808/553-3300**). The spacious restaurant/bar, which also offers free Wi-Fi and themed nightly specials (Chinese, barbecue, Mexican, and the like), has a newly roofed lanai with predominantly local acts onstage every night but Monday. You'll hear classic and contemporary Hawaiian music, country, even jazz (on Sat nights), usually 6:30 to 8:30pm, with a disco DJ keeping the party going from 9pm to midnight most Fridays.

LANAI

by Shannon Wianecki

anai is deliciously remote: The island's tiny airport doesn't accommodate direct flights from the Mainland and its closest neighbor is a 45-minute ferry ride away. It's almost as if this quiet, gentle oasis—known for both its small-town feel and celebrity appeal—demands that visitors go to great lengths to get here in order to better appreciate it.

With barely 30 miles of paved road and not a single stoplight, Lanai (pronounced "lah-*nigh*-ee") is unspoiled by what passes for progress. Much of the island is still untamed, except for a tiny 1920s-era plantation village—and two first-class luxury hotels where room rates average $400-plus a night.

Still, this nostalgic outpost manages to rank high among the world's top travel destinations. It's a place where people come looking for serenity, solitude, and the chance to connect with nature: hushed, empty beaches; dramatic sea cliffs; and skies dotted with stars. The chilled towels and fresh-muddled mojitos served up by the Four Seasons Resorts Lanai staff aren't bad, either.

This lesser-known Hawaiian island lures visitors with an abundance of activities: snorkeling and swimming in the marine preserve known as Hulopoe Bay, hiking on 100 miles of remote trails, "talking story" with the friendly locals, and beachcombing and whale-watching along stretches of otherwise deserted sand. Adventurers can ride horseback in the forest, scuba dive in caves, swing clubs on golf courses with jaw-dropping ocean views, or go four-wheeling for the day across wild plains where spotted deer run free.

Despite the increase in private jets and America's Cup yachts, courtesy of the island's newest owner, software tycoon Larry Ellison, Lanai is still a quaint, idiosyncratic throwback to older times. With a population of just over 3,000, everybody knows everybody. The minute you arrive on island, you'll feel the small-town coziness. People wave to passing cars, residents stop to talk with friends, fishing and gardening are considered top priorities in life, and leaving the keys in your car's ignition is standard practice.

Lanai residents might live in a rural setting, but they certainly aren't isolated. Honolulu's big-city bustle is just across the channel, and many islanders regularly commute to Oahu or Maui. But when the plane touches down on Palawai Basin, or the ferry rounds Puu Pehe (Sweetheart Rock) to pull into Manele Harbor, it's easy to relax into the leisurely pace of life that makes Lanai such a paradise.

GHOSTS TO GOLF COURSES

Lanai hasn't always been so welcoming. Early Hawaiians believed the island was haunted by Pahulu (the god of nightmares) and spirits so wily and vicious that no human could survive here. But many have, for the past 1,000 years. Remnants of ancient Hawaiian villages, temples, fish ponds, and petroglyphs decorate the shorelines and uplands of Lanai. King Kamehameha spent his summers here, at a cliffside palace overlooking the sunny southern coast.

Previous page: Shipwreck on the coast of

Lanai

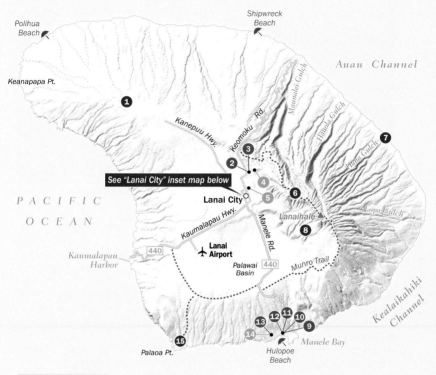

Shipwreck
Beach

Polihua
Beach

Keanapapa Pt.

Auau Channel

Kanepuu Hwy.

Keomoku Rd.

Maunalei Gulch

Hauola Gulch

Hiina Gulch

1

3

2

4

5

6

7

8

See "Lanai City" inset map below

Lanai City

Kaumalapau Hwy.

Manele Rd.

Lanaihale

Lopa Gulch

PACIFIC

OCEAN

Kaumalapau
Harbor

440

Lanai
✈ Airport

Palawai
Basin

440

Munro Trail

Kealaikahiki Channel

13 **12** **11** **10**

14 **9**

15

Palaoa Pt.

Hulopoe
Beach

Manele Bay

0   2 mi
0   2 km

Ilima Ave.

Jacaranda St.

Sixth St.

Houston St.

Gay St.

Nani St.

16

17 **18**

Seventh St.

19

Dole Park

20 **21**

Lanai Ave.

Koali St.

Eighth St.

Kiele St.

22

Fraser Ave.

23

Gay St.

Houston St.

Ninth St.

Ilima Ave.

Lanai City

ATTRACTIONS

Kaunolu Village **15**
Keahia Kawelo
  (Garden of the Gods) **1**
Keomoku Village **7**
Lanai Culture & Heritage
  Center **19**
Lanaihale **8**
Munro Trail **6**

HOTELS

Four Seasons Resort Lanai
  at Manele Bay **12**
Four Seasons Resort Lanai,
  The Lodge at Koele **2**
Hotel Lanai **20**

GOLF COURSES

Cavendish Golf Course **5**
The Challenge at Manele **14**
The Experience at Koele **4**

RESTAURANTS

Anuenue Juice Bar & Cafe **22**
Blue Ginger Cafe **17**
Canoes Lanai **18**
Coffee Works **16**
Kailani **11**
Lanai City Grille **21**
Main Dining Room **3**
Nobu Lanai **10**
One Forty **9**
Pele's Other Garden **23**
Terrace **3**
Views **13**

The 12th hole at the Experience at Koele golf course.

The island's arid landscape was once native forest—patches of which persist on the 3,379-foot summit of Lanaihale, along with native birds, insects, and jewel-like tree snails. But the 1800s brought foreign ambitions and foreign strife to Hawaii: Disease took more than half of her native people, Western commerce supplanted the islanders' subsistence culture, and new pests such as rats and mosquitos decimated native flora and fauna. Various entrepreneurs tried to make their fortune here, farming sugarcane, cotton, sisal, and sugar beets and launching enterprises such as a dairy and a piggery and raising sheep for wool. All failed, mostly for lack of water.

An unsuccessful ranching effort unleashed 40,000 sheep and goats on the island. In short order, these feral animals nibbled down the groundcover that held the soil. By 1911, when George Munro arrived from New Zealand to manage the Lanai Ranch, the island was eroding away. What little rain fell washed off the barren ground into the sea. Munro happened to notice that the tall Norfolk pine beside his house captured moisture from the misty air and sent it raining down onto his roof. That inspired him to plant thousands of Cook pines across Lanai, each of which collects 100 gallons of water a day from passing fog. It was a first step in restoring the island's battered watershed, work that continues today.

From Pineapple Patch to Luxury Destination

In 1917, Harry Baldwin, a missionary's grandson, bought Lanai for $588,000. He developed a 20-mile water pipeline between Koele and Manele, and sold the island 5 years later to Jim Dole for $1.1 million. Dole planted and irrigated 18,000 acres of pineapple. He built Lanai City, blasted out a harbor, and turned the island into a fancy fruit plantation. For 70 years, the island was essentially one big pineapple patch, owned and operated by Dole. Acres of prickly fields surrounded a tiny grid of workers' homes. Life in the 1960s was pretty much the same as in the 1930s. Dole enjoyed great success until cheaper pineapple production in Asia brought an end to Lanai's heyday.

In 1985, self-made billionaire David Murdock acquired the island in a merger—well, 98 percent of it anyway; the remaining 2 percent is owned by the government or longtime Lanai families. A new era was ushered in when Murdock built two grand hotels on the island (the **Lodge at Koele** and the **Four Seasons Resort Lanai at Manele Bay**), and almost overnight the plain, red-dirt pineapple plantation became one of the world's top travel destinations. Touting Lanai as the "private island," Murdock recycled the former field hands as waitstaff, even summoning a London butler to school residents in the fine art of service. He carved a pair of daunting golf courses, one in the island's interior and the other along the wave-lashed coast. Microsoft billionaire Bill Gates chose the island for his lavish wedding, booking all of its hotel rooms to fend off the press—helping put uncomplicated Lanai on the map as a vacation spot for the rich and powerful.

The Ellison Era

David Murdock's grand maneuver to replace agriculture with tourism never proved quite lucrative enough, however. In 2010, after years of six-figure losses, Murdock sold his share of the island to the third-richest person in the United States, Larry Ellison.

The software tycoon made some important first moves to endear himself to the tiny, tight-knit community. First, he reopened the public swimming pool, which had been closed for a decade. He built ball courts and a football field so that student athletes finally had somewhere to practice. And he hired someone born and raised on Lanai to act as chief operating officer of Lanai Resorts. Unemployment evaporated, as did available housing.

Mr. Ellison's ambitious plans for the future of Lanai include everything from sustainable agriculture to a third uber-exclusive resort at Halepalaoa, on the island's pristine eastern shore. He's currently developing a desalination plant and electric-car charging stations, and intends to endow a "sustainability laboratory" to make Lanai "the first economically viable 100-percent green community."

Longtime residents (who've seen it all before) are cautiously optimistic. Some have drawn the line against particularly intrusive developments, such as a massive wind farm that would provide power for Oahu. Lanaians for Sensible Growth advocates for affordable housing, alternative water systems, and civic improvements that benefit residents. In many ways, the island still resembles old photographs taken in the glory days of Dole. Having watched the other Hawaiian Islands attempt a balancing act of economic growth and island lifestyle, Lanai cautiously welcomes "progress," but at a rate its resilient community can digest.

ESSENTIALS

Arriving

BY PLANE If you're coming from outside of Hawaii, you'll have to make a connection on Oahu (Honolulu/HNL) or Maui (Kahului/OGG or Kapalua/JHM), where you can catch a blink-and-you'll-miss-it flight to Lanai's airport. You'll touch down in Palawai Basin, once the world's largest pineapple plantation; it's about 10 minutes by car to Lanai City and 25 minutes to Manele Bay.

Hawaiian Airlines (www.hawaiianairlines.com; ✆ **800/367-5320**) just launched 'Ohana by Hawaiian, a fleet of pretty new turboprop planes that fly twice daily between Honolulu to Lanai. **Island Air** (www.islandair.com; ✆ **800/652-6541**) runs five flights a day between Lanai and Honolulu. Unfortunately, this airline—currently the main conduit between Lanai and the world—is notorious for running late and stranding passengers mid-route. Direct complaints to its new owner, Larry Ellison.

Plantation houses in Lanai.

Mokulele Airlines (www.mokuleleairlines.com; ℂ 866/260-7070) offers service to Lanai from Honolulu, Kahului, Kapalua, Kona, and Molokai. Currently, it offers the best (and most hassle-free) flights, but availability is limited. The nine-passenger Cessna Grand Caravan planes are small; you'll board from the tarmac, and weight restrictions apply.

BY BOAT A round-trip on **Expeditions Lahaina/Lanai Passenger Ferry** (www.go-lanai.com; ℂ 800/695-2624) takes you between Maui and Lanai for $30 adults and $20 children, each way. The ferry runs five times a day, 365 days a year, between Lahaina (on Maui) and Lanai's Manele Bay harbor. The 9-mile channel crossing takes 45 minutes to an hour, depending on sea conditions. Reservations are strongly recommended; call or book online. Baggage is limited to two checked bags and one carry-on. *Tip:* During the winter months, taking the ferry amounts to a free whale-watch.

Visitor Information

Lanai Visitors Bureau, 1727 Wili Pa Loop, Wailuku, Maui 96793 (www.go hawaii.com/lanai; ℂ 800/947-4774 or 808/565-7600), and the **Hawaii Visitors & Convention Bureau** (www.gohawaii.com; ℂ 800/GO-HAWAII or 808/923-1811) provide brochures, maps, and island guides.

The Island in Brief

Inhabited Lanai is divided into two regions: Lanai City and Manele, and their corresponding climates—cool and misty and hot and dry.

Lanai City (pop. 3,200) sits at the heart of the island at 1,645 feet above sea level. It's the only place on Lanai that offers services. Built in 1924, this plantation village is a tidy grid of quaint tin-roofed cottages in bright pastels, with tropical gardens of banana, lilikoi, and papaya. Many of the residents are Filipino immigrants who once worked the pineapple fields. Their clapboard homes, now worth $500,000 or more (for a 1,500-sq.-ft. home, built in 1935, on a 6,000-sq.-ft. lot), are excellent examples of historic preservation; the whole town looks like it's been kept under a bell jar.

Around **Dole Park,** a charming village square lined with towering Norfolk and Cook pines, plantation buildings house general stores, a post office (where people stop to chat), two banks, a half-dozen restaurants, an art gallery, an art center, a whimsical shop, and a coffee shop that easily outshines any Starbucks. The local one-room police station displays a "jail" consisting of three padlocked, outhouse-size cells as a throwback to earlier times. The new station—a block away, with regulation-size jail cells—probably sees just as little action.

Just up the road from Dole Park is the Lodge at Koele (managed by the Four Seasons). The stately resort stands alone on a knoll overlooking pastures and the sea at the edge of a pine forest, like a grand European manor.

Manele is downhill, on the island's sunny southwestern coast. There you'll find the other bastion of extravagance, the Four Seasons Resort Lanai at Manele Bay. You'll see more of "typical" Hawaii here—beaches, swaying palms, and superlative sunsets.

GETTING AROUND

With so few paved roads on Lanai, you'll need a four-wheel-drive vehicle if you plan to explore the island's remote shores, wild interior, or forested summit, Mount Lanaihale.

Rabaca's Limousine Service (✆ 808/565-6670) is a terrific option for a short romp around the island. Knowledgeable local drivers will navigate the wild roads for you, visiting Shipwreck Beach, Garden of the Gods, and even Kaunolu Village in roomy Suburbans. Three-and-a-half-hour trips are $75 per person (minimum two guests). Or book the "4x4 Trekker Tour" package from **Expeditions,** which includes ferry travel to Lanai (www.go-lanai.com; ✆ 808/565-6670; from $186).

If you'd rather strike out on your own, **Dollar Rent A Car** at **Lanai Plantation Store/Lanai City Service,** 1036 Lanai Ave. (✆ 800/533-7808 for Dollar reservations; **808/565-7227** for Lanai Plantation Store) rents both standard cars and four-wheel-drive jeeps. Expect to pay about $139 a day (plus taxes) for a jeep. Keep in mind, however, that days of rain may render muddy roads impassable. Check with the Dollar office to see which roads are open and whether renting is worth your money! For slightly more coin, you can forge through just about anything in your very own Hummer. Jim Kaiser at **808 Hummers** will pick you up in one of his six-passenger behemoths for $199, fees included (www.808hummers.com; ✆ **808/286-9308**).

Warning: Gas is expensive on Lanai—upward of $5 a gallon—and off-road vehicles get lousy mileage. Spending $40 to $50 per day on gas isn't unheard of. Rent only for those days you want to explore the island's hinterlands; everything else is accessible by foot or shuttle.

Finally, it's entirely possible to enjoy Lanai without wheels. Hulopoe Beach is a short hike from the harbor, and everything within Lanai City is walking distance. Air-conditioned resort shuttles run on the half-hour between the two Four Seasons resorts, Lanai City, the airport, and the harbor. Four Seasons guests pay a one-time charge of $48 for unlimited rides; anyone else can hop on for $10 per day.

LANAI'S grand central station

Whether or not you rent a car, sooner or later you'll find yourself at the **Lanai Plantation Store,** 1036 Lanai Ave. (✆ **808/565-7227**). It's an all-in-one grocery, gas station, rental-car agency, and souvenir shop—you can pick up information, directions, maps, and all the local gossip here. It's also a good place to fill your water jugs: A reverse-osmosis water dispenser is just out front.

[FastFACTS] LANAI

Note: Lanai is part of Maui County.

Emergencies   In case of **emergencies,** call the police, fire department, or ambulance services at ✆ **911,** or the **Poison Control Center** at ✆ **800/222-1222.** For non-emergencies, call the **police** at ✆ **808/565-6428.**

Doctors & Dentists For emergency dental care, call **Dr. Nora Harmsen** (✆ **808/565-6418**). If you need a doctor, contact the **Straub Lanai Family Health Center** (✆ **808/565-6423**) or the **Lanai Community Hospital** (✆ **808/565-8450**).

Weather   For both land and sea conditions, visit the **National Weather Service** website (www.prh.noaa.gov) and type Lanai, Hawaii, in the search box.

EXPLORING LANAI

You'll need an off-road vehicle to reach the sights listed below. Four-wheel-drive rentals on Lanai are expensive—from $139 to $199 a day—but worth it. Rent just for the day (or days) you plan on sightseeing; otherwise, it's easy enough to get to the beach and around Lanai City without your own wheels. For details on vehicle rentals, see "Getting Around," above.

Note: You'll find the following attractions on the "Lanai" map on p. 393.

Keahiakawelo (Garden of the Gods) ★

A four-wheel-drive dirt road leads out of Lanai City, through fallow pineapple fields, past the Kanepuu Preserve (a dry-land forest preserve with rare native Hawaiian trees) to Keahiakawelo, the so-called Garden of the Gods out on Lanai's north shore. This rugged, beautiful place is full of boulders strewn by volcanic forces and sculpted by the elements into varying shapes and colors—brilliant reds, oranges, ochers, and yellows.

Garden of the Gods.

Take the dusty, bumpy drive out to Keahiakewalo early in the morning or just before sunset, when the light casts eerie shadows on the mysterious lava formations. Drive west from the Lodge on Polihua Road; in about 2 miles, you'll see a hand-painted sign pointing left down a one-lane, red-dirt road through a kiawe forest to the large stone sign.

The Munro Trail ★

In the first golden rays of dawn, when owls swoop silently over the abandoned pineapple fields, take a peek at **Mount Lanaihale,** the 3,370-foot summit of Lanai. If it's clear, hop into a 4×4 and head for the Munro Trail, the narrow, winding ridge trail that runs across Lanai's razorback spine to its peak. From here, you may get a rare treat: On a clear day, you can see most of the main islands in the Hawaiian chain.

But if it's raining, forget it. On rainy days, the Munro Trail becomes slick and boggy with major washouts. Rainy-day excursions often end with a rental jeep on the hook of the island's lone tow truck—and a $250 tow charge. You could even slide off into a major gulch and never be found, so don't try it. But in late August and September, when trade winds stop blowing and the air over the islands stalls in what's called a *kona* condition, Mount Lanaihale's suddenly visible summit becomes an irresistible attraction.

Look for a red-dirt road off Manele Road (Hwy. 440), about 5 miles south of Lanai City; turn left and head up the ridge line. No sign marks the peak, so you'll have to keep an eye out. Look for a wide spot in the road and a clearing that falls sharply to the sea. From here you can see Kahoolawe, Maui, the Big Island of Hawaii, and Molokini's tiny crescent. Even the summits show. You can also see the silver domes of Space City on Haleakala in Maui; Puu Moaulanui, the tongue-twisting summit of Kahoolawe; and, looming above the clouds, Mauna Kea on the Big Island. At another clearing farther along the thickly forested ridge, all of Molokai, including the 4,961-foot summit of Kamakou and the faint outline of Oahu (more than 30 miles across the sea), are visible. Once you could see all five islands in a single glance, but now a thriving pine forest blocks the view. For details on hiking the trail, see "Hiking" on p. 405.

Tide pool at Kaunolu Village site.

Kaunolu Village

Out on Lanai's nearly vertical, Gibraltar-like sea cliffs is an old royal compound and fishing village. Now a national historic landmark and one of Hawaii's most treasured ruins, it's believed to have been inhabited by King Kamehameha the Great and hundreds of his closest followers about 200 years ago. It's a hot, dry, dusty, slow-going, 3-mile 4×4 drive from Lanai City to Kaunolu, but the mini-expedition is worth it. Take plenty of water, don a hat for protection against the sun, and wear sturdy shoes.

Ruins of 86 house platforms and 35 stone shelters have been identified on both sides of Kaunolu Gulch. The residential complex also includes the **Halulu Heiau temple,** named after a mythical man-eating bird. The king's royal retreat is thought to have stood on the eastern edge of Kaunolu Gulch, overlooking the rocky shore facing Kahekili's Leap, a 62-foot-high bluff named for the mighty Maui chief who leaped off cliffs as a show of bravado. Nearby are **burial caves,** a **fishing shrine,** a **lookout tower,** and warrior-like stick figures—**petroglyphs**—carved on boulders. Just offshore stands the telltale fin of little **Shark Island,** a popular dive spot that teems with bright tropical fish and, frequently, sharks.

Excavations are underway to discover more about how ancient Hawaiians lived, worked, and worshiped on Lanai's leeward coast. Who knows? The royal fishing village may yet yield the bones of King Kamehameha. His burial site, according to legend, is known only to the moon and the stars.

Off the Tourist Trail: Keomoku Village

If it hasn't been raining heavily, venture out onto the dirt road to Keomoku, on Lanai's east coast. A ghost town since the mid-1950s, Keomoku village offers a trip back in time. This former ranching and fishing community of 2,000 was home to the first non-Hawaiian settlement on Lanai, but it dried up after droughts killed off the Maunalei Sugar Company. Check out **Ka Lanakila,** the

Ka Lanakila church.

sweetly restored church that dates back to 1903. Along the way you'll find excellent views across the 9-mile Auau Channel to Maui's crowded Kaanapali Beach, and empty beaches that are perfect for a picnic or a snorkel. Follow Keomoku Road for 8 miles to the coast, turn right on the sandy road, and keep going for 5¾ miles.

BEACHES

If you like big, wide, empty, gold-sand beaches and crystal-clear, cobalt-blue water full of bright tropical fish—and who doesn't?—go to Lanai. With 18 miles of sandy shoreline, Lanai has some of Hawaii's least crowded and most interesting beaches.

Hulopoe Beach ★★★

In 1997, Dr. Stephen Leatherman of the University of Maryland (a professional beach surveyor who's also known as "Dr. Beach") ranked Hulopoe the best beach in the United States. It's easy to see why. This palm-fringed, gold-sand beach is bordered by black-lava fingers, protecting swimmers from ocean currents. In summer, Hulopoe is perfect for swimming, snorkeling, or just lolling about; the water temperature is usually in the mid-70s (mid-20s Celsius). Swimming is generally safe, except when swells kick up in winter. The bay at the foot of the Four Seasons Resort Lanai at Manele Bay is a protected marine preserve, with schools of colorful fish and spinner dolphins. Humpback whales cruise by here in winter. Hulopoe is also Lanai's premier beach park, with a grassy lawn, picnic tables, barbecue grills, restrooms, showers, and ample parking. You can camp here, too.

HULOPOE'S TIDE POOLS ★★ Some of the best **lava-rock tide pools** in Hawaii are found along the south shore of Hulopoe Bay. These miniature Sea-Worlds are full of strange creatures such as asteroids (sea stars) and holothurians

401

Hulopoe Beach.

(sea cucumbers), not to mention spaghetti worms, Barber Pole shrimp, and Hawaii's favorite local delicacy, the opihi, a tasty morsel also known as the limpet. Youngsters enjoy swimming in the enlarged tide pool at the eastern edge of the bay. *A few tips:* When you explore tide pools, do so at low tide. Never turn your back on the waves. Wear tennis shoes or reef walkers, as wet rocks are slippery. Collecting specimens in this marine preserve is forbidden, so don't take any souvenirs home.

Polihua Beach ★

So many sea turtles once hauled themselves out of the water to lay their eggs in the sunbaked sand on Lanai's northwestern shore that Hawaiians named the

Polihua Beach.

beach here Polihua, or "egg nest." Although the endangered green sea turtles are making a comeback, they're seldom seen here now. You're more likely to spot an offshore whale (in season) or the perennial flotsam that washes up onto this deserted beach at the end of Polihua Road, a 4-mile jeep trail. This strand is ideal for beachcombing, fishing, or just being alone. It has no facilities except fishermen's huts and driftwood shelters. Bring water and sunscreen. Beware of strong currents, which make the water unsafe for swimming.

Shipwreck Beach ★

This 8-mile-long windswept strand on Lanai's northeastern shore—named for the rusty ship *Liberty* stuck on the coral reef—is a sailor's nightmare and a beachcomber's dream. The strong currents yield all sorts of sea debris, from Japanese hand-blown-glass fish floats and rare pelagic paper nautilus shells to lots of junk. This is also a great place to spot whales from December to April, when Pacific humpbacks cruise in from Alaska. The road to the beach is paved most of the way, but you really need a four-wheel-drive to get down here. At the end of the road, you'll find a trail that goes about 200 yards inland to the Kukui Point petroglyphs; follow the signs. Respect this historic site by not adding anything to it or taking anything away.

WATERSPORTS

Because Lanai lacks major development, it has Hawaii's best water clarity. It also has low rainfall and runoff, and its coast is washed clean daily by the sea current—known as "The Way to Tahiti". But the strong currents also pose a threat to swimmers, and there are few good surf breaks. Most of the aquatic adventures—swimming, snorkeling, scuba diving—are centered on the somewhat protected south shore, around Hulopoe Bay.

The main watersports outfitter is **Trilogy Lanai Ocean Sports ★★★** (Lanai-based trips: http://scubalanai.com; Maui-to-Lanai trips: http://sailtrilogy. com; ✆ **808/874-5649**). This Maui-based company has built a well-deserved reputation as the leader in sailing/snorkeling cruises in Hawaii. Trilogy's superb crew offers daylong snorkeling trips from Maui to Lanai, plus a few Lanai-based excursions. The latter are ideal: less crowded, less expensive, and less time spent en route, all of which adds up to more fun. But because of lack of demand, the Lanai-based trips aren't always available. Try booking online (for a 10-percent discount) or—your best bet—with the concierges at either Four Seasons resort. They usually know better than the Maui office folks which boats are sailing when.

SAILING & SNORKELING   **Trilogy Lanai Ocean Sports** (see above) offers wonderfully uncrowded morning and afternoon snorkel sailing trips on board its luxury catamarans and 32-foot jet-drive rigid aluminum inflatable vessel. Cruises along Lanai's protected coastline sail past hundreds of spinner dolphins and into some of the best snorkeling sites in the world ($189 adults, $142 teens 13–18, and $94 children 3–12). Breakfast and lunch are included, along with sodas, snorkel gear, and instruction.

If you just want to snorkel on your own, Hulopoe is Lanai's best snorkeling spot. Fish are abundant in the marine-life conservation area. Try the lava-rock points at either end of the beach and around the lava pools.

SCUBA DIVING   Two of Hawaii's best-known dive spots are found in Lanai's clear waters, just off the south shore: **Cathedrals I** and **II,** so named because

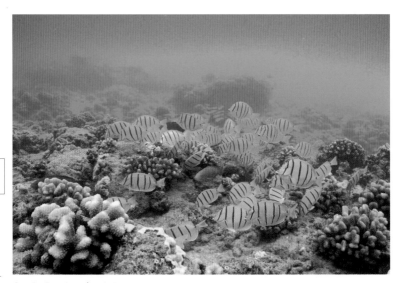

Convict Tang in Hulopoe Bay.

the sun lights up an underwater grotto like a magnificent church. **Trilogy Lanai Ocean Sports** (see above) offers its version of "sunrise services" at Cathedrals—not only is dawn the best time of day to dive this incredible area, but no other dive boats are here this early. For repeat guests, the captain has a dozen other excellent underwater destinations from which to choose. Divers have extra room to stretch out—trips on the *Manele Kai,* a 32-foot jet-drive Zodiac, are limited to six certified divers. A two-tank dive costs $212. For the same price, you can also learn to dive off the beach.

SPORT FISHING   **Spinning Dolphin Charters of Lanai** (www.sportfishing lanai.com; © **808/565-7676**) offers sport-fishing expeditions on *Fish-n-Chips,* a 36-foot Twin-V boat. It costs $700 for 4 hours for six passengers ($110 for each additional hour), or you can share a boat for $150 each for 4 hours.

SURFING   If you've ever wanted to learn how to surf, let instructor and surfing champion Nick Palumbo take you on a four-wheel-drive surfing safari to a secluded surf spot. He'll have you up and riding the waves in no time. His **Lanai Surf School & Surf Safari** (www.lanaisurfsafari.com; © **808/649-0739**) offers 2-hour surf or paddleboarding lessons, which include four-wheel-drive transportation, refreshments, and "a really good time," for $200 per person, minimum of two guests.

SUNSET/WHALE-WATCHING   **Trilogy Lanai Ocean Sports** (see above) offers a 2-hour ocean adventure on its sailing catamaran or jet-drive Zodiac. Cruise past sea cliffs and unspoiled coastline while watching schools of spinner dolphins and flying fish dart ahead of the bow. You'll arrive at Sweetheart Rock just in time for the best sunset shots. During whale season (Dec–Mar), North Pacific humpback whales put on impressive shows, breaching, slapping their pectoral fins, and singing complex melodies underwater. The captain and crew are certified naturalists who make each trip educational. The cost ($111 adults, $83 teens 13–18, and $55 children 3–12) includes soft drinks and snacks.

OTHER OUTDOOR ACTIVITIES

Biking

The **Lodge at Koele** (© 808/565-4552) rents street bikes for $10 an hour or $40 a day (sunrise to sunset) for resort guests. **Hotel Lanai** (© 800/795-7211) also offers cruisers (complete with cup holders!) free to guests.

Golf

Note that as we went to press, Jack Nicklaus was busy redesigning **The Experience at Koele** (www.fourseasons.com) golf course. We can't wait to see how he improves on the existing 18th hole, a par-5 grand finale featuring waterfalls that flow into a lake.

The Challenge at Manele ★★ This target-style, desert-links course, designed by Jack Nicklaus, is one of the most challenging courses in the state. Check out some of the course rules: no retrieving golf balls from the 150-foot cliffs on the ocean holes 12, 13, or 17, and all whales, axis deer, and other wild animals are considered immovable obstructions. That's just a hint of the unique experience you'll have on this course, which is routed among lava outcroppings, archaeological sites, kiawe groves, and ilima trees. The five sets of staggered tees pose a challenge to everyone from the casual golfer to the pro. Facilities include a clubhouse, pro shop, rentals, practice area, lockers, and showers.

Next to the Four Seasons Resort Lanai at Manele Bay. www.golfonlanai.com/manele. © **800/321-4666** or 808/565-2222. Greens fees $295 ($250 for guests).

Hiking

KOELE NATURE HIKE The leisurely 2-hour self-guided **Koele Nature Hike** starts by the reflecting pool in the backyard of the Lodge at Koele and takes you on a 5-mile loop through Norfolk Island pines, into Hulopoe Valley, past wild ginger, and up to Koloiki Ridge, with its panoramic view of Maunalei Valley and the islands of Molokai and Maui in the distance. You're welcome to take the hike even if you're not a guest at the Lodge. The path isn't clearly marked, so ask the concierge for a free map. Do this hike in the morning; by afternoon, the clouds usually roll in, marring visibility at the top and increasing your chance of being caught in a downpour. If you'd like to go with a local expert, check in at the front office at the **Lodge at Koele** (www.fourseasons.com/lanai; © **808/565-4000**). Guided hikes start at 11am daily and cost $35.

MUNRO TRAIL This tough, 11-mile (round-trip) uphill climb through groves of Norfolk pines is a lung-buster, but if you reach the top, you'll be rewarded with a breathtaking view of Molokai, Maui, Kahoolawe, the peaks of the Big Island, and—on a really clear day—Oahu in the distance. Figure on 7 hours. The trail begins at Lanai Cemetery along Keomoku Road (Hwy. 44) and follows Lanai's ancient caldera rim, ending up at the island's highest point, Lanaihale. Go in the morning for the best visibility. After 4 miles, you'll get a view of Lanai City. The weary retrace their steps from here, while the more determined go the last 1.25 miles to the top. Diehards head down Lanai's steep south-crater rim to join the highway to Manele Bay. For more details on the Munro Trail—including information on four-wheel-driving it to the top—see "The Munro Trail" (p. 399).

KAPIHAA TRAIL An old fisherman's trail snakes along the scenic coastline, starting at Manele Bay. This easy hike will expose you to Lanai's unique geography and many unusual native Hawaiian coastal plants. The back-and-forth trek

Maunalei Gulch.

takes around 90 minutes. Venture out on your own, or, if you're a hotel guest at the Four Seasons Resort Lanai at Manele Bay, arrange a complimentary guided hike through the concierge (www.fourseasons.com/lanai; ℂ **808/565-2000;** $10 donations accepted).

Horseback Riding

Explore much of Lanai's unique landscape that is otherwise unreachable on horseback. **Lanai Western Adventures** (http://lanaigrandadventures.com; ℂ **808/563-9385**) offers various rides with *paniolos* (cowboys) starting at $160. You'll meander through guava groves and ironwood trees; catch glimpses of axis deer, sheep, quail, and wild turkeys; and end with panoramic views of Maui and Lanai. Pony rides are available for pint-size *paniolos*. Wear clothes you're willing to sacrifice to Lanai's red dirt (long pants and closed-toe shoes are required) and bring a jacket (rain is frequent).

Sporting Clays

Even inexperienced shooters (like myself) love taking a crack at the clay targets on this beautiful 14-station course operated by **Lanai Western Adventures** (http://lanaigrandadventures.com; ℂ **808/563-9385**). Beginners are armed with 25 cartridges, a shotgun, safety glasses, vest, earplugs, golf cart, and an extremely helpful coach for $160. Advanced shooters can head out on their own golf carts. The course is on the ridge above the Lodge at Koele and rambles past ironwood trees, opening up to scenic vistas. Each station presents a fresh challenge—the skipping "rabbits" are the most fun. Aim to hit both at once.

Tennis

Public courts, lit for night play, are available in Lanai City at no charge; call ℂ **808/565-6979** for reservations. If you're staying at the Lodge at Koele or

Manele Bay, you can take advantage of the Lodge's three Premiere Cushion outdoor hard courts for free, with complimentary use of Prince rackets, balls, and bottled water—even shoes if you need.

WHERE TO STAY ON LANAI

Accommodations on Lanai are limited: You can go for broke at one (or both) of the luxurious Four Seasons properties, book a plantation-style room at the Hotel Lanai, or camp under the stars at Hulopoe Beach Park. When you stay with the Four Seasons, you're greeted at the airport or ferry with chilled towels and shuttled off in style. Later, if you move from one resort to the other, the staff will pack and deliver your luggage for you.

In addition to the above choices, the island offers a handful of vacation rentals. **Hale O Lanai,** in Lanai City (www.myhawaiibeachfront.com; ℂ **808/247-3637**), is a fully equipped two-bedroom plantation house that sleeps up to six. The bathroom is a little funky, but the hardwood floors and tropical accents are charming. Rates range from $125 to $150 plus an additional $65 cleaning fee.

Expensive

Four Seasons Resort Lanai, The Lodge at Koele ★★★   This elegant retreat sits against Lanaihale, the island's tallest peak, in the cool mist of the mountains. On 21 immaculately landscaped acres, it resembles a grand country estate, complete with croquet lawns, gazebos, orchid greenhouse, reflecting pond, and Chinese pagoda.

Inside, the Great Hall's beamed ceilings and enormous stone fireplaces evoke the atmosphere of a storied hunter's lodge. Leather couches, rustic footstools, and richly patterned ottomans are gathered invitingly around each fireplace—coveted spots during the nightly live music sessions.

The large guest rooms have an English countryside flair, with somewhat dizzying striped carpet, bright floral curtains above window seats, and plush fourposter beds. Whether you're in a standard room or fireplace suite, you'll have the benefit of a massive flatscreen TV, marble bathroom with oversize tub, Nespresso machine, and furnished lanai overlooking stately gardens.

At 1,700 feet above sea level, temperatures can drop into the 50s—especially during winter. Never fear, the rooms have heat as well as air-conditioning, there are extra blankets in the closet, and the cooler climate just makes everything cozier. This isn't your stereotypical Hawaiian vacation; people come to Koele to play golf on one of the world's most scenic courses, explore the hinterlands on horseback, hike up into the forested hillside, or simply put their feet up on the foyer's comfy rattan chairs and disappear into a novel.

Take afternoon tea in the Great Room or kick back with a whiskey in that swanky bar that Hemingway would likely approve of. Try your hand at lei-making, hula, or ukulele. Throughout the week, the Hookipa Cultural Program offers lessons—and a chance to get to know some of the good-natured, island-raised staff. And whenever you crave some beach time, Hulopoe is just a short shuttle ride away.

1 Keomoku Hwy., Lanai City. www.fourseasons.com/lanai. ℂ **800/321-4666** or 808/565-4000. 100 units; 7 suites. $339–$1,229 double; from $889 suite. Extra adult $100; free for children 17 and under. Numerous packages available. Airport and local shuttle $48 for unlimited trips. Free parking. **Amenities:** 3 restaurants; bar w/live music; babysitting; bike rentals; children's

program; concierge; croquet; fitness room; golf at Jack Nicklaus–designed Experience at Koele; self-guided hike; Jacuzzi; outdoor pool; room service; in-room spa treatments; tennis courts; watersports equipment; Wi-Fi (free or premium for $20 per day)

Four Seasons Resort Lanai at Manele Bay ★★★   It's pretty sweet, reclining on a chaise longue beneath a giant umbrella on a near-empty beach. Add to that a genuinely friendly attendant who delivers cucumber-scented oshibori towels, mini mango smoothies, and Evian spritzes, and you've entered a new dimension of pampered pleasure. This gracious resort on Lanai's south coast overlooks Hulopoe Beach—one of the finest stretches of sand in the state. As you meander through the open-air lobby to one of two oceanfront wings, you'll pass by lush gardens, waterfalls, and koi-filled lotus ponds. Rare Polynesian artifacts purchased from the Bishop Museum decorate the main lobby's lower level, which is home to two fantastic restaurants: **Nobu Lanai ★★★** and **One Forty ★★★**.

Oversize guest rooms have plush down comforters and pillows, huge marble bathrooms, 40-inch flatscreen TVs, and Nespresso machines. Each room has a semi-private lanai with a day bed from which you can gaze at the big blue Pacific to your heart's content. Other amenities sprinkled around the property include Adirondack chairs beneath swaying palms, binoculars for whale-watching, free popcorn and shuffleboard tables in the chic sports bar, and an exercise room with a view so grand you'll forget you're burning calories on a stationary cycle. The 1,500-square-foot fitness center has state-of-the-art cardiovascular equipment and a wood-floored studio for spinning, yoga, Pilates, and meditation classes.

Inspired by indigenous healing traditions, the resort's spa offers traditional lomi lomi Hawaiian massages, facials, scrubs, wraps, and salon services in serene treatment rooms or beachfront huts. Work with the spa's perfumier to design your own signature scent—an ideal souvenir. Guests have free access to the spa facility's cedar saunas, eucalyptus steam rooms, and rainforest showers. Slightly less formal than the Lodge at Koele up the hill, this resort has "Kids for All Seasons" child-care programs and a teen center with video games, a pool table, and a 54-inch TV.

1 Manele Bay Rd., Lanai City. www.fourseasons.com/lanai. © **800/321-4666** or 808/565-2000. 209 units, 33 suites. $489–$2,100 double; from $1,329 suite. Extra adult $100; free for children 17 and under. Numerous packages available. Airport and local shuttle $48 per person for unlimited use. **Amenities:** 4 restaurants; bar w/breathtaking views and live music; babysitting; children's program; concierge; fitness center w/classes; golf at Jack Nicklaus–designed Challenge at Manele; Jacuzzi; large outdoor pool; room service; full spa; tennis courts; watersports equipment; Wi-Fi (free or premium for $20 per day).

Moderate

Hotel Lanai ★   This boutique hotel in the heart of town is perfect for families and other vacationers who can't afford to spend $400-plus a night but still want to experience Lanai. If you're looking for the old-time aloha that the island is famous for, this clapboard relic is your place. Built in the 1920s, it has retained its quaint, plantation-era character.

That character comes at a price, however: Guest rooms are extremely small, and noise travels. But the comfy beds come with Hawaiian quilts, and the ceiling fans do a more than adequate job in the cooler climate. The popular lanai units share a furnished deck that faces Dole Park. The one-bedroom cottage is perfect for small families, with the added amenities of a TV, bathtub, and hammock. All of Lanai City is within walking distance, and complimentary bikes are available for longer forays. It has an excellent restaurant in **Lanai City Grille ★★**.

This social spot is where visitors might mingle with locals on the lanai, talking or playing the ukulele long into the night. While it lacks the luxury of the nearby resorts, Hotel Lanai offers an authentic, unpretentious peek into the island's Hawaiian heart.

828 Lanai Ave., Lanai City. www.hotellanai.com. © **800/795-7211** or 808/565-7211. 10 units, 1 cottage. $149–$199 double; $229 cottage. Extra adult $50. Rates include continental breakfast. Unlimited shuttle service for entire stay $35. Free parking. **Amenities:** Restaurant; bar; complimentary bikes; access to 2 resort golf courses on the island; complimentary snorkeling equipment; nearby tennis courts; Wi-Fi (free).

Camping at Hulopoe Beach Park ★★

There is only one legal place to camp on Lanai, but it's a beauty: **Hulopoe Beach Park.** To camp in this exquisite beach park, with its crescent-shape, white-sand beach bordered by a shady grass lawn, contact Tom Viera (© **808/215-1107**). There's a registration fee, plus a charge of $15 per person per night. Hulopoe has eight campsites, and each accommodates up to five people. Facilities include restrooms, showers, barbecues, and picnic tables.

WHERE TO EAT ON LANAI

Lanai offers dining experiences on two ends of the spectrum: from humble ma-and-pa eateries to world-class culinary adventures. The posh resort restaurants require deep pockets, and Lanai City has only a handful of other options.

Note: You'll find the restaurants reviewed in this chapter on the "Lanai" map on p. 393.

Very Expensive

Main Dining Room ★★★ NEW AMERICAN   Not too long ago, the Lodge's Main Dining Room was among the last restaurants in Hawaii to require men to wear a suit coat. That formality is gone, but the culinary excellence it suggested remains. Try Chef Guryel's four-course tasting menu, which might include Molokai venison roasted on a hot lava rock tableside, succulent Kona lobster, and artisanal Hawaii Island cheeses drizzled with kiawe honey. I've had some of the best lamb chops of my life here, served with juicy poha berries and roasted heirloom carrots. Subdued lighting and a crackling fire give this stately octagonal dining room a seductive ambience.

At the Four Seasons Resort Lanai, the Lodge at Koele, 1 Keomoku Hwy., Lanai City. www.four seasons.com/koele/dining. © **808/565-4580.** Main courses $43–$65; 4-course tasting menu $89. Fri–Tues 6–9:30pm.

Nobu Lanai ★★★ JAPANESE   What does Lanai have in common with New York, Milan, Budapest, and Mexico City? All have a Nobu restaurant—a measure of how fun a place is, according to pop singer Madonna. The best way to experience this epicurean phenomenon is to order the *omakase*—chef's tasting menu—for $120. Every dish is as delicious as it is artful: the Kona kampachi sashimi decorated with thin jalapeño discs, the masterfully seared Wagyu beef served with asparagus spears and lotus root, and the immaculate plates of nigiri sushi. Vegetarian? Nobu has a sophisticated menu just for you, featuring fusion tacos and tofu tobanyaki anticucho—a melting pot of Japanese and Peruvian flavors. The wine and cocktail list is topnotch, including YK35—chef Nobu's favorite sake—and a sassy caipirinha with Pisco, fresh lime, ginger beer, and sprigs of shiso.

At the Four Seasons Resort Lanai at Manele Bay, 1 Manele Bay Rd., Lanai City. www.fourseasons. com/manelebay/dining. ℂ **808/565-2290.** Main courses $12–$58; multi-course tasting menu $120. Fri–Tues 6–9:30pm.

One Forty ★★★ BREAKFAST/STEAK & SEAFOOD   The restaurant formerly known as Hulopoe Court has been reborn as a steakhouse. Thankfully, the breakfast buffet—probably the best in the state—stayed the same, while dinner improved tenfold. Weeks later I'm still fantasizing about breakfast overlooking sparkling Manele Bay. Imagine: a cornucopia of ripe tropical fruit; "make-your-own" omelet, waffle, and smoothie stations; artisan cheese, charcuterie, four types of sausages, brioche French toast, and eggs any which way. Not just lox but house-cured ono with toasted bagels—now *that* is what I call breakfast! Dinner is also stellar. The sesame-crusted ahi with edamame relish is perfectly on point, as is the wagyu rib-eye (it should be, for a staggering $67). More than one guest has snuck the kalua pork and dill mac-and-cheese back to their room.

At the Four Seasons Resort Lanai at Manele Bay, 1 Manele Bay Rd., Lanai City. www.fourseasons. com/manelebay/dining. ℂ **808/565-2290.** Breakfast main courses $17–$24; buffet $40; dinner $28–$66. Daily 7–10am and 6–9:30pm.

Terrace ★ AMERICAN   Tucked in the back of the Lodge's Great Hall, this semi-casual restaurant serves hearty dishes that match the atmosphere: wild boar Bolognese, braised lamb, and barbecued beef short ribs with sides of sautéed forest mushrooms and Molokai sweet potato. At lunch and breakfast, the large glass doors open to reveal the resort's manicured grounds. Start the day with a venison sausage and egg sandwich, the same brioche French toast served at Manele (this time with Surinam cherry compote), or lemon-ricotta pancakes with candied lemon cream.

At the Four Seasons Resort Lanai, the Lodge at Koele, 1 Keomoku Hwy., Lanai City. www.four seasons.com/koele. ℂ **808/565-4580.** Full breakfast $16–$24; dinner main courses $27–$50. Daily 7am–2pm and 6–9:30pm.

Moderate

Lanai City Grille ★★ HAWAII REGIONAL/COUNTRY   Celebrated Maui chef Bev Gannon (Haliimaile General Store, Joe's, and Gannon's on Maui) brings her comfort-food-gone-fancy to this bright and lovely dining room at the Hotel Lanai. The crab cake appetizer, baby back ribs with citrus barbecue sauce, and Joe's famous meatloaf—yes, meatloaf—are satisfying, lip-smacking indulgences. A special vegetarian menu has entrees like goat cheese ravioli and house-made gnocchi. On Friday, live entertainment packs the place—giving guests a chance to mingle with the community.

At the Hotel Lanai, 828 Lanai Ave., Lanai City. www.hotellanai.com. ℂ **808/565-7211.** Main courses $28–$42. Wed–Sun 5–9pm.

Views ★★ PACIFIC RIM   Take a stroll or hop the shuttle to the Challenge at Manele's clubhouse, the island's best spot for lunch, where the idyllic view of Puu Pehe and Hulopoe Bay is even better than at the resort proper—if you can fathom that. Sip a Lanai Mule (vodka with ginger beer and calamansi lime juice), nosh on a prawn B.L.T. (pita stuffed with fat prawns, Creole aioli, and caramelized onions), and crown your meal with a decadent ice cream sandwich. My fave: the gingersnap cookie loaded with pineapple coconut ice cream.

At the Challenge at Manele Golf Course, 1 Manele Bay Rd., Lanai City. www.fourseasons.com/manelebay/dining. ℂ **808/565-2230.** Main courses $19–$34. Daily 11am–3pm.

Inexpensive

Anuenue Juice Bar ★★ JUICE BAR Anuenue, the Hawaiian word for rainbow, is an apt name for this color-splashed juice bar. Owner Tammy Ringbauer answered a deep need on Lanai when she opened this health-conscious outpost. She sources Lanai-grown produce whenever possible for emerald-green smoothies, ruby-red beet juice, and golden turmeric shots. Her good-and-good-for-you daily specials include warm quinoa salad and Greek yogurt parfait. Create your own juice blend with extras like fresh ginger, chia seeds, bee pollen, or flax meal. Here for a few days? Borrow a refillable Mason jug.

338 Eighth St. (at Gay St.), Lanai City. www.anuenuejuicebar.com. ℂ **808/250-0633.** Most items $4–$20. Mon–Sat 8am–4pm; Sun on occasion.

Blue Ginger Cafe ★ COFFEE SHOP With its cheery curtains and oilcloth-covered tables, this humble eatery welcomes residents and locals alike in for eggs and Spam (yes, Spam is a beloved breakfast meat in Hawaii), adequate bowls of saimin, epic plates of fried rice, fried chicken katsu, and decent egg/tuna/chicken salad sandwiches on homemade bread. The kitchen staff bakes all of its own breads and pastries, so burgers and sandwiches taste especially fresh. Hot out of the oven, the blueberry turnovers, cinnamon buns, and cookies are legendary.

409 Seventh St. (at Ilima St.), Lanai City. www.bluegingercafelanai.com. ℂ **808/565-6363.** Breakfast and lunch items under $17; dinner main courses under $18. Cash only. Mon and Thurs–Fri 6am–8pm; Tues–Wed 6am–2pm; Sat–Sun 6:30am–8pm.

Canoes Lanai ★ LOCAL "Lanai's oldest eating establishment" opened in 1926 as a soda fountain. The Tanigawa family took it over in the 1950s and began selling their secret-recipe hamburgers, still on the menu. Today's favorites are *furikaki* chicken served with (of course) two scoops of rice and macaroni salad, and the Tanigawa loco moco: a monster pile of rice topped with that famous burger, a fried egg, and a slather of gravy.

419 Seventh St., Lanai City. **808/565-6537.** Breakfast items under $14; sandwiches $5–$8; burgers $3–$6. Cash only. Sun–Thurs 6:30am–1pm; Fri–Sat 6:30am–8pm.

Coffee Works ★ COFFEEHOUSE A biscuit's toss from Dole Park, this cozy coffeehouse churns out excellent espresso drinks, amply loaded lox and bagels, acai bowls, and ice cream. The renovated plantation home is the perfect place to fuel up in the morning. It's also Lanai City's local watering hole—expect to see your waiter from dinner last night chatting away on the wide wooden deck with the shuttle driver. As you wait for your cappuccino, browse the gift items opposite the counter: T-shirts to prove you were here, tea infusers and pots, island coffee beans, and CDs featuring music from the most recent Hawaiian slack key guitar festival.

604 Ilima St., Lanai City. www.coffeeworkshawaii.com. ℂ **808/565-6962.** Most items under $9. Mon–Fri 7am–3pm. Sat 8am–3pm.

Pele's Other Garden ★ DELI/BISTRO The checkered floor and vanity license plates decorating the walls set an upbeat tone at this casual bistro. For lunch, dig into an avocado and feta wrap or an Italian hoagie. Cheese lovers will swoon over the thin-crusted four-cheese pizza—a gooey medley of mozzarella, Parmesan, feta, and provolone. During happy hour, nosh on onion rings and coconut shrimp at one of Lanai City's only bars. Enjoy cocktails, wine by the glass, or one of the dozen brews on tap. The atmosphere grows slightly more romantic after sundown, with white linens on the tables and twinkle lights over the outdoor seating. Dole Park, 811 Houston St., Lanai City. www.pelesothergarden.com. ✆ **808/565-9628.** Main courses $9–$13 lunch, $17–$20 dinner; pizza from $9. Mon–Fri 11am–3pm and 5–8pm. Bar menu Mon–Sat 4:30–6:30pm.

LANAI SHOPPING

For such a tiny population, Lanai has some surprisingly great shopping. A stroll around Dole Park will yield original artwork, fashions, and souvenirs, and both Four Seasons resorts have excellent sundries shops. Just remember that groceries are delivered only once a week, so stock up accordingly.

Art

Lanai Art Center ★ Established in 1989, the Lanai Art Center showcases works by Lanai residents, including evocative watercolor paintings of local landmarks, silk-screened clothing, and necklaces made of polished shells and bone. Often, the artists are at work in back. Check out the center's reasonably priced workshops, where local and visiting artists offer instruction on everything from *raku* (Japanese pottery) to silk-printing, quilting, lei-making, felting, and *gyotaku* (printing a real fish on your own T-shirt). 339 Seventh St., Lanai City. www.lanaiart.org. ✆ **808/565-7503.**

Mike Carroll Gallery Oil painter Mike Carroll left a successful 22-year career as a professional artist in Chicago for a distinctly slower pace on Lanai. His gorgeous, color-saturated interpretations of local life and landscapes fill the walls of his eponymous gallery, which also sells original work by top Maui and Lanai artists, prints, and locally made, one-of-a-kind jewelry. 443 Seventh St., Lanai City. www.mikecarrollgallery.com. ✆ **808/565-7122.**

Edibles & Grocery Staples

Pine Isle Market This family-run grocery, three doors down from Richard's, carries everything that its competition doesn't. A visit to both will net you a fine haul. Pine Isle specializes in locally caught fresh fish, but you can also find ice cream, canned goods, fresh herbs, toys, diapers, paint, and other essentials. Take a spin through the fishing section to ogle every imaginable lure. The Hondas, who've operated the shop for 6 decades, still observe the "plantation days" tradition of closing for lunch on Tuesdays and Thursdays. 356 Eighth St., Lanai City. ✆ **808/565-6488.**

Richard's Market Since 1946, this family grocery has been the go-to for dry goods, frozen meats and vegetables, liquor, paper products, cosmetics, utensils, and other miscellany. It just got a major makeover, courtesy of Larry Ellison. Now the inside resembles a miniature Whole Foods and has a comparable array of fancy chocolates and fine wines, mixed in with aloha shirts, fold-up lauhala mats,

Dis 'N Dat shop.

and Central Bakery breads. Don't faint when you see that milk costs $9 a gallon; that's the price of paradise. Even still, the spiffy new shelves are often empty by the weekend. Wednesday is barge day, when the island's fresh merchandise is delivered. Plan your shopping accordingly. 434 Eighth St., Lanai City. © **808/565-3780.**

Saturday Market ★   From 7am to noon-ish each Saturday, the southeast corner of Dole Park turns into a farmer's market. Lanai residents bring their homegrown fruits and vegetables, freshly baked pastries, plate lunches, and handicrafts to sell. The best lunches sell out quickly—if you want one of Juanita's scrumptious pork flautas with a dollop of hot sauce, get here early.

Gifts & Souvenirs

Adore' ★★   Just try to resist this resort shop's bona fide (read: top-dollar) treasures, including delicately wrapped freshwater pearl and diamond bead necklaces by Jordan Alexander, the cutest-ever bikinis by Hawaii's own Le Tarte, and slinky dresses and housewares by Missoni (yes, you can fit that throw pillow in your suitcase). Four Seasons Resort Lanai at Manele Bay, 1 Manele Bay Rd. © **808/565-2093.**

Cory Labang Studio ★★   Local designer and artist Cory Labang scours thrift shops and rummage sales to find one-of-a-kind vintage treasures, which she sells at her studio for reasonable prices. She's got a keen eye for Hawaiiana and a knack for upcycling. Look for aloha shirts and Labang's must-have clutches, coin purses, and stash bags, the latter made from antique neon muumuus and fabric printed with her own photographs. 431 Jacaranda St., next to post office. www.corylabangstudio.com. © **808/315-6715.**

Dis 'N Dat ★★   This may be the best souvenir shop I've ever encountered. The chartreuse storefront with its singing chimes and '59 Nash Metropolitan parked out front are impossible to miss. Owners Barry (Dis) and Suzie (Dat) Osman comb international markets for cool stuff and have packed their small

CELEBRATING WITH LANAI festivals

Throughout the year, HawaiiOnTV.com and JazzAlleyTV.com bring world-class entertainers to little Lanai. These intimate annual festivals are worth planning your vacation around. The Four Seasons resorts even offer discounted room rates in conjunction with festival dates.

o In February, the 3-day **Lanai Hawaiian Culture Film & Musical Festival** (www.lanaifilmfestival.com) screens fascinating shorts, features, and documentaries about the people of the Pacific that you're not likely see anywhere else. Live music and cultural workshops round out the weekend.

o Jazz greats from as far as Kansas City descend on the island for the **Lanai Jazz Festival** (www.lanaijazzfestival.com) in March. Live performances pop up throughout Lanai City: Grammy-award-winning saxophonists serenade audiences in the Lodge at Koele's Great Hall while jazz guitars perform at the local juice bar.

o The "jumping flea," the quintessential instrument of the Islands, is celebrated

during the **Lanai Ukulele Festival** (www.lanaiukulelefestival.com) in June. This light-hearted musical weekend includes concerts under the stars and free clinics for beginning uke players.

o Dole Park is the site of fireworks, a parade, and all-day entertainment during the annual **Pineapple Festival,** generally held on the first Saturday in July (see "Hawaii Calendar of Events" on p. 511).

o The **Lanai Slack Key Guitar Festival** (www.lanaislackkeyfestival.com) in August is 3 days of superlative concerts and workshops led by Grammy and Na Hoku award-winning artists. Events are free and take place around Lanai City.

o The **Aloha Festival** (www.aloha festivals.com) takes place in September or the first week in October, and the **Christmas Festival** is held on the first Saturday in December. For details on these festivals, contact the **Lanai Visitors Bureau** (p. 396).

shop with mobiles and wind chimes, carved statues, batik scarves, dragonfly lamps, and sparkly pineapple pendants. 418 Eighth Ave., Lanai City. www.disndatshop. com. ℂ **866/DIS-N-DAT** [347-6328] or 808/565-9170.

The Local Gentry ★★ Jenna (Gentry) Majkus manages to outfit her small but wonderful boutique with every wardrobe essential, from fancy lingerie to stylish chapeaux, for the whole family. Browse the selection of OluKai sandals, Kahala aloha shirts, handmade onesies, and (best of all) T-shirts with Lanai-inspired silkscreens, including: what happens on lanai everybody knows. 363 Seventh St., Lanai City. ℂ **808/565-9130.**

LANAI NIGHTLIFE

The Four Seasons resorts and the Hotel Lanai are the island's mainstays for nightlife. Nightly, in the **Great Hall** at the Lodge at Koele, in Four Seasons Resort Lanai, 1 Keomoku Hwy. (www.fourseasons.com/koele; ℂ **808/565-4580**), various local musicians perform from 7 to 9pm. Sink into a plush chair by one of the manorial fireplaces and let them serenade you with lovely contemporary Hawaiian music. Uncle Kimo tickles the ivories of the grand piano and throws in a few show tunes for fun.

At **Kailani,** the poolside restaurant overlooking Manele Bay, at Four Seasons Resort Lanai at Manele Bay, 1 Manele Bay Rd. (www.fourseasons.com/manelebay; ℂ **808/565-2093**), nightly live music enhances the already romantic atmosphere. On Friday night, local musicians get together for jams at the **Lanai City Grille** ★★ at the Hotel Lanai, 828 Lanai Ave. (www.hotellanai.com; ℂ **800/795-7211** or 808/565-7211).

9

KAUAI

by Jeanne Cooper

T ime has been kind to Kauai, the oldest and northernmost of the Hawaiian Islands. Millions of years of erosion have carved fluted ridges, emerald valleys, and glistening waterfalls into the flanks of Waialeale, the extinct volcano at the center of this near-circular isle. Similar eons have created a ring of enticing sandy beaches and coral reefs. Kauai's wild beauty sometimes translates to rough seas and slippery trails, but with a little caution, anyone can safely revel in the island's natural grandeur.

ESSENTIALS
Arriving

BY PLANE A number of North American airlines offer regularly scheduled, nonstop service to Kauai's main airport in Lihue (airport code: LIH) from the Mainland, nearly all from the West Coast. (*Note:* From Los Angeles, flights generally take about 5½ hours heading to Kauai, but only 4½ hours on the return, due to prevailing winds.)

United Airlines (www.united.com; ℂ 800/225-5825) flies nonstop to Kauai daily from Los Angeles, San Francisco, and Denver. **American Airlines** (www.aa.com; ℂ 800/433-7300) and **Delta Airlines** (www.delta.com; ℂ 800/221-1212) each have nonstop flights from Los Angeles. **US Airways** (www.usairways.com; ℂ 800/428-4322), which at press time was preparing to merge with American Airlines, flies nonstop from Phoenix. American also codeshares on some routes of **Alaska Airlines,** which flies nonstop to Lihue from San Jose, Oakland, and San Diego in California as well as Portland and Seattle in the Pacific Northwest. *Tip:* Upgrading to first class is often easiest and cheapest on Alaska.

Other carriers' service varies by season. **WestJet** (www.westjet.com; ℂ 888/ 937-8538) offers its most frequent nonstop flights between Vancouver and Lihue December to March. From late June to mid-September, **Hawaiian Airlines** (www.hawaiianairlines.com; ℂ 800/367-5320) flies nonstop several times a week from Oakland and Los Angeles to Lihue.

You can also travel to Lihue via Oahu and Maui. **Hawaiian Airlines** (see above) flies to Kauai 16 to 20 times a day from Honolulu and four times a day from Kahului, Maui. The Honolulu route lasts about 35 minutes; the Maui route, about 10 minutes more, both using Boeing 717s that seat around 120. **Island Air** (www.islandair.com; ℂ 800/652-6541) flies twin-engine turboprops, with 64 passengers, from Honolulu six times a day; flights take just over 40 minutes.

Note: The view from either side of the plane as you land in Lihue, 2 miles east of the center of town, is arresting. On the left side, passengers have a close look at Haupu Ridge, separating the unspoiled beach of Kipu Kai (seen in "The Descendants") from busy Nawiliwili Harbor; on the right, shades of green demarcate former sugarcane fields, coconut groves, and the ridgeline of Nounou ("Sleeping Giant") to the north.

BY CRUISE SHIP   Several cruise lines call in Kauai's main port of Nawiliwili, but **Norwegian Cruise Lines** (www.ncl.com; ✆ 866/234-7350) is unusual in offering weekly Hawaii itineraries that include overnight stays on Kauai and Maui, allowing for multiple excursions.

Visitor Information

Before your trip begins, visit www.gohawaii.com/kauai, the website of **Kauai Visitors Bureau** (✆ 800/262-1400) and download or view its free "Kauai Vacation Planner." (**Note:** The bureau's location in Lihue's Watumull Plaza, 4334 Rice St., Suite 101, is not the most convenient area for drop-bys; it's open 8am–3pm weekdays.) Before and during your trip, consult the authoritative **Kauai Explorer** website (www.kauaiexplorer.com) for detailed descriptions of 18 of the island's most popular beaches (with or without lifeguards), plus a daily ocean report, surf forecasts, and safety tips. Hikers will also want to read Kauai Explorer's notes on 10 island trails, from easy to super-strenuous. Click on the "Visiting" link of **Kauai County**'s homepage (www.kauai.gov), for links to Kauai Explorer, the Visitors Bureau, bus schedules, camping information, local park and golf facility listings, a festival calendar, farmers' market schedules, and more.

The **Poipu Beach Resort Association** (www.poipubeach.org; ✆ 888/744-0888 or 808/742-7444) highlights accommodations, activities, shopping, and dining in the Poipu area; follow the "Contact Us" link to receive a free map of the Koloa and/or Mahaulepu heritage trails.

Check out **Midweek Kauai** (www.midweekkauai.com) online before you arrive and look for a free copy, distributed on Wednesday, once you're on Kauai, to take advantage of the latest entertainment listings and dining specials. The **Garden Island** daily newspaper (http://thegardenisland.com) also publishes events listings, found under the online "Visitors" link.

Napali Coast cliffs.

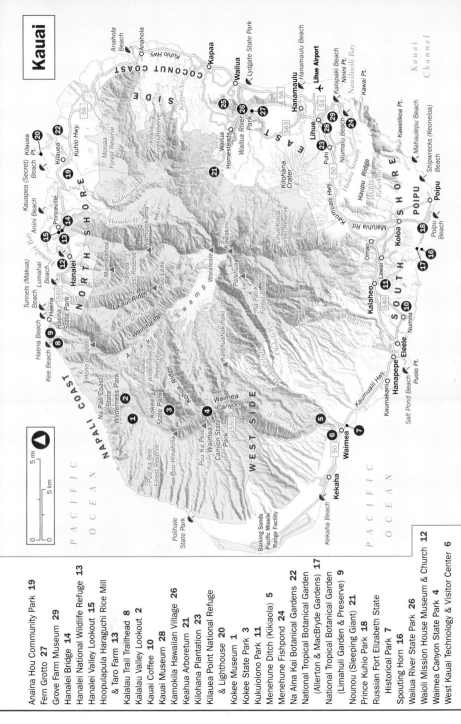

Kauai

The Island in Brief

EAST SIDE

Home to the airport, the main harbor, most of the civic and commercial buildings on the island, and the majority of its residents, Kauai's East Side has nevertheless preserved much of its rural character, with green ridges that lead to the shore, red-dirt roads crossing old sugarcane fields, and postcard-pretty waterfalls. Heading east from Lihue into the Coconut Coast strip of Wailua and Kapaa, the main highway changes its name and number from the Kaumualii Highway (Hwy. 50) to Kuhio Highway (Hwy. 56). More noticeable are the steady trade winds that riffle fronds of hundreds of coconut palms, part of the area's royal legacy; a long and broad (by Hawaii standards) river and easily accessed waterfalls; and the chock-a-block low-rise condos, budget hotels, and shopping centers, all adding to the East Side's significant rush-hour traffic jams.

LIHUE Bargain hunters will appreciate the county seat's many shopping, lodging, and dining options, but Lihue also boasts cultural assets, from the exhibits at the **Kauai Museum ★★** to hula shows, concerts, and festivals at the Kauai War Memorial Convention Hall and Kauai Community College's Performing Arts Center. Nearby outdoor attractions include **Kalapaki Beach ★★**, next to the cruise port of Nawiliwili; ATV, ziplining, hiking, and tubing excursions, the latter on old sugarcane irrigation flumes; and kayaking on Huleia River past the historic **Menehune Fish Pond ★**.

WAILUA **Wailua Falls ★** (seen in the opening credits of "Fantasy Island"), the twin cascades of **Opakeaa Falls ★★**, and a riverboat cruise to **Fern Grotto ★★** are highlights of this former royal compound, which includes remains of stone-walled heiau (places of worship), birthstones, and other ancient sites. Kayakers flock to **Wailua River,** which also offers wakeboarding and water-skiing opportunities; the municipal **Wailua Golf Course ★★** is routinely ranked as one of the top in the state; and hikers can choose from three trailheads to ascend Nounou (Sleeping Giant) mountain. Highway 56 also passes by the decaying structures of the Coco Palms resort, featured in Elvis Presley's "Blue Hawaii," closed after

MOA BETTER: chickens & roosters

One of the first things visitors notice about Kauai is the unusually large number of wild chickens. Mostly rural, Kauai has always had plenty of poultry, including the colorful jungle fowl known as *moa,* but after Hurricane Iniki blew through the island in 1992, they soon were everywhere, reproducing quickly and, in the case of roosters, crowing night and day. While resorts work tirelessly to trap or shoo them away, it's impossible to ensure you'll never be awakened by a rooster; if you're staying outside a resort, it's pretty much

guaranteed you will. Light sleepers should bring earplugs.

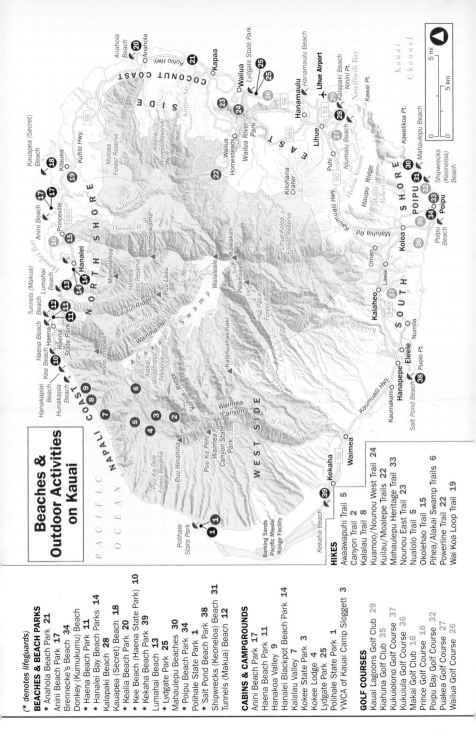

Beaches & Outdoor Activities on Kauai

(* denotes lifeguards)

BEACHES & BEACH PARKS

* Anahola Beach Park **21**
Anini Beach Park **17**
Brennecke's Beach **34**
Donkey (Kumukumu) Beach
* Haena Beach Park **11**
* Hanalei Bay Beach Parks **14**
Kalapaki Beach **28**
Kauapea (Secret) Beach **18**
* Kealia Beach Park **20**
* Kee Beach (Haena State Park) **10**
* Kekaha Beach Park **39**
Lumahai Beach **13**
* Lydgate Park **25**
Mahaulepu Beaches **30**
* Poipu Beach Park **34**
Polihale State Park **1**
* Salt Pond Beach Park **38**
Shipwrecks (Keoneloa) Beach **31**
Tunnels (Makua) Beach **12**

CABINS & CAMPGROUNDS

Anini Beach Park **17**
Haena Beach Park **11**
Hanakoa Valley **9**
Hanalei Blackpot Beach Park **14**
Kalalau Valley **7**
Kokee State Park **3**
Kokee Lodge **4**
Lydgate Park **25**
Polihale State Park **1**
YWCA of Kauai Camp Sloggett **3**

GOLF COURSES

Kauai Lagoons Golf Club **29**
Kiahuna Golf Club **35**
Kukuiolono Golf Course **37**
Kukuiula Golf Course **36**
Makai Golf Club **16**
Prince Golf Course **16**
Poipu Bay Golf Course **32**
Puakea Golf Course **27**
Wailua Golf Course **26**

HIKES

Awaawapuhi Trail **5**
Canyon Trail **2**
Kalalau Trail **8**
Kuamoo/Nounou West Trail **24**
Kuilau/Moalepe Trails **22**
Mahaulepu Heritage Trail **33**
Nounou East Trail **23**
Nualolo Trail **5**
Okolehao Trail **15**
Pihea/Alakai Swamp Trails **6**
Powerline Trail **22**
Wai Koa Loop Trail **19**

421

being damaged by Hurricane Iniki in 1992, and still awaiting restoration at press time. The family-friendly destination of **Lydgate Park** ★ connects with one leg of the popular **Ka Ala Hele Makalae coastal path** ★.

KAPAA The modern condos, motels, and shopping strips of Wailua and Waipouli along the Kuhio Highway eventually segue into **Old Kapaa Town,** where funky boutiques and cafes share plantation-era buildings with mom-and-pop groceries and restaurants. An all-ages hostel and other inexpensive lodgings attract many international and budget travelers, including scruffy hikers returning from Kalalau Valley, all of whom seem equally grateful for the laundromat, taquerias, and other signs of civilization. There are sandy beaches here, but they're hidden from the highway until the road rises past **Kealia Beach Park,** a boogie-boarding destination and northern terminus of the coastal bike path.

ANAHOLA Just before the East Side becomes the North Shore, the highway dips and passes through this predominantly Native Hawaiian community near Kalalea Mountain, more widely known as **King Kong Mountain,** or just Kong, for its famous profile. Farm stands, a convenience store with homemade goodies, and the roadside **Duane's Ono Char-Burger** ★★ can supply provisions for a weekday picnic at **Anahola Beach Park** ★ or Aliomanu Beach; weekends draw local crowds. (Give the poles and nets of local fishermen a wide berth.)

NORTH SHORE

On a sunny day, there may be no more beautiful place on earth than Kauai's North Shore. It's not half-bad even on a rainy day (more frequent in winter), when waterfalls almost magically appear on verdant mountains; once the showers stop, rainbows soar over farms, taro patches, and long, curving beaches. The speed limit, and pace of life, slow down dramatically as the Kuhio Highway traverses a series of one-lane bridges, climaxing at a suitably show-stopping beach and the trailhead for the breathtaking **Napali Coast.** Two quaint towns—one home to a lighthouse and a seabird preserve—plus the island's most luxurious resort provide ample lodging, dining, and shopping options to match the natural wonders. But it's far enough from the South Shore (minimum 1½ hr. away) that day-trippers may wish they had relocated for a night or two.

KILAUEA ★ A right turn going north on Kuhio Highway brings you to this village of quaint stone buildings and the plantation-vintage **Kong Lung Historic Market Center** ★, a cozy den of cafes, crafts makers, and boutiques. Kilauea Road heads *makai* (seaward) to **Kilauea Point National Wildlife Refuge** ★★★, a sanctuary for nene (the goose-like state bird) and other endangered species, and home to the

Kilauea Lighthouse.

Hanalei.

stubby, red-topped **Kilauea Lighthouse,** built in 1913. Shortly before the preserve is the turnoff for scenic but not-so-secret **Kauapea (Secret) Beach ★★,** a 15-minute hike from a dirt parking lot. Ben Stiller owns a home on the cliffs here; numerous farms, the island's only mini-golf course, and the extensive **Na Aina Kai Botanical Gardens ★★** are the area's other claims to fame.

ANINI BEACH ★★★   A 2-mile fringing reef—the longest on Kauai—creates a shallow, pond-like setting for swimmers, snorkelers, and (when conditions permit) windsurfers. The long beach is narrow but borders a grassy park with showers, restrooms, picnic tables, and campsites, across from a former polo field.

PRINCEVILLE ★   This 11,000-acre resort and residential development is home to two 18-hole golf courses, steep trails to pocket beaches, and gorgeous views of crescent-shaped Hanalei Bay and iconic **Makana,** the mountain that portrayed Bali Hai in "South Pacific." The **Princeville Shopping Center** holds a few bargain eateries as well as supplies for those staying in one of the many condo or timeshare units; money is generally no object for guests at the **St. Regis Princeville ★★,** Kauai's most luxurious hotel (formerly the Princeville Hotel), with elevator service to the beach below. Just before the highway drops into Hanalei Valley, a vista point offers a photo-worthy panorama of the Hanalei River winding through wetland taro patches under towering green peaks.

HANALEI ★★★   Waiting to cross the first of nine one-lane bridges on the northern stretch of the Kuhio Highway (now Hwy. 560) is a good introduction to the hang-loose ethos of the last real town before road's end. The fringing green mountains share their hue with the 1912 **Waioli Huiia Church ★** and other vintage wooden buildings, some of which house unique shops and moderately priced restaurants. Nearby, the 2-mile-long, half-moon **Hanalei Bay** attracts surfers year-round; during the calmer summer conditions, children splash in the water while parents lounge on the sand (a la "The Descendants.") Three county beach parks offer various facilities, including several lifeguard stations; the southernmost **Black Pot Beach Park ★★**, renowned for its 300-foot-long pier, allows camping on weekends and holidays.

HAENA ★★ Homes modest and grand hide in the lush greenery of Haena on either side of the Kuhio Highway as it undulates past rugged coves, tranquil beaches, and immense caves, finally dead-ending at **Kee Beach ★★**, gateway to the Napali Coast and a popular destination for snorkelers (when the surf permits) and campers. **Limahuli Garden and Preserve ★★**, the northern outpost of the National Tropical Botanical Garden, explains Haena's legends, rich cultural heritage, and ecological significance to visitors able to navigate its steep terraces in the shadow of Mounta Makana. Food trucks at **Haena Beach Park ★★** supplement the meager if popular dining options, such as Mediterranean Gourmet at the **Hanalei Colony Resort ★★** (p. 480), the only North Shore resort with rooms right on the sand.

NAPALI COAST ★★★ Often written as Na Pali ("the cliffs"), this dramatically crenellated region that bridges the North Shore and West Side begins not far from where the road ends. Hardy (and some foolhardy) hikers will cross five valleys as they follow the narrow, 11-mile Kalalau Trail to its end at beautiful **Kalalau Valley,** with tempting detours to waterfalls along the way. The less ambitious (or more sensible) will attempt shorter stretches, such as the 2-mile hike to Hanakapiai Beach. In summer, physically fit kayakers can spend a day exploring Napali's pristine reefs, sea caves, and hidden coves, which also come into view on catamaran and motorized raft tours (almost all departing from Kauai's West Side); helicopter tours from Lihue, Port Allen, or Princeville offer the quickest if most expensive way to explore Napali's stunning topography (see "Organized Tours," p.444).

SOUTH SHORE

After a short drive west from Lihue on Kaumualii Highway, a well-marked right turn leads to a mile-long **tree tunnel** of eucalyptus trees, planted in 1911. The well-shaded Maluhia Road is ironically the primary entrance to the sunniest of Kauai's resort areas, Poipu; the South Shore also generally has the calmest ocean conditions in winter. Among outdoor attractions are the geyser-like **Spouting**

Koloa eucalyptus tree tunnel.

Horn ★★, the McBryde and Allerton gardens at the **National Tropical Botanical Garden ★★**, family-friendly **Poipu Beach Park ★★★**, and other sandy beaches, including those in rugged **Mahaulepu ★★**. Pocket coves, surf breaks, and dive sites also make the area ideal for watersports. The only downside: The North Shore is at least 1½ hours away.

POIPU   Three of Kauai's best hotels—the lavish **Grand Hyatt Kauai Resort & Spa ★★★**, the family-friendly **Sheraton Kauai Resort ★★**, and the luxury boutique **Koa Kea Hotel & Resort ★★**—punctuate the many low-rise condos and vacation homes in the master-planned **Poipu Beach Resort.** Landlubbers can enjoy tennis, 36 holes of golf, and numerous options for dining and shopping, including those at the **Shops at Kukuiula** just outside the resort proper. (To access another 18 holes of golf and the island's best spa, both located in the luxurious Kukuiula residential community, you'll need to stay in one of its $1,000-plus-a-night **Club Cottages ★★**.)

KOLOA   Before the Poipu Bypass Road (Ala Kinoiki) was built, nearly every South Shore beachgoer drove through Hawaii's oldest sugar plantation town, founded in 1835. If you're staying elsewhere, it would be a shame not to visit at least once, to browse the shops and restaurants in quaint storefronts under towering monkeypod trees. Historical plaques on each building give glimpses into the lives of the predominantly Japanese-American families who created the first businesses there. Those staying in South Shore condos may find themselves making multiple trips, especially to stock up on produce at the "sunshine market" at noon Mondays, to buy fresh seafood from the **Koloa Fish Market ★**, or purchase other groceries from two locally owned supermarkets.

KALAHEO & LAWAI   These more residential communities on either side of the main highway are just a 15-minute drive to Poipu Beach Park. On the way, you'll pass through the green fields of rural Omao along Koloa Road (Hwy. 530). Visitors en route to or from Waimea Canyon often refuel at the locally oriented restaurants here; others find lodgings in the relatively inexpensive (but often unlicensed) bed-and-breakfasts. The higher elevations are mistier, with wild chickens roaming even more freely than on the manicured resorts below. On the west edge of Kalaheo, look for the turnoff for **Kauai Coffee ★★**, whose 3,100 acres produce a dizzying variety of coffees, with free samples at the visitor center.

WEST SIDE

This arid region may have the fewest lodgings, destination restaurants, or swimmable beaches, but the twin draws of **Waimea Canyon State Park ★★★** (rightly hailed as the "Grand Canyon of the Pacific") and the **Kalalau Overlook ★★★** in Kokee State Park make up for the long drive (80 min. to the latter from Poipu). Most Napali snorkel tours are also based here, not to mention two swinging bridges, a weekly art festival, and other good excuses to pull over. Those who can manage the bumpy, unpaved 5-mile road to **Polihale State Park ★** are rewarded with views of Niihau and Napali, as well as a 17-mile stretch of sand (including the restricted-access **Barking Sands Beach** on the Pacific Missile Range Facility).

ELEELE & PORT ALLEN   The main highway from Kalaheo passes by Eleele's plantation homes and several miles of coffee trees before the intersection with Waialo Road. Turn *makai* (seaward) and the road dead-ends a few blocks later at Port Allen, the island's second largest commercial harbor; nearly all boat tours launch from here. Although the area is fairly industrial—and its once-vaunted "Glass Beach" by the oil tanks no longer has enough polished sea glass left to recommend it—the affordable dining and shopping options in Port Allen and adjacent **Eleele Shopping Center** are worth exploring post-snorkel or pre-sunset cruise.

NIHAU Just 17 miles across the Kaulakahi Channel from the West Side of Kauai lies the arid island of Niihau (pronounced *"nee-ee-how"*), nicknamed "The Forbidden Island." Casual visitors are not allowed on this privately owned isle, once a cattle and sheep ranch that now supports fewer than 200 full-time residents, all living in the single town of Puuwai, and nearly all Native Hawaiians. Nonresidents can visit on hunting safaris and helicopter tours. Half-day **helicopter tours** ($385 per person, five-person minimum) depart from Kauai's West Side and include lunch and several hours on a beach snorkeling or swimming as well as shell-hunting. You're more likely to see the endangered Hawaiian monk seal than Niihauans, which is how they like it. For more about Niihau culture, visit **www.niihauheritage.org**.

HANAPEPE An easy detour off Kaumualii Highway, Hanapepe looks like an Old West town, with more than 2 dozen art galleries and quaint stores, plus a couple of cafes, behind rustic wooden facades that inspired Disney's "Lilo and Stitch." Musicians, food trucks, and other vendors truly animate the quiet town during the weekly "Art Night" on Fridays from 6 to 9pm. The other daytime attraction is the **swinging footbridge** ★ over Hanapepe River (rebuilt after 1992's Hurricane Iniki, and marked by a large sign of Hanapepe Rd.). On the other side of the highway, family-friendly **Salt Pond Beach** ★ is named for the traditional Hawaiian salt pans in the red dirt, which gives the salt (*'alae*) its distinctive color and flavor.

WAIMEA Hawaii's modern history officially begins here with the landing of British explorer Capt. James Cook on Dec. 20, 1778, 2 days after his ships sailed past Oahu. Despite Cook's orders to the contrary, his sailors quickly mingled with native women, introducing venereal disease to a long-isolated population. Foreigners kept coming to this enclave at the mouth of the Waimea ("reddish-water") River, including a German doctor who tried to claim Kauai for Russia in 1815, and American missionaries in 1820. Today Waimea is attuned to its more recent history of plantation and *paniolo* (cowboy) culture, as well as its Native Hawaiian roots, all of which can be explored at the **West Kauai Technology & Visitor Center** ★. Waimea Canyon and Kokee State Park hikers flock to Waimea's shave ice stands and moderately priced dining choices in the late afternoon, while locals seek

Hanapepe swinging footbridge.

out **Waimea Theater,** one of the island's few places to catch a movie or concert.

KEKAHA Travelers heading to or from Waimea Canyon may be tempted to go via Kokee Road (Hwy. 55) in Kekaha as a change of pace from Waimea Canyon Road. Don't bother. There's not much to see in this former sugar town, whose mill operated for 120 years before shutting down in 2000, other than **Kekaha Beach Park,** a long, narrow strand with often-rough waters suitable only for expert surfers. You do have to pass through Kekaha on the way to **Polihale State Park ★**; if the latter's access road is impassable, stop by Kekaha for a striking view of **Niihau,** 17 miles offshore, or a brilliant sunset. Just don't plan on sticking around for dinner.

GETTING AROUND

Unless you're on a fairly leisurely schedule, you'll need a car or other motorized vehicle to see and do everything on Kauai, which has one major road—one lane in each direction, in most places—that rings the island except along the Napali Coast. During rush hour, from about 6 to 9am and 3 to 6pm, the road between Lihue and Kapaa—the central business district—can turn into a giant parking lot, even with a third, "contra-flow" lane whose direction is determined by time of day. Bypass roads in Kipu (when heading north from Poipu) and Kapaa (when heading south) can alleviate some of the stress, but plan accordingly.

   Note: The top speed is 50mph, with many slower sections in residential and business areas. Addresses in this chapter will use Kaumualii Highway (Hwy. 50) and Kuhio Highway (Hwy. 56/560), following local convention. Since highway addresses can be hard to spot (if marked at all), directions may be given with mile marker numbers, cross streets, and/or the descriptors *mauka* (toward the mountains) and *makai* (toward the sea).

BY CAR All of the major car-rental agencies are represented on Kauai. At the airport baggage claim, cross the street to catch one of the frequent shuttle vans to the rental lots. **Avis** (www.avis.com; ✆ **800/230-4898**) also rents cars from the Grand Hyatt Kauai and the Princeville Airport. Be sure to book early for peak periods. **Discount Hawaii Car Rental** (www.discounthawaiicarrental.com; ✆ **800/292-1939**) may have cheaper options for last-minute bookings; it also offers free pickup for cruise passengers.

BY MOTORCYCLE, MOPED, OR SCOOTER Riders 21 and older with a heavyweight motorcycle license can rent a "hog" from **Kauai Harley-Davidson** (www.kauaiharley.com; ✆ **888/690-6233** or 808/212-9469) outside Lihue. Rates start at $179 for 24 hours, with unlimited mileage. Lihue's **Kaui Mopeds** (www.kauai-mopeds.com; ✆ **808/652-7407**) offers two-person scooters with similar age and license restrictions; daily rates start at $75 for models with a top speed of 52mph, and $110 for those reaching 75mph. For cruising back roads (directions provided), those 18 or older with a driver's license can rent a single-person moped with a top speed of 30mph for $65 a day.

BY TAXI OR SHUTTLE Set by the county, taxi meter rates start at $3, with an additional $3 per mile; it's about $50 to Poipu and $90 to Princeville from the airport, plus 40¢ per item of luggage, and $4 per bulky item. You can also arrange private tours by taxi starting at $120 for 2 hours. Call **Kauai Taxi Company** (✆ **808/246-9554**) for taxi, limousine, or airport shuttle service. From the airport, solo travelers will find it cheaper ($39 to Poipu, $67 to Princeville) to take the shared-ride **SpeediShuttle** (www.speedishuttle.com; ✆ **877/242-5777**), but be aware it may make multiple stops. **Pono Express** (http://ponoexpress.com; ☎ **800/258-6880**) offers private airport shuttles and sightseeing tours in vans accommodating one to 14 passengers; rate is by vehicle or by hour. Those staying in Poipu should take advantage of the free **Aloha Spirit Shuttle** (www.mykauai connection.com; ☎ **855/742-2260** or 808/742-2260); the 12-person open-air tram—a former Disneyland people-mover—shuttles locals and visitors around resorts and restaurants from 5 to 10pm daily.

BY BUS **Kauai Bus** (www.kauai.gov, click "Transportation"; ☎ **808/246-8110**) continues to expand bus service between Kekaha and Hanalei daily, including stops near several Poipu and Lihue hotels, the central Kapaa hotel corridor, the Princeville Shopping Center, and Hanalei. *Note:* There's also an airport stop, but suitcases, large backpacks, and surfboards are not allowed on the bus. The white-and-green buses, which have small bike racks in front, run more or less hourly from 5:30am to 10:30pm weekdays, and 6:30am to 6pm on weekends and holidays. The fare (exact change only) is $2 for adults and $1 for seniors and children 7 to 18.

BY BIKE Due to narrow (or nonexistent) shoulders along much of the main highway, relying on bicycles for transportation is generally unsafe. For recreational routes, including the coastal **Na Ala Hele Makalae** bike path, see "Biking," p. 462.

[Fast FACTS] KAUAI

Dentists Emergency dental care is available from **Dr. Mark A. Baird,** 4–9768 Kuhio Hwy. (at Keaka Rd.), Kapaa (☎ **808/822-9393**), and **Dr. Michael Furgeson,** 4347 Rice St., Lihue (☎ **808/246-6960**).

Doctors Walk-ins are accepted from 8am to 2pm daily for the **Kauai Medical Clinic's Urgent Care Clinic** (☎ **808/245-1532**), part of the Wilcox Memorial Hospital complex at 3-3420 Kuhio Hwy. (*makai* side, at Ehiku St.), Lihue. The clinic's non-urgent-care facility (☎ **808/245-1500**) is open for appointments 8am to 5pm weekdays and 8am to noon Saturday; Kauai Medical Clinic also has branches, with varying hours, in **Koloa,** 5371 Koloa Rd. (☎ **808/742-1621**); **Kapaa,** *mauka*

side of Kuhio Highway, north of Kuamoo Road (☎ **808/822-3431**); and **Eleele,** 4392 Waialo Rd. (☎ **808/335-0499**). **Hale Lea Medicine,** 2460 Oka St. (at Kilauea Rd.), in Kilauea (☎ **808/828-2885**), serves the North Shore, with appointments offered 9am to 5pm weekdays and 9am to 1pm Saturday.

Emergencies Dial ☎ **911** for police, fire, and ambulance service.

Hospitals **Wilcox Memorial Hospital,** 3-3420 Kuhio Hwy. (*makai* side, at Ehiku St.), Lihue (☎ **808/245-1100**), has emergency services (☎ **808/245-1010**) available 24 hours a day, as do the smaller **Mahelona Memorial Hospital,** 4800 Kawaihau Rd., Kapaa (www.smmh.hhsc.org; ☎ **808/**

823-4166), and **Kauai Veterans Memorial Hospital,** 4643 Waimea Canyon Dr. (www.kvmh.hhsc.org; ☎ **808/338-9431**).

Internet Access Numerous cafes (including Kauai's four **Starbucks** outlets; www.starbucks.com) offer free Wi-Fi hotspots; many hotels offer free Wi-Fi in public areas or for a fee in rooms. All Hawaii public libraries have free Wi-Fi but require a library card ($10 nonresidents, good for 3 months). Kauai's branches are in Hanapepe, Kapaa, Koloa, Lihue, Princeville, and Waimea; all are closed Sunday. See http://libraries-hawaii.org for details on locations, hours, and reserving a personal computer with Wi-Fi (click on "Services").

Police   For non-
emergencies, call
☎ 808/241-1711.

Post Office   The **main
post office** is at 4441 Rice
St., Lihue, open 8am to 4pm
weekdays and 9am to 1pm

Saturday; hours vary at the
14 other offices across the
island. To find the one nearest you, visit www.usps.com
or call **☎ 800/275-8777.**

Weather   For current
weather conditions and

forecasts, call the National
Weather Service at
☎ 808/245-6001. For the
daily ocean report, including surf advisories, visit
**www.kauaiexplorer.com/
ocean_report**.

EXPLORING KAUAI

Attractions & Points of Interest

EAST SIDE

Fern Grotto ★★ NATURAL ATTRACTION   The journey as much as the
destination has kept this tourist attraction popular since 1946, when the Smith
family first began offering boat trips 2 miles up the Wailua River to this lava-rock
cave with lush ferns hanging from its roof. The open-air barge cruises past royal
and sacred sites of antiquity, noted by a guide, until it arrives at a landing that's a
short walk from the grotto. Although you can no longer enter the cave, an observation deck provides a decent view, as well as the stage for a musician and hula
dancer to perform the "Hawaiian Wedding Song" (made famous by Elvis Presley's
1961 film "Blue Hawaii," filmed nearby at the Coco Palms.) The tour, a total of
80 minutes, includes music and hula on the return trip down Hawaii's longest
river (see "Wailua River State Park," below.) *Note:* Kayakers may visit Fern Grotto
on their own, as long as their arrival or departure doesn't overlap with those of the
tour boats; see "Kayaking" on p. 456 for rental information. **Kamokila Hawaiian**

9

KAUAI

Exploring Kauai

Fern Grotto.

Village (see below), across the river from the grotto, also offers guided outrigger canoe tours and kayak rentals.

2 miles inland from Wailua Marina State Park, south side of Wailua River off Hwy. 56 (Kuhio). Tours via **Smith's Motor Boats** (www.smithskauai.com; ✆ **808/821-6895**) depart at 9:30 and 11am, and 2 and 3:30pm. $20 adults, $10 children 3 to 12 (book online for 10 percent off).

Grove Farm Museum ★ HISTORIC SITE/MUSEUM AOL cofounder Steve Case may own Grove Farm now, but little else has changed at the 100-acre homestead of George N. Wilcox. The son of missionaries in Hanalei, Wilcox bought the original 900-acre Grove Farm from a German immigrant in 1864 and turned it into a successful sugar plantation. Two-hour guided tours start at the original plantation office and include the two-story main home, still furnished with vintage decor and Hawaiiana, plus extensive gardens and intriguing out-buildings, such as a Japanese teahouse built in 1898. **Note:** Tours may be canceled on rainy days. Contact the museum about its free rides on restored, plantation-era steam trains near the old Lihue Sugar Mill, usually offered the second Thursday of each month.

4050 Nawiliwili Rd. (Hwy. 58), at Pikaka St. (2 miles from Waapa Rd.), Lihue. http://grovefarm.org. ✆ **808/245-3202.** Admission $20 adults, $10 children 11 and under. Open only for tours Mon and Wed–Thurs at 10am and 1pm; reservations required.

Kamokila Hawaiian Village ★ CULTURAL ATTRACTION This family-run 4-acre compound of thatched huts and other replica structures, opened in 1979 on the site of an ancient village, always looks in need of more upkeep. Nevertheless, it serves as a pleasantly low-key introduction to traditional Hawaiian culture, especially for families. Peacocks and wild chickens roam around huts designated for healing, sleeping, eating, birthing, and more, all part of a self-guided tour, with displays inside some huts. You're also welcome to sample fruit hanging from the many labeled trees, including mountain apple, guava, and mango. A stand-in for an African village in the 1995 movie "Outbreak," Kamokila is known as having the fastest (and cheapest) access for paddling to **Uluwehi (Secret) Falls, Fern Grotto,** and several swimming holes.

Off Kuamoo Rd. (Hwy. 580), Kapaa. Look for sign across from Opaekaa Falls, 2 miles inland from Hwy. 56; entrance road is steep. http://villagekauai.com. ✆ **808/823-0559.** Admission $5 adults, $3 children 3–12. Daily canoe and kayak rentals $35 adults, $30 children 3–12. Guided outrigger canoe rides: **Secret Falls** $30 adults, $20 children 3–12; **swimming hole** $20 adults, $15 children 3–12; **Fern Grotto** $20 adults, $15 children 3–12. Daily 9am–5pm.

Kauai Museum ★★ MUSEUM The fascinating geological and cultural history of Kauai and Niihau are well-served in this compact museum that's just a little too good to save for a rainy day. Visitors enter through the Wilcox Building, the former county library built in 1924 with a somewhat incongruous Greco-Roman facade on its lava rock exterior. Inside are temporary exhibitions, a gift shop with an extensive book selection, and the Heritage Gallery of koa-lined cases brimming with exquisite Niihau shell lei and beautifully carved wooden bowls (*umeke*) and other furnishings that once belonged to royalty. (There's even a display of Iolani Palace china no doubt coveted by the Honolulu site's curators.)

The adjacent Rice Building, a two-story lava rock structure opened in 1960, tells "The Story of Kauai." The main floor's exhibits focus on the island's volcanic origins through the arrival of Polynesian voyagers and the beginning of Western contact, including the whalers and missionaries who quickly followed in Capt.

Cook's wake. Rare artifacts include a torn piece of a Niihau *makaloa* mat, a highly prized bed covering and art form that was essentially abandoned in the late 19th century. On the second floor, the story shifts to that of the plantation era, when waves of immigrants fomented the complex stew known as "local" culture, and continues through World War II. One display illuminates the little-known story of the Japanese pilot who crashed on Niihau during the Pearl Harbor attack, took captives, and was eventually overpowered by several Native Hawaiian islanders after others had rowed to Kauai to alert authorities.

Tip: Try to time a visit on the first Friday of the month, when the museum holds a traditional *paina* (feast) with a plate lunch, live music, and hula in the courtyard at 11:30am; admission is $20, reservations requested.

4428 Rice St., Lihue. www.kauaimuseum.org. ℂ **808/245-6931.** Admission $10 adults, $8 seniors, $6 students 13–17, $2 children 6–12 (free admission to gift shop). 1st Sat of every month admission $8 adults, $6 seniors, $2 students 13–17, $1 children 6–12. Mon–Sat 10am–5pm. Guided tours Mon–Fri 10:30am. Check "Events" listings online for frequent crafts workshops and festivals.

Keahua Arboretum ★ GARDEN   Part of the Lihue-Koloa Forest Reserve, this grove of rainbow eucalyptus (named for its colorful bark), monkeypod, and mango trees may not be well-maintained from an arborist's standpoint, but it's a nifty, family-friendly place to picnic and dip in a cool stream, particularly after a hike on the nearby **Kuilau Trail** (p. 467). A short loop trail leads to a "swimming hole" with a rope swing; be sure to wear mosquito repellent. Facilities include picnic tables, pavilions, and composting toilets. Part of the fun is getting here: The main parking area and picnic tables are across a spillway at the paved end of Kuamoo Road, about 5 miles inland from Opaekaa Falls. (Please use good judgment when deciding if it's safe to ford the stream.) This is also where adventurers will find the trailhead for the 13-mile **Powerline Trail** (p. 467), which ends near Princeville, and the extremely rugged, unpaved Wailua Forestry Management Road, the start of treks to the "Jurassic Park" gates (just poles now) and Waialeale's "Blue Hole."

End of Kuamoo Rd., Kapaa. 7 miles inland from intersection with Hwy. 56, Wailua. www.dlnr. hawaii.gov/forestry/frs/reserves/kauai/lihue-koloa. ℂ **808/274-3433.** Free admission. Daily during daylight hours.

Kilohana Plantation ★★ FARM/ATTRACTIONS   Longtime Kauai visitors might remember this 105-acre portion of a former sugar plantation for the unique shops tucked into a handsome 1930s mansion, its luau, or the courtyard Gaylord's restaurant, named for original owner Gaylord Wilcox. While all of those elements are still there, so many changes have happened in recent years that few should skip a visit here. In addition to sampling the wares of the **Mahiko Lounge,** the 2013 conversion of the mansion's former living room (see "Nightlife," p. 506), tipplers ages 21 and up can create their own mini mai tai around a gleaming wood bar in the **Koloa Rum Co.**'s tasting room (www.koloarum.com; ℂ **808/246-8900**). There's a 16-person maximum per free, half-hour tasting (see website for the varying hours), while an all-ages store sells the locally made spirits and non-alcoholic gifts.

The first new railroad to open on the island in almost 100 years, the **Kauai Plantation Railway** (www.kauaiplantationrailway.com; ℂ **808/245-7245**) uses a restored diesel locomotive to pull open-sided cars with trolley-style bench seats around a 2½-mile track. The train passes by Kilohana's gardens growing 50 varieties of fruit and vegetables and through flowering fields and forest on a

Kilohana Plantation.

40-minute narrated tour that includes a stop to feed goats, sheep, and wild pigs (watch your hands). It departs five times daily between 10am and 2pm. Tickets are $18 for adults and $14 for kids 3 to 12; reservations are not required, but you can receive a 15-percent discount by calling ahead and requesting the Web discount. On weekdays, you can also combine a train ride that starts at 9:30am with an easy hike, lunch, and orchard tour that costs $75 for adults and $65 for kids 3 to 12 (ask for the 15-percent Web discount when reserving.)

On Tuesday and Friday, the railway offers an "express train" package with **Luau Kalamaku** (www.luaukalamaku.com; 🕾 **808/833-3000**), a theatrical-style show with dinner buffet in a specially-built theater-in-the-round near the Wilcox mansion. The train-luau package is $117 for adults and $87 for kids 13 to 18, and $63 kids 3 to 12 (ask for Web discount of 10 percent when reserving). For the luau dinner and show only, it's $100 for adults, $70 for teens, and $40 for children.

3-2087 Kaumualii Hwy. (Hwy. 50), Lihue, just north of Kauai Community College and ½-mile south of Kukui Grove Shopping Center. www.kilohanakauai.com. 🕾 **808/245-5608.** Mansion opens at 10:30am daily; restaurant, lounge, and shop hours vary.

Lydgate Park ★ PARK   This is one of the rare beach parks in Hawaii where the facilities almost outshine the beach. Hidden behind the Aston Aloha Beach Resort, **Lydgate Beach ★** (p. 448) offers two rock-walled ponds for safe swimming and snorkeling. But many families also gravitate to the 58-acre, half-mile-long park for the immense **Kamalani Playground,** a sprawling wooden fantasy fortress decorated with ocean-themed ceramics. It was built by 7,000 volunteers in 1994; many returned 7 years later for the **Kamalani Kai Bridge** expansion, an equally whimsical structure that leads to observation decks and small pavilions in the dunes. Stroller pushers, joggers, and cyclists also pick up the 2.5-mile southern leg of the **Ka Ala Hele Makalae coastal path** here; Lydgate's northern end is next to **Hikinaakala Heiau,** part of Wailua River State Park (below). Facilities include picnic tables, restrooms, showers, pavilions, and campgrounds.

Leho Dr. at Nalu Rd., Wailua. From intersection of hwys. 56 and 51 outside of Lihue, head 2½ miles north to Leho Dr. and turn right. Turn right again on Nalu Rd. and follow to parking areas. Free admission. Daily during daylight hours.

Wailua River State Park ★★ PARK/HISTORIC SITE   Ancients called the Wailua River "the river of the great sacred spirit." Seven temples once stood along this 20-mile river, Hawaii's longest, fed by the some 450 inches of rain that fall annually on Waialeale at the island's center. The entire district from the river mouth to the summit of Waialeale was once royal land, originally claimed by Puna, a Tahitian priest said to have arrived in one of the first double-hulled voyaging canoes to come to Hawaii.

Cultural highlights include the remains of four major temples; royal birthing stones, used to support female *alii* in labor; a stone bell used to announce such births; and the ancient stone carvings known as petroglyphs, found on boulders near the mouth of the Wailua River when currents wash away enough sand. Many sites have **Wailua Heritage Trail** markers; go to www.wailuaheritagetrail.org for map and details. The **Hawaii State Parks website** (www.hawaiistateparks.org) also has downloadable brochures on two *heiau* (temples) that each enclosed an acre of land: Just north of Lydgate Park, next to the mouth of the Wailua River, **Hikinaakala Heiau** once hosted sunrise ceremonies; its name means "rising of the sun." Now reduced to its foundation stones, it's part of a sacred oceanfront complex that also appears to have been a place of refuge (*puuhonua*). Two miles up Kuamoo Road (Hwy. 580) from the main highway, **Poliahu Heiau** shares its name with the goddess of snow (admittedly a weather phenomenon more common to the Big Island). The 5×5-feet lava rock walls— attributed to *menehune,* and most likely erected by the 1600s—may have surrounded a *luakini,* used for human sacrifice. (Please don't stand on the rock walls, enter the center of the heiau, or leave "offerings," which is considered disrespectful.)

Across the road from Poliahu is an ample parking lot and sidewalk leading to the overlook of 40-foot-wide, 151-foot-tall **Opaekaa Falls** ★★. Named for the "rolling shrimp" that were once abundant here, this twin cascade glistens under the Makaleha ridge—but don't be tempted to try to find a way to swim beneath it. The danger keep out signs and wire fencing are there because two hikers fell to their deaths from the steep, slippery hillside in 2006.

You're allowed to wade at the base of the 100-foot **Uluwehi Falls,** widely known as Secret Falls, but first you'll need to paddle a kayak several miles to the narrow right fork of the Wailua River, and then hike about 30 to 45 minutes on a trail with a stream crossing. Many kayak rental companies offer guided tours here (see "Kayaking," p. 456)

Also part of the state park, but at the end of Maalo Road (Hwy. 583), 4 miles inland from the main highway in Kapaia, is equally scenic **Wailua Falls** ★. Pictured in the opening credits of "Fantasy Island," this double-barreled waterfall drops at least 80 feet (some say 113) into a large pool. Go early to avoid crowds and enjoy the morning light. ***Note:*** The state has also installed fencing here to block attempts at a hazardous descent.

Opaekaa Falls and **Poliahu Heiau:** Off Kuamoo Rd., 2 miles inland from intersection with Kuhio Hwy. just north of Wailua River Bridge. **Hikinaakala Heiau:** South side of Wailua River mouth; access from Lydgate Park (p. 432). **Wailua Falls:** end of Maalo Rd. (Hwy. 583), 4 miles north (inland) of intersection with Kuhio Hwy. in Kapaia, near Lihue. http://hawaiistateparks.org/parks/kauai. ✆ **808/274-3444.** Free admission. Daily during daylight hours.

NORTH SHORE
Anaina Hou Community Park ★ GARDEN/ATTRACTIONS   Anywhere else, a mini-golf park might be easily dismissed as a tourist trap. On Kauai, it's a

wonderful introduction for families to the Garden Island's tropical flora and cultural history, and just one of several visitor attractions in this inviting park. The well-landscaped, 18-hole **Kauai Mini Golf & Botanical Gardens** (www. kauaiminigolf.com; ✆ 808/828-2118) showcases native species, Polynesian introductions, plantation crops, Japanese and Chinese gardens, and modern plantings; it's open daily except Monday, and is quite popular on weekends. For a more natural experience, walk or mountain bike along the park's 5-mile **Wai Koa Loop Trail.** This unpaved, rolling path starts in a forest of albizia and Cook Island pines and passes through a working farm and mahogany orchard before reaching the highlights of the Kalihiwai Lagoon reservoirs and stone dam lookout. The trail is open during daylight hours and access is free, but because it crosses private property, you're asked to sign a waiver at the **Garden Cafe** (www. cgkauai.net; Tues–Sat 9am–3pm), where you can also rent a mountain bike for the day or longer. Donated by the founder of E-Trade and his wife, Bill and Joan Porter, the 500-acre community park also offers skateboard ramps, a dog park, and twice-weekly farmers markets. An elaborate children's playground is planned for 2015.

5-2723 Kuhio Hwy., Kilauea. Heading north from Lihue, pass the Shell station at Kolo Rd. turnoff to Kilauea; entrance is 500 yards farther on the left, at Kauai Mini Golf sign. www.anainahou.org. ✆ 808/828-2118. **Anaina Hou Community Park:** Free admission. **Kauai Mini Golf:** Tues–Sun 10am–8pm; admission $18 ages 11 and up, $10 children 5–10, free for children 4 and under. **Wai Koa Loop Trail:** Free admission.

Haena State Park ★★ NATURAL ATTRACTIONS   Besides snorkeling at pretty **Kee Beach** (p. 450), in the shadow of jutting Makana (Bali Hai) mountain, or camping, the main allure of this state park is that it's at the end of the road, the perfect place to witness sunset after a leisurely drive to the North Shore. It's also the start of the 11-mile **Kalalau Trail** (p. 467), meaning its large parking area can still fill up quickly—if so, just turn around and you'll find overflow parking farther away. At the western end of Kee Beach, an uphill path leads to an ancient hula platform and temple *(heiau),* where hula *halau* (schools) still conduct formal ceremonies; please be respectful by covering up before hiking up here, and leave any offerings undisturbed. Before the road's end, you'll also want to stop for a look at two **wet caves,** former sea caves left high but not dry when the ocean receded; chilly water percolates into them from a spring that's affected by the nearby tides. The larger **Waikanaloa** is just off the road, with parking in front. From there it's a short, uphill walk to the craggier **Waikapalae,** seen as the entrance to the Fountain of Youth in "Pirates of the Caribbean: On Stranger Tides." Note that swimming is not allowed or considered safe.

Northern end of Hwy. 560, Haena. www.hawaiistateparks.org. Free admission. Daily during daylight hours.

Hoopulapula Haraguchi Rice Mill & Taro Farm ★ FARM/MUSEUM Many of the green taro patches seen from the Hanalei Valley Overlook belong to the 30-acre **Haraguchi Farm,** where fifth-generation farmer Lyndsey Haraguchi-Nakayama, family members, and other laborers tend Hawaii's revered staple by hand. When the Haraguchis bought the farm in 1924, the wetlands were rice paddies, planted by Chinese immigrants in the 1800s. With the purchase came a wooden rice mill that stayed in operation until 1960, and is now the only such structure left in the state. Restored several times after fire and hurricanes, the **Hoopulapula Haraguchi Rice Mill** is now a nonprofit "agrarian museum," and, like the farm, is open to visitors only as part of a weekly guided tour. Adults will appreciate hearing Haraguchi-Nakayama's stories from the family's rice-growing days, when children would be tasked with keeping grain-hungry birds away; she'll also point out the endangered birds in this corner of the **Hanalei National Wildlife Refuge.** Current challenges include frequent floods and large apple snails that eat young shoots. Once you've begun to appreciate the hard work of cultivating *kalo,* as the Hawaiians call taro, it's time to sample fluffy, freshly pounded taro rolled in coconut. The tour begins at the family's roadside stand in Hanalei with a taro smoothie and ends there with a tasty lunch.

Check in at Hanalei Taro & Juice stand, 5-5070 Kuhio Hwy., Hanalei, 1¼ miles west of Hanalei Bridge. www.haraguchiricemill.org. © **808/651-3399.** Tours $65–$85; must book through hotel concierge. Wed 10am by reservation only.

Kilauea Point National Wildlife Refuge & Lighthouse ★★★ NATURE PRESERVE/LIGHTHOUSE   Two miles north of Kilauea's historic town center is a 200-acre headland habitat—the only wildlife refuge open to the public—that includes cliffs, two rocky wave-lashed bays, and a tiny islet serving as a jumping-off spot for seabirds. You can easily spot red-footed boobies, which nest in trees and shrubs, and wedge-tailed shearwaters, which burrow in nests along the cliffs between March and November (they spend winters at sea). Scan the skies for the great frigate bird, which has a 7-foot wingspan, and the red-tailed tropicbird, which performs aerial acrobatics during the breeding season of March through August. Endangered nene, the native goose reintroduced to Kauai in 1982, often stroll close to visitors, but please don't feed them. Mounted telescopes and loaner binoculars from the refuge's visitor center may bring into view the area's marine life, from spinner dolphins, Hawaiian monk seals, and green sea turtles year-round to humpback whales on their winter migrations. Nevertheless, the primary draw for many of the refuge's half-million visitors is the **Kilauea Point Lighthouse** (www.kilauealighthouse.org), built in 1913 and listed on the National Register of Historic Places. The 52-foot-tall white lighthouse wears a jaunty red cap above its 7,000-pound Fresnel lens, whose beam could be seen from 20 miles away before it was deactivated in 1976. Docents offer free tours of the beacon, officially renamed the Daniel K. Inouye Lighthouse in 2013, in memory of the state's late senator.

End of Kilauea Rd., Kilauea. www.fws.gov/refuge/kilauea_point. © **808/828-1413.** Admission $5 ages 16 and up; free for ages 15 and under. Tues–Sat 10am–4pm. Heading north on Kuhio Hwy., turn right on Kolo Rd., just past mile marker 23, then left on Kilauea Rd. and follow 2 miles to entrance.

Limahuli Garden and Preserve ★★ GARDEN   Out on Kauai's far North Shore, beyond Hanalei and the last wooden bridge, there's a mighty cleft in the coastal range where ancestral Hawaiians lived in what can only be called paradise. Carved by a waterfall stream known as Limahuli, the lush valley sits at the foot of steepled cliffs that Hollywood portrayed as Bali Hai in "South Pacific." This small, almost secret garden, part of the National Tropical Botanical Garden, is ecotourism at its best. Here botanists hope to save Kauai's endangered native plants, some of which grow in the 1,000-acre Limahuli Preserve behind the garden, an area that is off-limits to visitors. The self-guided tour encourages visitors to walk slowly up and down the garden's .75-mile loop trail (resting places provided) to view indigenous and "canoe" plants, which are identified in Hawaiian and English, as well as plantation-era imported flowers and fruits. From taro to sugarcane, the plants brought over in Polynesians' voyaging canoes (hence their nickname) tell the story of the people who cultivated them for food, medicine,

Na Aina Kai Botanical Gardens.

clothing, shelter, and decoration; note the traditional hut with a thatched roof made from the indigenous loulu palm. The tour booklet also shares some of the fascinating legends inspired by the area's dramatically perched rocks and Makana mountain, where men once hurled firebrands (*'oahi*) that floated far out to sea. You'll learn even more on one of the daily 2½-hour guided tours, but be sure to reserve well in advance.

5-8291 Kuhio Hwy., Haena, ½-mile past mile marker 9. www.ntbg.org/gardens/limahuli.php. ℂ **808/826-1053.** Self-guided tour $15 ages 13 and up; free for children 12 and under (Tues–Sat 9:30am–4pm). Guided tour $30 ages 13 and up; $15 for children 10–12; children 9 and under not permitted (Tues–Sat 10am by reservation only).

Na Aina Kai Botanical Gardens ★★ GARDEN   Off the North Shore's beaten path, this magical garden covers 240 acres, sprinkled with 70 life-size (some larger-than-life-size) whimsical bronze statues. It's the place for avid gardeners, as well as people who think they don't like botanical gardens. It has something for everyone: waterfalls, pools, arbors, topiaries, colonnades, gazebos, a poinciana maze, a lagoon with spouting fountains, a Japanese teahouse, and an enchanting path along a bubbling stream to the ocean. The imaginative, fairy-tale creativity that has gone into these grounds will be one of your fondest memories of Kauai. A host of different tours is available, from 1½ hours ($35) to 5 hours ($85) long, ranging from casual, guided strolls and rides in the covered CarTram to treks from one end of the gardens to the ocean. Currently, these tours are open only to adults and children 13 and older. Younger kids are invited on tours of the wonderful "Under the Rainbow" garden, featuring a gecko hedge maze, a tropical jungle gym, a pint-size railroad, a treehouse in a rubber tree, and a 16-foot-tall Jack-and-the-Beanstalk giant with a 33-foot wading pool below. The 2-hour tour is $35 for adults and $20 for kids 13 and under, and includes the maze and koi pond in the formal gardens. The last Saturday of each month is usually Keiki (Children's) Day, when the children's garden is open from 9am to noon for just

$10; check the website for other seasonal family activities. *Tip:* Most tours are limited to eight or nine guests, and the gardens are closed weekends and Monday, so book a tour before you arrive.

4101 Wailapa Rd., Kilauea. www.naainakai.com. © **808/828-0525.** Tours Tues–Fri; most tours start at 9am but hours vary. Reservations strongly recommended. From Lihue, drive north past mile marker 21 and turn right on Wailapa; from Princeville, drive south 6½ miles and take the 2nd left past mile marker 22 onto Wailapa. At the road's end, drive through the iron gates.

Napali Coast State Wilderness Park ★★★ PARK   This 15-mile-long crown of serrated ridges and lush valleys is the most impressive of Kauai's natural features—and also its most inaccessible. Only hardy, well-equipped hikers should attempt the full length of the 11-mile **Kalalau Trail,** which begins at Kee Beach and plunges up and down before ending at **Kalalau Valley.** The area's last Hawaiian community lived in this 3-mile-wide, 3-mile-deep valley until the early 1900s. The valley, which can also be viewed from an overlook in Kokee State Park (p. 441), is the setting for Jack London's 1912 short story "Koolau the Leper," based on a true tale of a man who hid from authorities determined to exile him to Molokai. (Today, the bohemian squatters bedevil rangers and others determined to protect the valley's cultural treasures.) Most visitors just huff and puff 4 miles round-trip from Kee Beach to **Hanakapiai Beach,** or make it a daylong adventure by adding a 4-mile, boulder-hopping slog to the waterfall (see "Hiking," p. 466).

In late spring and summer, kayakers may explore the sea caves and oceanside waterfalls of Napali, but landing is only allowed at Kalalau and **Milolii** valleys (see "Kayaking," p. 456). **Nualolo Kai,** the lower, seaside portion of another valley, has many archaeological sites, some under restoration, but only motorized raft (Zodiac) tours may land here (see "Boat & Raft [Zodiac] Tours," p. 454.) The natural arch at **Honopu Beach** is a highlight of the snorkel cruises passing by, but may be examined closely only by the few capable of swimming here from Kalalau or a moored kayak—a dicey proposition much of the year.

The easiest, and most expensive, way to survey Napali's stunning land- and seascape is by helicopter (see "Helicopter Tours," p. 445). However you experience it, though, you'll understand why Napali remains the star of countless calendars, postcards, and screen savers.

Between Kee Beach Park and Polihale State Park. www.hawaiistateparks.org/parks/kauai/napali. cfm. © **808/274-3444.**

Waioli Mission House Museum and Church ★ HISTORIC SITE/ MUSEUM   Many visitors passing through Hanalei pull over for a photo of **Waioli Huiia Church** (www.hanaleichurch.org; © **808/826-6253**), a 1912 American Gothic wooden church with a steep roof, forest-green walls, and belfry reflecting the shape and hues of the mountains behind it. Nearby is the timber-and-plaster **Mission Hall,** built in 1841 and the oldest surviving church building on Kauai. Follow the dirt road leading behind the church to the **Mission House,** erected in 1837 by the area's first missionaries, who traveled from Waimea via outrigger canoe. Teachers Abner and Lucy Wilcox and their four sons moved to this two-story, surprisingly airy home in 1846; four more sons were born here while the Wilcoxes instructed native students in English and the newly transliterated Hawaiian language. The homespun Americana—a still-ticking wall clock, braided rugs, and spinning wheel—is complemented by Hawaiian elements such as ohia wood floors, a lava rock chimney, and lanais. Restored in 1921, the house is open for first-come, first-served guided tours 3 days a week.

Waioli Huiia Church.

5-5363 Kuhio Hwy., Hanalei, mountain side, just behind the green Waioli Huiia Church. www. grovefarm.org/waiolimissionhouse. ℭ **808/245-3202.** Requested donation $10 adults, $5 children 5–12. Tours on demand Tues, Thurs, and Sat 9am–3pm.

SOUTH SHORE

Note: Addresses here for Poipu-area sites refer to Koloa, reflecting the official mailing address and convention used by GPS devices and online maps. You may seem them listed elsewhere as "Poipu" or "Poipu Beach," to distinguish them from Old Koloa Town.

Kauai Coffee ★★ FARM   Some 4 million coffee trees grow on 3,100 acres of former sugarcane fields from Lawai Valley to Eleele, making Kauai Coffee the largest producer of coffee in Hawaii—and the United States. Kona coffee fans might sniff at the fact that the beans are machine-harvested, but it's surprisingly sustainable for such massive production, with 2,500 miles of drip-irrigation tubes, water recycling, cherry-pulp mulching, and other practices. You can learn all about the coffee growing and roasting process on a free short, self-guided or guided tour, or from a video and displays in the free tasting area behind the gift shop on a covered porch. Let's face it, everyone heads to the latter first: How better to determine the difference between coffee varietals such as Blue Mountain, yellow catuai, or red catuai beans (to name a few) in an equally wide array of roasts and blends? A small snack bar in the tasting room helps take the edge off all that caffeine.

870 Halewili Rd. (Hwy. 540), Kalaheo. www.kauaicoffee.com. ℭ **808/335-0813.** Free admission. Daily 9am–5pm (till 5:30pm Sept–May). Free guided tours daily 10am, noon, and 2 and 4pm. From westbound Hwy. 50, drive through Kalaheo and look for Hwy. 540 on left just outside of

town. From the intersection with Hwy. 50, it's 2½ miles to the visitor center. Hwy. 540 rejoins Hwy. 50 another 1½ miles west.

Kukuiolono Park ★ HISTORIC SITE/GARDEN   Hawaiians once lit signal fires atop this Kalaheo hillside, perhaps to aid seafarers or warn of invaders approaching by sea. Most visitors are still in the dark about this unusual park, created by pineapple magnate Walter McBryde and then bequeathed to the public after his death in 1930. A mile off the main highway, the recently renovated park includes the 9-hole **Kukuiolono Golf Course ★★** (p. 465) and clubhouse restaurant, Birdie's; a well-manicured Japanese garden, where you might see weddings being held; a collection of intriguing Hawaiian lava rock artifacts (such as a rain-activated "mirror"), and several miles of wooded jogging paths. A new meditation pavilion and stone benches also provide excuses to enjoy the views.

854 Puu Rd., Kalaheo. ✆ **808/332-9151.** Free admission. Gates open daily 7am–6pm. From Lihue, take Hwy. 50 west into Kalaheo, turn left on Papalina Rd. and drive uphill for nearly a mile; look for sign at right—entrance has huge iron gates and stone pillars.

National Tropical Botanical Garden ★★ HISTORIC SITE/GARDEN   Formerly owned by the McBryde Sugar Company, who bought the land from Hawaii's Queen Emma in 1886, this lush swath of Lawai Valley contains three separate gardens worth visiting, as well as the headquarters and research facilities of the National Tropical Botanical Garden. The 186-acre **McBryde Garden,** open for self-guided tours, boasts the largest collection of rare and endangered Hawaiian plants in the world, plus numerous varieties of palms, tropical fruit trees, heliconias, orchids, and other colorful flowers. Its "Spice of Life" trail, which includes cacao and allspice trees, meanders past picturesque Maidenhair Falls. You'll want to allow at least 90 minutes to explore the area, most of which is unpaved.

Open only to guided tours, the captivating formal gardens of adjacent **Allerton Garden** are the legacy of wealthy Chicagoan Robert Allerton and his

Allerton Garden.

companion John Gregg, whom Allerton later adopted. Allerton bought the land from McBryde in 1938 and with Gregg designed a series of elegant outdoor "rooms," where fountains and European statuary bracket plants collected from Southeast Asia and the Pacific. Allerton Garden tours last about 2½ hours; the 3-hour sunset tours begin in the late afternoon and end with a peek inside the oceanfront Allerton estate (normally off-limits), plus appetizers and drinks served on the lanai.

Both the Allerton and McBryde garden tours require a tram ride down to the valley, and reservations (by credit card) are required. It's free, however, to tour the well-labeled **Southshore Visitors Center Garden,** where the trams depart. Its several acres include separate areas for ornamental flowers and trees, plants evocative of a plantation-era home garden, Hawaiian native plants, and the profusion of color and textures known as the Gates Garden, at the entrance. The well-stocked gift shop, where tour members check in, includes cuttings and seeds already cleared for export, as well as local arts, crafts, and food inspired by nature's bounty.

NTBG Southshore Visitors Center, 4425 Lawai Rd. (across the street from Spouting Horn), Poipu. www.ntbg.org. ✆ **808/742-2623. Visitors Center Garden:** Self-guided tours daily 8:30am–5pm; free admission. **McBryde Garden:** Self-guided tours daily 9:30am–5pm; admission $15 adults, $7.50 children 6–12, free for children 5 and under; reservations required. Trams leave once an hour on the half-hour, last tram 3:30pm; check-in minimum 30 min. in advance. **Allerton Garden:** Guided tours daily 9 and 10am, and 1, 2, and 3pm; admission $35 adults, $15 children 8–12, children 7 and under not permitted; reservations required.

A prince **OF A PRINCE**

With his name gracing half of Kauai's main highway as well as a popular beach and busy avenue in Waikiki, you could say **Prince Jonah Kuhio Kalanianaole** is all over the map, just as he was in life. The nephew and adopted son of King David Kalakaua and Queen Kapiolani, Prince Kuhio studied in California and England before the American-backed overthrow of the monarchy in 1893. He spent a year in prison after being arrested in 1895 for plotting to restore the kingdom, and later fought with the British in the Boer War. In 1903, he was elected as a territorial delegate to the U.S. Congress, where he served until his death in 1922, at age 50.

Along the way, Prince Kuhio founded the first Hawaiian Civic Club, restored the Royal Order of Kamehameha, created the Hawaiian Home Lands Commission (which awards long-term leases to Native Hawaiians), established national parks on Maui and the island of Hawaii, opened his Waikiki beachfront to the public, and popularized outrigger canoe racing—just to name a few of the reasons "the people's prince" is so revered. His March 26 birthday is a state holiday, which his home island of Kauai marks with 2 weeks of **festivities** (www.princekuhio.net).

His birthplace in Poipu is part of **Prince Kuhio Park,** a small, grassy compound off Lawai Road, not far from where surfers navigate "PK's," a break also named for the prince. The park holds the foundations of the family home, a fish pond that's still connected by a culvert to the sea, the remains of a *heiau* (shrine), and a monument that still receives floral tributes. **Note:** It's considered disrespectful to sit on the rock walls, as tempting as it might be to picnic or don snorkel gear for the nearby cove.

View from Kalalau Overlook.

Spouting Horn ★★ NATURAL ATTRACTION Hawaii's equivalent to Old Faithful—at least in regularity, if not temperature—is an impressive plume of seawater that jettisons 10 to 50 or so feet into the air above the rocky shoreline (fenced for safety reasons). The spout comes from the force of ocean swells funneling waves through a lava tube, with the most spectacular displays winter and other high-surf days. The *whoosh* of the spraying water is often followed by a load moaning sound, created by air pushing through from another nearby hole. There's an ample parking lot (as well as restrooms) on the site, but if you spot large tour buses in attendance, don't try to compete with the crowds for a Spouting Horn photo. Instead, browse the vendors of arts, crafts, and jewelry (from $5 bangles to Niihau shell leis costing hundreds of dollars) under the tents along the bluff, or watch the wild chickens put on a show, until the buses pull out 15 to 20 minutes later.

Ocean side of Lawai Rd., Poipu, 2 miles west of the traffic circle with Poipu Rd. Free admission. Daily during daylight hours.

WEST SIDE

Kokee State Park ★★★ PARK It's only 16 miles from Waimea to Kokee, but the two feel worlds apart: With 4,345 acres of rainforest, Kokee is another climate zone altogether, where the breeze has a bite and trees look quite continental. This is a cloud forest on the edge of the Alakai Swamp, the largest swamp in Hawaii, on the summit plateau of Kauai. Days are cool and wet, with intermittent bright sunshine, not unlike Seattle on a good day. Bring your sweater, and, if you're staying over, be sure you know how to light a fire (overnight lows dip into the 40s/single digits Celsius).

While invasive foreign plants such as strawberry guava, kahili ginger, and Australian tree ferns have crowded out native plants, the forest still holds many treasures, including several species that only grow on Kauai: mokihana trees, whose anise-scented green berries adorn the island's signature lei; iliau, a spiky plant similar to Maui's silversword; and the endangered white hibiscus, one of the few of its kind to have a fragrance.

Russian Fort.

Before exploring the area, though, be sure to stop by the **Kokee Natural History Museum ★★** (www.kokee.org; © **808/335-9975;** daily 9am–4:30pm). It's right next to the restaurant/gift shop of the Lodge at Kokee, in the meadow off Kokee Road (Hwy. 550), 5 miles past the first official Waimea Canyon lookout. Admission is free, but it deserves at least the $1 donation requested per person. This is the best place to learn about the forest and Alakai Swamp. The museum shop has great trail information as well as local books and maps, including the official park trail map; a .1-mile nature walk with labeled plants starts just behind the museum.

Another 2.7 miles up the road from Kokee Lodge is **Kalalau Overlook ★★★**, the spectacular climax of your drive through Waimea Canyon and Kokee—unless the gate is open to the Puu O Kila Lookout 1 mile farther, the true end of the road. The latter lookout is usually closed in inclement weather, which is frequent: Nearby Waialeale is playing catch for clouds that have crossed thousands of miles of ocean. The view from Kalalau Overlook can be Brigadoon-like, too, but when the mists part, it's breathtaking. Shadows dance cross the green cliffs dappled with red and orange, white tropicbirds soar over a valley almost 4,000 feet below, and the turquoise sea sparkles on the horizon. Just below the railing, look for the fluffy red *'apapane* honeycreepers darting among the scarlet-tufted ohia lehua trees. Mornings tend to offer the clearest views.

With so many trails to hike up here, including the boardwalk through the Alakai Swamp (p. 468), some choose to stay overnight, either by pitching a tent in one of several campsites (by permit only) or opting for one of the cabins run by the Lodge at Kokee or the YWCA's Camp Sloggett (see "Where to Stay," p. 472). You'll need to plan carefully, though, when it comes to food and drink: The lodge's restaurant (see "Where to Eat," p. 487) is open only from 9am to 2:30pm, with takeout till 3pm, but I've found it closes early when business is slow. In the late afternoon, your best hope may be a snack vendor at a Waimea Canyon overlook; otherwise, it's a winding 15-mile drive down to Waimea.

Kokee Rd., 7 miles north of its merge with Waimea Canyon Rd. (Hwy. 550). www.hawaiistate parks.org/parks/Kauai. © **808/274-3444.** Free admission. Daily during daylight hours.

Russian Fort Elizabeth State Historical Park ★ HISTORIC SITE   To the list of those who tried to conquer Hawaii, add the Russians. In 1815, a German doctor tried to claim Kauai for Russia. He even supervised the construction of this fort in Waimea, named for the wife of Czar Alexander I, but he and his handful of Russian companions were expelled by Kamehameha I a couple of years later. Only the walls remain today, built with stacked lava rocks in the shape of a star. For years the walls lay covered with grass and invasive kiawe trees, making the fort a stop only for diehard history buffs. Recent cleanup efforts, however, have brought the fort's perimeter and interior into sharper focus, with interpretive signs for a self-guided tour. The site also provides panoramic views of the west bank of the Waimea River, where Captain Cook landed, and the island of Niihau. **Note:** Restrooms make this a convenient pit stop.

Ocean side of Kaumualii Hwy., Waimea, just after mile marker 22, east of Waimea River. www. hawaiistateparks.org/parks/kauai. Free admission. Daily during daylight hours.

Waimea Canyon State Park ★★★ PARK/NATURAL ATTRACTION Often called "The Grand Canyon" of the Pacific—an analogy attributed to Mark Twain, although there's no record he ever visited—Waimea Canyon is indeed spectacular, albeit on a smaller scale. A mile wide, 3,600 feet deep, and 14 miles long, depending on whom you ask, Kauai's counterpart to Arizona's icon deserves accolades for its beauty alone. A jumble of red-orange pyramids, striped with gray bands of volcanic rock and stubbled with green and gold vegetation, Waimea Canyon was formed by a series of prehistoric lava flows, earthquakes, and erosion from wind and water, including the narrow Waimea River, still carving its way to the sea. You can stop by the road and look at the canyon, hike into it, admire it

Waimea Canyon.

from a downhill bicycle tour, or swoop through it in a helicopter. (For more information, see "Organized Tours" and "Other Outdoor Activities," below.)

By car, there are two ways to visit Waimea Canyon and reach Kokee State Park, 15 miles up from Waimea. From the main road of Kaumualii Highway, it's best to head up Waimea Canyon Drive (Hwy. 550) at Waimea town. You can also pass through Waimea and turn up Kokee Road (Hwy. 55) at Kekaha, but it's steeper—one reason it's preferred by the twice-daily downhill bike tours—and its vistas, though lovely, are not as eye-popping as those along Waimea Canyon Drive, the narrower rim road. The two routes merge about 7 miles up from the highway and continue as Kokee Road.

The first good vantage point is **Waimea Canyon Lookout,** between mile markers 10 and 11 on Kokee Road; there's a long, gently graded paved path for those who can't handle the stairs to the observation area. Far across the canyon, two-tiered **Waipoo Falls** cascades 800 feet, while you might spot a nimble mountain goat clambering on the precipices just below. From here, it's about another 5 miles to Kokee. A few more informal and formal lookout points along the way also offer noteworthy views. **Puu Ka Pele Lookout,** between mile markers 12 and 13, reveals the multiple ribbons of water coursing through Waipoo Falls. **Puu Hinahina Lookout,** between mile markers 13 and 14, actually has two different vista points, one with a sweeping view of the canyon down to the Pacific, and another of Niihau, lying 17 miles west.

Free admission.

West Kauai Technology & Visitor Center ★ MUSEUM   Although its hours are limited (and it's closed Wed and weekends), this museum's two free weekly activities and the small but well-curated cultural exhibitions merit a stop here before or after your Waimea Canyon expedition. The **"Keepers of the Culture"** permanent displays include vintage photos, artifacts, and panels tied to Waimea's natural and cultural history, from traditional Hawaiian practices such as salt-making and herbal medicine to the arrival of Captain Cook, the sugar plantation era, and the modern Pacific Missile Range Facility. Seasonal exhibits examine Waimea's *paniolo* (cowboy) culture; Kauai's last king, Kaumualii, and King Kamehameha IV's wife, Queen Emma; and the first Christmas in Waimea. Kids will more likely enjoy the **lei-making class,** which takes place at 9:30am Friday from early March to mid-November (when fresh blossoms are available); it's free, but you need to reserve by phone no later than noon the Thursday before. On Monday, a free **guided walking tour** of historic Waimea Town explores its ancient Hawaiian roots and modern history with stops at the Captain Cook monument, missionary churches, and picturesque Waimea Pier. It starts at 9:30am and lasts 2½ to 3 hours; reservations are required by noon the Friday before. (**Note:** The "technology" part of the center's name refers to computers with free Internet access.)

9565 Kaumualii Hwy. at Waimea Canyon Rd., Waimea. www.westkauaivisitorcenter.org. © **808/ 338-1332.** Free admission. Mon 12:30–4pm, Tues and Thurs 9:30am–4pm, Fri 9:30am–12:30pm.

Organized Tours

Farms, gardens, historic houses, and other points of interest that may be open only to guided tours are listed under "Attractions & Points of Interest," above. For boat, kayak, bicycle, hiking, and similar tours, see listings under "Other Outdoor Activities."

HELICOPTER TOURS ★★★

If you forgo touring Kauai by helicopter, you'll miss seeing the vast majority of its untouched ridgelines, emerald valleys, and exhilarating waterfalls. Yes, the rides are expensive ($200–$300 per person), but you'll take home memories—not to mention photos, videos, and/or a professional DVD—of the thrilling ride over Waimea Canyon, into Kalalau Valley on Kauai's wild Napali Coast, and across the green crater of Waialeale, laced with ribbons of water.

Most flights depart from Lihue, last about 55 to 75 minutes, and, regardless of advertising, offer essentially the same experience: narrated flights, noise-canceling headphones with two-way communication, and multi-camera videos of your ride or a pre-taped version (often a better souvenir). The risks are also about the same—Kauai's last crash involving a sightseeing helicopter was in 2007, with many thousands of flights safely flown since. (If your pilot chooses to bypass Waialeale due to bad weather, appreciate his or her caution.) So how to distinguish among the half-dozen major operators?

Given the noise inflicted on residents, wildlife, and tranquillity-seeking hikers by flights that hover as low as 500 feet, I recommend touring with the most eco-friendly of the bunch, and most luxurious: **Blue Hawaiian ★★★** (www.bluehawaiian.com; ✆ **800/745-2583** or 808/245-5800). Its American Eurocopter Eco-Star choppers have a unique tail design that reduces noise and fuel use, while the roomy interior has six business-class-style leather seats with premium views. The best seats are the two next to the pilot, but the raised row of rear seats won't disappoint (keep in mind seating is usually determined by weight distribution.) The 55-minute "Eco Adventure" ride from Lihue costs $239 ($211 when booked online at least 5 days in advance), which also makes Blue Hawaiian the best value.

For those staying on the North Shore, it may be more convenient to arrange a tour with **Sunshine Helicopters ★★** (www.helicopters-kauai.com; ✆ **866/501-7738** or 808/270-3999). Its 40- to 50-minute flights from Princeville Airport

Napali Coast viewed from helicopter.

hollywood **LOVES KAUAI**

More than 50 major Hollywood productions have been shot on Kauai since the studios discovered the island's spectacular natural beauty. Kauai's most recent star turn was in **"The Descendants";** locations included Hanalei Bay, Tahiti Nui in Hanalei, and the breathtaking overlook of Kipu Kai. You can visit a number of Kauai locations that made it to the silver screen—including the settings of such TV classics as "Fantasy Island" and "Gilligan's Island"—on the **Hawaii Movie Tour** from Roberts Hawaii (www.robertshawaii.com/kauai/hawaiimovietour.php; ☎ **800/831-5541**). Offered daily except Sunday, the narrated mini-bus tour features singalongs, video clips that play between sightseeing stops, and lunch at Tahiti Nui, where George Clooney's clan dined in "The Descendants." You'll likely see more of Kauai on this 6-hour tour, which includes exclusive access to the Coco Palms resort, than you could on your own. Tickets are $116 for adults and $64 for children 11 and under, including lunch and pickup/drop-off ($10 extra for Princeville lodgings). **Tip:** Book online for a substantial discount ($90 adults, $45 children), and reserve early.

are in quiet, roomy Whisper Star models, similar in design to Blue Hawaiian's Eco-Stars (it flies different craft out of Lihue.) Tours cost $289 for open seating, $364 if you want to reserve an even roomier "first class" seat in the front row; it's $249 and $324, respectively, if you book online, with an extra $10 off on flights before 8:30am or after 2pm.

Although its aircraft are not as quiet as those of Blue Hawaiian and Sunshine, two other companies have unique itineraries deserving of consideration. **Island Helicopters** (www.islandhelicopters.com; ☎ **800/829-5999** or 808/245-8588) has exclusive rights to land at remote 350-foot Manawaiopuna Falls, nicknamed "Jurassic Falls" for its movie cameo. During your 25 minutes on the ground, you'll hear about the geological history and rare native plants in this area of Hanapepe Valley, which like Niihau is owned by the Robinson family. In part due to landing fees and fuel costs, Island's 75- to 85-minute **Jurassic Falls Tour ★** costs a whopping $371 ($321 booked online, plus a 4-percent credit-card fee); it leaves from Lihue Airport. **Safari Helicopters** (www.safarihelicopters.com; ☎ **800/326-3356** or 808/246-0136) offers the 90-minute **Kauai Refuge Eco-Tour ★★**, which includes a 30- to 40-minute stopover at an otherwise inaccessible Robinson-owned site overlooking Olokele Canyon; Keith Robinson is occasionally on hand to explain his efforts to preserve rare, endemic plants here (which your landing fees subsidize). The tour costs $279 ($252 booked online) and departs from Lihue.

BEACHES

Note: You'll find relevant sites on the "Kauai" map, p. 419.

Beaches

Kauai's nearly 70 beaches include some of the most beautiful in the world, and all are open to the public, as required by state law. They are also in the middle of the vast, powerful Pacific, where currents and surf patterns are often quite different than those of Mainland beaches. The North Shore sees the highest surf in winter (Oct–Apr), thanks to swells originating in the Arctic that can also wrap around the West Side and turn the East Side's waters rough. In summer, Antarctic storms can send large swells to the South Shore that wrap around the West Side and churn up the East Side.

The good news is there's almost always a swimmable beach somewhere: You just need to know where to look. Start by asking your hotel concierge or checking the daily ocean report on **Kauaiexplorer.com** to find out current conditions. Nine beaches—all of them county or state parks—have lifeguards, who are keen to clue you in on safety.

Below are highlights of the Garden Isle's more accessible beaches. For detailed listings, including maps and videos, of virtually all strands and coves, see **www.kauaibeachscoop.com**.

EAST SIDE

Anahola Beach ★

Anahola is part of the Hawaiian Home Lands federal program, meaning that much of the land here is reserved for long-term leases by Native Hawaiians; you'll pass their modest homes on the road to this secluded, mostly reef-protected golden strand. The 1½-acre Anahola Beach Park on the south end feels like the neighborhood's back yard, particularly on weekends, with kids learning to surf or bodyboarding, a hula class on the grass, and picnickers. It's better to explore here during the week, when you might share it with just a few fishermen and campers (who may also be locals). There are sandy-bottomed pockets for swimming and reefy areas for snorkeling, safe except in high surf. The Anahola River, usually shallow enough to walk across, bisects the beach. Facilities include picnic tables, restrooms, and lifeguards.

From Kuhio Hwy. heading north, turn right on Anahola Rd. (between mile markers 13 and 14) and head ¾-mile to the beach park. You can also park north of the Anahola River by taking a right on Aliomanu Rd. ½-mile past Anahola Rd., just after Duane's Ono Char-Burger (p. 496).

Kalapaki Beach ★★

This quarter-mile-long swath of golden sand may seem like a private beach, given all the lounge chairs on its border with the Kauai Marriott Resort, which towers behind. But there's generally plenty of room to find your own space to sunbathe,

---

Safe Swimming on Kauai

"When in doubt, don't go out" is the mantra of local authorities, who repeat this and other important safety tips on a video loop at the Lihue baggage claim and on a local TV channel for visitors. That refers to going into unsafe waters, walking on slippery rocks and ledges that may be hit by high surf, or other heedless acts, such as disregarding beach closed signs in winter. Many of the unguarded beaches have waters that should only be enjoyed from the sand, or during calm conditions, which can change rapidly; keep in mind that large waves may come in sets as much as 20 minutes apart. While you might see locals seemingly ignoring the warning signs that note hazards such as strong currents, steep drop-offs, dangerous shorebreak, and the like, keep in mind they've had years to acclimatize. Don't be afraid to ask for their advice, though, since they'll tailor it for newcomers. By all means, *do* go out to Kauai's beaches; just bring prudence with you.

while the jetty stretching across much of Kalapaki Bay offers a protected place to swim or paddle; body-surfing and surfing are also possible at a small break. The view of the mossy-green Haupu Ridge rising out of Nawiliwili Bay is entrancing, as is watching massive cruise ships and Matson barges angle their way in and out of the nearby harbor. The water is a little murkier here, due to stream runoff. Facilities include restrooms and showers, with numerous shops and restaurants within a short walk.

From Lihue Airport, turn left onto Hwy. 51 to Rice St., turn left and look for Kauai Marriott Resort entrance on the left. Free beach access parking is in the upper lot, past the hotel's porte-cochère.

Kealia Beach ★

Only very experienced surfers and bodyboarders should try their hands on the usually powerful waves here, but everyone else can enjoy the show from the broad golden sand, a picnic table, or the nearby coastal path. The lifeguards can advise you if it's calm enough to go for a swim and where to do it. When the wind is up, which is often, you might see kite flyers. The 66-acre Kealia Beach Park is just off the main highway, often with food trucks and coconut vendors in the parking lot, making it a convenient place for an impromptu break. Facilities include restrooms and picnic shelters.

Off Kuhio Hwy. in Kapaa, just north of Kapaa River.

Lydgate Beach ★

Part of the family oasis of 58-acre **Lydgate Park ★** (p. 432) on the south side of the Wailua River mouth, Lydgate Beach has two rock-walled ponds that create the safest swimming and best snorkeling on the East Side—unless storms have pushed branches and other debris into the pond, which can take several days to clear. Families also gravitate here for the immense wooden play structure known as the **Kamalani Playground** and access to a 2.5-mile stretch of the **Ka Ala Hele Makalae coastal path,** suitable for strollers and bikes. Facilities include a pavilion, restrooms, outdoor showers, picnic tables, barbecue grills, lifeguards, and parking.

DEADLY BEAUTY: queen's bath

With so many lovely places to hike, swim, or snorkel in relative safety on Kauai, it's hard to understand why so many visitors put themselves in jeopardy at Queen's Bath, an oceanfront "pond" in the lava rocks below the Princeville cliffs, where 29 recorded drownings and numerous injuries have occurred. The site is most dangerous from October to April, but even on seemingly calm summer days, rogue waves can knock the unwary off ledges, or surge across the pond and pull swimmers into the open ocean, where they can drown long before help arrives. Others have broken limbs by falling on the steep, rough trail—which is extremely slippery when wet—or while trying to enter the rocky pond. (It doesn't help that local daredevils enjoy jumping into the turbulent water of a nearby inlet, which inspires numerous YouTube videos and hapless imitators.) Unlike the many blithe reviewers on TripAdvisor who happened to experience tranquil conditions, I cannot in good conscience direct visitors here. If nothing else will dissuade you, know that parking is tight and illegally parked cars can and will be booted.

Anini Beach.

Leho Dr. at Nalu Rd., Wailua. From the intersection of Kuhio Hwy. and Hwy. 51 outside of Lihue, head 2½ miles north to Leho Dr. and turn right, just before Aston Aloha Beach Resort. Turn right again on Nalu Rd. and follow to parking areas.

NORTH SHORE
Anini Beach ★★★

Anini is Kauai's safest beach for swimming and windsurfing, thanks to one of the longest, widest fringing reefs on Kauai, among the very largest in all of Hawaii. With shallow water 4 to 5 feet deep, it's also a good snorkel spot for beginners (the coral is sparse here, however, which means the fish varieties are more spectacular elsewhere). In summer months, divers are attracted to the 60-foot dropoff near the channel in the northwest corner of the nearly 3-mile-long reef. In winter, the channel creates a very dangerous rip current, although the near-shore waters generally stay calm; it can be fun to watch breakers pounding the distant reef from the bath-like lagoon. The well-shaded, sinuous beach is very narrow in some places, so keep walking if you'd like more privacy. The 13-acre **Anini Beach Park** on the southwestern end has restrooms, picnic facilities, and a boat-launch ramp.

From Lihue, follow Kuhio Hwy. past Kilauea to the 2nd Kalihiwai Rd. exit on right (the 1st Kahiliwai Rd.; dead-ends at Kalihiwai Beach). Head downhill ½-mile to a left on Anini Rd.

Hanalei Beach ★★★

Easily one of Hawaii's most majestic settings, unbelievably just a few blocks from the main road, Hanalei Beach is a gorgeous half-moon of golden-white sand, 2 miles long and 125 feet wide. Hanalei means "lei-shaped," and like a lei, the curving, ironwood-fringed sands adorn Hanalei Bay, the largest inlet on Kauai. While the cliffside St. Regis Princeville dominates the eastern vista, the view west is lush and green; behind you, emerald peaks streaked with waterfalls rise to 4,000 feet. Renowned for experts-only big surf in winter (Sept–May), Hanalei attracts attract beginners and old hands with steady, gentler waves the rest of the year. In summer, much of the bay turns into a virtual lake, creating ideal swimming conditions for kids. The county manages three different beach parks here, two with lifeguards.

Black Pot Beach Park, near the historic, 300-foot-long pier, is particularly good for swimming, snorkeling, surfing, and fishing, while you'll also see kayakers and stand-up paddleboarders coming in from the mouth of the Hanalei River—note that it can be difficult to find parking on weekends and during holiday periods. Facilities include restrooms, showers, picnic tables, and campgrounds. **Hanalei Pavilion Beach Park,** in the center of the bay, has wide-open swimming (in calm weather), surfing, and boogie-boarding, under the watchful eye of lifeguards; facilities include restrooms, showers, and pavilions (the local nickname for this surf spot). "Pine Trees" is the widely used moniker for **Waioli Beach Park,** shaded by ironwood trees towards the western edge of the bay. It's another popular surf spot—champions Andy and Bruce Irons grew up riding the waves here, and started the children's Pine Trees Classic held here every April. Check with lifeguards in winter about possible strong currents; facilities include showers and restrooms.

From Princeville heading north on Kuhio Hwy., enter Hanalei and turn right at Aku Rd. just after Tahiti Nui, then right on Weke Rd. Hanalei Pavilion Beach Park will be on your left; the road dead-ends at parking lot for Black Pot Beach Park. For Waioli Beach Park (Pine Trees), take Aku Rd. to a left on Weke Rd., then left on Hee Rd.

Kauapea (Secret) Beach ★★

Not exactly secret, but still wonderfully secluded, this long, broad stretch of light sand below forested bluffs lies snugly between rocky points, with only a few cliff-top homes and Kilauea Point Lighthouse to the east providing signs of civilization. Although strong currents and high surf, especially in winter, make the water unsafe, tide pools at the west end invite exploration when the surf is low, creating beguiling mini-lagoons; a small artesian waterfall to the east is perfect for washing off salt water. ***Note:*** Despite its reputation as a safe haven for nudists (who hang out at the more remote eastern end), Kauai County does occasionally enforce the "no public nudity" law here. And as with all destinations where your car will be out of sight for extended periods, be sure to take your valuables with you. It's a 15-minute walk downhill to the beach.

From Kuhio Hwy., pass Kilauea and take 1st Kalihiwai Rd. turnoff on right. Drive about 50 yards, then turn right on unmarked dirt road on right and follow to parking area. Trail at end of lot leads downhill to beach, about a 15-min. walk.

Kee Beach ★★

The road ends here at this iconic tropical beach, hugged by swaying palms and sheltering ironwoods, its pale dunes sloping into a cozy lagoon brimming with a kaleidoscope of reef fish. You could feel like a sardine during the peak summer period, when the ocean is at its most tranquil and the parking lot is full by 9am. To be fair, many cars are for hikers tackling all or part of the 11-mile **Kalalau Trail** (p. 467), whose trailhead is just before the beach, and some belong to campers. Kee (pronounced *"kay-eh"*) is also subject to high surf in winter, when rogue waves can grab unwitting spectators from the shoreline and dangerous currents form in a channel on the reef's western edge. It's best to avoid the channel year-round, and always check with the lifeguards about the safest areas for swimming or snorkeling. Part of **Haena State Park** (p. 434), Kee has restrooms and showers in the woodsy area east of the parking lot. This is also a spectacular place to observe sunset, but you won't be alone in that endeavor, either.

From Hanalei, take Kuhio Hwy. about 7½ miles past Hanalei to the road's end.

Lumahai Beach ★

Between lush tropical jungle of pandanus and ironwood trees and the brilliant blue ocean lie two crescents of inviting golden sand beach, separated by a rocky outcropping. Here is Kauai at its most captivating—and where you must exercise the most caution. Locals have nicknamed it "Luma-die," reflecting the sad tally of those drowned or seriously injured here. With no reef protection and a steeply sloping shore, the undertow and shorebreak are exceptionally strong, while the rocky ledges that seemingly invite exploration are often slapped by huge waves that knock sightseers into the tumbling surf and sharp rocks. Flash floods can also make the Lumahai River, which enters the ocean from the western beach, turn from a wading pool into a raging torrent. Plus, it has neither lifeguards nor facilities. So why would you even go here? When summer brings more tranquil surf, it's a gorgeous setting to stretch out on the sand—not too close to the shorebreak—and soak in the untamed beauty. *Note:* The eastern beach, reached by a short, steep trail from the highway, is where Mitzi Gaynor sang "I'm Gonna Wash That Man Right Outta My Hair" in "South Pacific."

From Hanalei, follow Kuhio Hwy. about 2½ miles west. Look for pullout on ocean side, near mile marker 4, for trail leading to eastern beach. For western beach, continue west (downhill) to larger, unpaved parking area on ocean side by mile marker 5.

Tunnels (Makua) Beach ★★★ & Haena Beach Park ★★

Tunnels Beach, more properly known as Makua, takes its English name from the labyrinth of lava tubes that wind through its inner and outer reef, making this Kauai's premiere snorkeling and diving site. The reefs mean the water is safe to enter nearly year-round. But as fascinating as the rainbow of tropical fish and the underwater tunnels, arches, and channels may be, they're more than matched by the beauty of what's above water. The last pinnacle in a row of velvety green mountains, Makana (Bali Hai) rises over the western end of a golden curved beach with a fringe of ironwood trees. The only problem: Where to park? The handful of spots on dirt access roads fill up first thing, and residents vigilantly enforce "no parking" zones.

Fortunately, a quarter-mile up the sand is **Haena Beach Park,** a county facility with plenty of parking—plus restrooms, showers, picnic tables, campgrounds, and lifeguards. During calm conditions, most frequent in summer, it offers good swimming and some snorkeling, though not as showy or enticing as at Tunnels. Winter brings enormous waves, rip currents, and a strong shorebreak, time to leave the water to the expert local surfers. Do walk across the road for a gander at **Maniniholo Dry Cave,** another former sea cave (see "Haena State Park," p. 434) but one where you can walk for yards and yards inside before it gets too dark and low (watch your noggin).

From Hanalei, Tunnels (Makua) is just after mile marker 8 on Kuhio Hwy., but not visible from the road. Continue ½-mile to Haena Beach Park and parking lot on right.

SOUTH SHORE

Mahaulepu Beaches ★★

Not far from Poipu's well-groomed resorts is a magical place to leave the crowds—and maybe the last few centuries—behind. To reach the three different beaches of Mahaulepu, framed by lithified sand dunes, former sugarcane fields, and the bold Haupu ridge, you'll have to drive at least 3 miles on an uneven dirt road through private land (gates close at 6pm), or hike the fascinating Mahaulepu Heritage Trail (p.467). The first tawny strand is **Mahaulepu Beach,** nicknamed Gillin's Beach after the former Grove Farm manager whose house is the only

Mahaulepu Beach.

modern structure you'll see for miles; the house is available for rent starting at $3,250 a week (www.gillinbeachhouse.com). Windsurfing is popular here; strong currents means it's generally not safe for swimming or snorkeling. If you're lucky, the sea will have swept away the sand normally covering the petroglyphs in Waiopili Stream at the beach. Around the point is **Kawailoa Bay,** also a windsurfing destination, with a rockier shoreline great for beachcombing and fishing. Wedged between dramatically carved ledges, **Haula Beach** is a picturesque pocket of sand with a rocky cove, best for solitude. *Note:* The coastline here can be very windy, and subject to high surf in summer.

By car: From Poipu Rd. in front of Grand Hyatt Kauai, continue on unpaved road 3 miles east, past the golf course and stables. Turn right at the T intersection, go 1 mile to big sand dune, turn left, and drive ½-mile to a small lot under the trees to reach **Mahaulepu Beach.** You can continue on dirt road (high-clearance 4WD recommended) another ¼-mile to **Kawailoa Bay,** then another ½-mile to short trail to **Ha'ula Beach. By foot:** Follow Mahaulepu Heritage Trail (www. hikemahaulepu.org) 2 miles from east end of Shipwrecks (Keoneloa) Beach; public access parking is just past Grand Hyatt Kauai, on Ainako St.

Poipu Beach ★★★

A perennial "best beach" winner, the long swath of Poipu is actually two beaches in one, divided by a tombolo, or sandbar point. On the left, a lava-rock jetty protects a sandy-bottom pool that's perfect for children most of the year; on the right, the open bay attracts swimmers, snorkelers, and surfers. (If the waves are up, check with the lifeguards for the safest place to swim.) The sandy area is not especially large, but 5½-acre **Poipu Beach Park** offers a spacious lawn for kids to run around, plus picnic shelters, play structures, restrooms, and showers. There are plenty of palm trees, but not much shade; bring a beach umbrella to stay cool. Given the resorts and condos nearby, Poipu understandably stays busy year-round, and on New Year's Eve, it becomes Kauai's version of Times Square, with a fireworks celebration. *Note:* A short walk east is **Brennecke's Beach,** a sandy cove beloved by body-surfers and boogie-boarders; be forewarned that waves can be large, especially in summer, and the rocky sides are always hazardous. There's no lifeguard in this area.

From Koloa, follow Poipu Rd. south to traffic circle and then east to a right turn on Hoowili Rd. Parking is on the left at intersection with Hoone Rd.

Shipwrecks (Keoneloa) Beach ★

Makawehi Point, a lithified sand dune, juts out from the eastern end of this beach, whose Hawaiian name means "the long sand." Harrison Ford and Anne Heche jumped off Makawehi in "Six Days, Seven Nights" (don't try it yourself), while body-surfers and boogie-boarders find the roiling waters equally exhilarating. Novices should enjoy their antics from the shore, or follow the ironwood trees to the path leading to the top of Makawehi Point, which is also the start of the Mahaulepu Heritage Trail (p. 467). A paved beach path in front of the Grand Hyatt Kauai leads west past tide pools to the blustery point at Makahuena, perfect for photographing Shipwrecks and Makawehi Point. Restrooms and showers are by the small parking lot on Ainako Street.

Public access from Ainako St., off Poipu Rd., just east of Grand Hyatt Kauai.

WEST SIDE

Salt Pond Beach ★

You'll see Hawaii's only salt ponds still in production across from Salt Pond Beach, just outside Hanapepe. Generations of Hawaiians have carefully tended the beds in which the sun turns seawater into salt crystals, *pa'akai*. Tinged with red clay, *'alae*, the salt is used as a health remedy as well as for seasoning food and drying fish. While the salt ponds are off-limits to visitors, 6-acre **Salt Pond Beach** is a great place to explore, offering a curved reddish-gold beach between two rocky points, a protective reef that creates lagoon-like conditions for swimming and snorkeling (talk to the lifeguard first if waves are up), tide pools, and a natural wading pool for kids. Locals flock here on weekends for individual recreation and large family gatherings, so go during the week for more quiet enjoyment. Facilities include showers, restrooms, a campground, and picnic areas.

From Lihue, take Kaumualii Hwy. to Hanapepe, cross Hanapepe Bridge, and look for Lele Rd. on left (½-mile ahead). Turn left, and follow Lele Rd. to a right turn on Lokokai Rd. Salt Pond Beach and parking lot is 1 mile ahead.

Polihale Beach ★

This mini-Sahara on the western end of the island is Hawaii's biggest beach: 17 miles long and as wide as three football fields in places. This is a wonderful place to get away from it all, but don't forget your flip-flops—the midday sand is hotter than a lava flow. The pale golden sands wrap around Kauai's northwestern shore from Kekaha plantation town, just beyond Waimea, to where the ridges of Napali begin. For military reasons, access is highly restricted for a 7-mile stretch along the southeastern end near the Pacific Missile Range Facility, including the famed **Barking Sands Beach,** known to Hawaiians as Nohili. You'll still have miles of sand to explore in 140-acre **Polihale State Park,** provided you (or your car) can handle the 5-mile, often very rutted dirt road leading there. (Avoid driving on the car-trapping sand, too.) The sheer expanse, plus views of Niihau and the first stark cliffs of Napali, make the arduous trek worth it for many. While strong rip currents and a heavy shorebreak make the water dangerous, especially in winter, **Queen's Pond,** a small, shallow, sandy-bottom inlet, is generally protected from the surf in summer. It has restrooms, showers, picnic tables, a state camping

Polihale State Park.

area, and drinking water (usually) but no lifeguards or any other facilities nearby, so plan accordingly. As in all remote areas, leave no valuables in your car.

From Kekaha, follow Kaumualii Hwy. 7 miles northwest past Pacific Missile Range Facility to fork at Kao Rd., bear right, and look for sign on left to Polihale. Follow dirt road 5 miles to main parking area, bearing to right at forks.

WATERSPORTS

Several outfitters on Kauai not only offer equipment rentals and tours, but also give out expert information on weather forecasts, sea and trail conditions, and other important matters for adventurers. Brothers Micco and Chino Godinez at **Kayak Kauai** (www.kayakkauai.com; © **888/596-3853** or 808/826-9844) are experts on paddling Kauai's rivers and coastline (as well as hiking and camping), offering guided tours and equipment rentals at their store in the Wailua River Marina. You can also learn about ocean and reef conditions and recommended boat operators at **Snorkel Bob's** (www.snorkelbob.com) two locations in Kapaa and Poipu (see "Snorkeling," below).

Boat & Raft (Zodiac) Tours

One of Hawaii's most spectacular natural attractions is Kauai's **Napali Coast.** Unless you're willing to make an arduous 22-mile round-trip hike (see "Hiking" on p. 466), there are only two ways to see it: by helicopter (see "Helicopter Tours" on p. 445) or by water. Cruising to Napali may involve a well-equipped yacht under full sail, a speedy powerboat, or for the very adventurous, a Zodiac inflatable raft, in which you may explore Napali's sea caves or even land at one of Napali's pristine valleys—be prepared to hang on for dear life (it can reach speeds of 60 miles an hour) and get very wet.

You're almost guaranteed daily sightings of pods of spinner dolphins on morning cruises. When the Pacific humpback whales make their annual visit to

Hawaii from late November to early April, they also swim right by Kauai. In season, both sailing and powerboats combine **whale-watching** with their regular adventures. **Sunset cruises,** with cocktails and/or dinner, are another way to get out on the water and appreciate Kauai's coastline from a different angle.

Note: In addition to Captain Andy's (details below), only two other companies have permits to land at Nualolo Kai, home to the ruins of an 800-year-old Hawaiian village below an elevated Napali valley: **Na Pali Explorer** (www. napali-explorer.com; ✆ **808/338-9999**) and **Kauai Sea Tours** (www.kauai seatours.com; ✆ **800/733-7997** or 808/826-7254). All trips are on rigid-hull inflatables, which unlike larger boats can pass through the reef opening.

Captain Andy's Sailing Adventures ★   Captain Andy has been sailing to Napali since 1980, with a fleet that now includes two sleek 55-foot custom catamarans, the *Spirit of Kauai* and *Akialoa;* a luxurious 65-foot catamaran, the *Southern Star;* and the 24-foot zippy Zodiac, which holds about a dozen thrillseekers. The 5½-hour **Napali catamaran cruise** costs $149 for adults and $109 for children 2 to 12 and includes continental breakfast, a deli-style lunch, snorkeling, and drinks; aboard the *Southern Star* ($160 adults, $119 children), a barbecue lunch replaces the deli fare. A 4-hour Napali Coast dinner cruise—which sails around the South Shore when Napali's waters are too rough—costs $119 for adults and $89 for children ($149/$109 on the *Southern Star*), with no snorkeling; all Napali catamaran cruises leave from Port Allen. The 2-hour **Poipu cocktail sunset sail** aboard the *Spirit of Kauai* or *Akialoa,* including drinks and *pupu* (appetizers), is $79 for adults and $49 for children; it sails Saturday only, from Kukuiula Small Boat Harbor near Poipu. **Napali Zodiac cruises** depart from Kikiaola Small Boat Harbor in Kekaha; the 4-hour version ($139 adults, $119 children 5–12) includes snorkeling and snacks, while the 6-hour version ($159/$119) adds a landing at Nualolo Kai (depending on conditions) and expands snacks to a picnic lunch. *Tip:* Book online for a $10-per-person discount.
www.napali.com. ✆ **800/535-0830** or 808/335-6833.

Holoholo Charters ★★   A 50-foot catamaran called *Leila,* licensed for 45 passengers but limited to just 37, serves Holoholo's 5-hour, year-round **Napali snorkel cruises:** They're $149 adults and $109 children 6 to 12, including continental breakfast and deli lunch, and post-snorkel beer and wine. The 65-foot *Holo* power catamaran, the island's largest, was built specifically to handle the channel crossing between Kauai and Niihau, where passengers snorkel after Napali sightseeing on 7-hour trips, also with two meals and post-snorkel libations ($195 adults, $139 children 6–12). The 3½-hour **sunset cruise** ($115 adults, $99 children 5–12), also aboard the *Holo,* offers heavy appetizers, cocktails, and, at sunset, a champagne toast. Both *Holo Holo* and *Leila* depart from Port Allen. April through November, Holoholo Charters also offers Napali snorkel tours from Hanalei on Kauai's most comfortable inflatable "rafts," really speedboats with fiberglass hulls, twin motors, stadium seats, freshwater shower, and a marine toilet (not to be undervalued on a 4-hr. trip that includes drinks and lunch). These tours cost $169 for adults and $139 for kids 6 to 12. *Tip:* Book online at least 3 days in advance for $15 to $20 off per person.
www.holoholocharters.com. ✆ **800/848-6130** or 808/335-0815.

Liko Kauai & Makana Charters ★   Born and raised on Kauai, from a Native Hawaiian family with roots on Niihau, Captain Liko offers more than just a

typical **whale-watching cruise;** this is a 5-hour combination Na Pali Coast tour/snorkel/historical lecture/whale-watching extravaganza with lunch. It all happens on power catamarans: the 49-foot *Na Pali Kai,* limited to 32 passengers, and the 32-foot *Makana,* with just 12 on board, both narrow enough to go in the sea caves normally only visited by inflatable craft. The 5-hour tours cost $139 for adults and $95 for children 4 to 12 (10-percent discount with online bookings). Boats depart twice daily from Kikiaola Small Boat Harbor in Kekaha; check in at 4516 Alawai Rd., Waimea (from Hwy. 50, turn right at Alawai just west of the Waimea River).
www.tournapali.com. © **888/732-5456** or 808/338-0333.

Bodysurfing & Boogie Boarding

The best places for beginners' bodysurfing and boogie boarding are **Kalapaki Beach** and **Poipu Beach;** only the more advanced should test the more powerful shorebreak at **Kealia, Shipwrecks (Keoneloa),** and **Brennecke's** beaches (see "Beaches," p. 446.) Boogie-board rentals are widely available at surf shops (see "Surfing," p. 466) and beachfront activity desks. On the South Shore, **Nukumoi Surf Shop** (www.nukumoisurf.com; © 808/742-8019), right across from Brennecke's Beach at 2100 Hoone Rd., Koloa, has the best rates and selections ($6 a day; $20 a week). On the North Shore, **Hanalei Surf Co.** (www.hanaleisurf.com; © **808/826-9000**), rents boogie boards for $5 a day, $20 a week, or $7 with fins, $22 weekly (3- and 5-day discounts also available); it's in Hanalei Center, 5–5161 Kuhio Hwy. (Hwy. 560), Hanalei.

Kayaking

With Hawaii's only navigable rivers, numerous bays, and the stunning Napali Coast, Kauai is made for kayaking. The most popular kayaking tour, guided or unguided, is up the Wailua River to Secret Falls (limited to permitted kayaks Mon–Sat), but you can also explore the Huleia and Hanalei rivers as they wind through wildlife reserves, go whale-watching in winter along the South Shore, or test your mettle in summer with an ultra-strenuous, 17-mile paddle from Hanalei to Polihale.

Kayak Kauai (www.kayakkauai.com; © **888/596-3853** or 808/826-9844), the premiere outfitter for all kinds of paddling, offers a range of rentals and tours from its store in Wailua River Marina, 3-5971 Kuhio Hwy., Kapaa (just south of the Wailua River Bridge). River kayak rental starts at $29 for a one-person kayak and $54 for a two-person kayak per day ($64 for Wailua River–permitted double kayaks), including paddles, life preservers, back rests, and car racks. Twice-daily, 5-hour guided Wailua River tours with a Secret Falls hike/swim and picnic lunch cost $85 for adults and $60 for children under 12; a 3-hour version that skips the waterfall hike but adds a swimming hole is $55 for adults and $45 for children. The 5-hour Blue Lagoon tour from the Hanalei River mouth, which includes a shuttle to/from the Wailua River Marina, features snorkeling, bird-watching, and beach time; it's $95 for adults and $85 for children.

Kayak Kauai's Napali tours ($240, including lunch), offered April through September, are only for the very fit (and those who aren't prone to seasickness); it requires 5 to 6 hours of paddling, often through ocean swells, in two-person kayaks. If you're up for its rigors, this will be the kayak trip of your life—co-owner Micco Godinez calls it "the Everest of sea kayaking." The 6-hour winter whale-watching tours ($145) along the South Shore are slightly less challenging but still a significant workout. If you need to brush up on your skills first, Kayak Kauai also gives 90-minute lessons in Wailua River and Hanalei Bay for $75 per person (two-person minimum).

Headquartered in Poipu, **Outfitters Kauai** (www.outfitterskauai.com; © **888/742-9887** or 808/742-9667) offers a similar variety of well-organized tours, from a Wailua kayak/waterfall hike ($106 adults, $86 children 5–14, including lunch) to a summer Napali tour ($234 ages 15 and older only) or a winter whale-watching paddle from Poipu to Port Allen ($156 adults, $126 children 12–14). The family-friendly Hidden Valley Falls tour heads 2 miles downwind on the Huleia River and includes a short hike to a swimming hole and a picnic by a small waterfall, with the bonus of a motorized canoe ride back; it's $116 for adults and $96 for children 3 to 14.

Sailing

Kalapaki Bay and Nawiliwili Harbor provide a well-protected if bustling place to learn to sail or, with sufficient experience, take a spin around the harbor yourself. In addition to surfing and stand-up paddleboarding lessons and rentals, **Kauai Beach Boys** (www.kauaibeachboys.com; © **808/246-6333**) offers 1-hour rides with an instructor ($39) and sailing lessons for $140 per hour on its two-person, 18-foot Hobie Tandem Island and six-person, 16-foot Hobie Getaway boats; skilled sailors can tool around Kalapaki Bay on their own for $95 an hour ($75 per additional hour, up to $195 a day), or go out on the ocean with an instructor.

Scuba Diving

Diving, like all watersports on Kauai, is dictated by the weather. In winter, when heavy swells and high winds hit the island, it's generally limited to the more protected South Shore. Probably the best-known site along the South Shore is **Caverns,** located off the Poipu Beach resort area. This site consists of a series of lava tubes interconnected by a chain of archways. A constant parade of fish streams by (even shy lionfish are spotted lurking in crevices), brightly hued Hawaiian lobsters hide in the lava's tiny holes, and turtles sometimes swim past.

In summer, the magnificent North Shore opens up, and you can take a boat dive locally known as the **Oceanarium,** northwest of Hanalei Bay, where you'll find a kaleidoscopic marine world in a horseshoe-shape cove. From the rare (long-handed spiny lobsters) to the more common (taape, conger eels, and nudibranchs), the resident population is one of the more diverse on the island. The topography, which features pinnacles, ridges, and archways, is covered with cup corals, black-coral trees, and nooks and crannies enough for a dozen dives.

Because the best dives on Kauai are offshore, including the crystal-clear waters off Napali and Niihau, I recommend booking a dive with **Bubbles Below Scuba Charters** (www.bubblesbelowkauai.com; © **808/332-7333**), specializing in highly personalized small-group dives with an emphasis on marine biology. Based in Port Allen, the 36-foot *Kaimanu* is a custom-built Radon dive boat that comes complete with a hot shower, accommodating up to eight passengers; the 31-foot, catamaran-hulled *Dive Rocket,* also custom-built, takes just six. Standard two-tank boat dives cost $130 (if booked directly); it's $240 for the two-tank dive along the Mana Crack, an 11-mile submerged barrier reef, that includes a Napali cruise. Bubbles Below offers a three-tank trip, for experienced divers only, to more challenging locations such as the "forbidden" island of Niihau, 90 minutes by boat from Kauai, and its nearby islets of Lehua and Kaula; locations vary by time of year and conditions. You should also be willing to share water space with the resident sharks. The all-day, three-tank trip costs $190 (booked directly), including tanks, weights, dive computer, lunch, drinks, and marine guide (if you need gear, it's $30 more). Ride-alongs for nondivers and crustacean-focused twilight/night dives are also available.

On the South Shore, the highly regarded **Fathom Five Adventures** (www. fathomfive.com; ✆ **808/742-6991**) offers customized boat dives for up to six passengers, starting at $125 for a two-tank dive up to $350 for a three-tank Niihau dive ($40 more for gear rental.)

GREAT SHORE DIVES Spectacular shoreline dive sites on the North Shore include beautiful **Kee Beach,** where the road ends and the dropoff near the reef begs for underwater exploration (check with lifeguards first). **Cannons,** east of Haena Beach Park, has lots of vibrant marine life in its sloping offshore reef. Another good bet is the intricate underwater topography off **Tunnels Beach,** also known as Makua Beach. The wide reef here makes for some fabulous snorkeling and diving, especially during the calm summer months. (See "Beaches" on p. 446 for location details.)

On the South Shore, head to the right of the tombolo (sand bar) splitting **Poipu Beach** if you want to catch a glimpse of sea turtles; it's officially known as Nukumoi Point but nicknamed Tortugas (Spanish for "turtle"). The former boat launch at **Koloa Landing** has a horseshoe-shape reef that's teeming with tropical fish. It's off Hoonani Road, about a quarter-mile south of Lawai Road near Poipu traffic circle. **Sheraton Caverns,** located off the Sheraton Kauai, is also popular—its three large underwater lava tubes are usually filled with marine life.

If you want a guided shore dive, **Fathom Five Adventures** (see above) will take you out for $75 for one tank and $90 for two tanks year-round on the South Shore; spring through fall, it offers two-dive shore dives at Tunnels for $165, with a one-tank night version for $100.

Snorkeling

You can buy snorkel gear at any number of stores on the island, but with luggage fees going up, I find it easier just to rent. Opened in late 2013, **Kauai Bound** (www.kauaiboundstore.com; ✆ **808/320-3779**) provides top-quality snorkel sets, including carrying bags, fish ID card, and no-fog drops, for $7.50 a day or $28 a week (child's version $5 daily, $20 weekly) at its store in Anchor Cove Shopping Center, 3366 Waapa Rd. (at Rice St.); you can also rent pro-level underwater cameras ($20–$30 a day), camera accessories, and other outdoor gear here.

Robert Wintner, the quirky founder of the statewide chain **Snorkel Bob's** (www.snorkelbob.com), is a tireless advocate for reef protection, funding campaigns for more legislation through the Snorkel Bob Foundation. His two stores here rent a great variety of snorkel gear, with the convenience factor of 24-hour and interisland drop-offs, plus discounts on reputable snorkeling cruises. The East Side location (✆ **808/823-9433**) is at 4-734 Kuhio Hwy. (Hwy. 56), Kapaa, just north of Coconut Marketplace, while the South Shore outlet (✆ **808/ 742-2206**) is at 3236 Poipu Rd., Koloa, just south of Old Koloa Town.

In general, North Shore snorkeling sites are safest in summer and South Shore sites in winter, but all are subject to changing conditions; check daily ocean reports such as those on **Kauaiexplorer.com** before venturing out. See "Boat & Raft (Zodiac) Tours" for snorkel cruises to the reefs off Napali and Niihau. The following shoreline recommendations apply in times of low surf (see "Beaches" on p. 446 for more detailed descriptions):

EAST SIDE   The two rock-walled ponds at **Lydgate Park,** just south of the Wailua River, are great for novices and young snorkelers.

NORTH SHORE   **Kee Beach,** located at the end of Highway 560, and **Tunnels (Makua) Beach,** about a mile before the end of Highway 560 in Haena, offer the greatest variety of fish. **Anini Beach,** located off the northern Kalihiwai Road, between mile markers 25 and 26 on Highway 56, south of Princeville, has the most protected waters.

SOUTH SHORE   The right side of the tombolo, the narrow strip of sand dividing **Poipu Beach** into two coves, has good snorkeling but can be crowded. You can also follow the beach path west past the Waiohai Marriott to the pocket cove in front of Koa Kea Hotel; if the tide is high (and calm) enough, you can observe its teeming marine life. A boat ramp leads into the rocky cove of **Koloa Landing** (see "Scuba Diving," above), where on clear days you'll spot large corals, turtles, and plenty of reef fish. (*Note:* Rain brings in stream runoff, which turns the water murky.) Tour groups often visit rock-studded **Lawai Beach** off Lawai Road, next to the Beach House Restaurant; watch out for sea urchins as you swim among parrotfish, Moorish idols, and other reef fish.

WEST SIDE   **Salt Pond Beach,** off Highway 50 near Hanapepe, has good snorkeling around the two rocky points, home to hundreds of tropical fish.

Sport Fishing

DEEP-SEA FISHING   Kauai's fishing fleet is smaller than others in the islands, but the fish are still out there. All you need to bring is your lunch and your luck. **Sportfish Hawaii** (www.sportfishhawaii.com; **℃ 877/388-1376** or 808/396-2607), which inspects and books boats on all the islands, has prices ranging from $1,250 to $1,495 for an 8-hour exclusive charter (up to six passengers), $950 to $1,195 for a 6-hour charter, and $675 to $795 for 4 hours. Rates may be better, though, booking directly through local operators such as Captain Lance Keener at **Ohana Fishing Charters** (www.fishingcharterskauai.com; **℃ 800/713-4682**); excursions on the wide and stable 30-foot *Hoo Maikai* out of Kapaa start at $140 per person for a 4-hour shared trip up to $1,250 for a private 8-hour trip (up to six passengers). Mindful of how weather can change over the course of the day, Captain Harry Shigekane of **Happy Hunter Sport Fishing** (www.happyhuntersportfishing.com; **℃ 808/639-4351**) offers only private 4-hour tours ($625) aboard his 41-foot Pacifica, the *Happy Hunter II,* out of Nawiliwili Small Boat Harbor.

FRESHWATER FISHING   Freshwater fishing is big on Kauai, thanks to the dozens of manmade reservoirs. They're full of largemouth, smallmouth, and peacock bass (also known as *tucunare*). The **Puu Lua Reservoir,** in Kokee State Park, also has rainbow trout and is stocked by the state every year, but has a limited season, in recent years mid-June to the end of September.

Sportfish Hawaii (www.sportfishhawaii.com; **℃ 877/388-1376** or 808/396-2607) offers guided bass-fishing trips starting at $265 for two people for a half-day and $375 for one person for a full day, beginning at 6:30am in Kapaa.

Whatever your catch, you're required to first have a **Hawaii Freshwater Fishing License,** available online through the **State Department of Land and Natural Resources** (http://freshwater.ehawaii.gov) or through fishing-supply stores such as **Wal-Mart,** 3–3300 Kuhio Hwy., Lihue (✆ **808/246-1599**), or **Waipouli Variety,** 4–901 1-A Kuhio Hwy., Kapaa (✆ **808/822-1014**). A 7-day nonresident license is $10 (plus a $1 convenience fee if purchased online).

Stand-Up Paddleboarding

Like everywhere else in Hawaii, stand-up paddleboarding (SUP) has taken off on Kauai. It's easily learned when the ocean is calm, and still easier than traditional surfing if waves are involved. Lessons and equipment are generally available at all beachfront activity desks and the island's surf shops (see "Surfing," below), while Kauai's numerous rivers provide even more opportunities to practice. Kauai native and pro surfer Chava Greenlee runs **Aloha Stand Up Paddle Lessons** (www.alohasuplessonskauai.com; ✆ **808/639-8614**) at Kalapaki Beach, where he first learned to stand-up paddle; the bay offers a large, lagoon-like section ideal for beginners, plus a small surf break for more advanced paddlers. He and his fellow instructors (all licensed lifeguards) also teach SUP in Poipu, just south of the Sheraton Kauai. Two-hour group lessons (eight-person maximum) cost $75 and include 30 minutes on land and 90 minutes on water, both with instructor; lessons are offered four times a day, year-round. Walk-ups are welcome, but reservations are recommended. **Kauai Beach Boys** (www.kauaibeachboys.com; ✆ **808/742-4442**) gives 90-minute lessons three times a day at Kalapaki and Poipu beaches; the $75 fee includes a board, leash, and a rash guard (which also helps prevent sunburn).

Once you've got the hang of it, **Nukumoi Surf Shop,** across from Brennecke's Beach (www.nukumoisurf.com; ✆ **808/742-8019**), will rent you boards with paddles for $20 an hour, $80 a day, or $250 a week. **Pedal 'n Paddle,** in Hanalei's Ching Young Village Shopping Center (www.pedalnpaddle.com; ✆ **808/826-9069**), directs paddleboarders up the Hanalei River or into the bay, depending upon conditions; the $40 daily rental includes board, paddle, leash, foam pads, and straps for easy carrying.

Outfitters Kauai (www.outfitterskauai.com; ✆ **808/742-9667**) combines a SUP lesson with a 2-mile, downwind paddle on the Huleia River and hike to a swimming hole; a motorized outrigger brings you back up the river. The half-day trip starts at 7:45am and costs $131 for adults and $100 for kids 4 to 12.

Surfing

With the global expansion in surfing's popularity, the most accessible breaks around the island have plenty of contenders. Practice patience and courtesy when lining up to catch a wave, and ask for advice from local surf shops before heading out on your own. **Hanalei Bay**'s winter surf is the most popular on the island, but it's for experts only. **Poipu Beach** is an excellent spot to learn to surf; the waves are generally smaller, and—best of all—nobody laughs when you wipe out. To find out where the surf's up, go to **Kauai Explorer Ocean Report** (www.kauaiexplorer.com/ocean_report) or call the **Weather Service** (✆ **808/245-3564**).

Poipu is also the site of numerous surfing schools; the oldest and best is **Margo Oberg's School of Surfing** (www.surfonkauai.com; ✆ **808/332-6100**),

Surfing near Poipu Beach.

at the Sheraton Kauai. A world surfing champion at age 15, Oberg founded the Poipu school in 1977 and now runs it with the help of eldest son Shane and friendly, young pro instructors. Two-hour lessons cost $68, including 90 minutes of group instruction (up to six students) and 30 minutes of additional practice, with soft-topped boards for beginners and booties provided. If you want to keep practicing, it's easy to rent from **Nukumoi Surf Shop** (www.nukumoisurf.com; © **808/742-8019**), right across from Brennecke's Beach at 2100 Hoone Rd., Koloa. Nukumoi charges $6 an hour, $25 a day, or $75 a week for soft boards; the hard (epoxy) boards, for experienced surfers, cost $8 an hour, $30 a day, or $90 a week.

If you're staying on the North Shore, consider a lesson from **Hawaiian Surfing Adventures** (www.hawaiiansurfingadventures.com; © **808/482-0749**), which offers smaller group lessons (maximum of four students) that include 90 minutes of instruction, up to an hour of practice, and soft boards for $65. The exact surf spot in Hanalei will vary by conditions; check-in for lessons is at the **Hawaiian Beach Boys Surf Shop,** 5-5134 Kuhio Hwy. (just south of Aku Rd., on the right when heading north). It also offers daily rentals starting at $20 for soft boards and $25 for the expert epoxy boards, with discounts for longer periods, as does **Hanalei Surf Co.** (www.hanaleisurf.com/rentals; © **808/826-9000**), 5–5161 Kuhio Hwy. (in Hanalei Center), Hanalei.

Tubing

Back in the days of the sugar plantations, local kids would grab inner tubes and jump in the irrigation ditches crisscrossing the cane fields for an exciting ride. Today you can enjoy this (formerly illegal) activity by "tubing" the flumes and ditches of the old Lihue Plantation with **Kauai Backcountry Adventures** (www.kauaibackcountry.com; © **888/270-0555** or 808/245-2506). Passengers are taken in 4WD vehicles high into the mountains above Lihue to look at vistas generally off-limits to the public. At the flumes, you will be outfitted with a giant tube, gloves, and headlamp (for the long passageways through the tunnels, hand-dug circa 1870). All you do is jump in the water, and the gentle flow will carry you through forests, into tunnels, and finally to a mountain swimming hole, where a picnic lunch is served. The 3-hour tours are $102, open to ages 5 and up (minimum height 43 in., maximum weight 300 pounds). Swimming is not necessary—all you do is relax and drift downstream—but do wear a hat, swimsuit, sunscreen, and shoes that can get wet, and bring a towel, change of clothing, and insect repellent. Tours are offered at 9 and 10am, and 1 and 2pm. *Tip:* The water is always cool, so starting later in the day might be more pleasant.

Windsurfing & Kite Surfing

With a long, fringing reef protecting shallow waters, the North Shore's Anini Beach is one of the safest places for beginners to learn windsurfing. Lessons and equipment rental are available at **Windsurf Kauai** (www.windsurf-kauai.com; © **808/828-6838**). Owner Celeste Harzel has been teaching windsurfing on Anini Beach for decades; she has special equipment to help beginners learn the sport, plus refresher and advanced classes. A 2-hour lesson is $100 and includes equipment and instruction. If you want to keep going, she'll rent the equipment for $25 an hour.

Serious windsurfers and kitesurfers (that is, those who travel with their own gear) will want to check out **Haena Beach Park** and **Tunnels Beach** on the North Shore, and the **Mahaulepu** coastline (including Mahaulepu/Gillin's Beach and Kawailoa Bay) on the South Shore.

OTHER OUTDOOR ACTIVITIES
Biking

Although the main highway has few stretches truly safe for cycling, there are several great places on Kauai for two-wheeling. The **Poipu** area has wide, flat paved roads and several dirt cane roads (especially around Mahaulepu), while the **East Side** has two completed legs of the **Ka Ala Hele Makalae** multi-use trail (www.kauaipath.org/kauaicoastalpath), eventually intended to extend from Anahola to the airport in Lihue. For now, the Lydgate Park leg stretches 2.5 miles south from the Wailua River, while another 4.1-mile leg links Kapaa's Lihi Park to Ahihi Point, just past Donkey (Kumukumu) Beach, 1.5 miles north of Kealia Beach Park. Mountain bikers can also ride the scenic 5-mile **Wai Koa Loop Trail** at the Anaina Hou Community Park (p. 433) in Kilauea, or attempt more challenging trails in actual mountains, if it's not too muddy.

Several places rent mountain bikes, road bikes, and beach cruisers, including helmets and locks, with sizeable discounts for multiday rentals. In Poipu, **Outfitters Kauai** (www.outfitterskauai.com; © **888/742-9887** or 808/742-9667) charges $25 a day for hybrid bikes and $45 for Kona brand off-road and road bikes; reservations are recommended. The shop is at 2827 Poipu Rd., Koloa, in the Kukuiula Market strip, 1¼ miles south of Koloa town, across from the fire station; look for the yellow mini-submarine out front. Outfitters Kauai also leads twice-daily, 4½-hour **downhill Waimea Canyon bicycle tours** ($110 adults, $90 kids 12 to 14) that follow the Kokee Road spur to Kekaha. Some find the experience memorable, but I think there are better places on Kauai to cycle and certainly better ways to see the canyon.

Kapaa has choices for both adventurers itching to explore the single-track trails in the mountains and vacationers just wanting to pedal the coastal path for a couple of hours. **Kauai Cycle** (www.kauaicycle.com; ✆ **808/821-2115**) offers cruisers for $20 a day, but specializes in road and mountain bikes for $30 a day ($45 full-suspension), with maps and advice customized to abilities and current trail conditions. No reservations are needed; just walk in to its store and repair shop, which also sells clothing and gear, at 4-934 Kuhio Hwy., Kapaa, north of Ala Road, on the ocean side (across from Taco Bell). Families in particular will want to take note of the shiny Trek beach cruisers, tandems, and trailers from **Coconut Coasters** (www.coconutcoasters.com; ✆ **808/822-7368**) at 4-1586 Kuhio Hwy., Kapaa, just north of Kou Street on the ocean side. Half-day rentals start at $18; reservations are recommended.

On the North Shore, **Pedal 'n Paddle** in Hanalei (www.pedalnpaddle. com; ✆ **808/826-9069**) rents beach cruisers for $15 a day and hybrids for $20; it's in the Ching Young Village Shopping Center, 5-5190 Kuhio Hwy., on the ocean side just past Aku Road. In Kilauea, the rental mountain bikes from **Namahana Cafe** (www.namahanacafe.org/bike-rentals; ✆ **808/828-2118**) in Ainana Hou Community Park can be used on the Wai Koa Loop Trail or taken elsewhere; the rate is $25 for 1 to 6 hours and $33 for 24 hours.

Birding

Kauai provides more than 80 species of birds—not counting the "wild" chickens seen at every roadside attraction. To identify what you're seeing, check out photographer Jim Denny's **www.kauaibirds.com** or buy his excellent "Birds of Kauai" handbook online or in local gift shops. Coastal and lowland areas, including the wildlife refuges at Kilauea Point (p. 435) and along the Hanalei River (p. 435), are home to introduced species and endangered native waterfowl and migratory shorebirds; the cooler uplands of Kokee State Park shelter native woodland species, who were able to escape mosquito-borne diseases that killed off lowland natives.

David Kuhn leads custom bird-watching excursions, pointing out Hawaii's rarest birds on his **Terran Tours** (www.soundshawaiian.com; ✆ **808/335-0398**), using a four-wheel-drive vehicle to access remote areas. Tours start at $300 for a half-day, with longer periods available. Carl Berg, who holds a PhD in zoology from University of Hawaii, offers personalized tours, starting at $50 per couple per hour; contact **Hawaiian Wildlife Tours** (www.hawaiianwildlife tours.com; ✆ **808/639-2968**).

Golf

It's no wonder that Kauai's exceptional beauty has inspired some exceptionally beautiful links. More surprising is the presence of two lovely, inexpensive public courses: the 9-hole **Kukuiolono** on the South Shore, and the even more impressive 18-hole **Wailua Golf Course** on the East Side; see details below.

Value-seekers who don't mind occasionally playing next to a Costco and suburban Lihue homes—amid many more panoramas of several soaring green ridges—will appreciate **Puakea** (www.puakeagolf.com; ✆ **808/245-8756**), part of AOL founder Steve Case's Grove Farm portfolio. Greens fees for 18 holes are $99, $59 after 11am, and $35 after 3pm; it's $35 for 9 holes anytime. It's centrally located, at 4150 Nuhou St., off Nawiliwili Road, Lihue. (Greens fees in this section include cart rentals unless noted.)

Bargain hunters may also call **Stand-by Golf** (www.hawaiistandbygolf. com; ☏ **888/645-2665**) between 7am and 10pm daily for discounted greens fees of up to 30 percent off same-day or future golfing at **Kauai Lagoons** and **Kiahuna golf clubs,** described below. Stand-by Golf says it can guarantee same-day tee times, too, for last-minute types.

To play the newest course on the Garden Island, you'll need to spring for one of the $1,000-plus-a-night Club Cottages and Club Villas at Kukuiula (www. parrishkauai.com/kukuiula; ☏ **800/325-5701**) or make friends with a member of **Kukuiula** (www.kukuiula.com; ☏ **855/742-0234**) with exclusive access to Tom Weiskopf's rolling 18-hole course through gardens, orchards, and South Shore grasslands. Money can't buy your way out of dealing with trade winds, wherever you play, so start early for best scores.

EAST SIDE

Kauai Lagoons Golf Club ★★ Jack Nicklaus designed the 18-hole Kiele Course in the late 1980s, and returned for a 2011 makeover that created a half-mile series of four oceanfront holes, said to be the longest such stretch in the state. Featuring beautiful mountain, harbor, and *moana* (ocean) views, they're now part of the **Kiele Moana Nine;** the former back 9 are named **Kiele Mauka Nine,** reflecting their *mauka* (toward the mountains) location, behind the Kauai Marriott Resort. Together they're known as the **Kiele Championship Course.** As part of the renovations, Nicklaus chose the top 9 holes from his former 18-hole Mokihana Course to create the **Kiele Waikahe Nine,** perfect for juniors or beginners, with lots of open fairways. There's a free shuttle from the airport, 5 minutes away. Facilities include a driving range, snack bar, a pro shop, practice greens, a clubhouse, and club and shoe rental.

3351 Hoolaulea Way, Lihue, next to Kauai Lagoons and Kauai Marriott Resort. www.kauailagoons golf.com. ☏ **800/634-6400** or 808/241-6000. Greens fees $205 ($150 for Marriott guests, $155 for guests of other select hotels), $115–$135 after noon; subsequent rounds $95. Juniors 6–17 $60 anytime. From the airport, take Hwy. 51 south to a left on Rice Rd. Turn left at entrance to Kauai Marriott Resort and drive past hotel. Golf parking area is 500 yards ahead, on the left; golf shop and bag drop are on the right.

Wailua Golf Course ★★ Highly rated by both "Golf Digest" and the Golf Channel, this coconut palm–dotted, largely seafront course in windy Wailua has hosted three U.S. amateur championships. Spread along the *makai* (ocean) side of the main highway, the first 9 holes were built in the 1930s; the late Kauai golf legend Toyo Shirai designed the second 9 in 1961. Nonresident rates start at just $48 (plus $20 for a cart) for 18 holes. Facilities include the **Over Park** snack bar/restaurant and bar, locker room with showers, driving range, practice greens, and club rentals.

3-5350 Kuhio Hwy. (Hwy. 56), Wailua, 3 miles north of Lihue airport. www.kauai.gov/golf. ☏ **808/241-6666.** Greens fees $48 weekdays, $60 weekends/holidays, half-price after 2pm or for back nine only in morning. Cart $20 ($11 for 9 holes).

NORTH SHORE

Prince Golf Course at Princeville ★★ Here's your chance to play one of the best courses in Hawaii. Reopened in 2012 after a $5-million renovation, this Robert Trent Jones, Jr.–designed devil of a course sits on 390 acres molded to create ocean views from every hole. Some holes have a waterfall backdrop to the greens, others shoot into the hillside, and the famous par-4 12th hole has a long tee shot off a cliff to a narrow, jungle-lined fairway 100 feet below. This is the most challenging course on Kauai; accuracy is key here, or your ball will land in lushly vegetated canyons and other tropical greenery. You can always console yourself later at the clubhouse's **Tavern at Princeville,** created by celebrated chef Roy Yamaguchi. The practice facility's Mini Prince Par 3 Course, a 6-hole, 424-yard course with larger putting cups (open daily 4pm), makes for a unique, inexpensive family outing before dinner. Other facilities include a clubhouse, locker rooms, golf shop, and club rentals.

5-3900 Kuhio Hwy. (Hwy. 56), Princeville. www.princeville.com/golf. ✆ **800/826-5001.** Greens fees $250; $165 after noon; online rates as low as $165–$190. Mini Prince: $15 adults, $5 unaccompanied juniors 12–17, including clubs; free for adults who played the Prince Course same day and juniors 17 and under with paying adult. From Kilauea, take Hwy. 56 north to mile marker 27; the course is on the right.

Makai Golf Club ★ Robert Trent Jones, Jr., returned in 2009 to redesign the 27 holes he created here in 1971, his very first course on Kauai. What emerged in 2010: the 18-hole championship Makai Course, which winds around ocean bluffs and tropical forest with compelling sea and mountain views, and the family-friendly 9-hole Woods Course, in the sylvan setting its name suggests. There's a "time par" of 4 hours, 18 minutes, here, to keep golfers on track. Other facilities include a clubhouse, a pro shop, practice facilities, a restaurant, and club rentals. **Note:** Guests of the St. Regis and Westin Princeville Ocean Resort Villas should inquire at the golf shop or through their respective concierges about special discounts.

4080 Lei O Papa Rd., Princeville. www.makaigolf.com. ✆ **808/826-1912.** Greens fees $239; $179 after noon. Woods 9 $55 for adults; $28 for juniors 16–17 and children 6–15 unaccompanied by adult; free for children 6–15 with paying adult. Take Hwy. 56 to the Princeville main entrance, turn right, go 1 mile and course is on the left.

SOUTH SHORE

Kiahuna Golf Club ★ This par-70, 6,353-yard course designed by Robert Trent Jones, Jr., is a veritable wildlife sanctuary, where black-crowned night herons, Hawaiian stilts, and moorhens fish along Waikomo Stream, and outcroppings of lava tubes by the second fairway hold rare blind spiders. You'll want to keep your eyes peeled for remains of a stone-walled *heiau* (temple) and a Portuguese home from the early 1800s, whose former inhabitants lie in a nearby crypt—and watch out for the mango tree on the par 4, 440-yard hole 6. Facilities include a driving range, practice greens, and a restaurant, **Joe's on the Green,** that's popular with locals.

2545 Kiahuna Plantation Dr. (off Poipu Rd.), Koloa. www.kiahunagolf.com. ✆ **808/742-9595.** Greens fees $105, $75 after 2pm. $47 for juniors 17 and under with paying adult.

Kukuiolono Golf Course ★★ Although not on a resort, this 9-hole hilltop course has unbeatable views to match an unbeatable price: $9 for all day, plus $9 for an optional cart. The course is part of woodsy **Kukuiolono Park** (p. 439), which includes a Japanese garden and Hawaiian rock artifacts; both the garden and the course were developed by pineapple tycoon Walter McBryde, who bequeathed it to the public in 1930. The course is well maintained, given the price, with relatively few fairway hazards (barring a wild pig now and then).

Facilities include a driving range, practice greens, club rental, and **Birdies** restaurant, in the handsome yet playful clubhouse, renovated in 2013.

Kukuiolono Park, 854 Puu Rd., Kalaheo. ℂ **808/332-9151.** Greens fees $9 per day, optional cart rental $9; cash only. From Lihue, take Hwy. 50 west into Kalaheo, turn left on Papalina Rd. and drive uphill for nearly a mile. Look for sign at right; the entrance has huge iron gates and stone pillars.

Poipu Bay Golf Course ★★ This 7,123-yard, par-72 course with a links-style layout was, for years, the home of the PGA Grand Slam of Golf. Designed by Robert Trent Jones, Jr., the challenging course features undulating greens and water hazards on 8 of the holes. The par-4 16th hole has the coastline weaving along the entire left side. The most striking hole is the 201-yard par-3 on the 17th, which has an elevated tee next to an ancient *heiau* (place of worship) and a Hawaiian rock wall along the fairway. Facilities include a restaurant, lounge, locker room, pro shop, club rentals, and practice facilities (off grass).

2250 Ainako St. (off Poipu Rd., across from the Grand Hyatt Kauai), Koloa. www.poipubaygolf. com. ℂ **808/742-8711.** Greens fees (includes $5 resort fee): $245 before noon ($170 for Grand Hyatt guests); $155 after noon; $100 after 2pm. Second (non-twilight) round within 10 days, $125.

Hiking

As beautiful as Kauai's drive-up beaches and waterfalls are, some of the island's most arresting sights aren't reachable by the road: You've got to hoof it. Highlights are listed below; for descriptions of the 34 trails in Kauai's state parks and forestry reserves, check out **Na Ala Hele Trail & Access System** (http://hawaiitrails. ehawaii.gov; ℂ **808/274-3433**).

Note: When heavy rains fall on Kauai, normally placid rivers and streams overflow, causing flash floods on some roads and trails. Check the weather forecast, especially November through March, and avoid dry streambeds, which flood quickly. Always bring more drinking water than you think you need, too. Stream water is unsafe to drink, due to the risk of leptospirosis.

Among the guides, Micco Godinez of **Kayak Kauai** (www.kayakkauai.com; ℂ **888/596-3853** or 808/826-9844) is just as expert on land as he is at sea. He and his savvy guides lead regular trips to Waipoo Falls through Kokee/Waimea Canyon ($126), Napali's Hanakapiai Beach ($126) and Hanakapiai Falls ($168), Kapaa's Sleeping Giant ($81), and the Awaawapuhi/Nualolo loop trail ($231) that starts in Kokee and leads to dazzling overlooks of Napali. Naturalists with **Kauai Nature Adventures** (www.kauainaturetours.com; ℂ **888/233-8365** or 808/742-8305) lead a similar variety of day hikes, focusing on Kauai's unique geology, environment, and culture; they're $135 to $165 adults and $100 to $135 for children 7 to 12, including lunch.

The Kauai chapter of the **Sierra Club** (http://hawaii.sierraclub.org/kauai) offers four to seven different guided hikes around the island each month, varying from easy 2-milers to 7-mile-plus treks for serious hikers only; they may include service work such as beach cleanups and trail clearing. Online listings include descriptions and local phone contacts; requested donation per hike is $5 adults and $1 for children under 18 and Sierra Club members.

EAST SIDE

The dappled green wooded ridges of the Lihue-Koloa and Nounou (Sleeping Giant) forest reserves provide the best hiking opportunities here. From Kuamoo Road (Hwy. 580) past Opaekaa Falls, you can park at the trailhead for the easy,

2-mile **Kuamoo Trail,** which connects with the steeper, 1.5-mile **Nounou West Trail;** both have picnic shelters. Stay on Kuamoo Road till just before the Keahua Arboretum to pick up the scenic, 2.1-mile **Kuilau Trail,** often used by horses, which can be linked with the more rugged, 2.5-mile **Moalepe Trail,** ending at the top of Olohena Road in Kapaa. In the arboretum, you'll find the trailhead for the challenging **Powerline Trail,** an unmaintained path that follows electric lines all the way to Princeville's Kapaka Street, on the mountain side of the Kuhio Highway (Hwy. 56); avoid if it's been raining (the mud can suck your sneakers off, or worse.). A steady climb, but worth the vista at the top, is the 2-mile **Nounou East Trail,** which takes you 960 feet up a mountain known as Sleeping Giant (that really does look like a giant resting on his back); the trail ends at a picnic shelter on his "chest," and connects with the west leg about 1.5 miles in. The east trailhead, which has parking, is on Kapaa's Haleilio Road; turn inland just past mile marker 6 on Kuhio Highway and head 1¼ miles uphill.

NORTH SHORE

Traversing Kauai's amazingly beautiful Napali Coast, the 11-mile (one-way) **Kalalau Trail** is the definition of breathtaking: Not only is the scenery magnificent, but even serious hikers will huff and puff over its extremely strenuous up-and-down route, made even trickier to negotiate by winter rains. It's on every serious hiker's bucket list, and a destination for seemingly every young backpacking bohemian on the island. That's one reason a camping permit ($20 per night; http://camping.ehawaii.gov) is required for those heading beyond the 2-mile mark of Hanakapiai Beach; the permits often sell out up to a year in advance (see "Camping & Cabins," p. 486).

People in good but not great physical shape can still tackle the 2-mile stretch from the trail head at Kee Beach to Hanakapiai, which starts with a mile-long climb; the reward of Napali vistas starts about .5 mile in. You'll see the occasional barefoot local surfer on the first 2 miles, but wear sturdy shoes (preferably hiking boots) and a hat, and carry plenty of water. The trail can be very narrow and slippery in places; don't bring children who might need to be carried. At Hanakapiai Beach, sandy in summer and mostly rocks in winter, strong currents have swept more than 80 visitors to their deaths over the years; best just to admire the view. Those able to rock-hop can clamber another 2 miles inland to the 120-foot Hanakapiai Falls, but only when it has not been raining heavily. Allow 3 to 4 hours for the round-trip trek to the beach, and 7 to 8 hours with the falls added in.

Nearly as beautiful, but much less demanding and much less crowded, is the 2.5-mile **Okolehao Trail** in Hanalei, which climbs 1,232 feet to a ridge overlooking Hanalei Bay and the verdant valley. It starts at a marked parking area off Ohiki Road, inland from Highway 560, just past the Hanalei Bridge.

SOUTH SHORE

At the end of Shipwrecks (Keoneloa) Beach, in front of the Grand Hyatt Kauai, the limestone headland of Makawehi Point marks the start of the **Mahaulepu Heritage Trail** (www.hikemahaulepu.org), an easy coastal walk—after the first few minutes uphill—along lithified sand dunes, pinnacles, craggy coves, and ancient Hawaiian rock structures. Inland lie the green swath of Poipu Bay Golf Course and the Haupu summit. Keep a safe distance from the fragile edges of cliffs, and give the green sea turtles and endangered Hawaiian monk seals a wide berth, too. It's 1.5 miles to the overlook of Mahaulepu (Gillin's) Beach, but you can keep on another 2 miles to windy Haula Beach.

WEST SIDE

Some of Hawaii's best hikes are found among the 45 miles of maintained trails in **Kokee State Park** (p. 441), 4,345 acres of rainforest with striking views of the Napali Coast from up to 4,000 feet above, and the drier but no less dazzling **Waimea Canyon State Park** (p. 443). Pick up a trail map and tips at the **Kokee Museum** (www.kokee.org; © **808/335-9975**), which also describes a number of trails in the two parks on its website.

The best way to experience the bold colors and stark formations of Waimea Canyon is on the **Canyon Trail,** which starts after a .8-mile forested walk down and up unpaved Halemanu Road, off Kokee Road (Hwy. 550) between mile markers 14 and 15. From there it's another mile to a small waterfall pool, lined with yellow ginger, that lies above the main cascade of 800-foot **Waipoo Falls;** you won't be able to see the latter, but you can hear it, and gaze far across the canyon to try to spot the lookout points you passed on the way up. On the way back, check out the short spur called the **Cliff Trail** for more vistas. (**Note:** Families can hike this trail, but be mindful of the steep dropoffs.)

Two more challenging hikes beckon in dry conditions. The 6.2-mile round-trip **Awaawapuhi Trail** takes at least 3 hours—1 hour down, 2 hours coming back up, depending on your fitness level—but it offers a jaw-dropping overlook for two Napali valleys, Awaawapuhi (named for the wild ginger blossom) and Nualolo. Usually well-maintained, it drops about 1,600 feet through native forests to a thin precipice with a guardrail at the overlook. (**Note:** The **Nualolo Cliff Trail** that connects with the even more strenuous 8-mile **Nualolo Trail** was closed at press time due to significant erosion.) The trail head is just past mile marker 17 on Kokee Road, at a clearing on the left.

Slippery mud can make the **Pihea Trail** impassable, but when the red clay is firm beneath your feet, it's another must-do for fit hikers. Starting at the end of the Puu O Kila Lookout at the end of Kokee Road (Hwy. 550), the trail provides fantastic views of Kalalau Valley and the distant ocean before turning into a boardwalk through a bog that connects with the **Alakai Swamp Trail,** which you'll want to follow to its end at the Kilohana Overlook; if it's not socked in with fog, you'll have an impressive view of Wainiha Valley and the North Shore. The Pihea-Alakai Swamp round-trip route is 8.6 miles; allow at least 4 hours, and be prepared for drizzle or rain.

Horseback Riding

Ride a horse across the wide-open pastures of a working ranch under volcanic peaks and rein up near a waterfall pool, or explore a pristine shoreline hidden by former sugarcane field: You'll see parts of Kauai many have missed, while helping keep its treasured *paniolo* (cowboy) culture alive. Be sure to pack a pair of jeans or long pants, and closed-toe shoes.

CJM Country Stables ★★ A trail ride through the rugged Mahaulepu region, passing through former plantation fields and natural landscape to the untrammeled sandy beaches under the shadow of Haupu Ridge, may well be the highlight of your trip. CJM's standard rides both include 2 hours of riding, but the Secret Beach Picnic Ride ($140) adds an hour for lunch and beach exploration; reserve early. Private rides, which allow paces faster than a walk, are also available. **Note:** CJM also hosts rodeos throughout the year that are open to the public (see www.princekuhio.net and www.koloaplantationdays.com for details).

9

Off Poipu Rd., Koloa. From Grand Hyatt Kauai, head 1½ miles east on unpaved Poipu Rd. and turn right at sign for stables. www.cjmstables.com. ℭ **808/742-6096. 2-hr. Mahaulepu Beach Ride:** $110; Mon–Sat 9:30am and 2pm. **3-hr Secret Beach Picnic Ride:** $140; Wed and Fri 1pm. Private rides from $140 per hour.

Princeville Ranch Adventures ★★   There's no nose-to-tail riding at this working North Shore ranch, owned by descendants of the area's first missionaries. Instead, horses amble across wide-open pastures with mountain and ocean views as you learn about Kauai's cowboy history and this distinctive landscape. The "ride n' glide" option ($145) takes you to a secluded valley that you traverse via ziplines (see "Ziplining," p. 470), while the Waterfall Picnic Ride ($135) leads to a short (but steep) hike down to a trail to a swimming pool at the base of an 80-foot waterfall; after a picnic lunch, you'll climb out via a 10-foot rock wall. Both rides last 3 hours, with 90 minutes in the saddle. Less exertion is required on the 2-hour Paniolo Ride ($99) through pastures and the occasional herd of cattle. **Note:** Tours go out rain or shine, just like the cowboys.

Check in ocean side of Hwy. 56, just north of mile marker 27, Princeville. www.princevilleranch. com. ℭ **888/955-7669** or 808/826-7669. Booking by phone required. **Ride N' Glide:** $145; Mon–Sat 1:30pm; ages 10 and older. **Waterfall Picnic Ride:** $135; Mon–Sat 9am, noon, and 1pm (8am June–Aug); ages 8 and older. **Paniolo Ride:** $99; Mon–Sat 10am; ages 8 and older.

Silver Falls Ranch Stables ★★   The falls here are not as impressive as those on Princeville Ranch—they're wide but not tall—but the swimming hole is equally refreshing and the scenery just as stimulating. The 300-acre ranch in Kalihiwai Valley features an 80-acre tropical garden and close-up views of the 2,800-foot Makaleha Range. The 2-hour Silver Falls Ride ($115) includes a barbecue picnic that's a cut above the usual sandwich fare on Kauai, plus a dip in the "refreshing" waterfall pool, while the 90-minute Hawaiian Discovery Ride ($99) flows flower-lined streams through the garden, home to more than 150 species of palms. Combine the two itineraries on the 3-hour Tropical Trail Adventure ($139). **Note:** At press time, **Esprit de Corps Riding Academy** (www.kauaihorses.com; ℭ **808/822-4688**), which offers rides for more advanced riders, had relocated to Silver Falls Ranch while the trail it normally uses in Wailua was awaiting repair.

Kamookoa Rd., Kilauea. From Lihue, take Hwy. 56 north past mile marker 24 to a left turn on Kahiliholo Rd. at Kahiliwai Ridge sign, follow 2¼ miles to a left on Kamookoa Rd. www.silver fallsranch.com. ℭ **808/828-6718. Discovery Ride:** $99. **Silver Falls Ride:** $115. **Tropical Trails:** $139. All rides offered 3 times daily 9am–3:30pm June–Aug, twice daily Sept–May.

Tennis

Public tennis courts are managed by the **Kauai County Parks and Recreation Department** (www.kauai.gov; click on "Government," then "Departments," then "Parks & Recreation" in the left column, and then "Parks Facilities"; ℭ **808/ 241-4460**). Its website lists the 24 public tennis courts around the island, 20 of which are lighted and all of which are free. Private courts that are open to the public include those of **Hanalei Bay Resort,** Princeville (www.hanaleibayresort.com; ℭ **808/821-8225**), which has eight courts available for $15 per person per day; the resort also offers private lessons, daily clinics, and a pro shop. Also in Princeville, the **Makai Club** (www.makaigolf.com; ℭ **808/826-1912**) charges the same per player on its four courts. The South Shore is brimming with resort courts—including those of **Sheraton Kauai, Grand Hyatt Kauai, Poipu Kai Resort**, **Nihi Kai Villas,** and **Kukuiula**—but they are restricted to overnight guests.

Ziplining

Kauai apparently has Costa Rica to thank for its profusion of ziplines, the metal cable-and-pulley systems that allow harness-wearing riders to "zip" over valleys, forests, and other beautiful but inaccessible areas. After reading a "National Geographic" article about Costa Rica's rainforest canopy tours, Outfitters Kauai co-founder Rick Haviland was inspired to build the Garden Isle's first zipline, on Kipu Ranch, in 2003. Others soon followed, with ever longer, higher, and faster options. It may seem like a splurge, but keep in mind that ziplines not only offer an exhilarating rush and breathtaking views, they also help keep the verdant landscape gloriously undeveloped.

Be sure to book ahead, especially for families or groups—because of the time spent on harness safety checks, tour sizes are limited—and read the fine print about height, age, and/or weight restrictions. Tours usually go out rain or shine, except in the most severe weather.

SOUTH SHORE   Opened in 2012, **Koloa Zipline** (www.koloazipline.com; © 877/ 707-7088 or 808/742-2894) has an eight-line course ($176) in Koloa that includes a 2,500-foot zip—Kauai's longest—over the Waita Reservoir. For just $10 more, the Flyin Kau'ian harness option allows you to fly like a superhero over most of the lines on the 3½- to 4-hour tour. Check in at the office at 3477-A Weliweli Rd., Koloa, behind the Old Koloa Town shops. Kauai's newest course, **Skyline Eco Adventures** (www.zipline.com; © 888/864-6947 or 808/878-8400) opened its eight-line course above Poipu in 2013 and shares a different legend of Kauai for each of the progressively longer, faster lines on the 2½- to 3-hour tour. The cost is $140 (with a 10-percent online discount); check in at the office at Shops at Kukuiula, 2829 Ala Kalanikaumaka St., Koloa.

EAST SIDE   **Outfitters Kauai** (www.outfitterskauai.com; © 888/742-9887 or 808/742-9667) updated its original zipline course on 4,000-acre Kipu Ranch in 2012; the nine-line course includes suspension bridges, tandem lines, and a "zippel" (a zipline/rappelling combo) over picturesque streams and waterfalls. The full-length, 6-hour course, called Zipline Trek Nui Nui Loa, costs $163 for adults and $142 for children 7 to 14; the six-line, 4-hour Lele Eono option is $116 for adults and $106 for children 7 to 14. My favorite, the all-day Kipu Zipline Safari ($186 adults, $146 children), includes two of the course's longest ziplines and a water zipline over a swimming hole, plus kayaking the Huleia River, hiking, swimming, and lunch. Check in at the Poipu office, 2827 Poipu Rd., Koloa, across from the fire station, or at the Outfitters Kayak Shack in Nawiliwili Small Boat Harbor at Wilcox and Niumalu roads, Lihue.

Kauai Backcountry Adventures (www.kauaibackcountry.com; © 888/ 270-0555 or 800/245-2506) is the only outfitter with excursions through 17,000 acres of former sugarcane plantation land above Lihue. In addition to its unique tubing ride (see "Tubing," p. 461), the company has a seven-line zip course leading from the lush mountainside to a bamboo grove, where you can take a dip in a swimming hole (book the 10am tour for the warmest swimming weather). The 3-hour tour costs $130 (check online for $99 special), with check-in at KBA's

ESPECIALLY FOR kids

Climbing the Wooden Jungle Gyms at Kamalani Playground (p. 432)   Located in Lydgate Park, Wailua, this unique playground has a maze of jungle gyms for kids of all ages, including an actual labyrinth. Spend an afternoon whipping down slides, exploring caves, hanging from bars, and climbing all over.

Exploring a Magical World (p. 436) **Na Aina Kai Botanical Gardens** sits on some 240 acres, sprinkled with around 70 life-size (or larger-than-life-size) whimsical bronze statues, hidden off the beaten path of the North Shore. The tropical children's garden features a gecko hedge maze, a tropical jungle gym, a treehouse in a rubber tree, and a 16-foot-tall Jack-and-the-Beanstalk giant with a 33-foot wading pool below. It's open Tuesday through Friday only, so book before you leave home to avoid disappointment.

Riding an Open-Sided Train (p. 431) The **Kauai Plantation Railway** at

Kilohana Plantation is a trip back in time (albeit on new tracks and replica cars) to the sugarcane era, with younger kids exhilarated just by the ride. Parents can justify it as an informal botany class, since passengers learn about the orchards, gardens, and forests they pass along the 2½-mile journey. Children of all ages will enjoy the stop to feed goats, chickens, and wild pigs (as long as they watch their fingers).

office at 3-4131 Kuhio Hwy. (Hwy. 56), Hanamaulu, between Hanamaulu Road and Laulima Street.

The ecology-focused **Just Live! Zipline Tours** (www.ziplinetourskauai. com; © **808/482-1295**) offers three tours ranging from 2½ to 4½ hours ($79–$125). All glide over forest canopy in multiple shades of green, and the longest includes a 60-foot rock climbing wall and 100-foot rappelling tower. The online-only Early Bird Special offers $20 to $30 off tours with 7 and 7:45am check-ins, held at the office/outdoor gear store in Anchor Cove Shopping Center, 3416 Rice St., Lihue, between the Kauai Marriott Resort and Nawiliwili Harbor.

NORTH SHORE   Princeville Ranch Adventures (www.princevilleranch.com; © **888/955-7669** or 808/826-7669) If you just want to zip the nine lines over this verdant valley, the 3½-hour Zip Express Tour ($125) is for you, but it would be a shame, particularly in summer, to miss the chance to swim in a waterfall pool offered by the 4½-hour Zip N' Dip ($145, including picnic lunch). The company also pairs ziplines with its popular horseback rides and kayak/hike excursions (3 and 4½ hours, respectively; $145). *Note:* The latter Jungle Valley Adventure is unique in that it allows children as young as 5 and weighing as little as 50 pounds to zip on the two 400-foot-plus lines included on the tour.

WHERE TO STAY ON KAUAI

To avoid long drives, it pays to base your lodgings on the kind of vacation you envision, and consider dividing your time among locations. The island's East Side makes the most sense for those planning to divide their time equally among island sights; however, the best resorts for families and winter weather are on the South Shore. The most gorgeous scenery and best summertime ocean conditions are on the North Shore. If you're planning more than 1 day of hiking in Waimea Canyon or Kokee, or just want to experience the low-key island lifestyle, the West Side will definitely suit.

Taxes of 13.42 percent are added to all hotel bills. Parking is free, and pools are outdoors unless otherwise noted. Parking, Internet, and resort fees where applicable are charged daily; "cleaning" fees refer to one-time charges for cleaning after your stay, not daily housekeeping—the latter may be available for an additional fee for condos and other vacation rentals.

East Side

Convenient to all parts of the island (except during rush hour), Lihue and the Coconut Coast have the greatest number of budget motels, affordable beachfront condos, and moderately priced hotel rooms, along with a couple of posh resorts. Bed-and-breakfasts and vacation rentals in rural and residential areas such as Anahola and upcountry Kapaa are outside the official "visitor destination

hot-button issue: VACATION RENTALS & B&BS

As on other Hawaiian Islands, vacation rentals and bed-and-breakfasts outside of areas zoned for tourism have become a hot-button issue for many on Kauai. Since 2008, owners of all such rentals and B&Bs have needed permits to operate, with special restrictions on agricultural land; the benefit for guests is knowing that your lodgings conform to planning and safety codes, the taxes you're paying are actually going to the county, and your stay won't be in jeopardy of a surprise shutdown. At press time, the county was not enforcing the rules for B&Bs as much as for vacation rentals, which among other requirements must display their permit number (often starting with "TVR" or "TVNC") on any online advertising, and post a sign on the premises listing that number, plus the name and phone number of an on-island emergency contact.

The Kauai Visitors Bureau also urges special caution when booking a vacation rental online from sources other than licensed agencies, such as those listed here. Some visitors, usually those who paid by check or money order, arrive on island only to discover their unit belongs to somebody else; they have no place to stay and no recourse to recover their payments.

When booking a condo, also keep in mind that companies that manage multiple properties in a complex may be able to find you another unit if you're dissatisfied with your view or problems arise during your stay—generally not the case for a unit booked on VRBO.com and other do-it-yourself rental sites. However, some management companies are eliminating daily maid service and other niceties to remain competitive; read the fine print before you arrive to know what to expect.

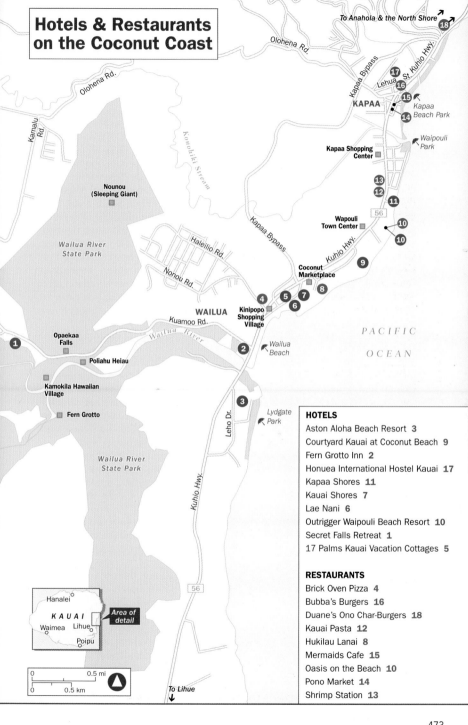

Hotels & Restaurants on the Coconut Coast

To Anahola & the North Shore

18

Olohena Rd.

Olohena Rd.

Kamalu Rd.

Kapaa Bypass

St. Kuhio Hwy.

Lehua

17
16

KAPAA

15

Kapaa Beach Park

14

Konohiki Stream

Waipouli Park

Nounou (Sleeping Giant)

Kapaa Shopping Center

13
12

11

Kapaa Bypass

56

Wailua River State Park

Haleilio Rd.

Wapouli Town Center

10

10

Kuhio Hwy.

Nonou Rd.

Coconut Marketplace

9

4 **5** **7** **8**
    6

WAILUA

Kuamoo Rd.

Kinipopo Shopping Village

PACIFIC

Opaekaa Falls

1

2

Wailua Beach

OCEAN

Poliahu Heiau

Wailua River

Kamokila Hawaiian Village

3

Fern Grotto

Lydgate Park

Leho Dr.

Wailua River State Park

Kuhio Hwy.

56

HOTELS

Aston Aloha Beach Resort **3**
Courtyard Kauai at Coconut Beach **9**
Fern Grotto Inn **2**
Honuea International Hostel Kauai **17**
Kapaa Shores **11**
Kauai Shores **7**
Lae Nani **6**
Outrigger Waipouli Beach Resort **10**
Secret Falls Retreat **1**
17 Palms Kauai Vacation Cottages **5**

RESTAURANTS

Brick Oven Pizza **4**
Bubba's Burgers **16**
Duane's Ono Char-Burgers **18**
Kauai Pasta **12**
Hukilau Lanai **8**
Mermaids Cafe **15**
Oasis on the Beach **10**
Pono Market **14**
Shrimp Station **13**

Hanalei

KAUAI

Area of detail

Waimea Lihue

Poipu

0   0.5 mi
0   0.5 km

To Lihue

473

area" and may not be licensed, although many have paid taxes and operated without complaints for years.

In addition to the properties below, consider renting a one- or two-bedroom oceanfront condo at one of two complexes in Kapaa. At the 84-unit **Kapaa Shores,** 900 Kuhio Hwy., the 10 units managed by Garden Island Properties (www.kauaiproperties.com; © **800/801-0378** or 808/822-4871) run from $800 to $1,050 a week (plus $100–$130 cleaning and $25–$50 reservation fees). At the slightly more upscale **Lae Nani,** 410 Papaloa Rd. (off Kuhio Hwy.), Outrigger (www.outrigger.com/laenani; © **866/956-4262** or 808/823-1401) manages about a quarter of the 83 spacious units ($189–$349 nightly; cleaning fees $95–$115); the beach here offers a rock-walled swimming area perfect for children.

If you prefer something more private, check out the two elegantly furnished (and licensed) cottages in a leafy setting known as **17 Palms Kauai Vacation Cottages** (www.17palmskauai.com; © **888/725-6799**), a block away from Wailua's beaches. Rates for the one-bedroom, one-bathroom Hale Iki (sleeps two adults, plus a small child) start at $165 a night, plus $100 cleaning; the two-bedroom, one-bathroom Meli Meli (sleeps four adults, plus a small child) starts at $245 (discounted 20 percent for couples), plus $125 cleaning. Tucked off Kapaa's busy Kuamoo Road, with easy access to the Wailua River, the pleasant compound known as the **Fern Grotto Inn** (www.ferngrottoinn.com; © **808/821-9836**) comprises five quaint cottages (most sleeping just two), for $110 to $195 a night, plus $75 to $100 cleaning, and one three-bedroom house (up to six adults) for $250 to $350 nightly and $175 to $225 cleaning.

EXPENSIVE

Kauai Marriott Resort ★★★ This 10-story, multi-wing hotel—the tallest on Kauai since opening in 1986—may be what prompted the local ordinance that no new structures be higher than a coconut tree, but it would be hard to imagine the Garden Island without it. Superlatives include Kauai's largest swimming pool, a sort of Greco-Roman fantasy that would fit in at Hearst Castle; its location on Kalapaki Beach, the best protected on the East Side for watersports; and one of the island's most popular restaurants, **Duke's Kauai** (p. 488), among other dining outlets. The long escalator to the central courtyard lagoon, the immense statuary, and handsome lobby sporting a koa outrigger canoe make you feel like you've arrived somewhere truly unique. Two shopping centers (Harbor Mall and Anchor Cove) and more restaurants are within a short walk; in the opposite direction lies the 18-hole championship course of the Kauai Lagoons Golf Club. Rooms tend to be on the smaller side, but feel plush and look chic, with hues of taupe and burnt umber. Try to get at least a partial ocean view—the rugged green Haupu ridge, the bay, and Nawiliwili Harbor provide a mesmerizing backdrop.

Note: The "vacation ownership" **Marriott's Kauai Beach Club** (www.marriott.com/lihka; © **800/845-5279** or 808/245-5050), which offers attractive studio, one-bedroom/two-bathroom, and two-bedroom/two-bathroom "villas" with kitchenettes ($309–$599 nightly), is on the same grounds and shares all the Kauai Marriott Resort's facilities, but there's no resort fee or charge for Wi-Fi or rollaway beds, while self-parking costs $16; it often has limited availability, due to the popularity of Hawaii properties in timeshare exchange programs. The newest development on the 800-acre resort is **Marriott's Kauai Lagoons—Kalanipuu,** 3325 Holokawelu Way, Lihue (www.marriott.com/lihkn; © **800/845-5279** or 808/632-8200), another timeshare with the possibility of nightly rentals, which

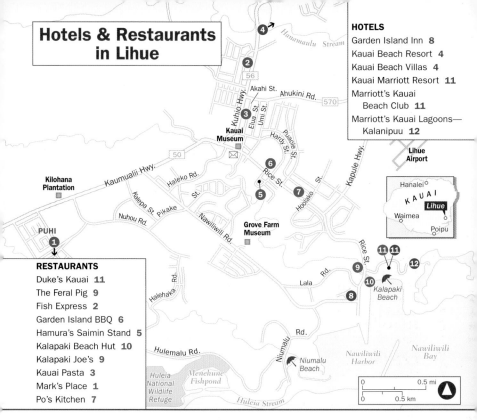

Hotels & Restaurants in Lihue

Kauai Museum

Kilohana Plantation

Grove Farm Museum

Lihue Airport

HANALEI○
K A U A I
Lihue
Waimea○
Poipu○

PUHI

Kalapaki Beach

Niumalu Beach

Huleia National Wildlife Refuge

Menehune Fishpond

Nawiliwili Harbor

Nawiliwili Bay

Huleia Stream

0   0.5 mi
0   0.5 km

---

opened in 2010. Its roomier two-bedroom/two-bathroom and three-bedroom/three-bathroom villas have full kitchens ($379–$679, including Wi-Fi and self-parking), but guests do not have privileges to use the Kauai Marriott Resort's sprawling pool or its lounge chairs at Kalapaki Beach (reached by free shuttle). As its name suggests, the Lagoons complex overlooks the Kauai Lagoons Golf Club; it's also home to the Ala Lani Spa & Tennis Club, with seven courts. Details below apply only to Kauai Marriott Resort only.

3610 Rice St. (at Kalapaki Beach), Lihue. www.marriott.com/lihhi. ⓒ **800/220-2925** or 808/245-5050. 356 units. $269–$484 double; check for online packages and discounts. Rollaway $25. $30 resort fee. $19 valet parking (self-parking included in resort fee). **Amenities:** 5 restaurants; 2 bars; free airport shuttle (on request); babysitting; children's program; concierge; fitness center; 5 Jacuzzis; pool; room service; watersports equipment rentals; Wi-Fi (included in resort fee).

Outrigger Waipouli Beach Resort ★★   Although its namesake beach is not good for swimming, kids and quite a number of adults are happy to spend all day in the heated fantasy pool here; it stretches across 2 acres with a lazily flowing river, sandy-bottomed hot tubs and children's pool, twin water slides, and waterfalls, amid lush landscaping. Inside the individually owned condos (mostly two-bedroom/three-bathroom units), adults will delight in the high-end kitchen appliances (SubZero fridge, Fisher & Paykel dishwasher drawers, Wolf glass cooktop) and luxurious finishes such as granite counters, Travertine stone tiles, and African mahogany cabinets. There's room for the whole family, too: Most of the two-bedroom units are 1,300 square feet, and a few corner penthouses run as large as 1,800 square feet. All units have washer-dryers and central A/C to boot. Opened in 2006, the $200-million complex covers 13 acres in Waipouli, between Wailua and Kapaa, conveniently across the street from Safeway, Longs Drugs, and other shops and restaurants—but you'll want to avoid the cheaper units facing the parking lot and highway due to noise. The owners' association approved a $12 daily resort fee in 2013; Outrigger, which manages the most units here, operates the front desk and charges one-time cleaning fees ($75–$115) similar or less than those of independently rented condos.

4–820 Kuhio Hwy., Kapaa. www.outrigger.com. 🅒 **877/418-0711** or 808/823-1401. 196 units. From $205 hotel double; $255–$385 1-bedroom/2-bathroom for 4; $295–$465 2-bedroom/3-bathroom for 6. Cleaning fee $75–$115. Resort fee $12. 2-night minimum. **Amenities:** Restaurant; business center; fitness center; pool; day spa; 3 outdoor whirlpools; Wi-Fi (included in resort fee).

MODERATE

Kauai Beach Resort ★★ Less than 5 minutes from the airport, but hidden from the highway by a long, palm-lined drive, this is the jewel in the crown of Aqua Hotels and Resorts' 15 moderately priced hotels in the islands, thanks to its extensive, beautifully sculpted pools—four in all, with adult and children's options, a 75-foot lava-tube water slide, whirlpools, waterfalls, and a sandy-bottomed beachfront lagoon. Decorated in a Balinese wood/Hawaiian plantation motif, rooms in the hotel itself are not particularly commodious, and some "mountain view" (odd-numbered rooms) units overlook parking lots, where wild chickens like to congregate. No matter: If you're not lingering by the pool, you can be walking for miles along the windswept beach (not recommended for swimming), which passes by the budget-friendly Wailua Golf Course, or indulging in a spa treatment or exploring nearby attractions.

Note: Aqua's hotel rates listed below reflect typical availability online; rack rates are higher. A number of hotel rooms are also individually owned "condos"; you'll find lower daily rates when booking through an owner, but you'll pay an extra $80 in resort/cleaning fees, with maid service upon request for $15 to $30 daily. The 25-acre resort is also home to the **Kauai Beach Villas,** spacious one- and two-bedroom condos operated as timeshares or privately owned rentals, all with access to the hotel's facilities; **Kauai Vacation Rentals** (www.kauaivacation rentals.com; 🅒 **800/367-5025** or 808/245-8841) manages the majority of the non-timeshare units, with daily rates and cleaning fees starting at $145 and $90, respectively, plus a $35 reservation fee.

4331 Kauai Beach Dr., Lihue (from airport, drive 2½ miles northeast on Hwy. 51/56 to a right turn on Kauai Beach Dr.). www.kauaibeachresorthawaii.com. 🅒 **866/536-7976** or 808/245-1955. 350 units. $189–$249 double; $349–$540 suite. Check for online specials. Extra person $45. Rollaway $20. Valet or self-parking $17. **Amenities:** 2 restaurants; cafe; lounge; poolside bar; free airport/golf shuttle; babysitting; concierge; fitness center; 2 Jacuzzis; laundry facilities; 4 saltwater pools; rental cars; room service; Hawaiian Rainforest Spa & Salon; high-speed Internet ($13 in room, free in lobby and restaurant).

Courtyard by Marriott Kauai at Coconut Beach ★

Under Marriott management since 2010, this centrally located hotel wins the most raves for its oceanfront courtyard and pool, offering firepits, fountains, and a large whirlpool spa. A well-manicured lawn separates the hotel from golden-sand Makaiwa

Beach, which is too reefy to do much swimming in, but just the ticket for long walks. Rooms, most of which are just 320 square feet, have lanais with cinnamon wood shutters to match the dark-veneered, Hawaiian-themed decor and two-thirds have at least partial ocean views. If you're looking for more space, book the executive oceanfront rooms, 528 square feet, with standard rates starting at $209. The $20 resort fee is more comprehensive than most and includes self-parking (plus first night of valet parking), Wi-Fi, two complimentary mai tais, free meals for children 12 and under with paying adults at the **Voyager** restaurant, yoga classes, and beach-gear rentals, among other perks.

650 Aleka Loop, Kapaa. www.courtyardkauai.com. © **877/997-6667** or 808/822-3455. 311 units. $139–$239 double; from $249 suite. Check for online packages. Extra person $25. Children 17 and under stay free in parent's room. Resort fee $20. Valet parking $5 after 1st free night. **Amenities:** Restaurant; bar; business center; fitness center; Jacuzzi; pool; room service; spa; basketball/tennis court; Wi-Fi (included in resort fee).

INEXPENSIVE

In addition to the hotels listed below, young backpackers and adventurous adults on a shoestring budget should consider **Honuea International Hostel Kauai** (www.kauaihostel.com; © **808/823-6142**) in historic Kapaa. Bunks in the three, 10-bed single-sex and co-ed dorm rooms (each sharing just one bathroom) start at $25 per person, including taxes; the two deluxe private rooms, which share a bathroom, have the nicest setting, in the main house, for $70 a night (single or double occupancy, taxes included). There's a 10pm curfew, but there's also little reason to stay out that late on Kauai.

B&B fans who don't mind having breakfast only on the first morning should consider the recently renovated **Secret Falls Retreat** (www.secretfallsretreat.com; © **808/823-6398**), formerly the Mohala Ke Ola Bed and Breakfast. On a quiet side street just past Opaekaa Falls in Kapaa, it offers five spacious rooms, all but one with private bathroom, for $99 to $140, with waterfall views and a large saltwater pool and hot tub adding to the serenity.

Aston Aloha Beach Resort ★ This 10-acre beachfront property is great for families: It's next to the protected swimming/snorkeling ponds of Lydgate Beach, the fanciful Kamalani Playground, and other park facilities, with an educational element added by the historic Hawaiian sites by the Wailua River. With tropical decor that includes Hawaiian quilt–print comforters and pineapple lamps, the larger-than-average rooms are unfortunately a little shabby around the edges—one reason the prices may be relatively low. By the time you read this, however, the management-promised "upgrades" should be completed throughout; currently, the north Maile wing appears to have the most updated units. *Note:* All rooms have mini-fridges, while junior suites and cottages also have microwaves; cottages are the only units with lanais (patios) and are closest to Kamalani Playground.

3–5920 Kuhio Hwy., Kapaa. www.astonalohabeachhotel.com. © **877/997-6667** or 808/823-6000. 216 units. $95–$119 double; $149–$166 1-bedroom cottage; $175–$189 suite. Resort fee $18 daily (includes self-parking, Internet, DVD/Playstation rentals, fruit platter, and more). Extra person $30. Children 18 and under stay free in parent's room. **Amenities:** 2 restaurants; bar; business center; fitness room; Jacuzzi; coin laundry; 2 pools; tennis court (free); Wi-Fi (included in resort fee).

Garden Island Inn ★★ Thrifty travelers will love this cheerily renovated, well-maintained motel within a short walk of Kalapaki Beach, shops, and restaurants, while families will appreciate the large suites (with up to one king-size bed with three twin beds) and extra guest fees of just $10 per person. It's easy to make breakfast on the cheap, too, thanks to the mini-fridge, microwave, wet bar, and kitchenware, in addition to the standard coffeemaker—there's free coffee and pie at the front desk, too. Other freebies include parking, Wi-Fi, and use of beach gear, not to mention happily given advice. Hanalei artist Camile Fontaine's bright, island-inspired murals and paintings make this a welcome antidote to neutral, cookie-cutter resort decor, while owners Lis and Steve Layne work tirelessly to improve their guests' comfort. Planned improvements include room-darkening blinds for better sleep (you'll still want to consider earplugs to offset street noise.)

3445 Wilcox Rd. (across the street from Kalapaki Beach, near Nawiliwili Harbor), Lihue. www. gardenislandinn.com. © **800/648-0154** or 808/245-7227. 21 units. $103–$170 double. Extra person $10. **Amenities:** Complimentary watersports equipment and beach gear; Wi-Fi (free).

Kauai Shores ★   A major overhaul of nearly all rooms and public areas was underway in 2014 at this 6-acre beachfront bargain, formerly known as Kauai Sands. But even with renovations only partly done, the benefit of new ownership (and management by Aqua Hotels and Resort) is already apparent. The small but functional updated rooms feature modern, slightly quirky, Ikea-style furnishings (curvy mirrors, square lamps) with orange and lime accents, bright blue geometric-patterned rugs, and compact but tidy baths, while updated landscaping, tiling, and pool furniture have made the oceanview pool especially inviting. A free continental breakfast (pastries, bananas, coffee/tea) is offered in the open-air lobby—at least until a new restaurant opens in the long-empty, beachfront half of the building. Swimming isn't safe here, but the rock-walled pool in front of neighboring Lae Nani is good for children, and the ponds at Lydgate Beach are just a short drive away. **Note:** Rack rates are substantially higher than rates typically available online, which are listed below.

420 Papaloa Rd., Kapaa (5 miles from airport, via Hwy. 51/56). http://kauaisandshotel.com. © **855/309-5483** or 808/822-4951. 206 rooms. $99–$209 double; junior suite with kitchenette $179–$229. Check for online discounts. Extra person $25. $8 parking. **Amenities:** 2 pools; barbecue grills; coin laundry; Wi-Fi (free).

North Shore

Despite this magical region's popularity with visitors, only Princeville is officially one of Kauai County's "visitor destination areas"; it's important to be aware that many rural bed-and-breakfasts and vacation rentals here are unlicensed. While the county may temporarily be leaving B&Bs alone, in 2014 the state abruptly shut down one longtime Hanalei B&B for building and operating in a conservation district, and unhappy neighbors of unlicensed rentals may report them to authorities. If you're not staying in one of the few hotels, I recommend booking through one of the following agencies, which manage only licensed properties and are known for their integrity.

Founded in 1978, **Kauai Vacation Rentals** (www.kauaivacationrentals. com; © **800/367-5025** or 808/245-8841) manages well-maintained homes and condos across the island, with the majority—102 at press time—on the North Shore. Most have a 3- to 5-night minimum that expands to 1 week or 2 weeks from December 15 to January 6. You can search online listings by location, size, view, and amenities such as air-conditioning (not so common where trade winds blow), swimming pool, and high-speed Internet access (increasingly more common); agents are happy to help you find the perfect match. In **Haena,** the non-holiday rate for a one-bedroom, one-bathroom garden-view cottage that's just a short walk to Tunnels (Makua) Beach is $250 a night or $1,250 a week; for an oceanview, two-bedroom, one-and-a-half-bathroom cottage right on **Anini Beach,** it's $360 a night or $1,800 a week—a good deal if you're splitting the expenses with another couple. For all rentals, you'll also pay a $35 reservation fee and a one-time cleaning fee that starts at $90 for a studio condo and can go as high as $565 for a sprawling, five-bedroom house.

Parrish Collection Kauai (www.parrishkauai.com; ☏ **800/325-5701** or 808/742-2000), which has made a name for itself with high-quality Poipu vacation rentals (see "Finding a Perfect Place in Poipu," p. 481), also represents 10 homes and cottages in Hanalei and nearly 50 properties (mostly condos) in Princeville. Many of the latter are in the **Hanalei Bay Resort,** which has spectacular views rivaling those of the St. Regis, air-conditioning in units, and a recently redone fantasy pool with waterfalls, slides, and so forth; rates start at $125 a night (five-night minimum) for a garden-view studio. If you can forgo an ocean view, Parrish's best values are in the **Plantation at Princeville,** roomy two- and three-bedroom air-conditioned units in a complex built in 2004 with a pool, spa, barbecues, and fitness center; rates start at $130 for a two-bedroom, two-bathroom unit. Not included in the rates are the $50 "processing" fee per booking and cleaning fees (starting at $100 for a studio and increasing by size).

Coldwell Banker Bali Hai Realty (www.balihai.com; ☏ **808/826-8000**) manages about 40 luxury vacation rentals, all of them licensed; expect a 7-night minimum June 1 to August 31 and December 15 to January 5, otherwise 4 to 5 nights. Its Princeville properties include 10 units at the desirable **Pali Ke Kua** and **Puu Poa** complexes, less than a half-mile from each other on the bluff above Hideaways Beach. At Pali Ke Kua, nightly rates start as low as $130 for a two-bedroom, two-bathroom mountain-view unit, and $160 for an oceanview one-bedroom unit with sleeper sofa that sleeps four. Its lowest rate at Puu Poa is $290 a night for a two-bedroom, two-bathroom oceanview unit (ideal for couples to share). For condo bookings, Bali Hai charges a reservation fee of $25 to $50 and a cleaning fee of $150 to $180.

A frequent resource for Hollywood movie crews on the island, Mike Lyons of **Kauai Style Vacation Rentals** (www.kauaistyleconcierge.com; ☏ **808/482-1572**) specializes in licensed properties on the North Shore; you won't find listings on his site because he prefers to work with clients individually. A passionate surfer, Lyons also enjoys escorting guests on ocean and trail adventures and can arrange private chefs and other services.

VERY EXPENSIVE

St. Regis Princeville ★★   Hawaii's first and only St. Regis—a brand renowned for its opulence and service—opened in late 2009, following a multimillion-dollar transformation of the Princeville Hotel. The dramatic cliffside layout didn't change: You still enter on the ninth floor, with a dazzling panorama of Hanalei Bay and Makana (the "Bali Hai" mountain) across the airy lobby and an elevator to take you down to the narrow but pleasant sandy beach and handsome, 5,000-square-foot infinity pool. The spacious (540 sq. ft. and up) rooms also still feature extra-large bedroom windows as well as "magic" bathroom windows, which toggle between clear and opaque. A welcome sheen of sophisticated

Hawaiiana has replaced the formerly palatial European decor, however, typified by the 11,000-square-foot Halelea Spa, which combines traditional Hawaiian healing practices and local botanicals with Western treatments and waterfall showers. Among the many lavish amenities are goose-down comforters, 42- and 52-inch flatscreen TVs, and, in junior suites on up, personal butler service. Golfers will enjoy easy access to the Prince and Makai golf courses, both designed by Robert Trent Jones, Jr., and recently renovated.

5520 Ka Haku Rd., Princeville. www.stregisprinceville.com. ℭ **877/787-3447** or 808/826-9644. 252 units. $525–$700 double; from $940 suite. Extra person $100. Children 17 and under stay free in parent's room. Parking (valet only) $30. **Amenities:** 3 restaurants; 3 bars; children's program; concierge; fitness center; golf; Jacuzzis; pool; room service; spa; watersports equipment rentals; Wi-Fi (free for basic, $22 for streaming/large file usage.)

EXPENSIVE

Hanalei Colony Resort ★★   With two bedrooms (separated by louvered wooden doors), one-and-a-half to two bathrooms, full kitchens, and living rooms, these 48 individually owned, updated condos are perfect for families—or anyone who can appreciate being as few as 10 feet from the beach, in the shadow of green peaks near the end of the road. It has no TVs, phones, or entertainment systems, although free Wi-Fi means guests don't disconnect quite as much as they used to. The beach is generally not safe for swimming, but you're less than a mile from Tunnels (Makua) Beach, and the garden-side pool and barbecue area boasts lush landscaping and a koi pond. In 2013, the resort added a 13-passenger shuttle that runs to Hanalei and beaches during the day, when it's free; in the evening, the shuttle takes guests to and from dining and entertainment destinations in Hanalei and Princeville for a $10 charge per unit. The independently run Ayurvedic-themed Hanalei Day Spa and the award-winning **Mediterranean Gourmet** restaurant are also on site.

5–7130 Kuhio Hwy., Hanalei. www.hcr.com. ℭ **800/628-3004** or 808/826-6235. 48 units. $256–$495 2-bedroom apt for 4. 2-night minimum; 7th night free. **Amenities:** Restaurant; coffee bar/art gallery; free weekly continental breakfast; babysitting; barbecues; concierge; Jacuzzi; coin laundry; pool; day spa; Wi-Fi (free).

Westin Princeville Ocean Villas ★★   A superb "vacation ownership" property that nonetheless offers nightly rentals, this 18½-acre bluffside resort is a winner with families and couples seeking condo-style units with resort furnishings and amenities. Besides Westin's justly famed "Heavenly Beds," the roomy studios and one-bedroom suites (which can be combined into two-bedroom units) have immaculate, well-stocked kitchens, washer-dryers, and huge bathrooms with separate glass showers and deep whirlpool tubs. Playful statuary and fountains mark the centrally located children's pool next to the main pool; adults will appreciate the quieter, bluff-side plunge pools. The indoor-outdoor **Nanea Restaurant and Bar,** one of the better hotel restaurants on Kauai, has substantial discounts for children 11 and younger, and the on-site deli has a tempting array of farm-fresh items. **Note:** The resort is near a steep, often muddy, unmaintained trail to Anini Beach, but most guests opt to take the free shuttle to the St. Regis Princeville, where they walk down nearly 200 steps to Puu Poa beach, or drive themselves to Anini or another nearby beach.

3838 Wyllie Rd., Princeville. www.westinprinceville.com. ℭ **808/827-8700.** 346 units. From $279–$370 studio (sleeps 2); $387–$497 1-bedroom (sleeps 4); $666–$1,078 2-bedroom (sleeps 8). $13 parking. **Amenities:** 2 restaurants, bar, deli/store; barbecues; children's program;

FINDING A PERFECT PLACE in poipu

The best way to find a high-quality, licensed vacation rental in Poipu is through **Parrish Collection Kauai** (www.parrishkauai.com; © **800/325-5701** or 808/742-2000). Parrish manages more than 200 units for 20 different islandwide condo developments, plus dozens of vacation houses ranging from quaint cottages to elite resort homes; about three-quarters are in Poipu, in a wide range of prices. The company sets resort-like standards for decor and maintenance, classifying its lodgings into four categories ("premium plus" is the highest, for new or completely renovated units), sending linens out for professional laundering, and providing signature bathroom amenities. At Parrish's flagship **Waikomo Stream Villas** and **Nihi Kai Villas** in Poipu, where the company manages about half the condos (75 in total), there's even concierge service—with no kickbacks for referrals, according to owner J. P. Parrish. "Our guides know the island really well and have no agenda; we only recommend what works and has good customer service," he notes.

Each well-equipped rental offers a full kitchen, washer/dryer, TV/DVD, phone, and free Wi-Fi; condo rates in the introductory Value Collection start as low as $100 a night; you'll pay cleaning but not resort or parking fees. At Nihi Kai Villas, which has a heated pool (a rarity here) and large floor plans, off-peak nightly rates start at $167 for a two-bedroom condo (sleeps six), plus $153 cleaning; at Waikomo Stream Villas, a one-bedroom condo (sleeps four) starts at $115 a night, plus $125 cleaning.

Parrish's vacation cottages range from $200 a night to $1,000-plus for sumptuous multimillion-dollar ocean estates and the cottages and bungalows at **Kukuiula** (exclusively rented by Parrish); the latter allow access to the exquisite and otherwise private Kukuiula spa, golf course, and clubhouse.

There's a 3- to 5-night minimum for condos, a 7-night minimum for houses, and no minimum at Kukuiula, except during winter holidays. For 5-night or longer stays, inquire about the **Frommer's Preferred Guest Discount,** good for 5 to 10 percent off; if a better deal is available, agents will let you know. The company also offers a price-match guarantee.

concierge; fitness room w/steam room and sauna, plus use of Makai Lap Pool and Fitness Center, 1 mile away; 4 pools; free resort shuttle; Wi-Fi (free).

MODERATE

The best values on the North Shore can be found among Princeville's many condo complexes, which vary widely in age and amenities; check the listings of the brokers mentioned above. I recommend either the dramatically perched **Hanalei Bay Resort** (www.hanaleibayresort.com; © **877/344-0688**) or the residential-style **Cliffs at Princeville** (www.cliffsatprinceville.com; © **808/826-6129**); both participate in timeshare and vacation rental programs but also allow direct bookings; both were also undergoing renovations in 2014. Nightly rates at the 22-acre Hanalei Bay Resort, just west of the St. Regis, start at $149 for a hotel-style unit with king-size bed, plus a $12 daily resort fee. At the posher, more tranquil Cliffs, on the northern edge of the Princeville bluff, one-bedroom, two-bathroom units (sleeping four) with full kitchen, living room, and lanai start at $227 nonrefundable ($324 standard), plus a weekly resort fee of $75.

South Shore

The most popular place to stay year-round, the resort area of Poipu Beach is definitely a "visitor destination area," with hundreds of rental condos, cottages, and houses vying with Kauai's best luxury resorts for families and a romantic boutique hotel. Upcountry Lawai and Kalaheo brim with more modest, not necessarily licensed, bed-and-breakfasts and vacation homes.

EXPENSIVE

Besides the resorts below, the 35-acre, green-lawned **Kiahuna Plantation Resort,** on the sandy beach next to the Sheraton, is also worth considering, although its 333 individually furnished, one- and two-bedroom condos vary widely in taste; they also rely on ceiling fans (and trade winds) for cooling, and there's no elevator in the three-story buildings. **Outrigger** (www.outrigger.com; ✆ **808/742-6411**) manages more than half of the units, but only those rented from **Castle Resorts** (www.castleresorts.com; ✆ **800/367-5004** or 808/545-5310) receive daily housekeeping and access to the tennis courts and resort-style pool of the Poipu Beach Athletic Club across the street. Outrigger's nightly rates for one-bedrooms start at $175 to $395 plus $70 cleaning, while Castle's start at $171 to $285, plus $35 to $70 cleaning; both include free Wi-Fi and parking in their rates.

Grand Hyatt Kauai Resort & Spa ★★★   Kauai's largest hotel aims to have one of the smallest carbon footprints. Renovated in 2011, its 602 luxurious rooms boast not only a fresh gold-and-green palette and pillow-top beds, but also eco-friendly elements such as low-flow toilets, recycled-yarn carpets, and plush robes made from recycled plastic bottles. Grass-covered roofs and solar panels reduce emissions, food scraps from dining outlets (such as the thatched-roof **Tidepools** restaurant) go to local pig farmers, and used cooking oil becomes biodiesel fuel. But that's just green icing on the cake of this sprawling, family-embracing resort, where the elaborate, multi-tiered fantasy pool and saltwater lagoon more than compensate for the rough waters of Shipwrecks (Keoneloa) Beach, and the 45,000-square-foot indoor/outdoor Anara Spa and adjacent Poipu Bay Golf Course offer excellent adult diversions. If you want to feel even more virtuous about splurging on a stay, check out the Hyatt's volunteer programs with National Tropical Botanical Garden and Kauai Humane Society (where you can cuddle cats or take dogs on field trips), among other nonprofits.

1571 Poipu Rd., Koloa. www.grandhyattkauai.com. ✆ **800/554-9288** or 808/742-1234. 602 units. $339–$409 double; from $497 Grand Club; from $729 suite. $25 resort fee includes self-parking, Wi-Fi, fitness classes, and more. Extra person $75. Children 17 and under stay free in parent's room. Packages available. Valet parking $15. **Amenities:** 4 restaurants; 4 bars; babysitting; bike and car rentals; children's program; club lounge; concierge; fitness center; golf course and clubhouse; 3 Jacuzzis; 1½-acre saltwater swimming lagoon; luau; 2 non-chlorinated pools connected by river pool; room service; spa; 3 tennis courts; watersports equipment rentals; Wi-Fi (included in resort fee.)

Koa Kea Hotel & Resort ★★   If everything seems to run like clockwork at this jewel box of a hotel, hidden between the sprawling Kiahuna Plantation Resort and the densely built Marriott Waiohai Beach Club, chalk it up to general manager Chris Steuri, whose Swiss family has been in the hotel business for generations. He oversaw the years-long, multimillion-dollar transformation of the old Poipu Beach Hotel (dormant since 1992's Hurricane Iniki) into a posh, boutique inn boasting the island's best hotel restaurant, **Red Salt** (p. 498), as well as a small but expertly staffed spa. *Ko'a kea* means "white coral," which inspires the white and coral accents in the sleek, modern decor; all rooms feature lanais, many with views of the rocky coast (a short walk from sandy beaches). Steuri's European flair shows in the Nespresso espresso machines and L'Occitane bath products, but his staff resounds with pure Hawaiian aloha. *Note:* At prices this steep, the "garden view" will disappoint—best to spring for at least a partial ocean view, and sign up for the free Preferred Hotels & Resorts loyalty program to check for specials.

2251 Poipu Rd., Koloa. www.koakea.com. (C) **888/898-8958** or 808/828-8888. 121 units. $475–$850 double; from $1,625 suite. Packages available. $26 resort fee includes valet parking, Wi-Fi, fitness center, and more. **Amenities:** Restaurant (Red Salt, p. 498); 2 bars; concierge; fitness room; Jacuzzi; pool; room service; spa; watersports equipment rentals; Wi-Fi (included in resort fee).

Poipu Kapili Resort ★ All of the 60 upscale, individually owned and furnished condos overlook the waves crashing on the rocky shoreline just across the little-traveled street. Floor plans start at 1,200 square feet for a one-bedroom unit with one-and-a-half to two bathrooms, all on the ground floor with pool and ocean views; the larger two-bedroom units come with either three bathrooms in two-level townhomes with ground-level entries, or with two bathrooms in third-floor penthouses accessed by elevator. The layouts are especially appealing to families, but couples will appreciate the high priority the management places on maintaining a tranquil atmosphere, especially around the central pool area; cooks should take note of the spacious kitchens and free herb garden. The online interactive map and detailed photos can help you pick the decor and locale that's just right for you.

2221 Kapili Rd., Koloa. www.poipukapili.com. (C) **800/443-7714** or 808/742-6449. 60 units. $255–$305 1-bedroom (sleeps up to 4); $385–$485 2-bedroom (up to 6); $485–$525 2-bedroom penthouse. Check online for longer-stay discounts and specials. **Amenities:** Barbecue area; pool; 2 tennis courts lit for night use; Wi-Fi (free).

Sheraton Kauai Resort ★★ Thanks to a $16-million remodel, this appealingly low-key resort is finally living up to its ideal beachfront location, where the western horizon sees a riot of color at sunset and rainbows arc over a rocky point after the occasional shower. The expanded oceanfront pool—with mini-slide, rock-lined whirlpool, and luxurious cabanas (for rent)—provides a much more inviting place for a dip, which conveniently makes the traditional pool in the garden wing a quieter oasis. Nights here are livelier, too, thanks to large firepits in the oceanview courtyard and the tasty libations and wine-tasting social hours at **RumFire Poipu Beach,** the resort's ambitious, island-inspired restaurant with walls of glass. *Tip:* Ask for a room on the ocean side, even if garden view, to avoid having to frequently cross the street; rooms in the ocean wings seem larger, too. Rack rates start at $499, but prices listed below are common online.

2440 Hoonani Rd., Koloa. www.sheraton-kauai.com. (C) **866/716-8109** or 808/742-1661. 394 units. $239–$429 double (prepaid as low as $199–$269); $429–$679 suite; 4 people maximum per room. $31 resort fee includes self-parking (and 1st night valet parking), Wi-Fi, use of fitness center, bicycles, Poipu shuttle, bottled water, and more. Extra person $70. Valet parking $10. **Amenities:** 3 restaurants; bar; babysitting; concierge; free computer use; fitness room; Jacuzzi;

beachfront luau; 2 pools; room service; spa services; 3 tennis courts (2 night-lit); watersports equipment rentals; Wi-Fi (included in resort fee).

MODERATE

Of the options outside of Poipu, **Kauai Banyan Inn** (www.kauaibanyan.com; ℂ 888/786-3855) in rural Lawai offers six airy suites and a cottage, all with gleaming wood floors, Hawaiian quilts, and kitchenettes or full kitchens, for $140 to $230 per night plus $45 cleaning. Although the inn is not licensed, co-owners Lorna and John Hoff, who live on the 11-acre compound that they helped build and now run as a bed-and-breakfast, say it's not in an agricultural zone, and accommodations taxes do go to the county.

Kauai Cove Cottages ★ Honeymooners and other romance seekers find a serene oasis in these three studios, limited to two guests each, featuring four-poster canopy queen-size beds under high vaulted ceilings, private bamboo-walled lanais with barbecue grills, flatscreen TVs with DVD players, and full kitchens. They're on a quiet lane just a few houses up from the snorkel spot of Koloa Landing and a short walk to a sandy cove known as Baby Beach. Since it can get hot in Poipu, the wall-unit A/Cs (along with ceiling fans) are a nice touch. Helpful owners E. J. and Diane Olsson live nearby in Poipu Kai, where they also rent out a studio and one-bedroom suite ($115–$185, plus $75 cleaning) that includes use of a pool and hot tub.

2672 Puuholo Rd., Koloa. www.kauaicove.com. ℂ **800/624-9945** or 808/742-2562. 3 units. $145–$175 double. Cleaning fee $75. **Amenities:** Wi-Fi (free).

Poipu Plantation B&B Inn and Vacation Rentals ★★★ This ultra-tranquil compound almost defies description. It's comprised of four adults-only, bed-and-breakfast suites of various sizes in a lovingly restored 1938 plantation house; seven vacation rental units in three modern cottage-style wings behind the B&B; and two one-bedroom condos across the street at the 35-unit Sunset Kahili complex. The B&B suites, fully renovated in 2013, feature handsome hardwood floors, sturdy vintage furnishings, bright tropical art, and (thankfully) modern bathrooms; the 700-square-foot Alii Suite also includes a wet bar, two-person whirlpool tub, and private lanai. The one- and two-bedroom cottage units on the foliage-rich 1-acre lot have less character, but offer more space and full kitchens; some have ocean views across the rooftops of Sunset Kahili, where the neatly maintained oceanview condos have use of a small pool (but no A/C). Innkeepers Chris and Javed Moore and their friendly staff delight in offering travel tips. **Note:** When comparing rates, consider that the units here have no cleaning, resort, parking, or Wi-Fi fees; plus, breakfasts for the B&B units include Kauai coffee, hot entrees, and fresh island fruit and juice.

1792 Pee Rd., Koloa. www.poipubeach.com. ℂ **800/643-0263** or 808/742-6757. 13 units. Cottages: $130–$200 1-bedroom (sleeps 2–3), $155–$235 2-bedroom (sleeps up to 5). Condos: $138–$265 (sleeps up to 3); additional person $20. Inn: $124–$270 (including breakfast and daily housekeeping); adults only (2 maximum); 3-night minimum (5 for winter holidays). **Amenities:** Use of beach gear; laundry facilities; Wi-Fi (free).

INEXPENSIVE

In pricey Poipu, staying anywhere for $150 a night—especially if fees and taxes are included—can be a real challenge. **Kauai Vacation Rentals** (www.kauai vacationrentals.com; ℂ **800/367-5025** or 808/245-8841) manages 10 garden- and oceanview studios in the well-kept **Prince Kuhio** complex across from

Lawai Beach that cost about $135 a night (5-night minimum), even with taxes and fees rolled in; it also has eight one-bedroom/one-bathroom units (some sleeping four) that, all told, cost about $170 a night. During spring and fall, **Suite Paradise** (www.suite-paradise.com; © **800/367-8020**) frequently has garden-view one-bedroom/one-bathroom units in the **Kahala** condominium on the 70-acre Poipu Kai resort for $145 to $155 a night, all inclusive.

Marjorie's Kauai Inn ★ In keeping with its hilltop pastoral setting in Lawai, this three-room bed-and-breakfast prides itself on green touches: energy-efficient appliances, eco-friendly cleaning products, and local organic produce (some of it grown on site). You're more likely to notice the sweeping valley views from your private lanais. All rooms have private entrances and kitchenettes. Sunset View, the largest, boasts its own hot tub in a gazebo and a fold-out couch for extra guests. Everyone can use the 50-foot-long main pool and hot tub, down a long flight of stairs (this isn't the best place for young children.) All rooms include TV with cable and DVD player, but following in the tradition of the original owner, Marjorie Ketcher, guests are encouraged to explore the island with a booklet of helpful suggestions and free use of bikes, a surfboard, a kayak, and beach gear, among other equipment.

Off Hailima Rd., Lawai. www.marjorieskauaiinn.com. © **800/717-8838** or 808/332-8838. 3 units. $150–$215 double, including continental breakfast. Extra person $20. **Amenities:** Barbecue; complimentary use of bikes, kayak, and beach gear; Jacuzzi; laundry facilities; pool; Wi-Fi (free).

West Side
EXPENSIVE

Waimea Plantation Cottages ★★ Serenity now: That's what you'll find at this 30-acre oceanfront enclave of restored vintage cottages, spread among large lawns dotted with coconut palms, banyan trees, and tropical flowers. The black-sand beach is not good for swimming (there's a pool for that), but it offers intriguing driftwood for beachcombers and mesmerizing sunset views. The charming cottages feature period-style furnishings, full kitchens, lanais, and modern perks such as Wi-Fi; they come in one- and two-bedroom units with one bathroom (594–726 sq. ft.) and three-bedroom, two-bathroom versions (1,088 sq. ft.). Owned by the heirs of Norwegian immigrant Hans Peter Faye, who ran a sugar plantation, the property also includes the four-bedroom, three-bathroom Jean Faye House and five-bedroom Manager's House, both oceanfront (1,250 and 4,240 sq. ft., respectively), and the five-bedroom, five-bathroom Kruse House (4,020 sq. ft.), which offers A/C in all the bedrooms and a kitchenette in the master suite. Opened in 2014, the on-site restaurant, **Kalapaki Joe's,** is also a popular sports bar. **Note:** Lower rates reflect garden-view units in non-peak periods—the prices for most stays definitely qualify for the "expensive" category.

9400 Kaumualii Hwy. (ocean side, west of Huakai Rd.), Waimea. www.waimea-plantation.com. © **866/774-2924** (Aston Hotels & Resorts) or 808/338-1625. 56 units. $199–$379 1-bedroom double; $255–$445 2-bedroom (sleeps up to 4); $280–$462 3-bedroom (sleeps up to 5); from $515 4-bedroom (up to 8); from $633 5-bedroom (up to 10). $18 resort fee. Children 17 and under stay free in parent's room. Check for online specials. **Amenities:** Restaurant; bar; laundry; pool; volleyball; Wi-Fi (included in resort fee).

MODERATE

The West Inn ★ The closest thing the West Side has to a Holiday Inn Express, the West Inn opened in 2011, and its clean, neutral-toned rooms with bright accents and stone counters still look new. One two-story wing of medium-size rooms is just off the highway across from Waimea Theater; some second-story rooms have an ocean view over corrugated metal roofs from the long, shared lanai, and all units have refrigerators, microwaves, A/C, coffeemakers, and cable TV. Another wing of one- and two-bedroom suites, designed for longer stays with full kitchens and living rooms, is tucked off to the side, with a small barbecue area between the wings. **Note:** There's no elevator; call ahead to arrange check-ins after 6pm.

9690 Kaumualii Hwy. (at Pokole Rd.), Waimea. http://thewestinn.com. ☎ **808/338-1107.** 20 units. $149–$198 king or double; $243 1-bedroom suite (5-night minimum), $359 2-bedroom suite (sleeps up to 4; 5-night minimum). **Amenities:** Barbecue grills, coin laundry, Wi-Fi (free).

INEXPENSIVE

Inn Waimea/West Kauai Lodging ★★   If you're looking for accommodations with both character and modern conveniences, check out the small lodge and four vacation rentals managed by West Kauai Lodging. A former parsonage that's also known as Halepule ("House of Prayer"), **Inn Waimea** is a Craftsman-style cottage in the center of quaint Waimea, with simple, tropical-tinged, plantation-era decor in its four wood-paneled suites, all but one with a separate living area. Updated in 2013 and under new management, the suites now offer flatscreen TVs, Wi-Fi, and (in summer) air-conditioning, as well as private bathrooms with pedestal sinks, coffeemakers, mini-fridges, and ceiling fans. Upstairs, the Banana Suite boasts a king-size bed separated from a large Jacuzzi tub by a banana leaf wrought-iron screen, while the Bamboo Suite has a partial ocean view. Bring eyeshades—most curtains are just sheers. West Kauai Lodging also manages three moderately priced two-bedroom cottages in Waimea (owned by the Faye family, which has deep roots on the island), plus the newly built three-bedroom **Hale La** beach house in Kekaha, all with full kitchen, laundry facilities, and summertime air-conditioning. The plantation-style **Beach Cottage,** which includes a claw-foot tub, bamboo furniture, and sunset views over the ocean and Waimea Pier, is closest to the inn; the homey, Craftsman-inspired **Ishihara Cottage,** which features exotic hardwoods and an eat-in kitchen, and the tree-shaded **Pali Cottage,** with vintage furnishings and an enclosed lanai, are above town, with sweeping views of ridges and the distant sea. New manager Patrick McLean, who owns Hale La, is a former Kauai bed-and-breakfast pro who loves to help visitors plan where to eat, when to take a boat tour, you name it.

4469 Halepule Rd. (off Hwy. 50), Waimea. www.westkauailodging.com. ☎ **808/338-0031.** Inn (4 units) $135–$150 ($25 for 3rd person). 3 cottages (sleep 4–6) $179, plus $125 cleaning fee. Hale La beach house (sleeps 8) $395, plus $200 cleaning. **Amenities:** Wi-Fi (free).

Camping & Cabins

Kauai offers tent camping in six county-run beach parks and, for extremely hardy and self-sufficient types, several state-managed, backcountry areas of the Napali Coast and Waimea Canyon. Tents and simple cabins are also available in the cooler elevations of Kokee State Park and remote **Polihale State Park;** I can't recommend camping in the latter, due to its rugged conditions and increased potential for crime.

All camping requires permits, which must be purchased in advance, and camping in vehicles is not allowed.

County campsites, often busy with local families on weekends, close one day each week for maintenance. The most recommended for visitors, both for scenery and relative safety, are at **Haena, Hanalei Blackpot, Anini,** and **Lydgate** beach parks. Go to **www.kauai.gov**, click on "Visiting," and then "Camping Information," for schedules and downloadable mail-in permit applications. Permits cost $3 per adult (free for children 17 and under, with adult), except for Lydgate, which is $25 per site. On island, visit the **Department of Parks and Recreation** permits office (© **808/241-4463**) in the Piikoi Building, 4444 Rice St., Lihue (across from the post office), between 8:15am and 4pm weekdays; the county website also has details on satellite permit offices with more limited hours.

For camping in state parks and forest reserves, Hawaii's **Department of Land and Natural Resources** (http://camping.ehawaii.gov; © **808/274-3444**) prefers to issue online permits; its office in Lihue, 3060 Eiwa St., Suite 306, is also open 8am to 3:30pm weekdays. **Napali Coast State Wilderness Park** allows camping at two sites along the 11-mile Kalalau Trail—Hanakoa Valley, 6 miles in, and Kalalau Valley, at trail's end—for a maximum of 5 nights (no more than 1 consecutive night at Hanakoa). Camping is also permitted at Milolii, for a maximum of 3 nights; it's reached only by kayak or authorized boats mid-May through early September. Although there's no drinking water, trash must be packed out, and composting toilets are not always in good repair, permits ($20 per night) often sell out a year in advance. (**Note:** Due to frequent overstays, rangers conduct periodic permit checks here, so make sure you have yours on hand.)

Permits for primitive campsites in eight backcountry areas of Waimea Canyon and nearby wilderness preserves cost $18 per night, with a 5-night maximum; see http://camping.ehawaii.gov for detailed descriptions.

In **Kokee State Park,** which gets quite chilly on winter nights, **Kokee Lodge** (www.thelodgeatkokee.net; © **808/335-6061**) offers 12 rustic cabins ($74–$94 a night) that sleep up to six and should be reserved 3 to 6 months in advance; ask for a newer, two-bedroom unit, such as quiet No. 12. Kokee Lodge also manages the nearby state campgrounds ($18 per night; see above for permits). Less than a mile away, down a dirt road, the YWCA of Kauai's **Camp Sloggett** (www.campingkauai.com; © **808/245-5959**) allows tent camping in its large forest clearing for $15 per tent per night, with toilets and hot showers available; there's also a four-person cottage ($120–$135). Groups may rent its bunkhouse ($160–$120) or lodge ($200–$225), both of which sleep up to 15.

If you don't want to lug all your gear to and from Kauai, **Just Live** (www.ziplinetourskauai.com; © **808/482-1295**) sells and rents top brands of tents, camping stoves, sleep sacks, and more at its storefront in the Anchor Cove Shopping Center, 3416 Rice St., Lihue. **Kayak Kauai** (www.kayakkauai.com; © **888/596-3853** or 808/826-9844) offers rentals, supplies, and even car and bag storage at its Wailua River Marina shop, 3-5971 Kuhio Hwy., Kapaa.

WHERE TO EAT ON KAUAI

Thanks to a proliferation of hamburger joints, plate-lunch counters, and food trucks, you'll find affordable (by local standards) choices in every town; even in pricey Princeville, the shopping center food court offers a few tasty bargains. At the gourmet end of the spectrum, Kauai's very expensive restaurants—both on and off the resorts—provide excellent service along with more complex but reliably executed dishes. And nearly every establishment trumpets its Kauai-grown ingredients, which help keeps the Garden Island green as well as the flavors fresh.

The challenge is finding exceptional quality in the moderate to expensive range. Costs are indeed higher here, and service is often slower; it's best not to arrive anywhere—even at one of the many food trucks—in a state of starvation. Patience and pleasantness on your part, however, will usually be rewarded. During peak holiday and summer seasons, avoid stress by booking online with **Open Table** (www.opentable.com), currently available for 32 restaurants and luaus. The listings below, not all of which are on Open Table, will note where reservations are recommended.

For those with access to a kitchen (or just a mini-fridge), check out "Farmers Markets & Fruit Stands" (p. 507). You're guaranteed farm-to-table cuisine at a good price—and pace.

East Side

Note: You'll find the restaurants in this section on either the "Hotels & Restaurants on the Coconut Coast" map (p. 473) or the "Hotels & Restaurants in Lihue" map (p. 475).

EXPENSIVE

Duke's Kauai ★ STEAK/SEAFOOD   The view of Kalapaki Beach, an indoor waterfall and koi pond, and a lively beachfront bar have as much, if not more, to do with the popularity of Kauai's outpost of the California-Hawaii TS Restaurants chain as do the fresh seafood, vast salad bar, and belt-straining Hula Pie (a macadamia nut ice cream confection built for sharing). The downstairs bar's lunch and dinner menu offers the best values, with burgers, hearty salads, and flatbread pizzas, but the dinner-only upstairs dining room shows local flair with Hanalei taro cakes, seared ahi with papaya mustard sauce, and Kauai Kunana Dairy goat cheese atop grilled New York steak—among other tasty but less ambitious dishes such as shrimp scampi and macnut-crusted mahimahi. All upstairs dinner entrees include a trip to Kauai's biggest salad bar ($17 as a stand-alone item).

At west end of Kauai Marriott Resort, 3610 Rice St., Lihue (valet parking at restaurant or self-parking in hotel lot). www.dukeskauai.com. ℂ **808/246-9599.** Reservations recommended for dinner. Main courses $11–$15 lunch, $22–$33 dinner. "Taco Tuesdays" 4–6pm, with $3 fish tacos and $5 draft beer. Barefoot Bar daily 11am–11pm; main dining room daily 5–9:30pm.

Hukilau Lanai ★★ SEAFOOD/ISLAND FARM   Although his restaurant is hidden inside the nondescript Kauai Coast Resort off the main highway in Kapaa, chef/owner Ron Miller has inspired residents and visitors to find their way here in droves since 2002. The lure: a hearty menu that's virtually all locally sourced—from Kauai whenever possible, and other islands when not—as well as expertly prepared and presented. Four to six seafood specials, incorporating local produce, are offered nightly; try the Kauai coffee-spiced candied ahi, or the hebi (short-billed spearfish) when available. When you're not in a mood for seafood, the local mushroom meatloaf packs a savory punch, thanks to grass-fed beef from Kauai's Sanchez Ranch and Big Island mushrooms. Look for wine pairings on the "20 Wines for $20 Something" list, which offers good values from Californian and European vintners. Reservations are strongly recommended, especially for oceanview seating; the lobby bar offers nightly music but less ambience. **Note:** Hukilau Lanai also has an extensive gluten-free menu.

In the Kauai Coast Resort, 520 Aleka Loop, Kapaa. www.hukilaukauai.com. ℂ **808/822-0600.** Reservations recommended. Main courses $18–$32. Tues–Sun 5–9pm; poolside happy hour daily 3–5pm.

MODERATE

The Feral Pig ★ GASTROPUB   Let's dispense with the atmosphere first: There really isn't any. The self-proclaimed "pub and diner" is next to a mini-mall, with bare tables and just a few photos and chalkboards on the wall. At first glance, the dinner and lunch menus are also not that impressive, emphasizing burgers, sandwiches, and fries. But look more closely, and you'll find an attention to Kauai ingredients—especially beef and pork—and a flair for German-inspired dishes, such as house-smoked pork loin with blue-cheese mashed potatoes and a vinegary coleslaw or the occasional special of schnitzel with spaetzle (handmade egg noodles.) The seafood and many of the vegetables are local, too, but as the name suggests, pig is preeminent. Meat lovers should try the off-the-menu Feral burger, a potent mix of ground Kauai beef and house-smoked pork shoulder, topped with pork belly, caramelized onions, and aioli. The former bar manager of Town in Honolulu, co-owner Dave Power has crafted a first-rate cocktail menu with a goodly number of specialty beers on tap. Service can be uneven; weekends can get loud (and crowded) with live music.

3501 Rice St., Lihue (next to Harbor Mall). www.theferalpigkauai.com. © **808/246-1100.** Main courses $9–$13 lunch, $9–$20 dinner. Daily 7:30am–9pm. Reservations recommended Fri–Sat nights.

Kauai Pasta ★★ ITALIAN   Anyone who's grown up on their Nonna's home-made pasta may wonder what all the fuss is about, particularly with a menu loaded with standards like chicken parm and fettuccine Alfredo. But few can discount the good value of $10 lunch specials and the rarity (on Kauai) of a late-night lounge, both offered at the Kapaa location (there's another branch in down-town Lihue). Besides pasta, the dinner menu includes *pizzetta* choices such as rosemary grilled chicken with Gorgonzola and daily specials such as sous-vide pork; try the butternut squash ravioli if available. Portions are generous but not enormous; plan to order at least one of the tasty "sides to share"—I recommend the cone of truffle parmesan fries or bacon sautéed green beans, both salty and crispy. The *keiki* (kids') menu is a good deal too, from $5 pastas to $10 for grilled shrimp with mashed potatoes and vegetable. Both locations fill up quickly for dinner; bear in mind you can also eat in the darkly lit lounge at the rear of the Kapaa site. *Note:* Brown rice pasta can be substituted for most dishes.

4-939 Kuhio Hwy., Kapaa (next to Taco Bell, just north of Kuamoo Rd.). © **808/822-7447.** Also 3-3142 Kuhio Hwy., Lihue (btw. Poinciana and Hardy sts., in the Garden Island Publishing building). © **808/245-2227.** www.kauaipasta.com. Main courses $12–$24 lunch, $12–$24 dinner. Restaurant daily 11am–9pm; Kapaa lounge Mon–Sat 11am–midnight, Sun 11am–10pm, happy hour daily 3–5pm. Dinner reservations recommended (not available at Lihue).

Oasis on the Beach ★★ SEAFOOD/ISLAND FARM   Though not actually on the sand, the oceanview, poolside setting at the Waipouli Beach Resort is still memorable, as are the daily fresh-catch (grilled or pan-seared) and curry specials, the grilled kale salad with whipped Brie, and soy-glazed short ribs with yummy truffle fried rice. Chef de cuisine Sean Smull proudly notes that 90 percent of ingredients come from Kauai. Presentation wins points, too: Witness the pretty flower of blackberry syrup in the pineapple martini syrup. Luckily, half portions of many dinner entrees make sharing a breeze; the sights and sounds of ocean surf also make the occasional wait (the kitchen is not that close by) worthwhile. Save room for the apple banana spring roll with salted caramel ice cream, or another seasonal gelato from Papalani, the island's premium ice cream. Wednesdays are an ideal time to discover this culinary oasis, with live music and a special "chef's choice" menu from 4 to 6pm.

If you haven't yet tried Hawaii's local staples of plate lunch, bento, or poke, Kauai is a good place to start. The plate lunch is more than a mere meal; it's embedded in the local culture.

A reflection of the appetites (huge) and ethnic palates (varied) of early-20th-century plantation workers, traditional **plate lunches** include two scoops of rice, potato or macaroni salad, and a beef, chicken, fish, or pork entree, often a cutlet served **katsu** style—breaded and fried—and slathered in a rich, salty gravy. Luckily, many lunch counters are now happy to swap brown rice for white or sub a mixed green salad for a starch. Still, it's best to be hungry when you order a plate lunch. A Japanese creation, **bentos** are takeout trays offering smaller portions of more items, often with pickled vegetables, edamame (soybeans), and other nibbles, and traditionally sold at lunch counters known as *okazuya*. Bento and plate lunches usually range from $8 to $12. **Poke** (*poh-kay*), Hawaiian for "to slice," covers any number of diced, usually raw seafood dishes (sometimes made with tofu or vegetables), although the most common is ahi tuna, drizzled with *shoyu* (soy sauce) and sesame oil, and seasoned with green onions and crunchy *ogo* seaweed. Poke is usually sold by the pound ($12–$16).

Here are some of Kauai's standouts for plate lunch, bento, and poke:

EAST SIDE On the Coconut Coast, the indispensable **Pono Market,** 4–1300 Kuhio Hwy., Kapaa (✆ **808/822-4581**),

has enticing counters of sashimi, poke, sushi, and a diverse assortment of takeout fare. The roast pork and the potato-macaroni salad are top sellers, but it's also known for plate lunches, including pork and chicken laulau (steamed in ti leaves), plus flaky *manju* (sweet potato and other fillings in baked crust). It's on the ocean side of the highway, between Inia and Kauwila streets (weekdays 6am–6pm, Sat 6am–4pm).

In Lihue, **Po's Kitchen,** 4100 Rice St. (✆ **808/246-8617**), packs a lot of goodies in its deluxe bentos, including shrimp tempura, chicken katsu, chow fun noodles, spaghetti mac salad, hot dog, ham, and rice balls. It's hidden behind Ace Hardware and open Monday to Saturday from 6am to 2pm (cash only). One block away, **Garden Island BBQ,** 4252-A Rice St. (www.garden islandbbq.com; ✆ **808/245-8868**), is the place for Chinese plate lunches, as well as soups and noodle dishes; it's open daily 10am to 9pm. Off the main highway across from Wal-Mart, **Fish Express,** 3343 Kuhio Hwy. (✆ **808/245-9918**), draws crowds for its wide assortment of poke (the ahi with spicy crab in a light mayo sauce is a favorite), pork laulau, Spam musubi, bentos, and plate lunches, including lighter entree options such as Cajun blackened ahi and smoked fish. The downside: no seating (but you can ask for directions to nearby

In the Waipouli Beach Resort, 4-820 Kuhio Hwy., Kapaa (across from Safeway). www.oasiskauai. com. ✆ **808/822-9332.** Reservations recommended. Main courses $15–$32. Mon–Sat 11:30am–3pm and 4–9pm; Sun brunch 10am–2pm; dinner 4–9pm.

INEXPENSIVE

Hamura's Saimin Stand ★★★ JAPANESE NOODLES Honored by the august James Beard Foundation in 2006 as one of "America's Classics," this hole in the wall has been satisfying local palates since 1951. Visitors have also now

Isenberg Park). It's open daily from 10am to 5pm.

Mark's Place, in Puhi Industrial Park at 1610 Haleukana St., Lihue (www. marksplacekauai.com; ✆ **808/245-2722**), fashions daily salad and entree specials with a California-healthy bent: for instance, shrimp and grilled-vegetable quinoa salad and cornmeal-crusted mahi with chipotle aioli. But it also serves island standards such as Korean-style chicken, beef stew, and chicken katsu and is famed for its baked goods, including butter mochi and lavosh. It's open weekdays from 10am to 8pm, with three picnic tables for seating.

NORTH SHORE Everything is pricier on the North Shore, and ahi poke and plate lunches are no exception at **Kilauea Fish Market,** 4270 Kilauea Rd., Kilauea (✆ **808/828-6244**). At $29 a pound, skip the former here, but do stop by for Korean BBQ or grilled teri chicken plates ($11–$12); the burrito-like ahi wrap ($11) is a messy but filling alternative. It's open Monday to Saturday from 11am to 8pm, with outdoor seating only; the entrance is off Keneke Street, across from Kong Lung Trading. Opened in late 2013, **Sushigirl Kauai,** 5-6607 Kuhio Hwy., near the end of the road in Wainiha (✆ **808/827-8171**), is a takeout counter with ahi poke bowls served on rice, local greens, or quinoa ($12), plus meal-size seafood and veggie sushi rolls ($12–$15); it's open Monday to Saturday from noon to 8pm and Sunday from noon to 4pm.

SOUTH SHORE The **Koloa Fish Market,** 5482 Koloa Rd. (✆ **808/742-6199**), in Old Town Koloa, is a tiny corner store with two stools on the veranda. Grab some excellent fresh fish poke (try the Korean-style ahi), plate lunches, or seared ahi to go, and don't forgo decadent desserts such as Okinawan sweet potato pie with *haupia* (coconut cream) on macadamia nut crust. You can also pick up raw seafood to grill. It's open weekdays from 10am to 6pm and Saturday from 10am to 5pm. Down the road is **Sueoka's Snack Shop** (✆ **808/742-1112**), the cash-only window counter of Sueoka grocery store, 5392 Koloa Rd. (www.sueokastore.com; ✆ **808/742-1611**). It has a bigger, cheaper selection of meat-based lunch plates, such as shoyu chicken or kalua pork for $6.25. It's open daily; hours vary.

WEST SIDE Ishihara Market, 9894 Kaumualii Hwy. (Hwy. 50), Waimea (✆ **808/338-1751**), just off the main highway, is well worth a stop heading to or from Waimea Canyon. A local favorite that may even surpass Pono Market in reputation, Ishihara's is a family grocery store, founded in 1934, that stocks an impressive variety of fresh poke (including hamachi, baby octopus, salmon, and cooked lobster). It also has a grill making plate lunches Tuesday to Saturday (check Facebook page for specials). Picnic at nearby Waimea Pier and Lucy Wright Beach Park.

caught on to the appeal of saimin: large bowls of ramen noodles in salty broth with green onion, cabbage, and slices of fish cake, hard-boiled eggs, and pork, for starters. Here the housemade noodles are served al dente, and sometimes brusquely: Figure out what you're going to order before seating yourself at one of the U-shape counters. The "special regular" includes wontons and diced ham; top off any dish with a barbecued chicken skewer. If your appetite isn't large, order a to-go slice of the ultra-fluffy *lilikoi* (passionfruit) chiffon pie, just as renowned as Haura's saimin (and maybe even more delectable). Shave ice is also delicious, but its separate counter isn't always open. **Note:** There's often a line inside and out; it moves fast, so keep track of your place in it.

2956 Kress St., Lihue (1 block west of Rice St., in small blue building on left; park farther down the street). © **808/245-3271.** All items under $10. No credit cards. Mon–Thurs 10am–10:30pm; Fri–Sat 10am–midnight; Sun 10am–9:30pm.

Mermaids Cafe ★ PAN-ASIAN   There are just a couple of picnic tables on a deck outside the kitchen window of this cheerily bohemian spot in Old Kapaa Town, so plan on ordering your food to go. The laidback Kapaa hippie vibe means waits are sometimes long, and the kitchen can be inconsistent, but when the stars align, it's a wonderfully Kauaian experience. The signature dish is the ahi nori wrap, a massive sushi burrito in a green tortilla: seared tuna with rice, cucumber, nori, wasabi cream sauce, pickled ginger, and soy sauce. Tofu and chicken are the only other proteins on the limited, mostly organic menu, which includes a mild yellow coconut curry with island vegetables and satay plates with peanut sauce. The hibiscus iced tea and lemonade are especially refreshing on a hot day.

4-1384 Kuhio Hwy., Kapaa (north of Kukui St., next to Java Kai). www.mermaidskauai.com. © **808/821-2026.** Main courses $10–$13. No credit cards. Daily 11am–9pm.

North Shore

Note: You'll find the restaurants in this section on the "Hotels & Restaurants on Kauai's North Shore" map (p. 493).

EXPENSIVE

Bar Acuda ★★★ TAPAS   Named one of "Food & Wine" magazine's "Top 10 New American Chefs" in 1996, when he was still working in San Francisco, chef/owner Jim Moffatt later decided to embrace a low-key lifestyle in Hanalei. But he hasn't relaxed his standards for expertly prepared food, in this case tapas—small plates inspired by several Mediterranean cuisines—enjoyed here on the torchlit veranda or in the sleek, warm-toned dining room. Given Bar Acuda's deliciously warm, crusty bread, ordering one hearty and one light dish per person, plus a starter of spiced olives or Marcona almonds per couple, should suffice. But ask the server for help in ordering the right amount—some dishes, such as the delicious seared single scallop on mashed potatoes, aren't really suitable for sharing. The menu changes to reflect seasonal tastes and availability but usually includes a seared local fish and grilled beef skewers. An excellent finish is a wedge of North Shore honeycomb with Humboldt Fog goat cheese and a slice of crisp apple. **Note:** Reservations are strongly recommended, and you'll find patrons more smartly dressed here than anywhere else in Hanalei, even if they're dining at the handsome teak bar.

In Hanalei Center, 5-5161 Kuhio Hwy., Hanalei. www.restaurantbaracuda.com. © **808/826-7081.** Reservations recommended. Hearty tapas $12–$26. Daily 5:30–9pm.

Mediterranean Gourmet ★ MEDITERRANEAN   Imad and Yarrow Beydoun's unlikely but delightful oasis between Hanalei and the end of the road provides a welcome respite from the usual macnut-crusted mahimahi. At lunch, add fresh grilled fish to one of several generous salads featuring Kauai-grown kale or mixed greens, or the tabbouleh made with quinoa instead of the usual bulgur wheat. Meat-and-potato lovers can chow down on the well-spiced beef and lamb gyros wrapped in fluffy pita. At dinner, seafood paella or rosemary rack of lamb for two can make a special occasion that much more special, although the classic chicken shish-kabobs are no slouch. Imad, the Lebanese-born chef, and his wife, Yarrow, a Hanalei native, draw from traditions of both regions for evening

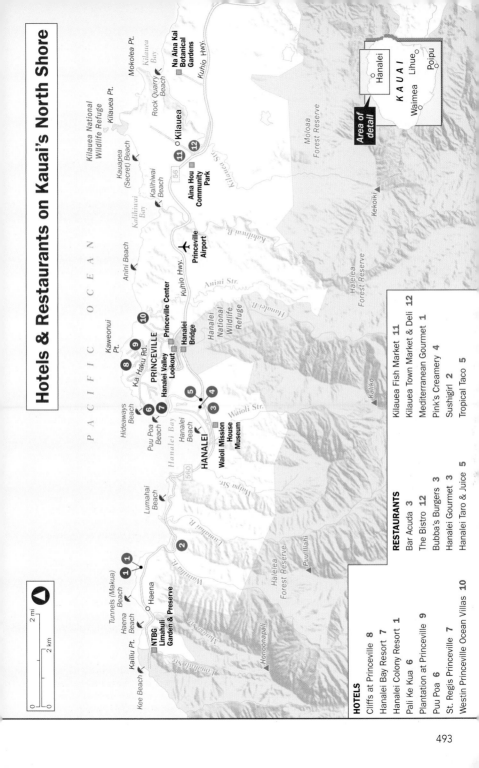

Hotels & Restaurants on Kauai's North Shore

HOTELS

Cliffs at Princeville **8**
Hanalei Bay Resort **7**
Hanalei Colony Resort **1**
Pali Ke Kua **6**
Plantation at Princeville **9**
Puu Poa **6**
St. Reg/s Princeville **7**
Westin Princeville Ocean Villas **10**

RESTAURANTS

Bar Acuda **3**
The Bistro **12**
Bubba's Burgers **3**
Hanalei Gourmet **3**
Hanalei Taro & Juice **5**
Kilauea Fish Market **11**
Kilauea Town Market & Deli **12**
Mediterranean Gourmet **1**
Pink's Creamery **4**
Sushigirl **2**
Tropical Taco **5**

entertainment, with belly dancing Thursday, a family-style luau (with Hawaiian buffet) Tuesday, and Hawaiian music and hula Sunday; more live music is offered the rest of the week. The dining room could use some updating, and the exceptional ocean view is better when windows are open—you're so close that salt peppers the glass. Reserve early to enjoy a sunset dinner.

Hanalei Colony Resort, 5–7132 Kuhio Hwy., Hanalei. www.kauaimedgourmet.com. © **808/826-9875.** Dinner reservations recommended. Main courses $11–$20 lunch, $24–$35 dinner. Lunch Mon–Sat 11am–3pm, Sun 10am–3pm (brunch 10am–1:30pm). Dinner Wed–Mon 4:30–8pm (light fare in lounge 3–4:30pm). Luau Tues 6pm.

MODERATE

The Bistro ★★ CONTEMPORARY AMERICAN/ISLAND FARM   John-Paul Gordon is yet another Kauai chef taking inspiration from the bounty of local fields and fishing grounds, with an admirably inventive palate and a well-practiced eye for presentation. Although his menu is largely seasonal, the "fish rockets" starter of seared ahi in lumpia wrappers with wasabi aioli is a signature dish; rich cuts of grass-fed beef from Kauai's Medeiros Farms are another standard, complemented by dill aioli, Gorgonzola cream sauce, or compound butter. If you crave something lighter, order the curly kale salad with local goat cheese and macadamia nuts, or the grilled fresh catch with white bean, arugula, and tomato ragu. Lunch includes simpler but satisfying options such as a Kauai beef burger and barbecued pork sandwich. The wine list is reasonably priced; ask about the $5 daily special. The intimate courtyard setting in the Kong Long Historic Market Center is also inviting. On Thursday slack key guitarist Pancho Graham performs from 6:30 to 9pm; there's also live music on Friday and Saturday. (If you're just looking for somewhere to use the restroom, know that non-patrons must pay $8—it's a long story.)

In Kong Lung Historic Market Center, Kilauea Rd. at Keneke St., Kilauea. © **808/828-0480.** Reservations recommended for parties of 6 or more. Lunch $11–$17; dinner main courses $15–$26. Daily noon–2:30pm and 5:30–9pm. Bar noon–9pm.

Hanalei Gourmet ★ AMERICAN   Located in a former Hanalei schoolhouse that's now a shopping center, this casual, decidedly non-gourmet spot offers the best values at lunch, with a variety of burgers and sandwiches on freshly baked bread starting at $8. The market-priced beer-battered fish and chips, accompanied by a suitably tart Asian slaw and soy wasabi sauce, is also notable. (If you want a half papaya, though, skip the $7 version here and walk a few steps to Harvest Market or across the street to the Big Save grocery.) Dinner has rather higher aspirations, not always met, as well as prices, but you can still order from much of the lunch menu. Although it has a soothing view of the Hanalei mountains, often with waterfalls, the atmosphere tends to be lively if not downright noisy, thanks to wooden floors, the popular bar, TV, and occasional live music, which draws an enthusiastic local crowd. Service is laidback but friendly.

In Hanalei Center, 5–5161 Kuhio Hwy., Hanalei. www.hanaleigourmet.com. © **808/826-2524.** Main courses $8–$13 lunch, $10–$29 dinner. Deli daily 8am–10:30pm; restaurant 11am–9:30pm; bar open until 10:30pm.

INEXPENSIVE

The best bargains in North Shore dining usually come from food trucks, often found at Anini, Hanalei, and Haena beach parks, but with fickle hours. One of the most reliable is **Hanalei Taro & Juice** (© **808/826-1059;** www.hanalei taro.com), on the right a mile past the Hanalei Bridge when heading into town.

It's open Monday to Saturday from 11am to 3pm, with most items under $10; be sure to sample the banana-bread-like taro butter mochi. Nearby, the tiny storefront **Pink's Creamery,** 4489 Aku Rd., is as equally renowned for its grilled cheese sandwiches with pineapple and optional kalua pork ($9, including chips) as it is for delicious tropical ice creams and housemade frozen yogurt; it's open daily 11am to 9pm. In Kilauea, chef A. J. Irons, a former Bar Acuda sous chef who also used to nourish beachgoers in Hanalei from his Opakapaka food truck, now prepares healthful, locally sourced takeout meals at **Kilauea Town Market and Deli** (www.kilaueatownmarket.com; ✆ **808/828-0021**), next to Kong Lung Historic Market Center at 2474 Keneke St.; it's open weekdays from 7am to 8pm and weekends from 8am to 8pm.

Tropical Taco ★ MEXICAN-SEAFOOD   Roger Kennedy operated a North Shore taco wagon for 20-odd years before taking up residence over a decade ago in this cottage-style building with a pleasant porch; dishes still come on paper plates. While the menu has a sprinkling of local/sustainable touches—the fresh seafood comes from North Shore fishermen, the lettuce mix is organic, and the fish and chips come with taro fries—the focus here is on satisfying hefty appetites. You might opt for the grilled fish special in soft corn tacos or as a crispy tostada rather than the gut-busting, deep-fried Fat Jack beef or veggie burrito, and be aware that any extras (cheese, sour cream, avocado) drive up prices quickly. **Note:** Hanalei has few places that are open for breakfast, so prepare to wait for your choice of one of four scrambled-egg burritos (try the taro and cheese).

In the Halelea Building, 5–5088 Kuhio Hwy. (Hwy. 560), Hanalei. http://tropicaltaco.com. ✆ **808/827-8226.** Most items $12–$14, breakfast burritos $6–$7. No credit cards. Mon–Fri 8am–8pm; Sat–Sun 11am–5pm.

South Shore

Note: You'll find the restaurants in this section on the "Hotels & Restaurants on Kauai's South Shore" map (p. 467).

EXPENSIVE

The Beach House ★★★ HAWAII REGIONAL   Call it dinner and a show: As sunset approaches, diners at this beloved oceanfront restaurant start leaping from their tables to pose for pictures on the grass-covered promontory, while nearby surfers try to catch one last wave. The genial waiters are as used to cameras being thrust upon them as they are reciting specials featuring local ingredients—a staple here long before "farm to table" became a culinary catchphrase. But there are plenty other good reasons to dine at the Beach House, whether you're splurging on dinner or sampling the more affordable lunch. Among them: the sherry-finished corn chowder, brimming with rock crab and fresh fish; the house ceviche of fish, prawns, and scallops in a citrus-lilikoi marinade, attractively served in a half coconut; the Kauai-grown beet salad; and any of the grilled fresh-catch dishes, such as black Thai rice, local green papaya salad, and red coconut curry sauce. (The sautéed preparations are also good, but on the sweet and rich side.) Desserts are less memorable than the well-crafted cocktails and wine list. **Note:** Vegan and gluten-free diners have good menu options.

5022 Lawai Rd., Poipu. www.the-beach-house.com. ✆ **808/742-1424.** Reservations recommended. Main courses $9–$19 lunch, $20–$48 dinner. Lunch daily 11am–3pm; light fare daily 3-5:30pm; dinner daily 5:30–10pm mid-Sept to mid-Mar (6–10pm mid-Mar to mid-Sept); lounge daily 11am–10pm.

CHEESEBURGERS in paradise

Delicious as Hawaii's fresh seafood is, sometimes what you're really looking for—in the words of Jimmy Buffett—is a cheeseburger in paradise. Luckily, Kauai boasts several inexpensive burger joints that are bound to satisfy.

The first thing to know about **Duane's Ono Char-Burger**, 4-4350 Kuhio Hwy., ocean side, Anahola (© **808/822-9181**), is that its burgers ($5–$8) are not made of the fish called ono (wahoo); they're just 'ono ("delicious" in Hawaiian.) The second thing to know is that waits can be long at this red roadside stand, opened in 1973, where wild chickens, cats, and birds are ready to share your meal with you. Duane's is open Monday to Saturday 10am to 6pm and Sunday 11am to 6pm. The founders of Duane's also run **Kalapaki Beach Hut,** 3474 Rice St., Lihue, near the west end of Kalapaki Beach (www.kalapakibeachhut.com; © **808/246-6330**). The two-story "hut" offers grass-fed Kauai beef burgers ($6–$10) and a unique taro burger ($7) made from organic taro grown in nearby Niumalu, Kauai sea salt, and Maui onions, among other ingredients; a taro bun is an option for 50¢ more.

Famed for its sassy slogans ("We Cheat Tourists, Drunks & Attorneys," among them) as much as for its Kauai beef burgers ($4–$7), **Bubba's** (www.bubbaburger.com/kauai.html) claims to have been around since 1936. It's certainly had time to develop a loyal following even while charging $1 for lettuce and tomato. Hearty appetites will want to try the Coors-spiked chili that comes on the open-face Slopper ($6) and with the Hubba Bubba ($7), in which it's poured over rice, a burger patty, and a grilled hot dog. The oldest Bubba's is in **Kapaa** (4-1421 Kuhio Hwy.; © **808/823-0069**), where the deck has a view of the ocean across Kapaa Beach Park. Bubba's other two locations are in **Hanalei** (5-5161 Kuhio Hwy., in Hanalei Center; © **808/826-7839**) and in **Poipu,** at the Shops at Kukuiula (2829 Ala Kalanikamauka, Koloa; (© **808/742-6900**). All three are open daily from 10:30am to 8pm, although the Kukuiula closing time may vary depending on business.

Josselin's Tapas Bar & Grill ★★ TAPAS   Other than Bar Acuda in Hanalei, this casual-chic bistro has the most New York/San Francisco urban vibe on Kauai. Chef Jean Marie Josselin, who closed his long-revered A Pacific Café in Kapaa in 2000 for a stint at Caesars Palace in Vegas, returned in 2010 with a radically different, rustic Asian-Mediterranean tapas concept in a lively (and sometimes very loud) atmosphere, on the second story of the upscale Shops at Kukuiula. When the sangria cart stops by your table, try the white lychee version—not too sweet—or, for nondrinkers, the strawberry pepper lemonade, while you peruse the eclectic and frequently changing menu. The "deconstructed ahi roll" may be a fancy way of saying poke on rice, but it's delicious, as are the unctuous slow-cooked butterfish and seared diver scallops. The wood-burning oven's use of *kiawe* (mesquite) adds smoky complexity to roasted cauliflower and other dishes. The tapas are designed for sharing, but ask one of the friendly waiters about portion sizes so you don't run up an even higher tab.

The Shops at Kukuiula, 2829 Ala Kalanikaumaka St., Poipu. www.josselins.com. © **808/742-7117.** Reservations recommended. Tapas $10–$32. Daily 5–10pm. Happy hour ($5 sangria/wine, $6–$10 tapas) 5–6:30pm. Live flamenco music Wed.

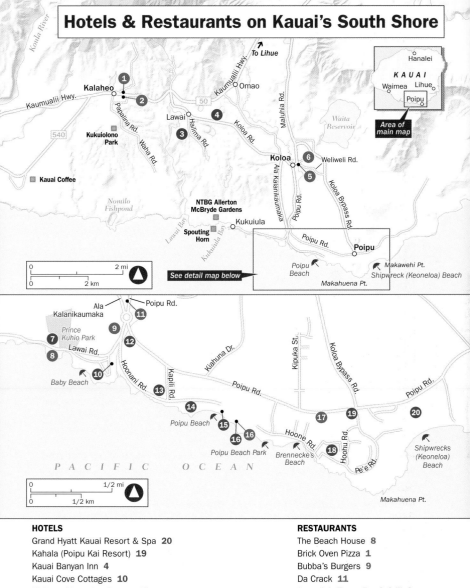

Hotels & Restaurants on Kauai's South Shore

KAUAI

Hanalei

Waimea Lihue

Poipu

Area of main map

To Lihue

Kaumualii Hwy.

Kalaheo

Kukuiolono Park

Kauai Coffee

Nomilo Fishpond

Omao

Lawai

Koloa

Weliweli Rd.

Koloa Bypass Rd.

NTBG Allerton McBryde Gardens

Kukuiula

Spouting Horn

Poipu Rd.

Poipu

Poipu Beach

Makawehi Pt.

Shipwreck (Keoneloa) Beach

Makahuena Pt.

Kaumualii Hwy.

Papalina Rd.

Waha Rd.

Hailima Rd.

Koloa Rd.

Maluhia Rd.

Waita Reservoir

Ala Kalanikaumaka

Poipu Rd.

| 0 | | 2 mi |
| 0 | | 2 km |

See detail map below

Ala Kalanikaumaka

Poipu Rd.

Prince Kuhio Park

Lawai Rd.

Baby Beach

Hoonani Rd.

Kapili Rd.

Kiahuna Dr.

Kipuka St.

Koloa Bypass Rd.

Poipu Rd.

Poipu Rd.

Poipu Beach

Poipu Beach Park

Hoone Rd.

Brennecke's Beach

Hoohu Rd.

Pe'e Rd.

Shipwrecks (Keoneloa) Beach

PACIFIC OCEAN

| 0 | | 1/2 mi |
| 0 | | 1/2 km |

Makahuena Pt.

HOTELS

Grand Hyatt Kauai Resort & Spa **20**
Kahala (Poipu Kai Resort) **19**
Kauai Banyan Inn **4**
Kauai Cove Cottages **10**
Kiahuna Plantation Resort **15**
Koa Kea Hotel & Resort **16**
Marjorie's Kauai Inn **3**
Nihi Kai Villas **18**
Poipu Kapili Resort **13**
Poipu Plantation B&B Inn & Vacation Rentals **18**
Prince Kuhio **7**
Sheraton Kauai Resort **14**
Waikomo Stream Villas **12**

RESTAURANTS

The Beach House **8**
Brick Oven Pizza **1**
Bubba's Burgers **9**
Da Crack **11**
Josselin's Tapas Bar & Grill **9**
Kalaheo Café & Coffee Co. **2**
Kalapaki Joe's **17**
Koloa Fish Market **6**
La Spezia **6**
Merriman's Gourmet Pizza & Burgers **9**
Red Salt **16**
Sueoka's Snack Shop **5**
Tortilla Republic **9**

Red Salt ★★★ HAWAII REGIONAL   The best hotel restaurant on Kauai may also be one of the smallest and hardest to find, tucked inside the discreetly located Koa Kea Hotel & Resort (p. 482). Although rivals offer arguably more dramatic ocean views in plusher settings, Red Salt consistently executes elegantly presented dishes from an intriguing menu designed by El Bulli–trained chef Ronnie Sanchez. Executive chef Adam Watten continues to showcase tender, moist fish with specials such as *onaga* (snapper) with giant snow peas and hearts of palm in a citrus curry or steamed *hapuupuu* (grouper) in a lemongrass shrimp broth with kabocha and Molokai sweet potatoes. The richer pan-roasted chicken and lobster saffron ravioli on the regular menu are equally compelling. A cloud of candlelit cotton candy (in varying flavors) makes a dramatic if sugary finish. **Note:** Exquisite sashimi and sushi are served most nights in the adjacent lounge. The more moderately priced breakfast and poolside lunch are less adventurous but no less thoughtfully prepared.

In the Koa Kea Hotel & Resort, 2251 Poipu Rd., Koloa. www.koakea.com. ✆ **808/828-8888.** Dinner reservations recommended. Valet parking. Main courses $14–$17 breakfast, $10–$21 lunch, $20–$50 dinner. Restaurant daily 6:30–11am and 6–10pm; poolside lunch daily 11am–6pm; sushi lounge Tues–Sat 5:30–9pm.

MODERATE

La Spezia ★★★ ITALIAN   The definition of charming, this much-needed stylish but cozy bistro in Old Koloa Town, opened in 2013, doesn't accept reservations for parties of fewer than six—reason enough to make a few friends at the pool to join you for dinner. Still, walk-ins will find it worth the possible wait for a table, handmade from wine crates by co-owner Dan Seltzer (formerly of Casablanca and Dali Deli); don't hesitate to sit at the small but handsome bar, either. Stalwarts on the seasonal, home-style menu include spicy veggie arrabbiata, ribsticking lasagne Bolognese, pan-roasted chicken, seared pork tenderloin with capers, and hanger steak with Gorgonzola polenta. At breakfast or the expanded Sunday brunch, French toast made with Hawaiian sweet bread, Brie, bacon, and raspberry jam provides the ultimate guilty pleasure, balanced by the Caprese-style egg-white frittata. **Note:** The gluten-free zucchini noodles are a great alternative no matter what your dietary requirements.

5492 Koloa Rd., Koloa (across from Koloa Post Office). www.laspeziakauai.com. ✆ **808/742-8824.** Reservations accepted for parties of 6 or more. Main courses $9–$12 breakfast, $12 Sun brunch, $14–$22 dinner. Tues–Sat 7:30–11am and 5–10pm; Sun 8am–1pm.

Merriman's Gourmet Pizza and Burgers ★★ AMERICAN/ISLAND FARM   A pioneer in Hawaii Regional Cuisine, Maui-based chef Peter Merriman first expanded onto Kauai with his even more gourmet (and very expensive) restaurant upstairs, now called Merriman's Fish House. While it's well worth a splurge, you're more likely to make repeat visits to his downstairs, much more casual Gourmet Pizza and Burgers. The thin-crust organic wheat pizzas ($1 more for gluten-free) are topped with such Hawaii-grown ingredients as roasted Hamakua mushrooms, kalua pork with grilled pineapple, or ahi with wasabi aioli (in lieu of cheese); the vegan version has a surprisingly decadent kale pesto and an array of hearty roasted vegetables. (Don't worry, you can still get pepperoni and sausage.) The similarly innovative burgers feature local grass-fed beef and lamb, although the turkey option, with Asian pear, white cheddar, and arugula, may be the most popular. Go elsewhere for fish tacos; fries are extra but worth it. (If you're not on a first date, order them with garlic and cilantro.)

In the Shops at Kukuiula, 2829 Ala Kalanikaumaka St., Poipu. www.merrimanshawaii.com. ✆ **808/742-8385.** Main courses $11–$17. Daily 11am–10pm. Live music Wed and Fri.

Tortilla Republic ★★ GOURMET MEXICAN   A smash with visitors and locals since opening in 2012, this vibrant, bi-level restaurant offers two ways to experience its modern, sophisticated take on Mexican cuisine: the upstairs **Grill** and the downstairs **TR Taqueria & Margarita Bar,** both with menus based on natural, organic, and local ingredients where possible. Open for dinner and Sunday brunch on the upstairs veranda (book for sunset), the Grill specializes in exotic-for-Kauai seasonings: Sautéed black tiger shrimp are served with a sauce of *pipián rojo* (red squash seeds), while the day's fresh catch comes rubbed in ancho chili and a serrano cilantro citrus sauce. Downstairs, the indoor/outdoor Taqueria & (often-mobbed) Margarita Bar offer simpler but still outstanding dishes, including a trio of guajillo-rubbed grilled fish tacos and a chicken quesadilla with roasted corn salsa and applewood smoked bacon. Service is congenial but sometimes slow; if you're dining upstairs, order the table-made guacamole for sheer entertainment value.

In the Shops at Kukuiula, 2829 Ala Kalanikaumaka St., Poipu. http://tortillarepublic.com. ℂ **808/742-8884.** Dinner/brunch reservations recommended. Grill main courses $19–$32 dinner, $10–$20 Sun brunch. Taqueria main courses $9–$15 breakfast, $11–$15 lunch and dinner. Grill: Mon–Sat 5:30–9pm; Sun 9am–2pm. Taqueria/bar: Mon–Sat 7:30am–5pm; daily 5–9pm. Happy hour daily 3–5pm.

INEXPENSIVE

Brick Oven Pizza ★ PIZZA   There's nothing gourmet or particularly Hawaiian about these pizzas, made with a hand-tossed, medium-thin, chewy crust (white with garlic butter or wheat) and mostly standard toppings (Portuguese sausage and barbecued chicken being the most unusual). Still, it's a local favorite (with another location on the East Side, in Wailua/Kapaa) and relatively easy on the budget—the large, 12-slice pizzas are genuinely large, and there's a bountiful, all-you-can-eat buffet from 5 to 9pm Monday and Thursday ($17 adults, $13 children 4–12). Pastas, subs, and salads are also fairly basic, but well-priced. If you're craving island flavors, order the kim chee tofu or guava-glazed smoked pork appetizers at the bar. **Note:** You can get pizza takeout and delivery through **Delivery Kauai** (www.deliverykauai.com; ℂ **808/755-5377**). Dining in, however, gives you the chance to work through the surprisingly broad beer list.

2–2555 Kaumualii Hwy., Kalaheo. www.brickovenpizzahi.com. ℂ **808/332-8561.** Also 4-4361 Kuhio Hwy., Kapaa (across from Kinipopo Shopping Village). ℂ **808/823-8561.** Sandwiches under $10; medium (10-slice) pizzas $17–$25. Daily 11am–9pm.

Da Crack ★ MEXICAN   Now *this* is a hole in the wall—hence the local nickname for a long-lived Mexican takeout window here, which the Kauai-reared Mexican-American chef Daniel Hurtado officially adopted in 2011. Portions are huge but ingredients are fresh, including housemade chips and guacamole. It's also relatively healthful: Beans are vegan and the rice is brown. Wasabi cream on the fresh fish taco (recommended) is about the only local twist; wash it down with a Mexican Coke or pop into neighboring Kukuiula Market for a smoothie from the juice bar at the rear. **Note:** Delivery is available from **Delivery Kauai** (www.deliverykauai.com; ℂ **808/755-5377**).

Next to Kukuiula Market, 2827 Poipu Rd., Koloa (north of the roundabout). www.dacrack.com. ℂ **808/742-9505.** Most items under $10. Mon–Sat 11am–8pm; Sun 11am–4pm.

Kalaheo Café & Coffee Co. ★★ BAKERY CAFE/ISLAND FARM   Whether you just grab a freshly baked cookie and cup of Kauai coffee to go or make a full meal of it, you'll quickly discover why visitors and locals jockey for parking spots at this casual restaurant and bakery. Early hours and hearty breakfasts (including convenient wraps to go) make the cafe a popular stop for folks on the way to snorkel cruises or Waimea Canyon hikes. About a 15-minute drive from Poipu, it also offers a great alternative to high-priced resort lunches; there's no view, but the plantation-style interior is bright and attractive. Greens grown nearby dominate the extensive salad list, while the rustic housemade buns pair nicely with grass-fed Kauai beef, veggie, or turkey burgers, among other plump sandwiches. Dinner is on the pricier side, but local seafood and produce shine, with island-style accompaniments such as stir-fried long beans and pohole ferns (similar to fiddleheads) and purple sweet potatoes.

2–2560 Kaumualii Hwy., Kalaheo (across the street from Brick Oven Pizza). www.kalaheo.com. ⓒ **808/332-5858.** Breakfast $5–$13, lunch $7–$13; dinner main courses $13–$29. Breakfast Mon–Sat 6:30–11:30am; Sun 6:30am–2pm. Lunch Mon–Sat 11am–2:30pm; Sun 11am–2pm. Dinner Tues–Thurs 5–8:30pm; Fri–Sat 5–9pm.

West Side

With fewer visitor lodgings and residents who can afford fine dining, the West Side offers mostly unassuming dining options. Other than the sites mentioned below, restaurants tend to be inconsistent at best, explaining why many visitors just stop at one of Waimea's several unrelated **Jo-Jo's Shave Ice stands** (I prefer the one at 9734 Kaumualii Hwy., across from the high school). **Ishihara Market** (see "Plate Lunch, Bento & Poke," p. 490) can also provide a quick lunch or picnic fare.

MODERATE

Kauai Island Brewery & Grill ★★ BREWPUB   The dry spell for Kauai brewpubs that began when the Waimea Brewing Company closed its doors in 2009 finally ended in 2012 when its former owners and beermaster celebrated the opening of their snazzy (but still sensibly priced) industrial/loft-style microbrewery and restaurant in Port Allen. The house lilikoi ale flavors the batter on fish and chips, but I prefer the excellent ahi poke with seaweed salad and the unique taro goat cheese spinach dip, which uses taro leaves (rather than the purple corm) with a dash of cayenne for seasoning. If the ample appetizers don't fill you up, the burgers, wraps, sandwiches, and beef and seafood platters certainly will. Up to 10 house beers are on tap, along with draft and bottled specials. The open-air mezzanine provides an angled view of sunset over the nearby harbor—and it can be mobbed when snorkel boats return mid-afternoon. **Note:** The kitchen closes around 9:30pm, but the bar often stays open past 10pm.

4350 Waialo Rd., Port Allen. www.kauaiislandbrewing.com. ⓒ **808/335-0006.** Main courses $11–$24. Daily 11am–10pm.

Kalapaki Joe's ★ AMERICAN/LOCAL   Opened in 2014 in the former Grove Café (and before that, the Waimea Brewing Co.) in the Aston Waimea Plantation Cottages compound of vintage wood-framed buildings, the newest of the three Kalapaki Joe's sports bar/restaurants boasts not only the best location but also the largest number of beers on tap (24). The list of burgers, sandwiches, meal-size salads, and Mexican items—tacos, quesadillas, enchiladas—is even more extensive; you can fill up just as easily from the appetizer menu. It's typical Mainland pub grub, but you can also order dishes with a local twist, such as kalua pork and seared cabbage with warm flour tortillas, the fresh ahi and avocado poke, or the fish of the day, grilled with a guava jelly glaze and topped with roasted macadamia nuts. Deep discounts at happy hour ($3 fish tacos, $1 shrimp tempura, and 25¢ chicken wings) and its convenience factor as the first pit stop heading back from Waimea Canyon mean it's often packed in late afternoons, as well as when any major sporting event is broadcast.

9400 Kaumualii Hwy., Waimea. www.kalapakijoes.com. ☎ **808/338-1666.** Also 1941 Poipu Rd., Koloa (☎ **808/742-6366**), and 3501 Rice St., Lihue (in Harbor Mall; ☎ **808/245-6266**). Main courses $11–$24. Daily 11am–10pm. Happy hour 3–6pm. Poipu location also serves breakfast on weekends 7–11am ($8–$14).

INEXPENSIVE

Kokee Lodge ★★ AMERICAN/LOCAL   It would be inexcusable to drive all the way up to Waimea Canyon or Kokee State Park and not schedule a meal here—at least if you order one of its hearty, local-fave specialties. The go-to entrees are Portuguese bean soup (add a giant hunk of cornbread for an extra $3.50), kalua pork (served with rice or on a sesame-seed bun), and loco moco (hamburger patty, two eggs over rice, and brown gravy). Vegetarians can opt for the broccoli-spinach quiche or a simple peanut butter and guava jelly sandwich (served with fruit, for under $4). Sadly, the limited hours don't make it easy for all-day hikers, but it's worth having at least one person circle back early to place a to-go order, especially for a generous slice of lilikoi chiffon pie or the warm, chocolate-bottomed coconut pie. With wooden tables and chairs, the dining room occupies the front half of a long cabin with picture windows overlooking the meadow next to the Kokee Museum; the rear gift shop is fun to peruse while waiting for food to arrive. Service is no-frills: Everything comes on paper plates, drinks and chips are self-serve, and you pay at the cashier.

9400 Kaumualii Hwy., Waimea. www.thelodgeatkokee.net. ☎ **808/335-6061.** Main courses $4–$8. Daily 9–2:30pm (takeout till 3pm).

Shrimp Station ★ SHRIMP   The name explains it all at this popular roadside stop on the way to or from Waimea Canyon and Polihale, with another branch in Kapaa. Shrimp plates—most featuring about 10 juicy shrimp in savory sauces with fries or two scoops of white rice—are the top draw, but you can also order chopped shrimp on large flour tacos or a fried shrimp burger. Order the latter, or the lightly battered fried coconut shrimp plate (including a zesty papaya ginger tartar sauce), if you don't want to get your hands messy from peeling shrimp, although the sweet chili and garlic sauces are indeed finger-licking good. The covered open-air picnic tables and trash cans can attract flies, so consider making yours a to-go order to eat at one of the nearby parks along the highway or on the beach. *Note:* The Kapaa location has a nicer dine-in area, though it still serves on paper plates.

9652 Kaumualii Hwy., Waimea (at Makeke Rd.). ☎ **808/338-1242.** Also 4-985 Kuhio Hwy., Kapaa (across from Chevron at Keaka Rd.). ☎ **808/821-0192.** Shrimp platters $12. Daily 11am–5pm.

KAUAI SHOPPING

Kaui has more than a dozen open-air shopping centers and historic districts well-suited to browsing, so souvenir and gift hunters are unlikely to leave the island empty-handed—though often it's with items made elsewhere. To find something unique to the Garden Isle, just look for the purple **kauai made** logo. The image of a *ho'okupu*, the ti-leaf wrapping for special presents, means the county certi-fies that these handicrafts and food items are made on the island using local materials where possible, and in relatively small batches. Some producers have their own storefronts, while other retailers post the logo to indicate they carry one or more Kauai Made lines; search the website, **http://kauaimade.net**, by type of product and region.

The similar but privately run **Kauai Grown** program, **www.kauaigrown. org**, showcases fresh and processed farm products (including cheese, chocolate, and soaps) containing at least 51 percent locally grown ingredients. Many of those items are available at local farmers markets; see p. 507 for listings. Below are some of the island's more distinctive boutiques and shopping enclaves.

East Side

LIHUE

The well-curated gift shop at the **Kauai Museum,** 4428 Rice St. (www.kauai museum.org; ✆ **808/245-6931**), carries the best selection of books about Kauai, plus exquisite artwork and handicrafts by local and other Hawaii artisans, from Niihau-shell lei to block-print fabrics.

While locals flock to the island's largest mall, **Kukui Grove Shopping Center,** Kaumualii Highway (Hwy. 50) at Nawiliwili Road (www.kukuigrove center.com), for department stores such as **Macy's** and **Sears,** visitors on a tight schedule or budget should browse the competitively priced, locally made food-stuffs (coffees, jams, cookies, and the like) at **Longs Drugs** (✆ **808/245-7785**). The family-run **Déjà Vu Surf Hawaii** (www.dejavusurf.com; ✆ **808/245-2174**) has a large selection of local and national brands.

The two small shopping centers near Nawiliwili Harbor mostly offer typical T-shirts, aloha wear, and souvenirs, but each has at least one store of note. At **Tropic Isle Music Co.** in **Anchor Cove,** 3416 Rice St. (www.tropicislemusic. com; ✆ **808/245-8700**), ignore the high-priced tourist trinkets and ask the friendly staff to find CDs matching your taste in the many subgenres of Hawaiian music. Across the street at **Harbor Mall,** 3501 Rice St. (www.harbormall.net),

Open-air shops in Kauai.

Twisted Turtles Yarn Shop (☏ 808/482-0122) sells colorful crocheted leis and other handmade item as well as a rainbow of yarns and supplies for needle-workers. Fans of tropical-print fabrics, batiks, and Hawaiian quilts will want to seek out **Kapaia Stitchery,** 3-3351 Kuhio Hwy. (Hwy. 56) at Laukini Road (www.kapaia-stitchery.com; ☏ 808/245-2281), which also offers ready-made aloha wear.

The 1930s mansion at **Kilohana Plantation,** 3-2087 Kaumualii Hwy. (www.kilohanakauai.com), next to Kauai Community College, provides a handsome setting for a half-dozen intimate boutiques selling locally made, Hawaiian-inspired artwork, jewelry, and confections, as well as unique clothing, accessories, and vintage Hawaiiana. Of them, **Grande's Gems** (www.grandesgemshawaii.com; ☏ 808/245-3445) also has stores in Princeville and at the Marriott resorts in Lihue and Poipu. The stand-alone **Koloa Rum Co.** (www.koloarum.com; ☏ 808/246-8900) carries a fun selection of logowear, rum-spiked goodies, and nonalcoholic treats, as well as five kinds of rum and a mai tai mix.

KAPAA

Parts of **Coconut MarketPlace,** 4-484 Kuhio Hwy. at Aleka Loop (www.coconutmarketplace.com), were under renovation at press time, and the rest of the open-air mall needed to be, but it remains a haven for lower-cost souvenirs. The most eclectic collection of native woodcarvings, jewelry, and island-themed tchotchkes lies in **Auntie Lynda's Treasures** (www.hawaiianjewelryandgift.com; ☏ 808/821-1780)—the staff is happy to chat, too. The mall's venerable vintage shop Bambulei was "on hiatus" at press time, but its sister store, **Pagoda,** 4-369 Kuhio Hwy. (www.pagodastore.com; ☏ 808/821-2172), north of Haleilio Road, ably fills its niche with Chinese antiques and curios, Hawaiiana, Asian-inspired decor, candles, soaps, and other gifts.

Although the sidewalks get crowded, the historic district of Kapaa offers an intriguing mix of shops, cafes, and galleries. Despite its name, **Hula Girl,** 4-1340 Kuhio Hwy. (www.ilovehulagirl.com; ☏ 808/822-1950), not only sells women's resort and aloha wear (much of it made in Hawaii), but also aloha shirts, board shorts, and other menswear, not to mention tiki-style barware, island-made soaps and salves, and accessories. Natural fibers rule the day at **Island Hemp & Cotton,** 4–1373 Kuhio Hwy. (☏ 808/821-0225), where the stylish men's and women's clothing lines also include linen, silk, and bamboo creations. Boho accessories include long flowery scarves, beaded purses, and leather bracelets.

North Shore

KILAUEA

On the way to Kauapea (Secret) Beach and the lighthouse, **Kong Lung Historic Market Center,** at the corner of Keneke Street and Kilauea Road (http://konglungkauai.com), deserves its own slot on the itinerary, with a handful of chic shops and cafes in vintage buildings to visit, historic market and photos to browse, and an umbrella cockatoo named Daphne to admire (not too closely). The flagship **Kong Lung Trading** (www.konglung.com; ☏ 808/828-1822) is an attractive, if pricey, showcase for ceramics, jewelry, stationery, books, and home accessories, including sake sets, tea sets, and hand-turned Hawaiian wood bowls. Souvenir seekers can find more budget options at the factory store of **Island Soap and Candle Works** (www.islandsoap.com; ☏ 808/828-1955), renowned for its Surfer's Salve, tropical soaps, and soy candles in coconut shells; it has another factory store in Old Koloa Town.

PRINCEVILLE

Island Soap also has a small store in **Princeville Center,** off Kuhio Highway just past the main Princeville entrance (www.princevillecenter.com). Although the two-level center is mostly known for its inexpensive dining options and resident-focused businesses, the **Hawaiian Music Store** kiosk (no phone) outside Foodland grocery has good deals on a large selection of CDs, while **Magic Dragon Toy & Art Supply** (© 808/826-9144) provides a wide array of rainy-day entertainment for kids.

HANALEI

As you enter Hanalei, look for **Ola's Hanalei,** on Kuhio Highway (Hwy. 560) next to the Dolphin restaurant by the river (© 808/826-6937). The jewel box of a gallery, opened in 1982 by award-winning artist Doug Britt and wife, Sharon, features Doug's whimsical paintings, wooden toy boats, and furniture made from *objets trouvés,* plus engaging jewelry, glassware, koa boxes, and other works by Hawaii and Mainland artisans.

The center of town reveals more of Hanalei's bohemian side, with two eclectic shopping and dining complexes in historic buildings facing each other on the Kuhio Highway. In the two-story rabbit warren of **Ching Young Village Shopping Center** (www.chingyoungvillage.com), **Divine Planet** (www.divine-planet.com; © 808/826-8970) brims with beads, star-shape lanterns, silver jewelry from Thailand and India, and Balinese quilts. **On the Road to Hanalei** (© 808/826-7360) also stocks unique gifts, from colorful pareos and clever figurines of Kauai roosters to Japanese pottery and African masks.

Across the street, the old Hanalei Schoolhouse is now the **Hanalei Center,** with two true gems tucked out of view: **Yellowfish Trading Company** (© 808/826-1227) and **Havaiki Oceanic and Tribal Art** (www.havaikiart. com; © 808/826-7606). At Yellowfish, retro hula girl lamps, vintage textiles and pottery, and collectible Hawaiiana mingle with reproduction signs, painted guitars, and other beach-shack musts, with ever-changing inventory. The owners of Havaiki have helpfully posted a "National Geographic" map of Oceania outside their gallery, all the better to appreciate the literal lengths they've gone to obtain the museum-quality collection of gleaming wood bowls and fishhooks, exotic masks, shell jewelry, and intricately carved weapons and paddles.

WAINIHA

Roughly halfway between Hanalei and the end of the road, next to the "last chance" **Wainiha General Store** (good for cold drinks and snacks), the **7 Artists Gallery,** 5-6607 Kuhio Hwy. (© 808/826-0044), always has at least one of the seven-plus local artists in residence. Look for Suzy Staulz's bold acrylics of local scenes, Lauren Johnson's garnet necklaces, and Alia DeVille's photographs of Kauai "sunrise" shells and other ocean treasures.

South Shore

KOLOA

Between the tree tunnel road and beaches of Poipu, **Old Koloa Town** (www. oldkoloa.com) has the usual tourist tees and trinkets, but also two sources of well-made local items and the island's best wine shop. The factory store of **Island Soap and Candle Works** (www.islandsoap.com; © 808/742-1945) is similar to the one in Kilauea (see above), while the **Koa Store** (www.thekoastore.com; © 808/742-1214) showcases boxes, picture frames, and other small pieces by local woodworkers using Hawaii's brilliantly hued native wood. **The Wine Shop** (www.thewineshopkauai.com; ☎ 808/742-7305) lives up to its name, but also sells high-quality locally made goodies such as Ko Bakery's *lilikoi* (passionfruit) white chocolate scones and Monkeypod Jam's Tahitian lime curd.

POIPU

Poipu Shopping Village, 2360 Kiahuna Plantation Dr. (www.poipushopping village.com), is home to a couple of independent clothing boutiques as well as local branches of Hawaii resort and surfwear chains. But the newer **Shops at Kukuiula,** just off the Poipu Road roundabout (www.kukuiula.com), has even more intriguing (often expensive) options spread among plantation-style cottages, flowering hibiscus, and greenery. **Palm** (www.palmpalmkauai.com; ☎ 808/742-1131) prides itself on exclusive, limited-edition collections of items such as vintage fabric handbags and glassware etched with tropical images, as well as women's designer clothing, jewelry, and other gifts. The airy boutique of **Malie Organics** (www.malie.com; ☎ 808/322-6220) offers its signature line of bath and beauty products, which use special distillations of island plants, including Kauai's native *maile* vine (not to be confused with *malie,* which means "calm" or "serene"); it also carries founder Dana Roberts' casual but tasteful resort wear in soft bamboo/cotton blends. Amid all the high-end chic, laidback surfers will feel right at home in **Poipu Surf** (www.poipusurf.com; ☎ 808/742-8797) and **Quiksilver** (run by local Déjà Vu Surf Hawaii; www.dejavusurf.com; ☎ 808/742-8088).

West Side

HANAPEPE

Known for its Art Night on Friday (see "Kauai Nightlife," p. 506), Hanapepe's dozen-plus art galleries in the historic town center are just as pleasant to peruse by day, especially the cheery paintings at the **Bright Side Gallery,** 3890 Hanapepe Rd. (www.thebrightsidegallery.com; ☎ 808/634-8671), and the playful tiles and other ceramics of **Banana Patch Studio,** 3865 Hanapepe Rd. (www.bananapatchstudio.com; ☎ 808/335-5944). The courtyard passage next to Little Fish Coffee leads to **MoonBow Magic Gift Gallery,** 3900 Hanapepe Rd. (www.moonbowmagic.com; ☎ 808/335-5890), which stocks an amazing potpourri of colorful baubles (including beaded geckos and Kauai chickens), Niihau shells, and other jewelry.

If the door is open, the store is open at tiny **Taro Ko Chips Factory,** 3940 Hanapepe Rd. (☎ 808/335-5586), where dry-land taro farmer Dale Nagamine slices and fries his harvest—along with potatoes, purple sweet potatoes, and breadfruit—into delectable chips, for $5 a bag (cash only). The wares of **Aloha Spice Company,** 3857 Hanapepe Rd. (www.alohaspice.com; ☎ 808/335-5960), include grill-ready seasonings with a base of Hawaiian sea salt, and Hawaiian cane sugar infused with hibiscus, vanilla, or lilikoi. Outside the historic strip are two other stores popular for more *omiyage,* the widely used Japanese term for food souvenirs. Flavored with guava, Kona coffee, macadamia nuts, and other tropical ingredients, the crisp butter cookies of the **Kauai Kookie Kompany** are ubiquitous in Hawaii, but a trip to the factory store at 1-3529 Kaumualii Hwy. (Hwy. 50) can be fun for kids (www.kauaikookie.com; ☎ 808/335-5003). Chocolate fiends need to try the luscious handmade truffles, fudge, and "opihi" (chocolate-covered shortbread, caramel, and macadamia nut) at

Kauai Chocolate Company in nearby Port Allen, 4341 Waialo Rd. (www.kauai chocolate.us; © **808/335-0448**).

WAIMEA

You have to plan ahead for a trip to the aptly named **Collectibles and Fine Junque,** 9821 Kaumualii Hwy., next to the fire station (© **808/338-9855**), since Rose Schweitzer only opens her jumble of vintage Hawaiiana and other finds from 11am to 4pm Monday to Thursday. Like Kauai Kookies, the passion-fruit products of **Aunty Lilikoi**—including jelly, butter, wasabi mustard, and salad dressing—are increasingly found around the state, but the factory store at 9875 Waimea Rd., across from the Captain Cook statue (www.auntylilikoi.com; © **808/338-1296**), is worth a peek.

When you head up to Kokee, leave time to pop into the gift shops of the **Kokee Museum** (www.kokee.org; © **808/335-9975**) and **Kokee Lodge** (www.thelodgeatkokee.net; © **808/335-6061**), the former for hundreds of Kauai- and nature-themed books, maps, and DVDs, and the latter for a judicious array of souvenirs, island foods, and locally made crafts.

KAUAI NIGHTLIFE

Kauai's nightlife is more suited to moonlight strolls than late-night partying, but if you're simply searching for live Hawaiian music, you're in luck. Virtually every hotel restaurant and lounge offers a slack key guitarist singing traditional and contemporary Hawaiian music on most nights, with many popular restaurants doing the same on the peak nights of Thursday to Saturday. You can occasionally hear other genres, too. **Kauai Music Scene** (www.kauaimusicscene.com) has a calendar you can search by date, type of music, and venue, among other filters.

Of the resort nightspots, **Duke's Barefoot Bar** (www.dukeskauai.com; © **808/246-9599**), inside the Kauai Marriott Resort, has long drawn a crowd of visitors and locals, especially at *pau hana* (end of work) on Friday. The downstairs bar features live Hawaiian music Wednesday through Monday from 4 to 6pm, and again Thursday through Saturday from 8:30 to 10:30pm.

The view isn't as memorable, but the *pupu* are tastier and the music more varied in the lounge of **Hukilau Lanai** (www.hukilaukauai.com; © **808/822-0600**) inside the Kauai Coast Resort, 520 Aleka Loop, Kapaa; top musicians playing Hawaiian, jazz, country, and blues perform Monday through Saturday from 6 to 9pm. *Note:* At the Grand Hyatt Kauai (www.grandhyattkauai.com; © **808/741-1234**), the book-lined **Stevenson's Library** sadly discontinued its live music (jazz) in 2014, but the resort's **Seaview Terrace** offers nightly Hawaiian music from 6 to 9pm, along with gorgeous sunset views.

You'll meet more locals—and pay a good deal less for your drinks—by leaving the resorts. Here are highlights from around the island:

EAST SIDE A combination sports bar, sushi bar, family restaurant, and nightclub, **Rob's Good Times Grill,** in the Rice Shopping Center, 4303 Rice St. (www.kauaisportsbarandgrill.com; © **808/246-0311**), bustles with live music Monday to Friday, swing dancing Tuesday, salsa dancing Wednesday, and DJs for club dancing Friday and Saturday. Provide your own live music via karaoke Sunday through Thursday. **Nawiliwili Tavern** (© **808/245-1781**), close to the Kauai Marriott Resort at 3488 Paena Loop (under the Hotel Kuboyama sign), is more of a dive bar, in a good way: It's got cheap drinks, two pool tables, and free karaoke. A sophisticated alternative, **Mahiko Lounge,** 3-2087 Kaumualii Hwy., is the swankily remodeled living room of the Kilohana Plantation mansion

farmers markets & FRUIT STANDS

Even if you're not staying in a place with a kitchen, a trip to one of the county-sponsored **Sunshine Markets** is a fun glimpse into island life, with shoppers queued up before the official start—listen for a yell or car honk—to buy fresh produce at rock-bottom prices. Markets end in 2 hours at the latest; arrive in time for the start, especially in Koloa and Kapaa. The weekly Sunshine Markets schedule:

- **Monday:** Noon, **Koloa Ball Park,** off Maluhia Rd. (Hwy. 520), on the left heading toward Old Town Koloa.

- **Tuesday:** 3pm, **Kalaheo Neighborhood Center,** Papalina Rd. off Kaumualii Hwy.

- **Wednesday:** 3pm, **Kapaa New Town Park,** Kahau St. at Olohena Rd. (Hwy. 581).

- **Thursday:** 3pm, **Hanapepe Park,** Kaumualii Hwy. at Lele Rd.; 4:30pm, **Kilauea Neighborhood Center,** Keneke St. off Kilauea (Lighthouse) Rd.

- **Friday:** 3pm, **Vidinha Stadium parking lot,** Hoolako and Halau sts. (off Hwy. 51), Lihue.

- **Saturday:** 9am, **Kekaha Neighborhood Center,** Elepaio Rd., between Alae and Amakihi roads (off Kaumualii Hwy.).

For the best selection of organic produce, visit North Shore farmers markets and fruit stands. In **Kilauea,** that includes the **Sunshine Market** and the privately run **Namahana Farmers Market**

(www.anainahou.org; © 808/828-2118) at Anaina Hou Community Park in Kilauea (off Kuhio Hwy., next to the mini-golf; Sat 9am–1pm and Mon 4pm–dusk). Next to Anaina Hou, on the same side of the highway, you'll see the bright yellow **Banana Joe's Fruit Stand** (www.bananajoekauai.com; © 808/828-1092). Its prices (ditto its expenses) are higher, but it's conveniently open Monday to Saturday from 9am to 5:30pm, with a great selection of exotic fruits, citrus, macadamia nuts, and locally made snacks.

In Hanalei, the popular **Waipa Farmers Market** (www.waipafoundation.org; © 808/826-9969) takes place every Tuesday at 2pm in an open field just west of Hanalei, on the mountain side of Kuhio Highway, between the Waioli and Waipa one-lane bridges. Some vendors also sell baked goods, jewelry, and other crafts. Hanalei community center **Hale Halawai** (www.halehalawai.org; © 808/826-1011) hosts a farmers market every Saturday from 9:30am to noon in its ballpark field (Kuhio Hwy. at Mahimahi Rd., next to the green Waioli Huiia church).

(www.kilohanakauai.com; © **808/245-5608**), offering cocktails made with freshly crushed sugarcane, live music, and terrific happy-hour specials (Mon–Sat 4–6:30pm) with dishes from adjacent Gaylord's.

NORTH SHORE Tiki Iniki (www.tikiiniki.com; © **808/431-4242**), tucked behind Ace Hardware in the Princeville Center, is a cheeky tiki bar/restaurant launched by Michele Rundgren (and her more famous rock-musician husband, Todd) in late 2013. Nightly cocktail specials and frequent theme nights have made it a big hit; table reservations are recommended. **Tahiti Nui,** 5-5134 Kuhio Hwy., Hanalei (www.thenui.com; © **808/826-6277**), opened in 1963, and is pretty much as it appears in "The Descendants": a great family-friendly restaurant and lounge with live Hawaiian music nightly. Another local hangout,

Hanapepe Art Night.

Hanalei Gourmet, in the Old Hanalei Schoolhouse, 5–5161 Kuhio Hwy. (✆ 808/826-2524), has live music Sunday at 6pm and Wednesday at 8pm.

SOUTH SHORE Keoki's Paradise, in the Poipu Shopping Village (www.keokisparadise.com; ✆ 808/742-7534), offers live music Tuesday to Saturday from 5 to 10pm and Sunday to Monday 7 to 9pm , with more dance-oriented music Thursday to Saturday. In the Shops at Kukuiula, **Merriman's Gourmet Pizza and Burgers** (www.merrimanshawaii.com; ✆ 808/742-8385) presents live music Wednesday and Friday nights, while the downstairs margarita bar, **Tortilla Republic** (www.tortillarepublic.com; ✆ 808/742-8884), is a lively scene.

WEST SIDE Kauai Island Brewery & Grill, 4350 Waialo Rd., Port Allen (www.kauaiislandbrewing.com; ✆ 808/335-0006), often hosts late-night live music and DJ "aftah" parties, starting at 10pm, and serves as a sports bar with five huge, high-definition TVs.

The *tutu kane* (granddaddy) of local art events is **Hanapepe Art Night** (www.hanapepe.org), every Friday from 6 to 9pm along Hanapepe Road. Food trucks, live music on the street and in stores, and brightly lit shops and galleries create a festive atmosphere. *Tip:* Drive cautiously when leaving—Hanapepe Road near the eastern Highway 50 turnoff can be very dark.

In 2013, the historic district of Kapaa (www.facebook.com/OldKapaaTown) debuted a similar **First Saturday Art Walk,** with sidewalk vendors, live entertainment, and extended shopping hours 5 to 9pm the first Saturday of the month. The **Kukuiula Art Walk** features the same format on the second Saturday of the month, from 6 to 9pm, at the Shops at Kukuiula.

PLANNING YOUR TRIP TO HAWAII

10

Hawaii is rich in natural and cultural wonders, and each island has something unique to offer. With so much vying for your attention, planning your trip can be bewildering. In this chapter, we've compiled everything you need to know before escaping to the Islands.

The first thing to do: Decide where you want to go. Read through each chapter (especially each chapter introduction) to see which islands fit the profile and offer the activities you're looking for. I strongly recommend that you **limit your island-hopping** to one island per week. If you decide to go to visit more than one in a week, be warned: You could spend much of your precious vacation time in airports and checking in and out of hotels. Not much fun!

My second tip is to **fly directly to the island of your choice;** doing so can save you a 2-hour layover in Honolulu and another plane ride. Oahu, the Big Island, Maui, and Kauai now all receive direct flights from the Mainland; if you're heading to Molokai or Lanai, you'll have the easiest connections if you fly into Honolulu.

So let's get on with the process of planning your trip. Searching out the best deals and planning your dream vacation to Hawaii should be half the fun.

For additional help in planning your trip and for more on-the-ground resources in Hawaii, turn to "Fast Facts: Hawaii," on p. 516.

GETTING THERE
By Plane

Most major U.S. and many international carriers fly to **Honolulu International Airport** (HNL), on Oahu. Some also offer direct flights to **Kahului Airport** (OGG), on Maui; **Lihue Airport** (LIH), on Kauai; and **Kona International Airport** (KOA) and **Hilo Airport** (ITO), on the Big Island. If you can fly directly to the island of your choice, you'll be spared a 2-hour layover in Honolulu and another plane ride. If you're heading to Molokai or Lanai, you'll have the easiest connections if you fly into Honolulu. See island chapters for detailed information on direct flights to each island.

Hawaiian Airlines offers flights from more mainland U.S. gateways than any other airline. Hawaiian's easy-to-navigate website makes finding the cheapest fares a cinch. Its closest competitor, price-wise, is **Alaska Airlines,** which offers daily nonstop flights from West Coast cities including Anchorage, Seattle, Portland, and Oakland. From points farther east, **United, American, Continental,** and **Delta** all fly to Hawaii with nonstop service to Honolulu and most neighbor islands. If you're having difficulty finding an affordable fare, try routing your flight through Las Vegas. It's a huge hub for traffic to and from the Islands.

For travel from beyond the U.S. mainland, check these airlines: Air Canada, Air New Zealand, Qantas Airways, Japan Air Lines, All Nippon Airways (ANA), the Taiwan-based China Airlines, Korean Air, and Philippine Airlines. Hawaiian

Previous page: Hawaiian sunset.

Airlines also flies nonstop to Australia, American Samoa, Philippines, Tahiti, South Korea, and Japan.

ARRIVING AT THE AIRPORT

IMMIGRATION & CUSTOMS CLEARANCE International visitors arriving by air should cultivate patience and resignation before setting foot on U.S. soil. U.S. airports have considerable security practices in place. Clearing Customs and Immigration can take as long as 2 hours.

AGRICULTURAL SCREENING AT THE AIRPORTS At Honolulu International and the neighbor-island airports, baggage and passengers bound for the Mainland must be screened by agriculture officials. Officials will confiscate local produce like fresh avocados, bananas, and mangoes, in the name of fruit-fly control. Pineapples, coconuts, and papayas inspected and certified for export; boxed flowers; leis without seeds; and processed foods (macadamia nuts, coffee, jams, dried fruit, and the like) will pass.

GETTING AROUND HAWAII

For additional advice on travel within each island, see "Getting Around" in the individual island chapters.

Interisland Flights

The major interisland carriers have cut way back on the number of interisland flights. The airlines warn you to show up at least 90 minutes before your flight and, believe me, with all the security inspections, you will need all 90 minutes to catch your flight.

Hawaii has one major interisland carrier, **Hawaiian Airlines** (www.hawaiian air.com; ✆ **800/367-5320**), and two commuter airlines, **Island Air** (www.island air.com; ✆ **800/323-3345**) and **Mokulele Airlines** (www.mokuleleairlines.com; ✆ **866/260-7070**). The commuter flights service the neighbor islands' more remote airports and tend to be on small planes; you'll board from the tarmac and weight restrictions apply.

By Car

The bottom line: You will likely need a car to get around the islands, especially if you plan to explore outside your resort—and you absolutely should. Public transit in the islands is spotty—Oahu has an adequate public transportation service, but even so, it's set up for residents, not tourists carrying coolers and beach toys (all carry-ons must fit under the bus seat). So plan to rent a car.

That said, Hawaii has some of the priciest car-rental rates in the country. The most expensive is the island of Lanai, where four-wheel-drive vehicles cost a small fortune. Keep in mind, too, that rental cars are often at a premium

---

A Weeklong Cruise Through the Islands

If you're looking for a taste of several islands in 7 days, consider **Norwegian Cruise Line** (www.ncl.com; ✆ **866/234-7350**), the only cruise line that operates year-round in Hawaii. NCL's 2,240-passenger ship *Pride of America* circles Hawaii, stopping on four islands: the Big Island, Maui, Kauai, and Oahu.

on Kauai, Molokai, and Lanai and may be sold out on any island over holiday weekends, so be sure to book well ahead. In fact, I recommend reserving your car as soon as you book your airfare.

To rent a car in Hawaii, you must be at least 25 years of age and have a valid driver's license and credit card. **Note:** If you're visiting from abroad and plan to rent a car in the United States, keep in mind that foreign driver's licenses are usually recognized in the U.S., but you should get an international one if your home license is not in English.

At Honolulu International Airport and most neighbor-island airports, you'll find many major car-rental agencies, including **Alamo, Avis, Budget, Dollar, Enterprise, Hertz, National,** and **Thrifty.** It's almost always cheaper to rent a car in Waikiki, or anywhere but at the airport, where you will pay a daily fee for the convenience of renting at the airport.

GASOLINE   Gas prices in Hawaii, always much higher than on the U.S. mainland, vary from island to island. Expect to pay around $4 a gallon, and as much as $5 a gallon on Lanai and Molokai. Check www.gasbuddy.com to find the cheapest gas in your area.

INSURANCE   Hawaii is a no-fault state, which means that if you don't have collision-damage insurance, you are required to pay for all damages before you leave the state, whether or not the accident was your fault. Your personal car insurance may provide rental-car coverage; check before you leave home. Bring your insurance identification card if you decline the optional insurance, which usually costs from $9 to $45 a day. Obtain the name of your company's local claim representative before you go. Some credit card companies also provide collision-damage insurance for their customers; check with yours before you rent.

DRIVING RULES   Hawaii state law mandates that all car passengers must wear a **seat belt** and all infants must be strapped into a car seat. You'll pay a $92 fine if you don't buckle up. **Pedestrians** always have the right of way, even if they're not in the crosswalk. You can turn **right on red** after a full and complete stop, unless otherwise posted.

ROAD MAPS   The best and most detailed maps for activities are published by **Franko Maps** (www.frankosmaps.com); these feature a host of island maps, plus a terrific "Hawaiian Reef Creatures Guide" for snorkelers curious about those fish they spot underwater. Free road maps are published by **"This Week Magazine,"** a visitor publication available on Oahu, the Big Island, Maui, and Kauai.

Another good source is the **University of Hawaii Press maps,** which include a detailed network of island roads, large-scale insets of towns, historical and contemporary points of interest, parks, beaches, and hiking trails. If you can't find them in a bookstore near you, contact **University of Hawaii Press,** 2840 Kolowalu St., Honolulu, HI 96822 (www.uhpress.hawaii.edu; © **888/UH-PRESS** [847-7377]). For topographic maps of the islands, go to the **U.S. Geological Survey** site (www.pubs.usgs.gov).

Stay off the Cellphone

Talking on a cellphone while driving in Hawaii is a big no-no. Fines range from $100 to $200, and double in school or construction zones. An Oahu woman was even ticketed for talking on her cellphone while parked on the side of the road! Save yourself the money; don't use a cell while you are driving.

SPECIAL-INTEREST TRIPS & TOURS

This section presents an overview of special-interest trips and tours and outdoor excursions in Hawaii. See individual island chapters for detailed information on the best local outfitters and tour-guide operators—as well as details for exploring on your own. Each island chapter discusses the best spots to set out on your own, from the top offshore snorkel and dive spots to great daylong hikes, as well as the federal, state, and county agencies that can help you with hikes on public property. I also list references for spotting birds, plants, and sea life. Always use the resources available to inquire about weather, trail, or surf conditions; water availability; and other conditions before you take off on your adventure.

Air Tours

Nothing beats getting a bird's-eye view of Hawaii. Some of the islands' most stunning scenery can't be seen any other way. You'll have your choice of aircraft here: **helicopter, small fixed-wing plane,** or, on Oahu, **seaplane.** For wide, open spaces such as the lava fields of Hawaii Volcanoes National Park, a fixed-wing plane is the safest and most affordable option. But for exploring tight canyons and valleys, helicopters have an advantage: They can hover. Only a helicopter can bring you face to face with waterfalls in remote places like Mount Waialeale on Kauai and Maui's little-known Wall of Tears, up near the summit of Puu Kukui.

Today's pilots are part Hawaiian historian, part DJ, part amusement-ride operator, and part tour guide, sharing anecdotes about Hawaii's flora, fauna, history, and culture. Top trips include:

o **Na Pali Coast,** Kauai, where you soar over the painted landscape of Waimea Canyon, known as the "Grand Canyon of the Pacific," and visit the cascading falls of Mount Waialeale, one of the wettest spots on Earth.

o **Haleakala National Park and West Maui,** where you skirt the edges of Haleakala's otherworldly crater before plunging into the deep, pristine valleys of the West Maui Mountains.

o **Hawaii Volcanoes National Park** on the Big Island, where you stare into the molten core of a live volcano and watch lava spill into the sea.

Flying High with Blue Hawaiian

Blue Hawaiian Helicopters (www.bluehawaiian.com; © **800/745-2583**) is the Cadillac of helicopter-tour companies, offering aerial excursions from Oahu, Maui, Kauai, and the Big Island. The high-tech, environmentally friendly (and quiet) Eco-Star helicopters are specially designed for air-tour operators and feature 60 square feet of panoramic windows. You can book 45- to 55-minute flights over Oahu or Kauai for just over $200. From Maui and the Big Island you have the option of visiting a second island as well. These spectacular 2-hour trips cost around $450. If you have somewhere specific you'd like to explore, private charters start at $1,860 per hour. **Tip:** Book on the website for substantial savings!

Farm Tours

Overalls and garden spades might not be the first images that come to mind when planning your Hawaii vacation, but a tour of a lush and bountiful island farm should be on your itinerary. **Agritourism** has become an important new income stream for Hawaii farmers, who often struggle with the rising costs of doing business in paradise. Farm tours benefit everyone: The farmer gets extra cash, visitors gain an intimate understanding of where and how their food is produced, and fertile farmlands stay in production—preserving Hawaii's rural heritage. There are so many diverse and inspiring farms to choose from: 100-year-old Kona coffee farms, bean-to-bar chocolate plantations, orchid nurseries, an award-winning goat dairy, and even a vodka farm!

With its massive cattle ranches, tropical flower nurseries, and coffee-covered hillsides, the **Big Island** is the agricultural heart of Hawaii. But each of the islands has farms worth visiting. Many agri-tours include sumptuous tasting sessions, fascinating historical accounts, and tips for growing your own food at home. You can visit farms independently (see each island's "Exploring" section for details) or book one of the following multifarm excursions.

On the Big Island, the nonprofit **Hawaii Agri-Tourism Association** (www.hawaiiagtours.com; ☏ **808/286-6559**) offers a full-day immersion in Hilo's flower, fruit, and coffee industries, with a stop at the Imiloa Astronomy Center for some cultural context. The educational tours cost $90 and take place Wednesday through Friday from 8:30am to 3:30pm.

Maui Country Farm Tours (www.mauicountryfarmtours.com; ☏ **808/283-9131**) offers a gorgeous overview of agriculture on the Valley Isle, traveling through working sugar and pineapple plantations and stopping at a lavender farm, goat dairy, and vodka distillery.

Guided Hikes

For hikers, a great alternative to hiring a private guide is taking a guided hike with the **Nature Conservancy** or the **Sierra Club.** Both organizations offer guided hikes in preserves and special areas during the year, as well as day- to weeklong volunteer work trips to restore habitats and trails and root out invasive plants. It might not sound like a dream vacation to everyone, but it's a chance to see the "real" Hawaii—including wilderness areas that are ordinarily off-limits.

All Nature Conservancy hikes and work trips are free (donations are appreciated). However, you must reserve a spot, and a deposit is required for guided hikes to ensure that you'll show up; your deposit is refunded when you do. The hikes are generally offered once a month on Maui and Molokai, and twice a month on Oahu. For all islands, call the Oahu office for reservations.

The Sierra Club offers half- or all-day hikes on Oahu, Kauai, the Big Island, and Maui. Hikes are led by certified Sierra Club volunteers and classified as easy, moderate, or strenuous. Donations of $1 for Sierra Club members and $5 for nonmembers (bring exact change) are recommended. You can find the latest edition of the club newsletter on the Sierra Club website (see below).

Contact the **Nature Conservancy of Hawaii** (www.nature.org/ourinitiatives/regions; ☏ **808/537-4508** on Oahu, ☏ 808/572-7849 on Maui, ☏ 808/553-5236 on Molokai, 808/246-0543 on Kauai, and 808/939-7171 on the Big Island); or the **Hawaii Chapter of the Sierra Club** (www.sierraclubhawaii.com; ☏ **808/538-6616** on Oahu).

Volunteer Vacations & Ecotourism

If you're looking to swap sunbathing for something more memorable on your next trip to Hawaii, consider volunteering while on vacation. Why not leave the islands a little nicer than when you arrived? Rewards include new friends and access to spectacular wilderness areas that are otherwise off-limits. To participate in beach and reef cleanups, or monitor nesting sea turtles, contact the **University of Hawaii Sea Grant College Program** (℅ 808/956-7031) or the **Hawaii Wildlife Fund** (www.wildhawaii.org; ℅ 808/280-8124). For land-based adventures, contact **Malama Hawaii** (www.malamahawaii.org/get_involved/volunteer. php), a statewide organization dedicated to *malama* (taking care) of the culture and environment of Hawaii. This site lists a range of opportunities on various islands, such as weeding and potting plants in botanical gardens, restoring taro patches, cleaning up mountain streams, bird-watching, and even hanging out at Waikiki Beach to help with a reef project.

For a truly novel experience, sign up on the waitlist to volunteer with **Kahoolawe Island Restoration Commission** (http://kahoolawe.hawaii.gov/volunteer.shtml or http://koolauwatershed.org; ℅ 808/243-5020). You'll travel by boat from Maui to Kahoolawe, an uninhabited island that the U.S. military used as target practice for decades. Plant by plant, volunteers are bringing life back to the barren island, once a significant site for Hawaiian navigators. A week here is a cultural immersion unlike any other.

Check out the **Hawaii Ecotourism Association** (www.hawaiiecotourism. org; ℅ 808/235-5431), a comprehensive site that lists ecotourism volunteer opportunities, such as seabird habitat restoration. Local ecotourism opportunities are also discussed in the individual island chapters.

Watersports Excursions

The same Pacific Ocean surrounds all of the Hawaiian Islands, but the varying topography of each shoreline makes certain spots superior for watersports. If **surfing** is your passion, head to Oahu. You'll find gentle waves at Waikiki and adrenaline-laced action on the famed North Shore. Maui has plenty of surf breaks, too, plus it's the birthplace of **windsurfing** and a top **kitesurfing** destination. Beginners and pros alike will find perfect conditions for catching air off of Maui's swells.

Kayaking is excellent statewide, particularly on Kauai, where you can take the adventurous Na Pali coast challenge, and on Molokai, where you can lazily paddle downwind past ancient fish ponds.

Sport fishing fans should make a beeline to the Big Island's Kona Coast, where billfish tournaments have reeled in monster Pacific blue marlins.

The deep blue Kona waters are also home to giant manta rays, and **scuba diving** among these gentle creatures is a magical experience. Scuba diving is also spectacular off the tiny island of Lanai, where ethereal caverns have formed in the reefs, and on Maui, on the back wall of Molokini Crater.

All of the islands have great **snorkeling** spots, but Maui's two harbors offer the widest range of snorkeling and diving boat tours. Book a half-day cruise out to fish-filled Molokini or an all-day adventure over to Lanai.

During the winter months, from November to April, **whale-watching** tours launch from every island. **Dolphin-spotting** is most reliable on Lanai at Manele Bay and on Hawaii at Kealakekua Bay, where the charismatic spinner dolphins come to rest.

View each island's "Watersports" sections for detailed information on watersports outfitters and tour providers.

[FastFACTS] HAWAII

Area Codes Hawaii's area code is 808; it applies to all islands. There is a long-distance charge when calling from one island to another.

Customs For details regarding U.S. Customs and Border Protection, consult your nearest U.S. embassy or consulate, or U.S. Customs (www.cbp.gov). You cannot take home fresh fruit, plants, or seeds (including some leis) unless they are sealed. You cannot seal and pack them yourself. For information on what you're allowed to bring home, contact one of the following agencies:

U.S. Citizens: U.S. Customs & Border Protection (CBP), 1300 Pennsylvania Ave., NW, Washington, DC 20229 (www.cbp.gov; ✆ 877/CBP-5511).

Canadian Citizens: Canada Border Services Agency (www.cbsa-asfc.gc.ca; ✆ 800/461-9999 in Canada, or 204/983-3500).

U.K. Citizens: HM Customs & Excise (www.hmce.gov.uk; ✆ 0845/010-9000 in the U.K., or 020/8929-0152).

Australian Citizens: Australian Customs Service (www.customs.gov.au; ✆ 1300/363-263).

New Zealand Citizens: New Zealand Customs, The Customhouse, 17–21 Whitmore St., Box 2218, Wellington (www.customs.govt.nz; ✆ 64/9-927-8036 outside of NZ, or 0800/428-786).

Electricity Like Canada, the United States uses 110 to 120 volts AC (60 cycles), compared to 220 to 240 volts AC (50 cycles) in most of Europe, Australia, and New Zealand. Downward converters that change 220–240 volts to 110–120 volts are difficult to find in the United States, so bring one with you if you're traveling to Hawaii from abroad.

Embassies & Consulates All embassies are in the nation's capital, Washington, D.C. Some consulates are in major U.S. cities, and most nations have a mission to the United Nations in New York City. If your country isn't listed below, check **www.embassy.org/ embassies** or call for directory information in Washington, D.C. (✆ **202/555-1212**).

The embassy of **Australia** is at 1601 Massachusetts Ave. NW, Washington, DC 20036 (www.usa.embassy.gov.au; ✆ **202/797-3000**). Consulates are in New York, Honolulu, Houston, Los Angeles, Denver, Atlanta, Chicago, and San Francisco.

The embassy of **Canada** is at 501 Pennsylvania Ave. NW, Washington, DC 20001 (www.canadainternational.gc.ca/washington; ✆ **202/682-1740**). Other Canadian consulates are in Chicago, Detroit, and San Diego.

The embassy of **Ireland** is at 2234 Massachusetts Ave. NW, Washington, DC 20008 (www.embassyofireland.org; ✆ **202/462-3939**). Irish consulates are in Boston, Chicago, New York, San Francisco, and other cities. See website for complete listing.

The embassy of **New Zealand** is at 37 Observatory Circle NW, Washington, DC 20008 (www.nzembassy.com; ✆ **202/328-4800**). New Zealand consulates are in Los Angeles, Salt Lake City, San Francisco, and Seattle.

The embassy of the **United Kingdom** is at 3100 Massachusetts Ave. NW, Washington, DC 20008 (http://ukinusa.fco.gov.uk; ✆ **202/588-6500**). Other British consulates are in Atlanta, Boston, Chicago, Cleveland, Houston, Los Angeles, New York, San Francisco, and Seattle.

Family Travel With beaches to build castles on, water to splash in, and amazing sights to see, Hawaii is paradise for children. Take a look at "The Best of Hawaii for Kids," in chapter 1. Be sure to check out the "Especially for Kids" boxes in each island chapter for suggested family activities.

The larger hotels and resorts offer supervised programs for children and can refer you to qualified babysitters. By state law, hotels can accept only children ages 5 to 12 in supervised activities programs, but can often accommodate younger kids by hiring babysitters to watch over them. Contact **People Attentive to Children (PATCH)** for referrals to babysitters who have taken a training course on childcare. On Oahu, call 🕻 **808/839-1988;** on the Big Island, call 🕻 **808/325-3864** in Kona or 🕻 **808/961-3169** in Hilo; on Maui, call 🕻 **808/242-9232;** on Kauai, call 🕻 **808/246-0622;** on Molokai and Lanai, call 🕻 **800/498-4145;** or visit www.patchhawaii.org. The **Nanny Connection** (www.thenanny connection.com; 🕻 **808/875-4777**) on Maui is a reputable business that sends experienced Mary Poppins-esque nannies to resorts and beaches to watch children for $19 per hour and up, depending on the number of children and holiday hours. Tutoring services are also available.

Baby's Away (www.babysaway.com) rents cribs, strollers, highchairs, playpens, infant seats, and the like on Oahu (🕻 **800/496-6386** or 808/640-6734), the Big Island (🕻 **800/996-9030** or 808/756-5800), and Maui (🕻 **800/942-9030** or 808/298-2745). The staff will deliver whatever you need to wherever you're staying and pick it up when you're done.

For a list of more family-friendly travel resources, turn to the experts at www.frommers.com.

Gasoline   Please see "By Car" under "Getting Around Hawaii," earlier in this chapter.

Gay & Lesbian Travelers   Hawaii welcomes all people with aloha. The number of gay- or lesbian-specific accommodations on the islands is limited, but most properties welcome gays and lesbians as they would any traveler. Since 1990, the state's capital has hosted the **Honolulu Pride Parade and Celebration.** Register to participate at www. honolulupride.org.

Gay Hawaii (www.gayhawaii.com) and **Pride Guide Hawaii** (www.gogayhawaii.com) are websites with gay and lesbian news, blogs, business recommendations, and other information for the entire state. Also check out the website for **Out in Hawaii** (www.outin hawaii.com), which calls itself "Queer Resources and Information for the State of Hawaii," with vacation ideas, a calendar of events, information on Hawaii, and even a chat room.

For more gay and lesbian travel resources, visit www.frommers.com.

Health   **Mosquitoes, Centipedes & Scorpions**   While insects can get a little close for comfort in Hawaii (expect to see ants, cockroaches, and other critters indoors, even in posh hotels) few of them cause serious trouble. Mosquitoes do not carry disease here (barring an isolated outbreak of dengue fever in 2001). Giant centipedes—as long as 8 inches—are occasionally seen; scorpions are rare. Around Hilo on the Big Island, little red fire ants can rain down from trees and sting unsuspecting passersby. If you are stung or bitten by an insect and experience extreme pain, swelling, nausea, or any other severe reaction, seek medical help immediately.

Hiking Safety   Before you set out on a hike, let someone know where you're heading and when you plan to return; too many hikers spend cold nights in the wilderness because they don't take this simple precaution. It's always a good idea to hike with a pal. Select your route based on your own fitness level. Check weather conditions with the **National Weather Service** (www.prh.noaa.gov/hnl; 🕻 **808/973-5286** on Oahu), even if it looks sunny: The weather here ranges from blistering hot to freezing cold and can change in a matter of hours or miles. Do *not* hike if rain or a storm is predicted; flash floods are common in Hawaii and have resulted in many preventable deaths. Plan to finish your hike at least an hour before sunset; because Hawaii is so close to the equator, it does not have a twilight period, and thus it gets dark quickly after the sun sets. Wear sturdy shoes, a hat, clothes to protect you from the sun and from getting scratches, and high-SPF sunscreen on all exposed areas. Take plenty of water, basic first aid, a snack, and a bag to pack out what you pack in. Watch your step. Loose lava rocks are famous for twisting ankles. Don't rely on cellphones; service isn't available in many remote places.

Vog   When molten lava from Kilauea pours into the ocean, gases are released, resulting in a brownish, volcanic haze that hovers at the horizon. Some people claim that exposure to the smog-like air causes headaches and bronchial ailments. To date, there's no evidence that vog causes lingering damage to healthy individuals. Vog primarily affects the Big Island—Kona, in particular—but is sometimes felt as far away as Maui and Oahu. You can minimize the effects of vog by closing your windows and using an air conditioner indoors. The University of Hawaii recommends draping a floor fan with a wet cloth saturated in a thin paste of baking soda and water, which captures and neutralizes the sulfur compounds. Cleansing your sinuses with a neti pot and saltwater is also helpful. ***One more word of caution:*** If you're pregnant or have heart or breathing problems, you should avoid exposure to the sulfuric fumes in and around Hawaii Volcanoes National Park.

Ocean Safety   Many people who visit Hawaii underestimate the power of the ocean. With just a few precautions, your Pacific experience can be a safe and happy one. Before getting into the water, take a moment to watch where others are swimming. Notice the pattern of the swells. If you get caught in big surf, dive underneath each wave until the swell subsides. Never turn your back to the ocean; rogue waves catch even experienced water folk unaware.

Note that sharks are not a big problem in Hawaii; in fact, local divers look forward to seeing them. Only 2 of the 40 shark species present in Hawaiian waters are known to bite humans, and then usually it's by accident. But here are the general rules for avoiding sharks: Don't swim at dusk or in murky water—sharks may mistake you for one of their usual meals. It should be obvious not to swim where there are bloody fish in the water, as sharks become aggressive around blood.

Seasickness   The waters in Hawaii can range from calm as glass (off the Kona Coast on the Big Island) to downright turbulent (in storm conditions); they usually fall somewhere in between. In general, expect rougher conditions in winter than in summer and on windward coastlines versus calm, leeward coastlines. If you've never been out on a boat, or if you've been seasick in the past, you might want to heed the following suggestions:

o   The day before you go out on the boat, avoid alcohol, caffeine, citrus and other acidic juices, and greasy, spicy, or hard-to-digest foods.

o   Get a good night's sleep the night before.

o   Take or use whatever seasickness prevention works best for you—medication, an acupressure wristband, ginger tea or capsules, or any combination. But do it ***before you board;*** once you set sail, it's generally too late.

o   While you're on the boat, stay as low and as near the center of the boat as possible. Avoid the fumes (especially if it's a diesel boat); stay out in the fresh air and watch the horizon. Do not read.

o   If you start to feel queasy, drink clear fluids like water, and eat something bland, such as a soda cracker.

Stings   The most common stings in Hawaii come from jellyfish, particularly Portuguese man-of-war and box jellyfish. Since the poisons they inject are very different, you'll need to treat each type of sting differently.

A bluish-purple floating bubble with a long tail, the **Portuguese man-of-war** is responsible for some 6,500 stings a year on Oahu alone. These stings, although painful and a nuisance, are rarely harmful; fewer than 1 in 1,000 requires medical treatment. The best prevention is to watch for these floating bubbles as you snorkel (look for the hanging tentacles below the surface). Get out of the water if anyone near you spots these jellyfish. Reactions to stings range from mild burning and reddening to severe welts and blisters. Most jellyfish stings disappear by themselves within 15 to 20 minutes if you do nothing at all to treat them. "All Stings Considered: First Aid and Medical Treatment of Hawaii's Marine Injuries," by Craig Thomas and Susan Scott (University of Hawaii Press, 1997), recommends the following treatment: First, pick off any visible tentacles with a gloved hand or a stick; then, rinse the sting with salt- or fresh water, and apply ice to prevent swelling. Avoid applying vinegar, baking soda, or urine to the wound; doing so may actually cause further damage. Be sure to see a doctor if pain persists or a rash or other symptoms develop.

Transparent, square-shaped **box jellyfish** are nearly impossible to see in the water. Fortunately, they seem to follow a monthly cycle: 8 to 10 days after the full moon, they appear in the waters on the leeward side of each island and hang around for about 3 days. Also, they seem to sting more in the morning, when they're on or near the surface. The stings from a box jellyfish can cause hive-like welts, blisters, and pain lasting from 10 minutes to 8 hours. "All Stings Considered" recommends the following treatment: First, pour regular household vinegar on the sting; this will stop additional burning. Do not rub the area. Pick off any vinegar-soaked tentacles with a stick and apply an ice pack. Seek medical treatment if you experience shortness of breath, weakness, palpitations, or any other severe symptoms.

Marine Life Awareness

Exploring the kaleidoscopic underwater world is the highlight of many Hawaiian vacations. Yet this salty environment is vulnerable to intrusion; swimmers can accidentally kill live coral colonies by stepping on or kicking them, or by introducing toxic sunscreen into the water. Chasing marine life such as dolphins, seals, or sea turtles prevents these animals from feeding and resting and can result in big fines. **Hawaii Wildlife Fund** (www.wildhawaii.org) and the **Coral Reef Alliance** (http://coral.org) are nonprofit agencies that strive to protect and conserve the marvelous marine life of Hawaii. Visit their websites to find out how you can protect yourself *and* the underwater critters you're hoping to ogle.

Punctures   Most sea-related punctures come from stepping on or brushing against the needle-like spines of sea urchins (known locally as *wana*). Be careful when you're in the water; don't put your foot down (even if you are wearing booties or fins) if you can't clearly see the bottom. Waves can push you into *wana* in a surge zone in shallow water. The spines can even puncture a wet suit. A sea urchin puncture can result in burning, aching, swelling, and discoloration (black or purple) around the area where the spines entered your skin. The best thing to do is to pull out any protruding spines. The body will absorb the spines within 24 hours to 3 weeks, or the remainder of the spines will work themselves out. Again, contrary to popular thought, urinating or pouring vinegar on the embedded spines will not help.

Cuts   Stay out of the ocean if you have an open cut, wound, or new tattoo. The high level of bacteria present in the water means that even small wounds can become infected. Staphylococcus, or "staph," infections start out as swollen, pinkish skin tissue around the wound that spreads and grows rather than dries and heals. Scrub any cuts well with fresh

PLANNING YOUR TRIP TO HAWAII

Health

water and avoid the ocean until they heal. Consult a doctor if your wound shows signs of infection.

Also see "Fast Facts" in the individual island chapters for listings of local **doctors, dentists, hospitals,** and **emergency numbers.**

Internet & Wi-Fi   In every island, branches of the **Hawaii State Public Library System** have free computers with Internet access. To find your closest library, check **www.librarieshawaii.org/sitemap.htm.** There is no charge for use of the computers, but you must have a Hawaii library card, which is free to Hawaii residents and members of the military. Visitors can visit any branch to purchase a $10 visitor card that is good for 3 months.

If you have your own laptop, every **Starbucks** in Hawaii has Wi-Fi. For a list of locations, go to **www.starbucks.com/retail/find/default.aspx.** Many, if not most, **hotel lobbies** have free Wi-Fi.

Most interisland airports have **Internet kiosks** that provide basic Web access for a per-minute fee that's usually higher than cybercafe prices. The **Honolulu International Airport** (http://hawaii.gov/hnl) provides **Wi-Fi access** for a fee through Shaka Net. Check out copy shops like FedEx Office, which offers computer stations with fully loaded software (as well as Wi-Fi).

Mail   At press time, domestic postage rates were 33¢ for a postcard and 49¢ for a letter. For international mail, a first-class postcard or letter up to 1 ounce costs $1.15. For more information go to **www.usps.com.**

If you aren't sure what your address will be in the United States, mail can be sent to you, in your name, c/o General Delivery at the main post office of the city or region where you expect to be. (Call ✆ **800/275-8777** for information on the nearest post office.) The addressee must pick up mail in person and must produce proof of identity (driver's license, passport, and the like). Most post offices will hold mail for up to 1 month, and are open Monday to Friday from 9am to 4pm, and Saturday from 9am to noon.

Always include zip codes when mailing items in the U.S. If you don't know your zip code, visit www.usps.com/zip4.

Medical Requirements   Unless you're arriving from an area known to be suffering from an epidemic (particularly cholera or yellow fever), inoculations or vaccinations are not required for entry into the United States.

Mobile Phones   Cellphone coverage is decent throughout Hawaii, but tends to be inconsistent in the more remote and mountainous regions of the Islands.

If you're not from the U.S., you'll be appalled at the poor reach of our **GSM (Global System for Mobile Communications) wireless network,** which is used by much of the rest of the world. You may or may not be able to send SMS (text messaging) home.

Do *not* use your cellphone while you are driving. Strict laws and heavy fines ($97–$150) are diligently enforced.

Money & Costs   Frommer's lists exact prices in the local currency. The currency conversions quoted below were correct at press time. However, rates fluctuate, so before departing consult a currency exchange website such as www.oanda.com or www.xe.com/ucc/convert/classic to check up-to-the-minute rates.

THE VALUE OF US$ VS. OTHER POPULAR CURRENCIES

1US$	Can$	UK£	Euro (€)	Aus$	NZ$
11	C$1.09	£.59	€.72	A$.992	NZ$1.15

	US$
Hamburger	6.00–19.00
Movie ticket (adult/child)	11.00/7.50
Taxi from Honolulu Airport to Waikiki	40.00
Entry to Bishop Museum (adult/child)	20.00/15.00
Entry to Wet 'n' Wild (adult/child)	48.00/38.00
Entry to Honolulu Zoo (adult/child)	14.00/6.00
Entry to Maui Ocean Center (adult/child)	27.00/20.00
Tour of Maui Tropical Plantation (adult/child)	16.00/6.00
Entry to Haleakala National Park (person/car)	5.00/10.00
Old Lahaina Luau (adult/child)	109.00/78.00
20-ounce soft drink at convenience store	2.50
16-ounce apple juice	3.50
Cup of coffee	3.00
Moderately priced three-course dinner without alcohol	60.00
Moderately priced Waikiki hotel room (double)	145.00–195.00

10

ATMs (cashpoints) are everywhere in Hawaii—at banks, supermarkets, Longs Drugs, and Honolulu International Airport, and in some resorts and shopping centers. The **Cirrus** (www.mastercard.com; ✆ **800/424-7787**) and **PLUS** (www.visa.com; ✆ **800/843-7587**) networks span the country; you can find them even in remote regions. Go to your bank-card's website to find ATM locations at your destination. Be sure you know your daily with-drawal limit before you depart.

Note: Many banks impose a fee every time you use a card at another bank's ATM, and that fee is often higher for international transactions (up to $5 or more) than for domestic ones (rarely more than $2.50). In addition, the bank from which you withdraw cash is likely to charge its own fee. Visitors from outside the U.S. should also find out whether their bank assesses a 1- to 3-percent fee on charges incurred abroad.

Credit cards are accepted everywhere except TheBus (on Oahu), most taxicabs (all islands), and some small restaurants and bed-and-breakfast accommodations.

Packing Tips   Hawaii is very informal. Shorts, T-shirts, and sandals will get you by at most restaurants and attractions; a casual dress or a polo shirt and long pants are fine even in the most expensive places. Jackets for men are required only in some of the fine-dining rooms of a very few ultra-exclusive resorts, such as the Halekulani on Oahu and the Big Island's Mauna Kea Beach Hotel—and they'll cordially provide men with a jacket if you don't bring your own. Aloha wear is acceptable everywhere, so you may want to plan on buying an aloha shirt or a Hawaiian-style dress while you're in the islands. If you plan on doing activities such hiking, horseback riding, or ziplining, bring close-toed shoes; they're required.

The tropical sun poses the greatest threat to anyone who ventures into the great outdoors, so pack **sun protection:** a good pair of sunglasses, strong sunscreen, a light hat, and a water bottle. Dehydration is common in the tropics.

One last thing: **It can get really cold in Hawaii.** If you plan to see the sunrise from the top of Maui's Haleakala Crater, venture into the Big Island's Hawaii Volcanoes National Park, or spend time in Kokee State Park on Kauai, bring a warm jacket. Temperatures "upcountry" (higher up the mountain) can sink to 40°F (4°C), even in summer when it's 80°F (27°C) at the beach. Bring a windbreaker, sweater, or light jacket. And if you'll be in Hawaii between November and March, toss some **rain gear** into your suitcase, too.

Passports   Virtually every air traveler entering the U.S. is required to show a passport. All persons, including U.S. citizens, traveling by air between the United States and Canada, Mexico, Central and South America, the Caribbean, and Bermuda are required to present a valid passport. **Note:** U.S. and Canadian citizens entering the U. S. at land and sea ports of entry from within the western hemisphere must now also present a passport or other documents compliant with the Western Hemisphere Travel Initiative (WHTI; check www.getyouhome.gov for details). Children 15 and under may continue entering with only a U.S. birth certificate, or other proof of U.S. citizenship.

Australia   Australian Passport Information Service (www.passports.gov.au; ✆ **131-232** in Australia).

Canada   Passport Office, Department of Foreign Affairs and International Trade, Ottawa, ON K1A 0G3 (www.ppt.gc.ca; ✆ **800/567-6868**).

Ireland   Passport Office, Setanta Centre, Molesworth Street, Dublin 2 (www.foreign affairs.gov.ie; ✆ **01/671-1633**).

New Zealand   Passports Office, Department of Internal Affairs, 47 Boulcott St., Wellington, 6011 (www.passports.govt.nz; ✆ **0800/225-050** in New Zealand or 04/474-8100).

United Kingdom   Visit your nearest passport office, major post office, or travel agency, or contact the **Identity and Passport Service (IPS),** 89 Eccleston Sq., London, SW1V 1PN (www.ips.gov.uk; ✆ **0300/222-0000**).

United States   To find your regional passport office, check the U.S. State Department website (http://travel.state.gov) or call the **National Passport Information Center** (✆ **877/487-2778**) for automated information.

Safety   Although tourist areas are generally safe, visitors should always stay alert, even in laidback Hawaii (and especially in Waikiki). It's wise to ask the island tourist office if you're in doubt about which neighborhoods are safe. Avoid deserted areas, especially at night. Don't go into any city park at night unless there's an event that attracts crowds—for example, the Waikiki Shell concerts in Kapiolani Park. Generally speaking, you can feel safe in areas where there are many people and open establishments.

Avoid carrying valuables with you on the street, and don't display expensive cameras or electronic equipment. Hold on to your pocketbook, and place your billfold in an inside pocket. In theaters, restaurants, and other public places, keep your possessions in sight.

Oahu has seen a series of purse-snatching incidents, in which thieves in slow-moving cars or on foot have snatched handbags from female pedestrians. The Honolulu police department advises women to carry purses on the shoulder away from the street or, better yet, to wear the strap across the chest instead of on one shoulder. Women with clutch bags should hold them close to their chest.

Remember also that hotels are open to the public and that security may not be able to screen everyone entering, particularly in large properties. Always lock your room door—don't assume that once inside your hotel you're automatically safe.

Burglaries of tourists' rental cars in hotel parking structures and at beach parking lots have become more common. Park in well-lighted and well-traveled areas, if possible. Never leave any packages or valuables visible in the car. If someone attempts to rob you or steal your car, do not try to resist the thief or carjacker—report the incident to the police department immediately. Ask your rental agency about personal safety, and get written directions or a map with the route to your destination clearly marked.

Generally, Hawaii has the same laws as the mainland United States. Nudity is illegal in Hawaii. There are *no* legal nude beaches (I don't care what you have read). If you are nude on a beach (or anywhere) in Hawaii, you can be arrested.

Smoking marijuana also is illegal. Yes, there are lots of "stories" claiming that marijuana is grown in Hawaii, but the drug is illegal; if you attempt to buy it or light up, you can be arrested.

Senior Travel   Discounts for seniors are available at almost all of Hawaii's major attractions and occasionally at hotels and restaurants. The Outrigger hotel chain, for instance, offers travelers ages 50 and older a 20-percent discount on regular published rates—and an additional 5 percent off for members of AARP. Always ask when making hotel reservations or buying tickets. And always carry identification with proof of your age—it can really pay off.

Smoking   It's against the law to smoke in public buildings, including airports, shopping malls, grocery stores, retail shops, buses, movie theaters, banks, convention facilities, and all government buildings and facilities. There is no smoking in restaurants, bars, and nightclubs. Most B&Bs prohibit smoking indoors, and more and more hotels and resorts are becoming nonsmoking even in public areas. Also, there is no smoking within 20 feet of a doorway, window, or ventilation intake (so no hanging around outside a bar to smoke—you must go 20 ft. away).

Taxes   The United States has no value-added tax (VAT) or other indirect tax at the national level. Every state, county, and city may levy its own local tax on all purchases, including hotel and restaurant checks and airline tickets. These taxes will not appear on price tags.

Hawaii state general excise tax is 4 percent. Hotel tax is 17.75 percent on Oahu and 17.25 percent on all the other islands. Oahu adds an additional .5 percent surcharge on all items purchased there (including hotel rooms) to pay for construction of an elevated public rail system.

Telephones   All calls on-island are local calls; calls from one island to another via a land line are long distance and you must dial 1, then the Hawaii area code (808), and then the phone number. Many convenience groceries and packaging services sell **prepaid calling cards** in denominations up to $50. Many public pay phones at airports now accept American Express, MasterCard, and Visa. **Local calls** made from most pay phones cost 50¢. Most long-distance and international calls can be dialed directly from any phone. **To make calls within the United States and to Canada,** dial 1, followed by the area code and the seven-digit number. **For other international calls,** dial 011, followed by the country code, city code, and the number you are calling.

Calls to area codes **800, 888, 877,** and **866** are toll-free. However, calls to area codes **700** and **900** (chat lines, bulletin boards, "dating" services, and so on) can be expensive—charges of 95¢ to $3 or more per minute. Some numbers have minimum charges that can run $15 or more.

For **reversed-charge or collect calls,** and for person-to-person calls, dial the number 0, then the area code and number; an operator will come on the line, and you should specify whether you are calling collect, person-to-person, or both. If your operator-assisted call is international, ask for the overseas operator.

For **directory assistance** ("Information"), dial 411 for local numbers and national numbers in the U.S. and Canada. For dedicated long-distance information, dial 1, then the appropriate area code plus 555-1212.

Time   The continental United States is divided into **four time zones:** Eastern Standard Time (EST), Central Standard Time (CST), Mountain Standard Time (MST), and Pacific Standard Time (PST). Alaska and Hawaii have their own zones. For example, when it's 7am in Honolulu (HST), it's 9am in Los Angeles (PST), 10am in Denver (MST), 11am in Chicago (CST), noon in New York City (EST), 5pm in London (GMT), and 2am the next day in Sydney.

Daylight saving time, in effect in most of the United States from 2am on the second Sunday in March to 2am on the first Sunday in November, is not observed in Hawaii, Arizona, the U.S. Virgin Islands, and Puerto Rico. Daylight saving time moves the clock 1 hour ahead of standard time.

Tipping   Tips are a major part of certain workers' income, and gratuities are the standard way of showing appreciation for services provided. (Tipping is certainly not compulsory if the service is poor!) In hotels, tip **bellhops** at least $2 per bag ($3–$5 if you have a lot of luggage) and tip the **housekeepers** $2 per person per day (more if you've left a disaster area for him or her to clean up). Tip the **doorman** or **concierge** only if he or she has provided you with some specific service (for example, calling a cab for you or obtaining difficult-to-get theater tickets). Tip the **valet-parking attendant** $2 to $5 every time you get your car.

In restaurants, bars, and nightclubs, tip **service staff** and **bartenders** 18 to 20 percent of the check, and tip **valet-parking attendants** $2 per vehicle.

As for other service personnel, tip **cab drivers** 15 percent of the fare; tip **skycaps** at airports at least $2 per bag ($3–$5 if you have a lot of luggage); and tip **hairdressers** and **barbers** 18 to 20 percent.

Toilets   You won't find public toilets or "restrooms" on the streets in Hawaii but they can be found in hotel lobbies, restaurants, museums, department stores, railway and bus stations, service stations, and at most beaches. Large hotels and fast-food restaurants are often the best bet for clean facilities. Restaurants and bars in heavily visited areas may reserve their restrooms for patrons.

Travelers with Disabilities   Travelers with disabilities are made to feel very welcome in Hawaii. There are more than 2,000 ramped curbs in Oahu alone, many hotels are equipped with wheelchair-accessible rooms and pools, and tour companies provide many special services. Beach wheelchairs are available at one beach on Maui (Kamaole I; ask lifeguard) and six beaches on Oahu. Call the **City and County of Honolulu Department of Parks and Recreation** (② **808/768-3027**) for locations.

For tips on accessible travel in Hawaii, go to the **Hawaii Tourism Authority** website (www.gohawaii.com/oahu/about/travel-tips/special-needs). The **Hawaii Center for Independent Living,** 200 N. Vineyard Blvd. A501, Honolulu, HI 96817 (www.cil-hawaii.org; ② **808/522-5400**), can provide additional information about accessibility throughout the Islands.

Access Aloha Travel (www.accessalohatravel.com; ✆ **800/480-1143**) specializes in accommodating travelers with disabilities. Agents book cruises, tours, rental vans (available on Maui and Oahu only), accommodations, and airfare (as part of a package only). On Maui and Kauai, **Gammie Homecare** (www.gammie.com; Maui: ✆ **808/877-4032;** Kauai: ✆ **808/632-2333**) rents everything from motorized scooters to shower chairs.

For more on organizations that offer resources to travelers with disabilities, go to www.frommers.com.

Visas   The U.S. State Department has a **Visa Waiver Program (VWP)** allowing citizens of the following countries to enter the United States without a visa for stays of up to 90 days: Andorra, Australia, Austria, Belgium, Brunei, Chile, Czech Republic, Denmark, Estonia, Finland, France, Germany, Greece, Hungary, Iceland, Ireland, Italy, Japan, Latvia, Liechtenstein, Lithuania, Luxembourg, Malta, Monaco, the Netherlands, New Zealand, Norway, Portugal, San Marino, Singapore, Slovakia, Slovenia, South Korea, Spain, Sweden, Switzerland, Taiwan, and the United Kingdom. (**Note:** This list was accurate at press time; for the most up-to-date list of countries in the VWP, consult http://usvisas.state.gov.) Even though a visa isn't necessary, in an effort to help U.S. officials check travelers against terror watch lists before they arrive at U.S. borders, visitors from VWP countries must register online through the Electronic System for Travel Authorization (ESTA) before boarding a plane or a boat to the U.S. Travelers must complete an electronic application providing basic personal and travel eligibility information. The Department of Homeland Security recommends filling out the form at least 3 days before traveling. Authorizations will be valid for up to 2 years or until the traveler's passport expires, whichever comes first. Currently, there is a US$14 fee for the online application. Existing ESTA registrations remain valid through their expiration dates. **Note:** Any passport issued on or after October 26, 2006, by a VWP country must be an **e-Passport** for VWP travelers to be eligible to enter the U.S. without a visa. Citizens of these nations also need to present a round-trip air or cruise ticket upon arrival. E-Passports contain computer chips capable of storing biometric information, such as the required digital photograph of the holder. If your passport doesn't have this feature, you can still travel without a visa if the valid passport was issued before October 26, 2005, and includes a machine-readable zone; or if the valid passport was issued between October 26, 2005, and October 25, 2006, and includes a digital photograph. For more information, go to **http://usvisas.state.gov**. Canadian citizens may enter the United States without a visa but will need to show a passport and proof of residence.

Citizens of all other countries must have (1) a valid passport that expires at least 6 months later than the scheduled end of their visit to the U.S., and (2) a tourist visa. For information about U.S. visas, go to **http://usvisas.state.gov**. Or go to one of the following:

Australian citizens can obtain up-to-date visa information from the **U.S. Embassy Canberra,** Moonah Place, Yarralumla, ACT 2600 (✆ **02/6214-5600**) or by checking the U.S. Diplomatic Mission's website at http://canberra.usembassy.gov/visas.html.

British subjects can obtain up-to-date visa information by calling the **U.S. Embassy Visa Information Line** (✆ **09042-450-100** from within the U.K. at £1.20 per min.; or ✆ **866/382-3589** from within the U.S. at a flat rate of $16, payable by credit card only) or by visiting the American Embassy London's website at http://london.usembassy.gov/visas.html.

Irish citizens can obtain up-to-date visa information through the **U.S. Embassy Dublin,** 42 Elgin Rd., Ballsbridge, Dublin 4 (http://dublin.usembassy.gov; ✆ **1580-47-VISA** [8472] from within the Republic of Ireland at €2.40 per min.).

Citizens of **New Zealand** can obtain up-to-date visa information by contacting the **U.S. Embassy New Zealand,** 29 Fitzherbert Terrace, Thorndon, Wellington (http://newzealand.usembassy.gov; ✆ **644/462-6000**).

Water   Generally the water in your hotel or at public drinking fountains is safe to drink (depending on the island, it may have more chlorine than you like).

Wi-Fi   See "Internet & Wi-Fi," earlier in this section.

Index

PHOTO CREDITS